Jürgen Habermas

Twentieth-Century Political Thinkers
Series Editors: Kenneth L. Deutsch and Jean Bethke Elshtain

Raymond Aron: The Recovery of the Political
    by Brian C. Anderson, American Enterprise Institute
Jacques Maritain: The Philosopher in Society
    by James V. Schall, Georgetown University
Martin Buber: The Hidden Dialogue
    by Dan Avnon, Hebrew University of Jerusalem
John Dewey: America's Philosopher of Democracy
    by David Fott, University of Nevada
Simone Weil: The Way of Justice as Compassion
    by Richard H. Bell, The College of Wooster
Gandhi: Struggling for Autonomy
    by Ronald J. Tercheck, University of Maryland at College Park
Paul Ricoeur: The Promise and Risk of Politics
    by Bernard P. Dauenhauer, University of Georgia
Carl Schmitt: The End of Law
    by William E. Scheuerman, University of Pittsburgh
Eric Voegelin: In Quest of Reality
    by Thomas W. Heilke, University of Kansas
Yves R. Simon: Real Democracy
    by Vukan Kuic, University of South Carolina
Jürgen Habermas: A Philosophical–Political Profile
    by Martin Beck Matuštík, Purdue University

Jürgen Habermas

A Philosophical–Political Profile

MARTIN BECK MATUŠTÍK

ROWMAN & LITTLEFIELD PUBLISHERS, INC.
Lanham • Boulder • New York • Oxford

ROWMAN & LITTLEFIELD PUBLISHERS, INC.

Published in the United States of America
by Rowman & Littlefield Publishers, Inc.
4720 Boston Way, Lanham, Maryland 20706
www.rowmanlittlefield.com

12 Hid's Copse Road
Cumnor Hill, Oxford OX2 9JJ, England

Copyright © 2001 by Rowman & Littlefield Publishers, Inc.

All rights reserved. No part of this publication may be reproduced,
stored in a retrieval system, or transmitted in any form or by any
means, electronic, mechanical, photocopying, recording, or otherwise,
without the prior permission of the publisher.

British Library Cataloging in Publication Information Available

Library of Congress Cataloging-in-Publication Data

Matuštík, Martin Beck, 1957–
   Jürgen Habermas : a philosophical-political profile / Martin J. Beck Matuštík.
     p. cm.—(Twentieth-century political thinkers)
   Includes bibliographical references and index.
   ISBN 0-7425-0796-3 (alk. paper)—ISBN 0-7425-0797-1 (pbk. : alk. paper)
   1. Habermas, Jürgen—Contributions in political science. 2. Critical theory. I. Title. II. Series.

JC63.H14 M38 2001
320'.01—dc21
                                                       00-065322

Printed in the United States of America

∞™ The paper used in this publication meets the minimum requirements of
American National Standard for Information Sciences—Permanence of Paper for
Printed Library Materials, ANSI/NISO Z39.48-1992.

To Jim Marsh
and to his
generation of great teachers and activists,
who spent the larger part of their lives in the twentieth century
pursuing the promise of a better world

CONTENTS

List of Tables and Figures	*ix*
Glossary of Abbreviations and Foreign Terms	*xi*
Introduction	*xiii*
Chronology	*xxix*
Part One: Situations	*1*
1 From Liberation to Restoration, 1945–1959	*3*
2 From Incubation to Revolt, 1960–1969	*35*
3 From Revision to Hope and Back Again, 1970–2000	*65*
Part Two: Profiles and Interventions	*87*
4 The Phantoms of 1968	*89*
5 The Ghosts of 1945	*125*
6 After 1989: In the Shadows of 1945 and under the Specters of 1968	*161*
Part Three: Impact and Discontents	*199*
7 Architectonic and Authorship	*201*
8 The Habermas Effect	*237*
9 At the Crossroads of a New Critical Theory	*277*
Habermas Bibliography and Abbreviations of Works Cited	*305*
References	*313*
Index	*327*
About the Author	*341*

TABLES AND FIGURES

TABLES

Table 1.1	Transmutations of 'Fascism' in the Generational Confrontations with the Nazi Past	6
Table 1.2	Impact of the Institutional Grounding of West Germany (FRG) on the Evolution of the First and Second Generations of Critical Theory in the 1950s	25
Table 2.1	Impact of the Institutional and Intellectual Groundings of West Germany (FRG) on the Evolution of the Student Movement, Marcuse, and Habermas	46
Table 7.1	Habermas' Integrative Concepts	203
Table 7.2	The Structure of Habermas' Authorship	221
Table 7.3	The Modes of Habermas' Authorship	222
Table 8.1	Habermas' Radical Pluralism	239
Table 8.2	The Structure of Unfinished Debates	246
Table 8.3	The Modes of Habermas' Learning and Blindness by Disaster	247

FIGURES

Figure 3.1	Habermas in the "German Autumn"	70
Figure 4.1	Habermas and Marcuse on Violence	116

GLOSSARY OF ABBREVIATIONS AND FOREIGN TERMS

APO	Ausserparlamentarische Opposition = Extraparliamentary Opposition
BRD	Bundesrepublik Deutschland = Federal Republic of Germany = West Germany (FRG)
CDU	Christlich-Demokratische Union = Christian Democratic Union (FRG)
CSU	Christlich-Soziale Union = Christian Social Union (FRG)
FDP	Freie Demokratische Partei = Free Democratic Party (FRG)
FRG	= BRD
GDR	German Democratic Republic (East Germany)
IfS	Institut für Sozialforschung = Institute for Social Research
NPD	Nationaldemokratische Partei Deutschlands = National Democratic Party of Germany (FRG)
NSDAP	Nazionalsozialistische Deutsche Arbeiterpartei = National Socialist German Labor Party (Third Reich)
SDS	Sozialistischer Deutscher Studentenbund = German Socialist Student League (FRG)
SED	Sozialistische Einheitspartei Deutschlands = Socialist Unity Party of Germany (GDR)
SPD	Sozialdemokratische Partei Deutschlands = Social Democratic Party of Germany (FRG)

INTRODUCTION

WALKING WITH HABERMAS THROUGH THE TWENTIETH CENTURY

Jürgen Habermas has acquired without any doubt a leading role among the most accomplished social and political theorists of the present age. In trying to witness and then sketch his genuine profile, I was ushered into an incredible engagement with the twentieth century. When I emerged from the forest of situations, thought streams, debates, and interventions—from Habermas' youth in Nazi Germany to his worldwide stature at the end of the twentieth century—with the draft of my book finished, I felt as if I were stepping onto home base. But finishing a home run is not necessarily winning the game. As I was settling down to do the revisions requested by the two anonymous reviewers of the manuscript, I came across new exciting analyses of those very situations, thought streams, debates, and interventions that so closely interweave throughout Habermas' life. I delved into three volumes with more than a thousand pages of Kraushaar's (1998) mind-boggling chronicle, documentation, and edited studies of the 1960s student movement in Germany. I poured breathlessly through penetrating discussions of the institutional 1950s and the intellectual 1960s founding of the Federal Republic of Germany in a volume authored by Albrecht and others (1999). On September 9, 1999, in an open letter to Habermas, Sloterdijk (1999a) pronounced this philosophical and political context of Germany's founding and of Habermas' lifework (what I describe later in this introduction as 'Critical Theory') all but "dead." Given such diametrically opposed assessments of postwar development—with Kraushaar's and Albrecht's volumes making a groundbreaking case for the importance of Critical Theory for the Federal Republic of Germany while Sloterdijk's contention degrades that very importance—I realized two things at once.

The first was the incontrovertible affirmation that the newly published German research by Kraushaar and Albrecht et al. validates my methodology and findings. Just as certain situations, thought streams, debates, and interventions can be reconstructed from their roles in the founding of the FRG and in the lives of its postwar generations (rather than through theoretical reconstructions alone), so too can Habermas' profile be reconstructed from his formative and intellectual life in postwar Germany and in relation to his generational sensibilities. Second, I became keenly aware that in my finished draft I had at best advanced through the thick forests at the foothills, only to discover that the mountain rose steeply in front of me. I thought to myself, considering what still needed to be done in crafting a genuine profile, that perhaps Habermas' century and lifework are too rich, too complex, too many-sided to allow me to give them justice. I had either to give up the climb right then and there or admit that I had not begun yet. True revisions required a deeper look at Habermas' formative postwar years, the German context of his young adult life in the 1950s, and the intensive peculiarity of the 1960s in West Germany—sending shock waves in 2001 through the generation of the '68ers and Germany's Red–Green coalition of Chancellor Gerhardt Schröder and Foreign Minister Joschka Fischer. I needed to address the multiple contemporary audiences that come to Habermas across the wide political and geographical spectrum of their interests.

I should declare at the outset that I did not come to Habermas out of nowhere or without a standpoint. While my pervasive concern lies in existential freedom and social liberation—working and waiting for a world wholly other than this unjust one—I realize that such sympathies (whether in radical socialist democracy or existential self-transformation) might not explicitly express the standpoint of all readers, not even of all Habermas' interpreters or the master himself. No matter where the readers and the author may stand, this profile reveals the full gamut of Habermas' complex legacy, weighing the pros and cons of various contentious issues, such as the student movement, the relationship between political and economic democracy, or the notion of a 'humanitarian' war of intervention. With this balance in view, very different readers will benefit from the book.

What the reader holds in hand is the fruit of my struggle to write an incomplete and yet earnest book: this must be an honestly unfinished book because Habermas' life is not over at this time and because any profile of a well-spent life cannot be as rich as the full life that shaped it. That an infinity qualifies every single human being makes the writing of a fully formed profile equally impossible and undesirable. I hope that the textured depth of the events surrounding this profile comes forth in rich colors, deep contours and contrasts, and with requisite dramatic flare. This book marks my encounter with the legacy of the twentieth century—both astonishingly beautiful and truly the most horrible imaginable. Journeying through that history with Habermas has been a most rewarding yet overwhelming, an enriching yet frustrating writing experience. If the reader catches some of this excitement, insight, and drama in traveling with Habermas through many a great theme of the twentieth century, then this effort will have been worth it and not just for me.

SELF-GUIDING SYLLABUS AND SYNOPSIS

This study interweaves three question areas across nine chapters. Rather than proceed didactically, I invite the participant in this journey to begin by making his or her own the three guiding *question areas* through which I approach Habermas' lifework. While this order of questioning is not exhaustive, linear, or even chronological, its rationale is to start from questions that are more immediate and familiar to *us* and move to matters of greater complexity.

- It might help to begin by situating Habermas' work in relation to the key formative events of his intellectual biography. This angle of *existential questioning* provides us with his formative *situations*.
- One might want to analyze next how Habermas' *philosophical-political questioning* emerges in responding to the crises of his era, its institutions, and its generations. These sketches proceed from the angle of the generational profiles of 1945 and 1968 to the formation of Habermas' own *profile and interventions*.
- In responding to theoretical debates in the social sciences, ethics, and politics, one might be able to approach Habermas' oeuvre by way of *critical questioning* about its *impact and discontents*. What does it mean to do social theory *today*?

The heuristic guides for approaching Habermas are fashioned with the help of the questioning areas of his formative beginnings: *existential, philosophical-political, and critical questions*. He has posed these and similar questions with ever-greater intensity since his youth:

- *Existentially*, how can modern discontented individuals, those we meet in adolescent crises or adult rebellions, those we meet after the destruction of long-cherished cultural continuities, become once again socially integrated? How can they find any renewed social integration, even after the numerous disasters of the twentieth century, particularly Auschwitz, with trust?
- *Philosophically-politically*, what form of life could communicatively, ethically, and democratically sustain nonoppressive communities, nonrepressive solidarities, and consensual procedures—given the historical catastrophes of *our* received traditions and institutions?

- *Critically,* granting the exhaustion of theory in its ability to motivate (in actuality and ideally) either social change or the hope of liberation, can *we* find adequate normative and empirical resources for emancipatory transformation of *our* societies towards a more rational (i.e., just) world?

By combining our approach to Habermas with his own questions, we get three angles through which to view and sketch his philosophical-political profile:

Questions	The angle of the profile
Existential questioning	Formative situations of Habermas' life
Philosophical-political questioning	Habermas' intellectual profile and his interventions in political events
Critical questioning	The impact and discontents of his lifework

These angles are suitable for beginning as well as continuing an in-depth study of Habermas' lifework. Because the foreshadowed guiding orientations do not commence from on high with theoretical grids or content presuppositions, but rather from bearing witness to the dramatic (historical, political, philosophical) contexts of his lifework, the guiding questions can (indeed must) be made one's own at one's pace and level of reflection. The nonlinear and open-ended nature of this self-guiding syllabus governs this entire study, and it recommends itself for teaching Habermas. These questions are to be adapted by individual readers, students, and teachers in each generation:

- *Situations:* What does it mean to become contemporary with another's work and the questions that arise in relation to the existential upheavals of his life's journey?
- *Profiles and interventions:* What does it mean to become contemporary with problems arising in the present age, with the crises of its institutions, and with the profiles and responses of its generations?
- *Impact and discontents:* What effects emerge for *us* theoretically if, from the present vantage point, *we* reconstruct normative responses to the existential and philosophical-political problems that one, as a thinker or an activist, faces in his or her lifetime?

Keeping this living syllabus or road map in the foreground, we can subdivide Habermas' lifework as thinker and activist into *political commentaries* on or interventions in various situations of the present age and his various *theoretical debates*. He conceives his social theory as well as his political involvements to be both multidisciplinary and collaborative. As theorist and activist, in the form and content of his work, he dialogues, writes, and reads by engaging in lively encounters with other thinkers, activists, and different theoretical disciplines. The division of the book follows from the foregoing statement of basic orienting questions and angles in terms of which we can view, sketch, and understand Habermas' profile.

Part One

The *existential question* of repairing social integration after the disasters of the twentieth century arises from the angle of Habermas' formative *situations*. Accordingly, this personal dimension of questioning emerges first for Habermas in his teens: he turns sixteen on June 18, 1945, only months after the end of World War II. This same questioning reenters the stage with his deep personal disappointment with Heidegger's unrepentant Nazi politics, elevating Heidegger's existential philosophy, perhaps ironically, into Habermas' own lifelong existential-political motivations. The question revisits Habermas in the 1960s with the youth rebellion against the silence of that generation's parents. Narrating the trajectory of this thinker's lifework from the vantage point of 1945, the existential question punctuates most if not all of his political and theoretical questioning in the subsequent formative situations: 1977 and 1983 (German Autumn), 1989 (the fall of the Berlin Wall), 1990 (unification of Germany), 1991 (the Persian Gulf War), 1993 (second German Autumn), and 1999 (NATO's bombing of Serbia).

In this fashion I traced Habermas' fundamental concerns with questions of social integration after the disaster of Auschwitz all the way to his mature *theory of communicative action* (sometimes also called *discourse theory*). Habermas adopts J. L. Austin's insight that by speaking with another human we are not just using words as instruments, but we are doing something in the world. This doing or speech *action* involves speakers and hearers in binding one another performatively by raising claims to the truth, rightness, and sincerity of each utterance. Habermas distills from this structure of speech acts, with which one speaker motivates another speaker rationally (i.e., by their mutual expectations of having to validate each claim if it is challenged), a *normative theory of communicative rationality*. It is deemed 'normative' insofar as the rational motivation and its fulfillment are validated in a discursive, publicly enacted argument.

With the accent of the book falling on the performance of questioning, I affirm a certain practical primacy of existential freedom and social liberation (e.g., Habermas' question of social integration) in motivating the specialized praxis of normative or political theorizing (e.g., his rational reconstruction of communicative action). *Habermas' beginnings*, viewed from this angle, are always already existential, whether they are theorized as such or not. In *our* becoming contemporary with a living profile of another person, Habermas in this case, *our beginnings* in the book must be likewise considered existentially.

Part Two

The *philosophical-political question* defines *the generational profiles and interventions* formed through responding to the key existential situations—formative years, events, and influences. My guiding concern here is how Habermas' philosophical-political profile itself becomes shaped through the practical engagements he conducts with the two dominant generations of his era: 1945 and 1968. This dimension of questioning shapes Habermas' own profile insofar as in all these formative situations he learns how the fragile liberal institutions of Weimar Germany and the postwar revisionist debates failed to adopt a sharp critical distance from Fascism. This concern for the generation of 1945 is heightened in the response he gives to the protesting generation of 1968. The student movement did not take kindly to being implicated by the charge of 'Left Fascism', however well-meaning Habermas' desire for deliberative democracy was. After 1970, he largely retreats from public political engagements. We witness his renewed political involvement in the "German Autumn" of 1977, when the state clamps down on the ultra-Left terrorist groups and in turn curtails civil freedoms. Habermas warns then against the rise of right-wing authoritarianism and the historical revisionism of the Nazi era. As the Berlin Wall crumbles in November 1989 and refugees stream west en masse, he protests West Germany's undemocratic basis for unifying two Cold War German states. He demands a liberal immigration policy with borders that would be open to asylum seekers. In 1991 and after, when it becomes known that West Germany's chemical production contributed to the deadly gas that Saddam Hussein used to threaten Israel, Habermas justifies the UN-sanctioned western military intervention against Iraq. To understand this not-uncontroversial stance, one must not separate Habermas' experience of 1991 from the ways his profile grows out of responding to the two postwar generations of 1945 and 1968. In light of the overwhelming opposition to the Persian Gulf War by the American Left, Habermas reintroduces some critical distinctions, obliquely echoing the key concerns of the 1960s, between the global democratic ideals of perpetual peace in international law and the economic and political imperialism of the industrialized west. He balances his 1999 defense of NATO's bombing of Serbia by conceding to criticisms of existing international relations.

Part Three

The *critical question* adopts an angle of *impact and discontents* through which Habermas' philosophical-political profile comes to be apprehended by others. One way to generate an ever-new intellectual and practical interest in Habermas is to show how his lifework addresses the key existential, philosophical-political, and critical concerns of the present age. This is the view through the impact he exercises on others as well as through the discontents that arise from his tremendous achievements. By focusing on core concerns of an era or an oeuvre, one can make even very difficult prose, which his writing often employs, come alive. In discussing the authorship, I step back from examining the formation of his authoring profile in order to evaluate both its positive and negative impact from the perspectives of his contemporaries. What is Habermas' effect on his contemporaries? What crossroads do his contemporaries and later generations face that were neither addressed by the architectonic and its answers nor anticipated by his life-defining questions?

This dimension of questioning is inscribed in his response to *the dialectic of enlightenment* (the tension between hope and crisis inscribed into European modernity). His normative preoccupations are raised again and again by various theoretical controversies. He carries on the continuing *rationality debates* with positivists, social scientists, rational-choice theorists, legal scholars, postmodern and poststructuralist thinkers, theologians, and recent analytical philosophers. In these rounds of discussion, he elaborates the *linguistic-communicative turn* as his response (this response adopts certain methods of analytic philosophy and the theory of communicative action, defined above, to overcome normative deficits in other philosophies of language). There is the *practical debate* between liberals (defending the primacy of individual rights) and communitarians (defending the primacy of the good life). In this controversy, Habermas squares a Kantian-Hegelian circle. In these rounds of discussion, he elaborates *communicative ethics* as his response (this response adopts communicative rationality, defined above, to ground normatively the specifically moral claims raised in practical discourse). There are *the struggles for recognition and justice*. In these rounds of discussion, Habermas works out a multicultural, postmetaphysical, formally pragmatic *communicative theory of democracy* as his response. (This response expands communicative reason, defined above, to ground normatively the specifically procedural claims raised in political discourse and to institutionalize basic moral intuitions and rational democratic procedures permanently in law.)

Habermas' mature social theory is thus grounded formally in analytical philosophy of language, along with North American pragmatism, and in a liberal political corpus drawing on these complex Anglo-American philosophical resources. His core motivating questions can be traced to existentially, politically, and critically situated forms of life. This core marks what *we* can witness as his lived existential beginnings. In this conversation with Habermas, my study bears such witness to his recurring returns to these beginnings. The book enters his conceptual architectonic through this integrative understanding of his core questions, and not the other way around. The reverse entry would commence abstractly, considering his theory from another theoretical angle, bracketing the context of dramatization.

An existentially motivated philosophical-political self-understanding gathers, in Habermas' own words uttered in 1984 (in what amounts to his self-choice disclosed in an interview), the "person I [Habermas] would wish to be" rather than "someone other" (NU 257/AS 185). He chooses to be the person who is engaged in the public political struggles for a more just social form of life. One can almost steal a glance at a mature philosophical-political profile of Habermas in his 1953 evaluation of Heidegger's unrequited Nazi infatuation. Habermas inveighs here against the perceived gaps between Heidegger's politics and philosophy occasioned by the latter's 1953 republication of the 1935 Nazi-flavored lectures. I discuss this event in chapter 1. Here I stress the striking continuity in Habermas' authoring and self-reading. His self-choice articulated in 1984 originates minimally in 1953 when he says that the "two universes which hardly touched one another"—what he calls in an almost early Augustinian fashion his "political and philosophical 'confessions'"—become for him in light of Heidegger a single philosophical-political universe (KPS 515/AS 80).

TWO AXES FOR VIEWING HABERMAS' PROFILE

I gave myself the task of creating a living profile. Like the program one peruses before a performance, this introduction will provide the reader or viewer with the notes for staging and comment on the author's position inside and outside of the dramatic whole. In each of the three major divisions of this study, I move along the two main axes—dramatic and structural—through which I apprehend and sketch Habermas' profile. I emphasize the *dramatic axis* of his formative situations in Part One and of his authoring in Part Three. And I focus on the *structural axis* of the generational profiles and interventions of Habermas' era in Part Two and on the structure of his authorship in Part Three. The last Part Three thus integrates the dramatic and structural axes.

Dramatic Axis: Situations and Authoring

One key decision I had to make at the outset was where and how far back and forward to set the stage and the observation platform for the author and the viewer. I had virtually no examples for my project within the published Habermas scholarship. Two of the most excellent historical works on this period by Jay (1973) and Kraushaar (1998; cf. 1990) temporally restrict themselves to key segments of twentieth-century German intellectual history: Jay's history ends in the 1950s and Kraushaar's three volumes remain within the three-year span of 1967–1969, with only some analysis devoted to the 1950s, 1970s, and 1980s. Wiggershaus (1989) and Albrecht et al. (1999) cover a much wider historical territory and do so remarkably well. But none of these four books focuses specifically on Habermas. McCarthy (1982) and Rasmussen (1990) write widely referenced studies on Habermas' work, but both of them leave out most political, historical, or existential considerations in discussing his theory. There are, to my knowledge, five salient exceptions to purely theoretical treatments of Habermas. In his excellent study, Holub (1991) guides the reader through six debates in which Habermas acted as a critical participant in the public sphere. Dews edits a collection of Habermas interviews (AS), which is a gold mine for most autobiographical reflections that are available in print. Horster's (1991) short book on Habermas discusses the links between his philosophy and politics. Pensky's four articles (1989, 1995, 1999, 2000) variously analyze the relationship between Habermas' theory and the task of writing after Auschwitz. Müller's (2000) study of postwar Germany highlights Habermas' pivotal, both progressive and ambivalent, role in the political struggle over national history, memory, and identity.

Besides consulting intellectual biographies of other thinkers, I had no models to follow in this undertaking, except what Habermas suggests about his life and work in published interviews. In this same general regard I benefited, but only indirectly, from my earlier conversations with him (Matuštík 1993, xv, 259–64; 2000, 339f.) as well as from my Fulbright Ph.D. studies with him in Frankfurt between 1989 and 1991. While I would be eager to learn from reading Habermas' intellectual autobiography, I did not want to write a standard biography either. (One reason why I was sorry that Habermas withdrew from the volume planned on him in the Library of Living Philosophers, edited by Lewis E. Hahn [see 2000], is the fact that all books in this distinguished series open with rather extensive intellectual autobiographies by invited thinkers writing in the maturity of their years.) As I worked without much outside help—save for encouragement or the occasional question from friends, 'how is the book?'—in my solitude facing the blank 'canvas' for Habermas' portrait, I was left in the end with the title 'philosophical-political profiles' that he gives to the book of sketches about his contemporaries (PpP). To be sure, I could only borrow that title.

In this philosophical-political profile, I undertake a study of the relationship between Habermas as a thinker and the defining experiences of his life, and between Habermas as a social theorist and his engagements in the present age. *Reading and writing existentially* about Habermas is not the same thing as *deriving a normative theory* from his *oeuvre*. The former attests to pervasive motives and core intuitions in the temporal trajectory of his *authoring*, the latter justifies the architectonic structures of his theoretical and political *authorship*. By keeping in mind the distinctness of these two methodologies—one focusing on authoring and the other on authorship—the reader will be able to keep at bay worries about the *naturalistic fallacy* (justifying Habermas' theory from the bare facts of his life) or about the *inductive problem* (arriving at a normative theory by gathering together an aggregate of experiential profiles). That we can discern and articulate some essential (eidetic, universal) structures within the dramatic profile variations (attending to patterns of life situations, experiences, and acts) does not, however, justify the charge of fallacy. On the contrary, I will establish an intelligible and communicable link, a lived coherence of a wholesome portrait, between Habermas' authoring and the structure of his authorship. The form of my approach and the substance of this study vouch for and become accountable to each other, both in their complementarity and in their mutual attestation and critical reconstruction.

I begin the chronology of events in 1871 and end it in 2000. Habermas is born on June 18, 1929. The dramatic line of his life, as staged in this profile, begins somewhere in 1944–1945, his early teens, and vanishes beyond 2000, the year in which this book ends but his and *our* lives continue. My integrative staging instructions for viewing Habermas' profile aim to place the observation platform in such a way that would allow one to move along with the dramatic axis of Habermas' evolving self-understanding.

Structural Axis: Profiles, Interventions, and Authorship

The structural axis refers to the historical, political, and philosophical contexts of dramatization. These dramaturgical notes provide helpful background references for understanding the encounters that shape the generational profiles and interventions during Habermas' life, and his philosophical-political profile in particular. Historically, Habermas is a key representative of the second postwar generation of what was at first known as the *Institute for Social Research* (IfS), later popularly granted a group name, the *Frankfurt School*, and what generally continues to be subsumed under the philosophical-political category of *Critical Theory*. Politically, there are waves of engagement and disengagements of the IfS members with the present age. Philosophically, we may distinguish stages or orientations, rather than generations or engagements, of Critical Theory.

In terms of *Habermas' historical context,* following Albrecht et al. (1999, chap. 14), I distinguish throughout the book three postwar generations of Germans: securing, skeptical, and protesting. It should be noted at the outset that 'generation' is a sociological term and that it can neither ascribe collective guilt nor exonerate individuals by depicting them as members of a generational cohort (see Mannheim 1993; Müller 2000, 6–10). There are other postwar generations—such as "members of a generation-in-between (or *Zaungäste*) who were too young for '68, still steeped in the sometimes nasty radical student politics of the 1970s, and too old for the relatively apolitical mid-to-late 1980s" (Müller 2000, 223), or the post-1989 "Berlin Generation" (259)—that do not form a central focus of my narrative. It is rather Habermas' skeptical generation (6–12, 37, 43, 48, 59, 63, 251, 259–65) that occupies the main dramatic stage of the book.

Habermas belongs to the skeptical generation of those who were too young to be soldiers or adult members of the Nazi apparatus during World War II but who, as teenagers, were old enough to be existentially affected by the events, their upbringing, and even by identifications they were compelled to assume during the war. This ambivalent intergenerational situation fosters, as the major generational sensibility, ongoing skepticism and distance toward inherited traditions. In all these regards, even by his own admission, Habermas is a typical example of his generation. His teacher, Adorno, and Adorno's coworker, Horkheimer, as well as Heidegger and Habermas' doctoral directors and parents, all belong to the preceding, securing generation. After 1945 this generation's dominant sensibility was to salvage what was left as valuable out of the debris of national and personal destruction. This cautious, restorative trend manifests itself very differently among the perpetrators of Nazism than it does among its victims. In any regard, Marcuse stands to be a generational exception to the securing preoccupation, running ahead to the protesting youth instead. In 1964 Habermas already holds a professorship in Frankfurt, and thus the first wave of his students belongs to the protesting generation of the 1960s. This protesting youth (Albrecht et al. 1999, 34f.), and not his later students or those from the last Frankfurt period between 1982 and 1994 (Critchley and Schroeder 1998, 407–13), form the representatives of the third generation of critical theorists and activists that recognizes Marcuse as the intellectual and generational 'father' of the worldwide student movement in the 1960s. The youth of the 1960s confronted the two postwar generations and their institutional investments with great intensity. While two key theoretical and activist student leaders, Hans-Jürgen Krahl (also Adorno's student) from Frankfurt and Rudi Dutschke from Berlin, died still young after the 1960s, other famous members of their generation (e.g., Joschka Fischer) partake at the turn of the twentieth century in the Red-Green coalitional government of unified Germany. Some of Marcuse's most distinguished U.S. students should be placed within this third generation, including Angela Davis, Andrew Feenberg, David Ingram, and Doug Kellner. The fourth and fifth generations of critical social theorists include those students of Habermas who, like myself, passed barely into their teens by 1969 and yet were formed under the impact of those rebellious years and shaped the later new social movements. (Axel Honneth, one of Habermas' talented postdoctoral assistants, filled the Frankfurt post of his mentor after 1994.) The fourth and even fifth generations of critical social theorists at the turn of the twentieth century encompass students of Habermas' students.

The *Institute for Social Research* (IfS) was founded in the early 1920s in Frankfurt, but it was neither known nor did it understand itself as a school at that time. It became recognized as the *Frankfurt School* only after its postwar return to Frankfurt from exile in the United States in 1949, and even then it was not truly known as a school until 1965, when Marcuse called it specifically by this name in his birthday praise for Horkheimer's founding role in its establishment (Albrecht et al. 1999, 32f.; cf. chaps. 7, 14). As with many such names (e.g., existentialism or postmodernism), the *Frankfurt School* is a retrospectively applied, in this instance geographical, label for certain philosophical and political orientations that emerged into greater focus over time. The historical context of what came to be designated as the 'Frankfurt School' runs from its incipience in the 'Café Marx' (168) in the Weimar Republic of the 1920s–1930s; develops into a pessimistic outlook under the impact of failed socialist revolutions and the victory of Fascism in World War II; severs its ties with radical prewar origins after returning from its U.S. exile into the cautious restorative Cold War climate of the FRG; then renews those radical ties with its inceptive sensibilities of the 1920s under the impact of the 1960s revolt and with Marcuse's rise to international prominence; and finally since the 1970s undergoes its transformation and worldwide reception thanks to Habermas' innovations, public involvement, and the great number of his productive students around the globe. The members of this history are more diverse than would allow any of them—even if only all students of Habermas were gathered here—to form a unified school of thought (30–35).

Habermas' political context parallels the historical stages of the IfS: its founding, its U.S. exile, its return to the FRG, its radical renewal in the 1960s, and its transformations after the 1970s. But the political context of this study is anchored dramatically in the key events that determine Habermas' situations, public interventions, and philosophical thinking: the defeat of Nazi Germany (liberation), the Cold War period of the 1950s (restoration), the student revolt of the 1960s (from incubation to revolt), the historical debates of the 1970s and 1980s (revisions), the fall of the Berlin Wall in 1989 (hope), and the post-Wall era (revisions). These political events function as the specific lenses through which to approach Habermas' political and philosophical development and understand his profile. Significant for evaluating Habermas' evolving public involvement become the contrasts between the radical vision of the early period of the IfS and its conservative turn during the Cold War period, between the student renewal of this early radicalism in the 1960s and Habermas' struggle against the revisionist trends that follow up to the present. I situate Habermas in each political context (1950s, 1960s, etc.) and refer later contexts back to the earlier ones (e.g., 1980s to 1950s) to get a more fine-tuned angle of vision. This context furnishes likewise a contrasting matrix against which to view the major political bottlenecks: the trauma of 1945, the discontents of 1968, the ambivalence of 1989. In an overarching political structure, if 1949 signifies the *institutional founding* of the Federal Republic of Germany and, with Horkheimer's and Adorno's return to Germany in the same year, the rebirth of the *Frankfurt School* that significantly contributed to the grounding of the state; then the rebellious years of 1967–1969 mark the *intellectual grounding* of the FRG and the radical rebirth of the *Frankfurt School*'s origins (Albrecht et al. 1999, 14–20). Coming to terms with the Nazi past—with its ongoing waves of trauma and discontents—retains the structural character of a political leitmotif or 'chorus' from 1945 to the present. Not even the 1968ers in the post-1998 German government seem to be out of reach of the shadows of that past (12f.).

Habermas' philosophical context is provided by the stages of 'theory' that inform the term 'Critical Theory'. Concerning terminology, I refer to *Critical Theory* when speaking specifically of the various intellectual phases of the IfS, the *Frankfurt School*, and the innovations introduced by Habermas. I will use *critical social theory* when speaking more broadly about an early and present philosophical orientation or a movement, without regard to its precise geography or genealogy. I am willing to expand that broader term to encompass some literary critical theory, at least insofar as the latter shares with the early *Frankfurt School*'s or the Marcusean origins in the 1960s an interest in multifaceted dimensions of liberation (anticolonial, gay, ecological, or women's liberation struggles). Albrecht et al. (1999, 35; cf. 25–30) use a convention in German that allows them to distinguish "Critical Theory" from "critical theory." The distinction between the prevalence of the latter (broader movement) in the 1930s–1940s and again the 1960s, and the canonization of the former (school) in the 1950s and against the horizon of the 1960s, parallels my usage in the book. I locate Habermas on the border between continuing the tradition of Critical Theory, where he occupies the place of an heir of the *Frankfurt School* tradition assigned to him by worldwide recognition of his accomplishments, and becoming a social theorist in his own rank who often situates himself outside of that very inheritance. This book stands at the crossroads of a *new critical theory* (to which I refer in chapter 9)—between Habermas as a twentieth-century political thinker in a distinct tradition of Critical Theory and the future prospects of critical social theory.

In a philosophical genealogy, I distinguish six main stages of theory on its way to becoming 'critical'. First, there is the Kantian critique of the conditions of the possibility of experience. In setting limits to reason from within its own resources (distinguishing its value spheres of science, morality and law, and aesthetics), one can learn to know what can be apprehended rationally and what can lead thought to unresolvable contradictions (antinomies). Second, Hegel searched for the historical conditions of the possibility of experience and made it difficult to tune one's rational instruments apart from attending to the rational whole of the cultural, social, and political institutions that form our very experience and thought. Hegel's 'critical theory' becomes a phenomenology of historical experience and a critique of its developmental conditions of possibility. Third, Marx studied the political economy of institutions and concept formations. Kant's critique of rational contradictions and Hegel's critique of the historical shapes of human understanding give way to Marx's critique of ideology. Genuine Marxian theory must be emancipatory, and in that sense philosophy yields to the concrete revolutionary praxis of those who can bring about social liberation. Fourth, liberation not only failed where it was promised (Soviet Union) or not only did not happen where it was supposed to take place (western democracies), but also those who are oppressed participate in their very enslavement (workers, colonized peoples, women). Classical Marxist theory provided no explanation for these depth dimensions of unfreedom. Western Marxists, such as Korsch, Lukács, Gramsci, or Sartre, theorized a more robust critique of this reified, self-enchaining consciousness. Fifth, the early movement of *critical social theory* arose as an amalgam of radical critique that learned from western Marxism as much as from Weber's, Nietzsche's, Freud's, and, I would add, Kierkegaard's, criticisms of self-deceiving forms of consciousness. Early critical social theorists of the 1920s and 1930s—Adorno, Benjamin, Horkheimer, and Marcuse among them—at the same time eschewed the dogmatic Soviet Marxism or the vanguardism of the Communist Party, but did so without giving up the liberation intent of radical social theory. Sixth, the path that begins as a movement and the IfS—from the 1920s to the World War II years in U.S. exile, to the restorative years of Critical Theory in the 1950s and 1960s under Horkheimer's and

Adorno's codirectorship of the IfS, to the renewal of the wider movement of social criticism in the 1960s with Marcuse in dominance, and finally to Habermas' ascendance as a key representative of both the movement and the inheritance of the tradition, from the late 1970s up to the present vantage point of the turn of the century—represents four stages internal to the genealogy of Critical Theory and the *Frankfurt School*.

As the main markers of the four internal developments within this sixth stage of critical social theory as a movement and Critical Theory as a tradition, I list the following key texts: Horkheimer's ([1937] 1972) classic that introduces the concept of Critical Theory and distinguishes it from Traditional Theory and Marcuse's "Philosophy and Critical Theory"* (1988, 134–58; written also in 1937); Horkheimer and Adorno's ([1944] 1987) fragments of critical social theory, namely, their gloomy diagnosis and prognosis for the present age in the 1940s; Marcuse's ([1964] 1991) critique of late industrial society; and Habermas' linguistic-communicative grounding of democratic social theory (TCA and FuG). In this last transformation of Critical Theory, Habermas exercises tremendous impact on its third and even more so its fourth and fifth postwar generations.

The Performative Inside and Outside of the Profile

In chapters that are devoted to Habermas' core situations and interventions (Parts One and Two), even when speaking of his action or positions taken prior to the present moment, I deliberately use *the historical present tense*. The purpose in setting the motion in this tense is not to grant those events and positions a problematic universality or some mythic quality, as if Habermas were a fictional character, like Hamlet, uttering dialogues and soliloquies in a timeless classic. I admit that this tense usage does imbue the presented events in the book with dramatic (if not a journalistic or motion picture) quality. If the historical present tense can comfortably accompany a photograph chronicle of 1968 (Ali and Watkins 1998), then the text about those or other events can bear witness to another, even though no author or dramaturge can live in another's mind and heart. At a second remove from actual events, where I stand vis-à-vis Habermas' skeptical generation, in the mode and style of a dramatic documentary, I want to communicate the living quality of his philosophical-political profile.

I found the present historical tense inviting for one more reason: I had in mind that reader—whether or not he or she is a critical social theorist, whether or not sharing Habermas' Left-liberalism or someone else's socialist critique of it, whether or not holding a more conservative position than either of the two—would be moved to personal engagement with the themes and events unfolded here. The emphasized *we* refers to the real as well as imagined community of readers and viewers of this profile. After all, even if the thinker were not alive at the time of this writing, as Habermas is, his past would not need to be considered closed for *us*. In writing this book, I was not interested in producing another commentary on Habermas, not even a year-by-year historical account. What motivated me in my work was to attest to the past and present of Critical Theory in order to rescue *our* future for a *new critical theory*. This book is in a crucial sense very much about *us* and *our* hope beyond the threshold of the twentieth century.

In the chronology that follows this introduction, I list the most significant years and events that give rise to the key formative situations in Habermas' still-living narrative. Each situation creates a cluster with preceding and consequent events. Accordingly, each cluster has one or more core events with a temporally circular, rather than temporally linear, retrospective-prospective movement of surrounding events. These key situations do not necessarily provide a final or definitive periodization of formative events and influences in Habermas' life. Their narrative account does, however, capture the ongoing preoccupations around which his thinking stabilizes or to which he repeatedly returns. The prologue to his life situations contains wider events preceding his biological birth and the first fourteen years of his youth. The curtain of the book opens with Habermas awakening from his living nightmare.

I would like to thank executive editor Steve Wrinn, editor in chief Jon Sisk, and general series editors Kenneth Deutsch and Jean Bethke Elstain for their enthusiastic support of this project, as well as Chrisona Schmidt for copyediting the book manuscript with superb professional skill and personal care. I am very grateful to close friends and associates for their unwavering encouragement. While no part of this book includes a reprint of my previous work, some ideas and formulations from the book informed my "The Critical Theorist as Witness: Habermas and the Holocaust," which appeared in Lewis Edwin Hahn, ed., *Perspectives on Habermas* (2000). I wrote that chapter after completing the book manuscript, even though the former was published before the appearance of the latter.

CHRONOLOGY: HABERMAS' FORMATIVE SITUATIONS AND INTERVENTIONS IN RETROSPECTIVE GLANCE

PROLOGUE

1871–90	Otto von Bismarck's *Deutsches Reich* (German empire).
1914	World War I begins.
1917	The Russian Bolshevik Revolution begins.
1918	World War I ends. The Weimar Republic is established. Horkheimer, Marcuse, and Pollock participate in the failed November Revolution in Germany.
1919	Rosa Luxemburg is murdered.
1922	The idea of founding the IfS is conceived by Felix J. Weil, with a memorandum of its founding issued by Kurt Albert Gerlach. Horkheimer receives a Ph.D., his dissertation on Kant.
1923	IfS is officially affiliated with the Frankfurt University. Marcuse receives a Ph.D., his dissertation on the *Künstlerroman*.
1924	June 22, Carl Grünberg dedicates the new IfS building in Frankfurt a/M. Adorno receives a Ph.D., his dissertation on Husserl's phenomenology.
1929	Habermas is born on June 18 in Düsseldorf and brought up in Gummersbach. Grandfather is a Protestant minister and a director of the seminary in Gummersbach. Father, Dr. Ernst Habermas, directs the Bureau of Trade and Industry in Gummersbach. Chair of social philosophy is established for Horkheimer at the Frankfurt University. Marcuse begins postdoctoral studies with Husserl and Heidegger in Freiburg.

1931   January 24, Horkheimer is officially inaugurated as the new director of IfS.
1932   Heidegger rejects Marcuse's *Habilitation* work on Hegel; with Husserl's intervention, Marcuse is recommended to Horkheimer who, with Adorno, admits him to join IfS in Geneva.
1933   January 30, the *Drittes Reich* of National Socialists under Adolf Hitler.
Habermas is four when the Nazis seize power.
March, IfS is closed down, library is confiscated by the Nazis; Horkheimer, followed by Leo Lowenthal, Marcuse, and others, flees to Geneva.
1939   Habermas is ten when the criminal world still appears 'normal'.

FROM LIBERATION TO RESTORATION (1945–1959)

The key event: May 8, 1945, Nazi Germany is defeated, when Habermas is fifteen.

1944–45   Habermas is about fifteen when he joins the Hitler Youth and is ordered to assist at western defenses.
1945   May 8, Germany is liberated from the Nazi regime: Habermas views the Holocaust film documentaries and the Nuremberg Tribunal proceedings.

The key event: July 25, 1953, Habermas parts with Martin Heidegger.

1945–49   Gymnasium studies: Habermas reads early Marx, Engels, Sartre (dramas).
1947   Group 47 is founded—a loose organization of progressive writers promoting new German literature.
1949   The first government of FRG is established under Chancellor Konrad Adenauer.
July, Horkheimer obtains a schair in social philosophy in Frankfurt a/M.
1949–54   Habermas studies at universities in Göttingen, Bonn, and Zurich; he reads Heidegger, Lukács, Marx, Sartre (philosophy), de Beauvoir.
1950   August, Horkheimer becomes the director of the renewed IfS.
1951   November 20, Horkheimer becomes rector of Johann Wolfgang Goethe University, Frankfurt a/M.
1951–53   Early student movement occurs against Veit Harlan's films about the Nazi period.

1952	January 9, student parliament of the Frankfurt University issues explanation entitled *About the Attitude toward the Jews*. Horkheimer praises the students.
1953	June 17, uprising occurs against the Soviet regime in GDR. "Mit Heidegger gegen Heidegger denken."
1954	Habermas writes his Ph.D. dissertation on Schelling, Bonn University, under the direction of Erich Rothacker.
1955	Adorno becomes Horkheimer's codirector of the IfS.
1956	Habermas attends Freud lectures in Frankfurt, discovers Marcuse's early essays.
1956–59	Habermas is Adorno's first assistant at the IfS: reads Adorno, Bloch, Benjamin, Durkheim, Horkheimer, Marx, Parsons, Weber.
1957	"Literaturbericht zur philosophischen Diskussion um Marx und den Marxismus."
1957–59	'Kampf dem Atomtod': antinuclear movement.
1958	May 20, "Unruhe, erste Bürgerpflicht" (Habermas speaks in front of 400 students in Frankfurt a/M in support of the antinuclear movement). September 27, Horkheimer criticizes Habermas' reception of Marx in a nine-page private letter to Adorno; Habermas departs from Frankfurt's IfS.
1959	Habermas works on his second doctorate with Abendroth in Marburg. Christmas, anti-Semitic acts of defamation occur in Köln. Adorno takes over the directorship of the IfS.
1959–60	Horkheimer responds to the wave of anti-Semitic events with fear and increasing pessimism and resignation.

FROM INCUBATION TO REVOLT (1960–1969)

The key events: 1964, Marcuse's One-Dimensional Man *published; November 1966, the Grand Coalition formed.*

1961	Habermas becomes *Privatdozent* in Marburg. Adolf Eichmann goes on trial in Jerusalem. August 13, construction begins on the Berlin Wall. *Student und Politik*. Fanon's *Wretched of the Earth* with Sartre's preface (French).
1962	Habermas is named Extraordinary Professor of Philosophy in Heidelberg.

	December 12, protest occurs against the *Spiegel* affair by Heidelberg professors.
	Strukturwandel der Öffentlichkeit (second doctorate or *Habilitation*).
1963	The Auschwitz trial.
	The end of Konrad Adenauer era: Ludwig Erhard is elected chancellor of FRG.
1964	Habermas succeeds Horkehimer as professor of philosophy and sociology.
	Marcuse's *One-Dimensional Man* is first published in English.
	December, 800 students arrested at a sit-in in Berkeley, California.
1965	May 7, the rector of Berlin's Free University bans a student event sponsored for the twentieth anniversary of the German defeat in 1945.
	June 28, "Knowledge and Human Interests," Habermas' Frankfurt inaugural lecture.
	Marcuse's "Repressive Tolerance" is first published in English.
1966	Kurt Georg Kiesinger is elected chancellor of FRG.
	Adorno's *Negative Dialectics* is published in German.
	Marcuse's "Repressive Tolerance" appears in German.
	Fanon's *Wretched of the Earth* with Sartre's preface appears in German.
	May 22, Vietnam—Analysis of a Model, a Frankfurt conference, is held with Habermas, Marcuse, and Negt as participants, followed by a massive anti–Vietnam War demonstration.
	June 23, first sit-in protest of 3,000 students in West Germany occurs against repressive measures at Berlin's Free University.
	November, the Grand Coalition of SPD with CDU/CSU is formed.

The key event: June 2, 1967, Benno Ohnesorg is shot by the Berlin police.

1967	May, Marcuse's *One-Dimensional Man* is published in German.
	May 7, Horkheimer at the opening of the German-American Friendship Week shows himself side by side with a U.S. general. In the evening at *America-Haus*, Horkheimer criticizes the anti–Vietnam War protest from the position of someone liberated by the Allies. SDS accuses him of making an apologetic for Fascism.
	June 2, the Germanist student Benno Ohnesorg is fatally wounded in an anti-shah student demonstration.
	June 5–6, Adorno declares his sympathy for Ohnesorg at the start of his classes.
	June 9, Habermas and Berlin's student leader, Rudi Dutschke, speak at the Hannover congress, "Hochschule und Demokratie"; in a question to Dutschke, Habermas warns against student 'actionism', i.e., 'Left Fascism'.

July 7, Adorno's lecture in Berlin is disturbed; one poster reads: "Berlin Leftist Fascists greet Teddy, the classicist." He departs to Frankfurt before Marcuse's arrival in Berlin.

July 10–13, at Berlin's Free University, in four lectures, Marcuse speaks of "the natural right" of the oppressed to resist ("Repressive Tolerance," 116). In the *Spiegel* journal, Dutschke defends student council democracy (Wiggershaus 1989, 692; 1998, 624).

November 4–8, the SDS conference is held in Frankfurt a/M. November 5, keynote address is given on the Organization of the protest by Dutschke and Krahl.

1968

February 17–18, anti–Vietnam War protests occur in Berlin; Dutschke is the main speaker.

February 25, Heinrich Lübke, Christian Democrat president of the FRG, must resign after his signature on the architect plan for a Nazi camp is revealed.

April 8, assassination attempt is made on Dutschke by Joseph Bachmann, followed by the Easter anti–Springer Press campaign throughout FRG.

May 3, Daniel Cohn-Bendit addresses the student rally at the Sorbonne.

May 10–11, the "Night of the Barricades" occurs in Paris.

May 13, one-million-strong march and general strike occurs in Paris.

May 29, right-wing demonstrators in Paris chant "France for the French," "Cohn-Bendit to Dachau" (Ali and Watkins 1998, 105).

May 31, Sartre interviews Cohn-Bendit and affirms that the protesting students extend the very field of possibility.

May 27–31, SDS calls for a general strike against the proposed state-of-emergency laws; students occupy the rector's offices in Frankfurt.

May 28–30, students rename the Frankfurt University as Karl Marx University. Political University is formed with teach-ins and twenty-three new seminars.

May 30, 6 A.M., at the request of the rector and mayor, 200 special police units come to clear out about thirty students; the police occupy the university. The legislation of emergency laws is passed by a vote of 384 to 100 (Kraushaar 1998, 1:340).

June 1, "Five Theses on the Direction and Aims of the Student Movement": Habermas' critique of the SDS is given at an evening presentation as a part of a two-day student conference at the Frankfurt University's Mensa.

August 21, the Soviet invasion of Czechoslovakia: Bloch, Habermas, Heller, Marcuse, and others, while at the Korčula summer school, issue three protest letters to Tito, Brezhnev, and the general public. September 22, Cohn-Bendit, Fischer, and Krahl are arrested at Frankfurt, where they were protesting the German publishers' Peace Award *(Friedenspreis)* being given to Senegalese President Senghor.

September 23, Authorities and Revolution, Haus Gallus, is the last constructive exchange between Critical Theorists Adorno, Habermas, and Friedeburg and student leaders Cohn-Bendit and Krahl (Kraushaar 1998, 1:28).

December 8-9, students take over Frankfurt's Sociology Department, rename it the "Spartacus Seminar"(Department), declare an active strike, and demand structural reforms of university education. December 18, 5 A.M., three police transports and one water cannon come to clear the Spartacus Department at Mylius Street 30.

Antworten auf Herbert Marcuse is edited and introduced by Habermas.

1969

January 24, the students again occupy rooms and administrative offices of the Sociology Department.

January 31, the entire department is closed in fear of further student protests; at that point the students move to the IfS next door. Adorno and Friedeburg call the police. Seventy-six students are detained; all but Adorno's former doctoral student, Krahl, are released; he is charged with breaking in and trespassing.

March, Gustav Heinemann becomes the federal president. Willy Brandt is elected chancellor of FRG.

April 22, Adorno's lectures are disrupted by, among others, female students who expose their breasts.

May 15–30, California Governor Ronald Reagan uses armed police and National Guard units to clear students from the People's Park in Berkeley.

July 18, twenty-six-year-old Krahl has a court hearing; Adorno is the main witness.

September, Chancellor Willy Brandt's socialist-liberal coalition wins election to the Bundestag; period of "greater democracy" and reforms begins (Wiggershaus 1989, 704f.; 1998, 635f.).

January 24–August 6, Adorno and Marcuse conduct intense correspondence about the student movement.

August 6, Adorno dies in Switzerland.

August 13, 2,000 people attend Adorno's funeral.

September 12, in an essay for Adorno's sixty-sixth birthday, Habermas criticizes Krahl.

Protestbewegung und Hochschulreform (Kleine politische Schriften, I–IV).

1970	February 14, Krahl dies in a car accident. March, SDS officially dissolves.

FROM REVISION TO HOPE AND BACK AGAIN (1970–2000)

The key event: 1977, "German Autumn" and the conservative turn

1971	Habermas leaves Frankfurt and, with Carl Friedrich von Weizsäcker, directs the Max Planck Institut in Starnberg.
1972	January, loyalty checks are instituted for state employees. December, Basic Treaty is made between FRG and GDR.
1974	Helmut Schmidt is elected chancellor of FRG.
1975	April 9, Habermas and Dutschke meet for the first time since 1967.
1977	April 7, Siegfried Buback is murdered by the Red Army Faction (RAF). June 30, Jürgen Ponto is killed by RAF. September 5–October 19, Hanns Martin Schleyer is kidnapped and murdered by RAF.
1979	*Stichworte zur "Geistigen Situation der Zeit"* (ed.). July 29, Marcuse (1898–1979) dies in Starnberg after his last visit with Habermas. December 24, Dutschke (1940–1979) dies.
1980	January 4, Habermas eulogizes Dutschke. Habermas receives the Adorno Prize from the city of Frankfurt.
1981	October 10, protests take place against stationing cruise missiles and Pershing 2 rockets in FRG. *Kleine politische Schriften, I–IV*.
1982	Habermas returns to Frankfurt as professor of philosophy and sociology. Helmut Kohl is elected chancellor of FRG.
1983	April 4, Habermas, in his first lecture in Frankfurt after returning there, distinguishes the roles of science and politics, the core polemic with the student movement. September, Habermas defends nonviolent civil disobedience at the forum of SPD: the era is compared to the "autumn of 1977." November 22, the high point of anti-NATO demonstrations is reached.
1985	May 5, Reagan provokes the Bitburg cemetery debacle. May 17, "Entsorgung der Vergangenheit." *Die neue Unübersichtlichkeit (Kleine politische Schriften, V)*.
1986	June 6, *Römerberggesprächen*, "Politische Kultur—heute?" June 7, Habermas begins the first round of the Historians' Debate.

1987	Copenhagen's Sonning's Prize: lecture on Kierkegaard.
	Eine Art Schadesabwicklung (Kleine politische Schriften, VI).
1988	*Nachmetaphysischses Denken*.

The key event: November 9, 1989, the fall of the Berlin Wall

1989	The Soviet postwar occupation of East and Central Europe collapses dramatically.
1990	*Die nachholende Revolution (Kleine politische Schriften, VII)*.
	March 30, "Der DM-Nationalismus."
	September 12, "2 + 4 Treaty"—the final settlement of World War II: terms of German unification are signed by the World War II Allies.
	October 3, the unification of East and West Germany.
	December 2, first all-German elections are held since the fall of the Weimar Republic in 1933. Kohl is reelected chancellor of unified Germany.

The key event: January 16–March 3, 1991, the Persian Gulf War

1991	February 8, "Ein Plädoyer für Zurückhaltung, aber nicht gegenüber Israel."
	September, a second "German Autumn" (attacks on foreigners in Germany).
	Vergangenheit als Zukunft (interviews).
1992	*Faktizität und Geltung*.
	November 9, lecture, "Die zweite Lebenslüge der Bundesrepublik."
1993	May 28, "Die Festung Europa und das neue Deutschland."
1994	Habermas retires from Frankfurt.
	"Struggles for Recognition."
1995	May 8, lecture, "1989 in the Shadow of 1945."
	Die Normalität einer Berliner Republik (Kleine politische Schriften, VIII).
	February 13, Detlef Claussen remembers Krahl on the twenty-fifth anniversary of his death.
1996	*Die Einbeziehung des Anderen*.
1997	"On the Public Use of History: Why a 'Democracy Prize' for Daniel Goldhagen?"
1998	Helmut Kohl's government defeated in the all-German elections.
	Gerhard Schröder is elected chancellor; and the one-time '68er "Sponti," Fischer, becomes the foreign minister.
	October 8, "Es gibt doch Alternativen!"
	October 11, Martin Walser receives the German publishers' Friedenspreis.
	Die postnationale Konstellation.

The key event: 1999, March 24–June 20, NATO's intervention against Serbia in the war over Kosovo/a (bombing suspended June 10)

1999	March 31, "Der Zeigefinger: Die Deutschen und ihr Denkmal."
	April 29, "Bestialität und Humanität: Ein Krieg an der Grenze zwischen Recht und Moral."
	May 18, "Zweifellos: Eine Antwort auf Peter Handke."
	July, Sloterdijk's lecture at the Bavarian castle in Elmau, "Regeln für den Menschenpark" (published September 16).
	September 2, Thomas Assheuer, "Das Zarathustra-Projekt."
	September 6, Reinhard Mohr, "Züchter der Übermenschen."
	September 9, Peter Sloterdijk, "Die Kritische Theorie ist tot."
	Wahrheit und Rechtfertigung.
2000	June, Erich Nolte receives the Konrad-Adenauer-Preis.
	June 29, Kohl, who is charged with illegal financial dealings, compares his plight to that of the Jews under Hitler.
	Fall quarter, "Kierkegaard's Ethics." Habermas teaches a seminar, Studies in Contemporary Philosophy, at Northwestern University, Chicago.

Note: I list here Habermas' formative situations and his writings only insofar as they arise from or relate to formative events. See the references for a full bibliography of Habermas' works cited.

Part One

SITUATIONS

What does it mean to become contemporary with Habermas' work and questions in relation to the existential and sociopolitical upheavals of his life's journey? In order to understand his thought, I will begin with his core questions. But to become contemporary with such questions, it is important to grasp the core situations that Habermas faces as a result of the defining upheavals of his life. When certain events play a formative role, their situations become the pacemakers of key existential and sociopolitical concerns.

In Part One, I focus on three key situation clusters that give rise to Habermas' defining orientations. These clusters are not neatly defined, even in terms of the years that they span; rather, each cluster is governed by the dominant contradictions or tensions of that era:

- the years of liberation and restoration (1945–1959)
- the years of incubation and revolt (1960–1969)
- the years of revision, hope, and renewed revision (1970–2000)

The angle from which I approach this dimension of questioning in Part One is given by Habermas' formative situations as outlined in the chronology that follows the introduction. In Part Two, the angle will shift to the question of how Habermas' defining situations contribute to forming his philosophical-political profile. The focus on Habermas' defining existential and sociopolitical situations will give way to his interventions: How does Habermas respond to his key situations—formative years, events, and influences? By establishing a link between existential and sociopolitical situations (Part One) and the active formation of a philosophical-political profile (Part Two), I show the emergence of a significant relation between their complementary core questions.

Chapter One

FROM LIBERATION TO RESTORATION, 1945–1959

NAZI GERMANY DEFEATED, HABERMAS AT FIFTEEN, MAY 8, 1945

I am . . . ambivalent because I have the impression that something is deeply amiss in the rational society in which I grew up and in which I now live. On the other hand, I have also retained something else from the experience of 1945 and after, namely that things got better. Things really got rather better. One must use that as a starting-point too; and I then go on to look for a prehistory which is too lightly disposed of with the concept of 'Enlightenment'. (NU 203f./AS 126)

What really determined my political views was the year 1945. At that point the rhythm of my personal development intersected with the great historical events of the time. . . . These experiences undoubtedly helped develop motifs which then further determined my thinking. (KPS 511/AS 77)

Gummersbach, where Habermas spends his youth and early school years, was a small provincial German town during World War II. Events connected with the war do not seem to directly invade Habermas' formative years in the German province. On the contrary, as a schoolboy, he enjoys a rather sheltered life. He is somewhat protected from the ravages and ambivalences of the war by his age. Habermas is only four when the Nazis seize power in 1933, and he is ten in 1939 at the peak of the criminal Nazi world, which to him still appears then to be part of daily normality. He leads an existence very much shielded from the horrors of the Nazi regime by the ordinary ways of conventional town life (KPS 511/AS 77). Most of all, he is individualized through socialization in the generally conformist or—to use Habermas' own description of his father's attitude—*sympathetic* relation of his own family to the Nazi powers that be. "My father . . . was certainly only considered to be a passive sympathizer" (i.e., *Mitläufer,* literally, a fellow traveler; NR 23/AS 231). In his parents' generation of Germans, one went along to get along and to survive: "The political climate in our family home was probably not unusual for the time. It was marked by a bourgeois adaptation to a political situation with which one did not fully identify, but which one didn't fully criticize either" (KPS 511/AS 77). This very pervasiveness of adaptation to the Nazi regime made the postwar de-Nazification of German culture and its educational institutions difficult.

Habermas joins the Hitler Youth toward the end of the war (KPS 512/AS 78). At the time of his recruitment to the main Nazi youth organization for boys, in 1944, he is probably fourteen and going on fifteen.[1] In an interview, Habermas also tells us that he was sent with his cohort to help at the western wall defenses. Anyone in the Hitler Youth in 1944–1945 who was near the Ruhr area would have had an unhappy experience of the ferocious yet losing battle. Given the protection offered by his family, town, and culture, Habermas' boyhood in the Nazi Germany is not out of the ordinary. In joining his school compatriots in the Hitler Youth, he along with others is deceived and, insofar as teenagers do exercise agency, he is also self-deceived, by his individualization through Nazi socialization. His postwar critical relation to tradition in general, and to German history in particular, has its affective origins in the traumatic experience of having been willingly, even if through deception of culture and family upbringing, a member of a criminal organization. The war ends on May 8, 1945. Habermas still recalls how beautiful that spring was! With the suddenness of a storm, the world historical events rush into his world. The trauma of Germany's catastrophe becomes a ground that opens him to a different world.

With this introductory cluster of situations, we can now better locate Habermas within his generation. According to Albrecht et al. (1999), we may distinguish four ideal-typical generational "cohorts" (500) born in Germany between 1900 and 1946. We can place Habermas within the third generation, born between 1926 and 1937. Albrecht calls this ideal type the "skeptical generation" (506) that takes over the educational task of coming to terms with the liability of the preceding generation.[2] The members of this group would have "experienced the end of the war partly [working] as antiaircraft artillery auxiliaries *[Flakhelfer]*, but their childhood and youth belong within the Third Reich and in greater part was still linked with the [Nazi] youth organizations." Habermas' generation thus differs from the preceding "securing generation" of World War II soldiers or adult sympathizers who are born between 1900 and 1925 and who conserve their postwar survival. His generation also differs from the following "protesting generation" (506), born between 1938 and 1946, which before the war's end neither could have made "politically interpretable life decisions" nor could have belonged to the existing Nazi organizations (500). Müller (2000, 7) defines the *Flakhelfergeneration* as "the teenagers drafted out of school at the end of the Second World War to assist in operating anti-aircraft batteries" *(Fliegerabwehrkanone)*. At the end of the war, in 1944, the *Flakhelfer* included most likely boys as young as twelve.

Had Habermas been born a year later, in 1930, he would have belonged within his skeptical cohort to one of its two subgroups, which, being too young to be recruited by the Hitler Youth between 1944 and the beginning of 1945, "itself had no experience of the war front" (504). In two generations—those born shortly before 1900 or between 1900 and 1925 (i.e., before Habermas' own skeptical generation of *Flakhelfer* is born between 1926 and 1937)—Habermas discovers that the great majority of his German philosophy professors, not just the notorious case of Heidegger, followed at some point a path of more or less eager sympathy for, if not direct collaboration with, the Nazis (see Leaman 1993). In the course of Habermas' adult life, we encounter numerous transmutations of the generational confrontations with the Nazi past. Each confrontation is marked by shifts of the main marker of the targeted face of perceived 'Fascism' (tab. 1.1).

A new *existential question* emerges for Habermas at first with the rupture of the cultural normality of his childhood. "Our problems were moral and existential in the first place," he writes, describing at once a social and personal situation that faces his generation (KPS 468/AS 44). From Habermas' own recollections, May 8, 1945, records the first and key time around which he casts a retrospective glance at the years of his early youth. His entire early socialization takes place up to that day under the Nazis and in his early teens; he now witnesses the collapse of the world into which he has been by then socialized.

May 8, 1945, marks what, for the lack of better words, I call *Habermas' existentially motivated birthday*. To be sure, for him, "living in a state of shock at the Nazi atrocities" (KPS 467/AS 43), it would be a peculiar birthday, whose ongoing commemoration of birth begins with and returns to a catastrophe. In a Cartesian turn of sorts, the external rubble of postwar Germany draws Habermas toward the path of self-reflective consciousness. This is thus his *existentially motivated philosophical birthday*. He is critical of the introverted postwar trend insofar as for him the postwar turn to the subject punctuates "our [Germany's] unsociological view of the world" (KPS 486/AS 44). For Habermas, on the other hand, this early move to self-reflection takes on an increasingly post-Cartesian orientation: no inwardness is untouched by the social tragedy, since one has been individualized in this very process of deceptive socialization.

We need to pause at this juncture of 1945 with an earnestness reminiscent of the respect held for the recently deceased and with the keen sensibility that the tragic past must not be closed off to *our* redemptive hope. The caesura of the liberation date signifies both death (Habermas' youthful trauma of Germany's disaster) and birth (Habermas' existential beginnings). One can only guess from today's safe historical distance what contents or emotive charges might have been invested in a memory of the Hitler Youth commanded to the western front. In a published interview, Habermas discloses this memory without any comment whatsoever and

Table 1.1 Transmutations of 'Fascism' in the Generational Confrontations with the Nazi Past

Generational Confrontation	Core Positive Orientation	Targeted Face of 'Fascism'
Horkheimer versus the Nazi past (1948–53)	sympathy for the early student movement (1951–53)	unmasks the Fascism of Veit Harlan's films
Habermas versus the restorative German politics of the 1950s	sympathy for socialist and democratic Left	unmasks the Fascist continuities of Adenauer era
Habermas versus his teachers who were either Nazis or Nazi sympathizers (1950s)	sympathy for Marx, western Marxism, Kierkegaard, Sartre, early Marcuse, and existential thought in general	unmasks the Fascist continuities in Heidegger's thought and acts (1953) and at German universities
Habermas versus the remilitarization and unification of Germany (1957–59), the *Spiegel* affair (1962), and the Grand Coalition (1966)	active support of the antinuclear movement, civil disobedience, the extraparliamentary opposition, and the lawful democratic state	unmasks the Fascist dangers of restorative regime, the politics of power, and a state of emergency imposed on democracy itself
Horkheimer versus Germany's Nazi past (1958–60)	fear of new anti-Semitic acts in Germany, worried about dangers to the IfS	unmasks the perceived dangers of Fascism in the antinuclear movement
the protesting generation of students versus the securing generation of parents (1960s)	the student movement for cultural and sociopolitical change in West Germany; support for Third World struggles	struggle against injustice and the continuity of Fascism in 'democracy' and imperial power politics
the protesting generation of students versus the exiled and securing generation (Adorno and Horkheimer) and the skeptical generation (Habermas) of their teachers (1967–69)	recovery of early critical theory and its integration with the new critical theory of Marcuse (the post-1960s writings); identification with Marcuse as the 'father' of the student movement	critique of the conservative 'democratic turn' of the restorative Critical Theory of the 1950s, of its separating theory from politics, and of its lacking transformative praxis orientation

Table 1.1 *Continued*

Generational Confrontation	Core Positive Orientation	Targeted Face of 'Fascism'
Habermas versus the anarchy of the protesting generation (1967–69)	sympathy with the student movement's unmasking of the entrenched Fascist continuity	fear of 'Left Fascism' (1967); critique of the phantom dimensions of the student movement; Stalinism-Fascism charge (1968–69)
Adorno versus the students (1969)	critical of the not guilty verdict of the police shooting of Benno Ohnesorg	has police clear protesting students from the IfS (January 1969)
Habermas versus the police state (Autumn 1977)	critical of the Red Army Faction terror	unmasks the new police state and defends the Frankfurt School against charges of inspiring terrorism
Habermas versus revisionist German historians (1980s)	appropriates the cultural critique of the student movement from the 1960s	unmasks the apologetics for Fascism by the new historians
Habermas versus new dangers of genocide (1990s)	appeals to the German duties toward the state of Israel (the Persian Gulf War); appeals to learning from the Holocaust (NATO bombing over Kosovo/a)	unmasks the "new faces of Fascism" in Iraq and Yugoslavia; publicly endorses the allied interventions against Iraq and Serbia; calls for restoring international law

as a brute fact of his life. Let us absorb the pregnant meaning of the full sentence: "I was in the Hitler Youth; at fifteen I was sent to man the western defenses" (KPS 512/AS 78). Period. We need not be shocked by this fact, which was so common for healthy and biologically fit German youth—those of his peers who were neither Jewish nor Roma and Sinti (Gypsy) and were not from the targeted dissident families. One could even compare Habermas' early teen memory with another common fact revealed by the 1989 time quake: "I was in the pioneers; and as a Socialist Youth, I was sent to defend Stalin's motherland"—someone could write about this more recent era.

More crucial for us becomes the consideration of the breach punctuated by May 8, 1945, at fifteen, marking Habermas' existential birthday. In Leni Riefenstahl's docudramas of the Third Reich we can witness the portraits of the German boys with cleaned-up haircuts, dressed in "cute" Nazi outfits, frenzied en masse, pledging their body and soul to the *Führer*. Is this portrait also part of Habermas' haunting, since once before self-deceived, memory? Mitscherlich (1975, 211) characterizes the typical depth dimension of adolescence in the Third Reich:

> Organizations associated with the cult of the leader, such as the Hitler Youth and the League of German Girls, met a genuine adolescence need for mutual identification through peer groups. Such mutual identifications give the young a sense of security in rejecting, or at any rate arguing with, their previous models. Moreover, at the time, all this usually took place with the blind agreement of the parents themselves. A mass idol such as Hitler, who to a large extent swept parental standards aside in order to dictate new ones, emanated powerful stimuli towards such group identifications.

From the written record, we can be sure, minimally, of two things: Habermas' wartime memory offers no Archimedean (i.e., asocial) point of inward safety from the traumatic past! This trauma defines the loss of something to which one once pledged one's life; indeed, trauma then means the loss of one's self and self-discovery of one's false self. Because there was such a radical loss, we can truly speak of liberation as an existential birthday. The residual trauma marks the traces of memory of one's willing self-deception.

The skeptical generation, unlike the preceding securing generation that is at first unable to mourn the loss of its superior destiny and great leader (Mitscherlich 1975), lives out its trauma with a pervasive ambivalence toward all acts that require new commitments and carry new risks. Habermas is very much aware of his ongoing radical ambivalence toward everything in life (NU 203f./AS 126). Yet, as he notes on numerous occasions, things do get better during his lifetime. *Traumatic loss* and *redemptive hope*—these are the two temporal dimensions that accompany Habermas on his lifelong journey.

May 8, 1945, signifies likewise Habermas' existentially motivated political birthday. Politically too the ruptured horizon of shared culture inspires Habermas to turn inwardly and self-reflectively to the subject. Yet again, he does so increasingly in a post-Cartesian manner: the inward turning is marked by his deliberate, existentially motivated, and socially communicated self-choice. The liberation of 1945 compels him for the first time to ask what sort of person he is and wants to be and to what sort of world he will dedicate his lifework. His self-choice aims to radically recreate the identity of the first fifteen years of his life. But for someone who has been individualized through socialization in the shadow of the Nazi ideology, an intellectually reflected and existentially motivated philosophical-political birthday cannot be a one-time deal that one celebrates conventionally, with birthday candles or toasts. This fact constitutes part of his complaint: "the intellectual and cultural provincialism we were plunged into by the Nazis was not overcome at a stroke, but relatively slowly" (KPS 470/AS 45). Neither the fifteen-year-old memory, which if anything must be traumatic, nor knowing of a radical discontinuity with those fifteen years can be erased; otherwise Habermas' self-transformation could not motivate his present. Rather, the traumatic memory of a loss, if worked through well, can be integrated into a new individualization through socialization. This individual and cultural questioning of what I or we are and want to be motivates Habermas' lifetime. He integrates the personal-social axis of this radically questioning self-choice. This integration characterizes the existentially motivated, philosophical-political dimensions of his self-adopted identity formation. Müller (2000) calls this integration a "Holocaust identity" (44f., 57, 76, 84f., 95, 119, 143, 246ff., 255f., 269, 273, 277). It is rather pronounced among the members of the skeptical generation. For Müller, this identity formation—precisely because of its universal moral charge, which can at times evolve into blind spots—marks a rather insecure political foundation for a post-Wall future of unified Germany.

The first documentaries about the concentration camps, the reports from the Nuremberg trials of the Nazi war criminals, the very facts of Auschwitz and the Holocaust, neither of these immediate post-1945 events leads to direct face-to-face or heart-to-heart exchanges with the securing generation of Habermas' parents and teachers. That securing generation remains mostly silent during the postwar years; their skeptical children (either because of embarrassment or trauma) do not ask what the parents did or what they failed to do during the war. Not until the 1960s does the unspoken policy of don't ask and don't tell—keeping the Fascist skeletons in the cultural closet—give way to a more direct intergenerational confrontation.

That in 1939 Habermas' ten-year-old world still seems quite normal is not hard to fathom. He does not say much about the impact of the Protestant milieu of his parents and his grandfather, who was a minister and a director of the regional seminary in Gummersbach. But we can trace at least one source of Habermas' ambivalence toward religion directly to this criminal world in which Germany's provincial, cultural Christianity neither provided a buffer to anti-Semitism nor prevented the Holocaust. Indeed, Habermas credits the exiled German-Jewish intellectuals and artists, and not the courage of his parents' generation, for the postwar transformation of thinking and culture in West Germany. His horror at the revelations of the criminal Nazi regime is echoed and even intensified with each new attempt to reestablish Germany's discredited prewar cultural continuity or to revise Germany's liability for the Holocaust. The surviving generation of German-Jewish intellectuals, whether those like Horkheimer and Adorno, who return from exile to teach Habermas and his contemporaries, or Marcuse, who exercises his influence by publishing and working abroad, play a unique position vis-à-vis Germany's traditions. Habermas appears to universalize his characterization of their tragic historical experience (of being rooted within German traditions but not unreflectively of them) into a regulative ideal of self-critical culture. He wants to learn from the German-Jewish experience how to foster a self-critical culture that would support his later political vision of the cosmopolitan world:

> Those who had long been part of German culture, without ever really belonging to it, taught us how to identify with our own, with German traditions, and yet while standing within them, to keep a certain distance from them, which enabled us to continue them in a self-critical spirit, with the skepticism and the clairvoyance of the man who has already once been fooled. (KPS 471/AS 46)

The one person who has already once been fooled by an uncritical individualization through socialization is (which is here implied quintessentially) Habermas before 1945. Furthermore, the generation of his parents and grandparents becomes implicated, even if not directly, in its uncritical identification with those German secular and Christian traditions that contributed to the national catastrophe. Finally, learning from his tragic history by becoming a secondhand witness to the assimilative, exiled, and, indeed, annihilated experience of German-Jewish relations, Habermas formulates later a critical cultural equivalent of this learning.

In his mature social theory, Habermas derives the notions of *posttraditional and postnational identity*—identity formed in reflective distance from one's traditions or national origins—with distinctive help from a Kierkegaardian radical *existential self-choice*. This self-choice defines responsible editing of one's biography, whereby I am asking myself the question, Who am I and who do I want to be as a self? That autobiographical, existential questioning of 1945 provides Habermas with an interpretative framework for his later theoretical examination of *ethical-political discourses* about those traditions we want to keep and those we must jettison. We thus find the model of an open and critical identity formation not only theorized and appropriated by Habermas through existential literature and Kierkegaard in particular, but also in his early considerations of its instantiations within the German-Jewish experience. Habermas embodies what Müller names, a Holocaust identity: a past-oriented horizon of Germany's catastrophe and a future-oriented, more universal striving for a postnational political culture. These two temporal dimensions stand in tension and yet they act as Habermas' bellwether correctives to the twin dangers of insular particularism and abstract universalism (cf. Müller 2000, 45, 76, 255f.).

The character of Habermas' active remembrance—working through the past and hoping for better future—of the historical trauma remains even in his mature writings *postmetaphysical* (see ND), which is another way of saying that ethical and political discourses on our past and future pertain to something lived or existential rather than abstractly speculative. Once one has been fooled by uncritical cultural and religious integrations, the future of neither traditions nor religions can be redeemed in terms of any one tradition or religion. Habermas' specific brand of *methodological atheism* (bracketing unexamined assumptions of theological or religious beliefs in raising critical questions) also has its roots in the shock of 1945. For that reason this sober atheism invokes a messianic-existential moment of redemptive hope: Benjamin's *anamnestic solidarity* with the victims of history (solidarity in remembrance that, and this is its messianic dimension, 'rescues' the past) and Kierkegaard's chosen as well as Marx's sociopolitical responsibility for our shared future. This at once redemptive and critical moment of Habermas' mature social theory reveals how he, still harkening back to his own traumatic memory, tries to hope against hope. We might call his paradoxical hope *dialectical atheism,* that is, a redemptive future orientation of disconsolate religiousness without the theistic guarantees of a religion. He offers one minimal clue for this reading: "How can the legacy of religion be salvaged for the secular world? For the moment we can only say: not *as* a religious legacy" (KPS 489/AS 61). The lived question of how to begin after Auschwitz becomes inevitably motivated by this postsecular, that is, messianic-existential, philosophical-political moment. This is the very same instant of Habermas' existentially motivated philosophical-political birthday of 1945.

HABERMAS' FIRST GREAT DISAPPOINTMENT, 1949

I myself am a product of "re-education." (KPS 513/AS 79)

Germany's inability to break with its ugly past in shaping its future-presents confronts Habermas with a continuing series of disappointments. If May 8, 1945, occasions his philosophical and political enlightenment, what I designated as his existentially motivated philosophical-political birthday, then the formation of the first postwar government in the Federal Republic of Germany marks his first great disappointment and second rude postwar awakening.

The Konrad Adenauer era begins in 1949 and lasts until 1963. Habermas dramatizes on several occasions a particularly upsetting memory from the first year of his university studies in Göttingen: the 1949 election meetings for the first Federal Parliament held by the German Conservative Party. He visualizes how the gathering place for the German Party chairman, Mr. H. Seebohm, is dressed up in the old German nationalistic paraphernalia with the colors of Prussia and the Third Reich—in black, white, and red. (I recall seeing these very same old colors and symbols on the streets of Frankfurt a/M after the fall of the Berlin Wall in 1989 when Germany won the World Soccer Cup.) Habermas describes a campaign meeting he attended in 1949: he runs out disgusted when he hears the first stanza of "Deutschland, Deutschland über Alles" solemnly intoned. Since the defeat in 1945, neither the old colors nor the first stanza of the song, "Germany, Germany above All," can be officially representative of postwar Germany (whether before or after its post-1989 unification). Seebohm becomes a minister of transportation in Adenauer's first postwar government. "The hopes I had at that time were so unrealistic that I cannot begin to relate them to the present day" (KPS 467/AS 43).

Habermas and his teenage peers from the skeptical generation hold out for a post-Fascist cultural renewal. If nothing more, the massive visual, spoken, and written information about the Nazi barbarism should have shaken the postwar generation, it should have punctured the seamless whole of the Fascist continuity. But not much more than protective silence and resentment of the securing generation take the place of this idealistic waiting for a new beginning. Indeed, the ruptured post-1945 continuities are desperately joined, glued, welded, and sealed together under the veneer of rebuilding the country. "I thought to myself, it's just not possible that someone [Seebohm] who embodies this historical continuity could be in the first cabinet" (KPS 513/AS 78).

The period of Habermas' Gymnasium studies from 1945 to 1949 and his university studies from 1949 to 1954 is shot through with an ambivalence of this Cold War era—the moral imperative that a decisive break with the Nazi times should occur and the de facto cultural continuity with these times. His later suspicion of the universality claim of hermeneutics (i.e., the Gadamerian privileging of historical experience and tradition as guarantors of ethical continuity) can be traced, in great part, to the ambivalence of his own postwar experience, a skepsis he retains toward any uncritical acceptance of any tradition. Habermas cautiously admits his teenage desire for a "spontaneous sweeping away" or an "explosive act" in order to wipe the space clean for a new identity formation (KPS 513/AS 79). This caution ripens with the maturing critical attitude of someone who constantly worries, in hindsight, that other fascisms could arise from any spontaneous cultural ruptures. Apart from these youthful postwar wishes for a radical transgressive break, we will never find Habermas celebrating dissensus and fragmentation for their own sake. Rather, we will witness his ongoing disappointment with Germany's accountability for its false intellectual traditions. As Habermas grows older, his protest against the political coverups of Germany's past will rise with unrestrained intensity.

Against the complicitous postwar silence exhibited by the securing generation of parents and teachers, Habermas mobilizes his at times traumatic memory of the past and at times skeptical attitude toward the present possibilities of radical change. This dual attitude gives way to his passionate and righteous anger. It likewise informs his public speeches and political writings. But this anger remains often unspeakable, hidden in a mute horror at the survival of those undying ghosts within the culture of his birth and the first fifteen years of his life. It should not surprise us to discover how much Habermas' lifework becomes self-consciously dedicated to breaking the false cultural and political continuities that gave birth to the Third Reich.[3]

HABERMAS' SECOND GREAT DISAPPOINTMENT: PARTING WITH MARTIN HEIDEGGER, 1953

> Until the appearance of Heidegger's Introduction to Metaphysics in 1953 my political and philosophical 'confessions', if you will, were two completely different things. (KPS 515/AS 80)

Habermas characterizes himself as "a thoroughgoing Heideggerian for three or four years" (AS 189). Which period of his life is he talking about? If the outer time frame for what he names as his 'Heideggerian phase' lasts until July 25, 1953, and we can objectively determine that, then we can retrace those four years back to about 1949. This temporal location marks the fourth and final year of his high school studies (1945–1949), which in a German Gymnasium culminated with his maturity examinations *(Abitur)*. Habermas' Heideggerian period falls between 1949 and 1953.

I want to focus on what occurs between 1952 and 1953, the fourth year of Habermas' university studies. On July 12, 1952, he publishes an essay, "Im Lichte Heideggers," in the *Frankfurter Allgemeine Zeitung*. This short review of Ludwig Landgrebe's *Philosophie der Gegenwart* might be his last unreservedly pro-Heideggerian piece. Not long after its publication, Heidegger occasions *Habermas' second great disappointment*. "Then I saw that Heidegger, in whose philosophy I had been living, had given this lecture in 1935 and published it without a word of explanation—that's what really disturbed me" (KPS 515/AS 80). Habermas recalls this, for him, dreadful event again in his foreword to the German translation of Victor Farias's book: "I was, as a student, at that time so impressed with *Being and Time* that reading these lectures, fascist down to their stylistic details, actually shocked me" (WaW 161). Yet what shocks Habermas is not that Heidegger had been a Nazi during the war (since those who were not implicated in Nazism in some fashion from Heidegger's entire securing generation of German philosophy professors represented a minority), but that he seemed to justify his "authentic" version of Nazism in 1953.

When in 1953 Heidegger republished his lectures from 1935, he did so without trying to hide his one-time infatuation with National Socialism. Maybe an ordinary attempt to refuse changing what one has written simply to please the current public trend could signify integrity, but in Heidegger's case the act might strike anyone else as utterly naive or politically stupid or morally base or self-deceived about one's mandarin place in human affairs. For Habermas, it is unacceptable to implicate oneself as an authentic mouthpiece of what had been in the 1930s regarded as the greatness of Nazism but had since been utterly discredited; and furthermore, to defend that defense with 'existential' honesty still in 1953, that is, long after the postwar de-Nazification proceedings, the Nuremberg Tribunal, and the Holocaust documentaries. Heidegger's republication communicated to Habermas more than humble silence, more than an expression of a fearful, securing generation; it was the historically revisionist implication of the act that elicited Habermas' public response.

In the 1930s, Heidegger, as the rector of Freiburg University, considered himself the philosophical *Führer* (leader) of the political *Führer*, Hitler. Thus, despite Hitler's aberration, Heidegger in his self-estimation came to espouse the *correct* version of National Socialism, the "inner truth and greatness of the Nazi movement." Even if in the 1930s the notion of some competing authentic movement might have been still someone's honest consideration, the Holocaust discredits that notion in 1953. The reality of the Hitler-Stalin pact, among others, discredits the ascription of 'authenticity' equally for Heidegger's movement and the Soviet Marxism, the latter being criticized by the social theorists associated with the Frankfurt School. The political Left had to come to terms with Stalin; Heidegger did not seem to account for Hitler.

We learn later that Heidegger's three assistants, who prepared the 1935 lectures for republication, were so appalled by his reference to the "inner truth and greatness of the Nazi movement" that they recommended that Heidegger delete it from the 1953 printing. He felt confident in his thinking and published it anyway. But he made changes elsewhere in the original lectures: he introduced two editorial interventions into the very controversial sentence. Heidegger replaced "greatness of the Nazi movement" with "greatness of this movement" and appended the parenthetical explanation for the inner truth and greatness of this [Nazi] movement: "the encounter between global technology and modern man" (Heidegger cited by Habermas, MHgH 68f., 157; my translation)[4]. Heidegger's sense in 1953 seems to be that this is what he meant in 1935 and that links between "this movement" and "the Nazi movement" represent historical aberrations and misunderstanding, not something for which he must be directly responsible.

On August 13, 1953, Lewalter responded in *Die Zeit* to Habermas' critical review of Heidegger, published in the *Frankfurter Allgemenine Zeitung* on July 25, 1953. Lewalter defended the self-distancing, private view of the movement that Heidegger ascribed to his action and with which he appealed to the inner Heidegger circle (i.e., those who can understand his meaning of greatness). Lewalter accused Habermas' review of being dogmatically Marxist and under the influence of the Frankfurt School. And yet none of this could have been fully true of Habermas at the time, even though he had been reading Marxist texts since attending Gymnasium (1945–1949). Habermas turns to the early Frankfurt School (as did Marcuse in 1933) only after his disillusioned engagement with Heidegger, that is, after he becomes Adorno's first assistant at the IfS (1956–1959) and after he discovers early Marcuse in 1956. Lewalter's charge from 1953, ironically, anticipates the radical turn Habermas is about to make.

It is not surprising that, in a letter published in *Die Zeit* on September 24, 1953, Heidegger confirmed Lewalter's apology by ignoring Habermas (just as he ignored Marcuse's repeated personal and earnest inquiries about the Nazi involvement) and by endorsing Lewalter's own response to Habermas. Heidegger declared that those who learn to think and hear (the inner circle) could grasp the true meaning of the sentence retained in the 1953 republication. While one may continue to learn much about true thinking from Heidegger—and Habermas never disputes the fact of Heidegger's own greatness as a thinker—the student Habermas must have been asking, What is there to think or hear in the greatness of the Nazi movement? What is one to do with *that* claim to greatness, viewing it as a German after May 8, 1945? Even the most initiated and the most honest of Heidegger's students, then and today, do not try to amplify this odd intransigence in the thinking and greatness of their teacher. Heidegger's silent protesting of his innocence becomes a liability. We can thus follow how Habermas' philosophical-political profile grows in great measure from a self-conscious reflection of the sharp contrasts with Heidegger's philosophical-political profile. Habermas perceives existential gaps or contradictions between the greatness of words and the cowardice of deeds. As much as he remains influenced by Heidegger's philosophical genius and by his core insights (e.g., in espousing *postmetaphysical thinking*), he never comes back to learn more from Heidegger, his first philosophical inspiration. Thus the year 1953 marks Habermas' radical break from Heidegger.

In the *Spiegel* interview he gave on September 1966 (which he permitted to be published only after his death in the spring of 1976) Heidegger clarified the controversial sentence and the parenthetical remark once more. When queried by the *Spiegel* interviewer as to the origin of the added parenthetical clause, Heidegger explained that while the clause could not have been spoken in the original 1935 lecture because of the student spies in the classroom, nonetheless it was meant in that original lecture the way he wrote it in 1953. Summarizing the affair, Habermas (WaW 162) concludes that Heidegger whitewashed the matter of the parenthetical clause three times: (1) in his 1953 publication, where the formulation was first added while the new preface made the readers believe that the clause had been originally part of the written lecture in 1935; (2) in Heidegger's indirect response to Habermas via the letter to *Die Zeit* in which he endorsed Lewalter's faulty interpretation (itself based on Heidegger's deceptive backward reading of his postwar critique of technology into his 1935 embrace of Nazism); and (3) in his 1966 *Spiegel* interview, published in 1976, where he is queried directly about the clause. In the end, Rainer Marten, one of the above-mentioned three assistants, testified in an essay published in 1987 and again in 1988 in a private letter to Habermas that in 1953 there had been no parenthetical clause in the original manuscript of Heidegger's 1935 lectures. Perhaps Heidegger thought the parenthetical addition in 1935 but wrote it down only in 1953? Possibly, but probably not—Habermas' summary indicates that much. Note finally Otto Pöggeler's report that the disputed original page is missing from the Heidegger archives since 1983.[5]

Once again, Habermas never disputes Heidegger's greatness as a philosopher. He even defends Heidegger's *Being and Time* from the Fascist imputations that are attributed to his later works. Habermas does not seek intrinsic connections between the philosophical texts (especially the early ones) of Heidegger and his Nazi politics (see GW). Finally, Habermas does not get particularly upset by that generation's Nazi sympathies and involvement in the 1930s. But he is markedly horrified by the unrepentant, concealing, double-minded philosophical-political profile that Heidegger exhibits after 1945. The great philosopher of existence sidesteps his *ontic* (i.e., existentially lived) responsibility for who he has been and wanted to be in relation to others into an noncommunicative evasion of responsibility. Is this posture of pregnant silence an act of letting go of one's fallen self (i.e., a way of accounting) or is it what it appears to be—an evasion of self-responsibility? One must truly appreciate Habermas' inner conflict about this question both because of his earlier attraction to Heidegger's existential philosophy and because of his own existential need to come to terms with his youthful past. This dual background can explain why Heidegger as a person, rather than a philosopher, remains more important for Habermas' ongoing self-questioning than many other thinkers of that era. To be sure, Heidegger's self-questioning about Being of beings does not enter Habermas' philosophical concerns.

Although Habermas says, "I'd rather not say terribly much about my youth" (KPS 511/AS 77), he has great deal to say against acts of reviving the Fascist sympathies that keep haunting the present from within their dark past. This central existential question of silence and unspeakability regarding the traumatic past will arise toward the end of this study.

Habermas' attraction to Heidegger is just as genuine as the public criticism of his first master is earnest. Had Heidegger in this instance really let go of his own conflicted self, as his later philosophy invites us to do, there would be no room for his double-mindedness—Habermas reaches this conclusion in his own life. While one need not follow Habermas in his total leave-taking of Heidegger's philosophical thinking, his young adult, risky, and quite selfless public act of confrontation with Heidegger remains a corrective milestone in the postwar German existential philosophy. The Heidegger case seems symptomatic of postwar Germany, of problems that his post-1945 securing generation failed to face. Habermas poses this case unequivocally in terms of an existentially anchored philosophical-political question (cf. MHgH 67, 74f.,156, 163), and he raises the stakes high for evaluating his own lifelong philosophical sobriety and political conduct.

> Heidegger's entanglement with National Socialism is one thing, which we can safely leave to the morally sober historical judgment of later generations. Quite another is Heidegger's apologetic conduct after the war, his retouchings and manipulations, his refusal publicly to detach himself from the regime to which he had publicly adhered. That affects us as his contemporaries. Insofar as we share a life-context and a history with others, we have the right to call one another to account. . . . In this regard, Heidegger remained bound by his generation and his time, the milieu of the Adenauer era of repression and silence. He acted no differently from others, was one of many. . . . As a contemporary, Heidegger is thrown into an ambiguous light, overtaken by his own past because when everything was finished and done he could not adequately relate to it. His behavior remained, even according to the standards of *Being and Time,* ahistorical. But what makes Heidegger into a manifestation, typical for his time, of a widely influential postwar mentality, concerns his person—not his work. (WaW 164f.)

Since his natural birth in 1929, and since his philosophical-political birthday in 1945, Habermas was fooled by his tradition essentially three times: by his primary school years and home environment up to the liberation day of 1945, by the first postwar government in 1949, and by Heidegger in 1953. The last two situations mark his two great disappointments, while the first represents a radical break in his socialized self-identity. If Habermas' existentially motivated philosophical and political birthday is punctuated by the rupture of 1945, then his formative education and his intellectual and moral enlightenment are measurable by the caesura of 1953. After parting with Heidegger, Habermas integrates his political-philosophical "confessions" into his lifework (KPS 515/AS 80).

If we place his radical break with Heidegger between the essay of July 12, 1952, and his July 25, 1953, publication of a critical review of Heidegger's 1935 lectures, then his Heideggerian years, 1949–1953, span the larger portion of his university studies, with a summer spent in Zurich and the regular semesters in Göttingen and Bonn. Habermas is twenty-four when he publicly parts with Heidegger. He takes this, by no means uncontroversial or even safe, stance only one year prior to defending his doctoral dissertation on Schelling (Bonn, February 24, 1954). I do not hesitate to name this performative event, following his philosophical-political birthday in 1945, *Habermas' signature*.

HABERMAS' POST-HEIDEGGERIAN INTELLECTUAL FORMATION, 1950s

> All the professors who had any importance to me were already professors before 1933. (KPS 514/AS 80) My own two teachers, under whom I wrote my dissertation—Ernst Rothacker and Oskar Becker—were cases in point. (AS 192)

Being fooled by an early socialization under the shadow of the Hitler Youth may not be the same thing as spending one's postwar adolescence on the path of a revered German *Existenz*-philosopher who, if only for several months,[6] intellectually as well as administratively, as a rector at the Freiburg University, supported the Nazi ideology. Even though Heidegger was a card-carrying member of the National Socialist Party (we have a photo of him with the swastika party pin on his lapel),[7] Habermas' self-ascription as a "thoroughgoing Heideggerian" might mislead us. Minimally, we need to situate that claim within two historical contexts of Habermas' circumstance. While a "thoroughgoing Heideggerian," Habermas (unlike political existentialists of the Nazi period and unlike many postwar German and non-German followers of Heidegger) never ignores the political implications of Heidegger's era for his own responsibility to it.

First, not only the 1949 Adenauer government or Heidegger's engagement during his rectorship but also the entire postwar educational system exhibited "an essential continuity" with the Nazi era, a continuity reaching all the way back to the Weimar Republic. "There was no break in terms of persons or courses,"

Habermas complains about his studies (AS 192). Germany's defeat seemed to have bypassed the culture of German universities. Professors of importance to Habermas who had been established before 1933 mostly remained at the universities until their retirement after 1945 (KPS 514/AS 80). Habermas recalls that during the four years of his university studies and while browsing books in the libraries and bookstores of Göttingen and Bonn, he accidentally discovered what Oskar Becker, Arnold Gehlen, Ernst Jünger, Erich Rothacker, Carl Schmitt, and others were thinking, writing, doing during the Nazi era. With Rothacker and Becker, his graduate teachers and two doctoral advisers, he could at least touch some of this hot topic, he concedes. Yet we do not have concrete reports even from these recollections.

How much does Habermas really know by 1954 about the past of his dissertation directors (German *Doktorvater* literally means a Ph.D. father), Rothacker and Becker? We read in the archival materials that Rothacker worked in 1933 in the Ministry of Propaganda, where he directed the department for popular education *(Volksbildung)*. He served likewise as a liaison for Joseph Goebbels's office on "action against the un-German spirit." This activity endeavored to bring ethnic Germans, *Volksdeutsche*, who were living abroad into the spirit of the new Germany (Leaman 1993, 73). In this role he was assigned as "a contact person for the students, who organized the burning of books" (Keulartz 1995, 121). Rothacker was a member of NSDAP since May 1, 1933. Weinreich ([1946] 1999, 16) singles out Rothacker's (1934) history of philosophy as an example of works by professors who early on showed scholarly enthusiasm for Hitler's intellectual contribution. Rothacker espoused a nonbiological notion of racist hierarchy. This caused him momentary troubles in 1937, when he was accused and then arrested by the Nazi security service because of attempting to "falsify the racial concept" by the idea that it would be possible to overcome one's race through will and lifestyle (Keulartz 1995, 127). Rothacker nonetheless supported the Nazi policies (Leaman 1993, 14), particularly those against Jews: "I am fully in agreement with all measures taken against Jews," he writes in March 1934 (cited in Keulartz 1995, 126). Becker, like Rothacker, ascribed to anti-Semitism and remained an active National Socialist until the Nazi defeat in 1945. Becker's racism (to trump that of Rothacker and Heidegger, both of whom in the 1930s still wanted to "lead the Leader") was "purely biological"—more intrinsically with the Nazi party line (Keulartz 1995, 126f.).[8]

Leaman's research shows that a radically antidemocratic and conservative line of thought had been widely entrenched at German universities and among German philosophers in particular. He gives evidence that nine out of 180 German philosophy professors teaching at universities when the Nazi regime took power in 1933 were connected to Left, social-democratic, or religiously socialist-oriented organizations. Of these nine Left-leaning professors, eight were fired in 1933 along with fourteen additional professors who were fired simply on account of their Jewish origins and not because of their views. The Aryan professors supported the dismissal of their colleagues of Jewish origin, Leaman says, with cheap excuses that Jewish academics could easily secure jobs abroad with help from various Jewish organizations. It is true that from among these nine, the three who were associated with the IfS in Frankfurt a/M (Theodor W. Adorno, Max Horkheimer, and Paul Tillich, who in 1931 directed Adorno's *Habilitation* on Kierkegaard) emigrated to the United States, where they were more or less gainfully employed during the war. Yet the case of Heidegger's teacher at the Freiburg University, Edmund Husserl, already falsifies the misguided excuse: the Husserl case shows the overall difficulty encountered by the Jewish intellectuals who stayed in Europe after 1933. This was the deep crisis of 'Europe' indirectly intimated in Husserl's lectures ([1935] 1970) in Vienna and Prague. Although Leaman lists Husserl as evangelical Christian and not Jewish, that conversion did not save Husserl from having to leave his post in Freiburg and did not allow him to get a new position at Charles University in Prague, his friendship with the former student and later Prague professor, Jan Patočka, notwithstanding. The Frankfurt School, along with the Vienna Circle (and that might seem ironic from today's ahistorical angle of the analytical-Continental split in the United States), was among the intellectual institutions targeted by the Nazis.

When Horkheimer (in the early summer of 1949) and Adorno later returned to Germany from their U.S. exile, they reestablished the Frankfurt Institute, which had been closed down in 1933.[9] Horkheimer obtained the chair in social philosophy in July 1949, and in August 1950 he became the director of the reopened IfS; in November 1951 he was named the rector (president) of the Johann Wolfgang Goethe-Universität in Frankfurt a/M. We encounter Habermas (after defending his Ph.D. in 1954) between 1956 and 1959 as Adorno's first assistant.[10]

Significantly, Marcuse (from 1928 to 1932 a postdoctoral student of Heidegger) rejoins the IfS in 1933 literally in flight from Nazi policies in Germany and only shortly after (but very long before Habermas in 1953) he breaks with Heidegger, who would not habilitate him in Freiburg in 1932. Husserl then intervened on Marcuse's behalf, helping secure him an introduction to Horkheimer in Frankfurt. Adorno and Horkheimer accept Marcuse to the IfS just as it is being relocated to Geneva. Marcuse, notably of Jewish origins, links up with Horkheimer and other Frankfurt colleagues on their way to Geneva, then to Paris, and finally to New York (TP 13). Unlike Horkheimer and Adorno, who return after the war's end to Germany, Marcuse remains teaching and writing in the United States. In 1956, with Adorno in Frankfurt, we find Habermas discovering the young Marcuse's essays of 1928–1932. Habermas is three when Marcuse finished the last of these essays, and he is twenty-seven when he discovers Marcuse in 1956. In the pre-1933 essays, Habermas can trace Marcuse's interrogations of Heidegger through Marcuse's own reading of the then published Paris *Manuscripts* of the young Marx. His discovery of the existential Marxist Marcuse helps Habermas to philosophically complete in 1956 his own departure from Heidegger, which he initiated existentially and politically in 1953 (AS 189f.).

Whether they had become Nazis through NSDAP membership or public pledges of allegiance to Hitler or privately held Nazi political beliefs, the philosophy professors of the Fascist era in general did not discuss their past. Rather than apologize or express sorrow for their actions or their passive acquiescence, that securing generation practiced silence—its predominant public norm. Habermas notes this with great regret (AS 192). This fact is no more true of Heidegger than of many of his contemporary sympathizers. However, for a renowned philosopher of authentic existence, an active engagement with the Nazis, followed by what to Habermas appears to be an actively deceptive and evasive (rather than selfless) silence, suggests an unexpected degree of existential inauthenticity. As an earlier philosopher of existence, Kierkegaard (1980), shows, not knowing or even denying one's despairing will-to-be in a defiant way (e.g., for the *Führer*), or in one's willing-not-to-be at all (silently irresponsible for one's existing), these are but two forms of despair. The *ontological* silence (silence before Being), if it oscillates between living now anxiously and now worshipfully before the mystery of Being, can also fail to come to terms with the *ontic* (lived) facticity of a possible despairing self-choice.

Only radical self-choice that can be disclosed in *communicative freedom* (see KFnT), that is, by securing its claims to truth, validity, and authenticity within the arena of communicative interaction and not in one's acommunicative privacy, Habermas reasons later, could be redeemed publicly. This is what, in the long citation about Heidegger (see the preceding section), Habermas means by the need for a public account for one's public acts. In light of Heidegger's entire generation of teachers, Habermas makes a radically democratic self-choice—joining the separate philosophical and political 'confessions' within a single philosophical-political life world. Here he follows in Kierkegaard's footsteps: after emerging from his precritical years and early teens in the Hitler Youth into the critical adolescence of the Gymnasium and university studies, at this juncture, Habermas breaks away from the German political existentialism of the 1930s.

The unbroken, falsely motivated philosophical and political continuity of postwar Germany, with its un-deconstructed past, thus sums up the basic situation of Habermas' young adult experience. In having been a Heideggerian of sorts, Habermas finds himself fooled by an intellectual tradition boasting the way of authentic existence. He can no longer rely on his inherited intellectual tradition's resources for renewal. Silence about Auschwitz signifies at best denial and at worst complicity. Parting with Heidegger, which had been an experience of being once fooled by *Existenzphilosophie*, defines for Habermas a living existential situation that opens him to a new philosophical-political horizon.

We must be aware of the distinction between the Nazi political existentialism of the 1930s and existential, philosophical-political questioning, or Habermas' own beginnings may escape us with the demotion of that failed existentialism. This flattening is much too common among the readers of Habermas and among the critics of Heidegger's politics. We can get a glimpse of the nuance between the antidemocratic, conservatively revolutionary existentialism and the questioning of existential-political beginnings, which are radically open and egalitarian. The former existentialism is defined by the *Führer* principle, which determines one's self-choice from without, and by a political *decisionism* that would define one's choices through the authoritarian state. The latter signifies communicative freedom of those who ask what sort of I or we they are and want to become (see Matuštík 1993, 1998a, 1999).

We should recall that Habermas sees German-Jewish thinkers in general and those of the Frankfurt School and western Marxists in particular as providing us a sober way to reckon with the traditions by which *we* have been fooled once before. Sobriety about cultures that once fooled us can be redemptive and democratic; otherwise no one could begin critically yet afresh. Habermas integrates philosophical and political 'confessions' into an existential sobriety about one's origins and into a self-choice regarding who one is and wants to be within them (KPS 515/AS 80).

This brings us to the second contextualization of Habermas' Heideggerianism. The aforementioned distinction between the political existentialism of the 1930s (harnessed on behalf of and by the Nazi ideologues as a decision or self-choice for the *Führer* or the fatherland) and existential sobriety (radical honesty about the difficulty of one's at once personal and social beginnings) proves to be crucial in situating Habermas' self-confessed Heideggerianism. We require this very distinction even more significantly to explain his departure from Heideggerianism. Habermas' formative educational influences shape both his reception of and breakup with Heidegger. My claim is that Habermas' latter move would have to strike us as fundamentally unintelligible if identified with a wholesale rejection of existential questioning. But this questioning has been continually informing Habermas' profile in its core! And in this regard we are not obliged to, and I am not compelled to, take Habermas' overtly stated considerations of existential*ism* at face value. Just like his misleading self-characterization as a thoroughgoing Heideggerian, these considerations too must be read for the most part in light of his break with Heidegger and with the emphatically antidemocratic career fathered by Germany's political existentialists (e.g., Carl Schmitt). First, Habermas cannot be a thoroughgoing Heideggerian in that critical sense since he has never espoused and does not hold out for an elitist *Führerdemokratie* (democracy that banks on a great leader). This type of elitism and provincial nationalism is well dramatized by Arendt (1965, 135ff.) in her report on Adolf Eichmann's self-defense at the trial in Jerusalem. Eichmann adopted a Nazi version of the Kantian-political existential imperative to act always in a way that your great Leader would approve. Second, Habermas has not become and is not someone who is no longer motivated by existential questioning. If he were such a person, then the issue of whether or not to continue a particular tradition could not arise for him in the first place. On the contrary, this issue of democratic and philosophical-political self-choice encapsulates his thinking repeatedly since 1945! Again, this is why Heidegger's case gains such a contrasting importance in Habermas' own self-assessment.

From 1945 to 1949, Habermas attends high school in Gummersbach. Starving from the postwar intellectual famine, he begins to read what he can get his hands on. He canvases the local Communist bookshops with books from the Rowohlt newspaper paperback series and from the Marxist-Leninist Library in East Berlin. He browses through the Gummersbach seminary library. He comes under the sway of expressionist painting and poetry, functionalism and the Bauhaus, existentialism in literature, drama, and postwar film. The film documents of the Holocaust only reinforce the process of his 'reeducation'. He carries on intellectual discussions with a circle of progressive friends. The hunger for learning and open debate issues from the totalitarian vacuum. His is not unlike that unsatiated intellectual hunger found in the Communist Eastern Europe right after November 1989. Those countries experienced their share of dogmatic teachers, proscribed or demolished books, and false continuities. Habermas' post-1945 reading list moves in the opposite direction of the post-1989 currents. By the time he completes his Gymnasium studies with maturity exams, he devours pamphlets by Marx and Engels, as well as books by Kafka, Rilke, Böll, Trakl, Thomas Mann, Hesse. He becomes excited by Sartre's plays.

In the midst of his university period from 1949 to 1954, when Habermas studies Sartre and de Beauvoir and now learns from them as philosophers, in 1953 he writes his *adieu* to Heidegger. At the same time he is introduced through Karl Löwith to the young Marx. (As already noted, he discovers Marx already in Gummersbach but forgets this early exposure and has to recover it.) He comes across Lukács's *History and Class Consciousness* in Bonn's seminary library.[11] Habermas' doctoral thesis on Schelling begins in 1952 under the impact of Heidegger's thought. With all those new influences and most significantly given the break of 1953, he pens in 1954 an introduction on the Young Hegelians to his completed thesis.

After completing his Ph.D. in 1954, Habermas turns in the next year to Horkheimer and Adorno's *Dialectic of Enlightenment*. Habermas' path to the early texts of critical social theory begins here. During his first postdoctoral year, in 1955, he is working as a freelance journalist. One year later, in the fall of 1956, Adorno invites Habermas to Frankfurt as his first research assistant. It is during this time, while holding a research grant for his work on the concept of ideology, that Habermas discovers Marcuse's early articles from 1928 to 1932. Habermas continues to devour at the same time more of Adorno, Bloch, Benjamin, and Marx; he gets immersed in the sociological works of Durkheim, Parsons, and Weber; and he attends an important Freud conference in Frankfurt—all taking place in 1956. But, and this is of great import, Habermas traces his mature philosophical-political break with Heidegger and his later turn toward the Hegelian, Freudian, and Weberian Marxism to the first 1956 impact of and, since the 1960s, to an ongoing "special affinity with the existentialist, i.e. the Marcusean, variant of Critical Theory" (NU 216/AS 150; cf. KPS 468f.; 512-16/AS 44f., 78-81; NR 24/AS 232; and AS 189f.).

HABERMAS' WAY TO THE FRANKFURT SCHOOL, THE IFS, AND CRITICAL THEORY, 1956–1959

> We have isolated Marcuse's analysis of the times—he himself presents in a quasi-redemptive framework. . . . Showing the courage to release utopian energies again . . . in times like ours makes a peculiarly strong impression. (TpS)

> Today one can wage wars, but one can no longer win them. . . . With what right have they demonstrated? With no other than the one pertaining to all citizens; but perhaps [also] with the obligation of intellectual honesty, which imposes on them their task. (UeB 105–6)

Three years after the early student movement (1951–1953),[12] and two years after receiving his Ph.D. in Bonn (1954), Habermas begins at the IfS in Frankfurt a/M as Adorno's first assistant (1956–1959). Habermas' tenure at the IfS itself falls into three distinct periods:

- 1956–1957: from the discovery of early Marcuse to the philosophical discussions of Marx
- 1957–1959: the period of active participation in the antinuclear movement
- 1959: from the break with Horkheimer and departure from the IfS to resumption of the second doctoral work *(Habilitation)* with Wolfgang Abendroth in Marburg

Shortly after Horkheimer assumes the directorship of the IfS (August 1950) and the rectorship of the Johann Wolfgang Goethe-Universität (November 20, 1951), protests and polemics break out against Veit Harlan's newly produced and distributed films. Harlan, who was known for his wartime anti-Semitic productions, releases in 1951 two films with unabashedly similar thematic of prejudice and sympathy for the Third Reich.[13] On January 9, 1952, the student parliament of the Goethe-Universität passes the statement that explains as well as educates about "The Attitude toward the Jews" (see "Haltung") in postwar Germany.[14] As part of Germany's material compensation for war crimes against Jews and a changed attitude toward them, students now demand the passage of antihate laws and the reform of the school curricula with the same intent. Horkheimer praises the student resolution and holds out great hopes for a new postwar student generation. He perceives in this early student protest a progressive chance for rupturing the conservative continuum entrenched at German universities (Kraushaar 1998, 2: doc.

26). Kraushaar (1:22) sums up the nature of the early student movement between 1951 and 1953. At its core, it was an idealistic, moral, anti-Fascist, and pro-Jewish movement of university students that took place largely and only at the universities.[15]

How did Horkheimer arrive at his later judgment, which he voiced in a private nine-page letter to Adorno (in Montagnola, September 27)? "Habermas takes as his model, what he considers at present for the most advanced, above all the writings of the young Marx and presumably a distorted view of Teddie [Adorno] and of our joint thoughts" (Horkheimer 1958c, 112). How do we reconcile Horkheimer's support for students in 1951–1953 with his growing conservatism in the postwar years and in the 1950s? A brief background of Critical Theory and the IfS in the 1950s is in order.

Albrecht and his coauthors, in their groundbreaking work on the history of influence of the Frankfurt School, distinguish two groundings of postwar Germany—the "institutional grounding," with the corresponding period of restoration (1949–1959, or until the end of the Adenauer regime in 1963), and the "intellectual grounding" of the upheaval period of 1967–1969 (Albrecht et al. 1999, 318f.; cf. 132f., chaps. 6–7).[16] First, there is a virtual disappearance of the early critical social theory from the postwar IfS; second, a 'securing' Critical Theory is deliberately fashioned (from the early to mid-1960s). The latter move transpires in the wake of Marcuse's ascendancy to prominence, at least since 1964, as an original representative of critical social theory and as the intellectual leader of the student movement in 1967–1969. Habermas' tenure at the IfS coincides with the peak of the first grounding up to the turning year of 1959. By situating him in relation to various currents and tensions of the 1950s, we can chart with considerable nuance his own path to Critical Theory and his later differences with the student movement of the 1960s.

The 1950s are marked by the tensions of fitting the original liberation project of the early critical social theory into an institutionally respectable Critical Theory and by "the changed political agenda of the Institute, of [its] 'turn to democracy'" (137; cf. 168). Horkheimer's aim in the Cold War context was to secure the renewed IfS "into the self-forming [German] state" (136). In this single aim, the returning Jewish exiles, Horkheimer and Adorno, did not differ *in form* of their response to the war trauma from the German cohorts of their securing generation. The sharp distinction remains, however, between wanting to restore western democratic institutions as opposed to restoring the Nazi continuities. Yet both forms of restoration in the 1950s—the revisionist-Fascist one and the conservative 'democratic turn'—went against any positive affirmation of socialism (132–35). The 1960s 'restoration' of the early critical social theory, along with Marcuse's new writings, differed from the postwar democratizing restoration (176–84).[17] The revolt of the 1960s renewed the socialist aspirations buried in the 1950s. The 'democratic turn' and the 'revolutionary turn' represent two distinct—institutional and intellectual—groundings of the postwar FRG. They represent, in the broader pos-

Table 1.2 Impact of the Institutional Grounding of West Germany (FRG) on the Evolution of the First and Second Generations of Critical Theory in the 1950s

Grounding of the FRG	Horkheimer/Adorno[a]	Habermas
institutional (restoration, 1949–63)	reeducation, democratization, west orientation	idea of radical participatory democracy
proto-intellectual (antinuclear movement, 1957–58)	coming to terms with the Nazi past/fear of Fascist revival	right and duty to protest; defense of civil disobedience and support for extraparliamentary opposition
Basic mode of Critical Theory	securing and restorative	skeptical and integrative

[a] Adorno's *Negative Dialectics* ([1966] 1973) eschews the restorative mode of the 1950s as much as the integrative mode of Habermas or the affirmative refusal of Marcuse. I am leaving Marcuse off this chart because he does not impact the intellectual grounding of the FRG and critical social theory until the 1960s.

itive sense preserved till the present, two—democratic and revolutionary—faces of 'Critical Theory' and 'critical social theory' (tab. 1.2).

In the 1950s, "Horkheimer and Adorno had no critical distance on the construction of German Federal institutions"; neither did they hope for some kind of "socialist change." The pressing issue was not socialism, but how the state came to terms with the Nazi past (145). The IfS of the 1950s was not some "esoteric refuge of Leftist thought with a distance to the Adenaurean state" (152). Rather, the goal was to achieve "democracy of western type, not a socialism of eastern dependency" (153). Along with the restorative democratic yet antisocialist turn of the 1950s comes the "ground consensus" to build "a new social science on the U.S. model in order to support democracy and overcome National Socialism" (167). No longer the early critical social theory, but the U.S. sociology served as their paradigm. In the 1950s, the early critical theory is "forgotten"; Adorno and Horkheimer seem to become classical Germanist philosophers and North American sociologists in Germany, not "Leftist intellectuals or even Marxists." There are two lines of conflicting publication histories of the IfS, those from the 1950s, which represent largely the above concerns, and those from 1930s and 1940s, which are reissued only after they are discovered by the new student movement and linked to Marcuse's new writings (28f.). That the early texts from Frankfurt and the U.S. exile could be used by prosocialist '68ers to hijack the image of Critical Theory toward revolutionary aims and even confront their authors might have prompted Horkheimer to "neutralize" the Marxist vocabulary in later editions (169, chap. 10). Habermas finds himself at the tip of this 'neutralization' by the time he decides to leave the IfS in 1959. Let me describe his situation at the IfS until his first departure from Frankfurt.

During the Freud conference in 1956, Habermas remains unaware of Marcuse's early links to the IfS or of his utopian synthesis of Freud and Marx: "Even as an associate of the Institute for Social Research, he [Habermas] had no sense of there being any Critical Theory that claimed to be systematic." Horkheimer kept early writings out of reach by his coworkers (Wiggershaus 1989, 604; 1998, 544). Habermas writes: "Critical Theory, a Frankfurt School—there was no such thing at the time.... Only some clever young people in the late 1960s discovered early Critical Theory and made it clearer in my mind that a theory of society should be systematic" (NU 170f./AS 98). In 1956, he discovers the early Marcuse's appropriation of young Marx, and thereby he in an ironic manner antedates the student discoveries from the 1960s. It is ironic insofar as in the 1960s his objections to the students echo Horkheimer's charges against Habermas in 1958 (Kraushaar 1998, 3:267).[18]

Under the impact of Marcuse's *One-Dimensional Man* (1964; German translation, 1967), whose project was undertaken sometime during 1958 at the time when Horkheimer attacked Habermas on account of his allegiance to Marxist revolution, the '68ers discovered the texts of early critical social theory and linked them with Marcuse's new work (Albrecht et al. 1999, 312–27, 292f.). Without this work, it is doubtful that there would ever have been known anything like the Frankfurt School or critical social theory. "Only when the political climate changed to the degree that there was more reputation to gain than to lose through [recovering] the old theories" and with Marcuse's independent German republication of his early essays, that "Adorno, his students, and Jürgen Habermas" took recourse to the early critical social theory "without Horkheimer's censorship" (176). In 1965, "Marcuse is the first one who brings such [Frankfurt] School into public discourse" (318). The 1960s movement in the end integrated into *its* history of the Frankfurt School three periods: the early Weimar visionary era, the second postwar-institutional founding of the IfS, and the revolutionary founding of critical social theory, itself initiated by Marcuse and spearheaded by the student protest of the 1960s.

We do not have distinct records of Habermas' awareness of the early student movement, but it is interesting that protests against Harlan fall roughly within the period of Habermas' turning away from Heidegger. With the exception of this 1953 public confrontation with Heidegger, we do not find Habermas[19] visibly involved in the protests of 1951–1953. Thus, of utmost significance for situating carefully Habermas' profile is Horkheimer's first and last public enthusiasm for the postwar generation of German students. We can benefit from placing Habermas' relationship to the later student movement in the 1960s between Horkheimer's short-lived support for the protests in 1952–1953 and his objections to Habermas' Marxist notion of revolution developed during the antinuclear movement of 1957–1959.

Habermas is finishing in 1958 the IfS joint interdisciplinary study, *Student und Politik*, and writes a far-reaching introduction to the book (RBpB). The project examines the political consciousness and specifically the democratic aspirations among the postwar generation of German university students. In September 1957 Habermas and his coauthors interviewed 171 Frankfurt students. To verify the reliability of the sample, in the spring of the next year, Friedeburg prepared a complementary questionnaire with which 550 additional students were interviewed (Kraushaar 1998, 3:268f.; Wiggershaus 1989, 608, 614; 1998, 547, 553). For our purpose of situating Habermas, of great importance are Wiggershaus's scattered reflections on the core of Habermas' early interest in developing a *radical democratic theory*:

- "*Students and Politics* continued Habermas's own interest in democracy, marked by the democratic 'reeducation' that took place after the war. This was democracy, however, *in a sense explicitly radicalized into an 'idea of democracy' by Habermas' proximity to Adorno and his encounter with Marcuse.*" (608/547; italics added)
- "What was also new was that the concept of democracy—which in *The Authoritarian Personality* [Adorno 1950], and even more so in *Group Experiment* [1953], had been a concession to research clients and the prevailing situation, concealing radically anti-capitalist, utopian-revolutionary criteria—*was invested with radical content by Habermas and overtly made into an explicit standard of measurement.*" (609/548; italics added)
- "[In the introduction to SuP] . . . Habermas appealed to the 'idea of democracy'—explicitly acknowledging his debt to [early] 'Critical Theory'. . . . The idea of democracy—that legitimate state power is mediated by the free and express consensus of all citizens—lay at the roots of the bourgeois constitutional state. It continued to give objective significance to existing institutions in Germany. . . . *Habermas thus succeeded in producing a sophisticated concept of political participation . . . democracy . . . seen as a historical process aimed at creating a society of responsible citizens and transforming social power into rational authority.*" (610f./550; italics added)
- "*The introduction stated that the only opportunity for participation in politics currently lay in 'extraparliamentary actions'*—by members of mass organizations who could put state organizations under pressure from the streets and by functional élites within the administrative apparatuses of industry, the state and lobbying organizations." (611/550; italics added)

Habermas' work under the auspices of the IfS and influences of early Adorno and Marcuse, the work so perceptively analyzed by Wiggershaus, situates him already in the late 1950s as an aspiring radical social democrat or Left liberal. This is the vantage point from which Habermas consistently embraces two of the protest movements: the antinuclear protests of the late 1950s and the mid-1980s. He values them for furthering the radical democratic project, but he reacts skeptically if not outright negatively to the perceived dangers of revolutionary or rebellious anarchy (1967–1969). Finally, he embraces the vision of social revolution (French 1789, Soviet 1917, German 1918, students 1960s, East-Central European 1989) insofar as he can integrate its challenge into a radical democratic project and insofar as he can reject it as pejoratively utopian when it frustrates such integration. His Critical Theory is at once skeptical and integrative, while Horkheimer's, and to some degree Adorno's in the 1950s, is securing and restorative (cf. tab. 1.2, na.).

We may, then, concur with Gunzelin S. Noerr (in Kraushaar 1998, vol. 3; cf. n. 18 above) that Horkheimer characterizes 'correctly' Habermas' application of the concept of revolution as "ahistorical" and "hyperidealistic" (269). Horkheimer objects to an "undifferentiated application of the revolutionary concepts from 1789 until 1848 to the present." He judges Habermas' novel elaboration of political democracy as "a cover for [these] old concepts of revolution" (268). Further, he complains in his letter to Adorno about "ahistorical use of revolutionary concepts, which remain untouched by social experiences" (270). Already in 1957, Habermas published a newspaper essay (LzDM), which antedated then some of the later themes of the book (SuP). In his letter to Adorno, Horkheimer objects now to the book, and to Habermas' introduction in particular (RBpB), while invoking Habermas' earlier piece: "The word [revolution] appears a hundred times in the article," but it makes no historical sense, he adds, the way Habermas enshrines the inherent meaning of philosophy in revolution (Horkheimer 1958c, 112).

Horkheimer can be viewed as 'correct' only with the irony of someone looking back at 1958 from the instant of 1968 when Habermas ascribes the very same generic notion of revolution to the new situation of rebelling students (Kraushaar 1998, 3:269). But as we read Horkheimer's nine-page letter to Adorno, we nonetheless get a portrait of Habermas as a radical Marxist theorist and activist. We should keep in mind that although in the 1950s Horkheimer accentuates cultural reeducation and the pro-American orientation of social sciences, Habermas neither defends socialism for postwar Europe nor takes on critical economic analysis. The latter two positions are more true for early critical social theory, early and late Marcuse, and the student leaders, like Hans-Jürgen Krahl or Rudi Dutschke or Oskar Negt in the course of the 1960s (cf. Albrecht et al. 1999, 130f.). "Habermas of 1957 was not anticipating Krahl, not proclaiming revolution here and now" (Kraushaar 1998, 3:269).[20] Habermas is already in the 1950s too skeptical or ambivalent to move single-heartedly from a "philosophical-epistemological" and generically critical (270) appropriation of Marxian revolutionary concepts to their practical elaboration for the specific situations by the revolting generation. In sum, what interests me about Horkheimer's worry is the discrepancy between, on the one hand, his objection to Habermas' uncritical use of the young Marx-inspired notion of revolution and to his reduction of all philosophy to serve this revolutionary aim (Horkheimer 1958c, 112); and, on other hand, Habermas' preoccupation with radical social democracy (Wiggershaus 1989, 607–11; 1998, 547–50) and with cognitive and philosophical "problem" of revolution (cf. Kraushaar 1998, 3:270). Such discrepancy sharpens the situation of Habermas as a sui generis representative of his skeptical generation.

After Horkheimer's objections, Habermas' book was published in 1961 without any reference to IfS. Consistently with his postwar fears, Horkheimer embraced the early student movement on account of its anti-Nazi and pro-Jewish protest. But he seeks Habermas' departure from the IfS in 1959 on account of his social democratic, Marxist orientation; and he will largely reject the critique and hope of the '68ers. In the complexities of the Cold War, we may appreciate the centrism of Habermas' evolving profile, without adjusting it in conservative or radical directions, by learning how it pivots between the student revolt of the 1960s and the conservative-democratic restoration of the 1950s. His mature turn to democratic theory, decades after the upheavals of the 1960s, preserves and transforms both types of grounding postwar Germany (institutional and cultural renewal) and the two faces of Critical Theory and critical social theory (focus on institutional and legal formation and focus on social critique). In 1953, he did not share the restorative aspirations of German conservatives; but neither does he share the aims of the IfS in 1956–1959.

In the letter to his codirector of the IfS, Adorno, Horkheimer had even more practical worry than Marxist theory on his mind: the twenty-nine-year-old assistant, Habermas, would damage the postwar reputation and institutional stability of the IfS, as well as its ability to influence policy and obtain the funding resources. Habermas' report on Marx (LzDM) already focused unwanted attention on the IfS, Horkheimer worries. "Habermas opened the cover of the [IfS] cellar box so far, that it can be read what had been hidden within it": Habermas discussed Marcuse's early discovery and interpretation of the young Marx from 1932 and named Horkheimer among the likes of Lukács and Bloch in the context of reviewing Marxist literature (Albrecht et al. 1999, 287). Horkheimer built the entire post-exile renewal of the IfS on a prowestern, pro-American, pro-Adenaurean platform. The IfS was to contribute to reeducating the German people and reforming the state institutions (119–31). Yet he continued living with great anxiety about the return of Germany's unrehabilitated Nazi past (with a special dispensation of the high U.S. commissioner, he kept his dual U.S.-German citizenship; see Kraushaar 1998, 1:18). Horkheimer's conserving goals were very distant from the radical ones of the prewar Frankfurt years or the critical ones of the early U.S. exile. After the United States entered World War II to defend democratic bourgeois institutions against Fascism, Horkheimer's earlier anti-imperialist position gave way to his pro-Allied, pro-American position (Albrecht et al. 1999, 108–14). The ideal targeted audiences for reeducating Germany were no longer social democrats but rather the "pious Catholics" (125). In the context of "the German-American politics . . . [of]

reeducation, democratization, and the Cold War" (128), Horkheimer can allow no revolutionary vocabulary to come out of the IfS. In the course of the 1950s, he was called upon to make unofficial recommendations to the cultural ministry regarding university hiring. This required sometimes discrediting a Nazi sympathizer, sometimes filling a new position strategically or with a friend (9f., 142f., 189–202; cf. 288ff.). His censoring letter to Adorno regarding the unsuitability of Habermas' work (RBpB) as an IfS publication and, consequently, his recommendation that Habermas depart from the IfS, both seem consistent with this directorship style.

It would seem premature for us to conclude, by projecting a contemporary judgment into an earlier historical instant, that Habermas internalizes Horkheimer's "lesson" from 1958 by shutting the Marxist box again and then transforming Critical Theory into a philosophy of social sciences, a species of rationality theory with a "historically sociological clothing" (Albrecht et al. 1999, 290). We can evaluate such claims, namely, whether or how significantly Habermas remains interested in Marx, from the vantage point of the student revolt of 1967–1969 and even better in the following periods of his present trajectory.

My account of Habermas' 1950s path to Critical Theory attains even sharper contours within the context of the spring events of 1958. That year marks his decidedly public support for the early antinuclear movement. The two main German political issues, notes Kraushaar (1998, 1:23), of the 1950s were unification and remilitarization. As Adenauer considered (on April 4, 1957) adding tactical nuclear arms to Germany's military arsenal, eighteen German nuclear physicists issued the *Göttingen Manifesto* against the nuclear deployment; and as the Bundestag (West German parliament) in March of the next year agreed arming the West German military with nuclear weapons under NATO's provision for all European member states, a massive wave of strikes and demonstrations took place all over West Germany (Wiggershaus 1989, 611f.; 1998, 551). The SPD, unsuccessful in stopping the nuclear armament procedurally, called on March 10, 1958, for an extraparliamentary action under the heading *Kampf dem Atomtod* (Struggle against nuclear annihilation; see Kraushaar 1998, 1:23).

Consistent with his evolving idea of radical democracy, Habermas takes an active role in the APO. This is the situation in April 1958, when more than 150,000 people march silently through Hamburg. On May 20, protests take place at fourteen different schools. In front of about 400 people at a student and faculty rally at the main Frankfurt square (Römerberg), Habermas (aged twenty-eight) speaks in support of the citizens' duty to act in civil disobedience (cf. CD) against the entrenched politics of power. This speech must have rubbed Horkheimer doubly the wrong way: as an antiestablishment, anti-NATO, and in key respects anti-U.S. critique of the politics of power; and as an affront to the chairman of the board of the IfS, Franz Böhm, a professor at Frankfurt's Goethe-Universität, a member of the conservative CDU, and an elected member of the Bundestag. In the same issue of the student paper that prints Habermas' speech (UeB), Böhm publishes an opposing view caricaturing the antinuclear movement and the APO as opening gates "for a new form of Nazism" (Wiggershaus 1989, 612; 1998, 551). Enter another historical irony: a conservative supporter of the IfS, Böhm, accuses the antimilitarist movement of inciting havoc and colluding with Fascism; in 1967, Habermas charges the APO of flirting with 'Left Fascism'.

Habermas unmasks in his antinuclear speech the Cold War politics of "Great Powers" (UeB 104). Wars can be waged, but they cannot be won (105); he presses his radicalized insight into Kant's idea of perpetual peace (cf. EdA). Nor can we prevent wars, he insists, by better preparing for them. He defends the early antinuclear movement against tendentious charges of its being a servant of Communist propaganda. This very charge is more indicative of Horkheimer's general estimation of the entire APO affair (1958a,b; cf. Albrecht et al. 1999, 151f.). Horkheimer compares the antinuclear movement to Egyptian president Gamal Nasser's support for the Lebanese uprising and to Russian nationalism. He imputes anti-American resentment to the participants in the antinuclear movement. Like Böhm, he worries about Fascism from this quarter rather than from the politics of power (Horkheimer 1958a, 103f.; 1958b, 111f.).

The neo-Nazi revival does not come to haunt Horkheimer from the Left but from the Right. In the year Habermas leaves the IfS, during the Christmas holidays of 1959, two junior members of a right-wing party desecrate with swastikas the newly opened synagogue and the memorial to the victims of the Nazi regime in Köln. Next January, some 685 anti-Semitic copycat acts follow in West and East Germany. As Germany's restoration is exposed to the whole world to see, with protests against the Adenauer regime taking place in the United States and Israel, Horkheimer still worries on January 6 about "Nasser and his Fascist advisors" and about "the dangers of liquidation of Israel" (Kraushaar 1998, 1:25; 2: doc. 55). The turn of 1959–1960 marks Horkheimer's growing paranoia and "resignation" from public involvement. He even considers returning to the United States (1:26). As Horkheimer retreats, Adorno takes over as the director of the IfS in 1959 (Critchley and Schroeder 1998, 374; Albrecht et al. 1999, 182).

NOTES

1. As we have virtually no membership records on the Hitler Youth or the League of German Girls preserved in the Berlin Document Center (Bundesarchiv Berlin-Lichterfelde and the BDC microfilms made recently available in the U.S. National Archives, College Park, Md.), I can rely only on Habermas' one public statement about this part of his youth. I found the only other reference to it in Keulartz (1995, 13): "During the war Habermas was a member of the 'Hitler Youth', the year 1944 he spent half a year on the 'Western Wall' and then several months with farmers in the countryside. Toward the end of the war he moved back with his family in Gummersbach, a small city near Düsseldorf where, as he himself ascertains, the structures of bourgeois society were conserved as if in a preserving jar."

2. Albrecht's chapter is called "Die Frankfurter Schule in der Geschichte der Bundesrepublik"(497–529); cf. Schelsky (1957). See n. 16 below.

3. For the discussion of the relationship between Habermas' theory and existential motives as well as a consideration of whether and how Auschwitz figures in his theory and politics, see chaps. 5, 7, and 8. On theory and practice, as well as philosophy and politics, see the discussions of the student movement in chaps. 2, 4 below.

4. The summer semester lecture text from 1935 reads: "Was heute vollends als Philosophie des Nationalsozialismus herumgeboten wird, aber mit dem inneren Wahrheit und Größe des Nationalsozialismus nicht das Geringste zu tun hat, das macht seine Fischzüge in diesen trüben Gewässern der 'Werte' und 'Ganzheiten'" (Heidegger 1953a, 152; 1959, 199). The second use of "Nationalsozialismus" was replaced in 1953 with "Bewegung."

5. For the response to Habermas, see Lewalter (1953). For an indirect response to Habermas, see Heidegger (1953b; [1966] 1976). For other sources on this affair, I draw on Leaman (1993, 109–49; 148 n. 42 citing Marten [1987]). Leaman claims that there were two students of Heidegger who asked him to delete the controversial sentence. Habermas mentions the 1988 private letter from Marten in WaW, n. 52 (three collaborators of Heidegger, not two students, are reportedly involved). Cf. Holub (1991, 16–19); Habermas' 1953 article (MHgH) and WaW 161–63.

6. One could compare the relative shortness of Heidegger's active and public involvement with the Nazis with the more substantive support that the prominent member of the former Yugoslav praxis philosophers Mihailo Marković gave to the genocidal regime of Serbian leader Slobodan Milošević. But this may not be a comparison, such as some supporters of NATO's bombing of Serbia utilized, between the Holocaust and ethnic cleansing. Comparing Marković with Heidegger has two merits. First, we can contrast their articulation of earnest praxis for social liberation and existential freedom, respectively. Praxis philosophy, like the early Marcuse, develops a notion of radical praxis out of existential phenomenology. Second, we can take Habermas' later intimate involvement with the praxis group and contrast it with the manifest rejection of existential approaches, the rejection found almost universally (with Marcuse and Habermas being two exceptions) among Critical Theorists. We must ask, then, whether or not these theorists, for all their criticism of Heidegger's politics and philosophy, lack an adequate self-critique of their own proximity to the failures of praxis philosophy. Has one theorized adequately the paths to multicultural social justice? Could not the theoretical failure to take seriously questions of nationality, race, and ethnicity have contributed to the present political disaster of Yugoslavia, as well as to the actual complicity of some former praxis philosophers with later nationalist fervor? Outlaw is one philosopher who pointed out, repeatedly and quite early on, the ongoing blindness of Habermasian Critical Theory to race issues (see the analyses by the one-time editor of *Praxis International*, Outlaw, 1996). Outlaw's thinking (and warning, I would say) stands virtually alone among social theorists of that time. On praxis philosophy and Yugoslavia, see Secor (1999).

7. Heidegger runs around Rome with the Nazi Party pin on his coat during his 1936 visit with Karl Löwith (see Leaman 1993, 114).

8. Rothacker directed Otto Pöggeler's and Karl-Otto Apel's dissertations, as well as those of Habermas. In his 1984 Starnberg interview with Habermas, Dews uses "Ernst" and not "Erich" as Rothacker's first name (see AS 192 and the index entry for Rothacker); whereas Josef Fruchtl in his 1991 question to Habermas employs the name "Erich" (see AS 217).

While both usages are printed in Dews's edited collection of interviews (AS), only "Erich" is correct. For an extensive discussion of Rothacker's cultural anthropology, National Socialism, and Habermas' thinking, particularly on the parallel interests of Rothacker and Heidegger to overhaul in 1933 the university education in the spirit of Nazi movement, see Keulartz (1995, 106–34). For Becker's views, see his work on Nietzsche from 1942. Keulartz cites Weber (1989, 139 and 152) for his discussion of Rothacker.

9. Horkheimer makes his first postwar visit to Germany in 1948 (Kraushaar 1998, 1:17).

10. Leaman (1993, 18f.; 52 on Husserl). For the list of nine professors, see Leaman (142 n. 4). Leaman (108) shows that the total ranks of philosophy professors between January 30, 1933, and May 8, 1945, grew from 180 to 214, out of which the number of immigrants in the same period was forty. Out of the 174 who did not emigrate, 115 philosophy professors (or 66 percent of the total) were members in various Nazi organizations (significantly, 78 were in the Nazi Party, NSDAP; 31 in SA; and 4 in SS). Jan Patočka, a one-time student of both Husserl and Heidegger, invited Husserl to Prague to give in 1935 his "Crisis" Lectures. He hoped then to find a position for him in Prague. Patočka himself was not allowed to teach during the Nazi occupation of Czechoslovakia.

11. See Wiggershaus (1989, 600; 1998, 539f.).

12. I am relying here almost entirely on the documentation provided by Kraushaar (1998, 1:21–23). The two other major studies of the Frankfurt School (Jay or Wiggershaus) do not discuss this topic.

13. Kraushaar (1998, 1:21) notes three films: *Jud Süß* (a wartime production, this film was shown also in the Soviet Union as part of German propaganda), *Unsterbliche Geliebte,* and *Hanna Amon* (1951 releases).

14. Cited in Kraushaar (1998, 1:21; cf. 77–90 on the chronology of events in 1952).

15. Horkheimer dedicated in Frankfurt the new International Student House on February 22, 1953, the ten-year anniversary of founding of the White Rose, the anti-Nazi student resistance group. High German and U.S. dignitaries were present at the opening (see Kraushaar 1998, 1:22).

16. Albrecht et al.'s (1999) extremely well-researched and timely volume is one of several new evaluative works on the Frankfurt School. It is composed of fifteen chapters, an introduction, and a concluding overview. I refer to the pages of the book, but note that Albrecht wrote chapters 1, 5–9, 12, 14, and the overview; Michael Bock wrote chapters 2, 15; Harald Homann wrote chapter 3; Friedrich H. Tenbruck wrote chapter 4; and Günther C. Behrmann wrote chapters 10–11, 13. I rely in my general historical narrative on their work, along with Kraushaar's edited trilogy (1998) and Wiggershaus's study (1989/1998). See also Müller (2000). On the early history of the IfS, its founding, exile, and immediate postwar years, Jay's pioneering study (1973) provides an excellent resource.

17. Wiggershaus (1989/1998) gives an appropriate heading to his chapter 6 on this period, "Critical Ornament of a Restoration Society."

18. The contributing essay is by Gunzelin Schmid Noer, "Horkheimer's-Habermas Kritik von 1958," in Kraushaar (1998, 3:267–72).

19. Kraushaar (1998, 1:22) notes that protests against the Harlan films took place also in Göttingen, which is one of the three universities Habermas attends between 1949 and 1954.

20. Krahl was Adorno's doctoral student and his later nemesis during the events of the 1960s. (See chaps. 2, 4 below.)

Chapter Two

FROM INCUBATION TO REVOLT, 1960–1969

The previous chapter took us to the end of the 1950s, when we found Habermas delivering a powerful speech in front of an antinuclear demonstration in Frankfurt. The concluding part of that presentation from 1958 signals the beginning of one of the most radical and critical phases of his trajectory. It is this situation, with Habermas at twenty-eight, that foreshadows his positive reception by progressive students and his ongoing critique of antidemocratic trends. In his speech from 1958 (UeB 106), Habermas

- argues for the right to demonstrate "extra muros" against the entrenched establishment of power[1]
- links one's right to critique and protest with the special "obligation" on part of the intellectuals
- challenges the hegemony of NATO within the international structures of great powers
- challenges "intra muros," those who passively do nothing against entrenched power
- praises the "civil courage" of the anxiety-free oppositional movement

The year 1959 marks a political and philosophical turn in several senses. Habermas leaves the IfS and begins to work with Abendroth on his second doctorate. His completed book (SÖ) is published in 1962 and soon becomes the core working text of the increasingly radicalized progressive students. Although the Adenauer era lasts until 1963, it is the anti-Semitic events of 1959–1960 that represent the watershed sea change, disclosing the intrinsic failure of that era's restoration. The shored-up sinister continuities underpinning the institutional grounding of the West German state will explode in an open generational rebellion in the 1960s, which Albrecht and his coauthors (1999) appropriately name postwar

Germany's "intellectual grounding." The sociology conference, held in May 1959, already displays the theoretical ruptures. "Released through the wave of the swastika desecrations 1959 began the politicization of the theory in renewed preoccupation with National Socialism, and it was sharpened by the phase of the rediscovery of the Marxist contents of Critical Theory" (170; cf. 180ff.).

We would be wise to place Habermas' yes and no to the student protest of the 1960s—the core situation to be discussed in this chapter and in chapter 4—between the preceding and the following two periods, the last of which will be the subject of chapters 3 and 5:

- the thaw or the incubation years, 1960–1966
- the upheaval years of the worldwide student revolt, 1967–1969
- the ice-hardening years of revision, 1977–1988

FROM THAW TO INCUBATION: HABERMAS' ASCENT TO THE INTELLECTUAL LEADERSHIP OF PROGRESSIVE GERMAN STUDENTS, 1960–1966

> The years between 1960 and 1967 were the incubation period, in which the cultural sphere, intellectual impulses, and non-institutionalized public opinion began to acquire political weight. The student movement was the subsequent explosion which no one foresaw, and which lasted for one or two years. (NR 22/AS 230)

Wiggershaus explains that Horkheimer laid down extensive research requests as preconditions for Habermas' second doctorate at the IfS. These demands would take Habermas off track and significantly delay his chances for *Habilitation* and a full-time teaching post. In fact, Horkheimer compelled Habermas in the end to leave the institute. Wiggershaus is also quite frank about Horkheimer's persistent animosity, if not rivalry, toward Habermas and about Adorno's vain attempt to mediate the conflict even after Habermas left the IfS. Horkheimer considered Habermas too far left for the Institute and was uncomfortable, as I explained in the previous chapter, with Habermas' work on *Student und Politik*. This successful sociological study of Frankfurt students develops a radically democratic variant of Critical Theory influenced equally by early Adorno and Marcuse and by Habermas' original elaboration of participatory democracy. Horkheimer reacted conservatively to various issues of the postwar era—the colonial war in Algeria, German rearmament, the U.S. war in Vietnam. This orientation matched neither the prewar work nor the early exile of the Frankfurt Institute, and it went against Habermas' overall social democratic orientation. Habermas offers his rather generous explanation for that period of his work at the IfS, drawing on Horkheimer's posthumously published diaries: he suggests that Horkheimer's growing conservatism arose from war trauma and from his renewed fear that radical thinking or public activism might compromise the work of the institute, making it impossible to keep it safe from the Cold War establishment. Horkheimer's postwar directorship of the IfS placed the Critical Theory of the 1950s in a protective "ditch," thereby smothering it for the sake of contributing to the restorative, institutional grounding of the postwar state (cf. McCumber 1996). If, as Habermas wants us to believe, Horkheimer's views were just a protective bubble with a more radical view hidden from the public eye, then there is no indication of this. Horkheimer neither gave Habermas a needed break during his assistant years in Frankfurt nor offered a private clarification of his political fears (AS 218–22).[2]

Utilizing the grant from the German Research Association, Habermas ventures on his own, away from the IfS, and turns his Marburg *Habilitation* into a book. He begins his research on this work while still associated with Horkheimer and Adorno at the IfS where, as already mentioned, he worked after his Ph.D. studies as Adorno's first research assistant from 1956 to 1959. Habermas at first intends to submit his research on the public sphere for his promotion in Frankfurt.[3] When it becomes apparent that he will not be able to proceed with this work under Horkheimer—Adorno's goodwill and interest to facilitate the process notwithstanding—Habermas completes his second doctorate with Abendroth, who was then professor of political science in Marburg. The manuscript is published with Luchterhand and dedicated to Abendroth. The original preface (Frankfurt, fall 1961) makes no mention of the Frankfurt Institute. In 1961, instead of taking up the post as a *Privatdozent* in Marburg and, more surprisingly, even before finishing his second doctorate, Habermas is called by Hans-Georg Gadamer and Karl Löwith (both one-time students of Heidegger) to take up the Extraordinary Professorship of Philosophy in Heidelberg. This skyrocketing path has its ironic culmination in Habermas' return to Frankfurt in 1964 as Horkheimer's successor (Wiggershaus 1989, 616f., 625; 1998, 555, 563).[4]

After his traumatic departure from the IfS, Habermas' star rises rapidly. It is worth reviewing his career in one glance:

- 1961, he becomes *Privatdozent* (associate professor) in Marburg.
- 1962, he is named Extraordinary Professor of Philosophy in Heidelberg even before completing his second doctorate in Marburg.
- 1964, he is appointed professor of philosophy and sociology in Frankfurt a/M to succeed none other than Horkheimer.

We may distinguish three Frankfurt periods punctuating Habermas' philosophical-political profile:

- 1956–1959, as Adorno's assistant at the IfS. This period covers the last segment of the Adenaurean era of restoration in the FRG (1959–1960).

- 1965, June 28 (the inaugural address) to 1971, as professor of philosophy and sociology. The period begins after the end of the Adenauer era (1963) and ends with the waning student movement (1969).
- 1982–1994, as professor of philosophy and sociology (retired from Frankfurt as professor emeritus since 1994). This period spans the antinuclear protests, the Historians' Debate (mid-1980s), and post-Wall Germany (1989–present), and it lasts from the beginning of Helmut Kohl's tenure as chancellor of the FRG (1982–1998).

When it comes to Habermas' work with Abendroth, two situation contexts are noteworthy. First, because of his illegal activities in the opposition to the Nazis, which began during his student years, Abendroth was sentenced in 1937 to four years in prison. Later he was forced to work in the special Punitive Battalion 999. After defecting to the Greek partisans, he became a British prisoner of war, being released in 1946. He earned his second doctorate while detained in the Soviet zone. In the immediate postwar years, Abendroth was one of the few openly socialist professors in Germany. Because of his progressive activities he almost fell into the hands of the Soviet secret service in December 1948. Abendroth left for West Germany, where he taught social science. Given the deadly continuity in postwar Germany, Abendroth, a unique case of a German partisan professor in the midst of Nazi sympathizers, represented a beacon of light to Habermas, even after the war's end (see PpP 249–52).[5]

Second, when Habermas could not get habilitated in Frankfurt due to Horkheimer's conservative postwar turn, Abendroth took him on without any hesitation. As Wiggershaus observes, Abendroth took notice of Habermas already at the time of his 1953 student publication of the critical essay on Heidegger. (Remember that Adorno also sides with Habermas in this regard and invites him in 1956 to work with the IfS in Frankfurt.) After the Marxist language and orientation are purged from the party platform of Social Democrats (at the SPD Bad Godesberg Conference, 1959), Habermas cofounds with Abendroth and several other progressive professors the Association of Socialist Sponsors of the Friends, Sponsors, and Former Members of the SDS (October 1961). Consequently, the student socialist organization, the SDS, is expelled from the SPD. This move spurs the gradual shift of the critical public sphere from Social Democrats to the more open structures of the student socialist organization. The SDS must now go through a period of incubation before it can became a springboard for the student movement.

This incubation situation of the progressive social forces is exactly what Habermas' work (SÖ) addresses, as well as what it itself calls into action. The significant extraparliamentary initiatives of the SDS begin to take place again during the years of the student revolt. His book on the public sphere turns its early attention to such extraparliamentary oppositional movements "to make it clear for myself and others that the political system of the Federal Republic has inherent weaknesses which can become dangerous" (KPS 517/AS 82). Thus, we would be remiss in not placing Habermas' first published monograph among the distinct positive influences on the student movement in West Germany. Not only sociologists and progressive philosophers but also the APO in Germany read and discuss his *Structural Transformation of the Public Sphere* (1962) during the incubation period. His work becomes very influential for the formation of the new oppositional movements, especially at German universities. Habermas views modern political public spheres—emerging from literary circles, salons, and cafes—as endowed with a potential for democratizing society. This potential is at the same time endangered. The student movement of the 1960s appropriates his analysis insofar as it targets the media monopoly, such as the one by the Springer Company or *Bildzeitung*, and the academic elitism with its unrepented Fascist past. But already in this work, Habermas shies away from a more radical questioning of the imperialist exploitation of Third World peoples by First World countries. Expressive of his skeptical generation's general attitude, Habermas will become less enthusiastic than the protesting generation about the revolutionary struggle, whether domestic or international. He will be much more eager to transform in a piecemeal fashion (i.e., while preserving) the achieved institutional grounding of postwar West Germany.

Habermas' unequivocal yes—and I mean the nonskeptical and enthusiastic half of his response—to the student protest crystallizes after the end of the Adenauer era (1963) and during the incubation years (1960–1966). The political consciousness of the new postwar generation was awakened in 1961 with the Israeli capture of Adolf Eichmann and his widely publicized trial in Jerusalem (cf. Arendt 1965). This was the year when the construction of the Berlin Wall began (August 13). In 1963, the Auschwitz trial took place in Frankfurt a/M, the Adenauer reign came to an end, and Ludwig Erhard became chancellor of the FRG. On May 18, 1965, the new West German parliament lifted the twenty-year limitation (from 1945) on prosecutions for murder. The Nazi war criminals could not become safer with the passage of time.

If Habermas' work on the public sphere contributed to the thaw, minimally within the progressive student movement and among the German Left already predisposed to it, then, reciprocally, his own positive incubation opening toward the events of the student revolt was formed in the context of two political situations of that period. The first event coincides with the completion of his book on the public sphere and with his Heidelberg appointment: the protest against the *Spiegel* affair by Heidelberg professors on December 12, 1962. The second, more prolonged, situation impacts the beginning of his professorship in Frankfurt: the formation of the Grand Coalition of Social Democrats (SPD) with the conservative Christian Democratic Union (CDU) and the Christian Social Union (CSU) in November 1966.

Der Spiegel was founded by Rudolph Augstein, its long-time publisher and editor, shortly after World War II as a nonpartisan, independently critical news weekly. Since then its circulation grew to over a million copies. In the estimation of one German historian, this political and cultural journal "has proved bolder than the parliamentary opposition in exposing the faults and abuses of government . . . and on occasions ministers have hit back" (Ardagh 1995, 362). This was the case with the so-called *Spiegel* affair in 1962. The journal published one of its famous in-depth and well-researched critical analyses of the defense policy of the FRG, implicating the minister of defense, Franz Josef Strauss. In October, the press offices as well as private residences were raided by the police; copies of the journal were confiscated; Augstein with several other editors were arrested and imprisoned; and the *Spiegel* correspondent for the Department of Defense, who was at the time on a trip in Spain, was detained by Franco's police and shipped under arrest to West Germany (Turner 1992, 135; Ardagh 1995, 362). One of the key charges was treason, which was justified by the claim that the *Spiegel* article disclosed confidential defense materials of the FRG illegally obtained by the press (Turner 1992, 135). Because the journal had scrutinized Strauss for some time, public suspicion about the origins of the police raid fell on him and Adenauer. There was an investigation of the matter in the parliament after the outcry at home and abroad, Strauss had to resign from the new cabinet, and Adenauer emerged from the entire mess considerably weaker. After the journal and all the accused editors were cleared of the charges against them, for which Augstein nonetheless paid with a fourteen-week imprisonment, Adenauer's fourteen-year-long postwar reign came to an end. He had to promise to step down in one year (136).

In his first year as the extraordinary Heidelberg professor, Habermas signs the protest declaration issued and sent to the parliament president, Eugen Gerstenmaier, by 285 professors, docents, and assistants at Heidelberg. The protest appeals to Article 17 of the Basic Law of the FRG and warns against police violations of parliamentary democracy and due legal process. The most significant point is addressed to the Adenauer regime, which is found responsible for the gangster tactics against the editors. The declaration invokes the historical context of the *Speigel* affair: "the failure of democratic continuity in Germany, the remembrance of the fall of the Weimar Republic [1933], and from that following breach of our tradition of lawful state during the Hitler period, [which] oblige all of us, to guard that the constitutional order and the rule of political decency are observed" ("Wir sind bestürzt, Herr Präsident" [We are disturbed, Mr. President, 1962], in Kraushaar 1998, 1:194). The context of the affair unmasks the contrast between the Fascist continuities surviving in the current regime and the face of postwar West German normality shown by Adenauer's restoration to the world. The affair signals the end of the Cold War restoration and reveals cracks in the icy veneer.

Perhaps recession accelerates the incubation in the mid-1960s just as Ludwig Erhard's era of Germany's postwar "economic miracle" ends. His chancellorship lasts barely three years, and the conservative coalition of the CSU/CDU and the FDP does not survive past the fall of 1966. The danger of the ultra-Right NPD gaining access to the government prompts the Social Democrats (SPD) to form the Grand Coalition with the CDU/CSU. The SPD's Godesberg Program purged the party in 1959 of the more radical platform planks and Marxist language. The SPD's "grand" compromise with the conservatives now wins the ministerial position for none other than Franz Josef Strauss of the *Spiegel* affair, something that is unacceptable to the FDP, which forced Strauss from the government in 1962. Kurt Georg Kiesinger, reeducated as a genuine democrat from being a member of the Nazi Party (since 1933) and a one-time employee in the Nazi Propaganda Ministry, is elected in 1966 the new chancellor of the FRG, with Willy Brandt serving as his foreign minister (Turner 1992, 142).

Habermas moved meanwhile back to Frankfurt in order to assume after Horkheimer the vacant professor chair in philosophy and sociology. Not even a year after his inaugural lecture, June 28, 1965, Habermas enters the beginning of the new political season of turmoil. On November 26, 1966, he signs an open letter of professors and assistants of the Johann Wolfgang Goethe-Universität to the SPD chairman, Brandt, which objects to the Grand Coalition. The charge of political opportunism characterizes the letter. On the same day at noon about 100 students demonstrate in the center of Frankfurt against the Grand Coalition. The poster for the event argues that only the extreme Right can gain from the coalition—the reverse of the SPD's self-justification for entering the coalition. Another student poster implicates the SPD in a sinister love affair with the CDU, whereby the political opposition goes to sleep—literally and sexually—with the enemy. Three days later 200 students demonstrate against the Grand Coalition and call for a minority coalition of the SPD with the FDP and Brandt as the chancellor (Kraushaar 1998, 1:239).

At a November panel discussion put together by the SDS, Habermas delivers "Theses against the Coalition of the Despondent with Dictators." In this sharply worded presentation, he opens with an emotion-laden wording: "The Social Democratic leaders [*Führer*]" have entered the Grand Coalition with the CDU/CSU. He does not just articulate an ordinary political distaste for the Grand Coalition, which emerges out of an "alibi" by Social Democrats that "a state of emergency" for such compromise with the two right-wing parties exists. Rather, the new regime will likely impose "a state of emergency on democracy" itself, he charges.[6] "We have reason to fear the new government more than the old one." He repeats and varies this key phrase at the opening of each of the next four short segments, employing the highly effective rhetorical skill of a preacher or an African American civil rights activist at a mass rally, but something rarely found in his other writings: "We have reason to fear the new government" (a) because of "the dangerous course" it charts ahead; (b) because it "endangers the foundations of parliamentary democracy"; (c) because the Social Democrats were willing to "pay any price for sharing power"; and (d) indeed, "we have reason to fear the new government," he ends the rhetorical series with an 'amen'. There is one hope, however, he concludes in this powerfully crafted speech, in content and form echoing Marx's critique of the SPD's Gotha Program from 1878 (cf. Wiggershaus 1989, 664; 1998, 598). This is truly a paradoxical hope. The hope is that the Grand Coalition of the despondent with the dictators will collapse and thereby shatter "the fateful spirit of self-destruction of a [Social Democratic] party with a great tradition" (TgKM 216f.). When Kiesinger's cabinet later introduces emergency powers *(Notstandgesetze)*, this event becomes one rallying point of the demonstrations in May 1968.

Turning to the formative influences on Habermas' ambivalent yes or his no— I mean here the skeptical and nonenthusiastic half of his response—to the student protest, I wish to pay attention to how the incubation events, leading up to the revolt, gradually overtake his own yearning, preparation, leadership role, and generally sympathetic rapport he has with the students. Parallel to the publication events of the works that made Habermas attractive to the progressive students (SuP [1961]; SÖ [1962]), and simultaneously with his June 28, 1965, Frankfurt inaugural lecture (EuI), there is another publication history. In his Frankfurt lecture, Habermas takes off from Horkheimer's ([1937] 1972) distinction between Traditional and Critical Theory in order to take up the task left by Husserl's lectures on *The Crisis of European Sciences* ([1935] 1970); but neither Critical Theory nor the Frankfurt School figure centrally in Habermas' lecture. And there is no sign of influence by Marcuse's critical social theory, coming from the discontented U.S. shores, on his programmatic research agenda (Albrecht et al. 1999, 32f., 317f.). More as a response to Husserl's theoretical demand for new foundations of sciences than to Marcuse's practical demand for social critique, transformation, and liberation, Habermas inaugurates in Frankfurt the theoretical program for the normative foundations of human and social sciences, not a new critical social theory in Marcuse's sense.

A few months before Habermas' public return to Frankfurt, on February 13, Marcuse (1965a) employs the concept of the Frankfurt School in a celebration essay for Horkheimer's seventieth birthday. Horkheimer, against all expectations, must be recognized as the founder of the Frankfurt School, Marcuse opens with praise. That founding spans the exile years of the IfS in 1932 and the end of World War II. Marcuse then slips in his own wider understanding of critical social theory. His wording differs quite sharply from Horkheimer's canonical version of Critical Theory in that it explodes the Cold War cover of the IfS altogether. "On both sides of the Iron Curtain it [the Frankfurt School] is for many in the younger generation the sign of possibility to apply a critical theory of society, as it was developed in the nineteenth century, to the contemporary phase of industrial society." Marcuse goes one step further in unlocking the treasure box of the early critical social theory hidden by Horkheimer in the basement of the postwar IfS. He shows how Horkheimer developed the concept of Critical Theory in the debates with positivism and metaphysics, but he then suggests that the concept was to serve only as "a cover for Marxism." For Horkheimer, and by association partly for Adorno, Critical Theory had been a cover of self-distancing from the early Marxism of the IfS. In the mid-1960s, Marcuse insists, "it is clear that critical theory announces likewise the critique of Marxian Theory" (Marcuse 1965a, 189).

In the case of Marcuse, two things are true: in his U.S. publication of *Eros and Civilization* ([1955] 1974), the concept of Critical Theory functions as a cover for reinterpreting Freud through Marx during the Cold War (and might function so for some today),[7] and now he develops a new critical theory out of critically engaging Marxism (see 1969a) and not rejecting it wholesale. We can situate Habermas' ambivalence toward the student revolt with a sharpness of a later evaluative hindsight. This ambivalence fits between Horkheimer's rejection of Habermas' early Marxist radicalism in 1958–1960 and Marcuse's departure from the Critical Theory of the 1950s into a new critical social theory of the 1960s. While Marcuse's dream of the postwar Frankfurt Institute was unrealizable in the conservative milieu of the 1950s (see Albrecht et al. 1999, 282f.), while this dream was dreamed by Habermas during the first Frankfurt period between 1956 and 1958 as he discovered early Marcuse, while the dream was then chased away by Horkheimer as a nightmare in 1959, Marcuse makes a self-conscious effort, at least since 1964, to nurture the return of the repressed dream to West Germany (290–93, 302–11). He defies his securing generation's preoccupations by jumping over the skepticism of Habermas' generation and by embracing the sensibilities of the revolting youth. He becomes that "'father' of the student movement" (317–27) who does not need to be transgressed in a generational struggle.

Fanon's revolutionary work was published in France in 1961. In his preface to the French edition of *The Wretched of the Earth*, Jean-Paul Sartre sides with the anticolonial struggle. Marcuse's *One-Dimensional Man,* written in exciting and accessible American prose, offers a severe indictment of western industrial societies, imperialism, and human willingness to participate in unfreedom and oppression. It appeared first in English in 1964, the year of the fourteenth Sociological Conference in Berlin. One main conference event is devoted to Max Weber's hundredth birthday. At the plenary panel, Marcuse is profiled with Talcott Parsons. The two North Americans could not have been more different. Marcuse's critique of Weber's sociological skepticism about the possibilities of social liberation draws against Parsons on Hegelian Marxism and the early critical social theory, and in both on his own new critique of the late industrial society. While Marcuse's presentation, as well as his book, is severely criticized from Parsonsian positions by Benjamin Nelson, this exchange marks an exact "place and time-point of the reimport of critical [social] theory" to Frankfurt—with Adorno, Habermas, Horkheimer, and Marcuse present in one place (Albrecht et al. 1999, 303).

The books by Fanon and Marcuse mentioned above attain the stature of manifestos of the 1960s revolt, although in very different ways. Marcuse's "Repressive

Tolerance," first published in English in the same year that Habermas gave his inaugural lecture in Frankfurt, establishes direct links between his and Fanon's (and by extension Sartre's) revolutionary intents (see Marcuse 1965b, 110). Moreover, Marcuse introduces here "a 'right of resistance' to the point of subversion" and characterizes it as "a 'natural right' of resistance for oppressed and overpowered minorities to use extralegal means if the legal ones have proved to be inadequate" (116). As the reader might have noticed at the opening of this chapter, when in 1958 Habermas (UeB) argued for 'civil duty' to take an APO action against the nuclear militarization of the West German army where parliamentary means to do so failed, he was not that far off from Marcuse's meaning of this 'right' to resist. But by the time students interpret Marcuse to legitimate their militancy, Habermas—as if needing to balance the scales of history—grows at first lukewarm and then quite cold and even harsh toward *any* such 'extralegal' militancy or 'violence' on the part of the student movement.[8]

All this hot literature arrives in West Germany at about the time when campuses in Berlin, Frankfurt, and elsewhere start to heat up. The original German—unembellished and uncensored—republication of Marcuse's essays from 1934–1938 appeared in 1965. In the opening paragraph of the foreword to his essays, Marcuse further corrects (i.e., radicalizes) the conservative reception of Critical Theory in Germany by linking the early critical social theory of the IfS to the present situation. "I have let them [essays] be republished unchanged. No revision could bridge the chasm that separates the period in which they were written from the present one. At that time, it was not yet clear that the powers that had defeated fascism by virtue of their technical and economic superiority would strengthen and streamline the social structure which had produced fascism" (1988, xvii). Commenting on this foreword, Günther C. Behrmann (in Albrecht et al. 1999, 309) suggests that Marcuse crafted this introductory text with Horkheimer and the postwar history of the IfS in mind. German readership, more than any other, would be able to appreciate these early essays, thereby fostering "the renewal of critical [social] theory" (311). Marcuse's publication history surpasses anything that the IfS produced in the postwar years. Behrmann lists the following data on West German sales: 80,000 copies of Marcuse's republished early essays, 60,000 copies of "Repressive Tolerance," and over 25,000 of his *Essay on Liberation*. Fanon's *Wretched of the Earth* with Sartre's preface was published in German in 1966, the same year as Adorno's *Negative Dialectics* and Marcuse's "Repressive Tolerance." *One-Dimensional Man* in German translation appeared a year later in May; by the end of the student movement, its worldwide sales in various languages reached 300,000 copies (290–93, 302–17; cf. Wiggershaus 1989, 676–83; 1998, 609–16).

By 1966, the thaw long gone, the incubation now sets the public stage for the next act.

THE STUDENT REVOLT: HABERMAS' YES AND NO TO THE MOVEMENT, 1967–1969

What 1945 signified in terms of a transformation of our constitutional status, 1968 signified for the loosening up of our political culture, for a liberalization in forms of living and in relationships which is only making its full effects felt today. (NR 28/AS 236)

The view of Habermas as someone who stood on the other side of the barricade erected by the student movement in West Germany in the 1960s or who consequently abandoned this revolt's hope for a more just social form of life is unnuanced and one-sided. At the very least, we must not seek Habermas' cautious side, or perhaps what some might dub as his conservative tendency, exclusively in the public responses he gave to the student rebellion at its peak. At the heyday of the protest in West Germany, Habermas is clearly recognized (even if less dramatically than Marcuse's work and voice are received within the New Left) by the students as their leading supporter and spokesperson. Within the established professorate in Germany, his active engagement with the student struggle has been more of a bright exception than a rule. Since the postwar conservative tenor of the West German academy was neither successfully disturbed nor radically democratized, the rupturing nature of the student upheaval took on the unfinished task of dislodging that conservative mentality. Habermas' later criticisms of the students' grasp of the era as well as their strategies and tactics notwithstanding, the movement challenged the status quo at its core. Habermas acknowledges this historical fact on numerous occasions. We should remind ourselves that his repeated complaints about the false continuities choking the academy and society provide one of the better justifications for the generational disobedience by the protesting students. If the youth revolt of the 1960s had occurred during Habermas' youth in the 1950s, would not Habermas have likely joined the revolt? His skeptical generation is stuck in a difficult predicament of coming of age too early for the social upheaval that did not happen and of growing too safe as well as fearful for the rebellion of the 1960s.

Habermas' active role in the student movement was more the exception than the rule, even among his own peers. Nonetheless, nobody can fully escape the hermeneutical horizon and the proclivities of one's era or socialization years. This sober concession need not be to Heidegger or Gadamer in their conservative nod to the primacy of tradition over critique. Hegel (along with Kierkegaard, Nietzsche, and Marx) already draws our attention to the limits of one's historical consciousness. Revolutionary consciousness, too, never emerges out of nowhere, in a temporal vacuum, as if ahead of itself. Otherwise particular social revolutions could come on the world historical stage at any time and under any and all conditions. But we know this to be false, not only from Marx's theorizing but also from historical experience. Habermas' skeptical generation, maturing after 1945, inherited from the securing generation of its parents the guilt and thereby its lifelong task to deal with the sense of shame. These two generational postwar situations do not match the revolutionary situations of the protesting generation of 1967–1969. If they could match them, then postwar Fascist continuities, which Habermas decries vis-à-vis Heidegger, Rothacker, and the entire Adenauer era, would not be able to hold fast until the 1960s. The absence of a generational match marks the sui generis situation of the rebellious youth (tab. 2.1).

How or why the years between 1960 and 1966 burst forth into a rebellious instant of 1967–1969 cannot be that easily explained. The incubation period alone fails to account for the unexpected birth of revolutionary spirit. If we could rationalize its emergence in a linear or an incremental fashion, then some quantitative measures would satisfy the question. Perhaps Sartre's dialectical analysis (1976) of the groups in fusion, with which he approaches the events of the French Revolution, offers one of the happier phenomenologies of qualitative change. Even this description, however, does not explain the rupture.

Who are the actors gradually populating the stage in Berlin and Frankfurt—the main centers of the West German student revolt? The two leading theorists

Table 2.1   Impact of the Institutional and Intellectual Groundings of West Germany (FRG) on the Evolution of the Student Movement, Marcuse, and Habermas

Impact of the Grounding of the FRG	Marcuse (1964–79) and the Student Movement (1967–69)	Habermas (1967–2000)
institutional and restorative (1949–63)	demand for radical democratization of institutions, extraparliamentary opposition, and critique of imperialism	discourse theory of democracy and law; cosmopolitan world citizenship, and new international world order
intellectual and critical (1967–69)	'natural right' to revolt against the restorative institutions of power; the struggle vs. Fascist culture; search for new modes of social and personal existence	ethico-political discourses on the future of our traditions; ongoing public interventions against neo-Nazi historical or political revisions
Basic Mode of Critical Theory	revolting and transformative	skeptical and integrative

and activists of the student revolt were Hans-Jürgen Krahl in Frankfurt a/M and Rudi Dutschke in West Berlin. Krahl was Adorno's doctoral student and a reader of Habermas' works; while Dutschke, originally from the GDR, was chiefly inspired by Marcuse and his own activist roots, first as a Christian conscientious objector to military service in the GDR and later in the group called Subversive Action (Wiggershaus 1989, 686; 1998, 618). Whereas Dutschke became Habermas' nemesis at the very outset of the revolt in 1967, Adorno's lawsuit against Krahl for trespassing the confines of the IfS marks the waning days of the student revolt, ending with Adorno's death in 1969.

Sometime in 1962 a student group called Subversive Action was formed (see Kraushaar 1998, 2: docs. 77, 83). In May 1964, the group issued and posted on the walls of several West German universities a "Suchanzeige" (wanted) ad notice (doc. 84)—seeking independent intellectuals who were dissatisfied with the status quo and wanted to come together to brainstorm about some ways out. The text of the poster juxtaposed various critical phrases reproduced from Adorno's published works with what the authors of the notice suggested was the existing uncritical praxis of Critical Theorists. Adorno's Frankfurt address was advertised on the very notice, recommending that he be contacted by those who object to the contradiction between Critical Theory and uncritical practice. Ernst Bloch, after Adorno sought to preserve both his own reputation and copyright, had one of his students help find the authors of the poster. The two identified ringleaders were later fined DM100 for the breach of Adorno's copyright (Kraushaar 1998, 1:26). This event might be of minor historical significance, even if it gives an early indication of the difference between Adorno's and Marcuse's attitudes toward the rebellious youth. But in Berlin, Dutschke is one of the students who responds to the ad. Dutschke first becomes active in the Subversive Action group and then ascends through the SDS ranks in Berlin to the position of student leader and theorist. To the degree that he wins Marcuse's friendship during the heat of the movement, Dutschke's activism and theoretical analyses distance him from the other members of the first and second generations of Critical Theorists.

The key events between the incubation period and the watershed turning point of June 2, 1967, follow with increasing intensity. On May 7, 1965, the rector of Berlin's Free University bans a panel discussion on the occasion of the twentieth anniversary of the German defeat in 1945. This event is organized by the students. The rector objects to the main invited speaker, the journalist Erich Kuby, because of his prior criticism of the university. Students hold the gathering anyway at a different Berlin campus. About one year later, on June 23,[9] this increasingly assertive student body organizes the first sit-in protest of 3,000 students in West Germany against the repressive measures at Berlin's Free University. This is just about two years after the December 1964 sit-in strike in Berkeley at which 800 students were arrested. Berlin becomes overnight the Berkeley of Germany (Wiggershaus 1989, 683, 678; 1998, 616, 611).

A conference called Vietnam—Analysis of a Model, with Habermas, Marcuse, and Oskar Negt as participants, takes place in Frankfurt on May 22, 1966. The conference, sponsored by the SDS, brings together about 2,000 participants. It opens with Marcuse's rousing speech and introduces the major themes of his new writings. Students link Marcuse's words with his support for the California-based student movement, and they join both in their minds to the fledgling West German student movement. The event is followed by a massive anti-Vietnam demonstration (681/614; Albrecht et al. 1999, 319f.).

Anti-Vietnam protests continue in Frankfurt the following year on February 4, 11, 18 and reach a turning point on May 7. On February 11, 150 students march to the U.S. consulate in Frankfurt. Some students burn a U.S. flag and several are arrested in skirmishes with the police (Kraushaar 1998, 1:245f.). At this time Angela Davis is a second-year student in Frankfurt where, since 1965, she attends classes with Adorno, Habermas, Negt, and Alfred Schmidt. She met Marcuse as the most captivating teacher during her undergraduate studies and discovered through him her love for philosophy and critical social theory. Marcuse volunteers to tutor the young Davis in weekly one-on-one sessions in the history of philosophy, starting with the pre-Socratics. Davis takes Marcuse's course on Kant's first critique and in 1964 is encouraged by him to take up her graduate studies in Frankfurt. She departs for Frankfurt a/M in the summer of 1965. In her reflections of the second year of her Frankfurt stay, Davis (1988, 143) recalls the heat of the situation on February 11, 1967: "After several hours of sitting and running, and a sizeable number of arrests, we made it to the Hauptwache, the center of the city, and listened to an arousing speech by Rudi Dutschke, the Chairman of S.D.S., who was later [April 1968] shot in the head by a would-be assassin who said he was inspired by the assassination of Martin Luther King."

On May 7, Horkheimer takes part at the opening of German-American Friendship Week. About 200 demonstrators from the SDS protest at Frankfurt's Römerberg against the military ceremony. At the beginning of the ceremony, Horkheimer, as the honorary guest of the city, parades himself "ostensively" side by side with a U.S. general (Kraushaar 1998, 1:27). As he arrives late to the tribune, the protesters whistle and shout at him to get out. At the end of the event he walks away from the podium hand in hand with the city mayor (252). In the evening, Horkheimer (1967; also in Kraushaar 1998, 1:252f., 27) presents a paper at the America-Haus, in which he criticizes the anti–Vietnam War protests from the position of someone who was liberated from the Nazi regime by the Allies. Without liberation by the United States in 1945, Germans would not be able to speak today freely, he contends against the anti-American sentiments of the protests. Raising a claim whose variation Habermas (BH) will formulate years later in the case of NATO's intervention in Kosovo/a, Horkheimer insists that when Americans go to war, it is to defend human rights and the constitution rather than to defend a fatherland. The SDS accuse him in turn of resignation dressed in a crude "apologetics for Fascism and imperialism" (Kraushaar 1998, 2: doc. 117; 1:27, 252f.).

Ludwig von Friedeburg (left the IfS in 1962 for Berlin), who is on his way to present the inaugural lecture as the newly installed professor in Frankfurt on May 8, passes by a huge wall poster announcing Horkheimer's fundamental contradiction: Horkheimer calls for tolerance toward the very Fascist terror that he fled in 1933 (253; cf. tab 2.1). While the protesting students dig out from the closet of restored history his and other radical writings of the early IfS, Horkheimer never comes to see the student movement otherwise than as anti-American and even pro-totalitarian (Wiggershaus 1989, 692; 1998, 624). A new discussion between Horkheimer and the antiauthoritarian students of the SDS takes place on June 12, but the events of June 2 overtake the central stage.

Given the distinctively progressive and activist tenor of Habermas' lifework all the way up to the instant of the student revolt, the breach with the progressive students could not have been foreseen or predicted. It might even be viewed from the angle of history as purely accidental. The trigger that occasions the break is itself a rather odd and relatively minor event on the sidelines of the major drama. When Habermas makes his infamous off-the-cuff pronouncement that the rebellious students might be flirting with 'Left Fascism',[10] the words send ripples through the entire student movement. He later partially retracts the offensive nature of the claim. I use the qualifier "partially" because he never comes to say, "I was essentially wrong in this my judgment about the movement." Rather, his later apology amounts to saying something like, "I was wrong in the way I said what and when I said it." The injury done by a mere two words—*Left Fascism*—is never adequately healed. During the course of the 1960s revolt, that comfort zone of familiarity and trust between Habermas' work and the revolutionary ideals of the radical democratic Left is never fully restored. Recall that the ideals of radical democracy inspired his postwar hunger for the works of Marx, western Marxists, and the early Frankfurt School; they in turn motivated his theoretical analysis in the early study (SuP) done while he was Adorno's assistant at the Frankfurt Institute. And they provided a background for the West German student Left insofar as it identified with Habermas' intellectual leadership and his analysis of the public sphere. But more than three decades after the 1960s, with the former activists growing into their mature years in unified Germany, the portion of the student Left within the new Green Party of the post-Kohl Red-Green coalition government will have moved closer to Habermas' reformist and Left-liberal thinking. And the seeds of that outlook are planted in his passage through the 1960s.

In the actual sequence of events, *preceding Habermas' two words*, history now passes at high speed. On June 2, 1967, the shah of Iran visits Berlin. Two thousand students stage a massive protest in front of city hall. Benno Ohnesorg, until then an unknown twenty-six-year-old student of German studies in Berlin, while fleeing to the parking lot from the skirmishes with the police units that intentionally pursue demonstrators, is fatally shot in the back by police officer Karl-Heinz Kurras. The Berlin police try to keep the case out of the public eye and even ask the city senate to forbid further demonstrations, in fact having the city impose undeclared emergency rule. Disobeying the ordinance, more than 6,000 students gather at Berlin's Free University on the next day. On the same day 2,500 students march silently in Frankfurt. The unstoppable wave of street marches and protest petitions over Ohnesorg's murder spreads to all West German campuses. On June 5, there is a teach-in attended by 3,000 students in Frankfurt, with the university rector and Habermas among the speakers supporting the students and demanding an investigation of the police shooting. Habermas warns that without public supervision of the police, there is a "danger that the democratic and lawful state silently turns into a police state" (Kraushaar 1998, 1:256; for documentation and photographs from the above events, see 254f., 27). On June 8, 8,000 students form a three-mile-long chain and silently march through Frankfurt for two hours. Friedeburg, now a sociology professor and Habermas' peer in Frankfurt, and Negt, the younger assistant professor of philosophy and a student activist leader, speak side by side to the students. Significantly, Negt, besides demanding with Habermas and Friedeburg an investigation of the shooting, objects to the undeclared imposition of Emergency Laws and defends "the rights [to engage in] an APO" (257; 2: doc. 124). During the same time period, Adorno twice opens his classes with his support for the students. On June 5, at his sociology seminar, he declares unequivocally that with Ohnesorg's death, German students have taken over the role of Jews (cited in 1:254). Next day, he starts his aesthetics lecture with a minute of silence for Ohnesorg and voices his support for the students as well as his worry about the state of democracy in West Germany (256f.; 2: doc. 123).

On June 9, as mourners accompany Ohnesorg's funeral procession from Berlin to Hannover for his burial there, a conference, University and Democracy: Conditions and Organization of Resistance, is held in Hannover. This is the D-Day of the protest movement, its radicalizing turning point, and the moment of breach between Habermas and the student Left. The conference, attended by 5,000 students and faculty, is charged with an explosive atmosphere and becomes the staging ground of struggle over the forms of resistance. It all turns on the generational struggle between the skeptics and the rebels, Habermas versus Dutschke and Krahl (1:258f.; KPS 205–15).[11]

Students invite Habermas to the conference as one of the seven main speakers. At this instant, the beginning of the conference day, he is still standing tall in their minds and in the foreground and as an essential ally. By the end of the conference the idol of the German student Left is shattered. In his main speech on June 9, Habermas discusses an extraparliamentary opposition and the tension between practice and theory. He affirms the critical role of the students in unmasking the dangers of the authoritarian state. But this corrective role has specific parameters. He defends his vintage position within Critical Theory, that is, the middle path between a mindless action (what he terms 'actionism') and abstract or traditional theory (intellectual indifference to the social circumstances that form the basic situation of one's thinking). The student leader from the Free University in Berlin, Dutschke, stresses in his speech direct and confrontational action vis-à-vis the entrenched establishment structures. In a not-so-veiled reference to Habermas' preceding lecture, Dutschke criticizes the objectivist social analysis that invokes enlightenment but without any transformative social action. Habermas returns to the microphone from his car in order to respond to Dutschke's rejoinder. Even though the shouts from the audience make it clear that Dutschke has meanwhile left the conference, Habermas introduces his last-minute rebuttal. It is almost an afterthought. But the sideline comment is the moment of the fateful blow when his two dreadful words break the camel's back:

> Mr. Dutschke has suggested as his concrete proposal that a sit-in should take place. That is a demonstration with nonviolent means. I ask myself why he did not name it so and why he spent 45 minutes on developing a voluntarist ideology which in 1848 one would have called utopian socialism, but which under today's circumstances one must call—in any case I believe to have reasons to suggest this terminology—'Left Fascism'. (KPS 214)

The news of Habermas' polemic spreads. We read in Dutschke's diary notes from June 10 that he finds out about the charge of "my Left Fascism" later that evening in Berlin as he goes out with friends to a local club. He feels somewhat "honored" by the charge as it, in his mind, shows how much Habermas is out of step with the activist student needs of the hour (Kraushaar 1998, 2: doc. 131).

Habermas' *two words* enter common usage overnight. When Adorno arrives in Berlin on July 7 for his previously scheduled lecture, one poster reads, "Berlin Left Fascists greet Teddy, the classicist" (Kraushaar 1998, 2: doc. 139). His lecture is interrupted by shouts and demonstrative walkouts by 200 students (1:265). Adorno and Marcuse miss each other in Berlin on the same day, and thus the key conversation about their different perceptions of the student movement in the United States and Germany does not take place (Wiggershaus 1989, 690; 1998, 622). As Adorno departs for Frankfurt, Marcuse arrives in Berlin for a four-day SDS event on July 10–13, signaling a change in content as well as tune.[12] Marcuse is welcomed each day at the Audimax auditorium of Berlin's Free University by 2,000–3,000 students. On the first two days he delivers two lectures, "The End of Utopia" and "The Problem of Violence in the Opposition." Krahl takes part in the ensuing discussions. On the third evening, Marcuse participates in a panel discussion entitled "Morality and Politics in Affluent Society"[13] and then on the last evening one called "Vietnam—The Third World and the Opposition in the Capital Cities." Dutschke participates in both panels (Kraushaar 1998, 1:265–67; Marcuse's second lecture in 2: doc. 143; and doc. 144 for the discussion of this lecture). In his second lecture, Marcuse raises the question of "a 'natural' right" of the oppressed to resist (1965b, 116), and he continues speaking with "Liberation from the Affluent Society" in London on July 28. Unlike Habermas, who increasingly argues for the need to keep science or philosophy and politics or action in their separate spheres, Marcuse defends an internal link between theory and political praxis, between education and social transformation (Kraushaar 1998, 2: doc. 147). This entire July sequence of events ends in London as it began in Berlin—with a symbolic coming and going. Marcuse meets with Angela Davis at the London conference on the dialectics of liberation just as she is returning from her Frankfurt studies with Adorno, who was going to direct her doctoral work in Frankfurt. She will join with the black liberation struggle in the United States and complete her Ph.D. at the University of California–San Diego under Marcuse's supervision.

In a *Spiegel* interview given before the Berlin lectures, Dutschke praises Marcuse and defends the student council democracy (Wiggershaus 1989, 692; 1998, 624).[14] Habermas takes issue with both Dutschke's interview and Marcuse's Berlin lectures, even while trying to contextualize his *two words*. In his July 26 letter to Erich Fried,[15] Habermas clarifies that the charge of Left Fascism was meant "purely hypothetically." He was "disturbed" by the type of "solidarization effect" that the week following Ohnesorg's shooting had exercised on the students and by the fact that Dutschke's militant approach had not been "relativized" as a "minority position" within the movement. He expands rather than diminishes his June 9 worry: Dutschke's "anarchistic" concept of action appears to share a family resemblance with the "Left tendencies of the early Italian Fascism such as [Georges] Sorel's" (BEE 278).[16] Habermas holds on to his conviction from June 9, namely, that the "psychological potential" of actionism, to which Dutschke appealed, is "highly ambivalent," since it can be "channeled equally well to the 'Right' as to the 'Left'." Habermas even invokes some firsthand experience from the U.S. student movement (which he "was able to examine on the Berkeley campus") in order to object to the "happening" character of a rebellion for rebellion's sake (i.e., not for some determined "political goals" out of which liberation is to be expected). His worries are not dispelled, even by Dutschke's well-argued *Spiegel* interview. Habermas concedes that in the current situation he would rather not voice these polemical reflections publicly. He tried, he says, to get in touch with the SDS and Dutschke after Hannover to speak of the "dangers" in blurring the distinction between the "nonrevolutionary situation" and its "demonstrative [method of] provocation," on the one hand, and "violent provocation" that belongs to a revolutionary situation, on the other hand. Habermas takes a swipe in the direction of Marcuse's Berlin lectures, concluding here and holding till his mature years, that Marcuse arbitrarily justified the use of violence, thereby playing into the hands of student actionism. Visibly embattled by criticisms from all corners of the activist student Left, Habermas defends himself at the end of his letter as a Leftist critic and supporter of the measured, rational, nonviolent student movement (BEE 279; see PK 232–39 and nn. 8, 17–18 in this chapter).

Following the September conference of the SDS,[17] the struggle against the enactment of Emergency Laws takes on new vitality. An excerpt from a flyer circulating on the Frankfurt University campus on November 20, 1967, paradoxically, yet appropriately, characterizes the complex and volatile situation arising since Habermas' utterance of the two fateful June 9 words. I say "paradoxically," since the flyer is written by his Frankfurt peers, eighteen faculty members in sociology and philosophy, who protest the university rector's ruthless handling—his imputation that "Fascist terror" is practiced by the students—of the growing anti-Emergency Laws movement on campus. (In November students planned a disruption of Prof. Carlo Schmid's political science lecture because he was a professor who as a minister in the Grand Coalition supported the legislation of the Emergency Laws.) I say "appropriately" because the flyer squarely turns the tables of Habermas' so-called Fascist charge from the rebelling students to the Frankfurt University rector. Echoing the opening of Marx's *Communist Manifesto*, the circular ends with an admonition:

> The specter is haunting Germany—the specter of Left Fascism. We protest with all resolve against the unreflective application of such concepts and against the defamation of uncomfortable minorities.... The terror should be sought where it really is exercised—[the terror] with deadly shootings and water canons, with prohibitions on demonstrations and the authoritarian curtailing of unlimited expression of meaning. (Kraushaar 1998, 2: doc. 169; 1:281)

With the movement against the Emergency Laws growing, against the stalled democratic university reform, and against the U.S. war in Vietnam that continues with the blessing and finances of the Grand Coalition, the end of November hurries to the climax of May 1968. On November 21, 1967, the West Berlin court clears Kurras, the police officer who shot Ohnesorg, of all charges. Two days later, Adorno protests the not guilty verdict at the beginning of his class. Krahl speaks at the gathering sponsored by the SDS in Frankfurt four days later—and 1,000 students gather in protest in front of the office of the rector, Walter Rüegg. Seven days earlier Rüegg had charged the students with Fascist tactics, filed formal charges against them, and threatened to suspend the SDS branch on campus. He is now requested to come to a "public discussion on the topic of Fascism." On the last day of November, Adorno raises critical questions to his student Krahl and to other students about the APO tactics (i.e., the disturbance of lectures given by Carló Schmid) (Kraushaar 1998, 1:282, 284). At about the same time, Habermas reports on the West German student movement in a lecture to the Goethe House in New York. In this very informative presentation he retraces various phases and root causes of the student protest from the 1950s, the early protest of 1951–1953, the antinuclear movement of 1958, the expulsion of the SDS from the SDP, to the present in 1967. Standing with Habermas on the observation platform of November 1967, his historical present at the time, we can relive the path taken with him from 1945 up to that moment. Habermas engages in a deep self-reflection on his and the students' generational experiences that occasioned different assessments of the key political event of June 2 (KPS 217–38/TRS 13–30).[18]

Habermas never fully reestablishes his prominent role within the student movement, despite his later attempts to contextualize, explain away, or retract what he might have meant by Left Fascism. While attempting to do all that explaining and while supporting the student movement in talks he gives in 1967 and at the beginning of 1968,[19] the problem from Hannover revisits him at the end of May 1968. On the heels of the large Berlin demonstration against the war in Vietnam (February 17–18) and the assassination attempt on Dutschke (April 8), over 60,000 people take part in the Easter boycott campaign (April 11–14) against the Springer publishing corporation, which is viewed as the source of public misinformation and manipulation. Dutschke is seriously wounded by Joseph Bachmann, "a 23-year-old unemployed house painter from Munich," who followed the example of the assassin who killed Martin Luther King Jr., as well as the daily hostility toward the student movement disseminated in the pages of *Bild Zeitung*, the main propaganda vehicle of the Axel Springer publishing conglomerate. Springer published hate speech with the "courtesy of the occupying armies of the West, in particular of the USA." Dutschke is shot by three bullets: in his face, chest, and brain (Ali and Watkins 1998, 78f.; see the photos of Dutschke, his assassin, and the Springer building). Wolf Bierman writes a song entitled "The Three Bullets at Rudi Dutschke," but East German authorities forbid him to perform it in West Berlin. (Recall that Dutschke fled East Germany.) On May 15, Bierman sings the song in his apartment to Marcuse, who is both impressed by its depth and appalled by East German socialist authoritarianism (see Kraushaar 1998, 1:326). Massive student and later also worker movement in Paris, the so-called May Events, erupt, just as Alexander Dubček's Prague Spring of '68 reaches its peak (were there really no objective conditions for revolutionary change in 1968?). At this time Germany's progressive forces embark on the struggle to stop the approval of the Emergency Laws. On May 11, over 100,000 people take to the streets in Bonn against the new legislation, and students occupy the Frankfurt university on May 27 (Wiggershaus 1989, 694; 1998, 626).

Here is a brief overview of the situation in Frankfurt between May 27 and June 1, 1968. After the April 8 assassination attempt on Dutschke and the Easter anti–Springer-Verlag campaign, universities in Berlin and throughout the FRG are occupied on May 20. (On the same day, Sartre agrees with Marcuse's Benjaminian conclusion to *One-Dimensional Man* that hope is given for the sake of those without it [Kraushaar 1998, 1:326].) On May 27 (Monday morning) the SDS calls for a general strike against the state of emergency laws soon to be approved by the Bundestag. An assembly of about 2,000 students votes to occupy the university. In the afternoon, 15,000 people demonstrate at the Römerberg in Frankfurt (333). Krahl in his speech unmasks the state terror in the proposed emergency legislation as a new form of Fascism. "The state is ready to make itself into a new Fascist Leader *[Führer]*"(334; 2: doc. 209).

Between May 28 (Tuesday) and 30 (Thursday), the students take over and rename Goethe University: It is now a liberated *Karl Marx Universität*. The curriculum of the political university is composed of twenty-three seminars, one general discussion, and a teach-in (Kraushaar 1998, 1:336 reproduces the full schedule of classes). As the students celebrate their liberated space on Wednesday night, some of them break into the rector's office and rummage through confidential documents. There is some alcohol consumption, and one student vomits on the carpet in the rector's office. On Thursday at 2 A.M., the rector informs the police headquarters about the situation, and at 6 A.M. the mayor requests the local state authority in Hessen to order the police forces to eject the students and occupy the university. When 200 riot police units arrive, there are only about thirty students on the scene; six of them are arrested. As the police occupy the university and the legislature in Bonn passes Emergency Laws (384–100) later that day, several thousand striking Frankfurt students gather to protest the police action (Kraushaar 1998, 1:335, 340). Krahl contests the rector's justification of the action, the seminars of the political university continue its parallel education, and in the afternoon students resolve to take further action (336).[20]

On June 1, almost one year after the murder of Ohnesorg, at the Frankfurt University Mensa (large cafeteria complex in which the majority of students eat their meals), Habermas presents to about 2,000 students his five theses on the student movement. (The sixth thesis is added to the published version.) This speech marks his most definitive yes-and-no position on the protest in West Germany (341–42, photos). The first two and the sixth theses mark Habermas' yes, the third, fourth, and fifth theses are his no. As he praises and yet criticizes the students at his evening presentation, itself part of a two-day student conference of the SDS, he adds to the repertoire of the polemical *two words* from June 9 of the previous year two more words—calling the student revolt a *phantom revolution* (SiK). This polemical part of his presentation undoubtedly caricatured the three student leaders: Krahl as agitator, Negt as mentor, and Hans Magnus Enzensberger as harlequin (343). Krahl and Negt criticize both the SDS and Habermas. They prefigure the answers to Habermas published by the group of progressive Leftists and edited by Negt (1968; cf. Kraushaar 1998, 2: doc. 221 [Krahl's paper]; doc. 222 [Negt's paper]; SiK).

I will return to Habermas' analysis and to the responses from the student Left in chapter 4 when I discuss his profile in light of the 1960s. Here I want to make general observations about the situation in which Habermas' complex thinking on these matters comes to birth. West Germany's effort to bring about the prerevolutionary thaw and incubation has been long and hard, and Habermas takes notice of this fact over and over, which together explain his skeptical, backward-looking caution in the 1960s (his partial no to aspects of the student movement). Yet his dangerous memory of false Fascist continuities also funds his forward-looking, integrative courage (his yes to the 1960s protest). It is this courage that repeatedly funds his ability to radically distance himself from bankrupt traditions. He values the student rebellion for breaking the silence of the postwar generation on Germany's Nazi past. He considers this historical change in social consciousness to be an irreversible achievement. "It [the student movement] brought about a certain rupture in the normative area, in attitudes, in the cultural value system" (KPS 520/AS 85). Habermas' ambivalent relation to the German student movement notwithstanding, his critical courage provides a repeated contrast to the conservative shifts following the rebellion of 1967–1969. I stress these two sides of Habermas' profile in order to balance my critical assessment of Habermas' break with the students, on the one hand, with my positive evaluation of his role as a public barometer of the returns of the repressed Fascist sympathies into the mainstream German culture, on the other hand.

On June 5, the police occupation of the Frankfurt University ends, but in a television discussion, the rector blames the students' self-defeating and debased activism for the failure of the political university (Kraushaar 1998, 1:344). On June 24, the rector forbids Krahl to enter the premises of the university because of his leadership position in the university takeover (346). In July the campaign to expel Marcuse from the University of San Diego begins (347). Meanwhile on July 20, in an essay for Marcuse's seventieth birthday, Habermas once again (as before in remarks regarding Marcuse's Berlin address) takes on the idea of the 'natural right to resist' and asks Marcuse to clarify the passages that appear to legitimate arbitrary violence (349f.; ZG 16).

Fascism—whether Left or Right—did not arrive at this moment from the direction Habermas anticipated. During 1968, an extraordinary year, the story of radically democratizing revolts and their violent repression repeats itself with greater or lesser intensity in other parts of the world. Not only in Paris and Frankfurt (May) and throughout the United States, but also in Prague (August 21) and in Tlatelolco, Mexico (October),[21] the movement for democratic change is violently suppressed, often massacred, by the established powers. Even after the collapse of the Soviet bloc in 1989, we still have not evaluated Czechoslovakia's attempt at radical democracy, which was crushed by Warsaw Pact armies (including East Germany's violation of the postwar prohibition on military actions outside of Germany) on August 21 1968, while the liberal west stood by. As the Soviet bloc armies invade Czechoslovakia, Habermas, Ernst Bloch, Agnes Heller, Marcuse, Svetozar Stojanović, and others find themselves on the beautiful Croatian island of Korčula at the fifth annual summer school of the Yugoslav praxis philosophy group. The conference topic is Marx and revolution. When the news of the brotherly invasion of Prague reaches them, they yield the scheduled program to composing three protest letters: to Josip Broz Tito (the Yugoslav president), Leonid Brezhnev (the Soviet chairman), and the general public (see Kraushaar 1998, 1:351f.). The students demonstrating against the invasion in Frankfurt carry a sign identifying their grasp of where the dangers of Fascism arise at present:

"Imperialism + Stalinism—the Enemies of Socialism" (353, for the photo)

Kraushaaur (1998, 1:28) underscores September 23 as the last public and earnest exchange between Critical Theorists—Adorno, Habermas, Friedeburg—and, among others, the student leader Krahl. On a previous day, Daniel Cohn-Bendit, Joschka Fischer, and Krahl are arrested at the Frankfurt protest against the Peace Award being given by the West German publishers to the pro-colonial Senegalese president Léopold Sédar Senghor. On the day of the exchange, Cohn-Bendit is still being interrogated, while in Haus Gallus a discussion entitled "Authorities and Revolution" takes place. Krahl praises Adorno as one of the only professors who came to visit the student sit-in several months ago, yet he criticizes the practical resignation of Critical Theory that Adorno represents (362). Günter Grass, present in the audience, is unimpressed by Krahl. In responding to a private critical letter from Grass, Adorno defends Krahl as one of his most talented students. At the same time he distances himself from the SDS and, using Habermas' terms, voices doubts about the "phantom revolution" of the students. Still (as on June 5, 1967), he identifies the present role of students and critical intellectuals with the Jews (2: doc. 238, p. 473; 1:28, 361f.; cf. 254).

The last chapter of the student movement in the FRG is written by the active strike in Frankfurt between December 8 and December 18, 1968. This drama reaches its afterclimax when police expel students from the IfS on January 31, 1969. The running leitmotif, or accompanying "chorus" to these events, is acted by the earnest letters that Adorno and Marcuse exchange (Adorno and Marcuse 1999; Leslie 1999) from January 24 to August 6, 1969. While corresponding, they repeatedly try and fail to meet to discuss their differences. Adorno dies on August 6, with the funeral held on August 13.

On Sunday evening, December 8, 1968, the students in Frankfurt take over the Sociology Department at Mylius Street 30. At night they set up the committees of the active political strike and formulate the demands for the structural reforms of university education. By Monday morning they rename the Sociology Department "Spartakus Department" (the photo of the huge sign for "Spartakus-Seminar," hung on the outside building walls, is reproduced in Kraushaar 1998, 1:377). The student strike takes its inspiration from the council movement.[22] One sign expressed this directly by declaring that all power should belong to the student councils. The strikers share all resources, they share solidarity in opposition, they daily rotate the membership of voluntary strike committees, and they form eleven working groups, each providing a basis for alternative seminars (377). On Monday, the strikers send Habermas a letter with the Negative Catalogue *(Negativkatalog)* of minimal demands for structural university reforms, such as recognition of the eleven working groups in the core curriculum plans and the democratization of the professorial ranks. "The university belongs to us!" declares the strike committee on December 11 (2: doc. 257). Three major professors—Adorno, Friedeburg, and Habermas—issue an explanation rejecting the Negative Catalogue of demands, which they deem "propagandistic." On the one hand, they claim to "support the protest"; on the other hand, they are bothered by the "violence" of the "technocrats of . . . the protest" that is "manipulated into new confrontations" (2: doc. 258, pp. 502–3). On December 12, at the start of his class on the philosophy of language (1:379f.), Habermas voices even sharper criticisms of the core striking group. In leveling with the students, he defends the domination-free discussion and the Enlightenment institutions against, what he finds to be, the danger of destroying both. Against the perceived possibility of the "Fascist or Stalinist prototypes" becoming now typified among the strikers—and this possibility reiterates the charge of Left Fascism raised on June 9, 1967—he argues for "the conditions of rational speech as the foundations of humanity" (2: doc. 259, p. 504). In his seminar theses from December 14 (doc. 260; KPS 261–64), Habermas rejects outright the students' demand to integrate the scientific or philosophical praxis of theory with the liberation praxis of political action. That is, he worries about the dogmatic politicization of scientific inquiry.

Habermas' insistence on separating theory from political practice goes hand in hand with his fear of Fascism-cum-Stalinism (i.e., Left Fascism). That this is the core difference with the students (and in this regard also with Marcuse) becomes clearer at the heated discussion on December 16 (Kraushaar 1998, 1:380–381, photo). Habermas repeats his defense of the institutional "basis of the Enlightenment" against the destruction that would make "enlightened political praxis impossible," and he repeats almost verbatim the "hypothetical" specter of Fascism-Stalinism (2: doc. 261, p. 507; at this very moment, a shout arises from the student audience: "[Here he goes] Once again!"). One of the participants, Reinhart Wolff, brings home that what differentiates students from Habermas is their hope for "uniting science with the strategy of liberation" (508). He rejects Habermas' implication of "Stalinism" and "Fascism" as a label that fits the students who hope to reform their education in order to promote radical democratic alternatives to capitalism (509–10). Krahl, who called for this forum in the first place, has the last word: he reiterates the principal demands of the Negative Catalogue and then rejects the charge of Stalinism-Fascism, even if Habermas meant it only "hypothetically." This charge, made for the second time since July 12 (as the earlier one from June 9, 1967), is a product of "demagogical infamy," as Krahl politely but firmly returns to Habermas his argument. In the end, Krahl concludes, Habermas' volatile criticisms help legitimate the existing institutional structures (512).[23]

On the next day, Habermas, Adorno, Friedeburg, and Alexander Mitschelrich issue a thinly veiled ultimatum to the students to clear out of the Sociology Department because, they contend, the occupation cannot be politically justified (doc. 264). On the same day, Adorno and Horkheimer write a complaining letter to Marcuse describing the situation in Frankfurt in which they can no longer offer normal classes (doc. 265). The police arrive with three transport vehicles and one water cannon on December 18 at 5 A.M. and take over the Spartakus-Seminar (1:381f.). In the student declaration issued later that day, Habermas is portrayed as a "classical betrayer." He and other Critical Theorists voice support, but in practice they work with the established authoritarian powers, with "the police action as the ultimate rationality," to crush any chances for the democratic reorganization of the university (2: doc. 266, p. 520). Even more significantly, on the same day nine assistant professors in sociology break, by generation as well as by rank, with full professors in the Sociology and Philosophy Departments of the Frankfurt University. They issue a strong protest directly implicating Adorno, Friedeburg, Habermas, and Mitscherlich in facilitating and legitimating, "from the beginning" of the Spartakus strike, the subsequent police action against the students. Through their double-mindedness, these full professors "radically destroyed" all possibilities for "the reorganization of the course of study" that still existed "in spite of the student occupation" of the department. And these full professors "place in question the [very] experiment in student self-organization of studies." The nine assistants cannot but "distance" themselves from "the authoritarian means" used against the students (doc. 267, p. 521). On the same day, the SDS issues its commentary on the events: The main representatives of Critical Theory and their current Frankfurt practices for the sake of pure theory and orderly institutional and administrative power—and their followers dubbed here as "Habermice" and "Adornites"—lead to "depoliticization" of the student movement. Those who unveil this contradiction between theory and practice, the commentary protests, are blackmailed (by the established professors) as "Stalinists and Fascists" (doc. 268, p. 521). The call for a teach-in to be held on the following day reiterates this criticism: The "Left intellectuals" and the "critical" professors of the Frankfurt School become now "the cops of the authoritarian state." Their authoritarian actions—employing something akin to the "Goebbels-like propaganda methods"—fragment the student movement (2: doc. 270, p. 527; 1:382f.).

The anticlimactic year 1969 opens on January 24 with a "modified" occupation of rooms and administrative offices of the Sociology Department in Frankfurt (1:29). Since on January 31, the rector closes the entire department, fearing the vandalism that occurred during city demonstrations a day before, the sociology students decide to move next door to the IfS building in order to use one of the empty rooms to plan the continued strike. Friedeburg at first tries to make them leave the institute premises, and then he and Adorno call the police to kick them out even though there was no indication of either student vandalism or other threat of takeover to the IfS. Seventy-six students are detained, and all but Krahl, Adorno's former doctoral student, are soon released. Krahl alone is held longer and charged with breaking in and trespassing. Adorno's lectures after his police stunt turn into sheer hell, and he remains deeply depressed about this event pretty much until his death on August 6. A famous case of class disruption takes place on April

22, when three female students throw flowers at Adorno just as they expose their breasts and attempt to kiss his cheeks. The flyer circulated at the same time in the classroom declares that "Adorno as an institution is dead" (418, for the text and an amateur photo of the incident). On July 18, the twenty-six-year-old Krahl has his court hearing (447ff.). Adorno, who could have dropped the charges against his student, is called as the main witness. He is cross-examined by Krahl (448, photo).

It is apparent that Adorno's reasons for calling the police stemmed mainly from his paranoid interpretation of the situation in light of the preceding Spartakus events. When on January 31, the protesting as well as defeated students moved to the IfS, they did so almost instinctively. Where else could they seek their natural home but in the institutional cradle of Critical Theory? At this moment, the students were disowned by these fathers of Critical Theory.

On August 6, as his secretary is typing his last letter to Marcuse, Adorno is dying of a heart attack after having ridden a cable car to a high Swiss mountain peak (455). On August 13, 2,000 people, Krahl and Habermas among them, attend Adorno's funeral (456, photo). Krahl intervenes against the extreme leather jacket faction of the SDS to prevent a provocation at the funeral (458). Even so, on September 12, Habermas severely criticizes Krahl without ever naming him (in an essay for Adorno's sixty-sixth birthday, PpP 172/102f.).[24] As in March of the same year Willy Brandt becomes the new chancellor of the FRG and in September his socialist-liberal coalition wins the elections to the Bundestag, the student movement might be failing to achieve a number of its immediate objectives. Two student protagonists die young: Krahl dies in a car accident on February 14, 1970, and Dutschke dies, most likely because of the delayed consequences of the shooting wounds in his brain, on December 24, 1979. Although the student revolt ends, and with it the postwar German restoration of the IfS and Critical Theory as well as the 1960s renewal of critical social theory, the period of "greater democracy" and reform is ushered in (Wiggershaus 1989, 704f.; 1998, 635f.). The protesting generation leaves its lasting mark on these progressive cultural shifts. It remains a vital force on the German Left in the 1970s and 1980s. And it comes of age in the 1990s, when it will have inhabited the new Green movement as well as formed the post-Kohl Red-Green coalition government.

Let me end this dramatic line with the leitmotif, or chorus, to the tragic downfall of the postwar restorative version of Critical Theory. The intensely genuine and deep correspondence about the student movement between Adorno and Marcuse (1999) takes place between January 24 and August 6, 1969. I shall return to some of this correspondence in chapter 4. Here I want to use four events from May 4 and 5 and June 4 to situate the front lines at the end of the student movement.

- On May 4, Marcuse argues in the *New York Times* that the student protest cannot be deemed violent next to the violence of the society in which it

occurs. He will maintain this position until his last conversation with Habermas before dying in 1979.
- In a letter from May 5 addressed to Marcuse, Adorno justifies his January 31 call for the police to clear the students from the IfS. Appealing to a familiarity of friendship and a shared history of struggle, Adorno implores Marcuse with the explanation that he was defending "our old Institute, Herbert." Adorno invokes the context of the Holocaust ("the murder of Jews") in which the exiled Critical Theorists did not become pure activists either. He chastises Marcuse's "self-deception" and (by implication agreeing here with Horkheimer) his anti-Americanism on account of joining the anti–Vietnam War protests. Adorno also defends Habermas' notion of Left Fascism as it befits student actionism and rejects the student challenge that he engage in self-criticism as their "pure Stalinism" (Kraushaar 1998, 1:426; 2: doc. 322, pp. 624f.).
- Also on May 5, Habermas sends a letter to Marcuse in which he reiterates that the December 1968 demands raised by the striking students were but "illusory partisan strategies" (2: doc. 323, p. 625). Would Marcuse let his seminar, department, or library fall into chaos, disorder, and pure "theater"? Habermas asks with entirely unmasked irritation in response to Marcuse's silent treatment of this point. The end of his letter implies core theoretical differences that exist between his views and Marcuse's *Essay on Liberation* (626), most notably on the issue of violence. As I noted before, Habermas retains till today his early conviction that Marcuse justified arbitrary uses of revolutionary violence (PK).
- On May 15–30, California governor Ronald Reagan dispatches armed police and National Guard units to clear students from the People's Park in Berkeley. Marcuse writes to Adorno on June 4 in strong terms. He rejects both the Habermasian charge of Left Fascism (or the implication that the students of the 1960s resemble those in the 1930s) and Adorno's recourse to the police force as a defense of their "old Institute" (Kraushaar 1998, 2: doc. 336, pp. 649f.).

NOTES

1. Compare Habermas' early radical claim with Marcuse's later claim (1965b) about a "'natural right' of resistance" (116) against oppression. Marcuse's later defense of his position, against those who suggest that he justifies blind violence, appeals to a radical idea of socialist democracy. See chapter 4 below.

2. Wiggershaus (1989, 607–17, 623ff., 628; 1998, 547–56, 561ff., 565f.).

3. *Habilitation* is required for full professorship with tenure at German universities.

4. *Privatdozent* is a rank roughly equivalent to associate professor, though only a full professor has tenure within the German university system. There are several levels of full professors.

5. Habermas' essay ("Partisanenprofessor im Lande der Mitläufer. Der Marburger Ordinarius Wolfgang Abendroth wird am 2. Mai sechzig Jahre alt," *Die Zeit,* April 29, 1966) appears only in the German edition of PpP. Significantly, Habermas uses the same word, *Mitläufer* (sympathizer, fellow traveler), both for his own father's relation to the Nazi regime (NR 23/AS 231 and the opening of chap. 1 above) and for that of most German philosophy professors. In the series of Habermas' formative father figures, Abendroth stands out as the only exception. Cf. Wiggershaus (1989, 617; 1998, 556).

6. On May 30, 1965, Habermas took part in the SDS congress, Demokratie vor dem Notstand (Democracy in emergency), which discussed the introduction of the Emergency Laws into postwar West German law (see Albrecht et al. 1999, 316f.).

7. Marcuse's (1974) work includes neither "Marx" nor "Critical Theory" in the word index.

8. On the question of violence, see chapter 4 below.

9. Wiggershaus (1989, 683; 1998, 616) dates this event on June 22, 1966. I follow Albrecht et al. (1999, 319) in listing the date as June 23.

10. On Habermas' two words, see KPS 214; on his later retractions and self-assessments, see KPS 215–16, 304–07, and 364–67; BEE; and interviews KPS 518–21/AS 83–85; NR 25/AS 233; and NC 185.

11. See Kraushaar 1998, 2: docs. 128–29, for direct transcripts of Habermas' two speeches in Hannover, and doc. 129, for Dutschke's response to the first of the two speeches.

12. Wiggershaus (1989, 690; 1998, 622) locates the start of the event on July 12, but I follow Kraushaar's (1998, 1:265) more precise documentation that situates the event between July 10 and 13, with Adorno departing Berlin on the afternoon of July 9 just as Marcuse is landing at the same airport.

13. The English rendition translates correctly the wrong word in the title, "Übergangensgesellschaft"—transitional society—of the first panel named by Wiggershaus (1989, 690; 1998, 622 n. 62). The word in the title should be "Überflußgesellschaft," affluent society (Kraushaar 1998, 2: doc. 147).

14. Bronner (1994, 14, 18–24, 75) discusses the council movement and its relation to Dutschke (23, 32, 89). The council movement not only influenced the November Revolution of 1918 in Germany, but also inspired the active strike that takes place in Frankfurt in December 1968.

15. Habermas' BEE is curiously absent from the KPS reprint of the relevant material surrounding the Hannover conference. The reprinted pages of PuH 137–52 exclude pages 149–51, and yet both the letter to C. Grossner from May 13, 1968, and to Fried from July 26, 1967, try to explain Left Fascism and what Habermas really wanted to say.

16. See Honneth (1992, chap. 7) for his reading of Sorel along with Marx and Sartre. Honneth, Habermas' former assistant, succeeded Habermas as a full professor in Frankfurt.

17. I discuss Dutschke and Krahl's keynote address delivered at this conference in chapter 4 below.

18. I return to this discussion in chapter 4 below.

19. In his two letters to a German poet, Erich Fried (PuH 149–51) (as a teenager, Fried protested the Nazis on the streets in Vienna and later fled abroad, see Ali and Watkins 1998, 48) and C. G. Grossner (KPS 215f.), Habermas tries to clarify and patch up the damage done by speaking of Left Fascism. In the October 10, 1977, *Spiegel* interview, he retracts his two

words as "overreaction" all too typical for the Leftists of his generation (KPS 365ff.). And he points back both to his early confrontation with Heidegger to balance out and thereby assure his proper credentials on the Left.

20. At 6 P.M., a group of students entered one of the Frankfurt theaters to ask actors for solidarity and the theater directors for "political asylum" (Kraushaar 1998, 1:336f.). In the context of the Czechoslovak Velvet Revolution on November 17, 1989, striking theaters became the first and very effective public political clubs.

21. See Sherman (1998). The recent student movement in Mexico City and its violent suppression by the Mexican government replays in a later, even more violent form, some of the drama from Frankfurt.

22. See note 14 above.

23. Habermas is repeatedly criticized for offering to the Right, even if hypothetically, an "enemy stereotype" (in a curiously Schmittian fashion) of the "Stalinist-Fascist" student activist (Kraushaar 1998, 2: doc. 263 [December 17, 1968], p. 515; and doc. 288 [January 25, 1969], p. 547). The relation between theory and practice is discussed (doc. 268 [December 18, 1968], p. 522; doc. 269 [December 18, 1968], p. 524; and doc. 296 [February 10, 1969], pp. 562–71; see also Habermas' delayed but significant response to this topic, and the entire period, in the first lecture of his third return to Frankfurt, doc. 428 [April 5, 1983]).

24. I will return to Habermas' harshness toward Krahl in chapter 4 below.

Chapter Three

FROM REVISION TO HOPE AND BACK AGAIN, 1970–2000

My concluding segment of the foregoing linear narrative covers a much longer trajectory than the 1960s revolt, which we traversed with intense attention to singular events running through a short time span. I want to restrict my account of Habermas' last thirty calendar years in the twentieth century to three historical revisions and the corresponding background situations that stage his defining interventions, which are profiled in Part Two:

- the terror of the Red Army Faction (RAF) and the rise of the new social movements: staging for Habermas' return to political analysis and active political involvement
- Bitburg ceremonies: staging for Habermas' entry to the Historians' Debate
- the fall of the Berlin Wall: staging for Habermas' ambivalence in unified Germany

While restricting my dramatic line in this chapter, I mainly devote Part Two to a profile of Habermas from the 1970s onward. The formative sketches in the periods between 1944 and 1970 gain the sharpness of a profile only after his passage through the 1960s. Moreover, his formed profile settles into distinct tones and contours during his third Frankfurt period starting in 1982, and it blossoms into a mature portrait in the post-Wall era. One segment of chapter 4 will take up Habermas' theory of nonviolent civil disobedience (formed out of his participation in the antinuclear movement of the 1980s and in response to the situations of the 1960s and 1970s). Chapter 5 will move from his observations on the 1970s to his engagement with revisionist German historians. Chapter 6 will sketch his ripened profile in light of the interventions affected by the situations of the recent post-Wall period.

Accomplishments of the student movement were overshadowed by the wrong lesson learned. This is the lesson of historical revision. Starting from the late 1970s up to the mid-1980s two great political-historical revisions of Germany's past take place; and with the end of the Cold War the third historical revision is attempted. Each of the three revisionary trends may be interpreted as a backlash against the student movement of the 1960s. The second revision, in addition, reacts against the new social movements (ecology, peace, women, gay) of the 1970s and 1980s. The third revisionist trend represents a post-Wall struggle between liberation and restoration. The following are the three revisions under discussion:

- 1977, the German Autumn
- 1985–1987, the Historians' Debate
- 1990, *re*/unification[1] of Germany, or "past as future"

FROM THE GERMAN AUTUMN TO ANTINUCLEAR PROTESTS: STAGING FOR HABERMAS' RETURN TO POLITICS, 1977–1983

There followed the counter-revolution, fed by hostility and resentment which has effectively lasted up to the present day [i.e., 1985]. (NR 22/AS 230)

Two years after Adorno died in August 1969, after the postwar era of the IfS waned, Habermas leaves Frankfurt for Starnberg, where, since 1971, he directs the Max Planck Institute with Carl Friedrich von Weizsäcker. After the student revolt officially ends, Habermas stays, so to speak, out of the public eye until 1977. The "German Autumn" of 1977 marks the first wave of revision as well as his comeback into the public sphere. He comes to Frankfurt—for the third and last time since his youth and for the second time as a professor of philosophy and sociology—only in 1982. In the German Autumn he detects and unmasks "a pogrom atmosphere" (AS 221; EgA 12/4; cf. OSSA xviii).[2] How does this pogrom come about? Does the student movement in West Germany, in its apparent defeat at the end of the 1960s and in its gradual replacement by the new terrorist radicalism of the RAF, unwittingly open a space for the return of the police state?

In September 1977 the RAF kidnaps and murders the president of the West German employers' federation, Hanns Martin Schleyer, and the fragile postwar liberal political culture in West Germany begins to erode.[3] As the public becomes more willing to take extreme measures in safeguarding law and order, the state enlists this willingness (its underlying fear of chaos) in its right-wing backlash against the Left. The remnants of the student movement, the Critical Theorists who sparred with them, progressive intellectuals and politicians, all are summarily lumped with and linked to the RAF terrorists. The Frankfurt School is singled out by name as the key origin of this terrorism (KPS 364). How ironic this must be, given the one-time Nazi targeting of the Frankfurt School along with the Vienna Circle! In hindsight Horkheimer's fears of triggering a new backlash against the IfS after its return from the U.S. exile do not appear unjustified. By 1977 it becomes clear that 'Left Fascism' (if such a danger ever existed in Germany since the signing of the Stalin-Hitler pact) did not represent the best choice of words to describe the student movement. But could it fit the goals and strategies of the terrorist Baader-Meinhof Gang? Let me follow the quick unfolding of the autumn events.

On April 7, Siegfried Buback, the chief federal prosecutor for prosecuting terrorism, his driver, and another member of Buback's court are murdered by the RAF in Karlsruhe. On June 30, Jürgen Ponto, a board member of the Dresdner Bank, is killed by the RAF. On September 5, the RAF kidnaps in Köln the German industrialist Schleyer. His driver and three policemen are shot dead at the abduction site. The RAF leaders demand the release of all their prisoners from the maximum security prison built for the terrorists in Stuttgart-Stammheim. On October 13, a collaborating Palestinian group hijacks a German-operated Lufthansa flight from Mallorca to Mogadishu, Somalia, in order to further pressure the West German government to release the prisoners. In the night between October 17 and 18, West Germany's special antiterrorist unit, GSG 9, rescues all eighty-six passengers and shoots dead three hijackers. On October 18, the imprisoned RAF members reportedly commit suicide in their cells in Stammheim. Schleyer is executed by the RAF on the next day (see Kraushaar 1998, 1:560ff., which includes a photo of the kidnapping site and a photo of Schleyer).

To get a better sense of this complex situation and of the distinct fault lines that emerged since the end of the 1960s, it might be worth reviewing some of the arguments made by Habermas next to those by the oppositional Left. I would like to compare both sets of arguments with the claims raised by the representatives of the conservative West German parties during the course of the German Autumn.

On September 17, 1977, the *Stuttgarter Zeitung* publishes an article, "How Leftist Is the Terrorist Actionism?—Jürgen Habermas on the Beginnings of the Protest Movement." This essay is composed from the collage of citations drawn from Habermas (PuH). The unnamed editor argues that in 1967 Habermas exposed the extreme actionist trends that gave rise to the later terrorist acts (Kraushaar 1998, 1:562, 564). But in his September 19 letter to Kurt Sontheimer, Habermas rejects the internal links between the theories of the New Left and the terrorist acts of 1977. The philosophical horizon of the 1960s and the political horizon of the RAF do not match each other, not even on a developmental scale. He differentiates the New Left and the student movement from various extreme groups known in history—Blanquists, Russian Anarchists, the Ultras (KPS 374). Even in June 1967, the discussion was about tomatoes and not weapons and human lives. In this retracing through recent history, he softens his own early warnings of Left Fascism. Ohnesorg was the only one then who was murdered by the state

(375). In his October 10 *Spiegel* essay, Habermas answers Alfred Dregger, the representative of the CDU from Hessen, who charged on October 5 (and repeated on October 28) that the Frankfurt School was the origin of the RAF terror. Again he draws sharp distinctions between the 1960s and the 1970s: he identifies himself and Adorno with the Frankfurt School and argues that the criticisms of the dangers of actionism in 1967–1969 set off the Frankfurt School clearly from the RAF (364–67). This last argument in *Spiegel*, however, weakens his rejoinder to Sontheimer, since it leaves the students open to the new charge by splitting their 1960s revolt off from the positions espoused then by Adorno and Habermas.

Entering this "terrorism debate" on November 2, Albrecht Wellmer writes an open letter to the CDU prime minister, Hans Karl Filbinger, from Baden-Württemberg, who on October 9 likewise implicated the Frankfurt School in RAF terrorism. Wellmer singles out the examples of Adorno and Habermas during the 1960s revolt and makes basically the same argument that Habermas made in *Spiegel*: Critical Theorists condemned already in the 1960s "the application of violence as a means of political struggle." This condemnation had something to do, intrinsically, with their versions of Critical Theory (Kraushaar 1998, 2: doc. 417, p. 820). Wellmer, however, raises another warning from history—the state terror practiced by Fascism and Stalinism (821). This is the Fascism-Stalinism charge, but it is turned against the permanent emergency situation of the state rather than invoked against the striking students. He finds the Emergency Laws unjustified in light of the small size of the RAF. Just as Eichmann misused Kant's ethics to justify himself, so any terrorist could take a mistaken recourse to Critical Theory, but such acts do not establish causal relations that condemn the theory. On the contrary, since democracy in the FRG remains a very fragile achievement, its suspension within the security state is even more dangerous here than elsewhere (822). Then something astonishing happens that almost never takes place in the United States: Filbinger, a politician, defends himself against Wellmer, a philosopher, in a November 26 essay (doc. 418). Filbinger basically holds on to his stated view. But he relies in addition on Cardinal Joseph Ratzinger's view that "the so-called 'critical theory' of the Frankfurt School contributed to the politicization of the university" and in that sense became part of the chain leading up to 1977 (823).

We get a sharper view of the situation existing on the Left from the one-time student activists who cannot defend themselves in 1977 by pointing to Habermas' criticisms of them in 1967. In their activist voices, we hear echoes of that strong criticism of oppressive social and economic forms of life, a critique that was prevalent in their analyses developed during the 1960s.

Dutschke condemns the acts of terror in his article for *Die Zeit*, "Criticism of Terror Must Become Clearer: Taking Distance from the RAF," published on September 16, 1977 (Kraushaar 1998, 2: doc. 412, pp. 805f.). He employs Marxist criticism of the economic and sociopolitical systems of exploitation in order to expose the terrorist acts against individual persons as unjustified. Buback and Ponto and others who were murdered are "alienated men, but still humans and not pigs ready for slaughter," he argues very much along the same lines as Kraushaar. In the chilling climate of 1977, Dutschke nonetheless presents himself as a committed socialist. With the same claim he defends the extraparliamentary opposition and condemns individual acts of terrorism. The most effective, then, is his appeal to the trigger event of the student revolt: "In 1967 we spoke unequivocally about the murder of Benno Ohnesorg" [the student shot by Berlin police in the anti-shah demonstration] (806). Marcuse, writing on the same page of *Die Zeit* (doc. 413, pp. 806f.), supplies a negative answer to his own two questions: whether terror weakens capitalist domination and whether terrorist acts are justified on the basis of revolutionary morality.

In his 1977 autumn analysis of the kidnapping and execution of Schleyer, "44 Days without Opposition" (from September 5 to October 19), Kraushaar (reprinted in 1990, 81–96) situates the oppositional Left between the RAF and the reactionary state. Schleyer embodied the continuity between the Nazi era and the capitalist present: as an SS member in Reinhard Heydrich's inner circle, he narrowly escaped death when Heydrich was assassinated in Prague in 1942. Later, as a top corporate member, he managed Daimler-Benz AG (Mercedes), the very company that produced the open car in which he rode through Prague with Heydrich. Everything that Habermas despises about such German continuities is concentrated in this linkage between the "SS technocracy" and the big-business management of a corporation that, after the ruin of 1945, emerged stronger through the German economic miracle. Yet, as Kraushaar notes, in Schleyer, the RAF terror trampled on a human face, not on a systemic offshoot of the Nazi continuity. Such acts of terror are inhuman (94). With Schleyer's murder, along with those of Buback and Ponto, the state justified its rightward shift. What followed was a witch-hunt in pursuit of everything that walks and moves like a Leftist (82f.). The RAF accomplished what the New Left never could have done: it destroyed moral dignity, imagination, and the legitimacy of the student protest, and it birthed the politics of anxiety as well as a permanent emergency situation within democracy (84). Now the state again displays *the* enemy before the public, thereby following Carl Schmitt in justifying its own existence (85). Citing Krahl, Kraushaar shows how democracy transfigures itself into emergency or, worse, how the present generation, like that of its wartime parents, unwittingly allows the return of Fascism within the "democratic" security state (89). The RAF hijacked the idea of direct extraparliamentary action, practiced in the 1960s by the student opposition, into assaults on military targets. The terrorist group and the terrorist state come to mirror each other (93). This is the moment to return to the street protest, Kraushaar concludes in the fall of 1977 (96).

We witnessed how in 1945 Habermas lacked the social order that could lead to implementing his desire, in a revolutionary way, to sweep away false Nazi continuities. He objected in the 1960s that the objective conditions for a social revolution did not exist. And he grew irritated that student anarchists of the 1960s did not respect legitimate law and order. Even in the extreme circumstances of 1977, designating the RAF terror as Left Fascism would require some support in terms of establishing objectively that a Fascist social order actually existed. Yet the existence of such a Fascist social order was far from being demonstrated by the major social groups around the RAF in the 1970s, as it was not objectively true in the 1960s. The RAF represented a minority, and the former student leaders never shared its theory or terror practices. Yet the RAF mirrored the objective climate of an increasingly authoritarian police state and a growing authoritarian culture. The fragile post-1945 democratic sensibilities yield at this time to the longing for law and order.[4] Habermas rightly detects in this turn the dangers of a new Fascism (fig. 3.1). Since objective conditions do not exist for Left Fascism in 1977, the RAF terror occasions a series of mismatches and misdiagnoses, regardless of whether they are introduced by Habermas, the uncritical public, or the West German security apparatus. Habermas' admonishments to the protesting students in the 1960s are taken to heart, ironically, by the wrong addressee, at a different constellation, and with pernicious excess. The West German state secures itself against the student or other progressive protest coming back to haunt it in the 1970s or in the foreseeable future, although the RAF, unlike the '68ers, is not a part of a new social movement for a more just society.

A coalition of Social Democrats (SPD) and Liberals (FDP) ruled West Germany from 1969 to 1982 (Willy Brandt, 1969–1974, and Helmut Schmidt, 1974–1982). In 1982 it was replaced by a conservative coalition of the CDU/CSU with the FDP and headed by Helmut Kohl. Christian Democrats continued in a coalition with Free Democrats from 1987. Helmut Kohl's era, which saw Germany's unification in 1990, ended with an electoral all-German defeat in 1998. Since a democratic constitution was imposed on defeated Germany by the Allies, thereby forming the second German Republic in Bonn, Habermas' awkward rhetorical question can be addressed appropriately only in terms of the conservative revisions of 1945: should West Germany not have "obtained" a different type of state (KPS 425/OSSA 13)? The new changes in the West German legal and administrative policies are introduced in reaction to the student movement, and these legal alterations anticipate future repeated challenges from the Left.

Figure 3.1. Habermas in the "German Autumn"

RAF	Student Left	Habermas	Social-Liberal Coalition	Neoconservatives

Note: The RAF (Red Army Faction) in the fall of 1977 kidnapped and murdered, among others, German industrialist Hanns Martin Schleyer.

Andrew Buchwalter, in his translator's introduction (1984, OSSA ix) to Habermas' edited volume, *Observations on "The Spiritual Situation of the Age"* (OSSA 1979), offers a succinct account of the political and legal shifts in the Federal Republic in the two decades after the decline of the student movement. I follow his analysis closely below. Buchwalter notes, concerning the first three changes listed, which are instituted by the coalition of Social Democrats and the Free Democrats, that they react to the student rebellion in the 1960s and to the RAF terror in the 1970s. Changes in the West German criminal code, proposed by the new coalition of Christian Democrats and Free Democrats, were meant to ward off the new peace and antinuclear protests of the 1980s, acts of civil disobedience, and resistance to U.S. Pershing 2 nuclear missiles being stationed in the Federal Republic of Germany.

1. In a vintage Foucaultean fashion, using modern computer technologies, the police apparatus introduced extensive forms of security surveillance.
2. Ironically, the state placed curbs on radical teachers rather than radical students. The authorities assumed that the latter social group would be inspired by the former (e.g., Habermas would be perceived among potentially dangerous radical teachers). Yet radical students worried Habermas (in 1967–1969). Hence there is an irony in the justification of the state measures. In the Decree against Radicals *(Radikalenerlass)*, the state instituted in January 1972 a de facto pledge of allegiance: all civil servants were obliged to profess the state religion ("a liberal democratic basic order," OSSA ix). About one-fifth of all adult citizens in West Germany (before the unification with the East) worked for the state. These employees included most of the secondary and university teachers in the predominantly public educational system. The Gymnasium teachers and doctor fathers (with a few doctor mothers among them) were obliged to procreate sons and daughters for the state or they would be found unfit to serve the fatherland as its public servants.
3. The 1972 provision for a proscription on work *(Berufsverbot)* put teeth in the pledge of allegiance. The provision grants the state the right to exclude from civil service (either not to hire or to fire) all individuals whose pronouncements or activities conflict with the pledge of allegiance to the state's basic order (KPS 523/AS 87).
4. Paragraph 88a of the Criminal Code criminalizes any advocacy, support for, or even sympathy with violent acts. The statute was introduced on April 22, 1976, and revoked on June 12, 1980 (KPS 523/AS 88, n. 9).
5. On September 30, 1977, the Ministry of Justice adopted changes in the Criminal Code and the legal statutes that abridged the rights of the suspected terrorists for a consultation with defense attorneys and that allowed for their solitary imprisonment *(Kontaktsperrgesetz)* if the ministry desired so (KPS 523/AS 87).

6. Other proposed changes in the Criminal Code required that activists who demonstrate in public must not mask their identities *(Vermummungsverbot)*; should any demonstration turn violent, participants could be charged unless they proved that they had not been involved in violent action. Such demonstrators were de facto guilty unless proved innocent.

One typical example of the hysteria and the big chill of the late 1970s is the so-called Buback affair. On April 7, 1977, the public prosecutor, Siegfried Buback, is ambushed and assassinated by Ulrike Meinhof of the RAF. The student newspaper in Göttingen then prints an article that sympathizes with the killing. Buback in his work as a prosecutor specialized in going after the terrorists. The student essay is published under a pseudonym, "Mescalero." The police take action against the students. The university teachers republish "Mescalero's" article in protest. Eduard Pestel, the minister of culture in Lower Saxony, compels eleven university professors who are implicated in the pen name "Mescalero" to sign a pledge of allegiance to the state that opposes all forms of violence (on this affair, see the conversation in KPS 523f./AS 87f.; cf. Kraushaar 1998, 1:560f.).

Thus, when Habermas asks, with thinly disguised sarcasm, whether or not Germany should "have obtained a *different* political system [eine *andere* Republik] after all?" he juxtaposes two forms of dogmatism. The student movement, he says, did not learn the lessons of his own generation, which exorcized Stalin's ghost at the end of the 1950s. And the new conservatives, following on the heels but in the opposite direction of the waning 1960s, brought back the old themes and arguments of the Nazi era. Neoconservatives developed a thoroughgoing "apologetic political theory" (KPS 425/OSSA 13). Habermas is repeatedly disappointed with these two forms of perceived dogmatism for some of the similar reasons that bother him about uncritical traditions and religiosity. Just as public figures of hope within *our* complex modern world so also symbols of politics must shed any aspirations to become a vanguard. Habermas holds out for a disconsolate ideal of hope and political liberation without absolutes. Is an undogmatic form of religiosity without religion possible, and does it serve as a parallel to Habermas' disconsolate social ideal? An affirmative answer to these related queries does not arise on Habermas' own grounds. But what we can say for sure in this connection is that he criticizes the dogmatic Left and the Right in light of his overall criticisms of unreconstructed religious dogmatism.

As the German Autumn of 1977 takes a chilling turn *(Wende),* the new climate sows icy seeds for the later German Historians' Debates of the mid-1980s and, even later, for the debates on Germany's re/unification in the 1990s. It is already apparent that Marcuse and Habermas do not agree on locating Fascist trends among the Leftist students in the movement days of the 1960s. Marcuse's leading role in the American New Left (both activist and theoretical) and Habermas' tarnished leadership role among the rebellious youth in West Germany took rather different turns. I would therefore qualify Detlef Horster's conclusion: "Because of his life's history, Habermas has a delicate sense for the signs of the Fascistic climate" (1991, 113). It would be more precise to say that Habermas attains and exercises this "delicate sense" after May 8, 1945, in the entire restoration period of the 1950s and during the three revisionist situations of 1977, the mid-1980s, and the 1990s. But in the key situation of 1967–1969, his diagnoses of the times are overdetermined, even if only "expressed hypothetically in 1968" (NR 25/AS 233). He is quite consistent, I would add on target, in detecting only and only that Fascism which more clearly resembles his own youth experience (tab. 1.1). Thus, after the 1960s, he comes to agree with Marcuse's analysis of the neoconservative outgrowth of the entrenched Nazi continuities:

> Marcuse's counterposing of revolt and counter-revolution fits the situation in the Bundesrepublik [i.e., the German Autumn of 1977] pretty well. It is as though the Right, discredited in the shadow of National Socialism, had only been waiting for a pretext to rise up against the "Ideas of 1789"; only this ghostly projection can explain the intensity of the emotions aroused. (NR 22/AS 230f.)

To the instantaneous rupture with the past (1967–1969), Habermas juxtaposes the reactionary rise of new conservatism (1977–1988). From 1977 until the present moment, he remains involved at the heart of the key political debates in Germany. He is uniquely situated between *witnessing critically* against the false continuities and yet suffering the inability of his own era, hence experiencing with pathos his own powerlessness, to break them. He, too, undergoes the movements of his own, the preceding, and the following generations: the postwar incubation, the real and the phantom revolutions, and the creeping return of conservatism. The generational perspectives do not neatly overlap, nor do they follow a linear pattern. Where at one historical instant Habermas finds himself in opposition to certain strategies and goals of the rebellious youth, at another he puts himself on the front lines against the rising power of the new conservatives. He puts himself on the line more than once:

- First, we witnessed his critique of Heidegger in 1953. This event he recalls in his 1977 *Spiegel* interview in the same breath while discussing his involvement with the student movement in the 1960s.
- Second, after withdrawing from the public to the Max Planck Institute in Starnberg in 1971, and just as the one-time activists begin to settle from the earlier "phantom revolt" into their middle-class plateaus, Habermas breaks his silence in 1977 (KPS 364–67).
- The third occasion for his active engagement comes after the student leaders from the 1960s once more shake hands with Habermas.

This third occasion brings us to the last encounters between Dutschke and Habermas. They meet for the first time since 1967 during a Frankfurt teach-in on

April 9, 1975. At this event they voice joint support for the persecuted praxis philosophers in Yugoslavia. They also discuss the new German curbs on critical intellectuals and compare these restrictions with the Joseph McCarthy era in the United States during the 1950s (see Kraushaar 1998, 1:545f.; 2: doc. 408, p. 792). Dutschke died at the age of thirty-nine on December 24, 1979, most likely a delayed consequence of the brain injury he received in the 1968 assassination attempt (1:576). In an obituary that appeared in *Die Zeit* on January 4, 1980 (KPS 304–7), Habermas echoes his reconciliation with Dutschke during their last meeting in 1979. In a later interview given in 1988, Habermas accentuates the hypothetical nature of his warning against Left Fascism in 1967. He recalls having retracted "this reproach" in the *Spiegel* interview in 1977, and he links the original warning and his later retraction of it to his last encounter with Dutschke in 1979. That Dutschke thanks Habermas in 1979 for this 1977 explanation published in the *Spiegel* interview indicates the genuineness of their personal reconciliation.

> On that occasion [the 1977 *Spiegel* interview] I sought to explain, in a biographical context, why Left intellectuals in the *Bundesrepublik* reacted in a more sensitive, scrupulous, irritated way to the first stirrings of a rhetoric of violence, and of the use of violence, than their friends in other countries. What is more—and this is something which gave me particular pleasure—Dutschke thanked me emphatically for this explanation, when we met in Starnberg after Marcuse's death [July 29, 1979]. (NR 25/AS 233; cf. NC 185f.)

Habermas returns to Frankfurt as professor of philosophy and sociology just as Helmut Kohl becomes the newly elected chancellor of the FRG. Even though Habermas brought the separate universes of philosophy and politics into one critical discourse when he came out against Heidegger in 1953, there is a politicization of theory that he rejected in principle both in the student experimental curriculum of political and critical universities of the 1960s and in the period of the active student strike in December of 1969 (Spartakus Department). He reiterates this rejection again in his inaugural lecture on April 4, 1983 (after his third and last inauguration in Frankfurt).

At about the same time, in a speech on civil disobedience (CD), originally given in September of 1983 to the cultural forum of the SPD and reformulated at the major panel at Frankfurt University on November 22 (Kraushaar 1998, 1:587), Habermas voices a very strong defense of nonviolent civil resistance. November records the peak number of anti-NATO peace demonstrations against stationing nuclear missiles on West German territory. The early antinuclear social movement dates back to 1957–1959, the first such protest movement from Habermas' youth; the new movement gains momentum on October 10, 1981, the day of the major gathering against the stationing of cruise missiles and Pershing 2 rockets in the FRG. The fall of 1983, which marks the last effort to stop nuclear weapons from coming to West Germany, is compared, in terms of the governmental rhetoric and antiprogressive legislation, to the pogrom climate of the German Autumn of 1977.[5]

THE BITBURG RITUAL: STAGING FOR HABERMAS' ENTRY TO THE HEAT OF THE HISTORIANS' DEBATE, MAY 5, 1985

> There is a desire to escape, finally, from the straitjacket of a life history revised after the fact, and so to be allowed once again to sing all the verses of the *Deutschlandlied* [German national anthem, 1922–1945; reinstated in the FRG in 1952, but with the first two stanzas forbidden]. (EV 264f./46f.)

Helmut Kohl's era comprises the second and third waves of conservative historical and political revisions. Kohl stages two dramatic plots for later events. In the first act he choreographs the ritual at Bitburg; the second casts him directly in the role of a new Bismarck, the *re*-unifier of two Germanies. What are we to make of the confused sense of history shared by Kohl, Ronald Reagan, and the retired U.S. and German generals who would select a German military cemetery in order to make amends for World War II enmity?

Kohl's dramatic act of May 5, 1985, was meant to comprise two parts. Part one represents a conceptual shift from the discourse of the Nazis' crimes, their defeat, and the liberation of Germany from Fascism to the discourse on "freedom or totalitarianism." In the revised discourse, one would no longer need to utter "Fascism" in the same sentence with "Germany." The FRG would become allied overnight with the United States in the struggle against worldwide Communism. The clear benefits of Bitburg are its retroactive projection of this alliance into the significance of 1945. Kohl was shunned on a prior occasion by the World War II Allies who gathered to celebrate V-E Day at the Normandy beach on May 8, 1984. French President François Mitterand had pity on Kohl that year and admitted him at the Verdun commemorations. However, World War I rituals cannot assuage the bad conscience over Auschwitz. Kohl needed his normalization success badly. Celebrating May 1945 at Bitburg would offer a tangible enactment of revised history. There, entombed immemorially, West Germany would remember its share of victims fallen to the worldwide struggle against Communism. The victorious march of Stalin's Red Army in 1945 would portend the dangers of the west's "defeat in [its] victory" in 1945 (EV 265f./47f.; trans. mine). Having an unsound historical memory of his own (or lacking one altogether), Reagan was all too willing to act as a character in Kohl's normalization-passion play. The lines were scripted by the new historians and utilized by Kohl's politics of memory.

Yet it is a badly written and choreographed theater play. Part two of the ritual turns into historical backpedaling: "the handshake of the German and American World War II generals next to the graves of the SS in Bitburg." The Bitburg handshake was meant to relieve West Germany from the weight of its past and foster a new cultural stability. Given NATO's stationing of the cruise missiles and the Pershing 2 rockets in West Germany after the antinuclear movement in 1981–1983 failed to stop this, the struggle against Communism would upgrade the defeated nation to its status interrupted in 1945. The kitsch character of this sentimental drama could not spare Kohl and Reagan from its fiasco ending. There were no U.S. soldiers buried at Bitburg (fiasco one), and snow covered the entire cemetery with its SS gravestones until spring (fiasco two). These fiascos became the two public relations reasons for needing to change the venue of the planned May celebration. That there were SS soldiers buried among ordinary German soldiers and that the SS graves would become visible as the snow melted with the arriving spring of liberation show how Kohl's intent to normalize West Germany was shattered not merely by poor planning or climate but by the SS ghosts of 1945 (EV 262f./44f.). That Reagan would hope to visit the Bergen-Belsen concentration camp and Bitburg on the same day, satisfying equally the memory of victims suffered by *all* sides, betrays either his naïveté or his stupidity, and likely both. Little did it matter that he turned his back on the SS graves while standing at Bitburg. Chancellor Kohl and President Reagan along with the generals shook hands in a joint offense and the stupidity of this revised historical normality (KNV 11).

Stepping back from the dramatic ritual, let me review the facts, which defy any revision. The forty-nine *Waffen Schutzstaffeln* (SS) troops are buried at the Bitburg military cemetery alongside other ordinary German soldiers killed during World War II.[6] In his informative introductory remarks, Wolin (in NC xxviii n. 15; cf. n. 16 on Reagan) discusses Raul Hilberg's analysis ("Bitburg as a Symbol," in Hartman 1986, 15–26): "Though most of the Bitburg debate has focused on the presence of the SS graves, Raul Hilberg has correctly pointed out that the German Wehrmacht, or regular army, was itself hardly an innocent bystander to the politics of genocide. It often provided logistical support to SS troops charged with exterminating the Jews. Its ranking officers (e.g., Field Marshall Keitel and General Jodl) were hanged as war criminals after the war. In truth, the German army was an integral part of Hitler's Reich and its crimes." Moreover, the SS soldiers buried at Bitburg were most likely responsible for mass murders somewhere in Heinrich Himmler's elite Nazi machinery of death.

The question is, What history is fashioned *now* by making amends *here*? What did Chancellor Kohl have in mind by staging at Bitburg a postwar reconciliation that would mark the FRG's return among "normal," civilized, and pacified Europeans? And was President Reagan thinking at all? Was he listening to the voices of Jewish survivors? Or was he out to lunch when he went to the concentration camp Bergen-Belsen in the morning (Reagan originally planned to violate Kohl's staging instructions and skip this part as too morbid for the late twentieth century) and to Bitburg later on that same day—May 5, 1985? The SS officers buried at Bitburg do not rise to the festive occasion of this liberation May parade. Yet as Benjamin

(1968, 255) intimates earlier, the dead victims are not safe from their dead enemies when the living enemies among us politically manipulate historical memory. The Bitburg debacle of 1985 casts ghoulish shadows over 1989 as well as over the late October unification of Germany in 1990. Just imagine, if the SS at Bitburg had risen from the dead to this normalizing occasion of resurrecting greater Germany, then a scary post-Wall revision would have taken place, a frightening continuity would have reestablished itself before *our* very eyes. The dates and places are both symbolic and material. Kohl's second major act raises the question, What sense of liberation do *we* invoke in the moment when the East-West Wall is being chiseled away? Does 1989 win *us* a new beginning or does it shore up a continuity of the narrative that was only briefly interrupted and mourned in 1945 (NBR 17, 171/12, 165)?

We encounter Habermas after 1977, through 1985–1987, and even more so from 1989 onward, immersed in the debates over Germany, in the controversies about the future of the European Union, and in discussing globalization issues. His responsible acts, his performance as a public intellectual and citizen, play their core role in shaping his philosophical-political profile, itself part of the larger living history in the making.

FROM HOPE TO NEW OBSCURITY: STAGING FOR HABERMAS' AMBIVALENCE IN UNIFIED GERMANY, NOVEMBER 9, 1989

> In unobtrusive ways, we are constantly learning from major traditions, but the question is whether we can also learn from *events* that reflect the failure of traditions. I refer particularly to situations in which the people involved find that their acquired approaches, interpretations, and abilities are not up to dealing with the problems that confront them; disappointing situations in which horizons of expectations—even the traditions themselves that stabilize expectations—are thrown into crisis. (NBR 15/11)

November 9, 1989, witnesses the fall of the Berlin Wall; November 9, 1938, witnesses the night of shattered glass *(Kristallnacht)*, the beginning of the intensified Nazi persecution of the Jews.

Given these two November events, what historical consciousness is punctuated by May 8, 1945? Was V-E Day a defeat, a moment ushering its contemporaries into a mourning of that past in the present; or was it an occasion to welcome liberation? If the latter is true, what kind of liberation is celebrated in 1945 and what sort of hope arrives with 1989 (NBR 167/161)? *Our* present age provokes these questions while the three (securing, skeptical, and protesting) postwar generations are now transported to the observation platform erected after 1989. So here and now someone could consider these to be silly and outdated questions. Müller

(2000, 256, 273, 277, 283f.) at times gives this negative impression by way of criticizing the so-called Holocaust identity and the very need for a continued coming to terms with the past as a way to critically apprehend the present. Let me admit that this questioning could nowadays appear to be at best anachronistic. And yet therein lies the staging ground of Habermas' ambivalence about the unification of two Germanies.

Taking a "Millennial" Perspective from Without

At the outset of this study, I took a certain liberty in designating May 8, 1945, as Habermas' existentially motivated philosophical and political birthday. Having set his beginnings in 1945 (and not in 1929, his biological birth), I shortened his life span by fifteen years. This would be presumptuous in any event, and certainly for the sole purpose of a profile or a book construction, had Habermas not given us permission to view history from the dual standpoint of "calendrical punctuation" and what I called the defining situations. By setting the beginning of the nineteenth century back in 1789 (the French Revolution) and extending it until 1914 (World War I), while abbreviating the twentieth century from its beginning in 1914 (World War I) to its end in 1989 (the fall of the Berlin Wall), Habermas effectively cut the twentieth century by twenty-five years. Thus condensing his life in that same shortened century by fifteen years is comparable within the reduced scale. This has been a short century, he agrees with the historians who introduce this convention. I should rest easy in taking my first perspectival screen cut of Habermas' profile in 1945, that is, fourteen or fifteen years after his biological birth, and in making the last defining cut of that era in the narrow trajectory of 1989. My staging of *Jürgen Habermas* is set between 1945 and 1989: Compressing his narrative into a forty-four-year-long dramatic perspective, after the first and before the last "calendrical turning point," each of which marks merely a "constructed chronology" (PK 65/LD 307) of our biological beginnings and ends, allows me to focus more specifically on the "physiognomies" of his moving philosophical-political profile (71/310).

While *we* are neither at the instant of this writing at the end of *our* century, but somewhere on either side of it, nor are *we* at the end of Habermas' life, *we* may join him and establish 1989 as the end point of this century and the last formative situation of his twentieth-century life. (It should be clear how arbitrary the beginning and end dates of *our* centuries are historically or philosophically, even if we knew exactly when the first day of Christmas rather than, say, the creation of the world, on the Jewish calendar, actually took place. If the calendrical millennium followed the Vatican *fiat*, then the twenty-first century would begin at some midnight, perhaps in Bethlehem, of December 31, 2000. This and similar calendrical punctuation marks represent mere conventions.) That year—1989—marks the culmination of Habermas' postwar situations, even if not the end of his intellectual life. The key physiognomies of his narrative, as we are staging the key situations of 1945, 1968, and 1989, are not the biologically or socially constructed beginnings and ends of *that* waning century or of one's life. Rather, each date is a segue carrying an existential sense of history and of this or that narrated philosophical-political profile. The trajectory for sketching a complete profile of Habermas is set by the staging of this short century. After 1989, *we* are thus viewing both events (the passing century and Habermas' life in it) as if from *outside*. Although he continues to write after 1989, this too happens with his view taken from *an outside* of *his and our* twentieth century, that is, as he understands the questions of that passing era. Inevitably even this *outside* end point (1989) is situated within another *inside*; however, *we* do not fathom the larger situation of this inside from *our* historical platform of 1989. What cannot be temporally fathomed or reconstructed does not raise an intelligible question for *us*. What cannot be questioned even as a known unknown—from that one cannot learn. Whereas in 1989, *we* can already gain a retrospective "diagnostic look back on the short 20th century" (PK 65/LD 307), *we* do not know yet how to vary the images of its failures to grasp the crux of *our* failures, how to get ourselves to the other side of doing the same thing over again. We suffer a peculiar millennial blindness (obscurity) of *our* defining situations.⁷

The three key "hermeneutical perspectives" by which Habermas defines "the conflict of the ideas which dominated the century" are Communism, Liberalism, and Fascism (71/310). For all his settlement into the gray post-Marxian fashion of the post-Wall days, in 1998, nine years into the new era, he affirms, and quite emphatically so, that there *are* alternatives (EgA)! There exist other untried alternatives both to the failures and to the exhaustion of the Occidental utopian energies (NÜ)! But he seems to catch the virus of exhausted imagination from the preceding (securing) as well as from his own (skeptical) generation. Both Habermas and these two generations, in different ways, gave up on the liberation project as something more than a formal idea of democracy. The securing and skeptical virus mutates first during the discontents with the '68ers; then its sedimented strain survives and mutates again in the 1970s and 1980s as a renewed trauma of 1945; and finally, combined, it is carried forward into the post-Wall era with its *humanitarian* wars of intervention (PK 86, n. 10/LD 318, n. 8).

Author's Interruption: A Backward-Looking Perspective within a Perspective

I now drop the perspective of a dramaturgical observer reconstructing Habermas' trajectory as a drama set in a historical present tense and enter the stage in person as its living participant. Only two weeks after I arrived in West Germany to study with Habermas as his international Fulbright student, the gates of history began to flood our seminar room with world historical events. The date was mid-September 1989. East Germans were storming western embassies in Prague and Budapest. And the more the television brought their pictures into the public sphere, the more the embassies filled up with refugees. Then the special trains from Czechoslovakia and Hungary were allowed to carry some of the human overflow to West Germany. Mass demonstrations were staged in East German cities, Dresden and Leipzig being among the most significant. While Erich Honecker tried to save the day with carrots and sticks, Mikhail Gorbachev looked the other way. Then in one instant, on November 9, the floodgates gave in and the Wall caved in. We did not know it then, but these revolutions in Central-East Europe (were they merely catch-up revolutions? cf. NR) announced Habermas' end of the twentieth century.

And something seemed to have culminated that fall in Habermas' lifework. The seeds of his later writings on law and democracy (the seeds were planted in his Thursday afternoon *Rechtsarbeitsgruppe*, a seminar including a mixed group of legal scholars, philosophers, and sociologists) matured in the heat of the revolutionary events. This revolutionary fall was neither 1918 nor 1968. And 1989 was only a catch-up revolution for Habermas; for some others, perhaps only a fallingback revolution. Habermas' thinking about democracy and postnational societies continued to evolve during the seminar discussions as well as in Dionysos, the Greek restaurant where he used to extend the Monday night Ph.D. seminar often well past the midnight hour. Our seminar group was a regular Monday night guest at Dionysos. We were given a large secluded room with a long wooden table, often seating twenty or more seminar participants. Students from Karl-Otto Apel's seminar, which was held next door to Habermas' classroom and at the same time as his colloquium on Mondays from 7 to 10 P.M., would at times join our group (though the students had to choose between Habermas' or Apel's seminar). Many nights we stayed until the closing hour. What we considered *after hours* was history in the making, advancing in a heated discussion (and ahead of our more formal classroom situation) the debates about constitutional patriotism, postnational political culture, asylum and immigration, democracy and law, the West German constitution, the meaning of the Central-East European revolutions, the future of socialism. In the smoke-filled room of the German-Greek pub, Habermas would speak his mind more frankly and express his heart more fully than he did in his classroom or his writings. He was passionate about political events, historical memory, his responsibility. I envision Jean-Paul Sartre at a café in France and Habermas at a pub in Germany fulfilling parallel nonmandarin roles of engaged teachers and public intellectuals. These roles are still more accepted in Europe and in some Latin American countries than they are in the United States. Václav Havel in neighboring Czechoslovakia and Adam Michnik in Poland played such public roles in situations not far from the crumbling Berlin Wall.

Habermas feared waking up one day once again in a nation-state that would not so much unify the two Germanies as glue together their false continuities. He voiced publicly and in print various strong objections to the process of West German administrative and economic annexation of East German territories. To be exact, he argued that people and not the government had to decide whether East Germans should be attached to the FRG according to Article 146 of the Basic Law *(Grundgesetz)* of the FRG, which considered all *Volksdeutsche,* all ethnic Germans, even those in the Slavic territories who no longer speak the language, as potential citizens, or whether a new constitution should be democratically established by all those affected. East Germans voted with their feet, and the only way to slow down the emigration tide seemed to be the expansion of the West German economic and administrative net eastward. DM nationalism (the East Germans' choice of the West German mark, the preferred hard currency) provided, however, little guarantee that the false continuities would not underwrite the unification (see DM). Habermas could not disagree in the final analysis with Günther Grass (echoing Karl Heinz Bohrer's publicly stated position on the purpose of reunification, see Müller 2000, 192, 258), who had declared in a remarkable Frankfurt lecture prior to unification that one virtue of unifying Germany would be that German *Volk* could remember Auschwitz together. This ongoing remembrance (retaining tradition in its crisis) is not the legacy that Kohl, the unification chancellor, reserved as his right in 1989, even as he was voted out of politics in the fall elections of 1998. Remembering Auschwitz as the heart of a new German identity does not seem to be included in the vision of the twenty-first century by the political generation of 1968 either: among them we find the foreign minister Joschka Fischer.[8]

Now let me take yet another step back from today, namely, from Habermas' end of the twentieth century in 1989, which I experienced on New Year's Eve in Prague's St. Wenceslas Square. I want to revisit one instant that reverses, in a feat of magic realism, the last two digits of Habermas' end of the twentieth century: the inverted numerology of 89 ushers us into 68.

I was eleven in 1968. This was the year of my intellectual and political awakening, and thereby *my precocious existentially philosophical and political birthday.* My encounter with Habermas' time line in the twentieth century is thus written from the perspective of these my beginnings. That year was for me unlike any other moment in *our* era. That year was set in as strange a time warp as Alexander Dubček's Prague Spring or the May Events in Paris or the student revolt in Mexico or Marcuse's exuberance in his *Essay on Liberation* (1969). The time quakes of 1968, as Kurt Vonnegut would call them, interrupt *our* time from its next century. My experience retains 1968 as a "now-time" from the future of the "not-yet." This is because the temporality of 1968 has been imbued with an uncharacteristic messianic hope of liberation. How far from *this* here and now lies the later new obscurity and exhaustion of the utopian energies? Students and workers dreamed and Marcuse wrote ahead of *their and our* time. The year 1968 comes from a century that might or might not be *ours* after this one ended in 1989. For an uncanny moment on New Year's Eve 1989, I thought as if the radical hope of 1968 welcomed us once again from the future. But in the instant following hope, revision returned with a vengeance.

The short-lived opening of 1968 was crushed violently. Should we still blame Marcuse and the students of 1968 for theorizing under these conditions both the nonviolent and the violent forms of disobedience (PK 237f.)?[9] Should we today blame the indigenous poor in Chiapas for wearing the rebel's mask? Who and from what historical stage has the luxury of making this charge? All too soon 1989 became exhausted by the gray neoliberal realities, and that is the real meaning of this century's end in the west—a dull ending with revised twenty-twenty vision and no hope. In the historical shifts of 1989 nobody had the strength to restart the unfinished dream of radical democracy once envisioned in 1968. At best we childishly played with the digits 68/89. But that is not what I am doing at this moment. The childishness does not come about because 1968 was a "phantom revolution" of 1989, the latter being just a "catch-up revolution"—catching up to complete the democratic socialization after 1945. That latter view defines Habermas' skeptical generational sensibilities and his perspective taken up from within them. Rather, I suggest, *we* have not-yet become capable of understanding what 1968 signifies. The seeming anachronism of 1968 bespeaks *our* ironic misreading of *our* own future, of the not-yet, even as *we* are nowadays already situated at its *outside* doorsteps (i.e., beyond 1989). For all his expressed support for and his valuation of the liberating potential of the new social movements in 1968, the 1980s, and after, Habermas' project (even post-1989) remains circumscribed by the twentieth century's problematic and by its preferred solutions. That vanishing horizon of 1989 with which the twenty-first century begins did not yet fathom the questions asked in 1968. That incomprehension of the question concerning *our* future, beyond the disasters of the passing era, indicates a peculiar millennial blindness too.

Habermas' Core Hope: The Self-Corrective Process of Learning

Can *we* learn? And what can *we* learn from history? From Habermas' generational perspective, May 8, 1945 (now viewed from outside of the twentieth century, after November 9, 1989), vanquishes one bankrupt tradition. In that instant, history is catapulted into a temporal point zero of mythical origins. But one must stay alert since these, as any other, origins are never innocent; human beginnings are always already part of traditions born in crisis!

> Certainly, it is from the perspective of a specific generation [of Jürgen Habermas] that 1945 appears in this way as a challenging break. From other perspectives, other dates appear just as decisive. The year 1989 is a break that also opened even the blindest eyes to the rise, fall, and crimes of the Soviet Union—a chain of events that is instructive concerning the failure of an unprecedented, and unprecedently irresponsible, human experiment. *Still written in the stars is the date that—one day—may mark the shipwreck of another regime exercised anonymously throughout the world market.* (NBR 17/12f.; italics added)

Such dates as September 12, 1990, when the final settlement of World War II and the terms of German unification are signed, and October 3, the day of unification, inevitably conjure up the horrors of a bankrupt tradition that is now refurbished in a renewed nation-state. For this reason, the years 1945, 1989, and 1990 (along with the *re-* in reunification) are populated with ghosts. The student movement of 1967–1969 and, even more, the Persian Gulf War of 1991 and the bombing of Serbia in 1999 provide the testing grounds and limit horizons for what one did or did not learn from history. The failures of one's history and, more significantly, one's attempts to redress them can produce blind spots. The long shadow of 1945, which worries Habermas so much, is cast not only over 1989 and 1990 but also from 1991 up to the last calendrical years of the second millennium (see NBR, chap. 6; cf. Müller 2000, 121, 216, 254f., 282).

When Saddam Hussein threatens Israel with chemical weapons produced with the aid of German companies, Habermas, traumatized by what 1945 signifies about Germany's historical debt to the Jewish people,[10] articulates his support for the Persian Gulf War (VaZ). And in 1999, recalling the memory of the Holocaust, he closes ranks with NATO and Germany's new Red-Green coalition in his, albeit ambivalent, approval of the bombing of Serbia (BH). Cognizant of his biography from 1945 to 1969, one must grasp Habermas' two moves in support of the western Allied wars of intervention as just examples of his consistent ambivalence toward everything. His yes-and-no act is the vintage seal of his skeptical generation. His stance is ambivalent but not necessarily nuanced, especially if it is contrasted with a clearer no voiced by others on the Left against the imperial underpinning of those two interventionist wars. Several North Americans were visiting with Habermas in Frankfurt during the heated period of the Gulf War hysteria. Suffering neither Germany's sense of guilt in regard to World War II nor the inability of some on the German Left to criticize the United States because of the Allied defeat of Germany in 1945, these U.S. visitors tried to argue Habermas out of his position. Although he stubbornly stuck to his guns, they did succeed over time in bringing a better argument to prevail over his support for the UN-sanctioned Allied intervention against Iraq, even if only after that war was over, even if only with the hindsight of that war's extreme brutality. We hear the echoes of this learning hindsight from the Gulf War in Habermas' later essay (BH) on the conflict in Kosovo. But even a careful theoretical position of his reflections on Kosovo, insofar as it ends supporting NATO's military action, is just that—an ambivalent and careful public act of legitimation.[11]

The postwar situation of Germany, Habermas convinces himself and us to hope against hope, occasioned definitive learning that now becomes part and parcel of the post-1945 socialization (NBR 17f./12f.). He learns different lessons from this catastrophe than does the generation of his parents and teachers, many of whom overprotected themselves from learning anything after 1945. The task

Habermas sets for critical social theory, integrating his postwar experience, is to preserve the valuative continuity of learning against the false continuities of traditions that once fooled us. One should like to believe that with his critical attitude, he continues to learn as he did from his hasty labeling of the student movement as Left Fascism. His self-corrective and dialogic efforts at learning differentiate him from postwar elitist silence about national failures. Indeed, what if it became obvious (also to Habermas) that the Persian Gulf War and the intervention in the Kosovo/a conflict, while the first one was procedurally legitimated in the Security Council of the United Nations and the second one was morally justified by certain appeals to universal human rights, had been at the core unjust orchestrations by one dominant superpower? Would not these wars be but new instances of situations that once fooled us (i.e., of one's own hope that the United Nations, as it now stands, or some international military police force, NATO, alone can protect us from bankrupt traditions)? Habermas was willing to admit that the cherished cultural consensus fooled the entire generation of the '45ers. He made some amends to his 1991, still rather German-centered, position on the Persian Gulf War (EdA 248/SR 119). His receptivity to refugees in the German asylum debates of 1991–1993 and his critical assessments of the global economic and postnational constellations (PK) of the neoliberal world order indicate, and I would say demand, the need to learn about a more robust notion of economic and anti-imperialist democracy. This ideal of inclusive political and economic democracy is contained in the most radical intuitions of the fifteen-year-old Habermas whom we met during his Gymnasium and university studies and still later at the IfS, in each instance reading Marx, western Marxists, and the early Frankfurt School authors.

I conclude these preliminary comments on Habermas' defining situations with a thought about his lifelong, tireless effort at intellectual honesty. His capacity for openness draws on his almost native learning hope that emerged within his reflective consciousness on the liberation day, May 8, 1945. Inspired by the Sartrean-Beauvoirean existential language, let me call this critical hope *Habermas' fundamental project*—an ideal of social transcendence or redemption on *this* side of the world. Transcending in the communicative immanence of one's/our coming to an understanding with another about something in the world, in communicative action with others in this world and not beyond it, we enter the heart, at once anxious and yearning, of Habermas' lifework. Justifiably, these returns to *the founding situation* of hope mark his existentially motivated, and at once philosophical and political, birthday. And therein I find the key that will help us, in what follows, to further unlock our understanding of Habermas' philosophical-political profile.

I traced Habermas' preoccupations with the conservative revisions of German history and identity from the German Autumn of 1977 to the Historians' Debate in the 1980s to the post-Wall controversies of the 1990s. The latter erupt with the drive to unify Germanies, and they continue in the second German Autumn of 1991–1993. These debates, Habermas insists in argument and by his public interventions, shatter any innocent veneer covering the surviving desire to refurbish the Nazi past. Notwithstanding the student disappointments with him during the heated days of 1967–1969, his situation and his indisputable legacy must be gathered from within a larger reach. I will not be saying that his philosophical-political profile could not harbor or does not exhibit a conservative side. My double-negative caution at this moment in the study is to ward off any premature judgment passed on a thinker and an activist whose singular existential pathos has been and is to foster radically democratic forms of life. If a conservative dimension in Habermas' profile were discovered, it would be found in places and in times in which his dominant concerns and strengths unravel into key blind spots and weaknesses.

Considering the blind spots of one's insights and the weaknesses of one's strengths in a manner that is not gratuitous or hasty, I must disclose how even blindness can motivate one's positive vision and speech, just as light and communication can vanish from one's horizon on the obverse side of the moon and still play their role. The effect of one's learning as well as one's consciously intended critical impact may at times inspire another's narrative of discontent. Such discontents indicate the limits of the lessons learned and of the impact exercised in the present age on its youngest generations.

NOTES

1. The italicized *re-* in reunification indicates the difference between two concepts. When Turner (1992) uses "reunification," he returns to a normalcy broken in 1945; when Habermas and others use "unification," they do not restore normalcy and speak instead of the need for new constitutional and symbolic beginnings.

2. Oskar Negt notes the "pogrom mood against the Left of all sorts" already in his essay from October 1971, "Zum Fall Baader-Meinhof" (in Kraushaar 1998, 2: doc. 394, p. 745).

3. Members of the Baader-Meinhof Gang were captured in 1972. The jail cell deaths of Andreas Baader, Gudrun Ensslin, and Jean-Carl Raspe in October 1977 were explained to the public as suicides, but this account remains suspicious (see OSSA 127f., 306 n. 8 by translator; Kraushaar 1998, 1:562). I use the spelling Hanns Martin Schleyer as the most consistently correct one, even though two other inconsistent versions of his first name appear in various texts: "Hans-Martin" (OSSA 26 n. 3 by translator; in Albrecht et al. 1999, 647, but that same book prints "Karl Martin" on p. 349); "Hanns-Martin" (Kraushaar 1998, 1:562, under the photo); but what I deem to be the correct version, "Hanns Martin," is used by Kraushaar on the same page in the text and again by Kraushaar (1990, 94) and Wiggershaus 727, 793 (1989, in German). But the English translation (1998) of Wiggershaus, 656 and 784, uses for some reason "Hans-Martin."

4. A collage of short films, *Deutschland im Herbst* (1978), captures seven weeks of the RAF terror and of reaction. It begins with the kidnapping of Schleyer and ends with the death of three Baader-Meinhof members. Lynne Cheney, a chairperson of the National Endowment for the Humanities (1986–1992), applied the term "liberal McCarthyism" against the "specter" of political correctness emerging at U.S. universities (see Kilian 2000).

5. I will return to Habermas' discussion of civil disobedience in chapter 4 below.

6. On Bitburg, see the chronology in Hartman 1986, xiii–xvi.

7. On blind spots in Habermas, see table 8.3 as well as references to Müller (2000) in n. 11 below.

8. Mohr 1998 and Bubis 1998, 54.

9. Cf. Wolin's lecture (1998).

10. Ertel et al. 1998; Habermas, PZ; ZLB.

11. Among the visitors to Habermas' seminar during the Persian Gulf War period were two U.S. Humboldt scholars in 1990–1991, James Bohman and Kenneth Baynes. Both are students of Tom McCarthy (one of the first American interpreters and translators of Habermas and the general editor of the major MIT series in which many of the newer translations of Habermas are published), and both urged Habermas to take a more clearly critical position against the U.S.-directed Allied war on Iraq. See also Müller (2000, on Habermas' blind spots, 8, 262, 282, as well as 12, 42, 45, and with reference to the wars of intervention, 121, 216, 227, 254f.).

Part Two

PROFILES AND INTERVENTIONS

What does it mean to become contemporary with the problems of the present age, the crises of its institutions, and the profiles of its generations? What does it mean to become contemporary with Habermas' present age? I will take up these questions by examining how Habermas' philosophical-political profile is formed in response to the key formative and generational situations of his era.

My core thesis, intimated in the opening citation for the second section of chapter 2, is that *Habermas' work and philosophical-political profile emerge integrally through debates and dialogues with his era's two generations—the securing generation of 1945 and the protesting generation of 1968*. The catastrophe ending in 1945 signifies the need for securing constitutional reform, lawful state, democratic institutions, and deliberative procedures; the protest of 1968 confronts Fascism at its symbolic and material roots surviving in postwar German culture, society, and politics. *The transformative-revolutionary core of 1968 undergirds the constitutional-democratic needs of 1945.* By discussing the formation of Habermas' profile in response to his defining situations, I will go forward biographically but in reverse historical order—in a temporally circular motion from

- the revolutionary "phantoms" of the 1960s
- to the echoes of 1945 during the "pogrom" atmosphere of the 1970s and the revisionist debates of the 1980s
- to a contemporary glance at how Habermas' mature post-1989 profile stabilizes in the shadows of 1945 and under the specters of 1968

Chapter Four

THE PHANTOMS OF 1968

> The '68 generation was probably the first in Germany which did not shy away from asking for face to face explanations—from parents, from older people in general, in front of the television set, and so on.... The student protest was the staging of a public... reckoning, also reaching into the private domain, with collective avoidance of the German responsibility, of the historical liability, for National Socialism and its horrors. (NR 23/AS 231)

After May 8, 1945, we found the young Habermas longing for some upheaval to open a clean postwar beginning. His confrontation with Heidegger's onetime philosophical and academic advocacy of the Nazi ideology and, even more so, with his ambiguous postwar silence about that conduct, represents in 1953 a relatively lonely voice in the cultural wilderness of postwar Germany. The false continuities have been melting for some time until they thawed in the 1960s and then suddenly erupted in 1967–1969. Even though he was one of the recognized intellectual leaders of the progressive Left in West Germany, Habermas too had to wait for the generation of the '68ers. The revolting students were the first generation that had the courage to face its parents and teachers in ways that neither Habermas' generation nor the preceding one did.

The crucial and interesting question for us lies in the evolution of Habermas' initial postwar situation from a life surrounded by the false continuities of his adolescence and young adulthood into the rupture of the 1960s. We should not be surprised that in the postwar era, he literally yearns for a radical revolutionary break with the Nazi past. Reflecting on the period after 1945, he intimates and, as if ahead of history, foreshadows that later Marcusean longing shared by many a student in 1967–1969. But his own passage through this time is haunted by nightmares, even as his desire to make a clean start bursts with increasing intensity through the seamless whole of postwar continuities. The language of radical memory he invokes makes his postwar years much closer to those later reevaluations of the past in 1968, the year that did not take place in his own youth. Again, we must ask, if a revolutionary break had taken place in 1945, would he not have embraced it with open arms, his self-restraint from a post-1968 hindsight notwithstanding? He offers us a glimpse into his Benjaminian yes-and-no relation to postwar beginnings:

> I thought then what one cannot say today without criticism: if only there had been some spontaneous sweeping away, some explosive act, which then could have served to begin the formation of a political entity. After such an eruption we would have at least known what we couldn't go back to. (KPS 513/AS 79)

In some regards, the protesting students are not that alien to the young Habermas. They do not think of their liberation struggle in a totally different way from his longing between 1945 and 1954. The perceived "phantom" nature of the revolutionary outburst in 1967–1969, which Habermas ascribes to the students, does not diminish the level of their achievement, which would have satisfied Habermas already in 1945! Students made possible something qualitatively new in the FRG. Habermas becomes gradually aware of this irreversible shift in social consciousness after 1945; he knows as much for sure by 1968.

But when Habermas reaches the age of twenty-four, the year is not 1968 but 1953—the height of the Cold War era. His public protest against Heidegger lacks broader social context and remains Habermas' personal revolution only. The early student movement and the antinuclear movements of the 1950s announced the upheaval to come. These movements were protointellectual, indicative of the needed radically corrective grounding of the FRG (tab. 1.2). The turn of the year 1959–1960 ends the restorative institutional grounding of the state and initiates the incubation period with the following period of the intellectual grounding of the FRG. The early student and protest movements were likewise preparatory for Habermas' full awakening to the dual—institutional and intellectual—dimensions of Critical Theory as a tradition and a movement (tab. 2.1).

He had to wait until 1967–1969 for the second act, which would make the revolutionary break concretely personal as well as social. Turning forty at the juncture when we locate Habermas in the 1960s, the middle-aged professor no longer agitates for an all-out "sweeping away." Like the later hippies moving from the 1960s into the second postwar restoration era of the late 1970s and 1980s (NC 186), he exercises already in 1967–1969 much greater caution. He leans on the constitutionally warranted and established institutional structures; he prefers channeling disagreements through respectful academic dialogue over agitating on the street corner. He has more to lose; and this means, in his argument, that the entire country has more to lose. The constitutional evolution of the postwar state into a functioning democracy was not easy. Given the long march through the institutions, which allowed for liberal democracy becoming at home in postwar West

Germany, Habermas is not about to throw this caution to the wind, no matter how much he itched for "some explosive act" in the youthful years. "There simply was no struggle," he remarks of that early era. From the observation platform of 1979, he adds: "I think it makes a difference whether one says that looking forward or looking back" (KPS 513/AS 79).

Habermas makes a rather rare personal admission about his intergenerational place in this passage of time:

> When I was a student, in 1953, I wrote a comparable article on Heidegger's 1935 lectures, because I was outraged by the inability of the protagonists (such as Heidegger, Carl Schmitt, Gehlen, and so on) to utter even one word admitting a political error. *But I avoided any confrontation with my father* [italics added], who was certainly only considered to be a passive sympathizer. In short, the generational clocks were set in such a way that the '68ers were able to insist, without any embarrassment, on a specific confrontation with the past. This confrontation had perhaps something abstract about it up until then. (NR 23/AS 231)

Habermas confronts the Nazi past of his philosophical icon, Heidegger, and even of one of his two doctoral advisers, Rothacker. But he must wait until the 1960s for the arrival of that social form of life which would embody the break with the false parental-national continuities they represent. Habermas comes to credit unequivocally the student movement for accomplishing this latter task. I employ this evolving turn of the phrase because in 1969 his own understanding of this matter seems rather murky. In a 1988 interview, however, he remembers his hurt and outrage when Inge Marcuse, at the Korčula summer school in 1969, proposed to him that the '68ers were the very first generation in West Germany with the courage to strip the Fascist culture down to its naked reality. "I experienced the suggestion as an injury." Habermas has his core identity invested in the formative years following 1945. He matures in the postwar milieu with his decidedly anti-Fascist new sensibilities. His Leftist friends and his future colleagues, as well as his left-wing university students, all represent either the primary relationships or the points of significant identification and self-realization. Habermas thinks of himself as one with their aspirations for a more just way of life. He invests his lifework in the constitutional reforms of postwar Germany and in its incorporation among "the six or seven most liberal countries in the world." I may sum up without hesitation his lifelong task as follows: to introduce "a sense of historical proportion," namely, *to integrate the constitutional needs of 1945 with the revolutionary core of 1968, while searching for an audience and the procedurally supported life forms that would receive this historical integration* (NR 23/AS 231; all citations above).

Habermas approaches his self-appointed task by way of internalized ambivalence. With regard to the student revolt, the outcome of this attitude becomes a series of skeptical interventions that prevent him from embracing *this* youth group and movement wholeheartedly (tab. 8.3). Accordingly, I will discuss the following profiles and interventions:

- Habermas' fear of revolutionary "phantoms"
- Krahl and Dutschke as the forgotten third-generation critical social theorists and activists
- the generational transmutations of the critical social theory and practice of violence and nonviolence

SPECTERS AND PHANTOMS OF REVOLUTION

Signs of Habermas' growing discomfort and caution with regard to the growing student protest appear, almost imperceptibly, at the Free University of Berlin on January 20, 1967. Different people speak on the topic of university and democracy, and Habermas presents a paper, "University in a Democracy—Democratization of the University" (KPS 134-56/TRS 1–12). He warns against anarchistic, irrational, provocative, and even violent trends as sheer political folly.[1] He recommends practicing forms of resistance that are appropriate to university life (nonviolent, domination-free discussion) and its freedom of research. He worries about West Germany's "masked states of emergency" that are accepted by the authorities as legitimate (e.g., in the *Spiegel* affair [153/11]), but he argues that unless university freedoms are endangered, the university should not be politicized as a springboard for the extraparliamentary opposition. His presentation is aired by the Hessische Rundfunk broadcast on April 11 as a contribution to contemporary issues (Kraushaar 1998, 1:244, 248).

Habermas credits the student movement for breathing a genuinely anti-Fascist new sensibility into West Germany's cultural ethos. But he never gives up his reservations either.

- "In one respect I was probably right, because for the most part the left-wing students had a rather clichéd notion of fascism."
- "At that time it cost a real effort to assert in public that the organs of state also carried out functions which helped to secure freedom . . ." (NR 23/AS 231; both citations above).
- Although Habermas avoids confronting his father during his own student years, the '68ers, who had the passion and daring for exactly this irreverent confrontation, "were already so removed from the Nazi period that they could no longer accept as obvious what was obvious for Marx—that there could be no socialist emancipation without the realization of the freedoms enshrined in bourgeois principles" (NR 25/AS 233).

My thesis about Habermas' profile is prescribed by his yes-and-no position, which is situated within the in-between generational space of 1958; his position embodies the 1945 need to institutionalize and democratize the revolutionary experience of 1968. The student movement in the FRG becomes at its peak a cup of strong coffee for Habermas. Given his shifting intergenerational sensibilities, some of his immediate political evaluations in 1968 overshoot the historical mean for integrating the needs of 1945 with the existential core of 1968. The '68ers confront their fathers and mothers, doctoral directors (in Germany these are often the adopted fathers of the second order), politicians, cultural heroes, and popular stars, and in the end the very socioeconomic foundations of the social compromise on which the postwar western establishments were formed. Habermas is for breaking the false Fascist continuities; in the same breath he vouches for keeping the new institutional continuities of the postwar constitutional democracy. But, as if instinctually, he shies away from student radicalism and seeks instead an institutional safety of democratic procedures, liberal freedoms, and constitutional law. By 1968 a form of life imbued with revolutionary spirit comes alive all around him: As the student movements overtake the main stages in Paris, Berlin, Berkeley, Prague, Frankfurt, and Mexico City, he gradually devolves from an intellectual leader of the progressive German Left into a reform-minded German professor, formal philosopher (more neo-Kantian and Hegelian than Marxian), and legal scholar.

One of the many paradoxes of Habermas' intergenerational sensibility is that his work on the public sphere (SÖ) functioned as a fundamental groundwork for his enthusiastic reception by the students as their key Left protagonist. His book stresses the role of the public cultural and political debate. The open public sphere represents the needed *institutional* foundation for the *intellectual* critique of politics, culture, and society. The student movement reverses this founding relation: the ongoing critique is necessary to secure the institutional foundations from authoritarianism (cf. the book title of Albrecht et al. 1999). Under the influence of Habermas' widely debated work, students aimed to democratize the university and the media. They aspired to link their academic public sphere, still quite a privileged domain, with the voices on the margins and, particularly, with the anti-imperialist struggles of the so-called Third World.

Like Habermas' work on the public sphere, Marcuse's *One-Dimensional Man* becomes a groundwork for the student movement and not only in the United States. But Habermas' and Marcuse's respective links to the student movements in the 1960s are far from similar. Marcuse's text is a rather sobering portrait of the failing options for liberating the post-Enlightenment industrial societies. The pessimistic tenor of Marcuse's book seems beside the point. It might have been precisely the tension between the reality exposed and the negating critique of his work that fueled the activist motion. The difference of notable significance lies, instead, in Habermas' embrace of the welfare state and reformist approach and

Marcuse's lifelong readiness to join revolutionary praxis. It is impossible to determine whether or not the historical fact that Marcuse was a Jew who had to flee Germany in 1933 can *explain* the more definitive degree in which he broke with the continuities of the modern state culturally and institutionally. Yet we would not be entirely wrong in contrasting Habermas' path away from social revolution to the institutional safety of democratic procedures, freedoms, and law with Marcuse's path away from sham democracy, institutions, and law to their outsiders who, like the persecuted Jews of the war period, exist on the margins (NR 27f./AS 235; PK 232–39).

When Marcuse finds himself in Paris during the May Events of 1968, he (like Daniel Cohn-Bendit)[2] is invited by the students to speak. He communicates the solidarity of the New Left in the United States with the social struggles in France. He goes out of his way to encourage the Paris students and other coalitional groups. He pours more fuel onto the fire by not sparing his critique of western establishments. In May 1968, under the impact of the Paris events, West German students take over Johann Wolfgang Goethe-Universität in Frankfurt and rename it *Karl Marx Universität*. They set up their own curriculum and carry on administrative duties, raising a red flag over the seminar, their microcosm of a liberated territory, in hopes of sending sparks from the transformative fire in the university to the society at large (cf. KPS 518/AS 83). Their optimism and courage, followed often by the other sectors of the society, embody an inverted Marxian scenario: students have the leisure or freedom to lose everything in breaking up the social chains. We find this happening again and again during 1968 in Paris, Berkeley, and Mexico City, during the 1989 revolts in Prague and Beijing's Tiananmen Square, and later in Belgrade.

The police step into the fray in Frankfurt when the student radical democrats encroach on the administrative core of state power—university documents. On June 1, 1968, at the Frankfurt Mensa, Habermas addresses the students. Unlike Marcuse or Cohn-Bendit in Paris, Habermas restricts his horizon to West Germany, where he deems social revolution untimely. Sounding cautious, he proposes piecemeal reformist aims within the established status quo. His yes and no to Marx accompanies his ambivalent posture toward student radicalism. His Kantian-Hegelian reevaluation of Marx undergirds some of the core theoretical reasons for his ambivalence toward the generation of the '68ers.

In his six theses on the strategies, goals, and political analyses of the oppositional youth, Habermas frames his evaluation of the evolving West German student movement after his fateful *two words* of June 9, 1967 (SiK).[3] The theses encapsulate his yes-and-no view of the student revolt. It is worth pondering the conceptual and metaphorical dimensions of his position. Conceptually, with a yes, Habermas affirms that the student movement in the FRG generated new cultural perspectives. With a no he warns against dogmatic dangers inherent in Marxism and, by extension, in certain dimensions of the movement. Metaphorically, his yes motivates the revolutionary confrontation with "the shadow of National Socialism" and with any future "ghostly projection" (NR 22/AS 230f.). His no arises out of the conclusion that the revolutionary specters of 1968 have become but "a laughable fantasy of power" (SiK 259), a mere "phantom revolution" (257f.).

The six theses divide into three affirmative and three critical positions. Theses 1, 2, and 6 mark Habermas' ongoing praise for the student generational achievement and its long-term positive implications for West Germany's ethical and cultural self-understanding. In theses 3-5, he articulates his differences with and direct criticisms of the student movement.

Thesis 1 (SiK 250–51): Habermas identifies among the immediate goals of the university and high school (Gymnasium) students to be the repoliticization of the public sphere and of the mainstream media (e.g., Springer-Verlag, which was one of the targets of the student protest). His own theoretical analyses of the rationality, legitimation, and motivation crises of late capitalist politics and economy (see SÖ and later LC) are as if mirrored in the students' aims. Students were inspired by Habermas' analyses of the public sphere. In this affirmative sense, the '68ers respond to the democratic needs arising from the best aspirations of the two postwar generations—securing and skeptical.

Thesis 2 (SiK 251–52): Habermas stresses the historical significance of new protest techniques. German students learn new forms of resistance from the U.S. civil rights struggles. Developed within popular culture, these protest styles make realistic inroads even against the disciplinary machinery of the state. Habermas is particularly impressed by the nonviolent character of the new oppositional techniques. He praises the ability of the street theater to rupture the false cultural continuities and the intact generational sensibilities.

Thesis 3 (253–54): Habermas analyzes the impetus behind the student movement. He differs with the explanations given by the student leaders and he indirectly criticizes their goals and strategies. He argues that the sources of the student protest cannot be economic but instead must be social, cultural, and psychological. He points out that the students embody a rather privileged group and lifestyle. They are part of a leisure class, if you will, even though in West Germany's welfare state, where education is paid by the state, not all students would necessarily have to come from wealth or an upper middle class. The revolting students detect the legitimation crises as one consequence of the failed promises of capitalism, but the Marcusean "new sensibility" (SiK 253) is born in the student ranks from the opportunities afforded to them by income and the educational environment itself, Habermas reasons.

He goes on the offensive in *thesis 4* (254–56): the movement relies on a very dubious (uncritical?) social theory, which he suspects to be an offspring of certain Marxist orthodoxy. Note that 'Marxism' and 'dogmatism' become at this juncture interchangeable terms for him insofar as (or because) he drops from his Critical Theory the following Marxian concepts:

- the labor theory of value as an explanation of the economic crises
- the existence of the class division of labor and the ensuing class struggle
- the analyzable (i.e., intelligible links) between the affluence of the First World and the immiseration of the Third World

Habermas enhances these revisions of Marx in his later writings (TP, chap. 7; LC; TCA, vol. 2; NR 177–204); his yes and no to Marx is already summed up under the three headings of thesis 4.[4]

Habermas locates the purported oversight of the student movement in its reliance on an unrevised (i.e., dogmatic) Marxism. In his characterization, students read off the crises of the capitalist social form of life directly from an analysis of its autonomously functioning economic system. They uncritically presuppose a holistic notion of liberation. Habermas argues at greater length later in his *Theory of Communicative Action* that we cannot directly translate the noncommunicative steering media, such as money or power, into the communicative and normative life world equivalents, as those found in the domains of ethics, morality, and politics. We can at best defend against the unwelcome disturbances in the life world brought about by the anonymous systems rationality of the economy and efficient administration. Since systems rationality (money and power) is here to stay, Habermas insists, a good market economy with corrective democratizing features is our best and only option to resist the unwelcome disturbances. We cannot liberate complex social forms altogether (holistically) from their reliance on the steering functionalism of money and administrative power. Marx's hope for such a liberation was naive, and students in 1968 followed his romantic suit, as Habermas concludes then and continues to hold today, thereby inscribing his view within his evolving revision, and some would say in the end his rejection, of Marx.

Habermas argues that the notion of the class struggle as a revolutionary strategy makes good sense only if the labor theory of value and the ensuing model of economic crises hold. With late capitalism's ability to adapt and establish class peace, such crises can be largely neutralized. Workers are no longer the sole revolutionary agency of social change. After 1989, more than in 1968, socialism in the form of radical critique and radical democratic reformism becomes Habermas' biblical "eye of the needle" for the narrow passage into a more just form of society (NR 203; cf. 187 and TP, chap. 6; NC 192).

Finally, Habermas concludes that with class peace established in western democracies, the imputed internal correlations between First World welfare and Third World exploitation also vanish. Any serious analysis of postwar Euro-American imperialism increasingly drops from Habermas' purview. In a 1984 interview entitled "A Philosophico-Political Profile," his answer to this issue is evasive but consistent with the missing critique of imperialism:

> [Question] *The Frankfurt School tradition as a whole has concentrated its analyses upon the most advanced capitalist societies, at the comparative expense of any consideration of capitalist societies as a global system. In your view, do conceptions of socialism developed in the course of anti-imperialist and anticapitalist struggles in the Third World have any bearing on the tasks of a democratic socialism in the advanced capitalist world? Conversely, does your own analysis of advanced capitalism have any lessons for socialist forces in the Third World?*
>
> [Habermas' answer] I am tempted to say 'no' in both cases. I am aware of the fact that this is a eurocentrically limited view. I would rather pass the question. (NU 255f./AS 183)

Habermas charges the revolting students with a certain naïveté that allows them, mistakenly he claims, to link their 1968 struggle with those waged by the wretched of the earth. Yet the liberal gallantry with which he himself moves over the greater part of the world, then and still now fighting against Euro-American imperialism, is inconsistent for the position of anyone who claims some roots in Marx and minimally the early critical social theory before its 1950s safe transmutations in West Germany (KPS 516–18/AS 81–83). Marcuse (1965b, 110; 1969b, 6–7), who was at one point inspired by Fanon (1963) and in part by Sartre (preface to Fanon 1963), encourages the very linkage to which Habermas objects as the unfounded romanticism of the students and of Marcuse (PK 232–39): that we join the struggles of the new social movements in the First World with those on its global margins.

Habermas articulates difficulties with one more oversight on the part of the rebelling students: besides their dogmatic Marxism, he reasons, they dream of being always and already a revolutionary movement. It is not clear, given his revisions of Marx, whether or not there could be in principle (ever) a genuine revolutionary movement. In either case, the students in West Germany were not it. Habermas is assured of this judgment at the height of their public confrontations with the state and the university establishment. Besides reminding students of their privileged life, imputed income, and class, Habermas stipulates that the objective conditions in the FRG were not ready for social revolution. Again, it is not clear whether or not there could ever be such conditions on Habermas' analysis. His preferential option for nonviolent forms of struggle within the confines of a bourgeois-democratic and lawful state, furthermore, his implied praise for class peace and the welfare state, and, finally, his own theoretical oversight of Eurocentrism and overt western imperialism, all suggest that Habermas criticizes students from an adopted social-democratic, politically liberal, and reformist platform.

In my discussion of Habermas' core situations in Part One of this volume, I cautioned against a premature critique of Habermas as someone who in the 1960s simply joined the opposition against the student barricades. If we now read the critical profiles of Habermas, written by the Leftist theorists and activists after their break with him in 1967, we might get precisely this unbalanced impression of Habermas as a champion for the conservative cause (NC 185; KPS 518ff./AS 83f.). Human profiles are never that simple, and this simplification is not my view of Habermas either. Such a prevailing view from the end of the 1960s would restrict us to a mere caricature, thereby precluding a more nuanced profile of him. We must not brush over his already stated reflective self-choice of himself as someone who is supportive of the students in their educational and democratic demands and who is even more enthusiastically for their cultural revolution against the lingering Fascist era. In 1984, Habermas does not exclude the future possibility of assuming again an active political place on the Left, a place that he occupied in the "Sozialistischer Bund" long before the student movement (i.e., in the 1950s): "Were I to rule that out [adopting publicly my place on the Left], I would be someone other than *the person I would wish to be*" (NU 257/AS 185; ital. added). Finally, we should accept at face value Habermas' categorical exception to the Leftist criticisms of the positions he adopts in June 1967 and in June 1968: "I'd like to challenge one premise—that I placed myself outside the framework of the student movement. I never saw it that way; I never intended it so" (KPS 518/AS 83).

A full accounting of Habermas' unequivocally affirmative relation with the protesting generation of students should even out any one-sided view of him:

- 1951–1953: Horkheimer (and most likely also Habermas) supports the early student movement.
- 1957–1959: Habermas is a vocal youth leader in the first antinuclear student movement; he acts against Horkheimer's opposition and consequently has to leave the IfS.
- 1966: Habermas takes part in the Frankfurt protests against the Vietnam War, again acting against Horkheimer's and Adorno's expressed views of these protests as anti-American.
- 1967: Habermas, like Adorno, protests the shooting of Ohnesorg and the not guilty verdict for the policeman accused of the killing.
- 1968: Adorno defends Krahl as his best student and compares the student role to that of the Jews.
- 1977: Habermas rejects implicating the Frankfurt School and the student generation in the terrorist acts of the RAF.
- 1979: Habermas and Dutschke reconcile their differences from the 1960s.
- 1981–1983: Habermas becomes a vocal supporter of the new social movements and nonviolent civil disobedience.

Habermas has a keen ability to listen, learn, and correct his views. "So I did perhaps react a shade too much like a bourgeois intellectual," he admits with remarkable honesty to an excessive tone of his *two words* (Left Fascism) by which he labeled, even if hypothetically, the students in 1967. Yet even with his conciliatory look back at his involvement during the heated days of 1967–1969, and contrary to his later self-stylization of carrying out an insider's critique of the movement, his objections to the student protest cannot be rendered fully intelligible as an immanent or *"internal* critique" of "student actionism" by a revolutionary-minded critical social theorist and activist (KPS 519/AS 84; NC 186, last citation). His position does not merely express the generational or personal difficulty of a professor who was unable to close ranks with the students during their most volatile moments. Rather, his critique records the view that arises from his deeper disagreements. While inspiring and joining the protesting youth for a long stretch of the road on the *inside* of the barricade, he thinks and speaks from *outside* the students' revolutionary aspirations. After the fateful turn of post-Weimar history, emerging from his own Hitler Youth experience into the liberation event of 1945, Habermas is perhaps too ambivalent and skeptical about social anarchy to be able to ever belong wholeheartedly, and specifically in the 1960s, to a protesting youth movement.

I think that Habermas remains consistent in this regard, and I am not unfairly characterizing him as someone thinking from a certain *outside* of 1968. At the same time, I may continue to accept at face value his own challenge to the Leftist caricatures of the position he holds in 1967–1969. Truth be told, Habermas develops a peculiarly Marx-inspired and Left-liberal social criticism of his own making. He is a critical social theorist committed to a nonviolent, reformist path of social democracy, constitutional state, and procedural law. "My Marxist friends are not entirely unjustified in accusing me of being a radical liberal" (NU 240f./AS 171). Insofar as he is a radical or Left-liberal and not a revolutionary-minded critical social theorist and activist, I may trace his roots back to the critical achievements of the bourgeois modernity adopted before him already by Marx and the early Frankfurt School. A Left-Rawlsian or a Left-Kantian and Hegelian position would not be entirely inconsistent with this achievement.

In sum, Habermas optimistically accepts the students' generational gains that once and for all challenged the false continuities of the Fascist culture. Yet his formal redemption of transformative praxis—into an ideal of socialism as critique (NR 202f.)—no longer trusts the economic and social-revolutionary aims of the '68ers, whether these hold out for democratic socialism without capital markets or for some form of market socialism. And this revision cannot situate him internally (i.e., disagreeing merely within) but rather places him on the right side of the student movement (i.e., disagreeing with and standing against) and its radical revolutionary project of social liberation.

For this very reason, *Thesis 5* (SiK 257–59) appears to be more radical than it in fact is. Habermas charges the rebellious students with leaping from their faulty economic and social analysis into adopting an unsuitable strategy. He brands their stratagem leap "actionism" and names the group outcome "phantom revolution."

The appearance of radicality in his thesis is given by his suspicion that the students were acting in isolation from other social groups (mainly workers) and thus elicited only a weak support for larger democratic change (cf. NC 186). But he psychologizes the situation and the motives behind the student movement, which betrays the overall ambivalent character of his belonging unreservedly to the possibility of social revolution as such. Had he elaborated an in-depth analysis of the 1968 events in Paris or Prague or Mexico, where more sectors of society were involved and where the objective situation provided different possibilities than it did in West Germany, his thesis could have become a form of immanent critique. Yet the platform of this thesis represents his reformist-affirmative position: he theorizes no other possibility of social revolution in contrast to the perceived failures of the students in the FRG. Other revolutionary options inhabit neither his counterfactual reasoning nor the vanishing point of his regulative ideal. His critique that the students conflate a symbolic phantom with the material reality says more about Habermas' philosophical-political profile within the established social order than about that of the '68ers.

With all his praise for the guerrilla street theater and the forms of protest that ruptured the faulty Fascist identity, Habermas concludes thesis 5 with a psychologizing portrait of the student revolt in West Germany as a revolutionary farce with three character masks. The *agitator* embodies an actionist's narcissism, the *mentor* represents an impractical observer, and the *harlequin* is staged as an irresponsible poet of the revolutionary mirage, if not a drifter or libertine who is clueless regarding the consequences of words and acts. With these nasty portraits of revolutionary specters (Hans-Jürgen Krahl, Oskar Negt, and Hans Magnus Enzensberger) turning to phantoms (agitator, mentor, and harlequin) between June 1967 and June 1968, does Habermas lose his nerve? Apparently he does, given the harsh fourteen responses he receives from student leaders and activists (Negt 1989; cf. KPS 518–22/AS 83–85).

Thesis 6 (SiK 259f.) charts the bold reformist program on the road from revolutionary upheavals to mass enlightenment. This plank evolves more for Habermas' own sake than that of the '68ers. Or to put this more constructively, his programmatic redirection of 1968 represents in a nutshell what I have called *Habermas' integral response to his era's two generations: the constitutional needs of 1945 and the revolutionary core of 1968*. The specter of social revolution, the unruly genie of liberation that in his imagination turns into a frightening phantom, immigrates within the normative confines of his communicative theory and becomes protected by the constitutional checks and balances of his democratic theory.

We should note here an almost imperceptible shift in the location of the ghosts and shadows that have worried Habermas since 1945. He continues to watch the Right and its negative reaction to any future return of the repressed "ideas of 1789" (NR 22/AS 231). We find Habermas fighting at the anti-Right barricades from about 1977 to 1987, and again after 1989. But in the 1960s, he warns that the

Left revolutionary specter can become a Fascist phantom, coming through the back door. He turns the table on the fallibility of the students' extraparliamentary opposition: not all state law and order can be identified with Fascist power (SiK 259; NR 22f./AS 231). Defending the validity of the lawful state against perceived dangers of student anarchism, he begins to search already in the 1960s for a legal space between facts and norms (FuG). This space of law and order is to integrate the revolutionary aims of 1968 with the constitutional needs of 1945.

We can only wonder how Habermas' analysis would develop had the '68ers anywhere managed to take and keep political power, thereby effecting in the 1960s (not as in Germany in the 1990s) long-lasting social change. In hindsight, Negt's softening introduction to the volume, in which the Left answers Habermas' six theses, can be read as ironic. Whereas Negt (1989, 32) eases up somewhat, the Left lambasts Habermas for being at worst a traitor and at best a Left-liberal social theorist of the welfare state establishment who gave up on radical liberation praxis. And yet Negt's conciliatory tone, or its driving assumption, becomes nowadays an ironic if not harsh reminder to Habermas how far his reception, mainly in the United States, moved him from the earlier, more socially emancipatory vision of his youth. The chorus of his critics in 1968 did not attempt to dislodge him from the Left but rather to protect him from his untrue friends on the Right. Whether or not Habermas desired such protection (or would want it today) is debatable. The benefits of getting this protection, even if Habermas did not ask for them, are obviously not harmful to the unsuspecting students of Critical Theory (cf. Holub 1991, 94).

In his November 1967 presentation at the Goethe House in New York, Habermas basically reiterates his six June theses. The essay is significant for its probing analysis of the root causes and development of the protest against West Germany's conservative continuities from the 1950s to the struggle against the Grand Coalition in 1966, as well as its historical glance at the entire year since Ohnesorg's murder on June 2, 1967. It is obvious from the structure of the presentation that Habermas' trajectory has a significant autobiographical undertone. For this reason, it represents a good comparative check and balance on the profile I have been crafting in this volume. Unlike his teachers in the Frankfurt Institute of the 1950s, Habermas identifies with the early progressive antinuclear movement. He joins with the ongoing struggles against the conservative (militaristic, pro-Fascist) trends in society, the co-opted SPD, the undemocratic university, and various affairs (e.g., the *Spiegel* affair) that signal authoritarian state intrusions into the public sphere. The most significant for my purpose is his generational self-assessment of what occurred on June 2, 1967:

> We of an older generation reacted to this event, which Günther Grass has called the first political murder of the Federal Republic of Germany, the way we reacted to the night-and-fog action against the *Spiegel*: as an additional symptom of the restriction of democratic rights and an alarm signal for a renewed defensive attempt. But for the active part of the student body, June 2 means something different.

These students belong to the first generation whose memory is not determined by the Nazi period . . . the first generation that did not witness the emergence of the institutional framework of the Federal Republic . . . the first generation that openly perceives the disproportion between the potential wealth and potential gratification of an industrially developed society. . . . the rising generation has developed a particular sensitivity to the untruth of prevailing legitimations. Outrage against the double standards of the older generation's morality is, of course, repeated in every generation. (KPS 231f./TRS 24f)

What is new about the student movement, he adds, is its "'neoanarchist worldview' and the predilection for direct action" (232/25). This predilection has such diverse sources as "a theory that somewhat existentializes Marx and Freud, as in the works of Herbert Marcuse" (235/28); Sorel's or Bergson's vitalism; and Mao's or Castro's anarchism. But these sources amount to the "fruitless violent acts of the actionists" (233/26). The students exaggerated the context of their struggle, imagining themselves to be part of a larger social revolution and the worldwide anti-imperialist struggle. "But," Habermas contends, "we have no ghettos that could possibly serve as the basis for urban guerrilla actions, and no students who are drafted to fight guerrillas in Southeast Asia" (234/27; cf. 271-303/31-49; an abridged English translation).

THE CRITICAL SOCIAL THEORISTS AND ACTIVISTS OF THE 1960s

Numerous people on the active student Left respond to Habermas' two interventions from June 9, 1967, and June 1, 1968 (Negt 1968). I focus on two responses by Krahl and Negt, then turn to the September 1967 position paper on the organization of the student movement coauthored by Krahl and Dutschke, and conclude with a comparison of these student leaders with the Leather Jacket faction of the 1960s movement. These texts and contrasts are significant for revealing a more differentiated theoretical position—an impression we will not get from what Habermas says or does not say about Krahl or other student leaders whom he stylizes as immediacy-seeking anarchists and decisionists who politicize theory and university and who pursue action for its own sake. Wolf Lepeniens can write in 1967, after the Hannover conference and Marcuse's Berlin lecture series, about the break between the prominent Frankfurt fathers of Critical Theory and their children as well as about Marcuse's rise to notoriety: "Adorno and Horkheimer are considered passé. Habermas, speaking of Left Fascism, has committed in Hannover a sacrilege—Marcuse remains" (in Albrecht et al. 1999, 335). As the 1960s end, it is not just the premature deaths of Krahl (1970) and Dutschke (1979), not just the militancy of the ultra-Left terrorist group, RAF, but the ascending Frankfurt position of Habermas and his students, nowadays placed at universities worldwide, that contribute to the eclipse of critical social theorists and activists of the third, protesting, generation. With the death of Adorno in 1969 and Marcuse in 1979, Habermas' great innovation and productivity in the fields linked more or less to the Frankfurt School continued unmatched.

Krahl responds to Habermas' presentation in Frankfurt on June 1, 1968 (Kraushaar 1998, 1: 343; 2: doc. 221). First, Krahl launches a critique of the dogmatic class theory held by the student platform of the SDS. Second, he objects that Habermas simplifies the international orientation of the student movement, that he undervalues its social protest potential, and finally that he projects pathological motives onto the extraparliamentary opposition. The triple objection suggests that Habermas fails to admit the possibility of a unified movement composed of students and workers. The first point is important because it suggests that Habermas' theses rely on an undifferentiated view of Marxism (something, as I noted in chap. 1, Horkheimer objected to in Habermas for quite different reasons in the 1950s) as well as the sophisticated theoretical debate among the activist students within the SDS (2: doc. 221, p. 413). This old-fashioned Marxism, then, leads Habermas to a *theoretical* failure to develop a critical social theory of anticolonial struggle with a wider base of international solidarity. Krahl praises Habermas' capacity to learn, only to show that he did not learn enough: "What a year ago, Habermas denounced as Left Fascism, he celebrates today as an imaginatively rich demonstration technique. The learning process he has absolved since then is gratifying. At the same time he holds firmly to an academic schema of praxis: first comes the enlightenment, then action. But this model has been since long overhauled" (414). Krahl's rejoinder represents that critical social theory which reveals a much greater theoretical sophistication of the student movement than Habermas' critique of its activists admits. Habermas' theses give no credit to the student leaders as selfstanding and original critical social theorists. But Krahl's way of thinking represents in 1968 a trend that, in spite of his accidental death in 1970, becomes much more pronounced in the new social movements of the 1980s and in the wider forms of solidarity emerging in the Seattle (November 1999), Washington, D.C. (April 2000), and Prague (September 2000) protests against the debilitating effects of globalization spreading at the expense of economic democracy. The move from a critique of imperialism and globalization in the 1990s to greater solidarity formed across class, gender, sex, race, and national borders validates the visionary thinking emerging within the 1960s student movement, rather than Habermas' restrictive polemics.

Negt (Kraushaar 1998, 2: doc. 218) writes in June 1968 that Habermas' charge of Left Fascism expresses "liberal-bourgeois consciousness" that ascribes this problem to the students when the charge really applies to the leadership groups of West German society and their aspiration to pass the new Emergency Laws (pp. 406f.). Negt perceptively drives home the context of Habermas' ambivalence: "The liberal public [in the Federal Republic] was always only then capable of mobilization, when the issue was obvious violation of laws and rules—such as in the *Spiegel-Affair*, such as after June 2 [1967]." Habermas' critique, however, suffers from a "fatal illusion" insofar as "he believes in the viability of a democracy without democrats" (407). In his introduction to the volume of the Left's answers to Habermas, Negt (doc. 223, pp. 417–25; cf. 1968) confirms Krahl's characterizations of Habermas' disappointed orthodox Marxism-Leninism. He reiterates his insights into Habermas' liberal-bourgeois standpoint, into the sources of his consistently vigorous defense of democratic rules, and into his ongoing skepticism toward and growing fear of extraparliamentary protest.

Dutschke and Krahl's programmatic paper on the "organization" of the protest movement in West Germany, delivered to the twenty-second delegate conference of the SDS (Frankfurt Mensa, September 4–8, 1967) provides a deep analysis of the historical precedents, present sociopolitical conditions, and strategic thinking demanded by the situation (Kraushaar 1998, 2: doc. 152, paper from September 5). In his detailed commentary, Kraushaar (1990) compares the situations of the student organization (SDS) and the actual student movement with the Frankfurt School's vibrancy in exile and its institutionalization in the 1950s: both organizations in their name no longer fit the reality (57). Reacting to the Fascist continuities, the 1960s emerged from restoration into the Grand Coalition between progressives and conservatives. Integration of oppositional parties in 1966 left no clear parliamentary opposition. The Communists were forbidden in 1956, the SPD purged itself of progressive agenda and language in 1959, and both the *Spiegel* affair in 1962 and the murder of Ohnesorg in 1967 contributed to the impression that in a one-dimensional society without opposition (pace Marcuse 1991), Fascism could return by way of West German parliamentarism as it once did in the Weimar Republic (Krausaar 1990, 59–61).

The keynote by Dutschke and Krahl addresses itself directly to the growing tension between the socialist student organization (SDS) and the protest movement (Kraushaar 1998, doc. 152, 287). The protest arises against a new system of "integral etatism," namely, the constellation of monopoly capitalism, in which the state regulates the economy and utilizes a full monopoly on violence as its major tool of domination (288). Against Habermas' June 9 anxiety about possible Left Fascism, the student leaders theorize on September 5 the existing "internalization" of Fascism within liberal democracy; against his forthcoming June 1, 1968, fear of "phantom revolution," they warn a year before of "phantom liberalism" *(Scheinliberalismus)* and "phantom democracy" *(Scheinparliamentarismus)*. The state assumes the integral roles of universal capitalist and manipulator of public opinion; it admits permanent structural unemployment. Unlike an overtly Fascist regime, this state controls without utilizing "physical terror" (289; last citation from Kraushaar 1990, 66).

If the problem is internalization of domination within democratic procedures, then the question for critical social theory and practice alike cannot be about institutionalizing liberal democracy but rather forms of struggle to break through what distorts democracy from within. Clearly, Dutschke and Krahl do not seek some empty, unmediated, unthinking anarchism (as if any anarchism were always and already that empty action in place of theory). Rather, they present an alternative critical social theory to that of Habermas and they draw different consequences for action—in their constellation—than liberal reformism.

The role of "agitator" presented here does not correspond to the caricature sketched a year later by Habermas (SiK). The task of the critical theorist and activist is to raise consciousness and offer evidence against the "global one-dimensionalization of all economic and social differences" (Kraushaar 1998, 2: doc. 152, p. 289). Such "visible irregular action against the abstract power of the system" of oppression would create tension within the internalized forms of this oppression and it would act as a catalyst within the consciousness of passive, uncritical consumers. The purpose of nonlegal and even anarchist acts by the "urban guerrilla" is to break open the closed social consciousness of "passive and suffering masses." While the theorist and activist leaders of the 1960s focused on universities as their main "social basis" and "security zone" for the social struggle (290), *we* witnessed in the 1999 Seattle protest against the World Trade Organization a much enlarged zone of struggle that now includes all levels of students, workers, ecology, women, and anticolonial activists. Contrary to Habermas' simplified characterization of anarchists, these groups, in Seattle and again in the Washington, D.C., protests in April 2000 and the Prague protests in September 2000, were theoretically savvy, organized, and effective in achieving and helping others achieve concrete protest aims (raising public awareness about globalization, communication with the media, producing independent media, closing down the meeting).[5] Kraushaar (1990, 67) underscores that this paper is the first one in West Germany in which the notion of "urban guerrilla" is discussed, "grounded," "deduced," and "demanded" as necessary. And yet this rehabilitation of Bakunin against Marx (and Habermas) cannot be judged as the intellectual origin of the RAF terror in the 1970s (68). Habermas agrees with this assessment, even though he cites his own (and Adorno's) critique of the student activists in 1967–1969 as the primary evidence against the charges that the Frankfurt School inspired red terror. Hence, for this very reason, he could not highlight these activists and theorists, exemplified here by Dutschke and Krahl, for their integrity and sophistication. The point of my discussion is to bring home this nuance. Kraushaar (1990) confirms this conclusion:

> Dutschke and Krahl define the urban guerrilla as an element of consciousness-raising strategy. The value of militancy arises from its propagandistic function, not vice versa. The sense of irregular action does not lie in the materially destructive power of violence. . . . The function of the urban guerrilla . . . is seen [by them] in the consciousness constituting role of the provocative act that breaks through the hermetically sealed system of manipulation. (68)

Kraushaar links the antiauthoritarian impulse of the early Frankfurt School's struggle against Auschwitz with the student struggle against Fascist trends within liberal democracy (71). Horkheimer relied in the 1930s, given the failure of social democracy to stop Fascism, on the free association of individuals to break through the integral etatist regime (72). Student theorists bridged these early analyses with Marcuse's new analysis of one-dimensional society, and both with their experience of the West German political scene bereft of democratic opposition. "The idea of direct action lives at its core from the existential indignation at Fascism . . . and the disappearance [of this indignation] in the postwar period" (75). Early critical theorists despaired over the possibility of liberation, but out of the most hopeless situation of the Holocaust, in the student ranks, they gave an "indirect" intellectual impetus to the idea of an urban guerrilla, Kraushaar concludes. I noted already how Habermas (KPS 364–87, 411–41/OSSA 1–28) and Wellmer (Kraushaar 1998, 2: doc. 417; OSSA 283–307) forcefully assessed the difference between the origins of the Frankfurt School and the RAF terror in the 1970s. Yet they failed to clarify the deeper motives shared by the early critical social theory and the antiauthoritarian student movement. Marcuse's notion of the 'great refusal' and students' application of it clearly were inspired by the struggle against Fascism and by the 1960s transmutation of that struggle—not, therefore, by the 1950s and some sovereign authoritarian decision promoted by Carl Schmitt (Kraushaar 1990, 78; Matuštík 1998a). "Marcuse's messages did not come . . . from the Big Sur. They came from Berlin of the November Revolution [his youth], from Heidegger's Freiburg, from the Germany of totalitarian ideologies and of total suspicion of ideologies" (Albrecht et al. 1999, 347).

Kraushaar honestly analyzes the critical implosion of the student movement. The revolt gave way to a homegrown antiliberal intolerance and self-hatred, and it flirted with sham radicalism. He underscores that not much remains from the 1960s Left except the motives and conflicts between the organizational structure of the movement and its active forms of protest. If his criticism of Habermas' oversight is correct, then we must learn from it as much as from the 1960s lest we misunderstand struggles of today (Kraushaar 1990, 79). This learning defines in the end what Dutschke and Krahl theorized under the rubric of "the problem of organization as a problem of revolutionary existence" (Kraushaar 1998, 2: doc. 152, p. 290).

A contrast between the student leaders, such as Dutschke and Krahl, and the ultra-activist SDS Leather Jacket faction can help focus this discussion. In March 1969, some members of *Lederjackenfraktion* decide to demolish the dorm room of a philosophy student from Krahl's circle. They throw books on the floor and spray-paint the walls. One of the signs painted on the wall reads: "Into the concentration camp with the gang of intellectuals" (Kraushaar 1998, 1:29). This event takes place after Adorno called the police to clear out the Frankfurt Institute and after Krahl was detained and formally charged. It should be clear by now that Krahl's circle comprised political activists who insisted on the necessity of independent theoretical work. Adorno after all called him his best student, and Krahl, in spite of his dramatic differences with his mentor, never turned against Adorno's high valuation of a sustained theoretical analysis. Rather, Krahl resisted the Leather Jackets both in abdicating critical social theory and in *their* mindless actionism (e.g., when they wanted to disrupt Adorno's funeral by throwing eggs, 458). There is no record of Krahl ever participating in the Leather Jackets' classroom stunts.

In these and similar regards, Habermas' profile that emerges from his various interventions against the protesting student generation of critical social theorists and activists appears to be

- overdetermined (charge of Left Fascism, June 9, 1967)
- prone to biting sarcasm (caricature of student leaders, June 1, 1968)
- bitterly nasty (attack on Krahl without naming him, September 12, 1969, see PpP 172/103f.)
- self-serving (1977, in defending Critical Theory against the right-wing accusations of sponsoring the RAF terror, Habermas cites his prior critique of the student activists in the 1960s)

When Habermas publishes a collection of philosophical-political profiles, Krahl is not included in the pantheon of distinguished intellectuals. But Habermas does not shy away from attacking Krahl's personal and intellectual integrity:

> One of Adorno's students called into the master's open grave, "He practiced an irresistible critique of the bourgeois individual, and yet he was himself caught within its ruins." That is quite true. To respond that "whatever is capable of falling down ought to be knocked down" and to say that Adorno should have had the power to strip away the last layer of his "radicalized bourgeois character" and go before the parade of activists carrying a flag demonstrates not only political and psychological foolhardiness but also a lack of philosophical understanding. (PpP 172/103)

Habermas' essay never mentions Krahl by name. The German original of the book collection does not include it even in the index of names. Kraushaar (1998, 1:460) perceptively remarks that the funeral oration attributed by Habermas to "one of Adorno's students" is related to an earlier panel discussion at Gallus Haus on September 23, 1968. But at that time, recall, Adorno, in a letter written to G. Grass, praised Krahl as his prize student! Krahl, being deceased, cannot defend himself against being reduced to anonymity or against a distorted attribution of his thought and action. When Habermas reprints his September 12, 1969, text from *Die Zeit*, it is shortly after Krahl's accidental death on February 14, 1970.

On August 13, 1969, the day of Adorno's funeral, Krahl warns of Fascism within democracy, and he cites approvingly the famous text in which Adorno ([1959] 1986, 115) speaks about the dangers of Fascism *within* democracy being greater than those against democracy. Krahl warns that Adorno's progressive fear of Fascism within democracy turns now into a regressive anxiety about practical forms of resistance against Fascism. Krahl thinks with Adorno against Adorno—and Habermas—when he analyzes a sophisticated tension between the theory and practice of democracy. Adorno "shares the ambivalence of political consciousness among many critical intellectuals in Germany, who project [the fear] that the socialist action from the Left presents a potential of Fascist terror from the Right, which it for the very first time freely combats" (in Kraushaar 1998, 2: doc. 352, p. 674 = Krahl 1971, 285; see vol. 3, essay by Claussen, 66).[6] This insight is neither discussed nor acknowledged in Habermas' indirect polemic with Krahl, and yet it goes to the heart of the differences between students as critical social theorists and activists and both Habermas' skeptical and Adorno's securing generations.

Krahl detects that weakness within democracy which requires a more complex critical analysis and practice than opposing Fascism by procedural democracy alone. If Krahl's innovation on Adorno is correct, then even Habermas' sophisticated communicative version of radical democracy will not suffice. This difference in their respective analyses represents a generational break, as Claussen (Kraushaar 1998, vol. 3) suggests, between Habermas' Critical Theory as a theoretical or an academic project and a critical social theory of the third, protesting generation with its explicit practical and political interest in liberation. With Krahl's death in 1970, the interest in a critical social theory, and the institutions that house it, to be decidedly partial to human liberation and well-being, this direction of theory and practice is pushed to the sidelines in West Germany. What is lost with Krahl is not some desire to control others that a "Stalinist party chief" might have or that Habermas and Adorno might misperceive among the students in the 1960s (p. 66). What is lost is an integration of antiauthoritarian spontaneity, solidarity, and critical social theory (67) that characterized this generation's (and Marcuse's) new sensibility. Krahl's theory of emancipatory praxis moved beyond both Soviet orthodoxy and social democratic reformism; he sought emancipation beyond mere technical-instrumental progress; he defined social revolution otherwise than by parameters of industrial revolution (68f.). Although the history books lack the "philosophical-political profile of Krahl" (70) or others of this third generation of critical social theorists, perhaps the new movements of protest against undemocratic globalization can recover this early sensibility with even greater depth.

As irritating as Krahl's or Dutschke's or similar positions of the protesting theorists and activists might have been at their time, Habermas' criticisms of their mindless actionism befits better the Leather Jackets who provide a solid contrasting case to Krahl and other student leaders. If we take the Fascist past of Germany as the core trauma variously lived through, inherited, and shared, then Adorno's misunderstanding of the students as much as Horkheimer's paranoia and Habermas' skeptical ambivalence must be viewed in light of their experiential horizons. Habermas shares with the securing generation the struggle to overcome the Fascist continuity by buttressing established postwar democracy from within; students worry about Fascism within democracy and they *misread* that securing caution against chaos and that preference for institutionalized democracy as conservative, not safe or even skeptical, moves. The multiple uses of targeted faces of 'Fascism' (see tabs. 1.1 and 8.3)—often bordering on overdetermined outbursts of hysteria about 'Fascist-Stalinists' hiding in every closet—are explainable by the varied generational backgrounds within the shared postwar German history. (See also references to Müller 2000 in chaps. 1 and 3 above.)

ON NON/VIOLENCE: GENERATIONAL TRANSMUTATIONS OF CRITICAL SOCIAL THEORY AND PRACTICE

In his *Spiegel* interview of October 10, 1977 (see KPS 364–67),[7] Habermas acknowledges that his great sensitivity to the rhetoric and uses of violence is typical for the Left of his generation and of his biographical background. This telling admission remains to date his most direct and sensible self-assessment on this topic. Against the charges, made on West German national television by the Christian Democrat Alfred Dregger that the Frankfurt School directly inspired the Left terror of the RAF, Habermas finds himself biographically somewhat "justified . . . by opposing between 1961 and 1969 . . . *every form* of violence in our country." Habermas erects in his 1977 accounting a self-chosen profile bridge (a public act that is both self-responsible and self-justificatory) between his critique of Heidegger in 1953 and his later intervention in the "student actionism" of 1967 and 1968. Habermas took over the very notion of 'actionism' from Adorno, though his charge of Left Fascism had been, as he confessed in the German Autumn of 1977, a generational "overreaction" of his own making (KPS 364f.).

I do not wish to imply that Habermas holds a simplistic thesis of the convergence between two forms of dogmatism and violence—the form that took place during Heidegger's Nazi period and the form that emerged in student 'actionism'. His explanation about the political Right in 1977 cannot be simply pinned retrogressively on the dogmatic Left of 1968. Indeed, in his September response to Kurt Sontheimer, he precludes that conflation: "The Nazis have so fundamentally discredited this [conservative] tradition that in West Germany . . . there can be no longer any 'authentic conservatism'" (KPS 386).[8]

Nonetheless, even this ruthless criticism of existing conservatism does not help us get a better sense of Habermas' position. Is questioning whether or not to oppose *every form of violence* in the FRG the same as asking *how to bring about greater social justice?* Maybe the former query shows how charged or ambivalent and confusing the relationship to violence in any form still is in postwar Germany and in Habermas' generation in particular. An outsider to these sensibilities cannot discern easily from the present historical vantage point the difference between Habermas' words "I was against all forms of violence during the period of 1961–1969" and the changes in the West German Criminal Code that were to preclude, after the events of 1977 (at least on paper), all forms of violence. Officially, the Federal Republic was against all violence. But was not the antiviolence of this state a mere *phantom nonviolence*? Ironically (again), the new statutes criminalized all forms of violence except the state monopoly on it. West Germany's target remained an internal enemy. In spite of perceived student 'actionism' in 1968 or the RAF terror in 1977, in spite of Habermas' worries that in 1967 students confused violent resistance with nonviolent civil disobedience, West Germany's publicly feared "enemy" has never been the authoritarianism under its own nose. It has always been the specter of the revolutionary Left.[9]

Habermas brings some measure of balance into this skewed picture in his letter to Sontheimer dated September 19, 1977. By distinguishing between the radical student protest of the 1960s and the RAF terror of the 1970s, he can clarify his position with a new sensibility that he lacked between 1967 and 1969.

> A moment of youth revolt was then enough to initiate years of reactionary action, a reactionary movement that apparently feels that its time has come to kill two birds with one stone: [1] to cleanse conservatism from the stain of its involvement with bureaucratic terror and [2] to banish radical enlightenment into the very realm that is morally discredited, the legitimate concern of the young conservative heritage of all-too-German traditions, by insinuating a connection with individual acts of terror of the RAF. (KPS 386)

I wish to support Habermas' superbly sharp reflection on the present age, first, by drawing on a biographical intervention from another student nemesis, Negt, and then by discussing an essay on civil disobedience (CD), in which Habermas addresses the issue of violence and nonviolence more directly.

Recall that Negt (1968), one of Habermas' assistants, was the student leader in the 1960s and that he edited the famously infamous volume of the Left answering Habermas' polemic with the students. In his newspaper article, written on the occasion of Habermas' sixtieth birthday (which was on Sunday, June 18, 1989), Negt (1989) accepts Habermas' public self-criticism about his conduct in the 1960s: that by bringing in one phrase the *topos* of Fascism and the Left student movement, he overreacted to the upheaval of 1967. In Negt's very acknowledgment of Habermas, in his existential and public comportment, it becomes unequivocal to all concerned that politically Habermas stood and stands elsewhere than Heidegger or Schmitt. The latter two made terrible public pronouncements and taught terrible things in support of the Nazi ideology and state. Yet after 1945 neither one of them made a clear public apology or offered some philosophical-political explanation for their one-time Nazi complicity (KPS 365). Following Habermas' public self-criticism, Negt (1989) in turn prints his own apology for having published in 1968 the book in which the Left not only attacked Habermas but also carved in stone an erroneous impression: "as if Habermas no longer belonged to the Left."[10]

Of great interest becomes Negt's (1989) reflection on the relationship between force or violence and language. He introduces three pivotal insights into Habermas' thinking and conduct. All three go to the heart of Habermas' profile, as I charted its historical course in Part One:

1. "The original impulse for the language and communicative theory of Jürgen Habermas is a *political* impulse."
2. "The development of *forms* of the reason oriented to an understanding [with another] is under these conditions ['after Auschwitz, War, and Stalinism'] an existential problem, and *democracy* is a question of survival."
3. "One cannot understand the systematic writings of Habermas at all if one has not read and understood his small *political* writings" (seine kleinen *politische* Schriften).

With Negt's three claims, I can support my corresponding insights into Habermas' profile:

1. May 8, 1945, marks his existential and philosophical-political birthday.
2. His philosophical-political profile develops in response to the key formative situations of the postwar generation struggling for a new democratic form of life.
3. His fundamental project responds to two postwar generations: the constitutional needs of the securing '45ers and the revolutionary core of the protesting '68ers.

I still want to argue, however, that we need to establish Habermas' true position on progressive social revolution or on violence, and do both with a more determinate sensitivity afforded by the above insights into his overall trajectory. This means minimally two things. First, within his immediate national context, he prefers quite consistently and almost instinctually nonviolent forms of conflict resolution. This inclination to nonviolence comprises various forms of progressive social and democratic change. In Part Three I will survey the sources of his communicative theory and note how the possibilities of progressive revolution migrate into the core of formal pragmatics. Habermas' postwar predilections for nonviolence on the home front are inscribed into an unforced force of the better argument.

Second, his nonviolent inclination, especially as it is manifest during the 1960s, cannot be read, using Negt's (1989) characterization, "as if Habermas no longer belonged to the Left." Negt helps us reinterpret Habermas' confrontation with the students in light of a threefold insight into his political impulse, existential problem, and the overall philosophical-political motivation. From this hindsight,

Negt explains that Habermas objects to human rights violations (here still on the home front) because they collapse the nonviolent force of communication into the decisionistic use of force. "We all, as the leaders of the protest movement, did not want to grasp [in 1967] what Habermas meant; . . . [one year later in 1968] none of us was more ready to perceive the differentiations that were involved in this [Habermas'] indirect plea for the true revolutionary process."

Negt brings a second-level reflection into his already differentiated account: a larger social climate of violence was "made explicit" but not "produced" by the protest movement. But then he neither draws out larger implications nor further develops this last distinction. Remember that Habermas (SiK) plays down the links between the student protest and the worldwide struggles of the wretched of the earth. In his Left-liberal plea to the students, he cannot but fail to distinguish between *two forms of violence*: violence against the poor, women, minorities (e.g., blacks or Vietnamese), social reformers, and so on, and the violence resulting as a secondary effect from the struggle against these structural and pervasive forms of oppression. Whether Negt is right that "the phantom revolutionaries . . . with a cynical form of violent praxis" were already within the student ranks in the 1960s or whether they only surfaced with the RAF in the 1970s, this seems besides the point. We may accept Negt's conciliatory suggestion that Habermas differentiated what the students collapsed: revolutionary struggle for a free realization of the human potential and perverted revolutionary violence as the means to this realization. We may further agree that supporting nonviolent conflict resolution or social change does not mean that Habermas can no longer stand with the Left. But we may still want to distinguish with Fanon (1963, 35–106) and Marcuse between *structural violence against the wretched of the earth* (domination) and *violence done to the oppressors as a result of decolonization* (resistance against domination). Habermas never draws out this difference.[11]

Instead, Habermas introduces another distinction: between nonviolent civil disobedience and legitimate resistance or revolutionary praxis (CD). He writes his powerful piece on civil disobedience in an ongoing conservative climate. The fall of 1983, the year when his essay appears, inspires the name given to the "pogrom" of 1977—the German Autumn (OSSA xvii).[12] West Germany, practicing its monopoly on violence, brands all resistance to itself, in the sense articulated by Schmitt, as an internal enemy. In this atmosphere of suspicion, the distinction between nonviolent disobedience and resistance or revolution inevitably goes by the wayside. All attention falls on defending nonviolent civil disobedience as the last vestige of extraparliamentary legitimate opposition within constitutional democracy. Under the "shadow" of the big chill, with one's "back to the wall," when "even nonviolent civil disobedience is illegal," Habermas' robust response to this one-sidedness understandably becomes one-sided. He defends both the unforced force of the better argument and the "unconventional means of influencing the formation of political will." West Germany's new etatist legal thinking classifies the latter too as "actual violent acts." This is the extreme context in which Habermas sets his argument (NU 79/CD 96).

"The peaceful demonstrator . . . appears as the only alternative to the troublemaker and agitator, to the violent criminal" (NU 79/CD 97). Habermas hopes to break this narrow view espoused by the state. This intervention starkly contrasts with his caricature of agitating students (SiK, thesis 5) in the 1960s. He writes in 1983: "The protest scene in the Federal Republic has indeed changed since the Easter Marches of the early sixties." And he reiterates his earlier affirmation (from thesis 2 of SiK) of the new demonstration techniques developed in the U.S. civil rights struggle. These novel forms of extraparliamentary protest have been expanded and integrated into the peace, ecology, and women's movements and into direct actions of nonviolent civil disobedience. Habermas draws in 1983 the line that might have been quite relevant in 1967–1969:

> Even clearer—and more strongly invested with emotion—is our recollection of the terrorist underground actions of the RAF, which very quickly clarified the distinction between criminal acts and civil disobedience—even, finally, in the heads of those for whom these concepts had remained confused after years of hard, protracted internal discussions. (NU 80/CD 97, all citations above)[13]

As on October 10, 1981, the marchers move through West German cities to oppose NATO's decision to station cruise missiles and Pershing 2 rockets on German soil, Habermas finds his place within the peace movement with its subculture and alternative lifestyle and opposition to NATO. Gone is his prior reluctance to even consider taking part in confrontational encounters with the police and the state. Among the acts of civil disobedience practiced by the social movements he enlists with approval—or minimally with a remarkable absence of doubt raised in the 1960s—the following (NU 81/CD 98):

- trespass, occupation, or blockade of nuclear power plants and missile construction sites
- construction of the tent cities or an "antiatom village" built to provide a contrast to the nuclear projects
- squatting in or taking over houses in poor and exploited areas, such as Kreuzberg in Berlin
- "human chains designed to disrupt traffic"
- "die-ins"

We have already met this passionate Habermas of the 1980s "hot autumn" protests in his emotional awakening of 1945, in his confrontation with Heidegger in 1953, and at the peak of the first antinuclear protests in 1959. It is *as if* Habermas finds, at least since the mid-1970s, his own *catch-up Leftist protest movement* (see the title of NR): a new movement that did not yet exist in 1945, that scarred him even as it passed him over in the 1960s, but a movement with which he can fully identify in greater comfort after the German Autumn of 1977. His breach of silence in that "pogrom-like" autumn of 1977 (EgA 12/4; cf. AS 221/EAS) is marked by an intensified return to public action.

I want to stress that Habermas' sympathy lies with the broadly based and pluralistic character of the new movements. In place of a perceived party or class dogma, he warms up now to the nonpartisan and undogmatic tenor of the peace, ecology, and women's movements (note, however, that gay, lesbian, and antiracist movements do not yet make it directly into Habermas' expressed purview):

> What is common to all these actions is that they have been initiated by spontaneously organized, heterogeneously constituted, and widely dispersed citizens' groups working in a decentralized fashion. This amalgam of peace movement, environmental movement, and women's movement is nothing that could be prohibited like a party. (NU 81/CD 98)

Furthermore, Habermas discovers something *new* about the new social movements that was not available to the political consciousness of the student protest in the 1960s. We could surmise that he might be self-justifying retrospectively his past reluctance and present enthusiasm.

> As the comparison with the student movement reveals, the contemporary protest movement offers the first chance to comprehend civil disobedience even in Germany as an element of a mature political culture. Every constitutional democracy that is sure of itself considers civil disobedience as a normalized—because necessary—component of its political culture. (NU 81/CD 98f.)

The internal relationship between civil disobedience and constitutional democracy, which Habermas emphatically defends here, lies at *the heart of my thesis that his philosophical-political profile develops in response to the key issues facing two postwar generations: the constitutional needs of the securing generation (1945) and the revolutionary core of the revolting generation (1968)*. Their integration failed in 1967–1969:

> In my experience during the years of the student revolts, I found that the self-understanding of many of the actors was inspired by false revolutionary ideals. (NU 81f./CD 99)

In other words, the cultural and social *facticity* of the student revolt in 1968 did not meet the constitutional *normativity* expected in the needs of 1945. Habermas adopts the middle in-between space (see FuG).

> Or, at least, they lacked the identification with the constitutional principles of a democratic republic that is necessary to comprehend *the exclusively symbolic character of an act of protest*, even when that acts oversteps the bounds of the legally permissible. (NU 82/CD 99; italics added)

Habermas emphasizes the "symbolic character" of nonviolent protest. Protest may violate accepted norms, but "solely with the intention of appealing to the capacity of reason and sense of justice of the majority in each particular case." The student leadership in 1967–1969, unlike the peace movement of the 1980s, conflated nonviolent protest with violent resistance, becoming "the strategists of a phantom revolution" (NU 82/CD 99; my translation). The peace movement is, by definition, intrinsically committed to pacifism. Its violation of accepted social and legal norms is symbolic or derivative of democratic decision making.

Habermas' theory of communicative action and ethics resonates with this original commitment to nonviolence. The originary mode of language is oriented to communication (i.e., to an understanding with another about something in the world) rather than to a strategic manipulation. Hence strategies and tactics are derivative of understanding, strategic force is derivative of the unforced force of the better argument, and in the same way violence cannot be a goal in itself but remains derivative of nonviolent forms of social integration.

Habermas agrees that some decisions of "existential importance" cannot be achieved without mass political action. But to what degree he allows that conditions might exist for a justified violent or even armed resistance, one that moves from a *symbolic* challenge to a *material* confrontation of the constitutional liberal state, does not enter his considerations. He mentions the constitutional right to "nonviolent *resistance*"—recorded in article 20, paragraph 4 of the Basic Law in the Federal Republic but quickly notes that nowadays objective conditions for such *resistance* do not exist. He says that even nonviolent protest of a lesser sort (civil disobedience) than resistance could be legitimated only by its appeal to the unfulfilled constitutional foundations of the established democratic republic. One can, paradoxically, transgress with legitimacy an established legal order—face prosecution for moral acts—when all other avenues of challenging even legitimate rules or their (ab)use are exhausted. Echoing his reservations toward the actual possibility of social revolution advocated in the 1960s, but in the 1980s standing in the shadow of the security state borne from the Autumn of 1977, Habermas only skirts the question of whether or not conditions for legitimate progressive revolution could exist and what they would be (NU 97/CD 112). Can we ever legitimately upgrade civil into an uncivil disobedience, rebel in ways that *matter* beyond *symbolic* challenges to existing order (NU 82f.; cf. 87, 89ff., 95f./CD 99f.; cf.103, 105f., 110f.)?[14]

A fair and open profile of Habermas' ambivalence regarding violence and the relationship between philosophy (critical social theory) and politics (liberation practice) can get some help from control cases. I want to read that profile briefly against three such cases: the Mayan uprising in Chiapas, the recent student movement in Mexico, and Marcuse's and the protesting students' position on violence and the relation between theory and practice. My third control case further opens onto two falsifying tests for Habermas' criticism of Marcuse and the students regarding violence as well as for his homefront predilection toward nonviolence. These are the two previously cited examples of the Persian Gulf War and NATO bombing of Kosovo (fig. 4.1).

The Mayan uprising of the indigenous peoples in Chiapas, Mexico, started in January 1994 with a demand that the Zapatista Army of National Liberation be recognized as a belligerent force, only to subsume in August of the same year the Zapatistas' revolutionary command to the civil leadership of the autonomous communities in resistance. The initial act of revolutionary violence, when masked Zapatistas took over several major cities in Chiapas, has since then become a consistently self-restraining symbolic presence of force in the service of civil society, indigenous leadership, and Mexican constitutional reform. *This is the sought-after control case regarding violence and nonviolence:* Zapatistas are consistently prodemocratic, antivanguardist (from below), antiterror, and imaginative in nonviolent forms of resistance. They never broke the cease-fire signed with the Mexican government—not in the face of the growing militarization of Chiapas by over 60,000 Mexican federal troops, not in response to genocidal massacres carried out by the paramilitary units operating with the government's silent consent. Yet they affirm

Figure 4.1. Habermas and Marcuse on Violence

Marcuse	*Habermas*
"'natural right' of resistance for oppressed and overpowered minorities" (1965b, 115)	"Making the best of the Gulf War" (Vaz 18/11); 'humanitarian' "war on the border between legality and morality" (BH 1/263)
no right of others to tell the oppressed whether or not they are allowed to resort to violent resistance	affirmative duty to defend universal moral human rights on behalf of others even by violent means
CRITIQUE OF IMPERIALISM CRITICAL OF FASCISM WITHIN DEMOCRACY	CRITIQUE OF GENOCIDE CRITICAL OF VIOLENCE RESULTING IN REVOLUTIONARY STRUGGLE
SOLIDARITY OF THE FIRST WORLD'S NEW SOCIAL MOVEMENTS WITH THE THIRD WORLD'S LIBERATION STRUGGLES	SUPPORT FOR INTERNATIONAL LAW: THE U.N., EUROPEAN INTEGRATION, 'PEACEFUL' AND DEMOCRATIC STATES
Margin of allowable violence: URBAN & THIRD WORLD RESISTANCE	*Margin of allowable violence:* INTERNATIONAL POLICE FORCE
The ideal standpoint of nonviolence: INTERNATIONAL SOLIDARITY/ DEMOCRATIC SOCIALISM	*The ideal standpoint of nonviolence:* COSMOPOLITAN WORLD CITIZENSHIP/GLOBAL DOMESTIC POLICY

the principle of the right to resist (even with arms) conditions of immiseration, oppression, and outright erasure from memory and existence by the established powers of liberal democracy. The movement is also consistently in solidarity with worldwide struggles of the oppressed and struggles against indiscriminate violence (e.g., Zapatistas both criticized Serbian oppression of Albanian Kosovars and condemned NATO's bombing of Serbia).

Mexico has had a continuous student movement, and for sure since the 1968 massacre in Tlatelolco with its hundreds of students dead and wounded (Sherman 1998). The UNAM (National Autonomous University of Mexico) strike in 1999 and the continuing student movement in 2000 represent a distinct new development (I rely below largely on Sherman 2000). UNAM is boasting 270,000 students, institutional autonomy, and a prominent history and role in Mexico. It embarked upon a period of upheaval when its rector, Francisco Barnés, decided in February 1999 to scrap the constitutionally guaranteed radical economic democracy with regard to student admissions: the 2 cents tuition was to be raised to about $150 per year. This plan was part of economic globalization and the privatization pressures from the World Bank, among others. After March 15, the University Council attempted to vote in the tuition hike despite student opposition, and on April 20 more than two-thirds of the UNAM schools went on strike, 223,000 students taking part (34). They occupied the UNAM buildings, shared resources, formed committees, issued demands for democratic restructuring of the institution and dropping the student fee—all pretty much like the scene we witnessed in the 1960s student movements. The strike continued for two months until the rector abandoned the tuition hike on June 7, only to permit the schools and departments to charge various fees of their own. To be sure, many of the students could hardly afford money for public transportation and books, let alone tuition; many of them had to work to support their poor families. The determined wing of the movement, later reinforced by the entering high school class, voted to continue the strike to meet all the demands, and some of their tactics became more forceful, though not injurious to persons or property. The turn toward splintering the students' resolve and ranks was banked on and exploited by the rector and the government. The press created the impression of division between moderates and irrational ultras, and by October only the latter remained (35).

This is the sought-after control case regarding theory and practice and the question of politicizing theory and the university: On February 3, 2000, eighty-nine prominent progressive Mexican intellectuals published a petition in major dailies that was critical of the militant student minority. They demanded that the strikers surrender the occupied buildings and accept the prior plebiscite organized by the rector (the January plebiscite voted returning to classes, but the strikers claimed the vote was rigged and put forward a contrary result from their own university-wide plebiscite). The ad letter was paid for by the UNAM rector. On February 6, in the early morning hours, over 2,000 riot police stormed the UNAM campus and arrested over 700 students, while reportedly beating and torturing some of them (36). The liberal-Left petition was a form of the Critical Theory used by the Mexican regime to legitimate the military solution without any opposition (37). Little did it matter that some of the signatories repented their act in horror or that on February 9, 100,000 marched in protest against state violence (36); the students' manifestly felt betrayal by established Left intellectuals has not healed since then. Just as by the end of the 1960s revolt only Marcuse from his generation could claim a total mutual trust with the students, in the UNAM strike only one political science professor, Luis Javier Garrido, played this role. What distinguished him, just as much as Marcuse, was that he valued immensely the students' vision, courage, and generosity, as well as the hope they offered to the tired and compromised generations, instead of being offended by the experimentally uncompromising even if fallible nature of the student protest. Noting undemocratic globalization trends reflected in the tuition hike and noting that all strikers were exempt from this hike affecting their studies retroactively, Garrido affirmed that "they are fighting for future generations, not for themselves" (37).

Since violence and nonviolence as universal concepts do not carry predetermined flags for concrete situations, they require contextualization. *In the periods contemporary with Habermas' own polemic with the students and with his later endorsements of the humanitarian wars of intervention, we find the third and most direct control case for critical social theory and practice of nonviolence.* Marcuse is more sensitive to this nuance when he indicates already in the 1930s that the liberal tolerance of immiseration *can* be itself but one step removed from Fascism. Fanon echoes Marcuse's sensibility from the opposite direction when he shows that decolonization is never a painless (abstract, disembodied sense of nonviolent) change.[15] Decolonization could never be pain-free for the whites who want to hold on to their privilege. Finally, in the 1960s Martin Luther King Jr., the champion of nonviolence, does not shy away from engaging in direct street action and confronting the white liberal establishment, even when his white progressive allies would prefer that blacks use slower and reformist means. When Rosa Parks one day refused to sit in the back of the bus in one southern U.S. town, there was no obviously objective revolutionary situation anywhere in the United States. Her right to resist oppression is consistent with the best traditions of religious pacifism as well as with secular forms of nonviolence, and it is consistent with a self-limiting adoption of militant defense of one's bare existence.

Habermas is neither an absolute nor even a partial pacifist. Yet he contributed to suspicions that Marcuse legitimated arbitrary revolutionary violence, even if not providing grounds for the later rise of the RAF terror (see Albrecht et al. 1999, 346f.). He never comes to share Marcuse's (1965b, 103) distinction between "revolutionary and reactionary violence, between violence practiced by the oppressed and by the oppressor," at least not as far as the marginal struggles (as opposed to NATO's Allied military interventions in the 1990s) are concerned. Marcuse's Berlin lecture from July 11, 1967, "The Problem of Violence in the Opposition" (Kraushaar 1998, 2: doc. 143; doc. 144, discussion), makes abundantly clear that he opposes arbitrary violence. He calls not for violent acts but rather for a new critical theory of liberation that envisions transforming the entirety of human existence. As Wiggershaus (1989, 691/1998, 623; also Albrecht et al. 1999, 326f.) perceptively drives home, on this very point there seems to be no great difference between Adorno overall, Habermas in Hannover, or Marcuse in Berlin. Marcuse has no theoretical blueprints of utopia for unmediated action either.

What this controlling case suggests is that Marcuse's stance can be consistently justified and contextualized across a wide historical continuum: he supports the student international solidarity and struggle for another than this unjust world; he rejects all terror aimed at single persons or institutions as such; and for both reasons he affirms the right to resist oppression, even in belligerent forms that it might take as the last resort against the state monopoly on violence and obliteration. The NATO-led *humanitarian* wars of intervention in the Persian Gulf and Serbia would qualify with great difficulty as instantiation of this resistance, just as the U.S. war against North Vietnam had great difficulty in legitimating itself. Preceding Garrido in today's Mexico, Marcuse intuitively found it repulsive to defend his safe institutional tenure and break ranks with the students, who, like the Mayans in Chiapas (no matter how volatile, vocal, and even uncivil they appear to be to those who love peace and order), never posed any real danger to the state. On the contrary, siding with the state monopolies on violence (preparing with words or public statements needed legitimation for or directly calling the police) against such resistance tips the scales of power in the direction of what critics of rebellions worry about most—Fascism.

In his 1969 correspondence with Adorno, already introduced in chapter 2, Marcuse refutes the arguments that justify Adorno's (by implication Habermas') recourse to the police; he refutes the arguments that place Adorno (and by implication Habermas) as champions of the old Frankfurt Institute and its critical social theory; and he refutes the arguments that blackmail his commitment to action as his or students' unmediated (uncritical) endorsement of unthinking practice.

From April 5, 1969 (Adorno and Marcuse 1999, 125; all following citations):

- "To put it brutally: if the alternative is the police or the left-wing students, then I am with the students—with one crucial exception, namely, if my life is threatened or if violence is threatened against my person and my friends, and that threat is a serious one. Occupation of rooms (apart from my own apartment) without such a threat of violence would not be a reason for me to call the police."
- "You know me well enough to know that I reject the unmediated translation of theory into praxis. . . . There are situations . . . in which theory is pushed on further by praxis . . . in which theory that is kept separate from praxis becomes untrue to itself."
- "And this fresh air is not that of 'left fascism' (*contradictio in adjecto!*)."

From June 4, 1969 (Kraushaar 1998, 2: doc. 336; Adorno and Marcuse 1999):

- "No Teddy, it is not our old Institute, into which the students have infiltrated." (649/128)
- "You know that we are united in the rejection of any unmediated politicization of theory." (649/129)
- "To say that one may not protest against the agony of imperialism, without in the same breath accusing those who desperately fight against this hell, by whatever means they can, seems to me be somehow inhuman." (650/129)
- "The (authentic) Left is not able to transform itself into the Right 'by the force of its immanent antinomies,' without decisively changing its social basis and objectives. Nothing in the student movement indicates such a change." (650/129)

From July 21, 1969 (Kraushaar 1998, 2: doc. 340; Adorno and Marcuse 1999):

- "'The crux of our controversy'. I certainly do believe that the student movement does have the prospect of 'effecting a social intervention'. I am thinking here mainly of the United States, but also France (my stay in Paris reinforced that once again) and South America. Of course, the causes that set off the process are all very different, *but unlike Habermas*, it seems to me that, despite all the differences, the driving motivation aims for the same goal. . . . a protest against capitalism, which cuts to the roots of its existence, against its henchmen in the Third World, its culture, its morality." (653/133; italics added)
- "We should have the theoretical courage not to identify the violence of liberation with the violence of repression, all subsumed under the general category of dictatorship." (655/135)

If any doubts linger from the 1960s as to what Dutschke, other student leaders, or Marcuse held about violence—and these were very much the doubts stirred up in 1967 by Habermas' hypothetical charge of Left Fascism—then the situation of 1977 and their public reaction to it make the borders between the student leaders from the 1960s and their forefather, on the one side, and the RAF, on the other, utterly clear. At Frankurt's annual book trade fair, on October 15, 1977, the league of Left publishers organized a panel discussion about the hunt on the so-called sympathizers of the red terror. The event was given an appropriate title: "Sympathy for the Devil—The Witch-Hunt on the Left." Daniel Cohn-Bendit, who took active part in the Paris Events of May 1968, argues here that the oppositional Left must break through from its present predicament in a way that will distinguish it from both the RAF and the state (Kraushaar 1998, 1, 565). The actions of the RAF qualify as what they are: ruthless violence targeted at the representatives of the ruling West German elite. Marcuse reiterates his position from September 16, 1977 (Kraushaar 1998, 2: doc. 413) in a later interview granted on his eightieth birthday, July 19, 1978 (doc. 421, p. 828): "I have never preached either individual or group terror." And just as he said in an earlier interview on April 28, 1975 (doc. 409, p. 793), he insists again in 1978 that the "natural right to resistance" is as old as western civilization and constitutes "the core of the mediaeval Catholic philosophy." Catholic teachings of the Middle Ages justified murdering a tyrant, and this is how the attempt to assassinate Hitler was justified, Marcuse explains, by a "natural right to resist" him. The right to resistance is always the way of the last resort. But in either case, terrorist acts or torture by SS officers cannot be compared with throwing tomatoes or even with revolutionary violence, which "is directed against conditions," not "primarily against persons" (doc. 421, p. 828).

In what, then, lies the danger of Fascism, whether Left or Right? To fear that Fascism can objectively migrate to this repeated outrage (by student rebels or civil rights activists) at the structural and systematically deployed violence (that 'false continuity' surviving in democratic establishments around the globe), no matter how otherwise objectively utopian the form of this outrage might take—is this fear not an odd thing for a progressive social critic to entertain in the 1960s?[16] What still seems odd about Habermas' explosive remarks from Hannover, as Holub (1991, 84f.) suggests, is the contrast it casts with Marx's *Communist Manifesto* of 1848. Habermas worries about students' presumed preference for an anarchistic (read here: violent) disruption of democratic rules. He manifests his generational predilection (entrenched in modern German history, which never had a successful social revolution) for a reformist process of gradual enlightenment. But for Marx and Engels of 1848, the generalized preference for nonviolence could just as well mask social positioning, which does not have to suffer institutionalized, rule-governed forms of violence. This decision for gradualism is often espoused by those in the established power structures who have a lot to lose from granting the stage to "disruptive" claims by blacks, women, gays, and the immiserated. The question for Marx is not essentially to opt for violence or for nonviolence, but rather to ask oneself which kind of each should one worry about, given that oppression is often a democratically established and legitimate form of violence. The utopian socialists of 1848 lacked ties to social struggles of the day and jettisoned revolutionary action, and this is what worries Marx in the *Manifesto*. But the students in 1967–1969 do not distinctly exhibit these flaws, regardless of what other weaknesses their movement might have had. So whatever Habermas could have legitimately meant by 'Left Fascism' or 'phantom revolution' in the context of the 1960s (the ghost of Stalin? the shadow of East Germany next door?), the motives he imputes to students, and to Dutschke or Krahl in particular, directly contradict Marx's and Engels's worries about and descriptions of the utopian socialists of 1848. The utopian socialists share little in context with the Fascists in the 1930s—whether one finds them in Germany or Italy. Habermas' analogy between the imputed dangers of student anarchy in the 1960s, the extremism of the Weimar Republic, and the Italian Fascist students influenced by Sorel and Mussolini breaks down. His view is just as marked by the generational-experiential horizon of expectations as is Horkheimer's reaction to the perceived anti-Americanism of the protests against the Vietnam War (Albrecht et al. 1999, 324). Minimally, the fear of belonging to a passionate student movement is overdetermined by Habermas' own traumatic youth memories. In this sense, "all and everything could fall under the suspicion of Fascism or could concern itself with charges of Fascism" (325). At worst, "in his reply [to the students], Habermas takes just that [conservative, reactionary] position, which was not long ago [1959] brought out against him by Horkheimer" (322).

As I intimated in my concluding reflections to Part One and as I will resume in the conclusion to Part Three, I want to suggest here that *perhaps there are two intergenerational middle points between the democratic needs of 1945 and the revolutionary core of 1968*. One lies on the axis of Habermas' integration, the other is situated on the Left of his middle, or nearer to Marcuse's new sensibility. With these alignments, there emerges a new question that points beyond the scope of Habermas' profile: Which integration of the democratic needs with the revolutionary core would deliver *us* to a genuine vanishing point of *our* post-1989 hope for liberation? Even if this sort of query comes *to us* (after 1989) from the still-unknown questions of the new century, we will not go wrong to envision it as *our* present horizon. At the end of the previous chapter I had Habermas locate the beginning of the twenty-first century already in *our* post-1989 times. Even as *we* ward off with him the phantom limbs of the revolutionary era of 1968 and even as we next confront with him the shadows and the ghosts of 1945, the question of the genuine specters of liberation persists (Matuštík 1998a).

NOTES

1. Habermas worries here about the direct action strategies developed by the SDS, such as those by the activist subgroups of "Sponties" (Joschka Fischer belonged once to this group) or "Provos" (for example, on February 18, 1967, they danced in front of the U.S. consulate in Frankfurt against the war in Vietnam).

2. See Cohn-Bendit's photo from the Paris rally in May 1968 in Ali and Watkins 1998, 89.

3. The first five theses were presented in Frankfurt on June 1, 1968; the essay, with the sixth thesis added, was published in the *Frankfurter Rundschau* (June 5, 1968).

4. Cf. Love 1995.

5. See "Showdown in Seattle" (1999).

6. Cited by Detlev Claussen, "Hans-Jürgen Krahl: Ein philosophisch-politisches Profil" (written in 1985 and reprinted in Kraushaar 1998, 3:65–70). Claussen lists the wrong date for Krahl's essay as June 13.

7. The interview was published as "Probe für Volksjustiz," *Der Spiegel* (October 10, 1977).

8. Habermas' letter to Kurt Sontheimer (KPS 367–87) was dated September 19, 1977, and published as "Die Bühne des Terrors" in *Merkur* 31, no. 353 (1977): 944–58.

9. Carl Schmitt fostered the notion of the internal enemy as necessary for the political cohesion of the state. This political theology immigrated into the chill of the 1970s and 1980s.

10. Negt 1989; all cited references are from page 3.

11. Cf. Gordon 1995b, 67–83; and Matuštík 1998a, 221–24.

12. Distinguish this name from "a second 'German Autumn,'" which refers to the asylum debate of 1991–1993 (see "The Asylum Debate," in the English translation of VAZ 127 and translator's note 5).

13. The context of this essay does not make it clear, however, whose heads were confused in the 1960s: those of the student Left, Habermas, or both.

14. Habermas identifies with Rawls's (1971) definition of civil disobedience (NU 83–86/CD 100–3).

15. Marcuse [1965] 1988: "The Struggle against Liberalism in the Totalitarian View of the State," 3–42 (This essay was first published in 1934). Matuštík 1998a, 220–24.

16. Habermas is not the last one to worry about Fascism on the Left: Wolin (1996; his 1998 presentation at the UC Berkeley centennial celebration of Marcuse) insinuates that Marcuse suffered from these tendencies in the 1960s.

Chapter Five

THE GHOSTS OF 1945

Had not Habermas become the target of the conservatives in the mid-1970s and after, the reproach leveled against him by the Left in 1968 for "supporting the conservative cause" (NC 185) could have come to define his overall philosophical-political profile. This one-sided impression is reinforced by objective as well as subjective factors. Among the objective factors is the rise of the authoritarian state formed in great part by reacting to the 1960s student protest. Habermas pleaded with the students that not everything about law and order, that not all power of the state, can be lumped together with the Fascist ghosts. The students are deceived, he pressed his point at that time, in conflating the self-defense of a legitimate constitutional state with "the naked repression of the Fascist power" (SiK 259). The state should be able to legitimately defend the valid norms of democracy against *uncivil* (read: undemocratic, unprocedural, or violent) forms of protest (CD; NU 100–117; cf. NR 22f./AS 231). By the time Habermas comes out of his self-imposed political seclusion in Starnberg (1971–1977), West Germany has grown (once again) into a police state.

After his confrontation with the student movement in the 1960s, Habermas not only leaves Frankfurt for the second time since Horkheimer occasioned his departure in the late 1950s but also retreats from the public sphere. In the fall of 1977 he comes out of the private political retreat and breaks his silence. In this new constellation, the radical Left answer given to Habermas in 1968 cannot save him from his false friends on the Right (Negt 1968, 32). Ironically, he can thank the German Autumn of 1977, its repetition in 1983, and the Historians' Debate of 1985–1987—these bona fide ghosts of 1945—for the opportunity to clear up an unwanted impression of himself lingering from the 1960s (NC 185f.). The historical occasions of repeated revisions reverse the constellations of the 1960s and thereby allow him to reconnect the silver lining around his philosophical-political self-portrait. From the observation platform of the 1980s, Habermas can situate himself as someone who has been always and already (at least since 1953, if not at fifteen in 1945) "a red flag" (NC 186) erected on the Left side of Heidegger, Schmitt, and West Germany's resurgent conservative turns.

I affirmed Horster's (1991, 113) insight that historical events had cultivated in Habermas a keen sensibility to the signs of the incoming Fascist climate and I qualified this fair judgment against Habermas' overdetermined relation to the 1960s. When he stands face-to-face with the prospects of a progressive social movement and when he grows fearful of what he perceives in it (i.e., the phantoms), then how reliable are his anti-Fascist antennas? He did not have in 1967–1969 the sensibility that funds his evaluation of the conservative turn of the 1970s and 1980s: he complains now that the FRG "has never experienced a [progressive] revolution" (NC 187)! This experiential gap (of not having had a successful progressive revolution) makes Germany, from 1789 (the French Revolution) onward, and for sure since 1933, susceptible to renewed conservative revolutions (i.e., historical revisions). Such reactionary revolutions are accompanied by irrational fears of progressive social change. Habermas' key public interventions from June 1967 to December 1968 occurred in a strange historical vacuum, recording virtually nothing about concurrent revolutionary events in all of France, Czechoslovakia, the United States, Mexico, and elsewhere. Given his nation's historical blindness in worrying consistently about the wrong thing (i.e., progressive change), Habermas worries in 1967 about 'Left Fascism' and in 1968 about 'phantom revolution'—but would not these be addressed more appropriately to another place and time? Enter this double irony: The West German state in the autumn of 1977 and 1983 and revisionist historians share Habermas' worry from the 1960s! Never mind that they, unlike him, have their own antidemocratic and historically revisionist reasons for their fears. Here comes the ironic twist. Thanks to the conservative trend *(Tendenzwende)* in West Germany's politics, law, and culture, Habermas, along with the Frankfurt School (KPS 364), was made responsible for the ideological origins of the Left terror in the 1970s. One interviewer drives home the paradoxical (damned if you do and damned if you don't) situation of Habermas: "To be made responsible, first by the Left and now by the conservatives, for things with which you really have nothing to do" (NC 186)! Habermas' ironic constellation not only affords him a historical correction but also gives us a fine-tuning of his philosophical-political profile.

From the time of the Bitburg embarrassment (May 5, 1985) and commencing with his challenge to the historians (1985–1987), Habermas exhibits a marked degree of existential pathos. He introduces Karl Jaspers's existential critique of the present age, already employed by Habermas in 1979 against the first wave of the "German Autumn," to preserve the postwar gains of constitutional democracy. Minimally since the lecture given in Copenhagen on the occasion of receiving the Sonning Prize (May 14, 1987), and as late as the seminar he teaches in the fall of 2000 (KE), he takes extensive recourse to Kierkegaard's existential ethics. He links this existential ethics to Walter Benjamin's *anamnestic solidarity* (solidarity rooted in

The Ghosts of 1945   127

redemptive remembrance) with the victims of history. Habermas' recurring existential interests invite me to deepen the thesis about the formation of his philosophical-political profile introduced in chapter 4. *One of Habermas' core questions is how to integrate socially the rebelling individuals (the intellectual grounding of '68ers and the new social movements of the 1970s and 1980s) into a radical democratic and constitutional republic (the institutional grounding of the post-1945 generation).*

I will approach this question under four conceptual clusters:

- critique of and intervention in the present age
- critical and revisionist notions of 'normality'
- collective liability for the criminal past and the *anamnestic solidarity* with the victims of history
- public discourse and enactment of an either/or choice, whereby life-giving traditions are affirmed and disastrous ones are jettisoned

These four clusters run across Habermas' interventions in the public sphere after the 1960s. The key interventions, in turn, define his mature profile, itself formed in responding to the institutional (1945) and the existential needs (1960s) of his present age.

The Big Chill Arrives in the "German Autumn":

> With this letter I am appealing to German writers, critics, artists, social scientists, and philosophers who combine the following three attributes: those whose identity was formed only after the end of the war; those who have exercised a certain intellectual influence in the Federal Republic of Germany; and those who stand committed to the traditions against which a German regime established itself in 1933. (KPS 412/OSSA 2f.)

After Adorno's death in 1969 and after Habermas' departure from Frankfurt in 1971, the Frankfurt vacuum is gradually inhabited by the ghosts banished in 1945. A climactic swing to the Right brings in 1977 the early autumn chill; the terror acts by the RAF elicit a "pogrom" reaction from the state apparatus (AS 221; EgA 12/4; cf. OSSA xviii). This more than symbolic sea change (*Tendenzwende,* or ideological shift) prompts Habermas to hearken back to Karl Jaspers's cultural criticism of late Weimar Germany.

Curious as it might sound, in his lecture given at the time of receiving the Adorno Prize from the city of Frankfurt (September 1980), Habermas espouses the thesis of a convergence between the Left and the Right dimensions of the *Tendenzwende.* He does not mean that the Left as such moved to the Right as we know it, but he implicates the new attacks on the Enlightenment rationality, insofar as these are joined by the poststructuralist and postmodern Left, in complicity with the neoconservative cultural swing. Enter the Left version of the *Tendenzwende.* Even more curious become some of the presumed anti-Enlightenment bedfellows:

Heidegger and Nietzsche with Foucault and Derrida with Adorno and Horkheimer (as authors of *Dialectic of Enlightenment*)—to offer just a sampling of these (PDM; OSSA xviii, xx). More curiously still, Habermas links the Left/Right convergence in the *Tendenzwende* to the counterculture emerging out of the 1960s. The 1970s reaction to the 1960s is discernible in conservative moral majorities and among social authoritarians. The direct linkage of this reaction to the postmodern turn, implied by Habermas, is at best murky:

> I fear that the ideas of anti-modernity, together with an additional touch of premodernity, are becoming popular in the circles of alternative culture. When one observes the transformations of consciousness within political parties in Germany, a new ideological shift (*Tendenzwende*) becomes visible. And this is the alliance of postmodernists with premodernists. (MP 14; cf. PDM xix)

Speaking of "the alliance of postmodernists with premodernists," Habermas is not without a kernel of truth when it comes to certain Heideggerian offspring. Yet this position—which he takes in 1980 and expands upon his return to Frankfurt and later in his Paris lectures of 1983 (PDM)—lacks his native sensibility to a rising Fascist climate. His cultivated strengths become his weaknesses as he navigates once more the seas of the post-1960s, postmodern, anarchist countercultures. Postmodern criticisms of western modernity's underside are one thing; the chill of 1977 or 1983–1985 is quite another. Habermas is out of his league altogether when he ventures an overall convergence diagnosis of the *Tendenzwende* between the "postmodern culture" and the waves of the political big chill. That is, his diagnosis overlooks entirely the pivotal alliances of postmodern critical social theory with postcolonial and antipatriarchal new social movements. Those very movements, which he praises in 1983, evolved with certain postmodern sensibilities also from the student movements of the 1960s.

When we return from these abstract speculations made in 1980 to the Jaspersian *Observations on "The Spiritual Situation of the [Present] Age,"* Habermas' intervention is remarkably concrete and on target. Habermas conceives this two-volume project with thirty-two contemporary Leftist intellectuals as publication 1,000 of the *Edition Suhrkamp*. It is published on the thirtieth anniversary of the Federal Republic of Germany (1979). The public intervention that this book is *to perform* is to revitalize the *Suhrkamp* political culture. Habermas finds the existence of the democratic political culture, based on collective meaning and will formation, necessary for the preservation of postwar constitutional gains in West Germany. Democratic political culture fulfills a core prerequisite for any lasting progressive social change, and for Habermas this includes, as I discussed in a previous chapter, also protest, civil disobedience, and resistance. In soliciting new essays for this project of resistance, he provides Jaspers's cultural criticism of late Weimar Germany, *Die geistige Situation der Gegenwart*, appearing only two years (1931) prior to Hitler's rise to power, as a paradigm for the type of theoretical and practical diagnosis of the present age needed to challenge the *Tendenzwende* in the contemporary Federal Republic of Germany (KPS 411–14/OSSA 1–4).[1]

Three tasks distinguish Habermas' proposal in 1979 from Jaspers's standpoint in 1931. The first two pertain to methodology, and the latter raises a normative issue. Thus Habermas explains why he inserts quotation marks within the title for this volume. First, Jaspers adopted "the absolute perspective of the great philosopher"; today we must abandon the search for an absolute fusion of reason and history. We can ascertain no grounds for a grand philosophical theory. Instead, Habermas argues, social criticism ought to become cognizant of its fallible grounds and precarious achievement. Second, critique of the present age cannot be directed by one individual from on high. We must rely on the collaborative work of inquirers. Such a collaboration inevitably shifts from the monological to dialogic reason. Third, with this shift from grand metaphysical narratives to fallible, postmetaphysical, and *communicative reason,* the critical angle of the book must differentiate between the pathologies of the present age and the emancipatory potential of critical enlightenment (KPS 411–14/OSSA 1–4).

Habermas' communicative approach structures the composition of this collection. Since the critique of the age does not assume a grand metanarrative about the situation of the present, the editor cannot be its sole author. The emancipatory possibilities of adopting a critical attitude toward the present lie in the renewed enlightenment ideal. In spite of his emerging convergence thesis, which brings the reactionary Right and the postmodern Left under one neoconservative roof, Habermas finds salient agreements with Foucault in their retelling of Kant's question, What is Enlightenment? The recent political writings in which Derrida defends a new enlightenment warrant this positive confluence of critical and postmodern social theory with the historic Enlightenment (i.e., ideas of 1789).[2]

Habermas' *regulative ideal of communicative reason,* as defined in my introduction, neither dwells in a metaphysical heaven nor drowns in facticity. Between facts and norms, there pivots a concretely operative ideality invoked by human speech acts and variously employed by all participants in these *Observations.* Such an ideal of speech is as concrete as natural languages in which speakers and hearers raise and defend claims. The regulative ideal is presupposed pragmatically and communicatively by the actual practices of those involved here and now in an actual communication community. Habermas' book itself projects this ideal, yet as such it neither calls for a closure nor an exclusion. Rather, the book's aim lies in an open-ended permanence of the operative ideal: the radically democratic republic. This type of revolutionary radicality of a democratic republic, intimated by him already in the late 1950s, Habermas sharply differentiates from that *other* republic, which is brought back by the autumn chill.

The *Observations* are to offset the reactionary spirit of the German Autumn of 1977. Therefore, they exhibit the typical one-sidedness of a corrective. All contributors come from the undogmatic Left. All defend the critical task of modernity, the values of reason, democratic constitution and institutions, and posttraditional forms of culture and identity formation. The one-sidedness plays the pedagogical role of reversing the falsely totalizing discourse of the age. Just as in 1931 Jaspers engaged in cultural criticism of Weimar Republic, so now

> it is the duty of the intellectuals to treat with partiality and objectivity, with sensitivity and incorruptibility, to movements, developmental tendencies, dangers, and critical moments. It is the task of intellectuals to make conscious a murky reality. We should not concede this to people for whom the word "intellectual" is itself a term of abuse. (KPS 413/OSSA 3)

I already discussed two out of the three thematic areas covered by the contributors to the *Observations*. All three are summarized very nicely both in Habermas' introduction (KPS 411–41/OSSA 1–28) to the book and in Buchwalter's translator's introduction (OSSA vii–xxxvii). The first area comprises a threefold anxiety, despair, and doubt regarding the West German state with its established postwar institutions and its economic future. These complex attitudes of insecurity emerge from the autumn of 1977, continue into the echoes of the autumn of 1983, and linger through the Historians' Debate. They find their expressions of resistance in the struggles waged by the new social movements (the peace, ecology, and women's movements). The second area of themes focuses on the state's surveillance of its progressive citizens, which increased in the mid-1970s in retaliation to the terrorism by the Red Army Faction. In chapter 3, I noted how the state introduced the new Criminal Code in order to curb acts of civil disobedience by the new antinuclear and other protest movements. The code was meant to secure legitimation from the citizens who are no longer willing to grant it in blind faith. Habermas' essay on civil disobedience (CD) along with these earlier observations both represent his forceful interventions in the two waves of the German Autumn.

The third area of themes leads to my next discussion concerning the struggles over historical memory, national identity, and traditions. After the 1963 Auschwitz trial in Frankfurt and following the cultural upheaval of the 1960s, the debate about national identity reemerges with a new intensity in 1979 right in the wake of the four-part U.S. television miniseries *Holocaust*, which was shown on West German television. The question of German identity quickly moves to center stage with the Historians' Debate. Identity questions carry in both Germanies many signs of a maladjusted and unmourned historical and national trauma—the loss of self-esteem invested in a love object that can never again be had innocently: *der Führer*. With the continued division of two Germanies in the 1980s, the unfulfilled nostalgic longing for the renewal of national spirit persists until the collapse of the Berlin Wall in 1989 and the unification of Germany in 1990. Yet an almost obsessive, at times hysterical melancholy to revise or sidestep the unmourned German past "before it gets us" is motivated by the ghosts of 1945. Some historians, along with some politicians, think that they can cure this condition, once and for all, by resurrecting the defeated Berlin eagle of that *other* republic.

By having us return to the unloading ramp in Auschwitz, as a 'second-degree witness' to the Holocaust who is neither a survivor nor related to the victims but is at best a 'witness of witnesses' or 'witness of testimonies' (Felman and Laub 1992, 213), Habermas presses his voice and pen against the forgetful revisions of national history, memory, and identity.[3]

THE HISTORIANS' DEBATE: REVISIONIST NORMALITY OR THE MANSION OF CULTURE BUILT ON DOG SHIT[4]

> Contemporary history remains fixated on the period between 1933 and 1945. It does not move beyond the horizon of its own life-history; it remains tied up in sensitivities and reactions that . . . still always have the same point of departure: the images of that unloading ramp at Auschwitz. (EAS 137/NC 229)

Habermas correctly assesses the relation between 1968 and 1985–1987 when he claims that "the 'Historians' Debate' [1985–1987] was the test of the political culture that aroused in the Federal Republic after 1968." Only with the hindsight of his 1988 interview can he make that judgment. And he can add the following reflection: "And it [1968] stood the test well" (NC 193). If doubts still linger regarding which of the lessons Habermas learned in the heat of the student struggle in 1967–1969, no doubts persist as to where he stands in the climate of new historical revisions. Habermas' active hope for things getting better offsets his generational skepticism and funds his persistent and relentless resistance to any masking of the German catastrophe or of its impact for the present formation of social institutions and national identity.

The Historians' Debate has dramatic antecedents in the U.S.-German joint state celebrations of the fortieth anniversary of the end of World War II. In chapter 3, the staging for Habermas' intervention was prefigured by the two visits scheduled for May 5, 1985: in the morning at the Bergen-Belsen concentration camp and in the afternoon at the Kolmeshöhe military cemetery in Bitburg. The anniversary of V-E Day continued on May 8 in the West German capital, Bonn.[5] The Historians' Debate has dramatic consequents leading up to the fall of the Berlin Wall, German unification, debates on World War II memorials in Berlin, and the new millennial controversy whether Germans must remember the Holocaust in their new historical present.[6] I consider Habermas' interventions in the post-Wall era in the following chapter.

The historical and political revisions effected in the 1980s intensified and entrenched the cultural and ideological *Tendenzwende* initiated in the 1970s.[7] The guiding concept and metaphor for this political and cultural revision is *normality*.

Common sense defines normality as the mainstream flow of stable continuities. Yet there are two kinds of being 'normal' and two sorts of continuities that go with each: that continuity is false which is achieved by a cover-up of pernicious breaches. As Brecht reminds us, something cannot be deemed 'normal' in the ordinary sense if its mansion is built on a pile of shit. This normality becomes loaded with stinking ambivalence. Deceptive normality and false continuities require radical surgeries. In the shadows of 1945, the living-dead ghosts are wearing the Halloween masks of innocent historical origins and nationalist belongings, thereby exuding a deceptive aura of innocence. Tradition that cannot mourn its gaps becomes *normal* with this deceptive measure of innocence (EV; KNV; cf. NC 190; ZLB).

It might be helpful to replay the resonances of Habermas' prior interventions as they echo in his present drama. When we encountered Habermas at fifteen on May 8, 1945, it was the day of his existential, philosophical-political birthday. His young adult struggle was marked by futile attempts to break through the false "German continuities" (EV 262–263, 265–266/44–45, 47–48), which were espoused from the war through the 1950s by his teachers, doctoral fathers, contemporary politicians, and cultural icons. In 1949 Habermas started his university studies in Göttingen. There he stormed out of the electoral assembly of the first Federal Parliament. Not only was the national-conservative German Party meeting for Mr. Seebohm, the future minister of transport in the Adenauer federal government, decked out in black, red, and white, the colors of the Third Reich, but the assembly intoned the first nationalistic stanza of the West German national anthem. We met Habermas in 1953 confronting his and Germany's postwar philosophical influence, Heidegger, but refraining at the same time from confronting his own father. It should be fitting that Habermas celebrates and defends May 8, 1945, as a day of national and personal liberation!

Yet the revisionary normality—initiated by the Bitburg drama as a staging of forty years after liberation—represents a terrifying déjà vu, a syndrome of cultural-social neurosis with obsessive compulsive repetition. Habermas analyzes numerous clinical terms invoked by the ensuing Historians' Debate:

- the past that has not passed or no longer matters (cf. EV; NC 193), the normalized past (cf. KNV)
- the repressed past that has not been addressed (NBR, chap. 2; Wolin, in NC ix–xiv, nn. 7–9)
- the past that has not been mourned (EAS 121/NC 213)
- the past haunting our future (cf. VaZ; LD)[8]

It is as if in 1985 the previous forty years (KNV 11) just about vanished to a time before May 1945. In this instant of regression, it is as if Habermas were not yet, or even worse—never arrived, at that zero point of his philosophical-political birthday; it is as if he were buried by his contemporaries before having had a chance to begin. Such resonances are conjured up by the ghosts haunting bad, anxiety-ridden dreams. This is now his historical reality or the past fashioned by revisionist historians. Habermas mirrors to the public that its waking reality has become a nightmare—once again.

A certain ahistorical yet redeeming irony comes to Habermas' historical rescue from an unexpected angle: West German revisionist historians! Just as during the German Autumn of 1977, some perceive Habermas' attack on the revisionist historians as an echo of the extremist Left of the 1960s. These conservative historians, and not the progressive activists and theoreticians, unwittingly rehabilitate his present intervention as an attempt to define his prominent place on the Left. This judgment is consistent with the portrait of Habermas I have been sketching, even though his primary objective is always to stop the revisionist train from running back to the Nazi past and not, therefore, to rehabilitate himself on the Left side of German national history. The pronouncement on Habermas' Leftist profile, as it is coming from a conservative historian (even if such a historian failed to study the history of Habermas' complex involvement with the student movement), carries the credibility of a nonbeliever (i.e., someone who never stood on the Left). It is worth citing one particular passage from Hillgruber, to which Maier draws our attention, since it reads in this constellation as a convex mirror of Habermas' fifth thesis with which he characterized the rebellious students in 1968. Hillgruber's own caricature of Habermas, given the latter's one-time caricature of the students as failed agitators, mentors, and clowns (SiK 258), serves not only ironic but also poetic justice: "If it is Habermas' goal to recreate the intolerable atmosphere that then [1967–1969] prevailed in the West German universities, he is deceived. History does not repeat itself at will according to the imagination and desires of failed 'prophets' and political agitators."[9]

In the shadow of Bitburg's normalization, in 1985 Habermas (EV) resumes Adorno's vintage preoccupations with *defusing the Nazi past*.[10] Habermas recalls Lübbe's (1983) earlier contention. Lübbe insinuates against the rebelling youth and the Left that in the 1960s they stripped the "discretion" of the cultural veil placed by the prior generation on the Nazi past and that by this obscene, denuding act they destabilized the Federal Republic. For Habermas—let us refresh our narrative of his profile from the 1960s—the transgressing cultural impact of the student revolt on the Nazi past was good news! Against this, we must reflect on his positioning during the Bitburg events. When West German Chancellor Helmut Kohl "learned from history," he endeavored to return the FRG symbolically, as well as in real political terms, to the new "normality" (EV 261/42) of *German continuities*. Enter a misplaced 'mourning' at Bitburg.[11]

From a distance of one year Habermas writes a script for three one-act plays acted out at Bitburg on May 5, 1985:

> Three moments had already come together into play in the Bitburg scenario:
> The aura of the military cemetery was to awaken national sentiment and thereby

"historical consciousness"; the juxtaposition of the mass graves in the concentration camp and the SS graves in the cemetery for those buried with honors, Bergen-Belsen in the morning and Bitburg in the afternoon, implicitly contested the uniqueness of the Nazi criminals; and the handshake of the veteran generals in the presence of the American president finally confirmed that we had always been on the right side in the fight against Bolshevism. (EAS 139/NC 231)

These three dramatic axes lead us back to the zero point of Germany's postwar beginnings and continuing trauma. The hard historical truth is that "many Germans did not experience the spring of 1945 as a liberation" (EAS 153/NC 243). Thus defeat and not liberation was more at home in the experiential repertoire of normality admissible into the postwar German historical consciousness. Habermas' intervention against the revisionist normalizers in the 1980s aims to reintroduce this experiential core of liberation to a wide-ranging political culture. His public intervention coincides with an existential struggle he wages for a preservation of his own philosophical-political birthday. His project communicates at once existential and social insight that one can never be done with giving birth to oneself! In the postwar Federal Republic of Germany, Habermas continues to beget himself by becoming a midwife to the radically democratic republic. Without the latter, he would lack that social form of life in which his own existentially motivated, philosophical and political birth could take place and stabilize.

Habermas' critical sense of normality is summed up by the move in the opposite direction of the events set in motion by the fortieth anniversary of his philosophical-political birthday:

> From this May 8, 1985, that is, from the performance at Bitburg, there is a direct line to the standard election speech with which [the Christian Socialist leader] Franz Joseph Strauss toured the country. In that speech he says: "It is now high time for us to step out of the *shadow* of the Third Reich and the *aura* of Hitler and become a normal nation again. . . . Without a national identity in which Germans can find their relationship to themselves and their past, but also to their future, the German people cannot fulfill their mission in the world." (EAS 157/NC 246; brackets above are in the English translation; ellipses are in the German original; italics are added)[12]

What is meant by "a national identity in which Germans can find their relationship to themselves and their past, but also to their future"? What is meant by the *normality* freed up from the shadows of 1945 and from the aura of "the great leader"? Unless we distinguish between an unmourned and a mourned normality, identity issues are drowned by the ghosts, at once melancholy and manic, whom one would wish to banish once and for all.[13]

The Historians' Debate must be understood as an ambivalent *settling of accounts and damages*. The historical revision names a singularly orchestrated collective attempt to pay an insurance premium for a shady past but without having to "work off" (see NBR, chap. 2) its core trauma. The politicians' Bitburg is followed chronologically by the historians' self-induced amnesia. Yet, anachronistically, the order of legitimation becomes reversed when history is written to reshape the present and the future. Franz Josef Strauss pleads in political speeches for the normality of the postwar state in ways that imitate Kohl and Reagan, who blurred all distinctions between the SS graves in Bitburg and the victims of the Holocaust in Bergen-Belsen. Alfred Dregger, West Germany's Christian Democratic parliamentary president, descends to Reagan's level of stupidity when in April 1986 he literally erases all difference between the victims and the perpetrators of Nazism. In Dregger's case, one has no longer any need for Bitburgs, one can argue in the West German Bundestag how to build war memorials in the image of one's innocent and normal nation, thereby creating historical memory ex nihilo (as a god, out of nothing). Kohl, Reagan, Strauss, Dregger, and their ilk need to recruit willing historians to retroactively justify these politicians' "bureaucratic creation of meaning" (EAS 123/NC 215). Historiography becomes a handmaiden of ideology. After Auschwitz, writing history unself-consciously cannot but be an ideological act, and this is meant in the pejorative sense with which Marx invested the word 'ideology' (see EAS 122, 137f., 145f., 156/NC 214, 230, 239, 246 on victims and perpetrators; cf. Wolin's introduction in NC xiv, xxviii).

Habermas' polemic with the revisionist German historians—Joachim Fest, Klaus Hildebrand, Andreas Hillgruber, Ernst Nolte, and Michael Stürmer—appears in several essays from 1986 to 1987 (EAS 115–58/NC 207–48).[14] At least four of them Habermas engages at some length. All exchanges are conducted in full public view and in the major West German press. Stürmer, not accidentally at that time Kohl's speechwriter and political adviser,[15] sets the stage for the first round of the debate by establishing internal links between ideology and history. Unabashedly, he adopts his handmaiden's service for the state. After the destruction of history (for him both modernity and Auschwitz represent this at their peak) the task of historians is to create the future by redrafting the past. Stürmer answers the core Habermasian question: How can rebelling and alienating modern individuals, who suffer from existential identity crises, become socially integrated?[16] Yet Stürmer, unlike Habermas (see TCA, vol. 2, chap. 5, sec. 3), would not welcome the critical *linguistification* (rendering the unquestioned contents of traditions available to articulated discussion) of sacred traditions. Stürmer's modernist project is functionalist: instead of defending the Enlightenment, he embarks on creating social meanings instrumentally. His instrumentalism is executed in a manner once before accomplished by religious integrations. Nationalism comes handy as the prime candidate for our tired postmodern times. The need to keep sober distinctions between historiographical scholarship and the crafting of meaning vanishes along with the handmaiden's role of the historians whom it behooves now to manipulate and retrogressively implant memory (EAS 123f./NC 215f.; Stürmer 1986a,b,c).

Habermas finds it ironic that, given Stürmer's legitimation of the ideological settling of historical accounts, Fest, the editor of the conservative *Frankfurter*

Allgemeine Zeitung, would fault professors in their ivory towers for "deciding who the victims were." The new ideologues in the historians' clothing seem anything but politically disengaged ivory towers. Still, they, and not critically thinking intellectuals, have become the Pirandelloesque servants of the state in search of its legitimacy and innocent identity (EAS 146/NC 238).[17]

Hillgruber's *Zweierlei Untergang* (1986c) creates the historical memory about two distinct kinds of destruction that took place on the German eastern front in the last year of World War II. One part of his work treats the destruction in the east, the other the destruction of the European Jews. In Hillgruber's analysis these historical events are recreated as two separate destructions. Habermas is "bewildered" by Hillgruber's determinate choice to adopt in his writing *a fictitious first-person perspective* of the self-sacrificing German combatants in the army and navy, of suffering civilians, and of the Nazi officials on the eastern front. Such dishonest perspectival shifts, Habermas worries, recreate history while irresponsibly dodging *an actual first-person perspective* of writing in 1986. Yet a "'normal' point of view" of the Holocaust, especially as its Final Solution continued with a heightened speed in the last year of the war, is absent from Hillgruber's *normality* based on a nationalist revision (EAS 124–28/NC 216–20).[18]

Following Stürmer's reading of history—stylized in the manner of an ideologically inflected political existentialism, in which the meaning that the historian creates and decides *for us* precedes any actual history that people live—Hillgruber writes a script for the future staging of Bitburgs and for installing the World War II memorials. He prompts patriotic German readers toward self-identification with the ordinary foot soldier: German soldiers saved the populations of the German east from the onslaught of Stalin's Red Army, even as they could not prevail and save either the German east or Western Europe from "the catastrophe of 1945."[19] This is but "a wishful interpretation of May 8, 1945," Habermas retorts. The identification with the foot soldier is not warranted by the methodological needs of objective historiography, no matter how much the revisionist historians protest against Habermas' presumed lack of graduate education in historical scholarship. Hillgruber's selective retelling of the last year of World War II through the eyes of the German soldier on the eastern front, sentimental and patriotic as it sounds, is a willful diffusion of that past which refuses to go away even from the vantage point of 1985. Habermas rejects such historical revisions of his and Germany's philosophical-political starting point—the existential birthday of May 8, 1945 (EAS 126/NC 218).

Hillgruber adds further insult to injury when he casts the Holocaust as the invention of a single mind, executed by one madman, Hitler, on the basis of his "radical race doctrine." Habermas introduces doubt for the sake of ironical distance when he inquires whether or not here too "the historian has assumed the perspective of the participant" (I presume, inside of Hitler's sick mind) to make his scholarly case (EAS 127/NC 219). One might make a case for studying the first-person plural perspective of "the bulk of the population [which] . . . kept quiet while it all went on."[20] This perspective, Habermas says, "Hillberger certainly assumes," if not in what he overtly writes, then in what he omits by silence. Like Heidegger in 1953, the silence of this "laborious revision" remains complicitous with the unatoned mass murder (EAS 127f./NC 220).[21]

In the conservative constellations of his age,[22] unlike the heat of the student revolt, Habermas finds himself called upon to remind his fellow Germans of their (failed) progressive revolution: "In a country that has never experienced a revolution, a right-wing intelligentsia—from Carl Schmitt to Ernst Nolte—stirs up the citizens' fear of civil war and constructs theories based upon it" (NC 187). When on June 6, 1986, Nolte, a one-time student of Heidegger, turns Hillgruber's silence and Stürmer's ideologically political existentialism into an unashamed apologetic offensive, Habermas jumps right into the fray the very next day.[23] His dethroning of Nolte's version of history is ruthless, it pulls all punches, it holds nothing back:

> Ernst Nolte's article in the *Frankfurter Allgemeine Zeitung,* which I read yesterday [June 6, 1986] . . . I consider astonishing. At least that was my first reaction. What is involved here is to make Auschwitz unexceptional by remarking, among other things, that with the sole exception of the technical procedure of gassing, what the Nazis did had already been described in an extensive literature dating from the early 1920s. With the lovely, almost Heideggerian words, "Was not the Gulag Archipelago more original than Auschwitz?" Nolte presents German fascism, even in its "aberrations," as merely a response and reaction to the Bolshevist threat of annihilation. One can see the revival of anticommunism as the reverse side of the same argument. (EAS 119/NC 211; internal citations are from Nolte 1986a)

Nolte's June 6 article (1986a) develops an earlier essay (1985) in which he already conflated the annihilation threatened by Hitler with the threat to Hitler by his enemies. Habermas links Stürmer's historiography, which invents historical meaning, with Nolte's apologetics, which justifies it now for the politicians:

> He [Nolte] resolves Stürmer's dilemma of scholarship *vs.* the creation of meaning with a bold decision and chooses as the point of reference for his account the terror of [the] Pol Pot regime in Cambodia. From there he reconstructs a prehistory that extends from the "gulag," the expulsion of the kulaks by Stalin and the Bolshevist revolution, back to Babeuf, the early socialists, and the English agrarian reformers of the early nineteenth century—a line of revolt against cultural and social modernization fueled by an illusory nostalgia for the return of a comprehensible, self-sufficient world. In this context of horror the destruction of the Jews appears as only the regrettable result of a nevertheless understandable reaction to what Hitler must have experienced as a threat of annihilation: "The so-called [sic] annihilation of the Jews during the Third Reich was a reaction or a distorted copy and not a first act or an original." (EAS 129/NC 221f.; Nolte 1985, 36)

The victors wrote the history of that era, and Nolte, later with help from Fest, only exercises a balancing act (on Fest's [1986] defense of Nolte, see EAS 146–48/NC 238–40).

Habermas unmasks the selectivity of Nolte's learning from the history of Auschwitz. Nolte's very perception is affected in its epistemic capacities to hear and see, for example, Claude Lanzmann's film *Shoah,* introduced at that time to the viewing public.[24] If after nine and a half hours of Lanzmann's uninterpreted interviews with the victims, accomplices, observers, and administrators of the Final Solution, Nolte learned only that the SS in the camps should be considered as sui generis victims, then there must be something decaying within *this* German's postwar historical consciousness. The putrefying smell is none other than Brecht's dog shit on which Nolte, echoing Stürmer, plans a revival of German national identity (EAS 131/NC 223). Habermas closes the circle on Nolte with a rather sinister account of bad faith:

> Nolte's theory has a great advantage for [the] purposes of this manipulation. He kills two birds with one stone: The Nazi crimes lose their uniqueness by being made at least understandable as a response to (now permanent) Bolshevist threats of annihilation. Auschwitz is reduced to the format of a technical innovation and explained through the "Asiatic" threat of an enemy who is still at our doors. (EAS 131/NC 224; Habermas refers to Nolte's [1986a] essay from June 6, 1986)

Nolte's sentence is worth citing in full:

> Could it be that the Nazis, that Hitler carried out an "Asiatic" deed only because they regarded themselves and those like them as potential or actual victims of an "Asiatic" deed? (Cited as the epigraph in EAS 120/NC 212; cf. EAS 145–48/NC 238–40)

The revisionist historians attempt to erase the past by making it irrelevant (EV), by settling accounts with it without being accountable to it (EAS), by normalizing it altogether (KNV), by mastering it for the future generations (VaZ) and future national identity (NBR). Habermas' closing remarks from the Historians' Debate sum up succinctly the "three operations" of historical amnesia involved in this major revamping of Europe's postwar memory: "[1] the identification of the historian with the Germans in combat, [2] the normalizing view of the opposition between Allied war aims and German interests, and [3] the trivializing of the German Resistance" (EAS 156/NC 246).

The purpose of this triple act is not historical but prescriptive. The task set by the revisionist politicians and historians alike is to escape the shadow of May 8, 1945, in order to gain a *normal* identity. One commits national misdeeds in the major press and in the daylight only to win back one's innocent face on illicit grounds—by "a redistribution of the moral weight between what the German nation suffered . . . and the suffering that German troops and German terror had caused others" (EAS 156/NC 246). Habermas raises against this misdeed his dangerous memory. Everything is existentially at stake for him when his philosophical-political birthday is threatened by the dangers of losing the future by way of forgetting the past. The twentieth century puts at risk its future by not learning from—by badly forgetting—its own disaster (LD).

THE MORAL CATASTROPHE, GUILT, AND *ANAMNESTIC SOLIDARITY*, OR, LEARNING AFTER AUSCHWITZ?[25]

> The anamnestic redemption of an injustice, which cannot of course be undone but can at least be virtually reconciled through remembering, ties up the present with the communicative context of a universal historical solidarity. (PDM 26/15)

Habermas' existential question returns as a refrain: Can we learn from disaster? This question provides an exciting entry into his profile and allows one to reconstruct it from his responses to the legacy of the early critical social theory and the defining sociopolitical situations of his era. As the twentieth century reaches its calendrical end, Habermas' millennial reflections from 1998 echo Horkheimer and Adorno's (1987, xi) concerns from the 1940s: "why [is] mankind, instead of entering into a truly human condition, . . . sinking into a new kind of barbarism"? Are the Enlightenment's emancipatory aims at best a myth we tell ourselves as a way of banishing the past ghosts and creating a future, or is Euro-American modernity self-destructive in forgetting its disasters? Citing Habermas' tragic sense of this waning age in unison with Horkheimer and Adorno's fragments from 1944, and pairing both with Foucault, Derrida, and Baudrillard in their somberness, may prove to be productive:

> This century has "produced" more victims, more dead soldiers, more murdered citizens, more killed civilians and displaced minorities, more dead by torture, maltreatment, hunger, and cold, more political prisoners and refugees than previously were even imaginable. Phenomena of violence and barbarism define the signature of the age. (PK 73f./LD 311)

These are "the cruel features of an age which 'invented' gas chambers and total war, state-conducted genocide and terrorism, death camps, brainwashing, and panoptical control of whole populations" (PK 73f./LD 311).

What distinguishes Habermas from an ordinary millennial apocalyptic is, however, his vital hope in the abilities of humans to learn. The defining feature of Habermas' mature profile, to be sure emerging from the early postwar experiences, is profound skeptical ambivalence coupled with secular yet undying redemptive hope. He rejects the Schmittian notion of a "worldwide civil war" between "world democracy [Wilson] and world revolution [Lenin]," the one-sided postmodern trends that debunk all of Enlightenment reason, and Nolte's style of "right-wing critique of ideology," which is typical for the revisionist historians (PC 72/LD 311). We can hear in Habermas' dialectical thinking another echo of early Horkheimer and Adorno. The one-sided rejection of the emancipatory promise of 1789 emerges from the blindness inflicted by "the horror of the images." The blinded critics fail "to see the reverse side of disaster" (PC 74/LD 312), Habermas warns. Enter the silver lining wrapped around Habermas' lifework, leading us from his existential birthday in 1945 back and forward to the revolutionary heart of modernity in 1789—the zero point of emancipatory hope that he affirms:

> For the nations that in 1914 embroiled the world in a war that was waged on a new scale of military technology, and for the populations who after 1939 were confronted with mass crimes of an ideologically unbounded war of destruction, the year 1945 also marks a turning point—*a change for the better*, taming those barbarian forces that in Germany had burst from the very ground of a developed civilization. *Could it be that we have learned something after all from the disasters of the first half of the century?* ... The victory and defeat of 1945 brought lasting discredit to the myths which since the end of the nineteenth century had been mobilized, along a wide front, against the heritage of 1789. (PK 74–75/LD 312; italics added)

If we move from *our* observation platform to the point in time when Habermas at fifteen found the continuities of German identity largely impenetrable, we witness Germany lying in total physical ruin. Neither the anti-Enlightenment transgressions nor the new historians can exonerate ex post facto the false sense of German universalism, even as West Germany undergoes its postwar economic miracle. The unmourned, at times melancholic and at times manic and often hysterical, collective identity is stuck in time as if in a compulsive repetition of repressed memory. There are legitimate places and times for performing transgressions; but Habermas encounters these already written in the flesh of the victims of history. He identifies the key negative event of transgression as "the moral catastrophe (Auschwitz, in other words) that made it definitively impossible to carry on with the continuities in a naive fashion." Thus "this moral catastrophe brought with it completely different opportunities." That disaster, if it is shunned in the horror of waking responsibility, cannot be reflexively admitted into a living memory. In their overdetermining impact on the historical present, the repressed contents remain the rejected/abjected cornerstones of recovery, or they are the ghosts haunting the fake normality (EAS 117/NC 210).

We *can* learn by disaster, Habermas emphatically foreshadows in 1986 his yes to a question he raises in a more direct fashion only in 1998. We *can* learn, if this learning is integrated into the Gadamerian receptivity of traditions along with their critical evaluation. Traditions in themselves do not carry preinterpreted flags that tell us which of them will lead us to justice and which to disaster. The hermeneutics (interpretation) of recovering traditions without the accompanying hermeneutics of suspecting their pernicious dimensions, this naïveté of understanding entrenches the conservatism that keeps driving the historical revisionists. In learning from disastrous traditions, *we* let ourselves be guided by what Ricoeur (1970) named the hermeneutics of suspicion: this is "a gaze educated by the moral catastrophe, a gaze that is, in a word, suspicious" (EAS 142/NC 234).

That the contradictory attitudes toward one's past do coexist within a single historical consciousness of individuals or groups only indicates an ongoing inability to come to terms with the disastrous parts of the past. The accompanying guilt and shame are symptomatic of the past that was not worked through, that was not mourned, that motivates the present self-destructively in the surviving victims or through other denials mixed with the skewed commemorations of "collective fates" among the surviving perpetrators. The Bitburg drama and the historical revisions indicate that there exists the repressed and misplaced guilt. The desire for artificial normality, with amnesia about the painful past, shows the aggravated nature of the hidden contradiction. "One cannot simultaneously undertake a moral abstraction and insist on historical concreteness. Someone who nevertheless persists in mourning collective fates without distinguishing between perpetrators and victims must be up to something else" (EAS 121–122/NC 213–214).

That 'something else' is a mourning act of the lost continuities that held together one's (nation's) identity and that cannot return with its original aura of innocence. This lost innocence about ourselves will not come back once it has been denuded and utterly discredited. There results a temporal identity gap. Without crossing its Rubicon, one remains bound to repeat compulsively only this destructive, melancholy emptiness. The origins of guilt and shame are, therefore, twofold. First, there are those who wish to revise the loss they cannot face now; they make an effort to refurbish the false continuity in some future form. "Thus one German spelling of 'survival' is 'continuity,'" as Geyer and Hansen (Hartman 1994, 189) succinctly point out.[26] Second, there are those who feel an inexplicable shame for having escaped the catastrophe even though they were innocent of complicity in it. A sense of having escaped carries forward the past that one has lived through or has inherited as a child of the next generation of survivors.[27]

We return to *our* beginnings through a full circle of remembering: Is there only a melancholy recollection of the past that neither lets itself be mourned nor allows itself to pass away? Can the traumatic past be worked off and remembered *today* rather than worked over and normalized by revisionist historians, museum archivalists, politicians? To answer this question, we must grasp the nature of an "intersubjective liability" for the injurious past (EAS 164, 174; cf. 141, 144/NC 252, 262f.; cf. 233, 236f.). *We* each face a dual task: (1) *anamnestic solidarity* with the victims of history and (2) a future-oriented critical praxis.[28]

In his 1987 Kierkegaardian address to a Danish audience, Habermas makes a key distinction between *collective liability and personal guilt*.[29]

> Some of us are heirs of the victims and of those who helped the intended victims of offered resistance. Others are the heirs of the perpetrators or of those who kept quiet. For those born later, this *divided* legacy establishes neither personal merit nor personal guilt. Beyond guilt that can be ascribed to individuals, however, different contexts can mean different historical burdens. With the life forms into which we were born and which have stamped our identity we take on very different sorts of *historical liability* (in Jaspers' sense). For the way we continue the traditions in which we find ourselves is up to us. (EAS 163/NC 251; second italics added)

Habermas intensifies his reflection on collective liability and personal guilt by reiterating that neither the victims nor their heirs, nor even the heirs of the Nazi criminals, could ground their personal feelings of shame (however real and psychoanalytically true all feelings may be) by the morally assignable criteria of personal guilt. Yet this sigh of relief from not being condemnable merely on account of one's inherited association with a criminal organization, this relief, may not revise the past by equalizing the status of victims and perpetrators. The ascription of collective guilt is not implied in the notion of generational cohorts. In our present memory work, likewise we cannot easily rely on the equalizing role of human mortality or the acts of divine Judgment Day. Habermas offers here a piece of postmetaphysical theological advice. The residual depth dimension of unmourned memory, which revisits us today with its melancholy undersides, teaches us how we may speak of radical evil and the need for redemption in the absence of theodicy (metaphysical justifications of God in light of existing evil). In sum, the melancholy mourning of the disastrous past that will not pass away is symptomatic both of radical evil and of the need for redemption (EAS 120f./NC 212f.).

The depth symptoms of evil and redemption are of two sorts. And this distinction puts at rest all revisionist (secular or theological) equalizations of the victims with perpetrators. On the one hand, there is the evasive melancholy of those who wish to recapture—in some renewed normality (Bitburg, war memorials and museums, historical settling of accounts and damages)—the lost identifications with defeated or utterly bankrupt narrative continuities. In the words of Geyer and Hansen (Hartman 1994, 176), in the acts of fake normalizations, revisionists "remember *in order to forget*." In more sinister scenarios, some "have begun to remember as to prepare revenge." Without learning how to remember and without having mourned the historical instances of self-deception and destruction in the first place, the future cannot redeem the problematic past dimensions of the received traditions by rendering them harmless.

On the other hand, melancholy—"that strangely archaic feeling of shame in the face of the catastrophe that one has survived not through one's own efforts but by chance" (EAS 163/NC 252)—often accompanies the traumatic narratives of the first, second, and now third generations of Holocaust survivors. The active evocations of the past suffering and the melancholy shame suffered by the innocents—

these acts on their own cannot redeem the victims of history either. Habermas argues in his Danish address that given the active melancholy suffered on account of the victims of history, "whose suffering cannot be made good ... [this very] melancholy places us under an obligation" (EAS 174/NC 263). Making *our* own this obligation allows *us* to transform the melancholy residues of the absolute past—radical evil of innocent suffering. This transformation of melancholy has two temporal dimensions, noted above as part of the existential-political task. The temporal indices run through the lives of contemporaries in all generations (1) as their critical remembrance of the past (2) for the sake of redeeming a more just future.

Before proceeding further, I need to call attention to Habermas' almost imperceptible identification with the victims of history. On a close reading, we discover this unique dimension of his philosophical-political profile. I offer this fitting title to underscore the depth dimension of his profile: *the critical theorist as witness* (Matuštík 2000). Everything Habermas says, does, and writes can be rendered intelligible by this one core referent, *the Holocaust*. It defines the depth axis motivating and shaping his life from his traumatic personal prehistory in 1929–1944, through his first awakening on May 8, 1945, and all the way to the significant political end point, which he assigns, as I discussed at the end of chapter 3, in the short twentieth century—to the year 1989. For Müller (2000), unlike for Habermas, the so-called Holocaust identity signals a problematic political foundation for a future development of critical culture in unified Germany.

One very important objection to my characterization of Habermas' profile comes from Johann Baptist Metz, a well-known German political theologian. Metz et al. (1997, 152f.) argue that there is a contemporary triumph of amnesia regarding Auschwitz. Among the three examples he gives, the third refers to Habermas as a representative of the notion of "science that heals all wounds." In his essay on Israel and Athens (IuA), Habermas debates with Metz that the spirit of remembrance, found in the biblical traditions, had long since migrated (through *linguistification* of sacred contents) into the secular heart of Enlightenment, discursive rationality. Metz objects that in Habermas' case, however, the "catastrophe of Auschwitz" plays a visibly influential role only in his various political writings, but that there is no impact, indeed, "not a word" about Auschwitz "in his great philosophical writings about communicative reason. Does communicative theory also somehow heal all wounds?" Metz asks. How can we *speak* about that which should not "get lost in cultural amnesia," which should not be simply transformed into a "normality" of rational and enlightened theorizing? How can communicative theory heal the wounds that are not healed perhaps even with the ordinary passage of time? I am aware of this objection from the beginning (see chap. 1 n. 3 above) when I established the thesis of a close internal link between Habermas' core situations and his philosophical-political profile. I will continue reconstructing his profile as an example of that theorist and activist whose preoccupations with the German catastrophe mark his entire life journey. I will return to Metz's disquiet with Habermas in chapters 7 and 9, when I ask about the unspeakable dimension of communication. The issue I postpone until Part Three is, thus, how Habermas learns by disaster, and whether or not in this learning he is aware that disaster may affect his very theoretical authorship and political praxis.[30]

Returning to Habermas' role, which I characterize as that of a critical theorist in the position of a second-degree witness to the Holocaust, we find him speaking of his postwar encounter with shame in Holocaust survivors:

> I first observed this reaction in others—in those who had escaped the concentration camps, who had gone into hiding or emigrated—and who could show solidarity with those who did not survive the extermination operations only in an inexplicably self-tormenting way. (EAS 163f./NC 252)

Grammatically, Habermas does not go on to say: 'later I observed this in myself'. Yet his entire narrative construction indicates both his identification with (however plausible and even ambivalent this act itself might be) and his assumed liability for the Holocaust legacy. He is careful not to blur the distinction between the Holocaust victims or survivors and those, like him in Germany, who are neither of Jewish origin nor victims or descendants of the survivors in the literal sense: "I do not want to deny the specificity of this phenomenon" (i.e., the shame and remembrance through shared suffering). Immediately after that disclaimer, he identifies with Germany's disaster as experientially his own and extends the liability for Germany's Holocaust legacy. He erects a bridge between Ricoeur's hermeneutics of suspicion (critical interpretation of tradition), Jaspers's question of guilt versus liability, and Benjamin's dangerous memory and *anamnestic solidarity*. The text echoes the addendum that is implied, even if unsaid and unwritten—'later I observed this in myself':

> But since that moral catastrophe doesn't the survival of all of us stand under the curse, in attenuated form, of having merely escaped? And doesn't the fortuitousness of unmerited escape establish an *intersubjective liability—a liability* for distorted life circumstances that grant happiness, or even mere existence, to some only at the cost of destroying the happiness of others, denying them life and causing them suffering? (EAS 164/NC 252; italics added)

Avoiding easy universalization of Germany's particular experience, Habermas nonetheless names Auschwitz as the disastrous signature event of the twentieth century that shattered our unquestioned trust in "a deep layer of solidarity among all who have a human face" (EAS 263/NC 251).[31] With this strikingly Lévinasian formulation, Habermas as a critical social theorist adopts the position of a witness—he restores the shattered solidarity in acts of dangerous remembrance. The danger does not consist in bringing the victims back from history, but in the emancipatory promise that the present generation enacts on behalf of the past and future generations. With acts of *anamnestic solidarity* one assumes liability. Both this past-oriented solidary remembrance and the future-oriented responsibility jointly motivate the task of social critique and transformation.

The task of *the critical theorist as witness* takes on this work of memory, critique, and liberation. As I underscored, invoking *intersubjective liability* cannot mean the same thing as espousing the notion of collective guilt. In all his contributions to the Historians' Debate and, most notably, in his Copenhagen lecture, Habermas rejects the notion of collective guilt, and yet he affirms collective liability, which in turn requires collective responsibility. The liability for past injuries orients *us*, the contemporaries in each succeeding generation, forward. Remembering is a public, not merely private, act, a task, "a historical force."[32] This existential repetition forward, to recall Kierkegaard's (1985) transformation of the Platonic metaphysical recollection *(anamensis)* backward, moves by virtue of the dangerous memory of the past injustices; it moves in an *anamnestic solidarity* with the victims of history. Habermas shares this search for an existential, for him at once Kierkegaardian and Benjaminian, dimension of social theory with thinkers from Sartre to Jaspers to Marcuse to Martin Luther King Jr. to Metz to Havel. The dilemmas of de-Nazification, de-Stalinization, or a broad detoxification of racist thinking are not the same. Yet in all three regards, we can jettison the faulty notion of collective guilt for the past acts inflicted by one's traditions on innocents and assume collective liability for such acts, and, indeed, have the latter motivate *our* active responsibility for the shared future (EAS 118/NC 211).

> Kierkegaard places the art of choosing oneself wholly under the viewpoint of moral justification. But it's only what we can attribute to an individual person that is subject to moral evaluation; we cannot feel responsible for historical processes in the same sense. For those born later, only a kind of *intersubjective liability* arises from the historical complex of forms of life that have been passed on from generation to generation. (EAS 174/NC 262f.; italics added)

Thus joint liability is intrinsically at once an existential and social issue. The 'existential' always and already carries its coterminous 'social' meaning:[33] "We have to stand by our traditions, then, if we do not want to disavow ourselves.... There are no grounds for such evasive maneuvers." Habermas goes on to question the implication of such existential-social links:

> But what follows from this existential connection between traditions and forms of life that have been poisoned by unspeakable crimes? At one time a whole civilized population, proud of its constitutional state and its humanistic culture, could be made liable for these crimes—in Jaspers's sense of a *collective joint liability*.

Does a criminal past into which we may be born pass on to the future as our collective guilt? "Does something of this *liability* carry over to the next generation and the one after that as well?" (EAS 140f./NC 233; all citations above; all italics added).

Habermas answers with a 'yes'—something of the liability does carry over—and still, he agrees with existential thinkers that responsibility can be ascribed only to the individuals in actual social forms of life who are acting in their historical present. We cannot be held guilty for acts completed in the past by others or even by the entire collectivity of our shared cultural tradition. Yet there is something like a *"historical liability* for the form of life in which Auschwitz was possible" (EAS 144/NC 236; italics added). How can my not being guilty and also my being liable coexist in the same historical consciousness without a contradiction?

The divided liability for a disastrous past cannot be resolved in a syllogistic manner. Yet the contradictory memory can be worked off (rather than worked over) or borne in one's active existential responsibility for the future. Because "memory ... has not become correspondingly [to the succeeding generations after the Holocaust] distantiated," Habermas keeps starting over and over from the positionality of a witness: "the same point of departure: the images of that unloading ramp at Auschwitz." This refusal to pass over the memory of disaster differs from the compulsion-repetition of a historical present, which is motivated by an unmourned past trauma. The memory of the catastrophe as a present departure becomes the dangerous, subversive memory. We can grasp Habermas' intervention in the Historians' Debate as the struggle over the memory of January 30, 1933 (the Nazi seizure of power), and May 8, 1945 (liberation). In the antecedents and the consequents of the struggle to remember, he performs the role of a public witness: "this traumatic refusal to pass away of a moral imperfect past tense that has been burned into our national history entered the consciousness of the general population only in the 1980s" (EAS 137/NC 229f.).

Habermas often refers to the critical mythology depicted in the Schwäbian tradition of mystical pietism as well as the Jewish Cabala: In *this* age when 'God' is increasingly becoming dead, humans share in their responsibility to cocreate, indeed, hasten the coming of the messiah. This redemptive responsibility marks the postsecular thought of liberation. The *anamnestic solidarity* with the victims of history cannot be relegated to a 'God' who alone is made responsible for saving us. Rather, an active solidarity turns into liberation praxis. In this recourse to myth we meet Habermas' peculiar dialectical atheism. He appropriates religious themes—Benjamin's or Metz's redemptive solidarity and dangerous memory with the victims of history—and integrates them into a more secular mode of public discourses on the future of our traditions (KPS 488f./AS 60f.; VsE 98–111; cf. PDM 24/14).[34]

But his *linguistified* (discursive, communicative) solidarity, albeit *postsecular* (it integrates religious themes) and socially existential in its intuition, is not a new religion. Habermas wants to avoid the irksome problems of uncritical mythologizing. With Grass, Adorno, Lévinas, and others, he joins actively in remembering the portrait of the Santa Claus who once fooled us by becoming a gas man. After Auschwitz, can anyone say with ease that only a "God save us now"? Which "God," which revolution will not turn out to be an evil genius? To raise such questions means to assume Habermas' critical-witness posture to the disaster of the Holocaust; it is to accept his communicative grounds for the very possibility of redemptive liberation. And waiting for the messianic redemption—whether it is conceived in religious or secular or postsecular language—goes hand in hand with *our* actively working for and hastening its remembrance now.

The existential link between received traditions and moral disasters that can befall them from within shows, thus, that the *anamnestic solidarity* with the victims of history provides the sui generis way for healing painful memories without screening them through the melancholy forms of paralysis, manic denial, or ill-motivated revision. Under the postmetaphysical conditions of secular modernity, the received ideas of 'God' become more and more moribund in our midst. This is true even if many a tradition today resurrects divinity in fundamentalist or nationalist colors. "Whether or not we view this *historical liability* as broadly as Benjamin did, today we bear a greater responsibility than ever for the proportion of continuity and discontinuity in the forms of life we pass on" (EAS 174/NC 263; italics added).

But can there be witnesses to the disaster of tradition if the past is closed? The Adornian task of working through the traumatic past rises or falls with the possibility of bearing witness to it. The question, How can one bear witness to the Holocaust if this is an event without witnesses (Felman and Laub 1992), whether in the first or second degree, brings us face-to-face with the Benjaminian issue whether or not the past is closed or open to liberation or, if you prefer his more postsecular language, to messianic redemption. Neither critical theorists in general, nor Habermas in particular, would be able to be a critical witness if the traumatic past were irretrievably closed. *My claim is that Habermas' life and his philosophical-political profile, and, with some qualifications, his reflective answer to the Benjaminian issue of the past, testify to the openness of history.*

Before making good on my claim, I need to sum up the Benjaminian outcome of the highly debated issue of the past and Habermas' most current position on it. The issue of the open or closed status of the past, especially of the injurious one, arises out of Benjamin's claim that "the work of the past remains uncompleted for historical materialists" ([1937] 1982, 233; 1955, 311; cf. Peukert 1986, 206). In a letter from March 16, 1937, Horkheimer rebuts the above claim with this either/or: history is either closed or it requires an ahistorical, theological explanation. In the *Passagen-Werk* for the *Arcades* project, Benjamin (1989, 61) cites from Horkheimer's letter: "Past injustice has occurred and is done with. The murdered are really murdered.... If one takes incompleteness completely seriously, one has to believe in the Last Judgment...." And Benjamin appends this "corrective" to any scientistic orthodoxy of 'historical materialism': "history is not just a science but also a form of memoration. What science has 'established', memoration can modify. Memoration can make the incomplete (happiness) into something complete, and the complete (suffering) into something incomplete." Redemptive criticism and commemoration of the injurious past are "theology," even if not theologically dogmatic.

Still, Benjamin's correction embraces materialist historiography. His corrective, moreover, wields a two-edged sword. First, having discovered that human history never had innocent origins, one must face the difficulty of its beginnings. "Barbarism inheres in the very conception of culture" (1989, 56; cf. 1968, 256; 1982, 233). Second, the history written from the view of its victorious progress "is a kind of transmission that is a catastrophe." Redemptive criticism and materialist commemoration are to "rescue" tradition from this double catastrophe—an inherited presumption of innocence and progress (1989, 63; cf. 81).

In his last completed work from 1940, Benjamin (1968) differentiates a progressivist "historical materialism" (253) from a messianic remembrance integrated with historical revolution. Rolf Tiedemann (1989, 175–209) emphatically reminds us that even as Benjamin invokes messianic time, redeeming the claims made by the victims of history on present generations, his theological concepts are thoroughly materialist. Benjaminian messianic hope enters through the gates of human history for the sake of those without hope, and Marcuse echoes this postsecular claim on the closing pages of *One-Dimensional Man*.

> The past carries with it a temporal index by which it is referred to redemption. There is a secret agreement between past generations and the present one. Our coming was expected on earth. Like every generation that preceded us, we have been endowed with a *weak* Messianic power, a power to which the past has a claim. The claim cannot be settled cheaply. Historical materialists are aware of that. (Benjamin 1968, 254)

Because of *our weak messianic power*—the phrase to be repeated and transmuted by Habermas on numerous occasions—witnessing to the past disaster becomes possible. And it becomes necessary because without witnessing to the unspeakable (i.e., traumatic), *"even the dead"* will not be safe from the enemy if he wins" (Benjamin 1968, 255). The past remains open through the temporal trajectory of the now time *(Jetztzeit)*, "of the present as the 'time of the now' which is shot through with chips of Messianic time" (263; cf. 261). By remembering the victims, *we* endow revolutionary praxis with the dangerous memory of the messianic promise of liberation. The critical historiographer must resist homogenizing the past. Against blueprints or idols of future progress, Benjamin witnesses to discontinuous, redemptive time as our present experience of the past. One can inhabit time which is no longer empty, knowing that "every second of time . . . [is] the strait gate through which the Messiah might enter" (264).

The issues separating Horkheimer and Benjamin are revisited by Peukert (1986, 206–10), Lenhardt (1975), Metz (1989), at one end, and Habermas at the other. It is in fact Lenhardt who introduces *anamnestic solidarity*, now a widely used term, to argue that future, thus present, generations may not consciously accept their liberation and happiness as brought about by those in history whose oppression and unhappiness stay without redress. Peukert (1986, 209f.) and Metz (1989,

736f.) insist that, short of willed amnesia, Habermas' communicative ethics presupposes *anamnestic solidarity* as the condition of its possibility.

In the end, Habermas parts with Horkheimer's rebuttal to Benjamin and accepts instead a secularized variation of Peukert's (1986, 210) formulation of the Jewish tradition: "The paradox of an existence that refuses to extinguish the memory of the victims of history in order to be happy." But Habermas does not share Peukert's reinterpretation of communicative action through Christian fundamental theology. Rather than Peukert's Christian theological or Horkheimer's despairing positions, he adopts a communicative rendition of the Judaic claim laid by past generations to *our* emancipatory remembrance. Benjamin's (1968, 254) *weak Messianic power* (see PDM 24f./14f.) becomes Habermas' *weak anamnestic power* (EAS 141/NC 233).

Anamnestic solidarity is beyond despair, yet it sheds theological pretensions: "social theory offers no consolation, has no bearing on the individual's need for salvation" (KPS 489/AS 60). He speaks now of "the dead who have a claim to the weak anamnestic power of . . . [our] solidarity" (EAS 141/NC 233).

I can safely conclude that Habermas' mature profile situates him between Benjamin and Horkheimer and, with a more nuanced reading, closer to the former.

> Now our responsibility extends to the past as well. This cannot simply be accepted as something fixed and over and done with. Walter Benjamin has probably defined most precisely the claim which is made by the dead on the anamnesic [sic] power of living generations. Certainly, we cannot make good past suffering and injustice done; but we have *the weak power of an atoning remembrance*. Only our sensitivity toward the innocently martyred, from whose inheritance we live, can generate a reflexive distance from our own traditions, a sensitivity to the profound ambivalences of the traditions which have formed our own identity. (NR 155/AS 242f.; italics added)[35]

I can now affirm my claim about Habermas' profile from his own Benjaminian affirmation: because the past is not closed, witnessing to disasters is not impossible; ergo, present and future generations can face their traumas. Whether in first- or, as in Habermas' case, second-degree proximity to Germany's catastrophe, witnessing empowers *our anamnestic solidarity* with the victims of history. If "the catastrophes of our century have . . . altered . . . [our] awareness of time" (NR 155/AS 242; cf. LD), as Habermas admits, then they must have altered, existentially speaking, our communicative competencies. Thus I will argue in Part Three when discussing Metz's objection also introduced in this chapter, *this century taught us that communicative action is possible because one can bear witness to the unspeakable. Learning this communicative competence from history alters our awareness of the possibility of disaster in our theory and practice alike.*

Regardless how the argument about 'God' is settled, Habermas accepts two of Benjamin's claims made upon the living from beyond the grave. First, even in the world with an absent 'God', the Holocaust represents radical evil: it marks the breach of the human solidary bonds, of that basic horizon of trust necessary for one's identity formation, communicative competencies, and social well-being. Second, there is the memory of those innocents killed by human hands, and "these dead ... have a claim to the *weak anamnestic power* of a solidarity that later generations can continue to practice only in the medium of remembrance that is repeatedly renewed, often desperate, and continually on one's mind." This *anamnestic* praxis exercises a solidary-redemptive role in the present vis-à-vis the past. The descendants of victims who live in our midst cannot restore their bonds to the human community without shared memory of suffering. The critical witness hastens a more just future to come now by extending solidary remembrance to the past (EAS 141/NC 233; italics added).

The dual past-and-future-oriented role of the *anamnestic solidarity* and redemptive praxis addresses the divided liability of the Holocaust. Nothing can once and for all settle accounts for the past pain, hence there is no easy redemptive normality. Yet we can continue our traditions "through remembrance, practiced in solidarity, of what cannot be made good, other than through a reflexive, scrutinizing attitude toward one's own identity-forming traditions." The uniqueness of the Holocaust is only historical and not universal (there have been other genocides and holocausts, and there are multiple commemorations). Indeed, the claim to this uniqueness lies in the particular liability of Germans of all present and future generations, a liability now transformed into active responsibility, which cannot be done away with once and for all or by passing it to others (EAS 144/NC 236f.). Since it is from the shared experience and memory—including that of happiness and suffering—that traditions are formed, only "mourning and remembrance, practiced communally, secure these traditions." The normality that would allow one generation to skip this communal memory must be illusory in its origins, neurotic in the present, and dangerous for the future. "Suffering is always concrete suffering; it cannot be detached from its context." The joint work of sober memory—waiting in witness, witnessing in critical praxis—provides the modicum of hope for a communal recovery from disaster (EAS 121/NC 213).

EXISTENTIAL EITHER/OR AS THE PUBLIC CHOICE OF OUR TRADITIONS

> Kierkegaard was the first to illuminate the postmetaphysical condition in which formal questions of personal identity replaced earlier, more substantive notions of an ethical life (in one or another version). (KE)

Writing in the wake of the German Autumn of 1977, neither Habermas nor the reviewers of his *Observations* (OSSA) let us know that Jaspers's (1931) cultural critique adopts for its prototype of social criticism Kierkegaard's *Two Ages* (1978, written in 1846). Habermas objects for his own, otherwise salutary, reasons that

Jaspers's culture critique from the 1930s follows Hegel and relies on a narrative of the great philosopher. Yet to his detriment, Habermas overlooks that Jaspers agrees with Kierkegaard's existential approach to history rather than with Hegel's universal view of history: "Kierkegaard was the first to undertake a comprehensive critique of his time, one distinguished from all previous attempts by its earnestness. This critique of his was the first to be applicable to the age in which we are now living, and reads as if it were written but yesterday" (Jaspers 1933, 10f.).[36]

Both Jaspers and Habermas oppose invidious nationalism. Habermas might agree with Jaspers's rather Kierkegaardian claim that "nationalist movements throughout the world are more intolerant than ever, and yet in them 'nation' is nothing more than the existence of a common speech in conjunction with a levelling type" (123f.). Habermas aims at a postnational identity integrated procedurally into a democratic republic; but Jaspers anchors resistance to an oppressive nation-state, situation, or age ultimately in the actions of individuals:

> It is true that life-order existent through the power of a state can never be surrendered or sacrificed, for therewith everything would go to ruin; but a life in radical opposition to the state may arise, under stress of the fundamental question how the conquest of the life-order is once more to be achieved. (129)

Habermas is preoccupied with at once radically democratic and ethically existential question of cultural continuities. My core thesis about the formation of his philosophical-political profile can be now enhanced as follows: *Habermas integrates the Jaspersian-Kierkegaardian existential accents placed on radical self-choice (via what he positively learned from the revolutionary student revolt of the 1960s and its intellectual grounding of radical democracy) with the postwar constitutional grounding needs of his own skeptical generation.* His radical democratic-existential either/or question posed now from within the trajectory of the 1980s and 1990s reads as follows: Which of our traditions shall we continue and which shall we jettison? "The shift of power at the turn of the sixties came after a decade of dogged intellectual opposition and another decade of active political confrontation with its legacy. So the political shift was the eventual outcome of a deeper change in the cultural climate" (EgA 12/4).

Habermas brings this either/or questioning into the public sphere, thereby radically democratizing the individual practices of self-choice—a choice customarily portrayed in textbooks on existentialism as one's solipsist affair. His communicative approach brings the debates concerning the shared ethical and social continuities into the full public view. No longer can cultural mandarins or leaders of nationalistic marches determine for others their existential choices. Nor must existential philosophy be a matter of something that issues behind our backs or in front of our noses, while we silently and passively wait for the invisible market hands or the forces of nationalism or other unreflected myths to deliver us from our follies. The messianic waiting for the wholly other than this unjust world, as inspired by Benjamin's historically materialist Jewish theology, and our being-in-the-world, as now socially and critically understood by Habermas, these notions of redemptive waiting and solidarity cannot be divorced from creatively hastening liberation.

Note, however, that Kierkegaard's genuine either/or choice is not about choosing this or that cultural value sphere. Rather, prior to any decision about values or paths, a fundamental choice pertains to an existential self-choice of oneself as capable of raising the ethical questions of good and bad and the moral question of right and wrong in the first place. Even a small dose of this competence, if harnessed by ordinary citizens, would be subversive to any authoritarian state! Only by presupposing or having at his disposal this reflexive quality of existential questioning (citizens capable of this attitude) can Habermas develop its communicative and radically democratic equivalents. To enter into an *anamnestic solidarity* with the victims of history presupposes that this highly reflexive existential self-choice already funds one's core attitude toward received traditions. The Kierkegaardian existential self-choice, harnessed into the Benjaminian sense of *anamnestic solidarity*, thus prompts Habermas to envision a public forum on the past and future of our inherited problematic traditions. His truly innovative move is that he introduces the futural-existential and the remembering-*anamnestic* dimensions of emancipatory praxis into radical democratic deliberations. This integrative move marks to date Habermas' most concrete synthesis of the democratic needs of 1945 with the revolutionary core of the '68ers. After Marcuse seemed to have abandoned his early project of *the existential variants of Critical Theory* (NU 216/AS 150), and even after Sartre's lifelong search for and his unstable integration of Marxism with existentialism, *Habermas' unique version of witnessing ethics, which he develops more clearly since the 1980s, represents one of the most original attempts at the synthesis of existential philosophy with a communicative model of Critical Theory.*[37]

Habermas facilitates this synthesis by rendering the first-person singular perspective of existential self-choice through *the linguistic-communicative turn* (the philosophical shift in methodology that starts with language and communication as the primary domains of analysis). The assumption of collective liability for the past in the form of collective responsibility for the present and the future must be "conducted from the first-person point of view. This arena, in which none of us can be nonparticipants, should not be confused with discussion among scientists and scholars who have to take the observational perspective of a third person in their work" (EAS 144/NC 237). In the Historians' Debate, and its side debates, the debating public confronts the either/or questions pertaining to the present future of inherited traditions. The valid question of personal guilt for the past moral disaster shifts thus to the terrain of an intersubjective liability for the shared communal future. If memory is at once individual and social, then the "working off" of the damaged intersubjectivity must be at once an existential and social task. Self-choice with regard to one's singular social memory cannot be separated from the historical situations of this memory.

Jaspers questioned the group labels assignable for past crimes and he assumed collective responsibility for the future. Habermas accepts both moves and shifts away from Heidegger's and Schmitt's political-decisionist existentialism of the 1930s. The latter two, in their one-time historically material realization of existential choice, confuse self-choice with a followership of the *Führer* or of the authoritarian state. German political existentialism of the 1930s abdicates personal responsibility to the great leader. And after the war and after that authority becomes dethroned, this prior pseudo-existential approach makes one incapable to mourn one's identity deposed along with those dethroned gods. Habermas' recourse to Kierkegaard's existential ethics allows him to develop a witnessing ethics as part of his communicative transformation of Critical Theory. With this innovation, he is even more successful in unmasking the revisionist historians whose fake existential pathos rings hollow.

Let us not forget that Habermas discovered the core of this Kierkegaardian existential-communicative ethics already in 1953 in his polemic with Heidegger's momentary 'inauthentic authenticity'. Habermas also retained from the student rebellion of 1968 an existential-revolutionary core of their cultural critique of Germany's false continuities. And at the present juncture of our profile reconstruction, in his 1987 Danish address, he resumes the existential critique of abstract existentialism from 1953 and positively appropriates the cultural critique of the 1960s. *At the peak of the polemic with the revisionist ghosts of 1945, Habermas integrates the existential-revolutionary core of the revolting generation into his lifelong integrative project of radical democracy.*[38]

Geyer and Hansen (Hartman 1994, 183) argue that the struggle over memory and identity represents one of the most recent "new social movements." That struggle emerges along with other post-1960s social forms of life. They note how Habermas' Copenhagen lecture from 1987 intervenes in this struggle at its peak, that is, in an almost three-decades-long (1960s–1980s) "memory movement." His intervention contains a two-pronged dimension. First, the communicative rendition of the existential either/or provides an alternative to Stürmer's ideological constructions of the past and present national meanings and identity formations.[39] *The critical theorist as witness* offers the existential check-and-balance element that is absent from the revisionist arbitrations of historical memory. The question cannot ask, To construct or not to construct meaningful narratives? Rather, the question becomes, How to narrate one's/*our* past? To answer this latter query for ourselves and within the debating public sphere, *we* must become at once receptive to the memory of innocent suffering (the role of the solidary witness who does not simply speak for the victims or for their survivors) and suspicious of the traditions *we* need to jettison (the role of critical witness) while *remembering* their fragile lifelines.

Second, Habermas' intervention brings this intersubjective dimension of narrating *our* collective lives into the foreground. In common, *we* can learn to resist blind forms of group identity formations that tempt us in the present to abdicate responsibility to witness critically the painful chapters of the past. Habermas names this persisting attitude *postconventional identity* (sometimes this notion includes or is synonymous with *posttraditional and postnational identity*). Resisting conventionalism, traditionalism, and nationalism would mean, in other words, becoming suspicious, particularly of those identity narratives that revisionists like Stürmer, Nolte, Hillgruber, Hildebrand, and other German mandarins, Schmitt and at one time also Heidegger, prized as the very best in their tradition. In place of celebrating political authoritarianism, Habermas defends *constitutional patriotism* (friendly bonds toward one's democratic institutions rather than uncritically accepted symbols like colors, flags, anthems); in place of nationalist and fundamentalist belonging, he nurtures community bonds that grow from existential valuations of traditions (i.e., in responsible distancing from and critical belonging to one's historical and life world situations).

Habermas' critically witnessing sense of an *either/or* choice must be distinguished from a decisionistic (i.e., uncritically receptive and ideologically constructivist) *either-or*. The latter, flattened either-or is practiced by the historical revisionists of meaning like Stürmer and Nolte (EAS 129/NC 221) or in "the struggle to reclaim encumbered traditions" (EAS 143/NC 236), which Habermas critically exposes in Hillgruber's separation of the two sorts of destruction (Jewish and German); in the proactive, vintage decisionistic, settling of accounts at Bitburg; or in the anti-Enlightenment "balancing of accounts that Nolte and Fest are conducting in full public view" (EAS 147/NC 240). Both the critical either/or and the decisionistic either-or have their social and public equivalents. Otherwise one could not speak of the Nazi political existentialism of the 1930s, or of an existential decision for the *Führer*; otherwise Nazi sensibilities could not be resurrected in the revisionist manipulations of identity and meaning of the 1980s. Yet we can unmask, with Habermas' unique communicative-existential ethics and witnessing Critical Theory, that either-or as false (i.e., as the very opposite of existential either/or), which puts a fake façade over the historical cracks in the wall. The ideological motives of manipulated memory are the very opposite of open communication; the flat either-or is "to historicize the Nazi period for the public in such a way that it is normalized and distanced" (EAS 178/NC 266).

Habermas' public enhancement of an existential either/or choice pertains to "the deeper question of what attitude we want to take toward the continuities of German history." In distinguishing conventional from postconventional (posttraditional, postnational) attitudes, the former describes a traditionalist relation to received meanings, whereas the latter emerges from a refracted experience. Postconventional and existential attitudes are complementary insofar as both are to be distinguished from a precritical attitude. Any existential ontology (analysis of the structures of existence), insofar as it is not subject to *ontic* (lived) questioning concerning who we are and want to be, has little in common with this integrated existential-postconventional attitude. The latter attitude has everything to do with such questioning. "Can we, and do we want to, give up the comforts and the dangers of a conventional identity that is incompatible with a *critical* appropriation of traditions?" Habermas asks (NC 193). Could one's unreconstructed silence on these *ontic* questions be interpreted after Auschwitz as an existentially authentic (solidary as well as critical) form of witnessing (see EAS 117f./NC 210)?

An uncritical silence of amnesia, as opposed to the silence of redemptive waiting, is unacceptable in the culture in which Auschwitz was possible, Habermas agrees with Adorno and Lévinas alike. With regard to the Holocaust, the 'critical theorist as witness' embodies two sides of the profiled face, and in Habermas' profile these sides in crucial instances come together. In his 1989 interview on the Historians' Debate, he explains the impossibility of an authentic silence on one's being-in-traditions that have deceived us. After Auschwitz only a critical silence (i.e., the redemptive waiting of a solidary witness to the disaster) can ward off the *deus malignus*—that evil genius invading even our silent trust in Being.

> [The] basis of trust . . . was destroyed before the gas chambers. The complex preparation and extensive organization of a coldly calculated mass murder, in which hundreds of thousands—indirectly a whole people—were involved, took place, after all, with the appearance of normality preserved, and was even depended on the normality of highly civilized social intercourse. The monstrous occurred, without interrupting the steady respiration of everyday life. Ever since, a *self-conscious* life has no longer been possible without suspicion of those continuities which are sustained unquestioningly, and which seek to draw their validity from their unquestionability. (NR 150/AS 238; cf. KPS 470f./AS 46)

From another angle, Geyer and Hansen explain the lived difference between the abstract absenting or presencing of Being and one's historical witnessing of the loss that occasions one's awareness of such absence or presence. An ahistorical silence before absent or present Being does not in itself require self-transformation; the generic sense of one's being-toward-death can still allow for a sentimental Bitburg spectacle; the mastered memory of the past can become available as a museumized monumental commodity. The postwar silence on Auschwitz safeguards deceptively "an affirmation of continuity in the face of its extreme rupture." And such silence comes to function, once again, as what Habermas calls, even in *this* postmetaphysical age, an evil genius. In Geyer and Hansen's words: "This way of remembering runs the danger of accepting the absence of the Jews, even of cannibalizing the memory of victims for the purpose of reconstructing German history." But the critical silence of redemptive waiting cannot preserve continuity in discontinuity; rather, it must distinguish the historical loss and affirm the victims in "the remembrance of absence." In a postmetaphysical, living historical memory, Geyer and Hansen find the Shoah "written into the act of representation itself. It is inscribed there as the remembrance of past lives and their mass death: as the reimagining of an unimaginable 'violence of linkage' . . . that holds Germans and Jews together ever since the moment of genocide" (Hartman 1994, 189f., n. 23, all citations; internal citation is from Negt and Kluge 1981, 771).

Habermas practices, at least since his 1953 student intervention against Heidegger, critical social theory as a countermonumental form of responsible witnessing to Germany's disaster. With his unique pathos, he denudes all convolutions of Germany's self-deceived individual or group consciousness. Taking part in the Historians' Debate: "After Auschwitz our national self-consciousness can be derived only from the better traditions in our history, a history that is not unexamined but instead appropriated critically." The public struggle over historical memory cannot be an archival matter, and the suffering of innocents cannot be met by an ontologically aloof silence. The public debate pertains to "the more narcissistic question of the attitude we are to take—for our own sake—toward our own traditions" (EAS 141f./NC 234). With Auschwitz, the either/or self-choice becomes a matter of *our* communal future. "At the center of the debate stands the question *how* the Nazi period is being dealt with historically in the public consciousness" (137/229).

One alternative to the Historians' Debate, with its ideological creation of meaning and with its "reticence with regard to our own past," must be a publicly conducted open debate. In the conclusion to his Danish lecture, Habermas, as a critical social theorist in the second-degree existential witness to the Holocaust, operates with the following either/or: "either to explicitly problematize a past that we no longer shunt aside, or to affirm, still a little defiantly, continuities that extend on through the Nazi period." That defiant affirmation of false continuities marks an obverse side of unmourned yet already broken identity. Kierkegaard, anticipating Freud's depth analysis of motivated ignorance (repression), characterizes defiance as one's going beyond an ordinary anxious being-toward-death: in defiance, one in despair wills to be oneself. This depth motivation of one's refusal to come to terms with one's problematic past and with one's ambivalent present indicates another reason why a witness in solidarity with the victims of history must employ an existential ethic and critical praxis to confront this repression. The critical social theorist as witness invokes the Kierkegaardian either/or as well as the Benjaminian dangerous memory rooted in redemptive solidarity. This memory becomes critically dangerous to one's despairing forgetfulness of disaster. It becomes redemptively dangerous to any actively defiant, present and future, working to cover or hide from one's memory.

> Kierkegaard's *Either/Or* is concerned with the way responsibility for a piece of history is assumed *consciously*. Nor should our postwar history be abandoned to hollow lip service in its decisive point, the renunciation of our disastrous traditions. (178/266; all citations above)[40]

NOTES

1. For a comparative analysis of the three critiques of the present age made by Jaspers, Kierkegaard, and Habermas, see Matuštík 1988; 1993, 230–33, 239.
2. Kelly 1994; Foucault's (1984) and Kant's (1959) essays "What Is Enlightenment?" On Derrida and Critical Theory, see Matuštík 1998a, chap. 3, "Multicultural Enlightenment."
3. Discussion in this chapter expands an essay that I wrote after this book, Matuštík 2000; it was published earlier. Compare and contrast my analysis with the critique of the "Holocaust identity" (Müller 2000, 44f., 57, 95, 119, 143, 246, 248, 255ff., 269, 273, 277).
4. The notion of the Fascist tradition as "the mansion of culture built . . . on dog shit" is from Bertolt Brecht; the reference is given by Jay 1984, 19.
5. See chapter 3 above, the chronology of events in Hartman 1986, xiii–xvi; and Maier 1997, chap. 1.
6. Mohr 1998; Bubis 1998; and Ertel et al. 1998.
7. On this, see Wolin's introduction to Habermas (NC viii).
8. See Adorno 1986; Mitscherlich and Mitscherlich, 1975.
9. Hillgruber 1986b, 733–36, cited in Maier 1997, 48f.; cf. 2. See also Hildebrand 1986b.
10. Adorno's essay ([1959] 1986) resonates in Habermas' NBR, chap. 2; and LD.
11. Mitscherlich and Mitscherlich, 1975, chap. 1, sec. 3, "Successful Defense against Mass Melancholia," and sec. 5, "Wounded Narcissism."
12. Habermas cites Strauss's essay from the *Frankfurter Rundschau*, January 4, 1987.
13. See Mitscherlich and Mitscherlich, 1975, chap. 1, sec. 9: "Is There Another Way to Mourn?"
14. The entire section on the Historians' Debate in EAS/NC is called *Eine Art Schadensabwicklung* [A kind of settling of damages] (the connotation of this notion refers to an insurance settlement for damages). Two of the four pieces gathered by Habermas are newspaper articles. In response to Nolte (June 6, 1986a), Habermas publishes "Eine Art Schadensabwicklung: Die apologetischen Tendenzen in der deutschen Zeitgeschichtsschreibung" [A kind of settling of damages: The apologetic tendencies in German historiography], *Die Zeit*, July 11, 1986 (this essay in EAS 120–36/NC 212–28 carries a new title, "Apologetische Tendenzen"/ "Apologetic Tendencies"). There follow sharp responses to Habermas in the *Frankfurter Allgemeine Zeitung;* see Hillgruber's letter (August 23, 1986a); Hildebrand (July 31, 1986a); and Habermas' rebuttals: to Hildebrand (see Habermas, Hil; August 11, 1986) and to Hillgruber (in "Von öffentlichen Gebrauch der Historie" [On the public use of history], *Die Zeit*, November 7, 1986, cited from EAS 137–48/NC 229–40). Cf. the critique of Hillgruber's book and of Nolte by two editors of *Der Spiegel*: Augstein (October 6, 1986) and Malanowski (September 1, 1986); more rebuttals to Habermas: Hillgruber (December 1986b) and Nolte's letter to the *Frankfurter Allgemeine Zeitung* (December 6, 1986b). Cf. Hildebrand (November 22, 1986b). In the previously unpublished "Nachspiel"/"Closing Remarks" (EAS 149–58/NC 241–48), from February 23, 1987, Habermas responds to Hillgruber. The entire section is introduced by Habermas' remarks ("Eine Diskussionsbemerkung"/"Remarks from the Römerberg Colloquium," June 7, 1986, cited from EAS 117–19/NC 209–11, previously published in Hoffman 1987) on Wolfgang Mommsen's first response to the essay by Nolte 1986a. On the Historians' Debate, Geiss 1988; and Maier 1997, chap. 2, pp. 34–65. See note 23 below.

15. See Maier 1997, 43–45; cf. Wolin in NC xxviii n. 18.

16. See the thesis that opens this chapter; see also Habermas' 1987 Copenhagen lecture, last chapter in EAS/NC; and the in-depth analysis of Habermas' question and lecture in Matuštík 1993.

17. Habermas refers to Fest 1986; cf. Maier 1997, 51f.; Stürmer 1986a,b,c; and Pirandello 1958.

18. On Hillgruber, see also Maier 1997, 19–25.

19. Hillgruber 1986c, 74, cited in Habermas, EAS 126/NC 218.

20. Cf. Goldhagen's (1996) critical angle of the first-person plural and Klemperer's (1999) first-person singular perspectives of witnessing.

21. See Mitscherlich 1975, chap. 1, sec. 2, "The Führer Is to Blame for Everything," and sec. 8, "Infatuation with the Führer."

22. The notion of 'constellation' comes from Walter Benjamin via Adorno to indicate open or converging situations rather than a closed totality.

23. Nolte publishes his article (1986a) in the Feuilleton section of the *Frankfurter Allgemeine Zeitung* on June 6, 1986; Habermas makes his first remarks about this piece in comments on Wolfgang Mommsen's talk at the Römerberg Colloquium in Frankfurt on June 7. Nolte does not to take part in the colloquium (he alleges that he was not allowed to come). Habermas develops these remarks a month later in an article published in the *Die Zeit* on July 11, 1986. On August 29 the editor of the *Frankfurter Allgemeine Zeitung*, Joachim Fest (1986), offers an anti-Habermas defense of Nolte. Nolte is supported by the Bonn historian Klaus Hilderbrand. On this, see also Maier 1997, 25–30. See note 14 above.

24. See Lanzmann 1985; cf. Felman 1994. On the epistemic effects of racism, see Butler 1993b and Matuštík 1998a, 114, 121.

25. Cf. Adorno 1984, 34.

26. Michael Geyer and Miriam Hansen, "German-Jewish Memory and National Consciousness."

27. Hass 1990.

28. Geyer and Hansen (Hartman 1994, 184). Cf. Maier 1997, on identity and Habermas' Copenhagen lecture, 151–59. See also Evans 1989, Mitscherlich 1975, Adorno 1986, and Habermas' resumption of Adorno's questioning in EV; NBR chap. 2; and LD.

29. Max Pensky's (1989) excellent analysis of Habermas' inspiration by Benjamin during the Historians' Debate is distorted by ascribing to Habermas the faulty view of 'collective guilt'. This misreading of Habermas runs consistently throughout Pensky's essay (1989, 352, 353, 355, 356, 357, 358, 375, 376). Duvenage's innovative work on apartheid (1999, 7, 11, 21) reproduces Pensky's error. One of Habermas' clearest rejections of collective guilt is in UöGH 25, 27/24, 26 (and this essay from 1997 is translated by Pensky; but Pensky's essay from 1995 [73, cf. 90] still contains unclear or minimally ambiguous language regarding Habermas' presumed view of collective guilt, a view Habermas explicitly rejects as untenable). As noted in the introduction, the sociological notion of 'generational cohorts' does not imply the view of collective guilt or merit.

30. I thank Peter Zeillinger for bringing Metz's objection to my close attention.

31. Müller (2000, 44f., 76–82, 255ff., 277, 283) analyzes an ambiguous tension existing between the particularist and universalist accents placed on German historical experience in the twentieth century. He argues that the Left and Right equally oscillate between na-

tionalist and postnational perspectives. Even Habermas' idea of a postconventional political culture does not escape being blinded by the context of its so-called Holocaust identity—its very particular historical point of departure for making moral and political judgments.

32. Geyer and Hansen, in Hartman 1994, 184. Müller (2000, 226–65; also 27ff., 281–85) partially endorses Martin Walser's argument for the privatization of remembrance as an act that would transform Jaspers's existential responsibility toward and Benjamin's *anamnestic* solidarity with the victims of history. This transformation would affect Habermas' fundamental project of forging a political culture of public atonement and critical deliberation as well as the sensibilities of his skeptical generation. Müller endorses a certain need to overcome the so-called Holocaust identity, which he finds at best an ambiguous blessing for politics. He proposes that a future-oriented critical consciousness, *especially after Germany's unification*, need not be anchored primarily in coming to terms with the past German trauma. He judges Habermas' (Jaspersian-Benjaminian), even Grass's or Bohrer's, call for an ongoing public commemoration of Germany's catastrophe inscribed into the particular ambivalence of the skeptical generation to be something the new postunification cohorts (perhaps the so-called Berlin generation), for better or worse, no longer share.

33. This communicative and social rethinking of existential categories, and vice versa, developing an existentially inflected communicative theory, is undertaken in greater depth in Matuštík 1993.

34. On Habermas' recourse to Protestant-Jewish mysticism, see also Part Three below.

35. For all of Habermas' references to Benjamin with existential variations on the same insight, see chronologically "Walter Benjamin: Consciousness Raising or Rescuing Critique" (1972), in PpP; KPS 488f./AS 60f.; RC 246f.; PDM, chap. 1, "Excursus on Benjamin's Theses on the Philosophy of History"; EAS 141/NC 233; VV 606, 630/468, 490; NR 155f./AS 242f.; TiTD; KFnT; and indirect discussion of Benjaminian themes via Metz in IuA.

36. I follow closely the previously published material in Matuštík 1993, 232ff.

37. On bringing these attempts to fruition, see Matuštík 1993; 1998a (on Kierkegaard, Critical Theory, and deconstruction, see chaps. 2–4; and on Marcuse, chaps. 6–7, 9); further 1999 on Habermas' original insight as well as his failure to drive home its implications. Cf. Flynn 1984.

38. On the trajectory of Habermas' existential interests, see Matuštík 1999 as well as 1993, introduction and Appendix A. These interests arrive in Habermas' seminar even more directly in the fall of 2000 (KE).

39. This point is brought up by Maier 1997, 151f.

40. Kierkegaard (1980b) analyzes an aggravated despair beyond the ordinary anxious state of being-toward-death (1980a). Cf. Patricia Huntington, "Heidegger's Reading of Kierkegaard Revisited: From Ontological Abstraction to Ethical Concretion," in Matuštík and Westphal 1995, 43–65. For a detailed analysis of Habermas' use of Kierkegaard's existential ethics (in EAS/NC, sec. IV–V, and in ND chap.7/chap. 8), see Matuštík 1993, pt. 1; and 1998a, chaps. 2–4; cf. 1999.

Chapter Six

AFTER 1989: IN THE SHADOWS OF 1945 AND UNDER THE SPECTERS OF 1968

We arrive at last in *our* contemporaneity with Habermas' life in the post-Wall era. *Our* vantage point reduplicates now, as if in an accelerated mode, the temporal structure of Habermas' previously traversed path, which *we* too have undertaken in the *historical present tense* of his situations.

- To begin within *Habermas' contemporaneity today, we* must enter into his questioning: *What does it mean for Habermas to come to terms with the past today*—after 1989?
- To begin within *the question of Habermas' repeated beginnings* (May 8, 1945), *we* must follow the transformations of his ever-new historical present: *What does it mean for Habermas to learn from the disastrous events of today*—in the post-Wall era?
- Since no beginnings are innocent, critical questioning opens to what remains *unspeakable* in them: *What does coming to terms with the past mean today?*

Habermas' profile meets its own and *our* contemporary beginnings with this chapter. The first two questions raised above will be discussed in this chapter. In Part Three of this study, I intend *to step back* in order to evaluate his profile from the perspectives of its architectonic and authorship (chap. 7), its receptive and polemical effect (chap. 8), and its relationship to the critical social theory to come (chap. 9). *Our* historical presents project their trajectories into the future, which is not yet even conceivable as a future present. Every historical present must continue interrogating its own beginnings—their presumed innocence. And at that vanishing futural point of *today*, the last of the above three questions, intimated already in the intervening concluding reflections of Part One and to be revisited in the last chapter, captures the larger concerns that go beyond Habermas' philosophical-political profile and his generation.

HABERMAS' BEGINNINGS TODAY: COMING TO TERMS WITH THE PAST AFTER 1989

> One wants to get free of the past: rightly so, since one cannot live in its shadow. ... But wrongly so, since the past one wishes to evade is still so intensely alive. National Socialism lives on, and to this day we don't know whether it is only the ghost of what was so monstrous that it didn't even die off with its own death, or whether it never died in the first place—whether the readiness for unspeakable actions survives in people, as in the social conditions that hem them in. (Adorno [1959] 1986, 115)

Adorno's essay "What Does Coming to Terms with the Past Mean?" functions as Habermas' self-chosen point of departure. Such self-consciously adopted existential beginnings provide a pivot around which he measures both the integrity of his own philosophical maturation and the responsibility for his ongoing interventions in public debates. Habermas returns to Adorno's essay at crucial historical occasions:

- 1985, in the heat of the Bitburg and Historians' controversies (EV and EAS 11–17)
- 1992, at the time of uncertainties arising from the fall of the Berlin Wall as well as from Germany's unification (NBR, chaps. 2, 6)
- 1998, in reflecting on the passing of the twentieth century (LD)

Adorno's *Aufarbeitung* is translated as "coming to terms with," but it also means working through, working up, or working off the past (1986, 116). With regard to the traumatic past this term marks a highly contested terrain of individual and group memory. In chapters 3 and 5, I examined the German Autumn of 1977 and the Historians' Debate, as both these events exhibit typical resistances to a hypocritically mourned or unmourned trauma stemming from the disastrous German past. If only the disastrous past could be eliminated from memory, if only victims could forgive or forget injuries, if only accounts could be settled (cf. EV and EAS)! Then the *Aufarbeitung* would be free from all present ambiguities and shame! Yet the ghosts of the Nazi past cast shadows and thereby conjure up the reality that revisits the present from our future. Adorno intensifies the image of haunting ghosts by suggesting that they beget something so monstrous that it is unable to "die off" (1986, 116) with their own death. The inability to die off with one's own death Kierkegaard (1980b) names despair or (as in his book title) the sickness unto death. The ghostly immortality punctuated by hell: in it ghosts live on as waking nightmares.

Adorno sharpens his pen against the social neuroses in which social groups defend the false memory suffused with frightening forgetting. This strategic destruction of truthful historical memory secures its achievement of willed ignorance; it is never a result of an accident. "The murdered are to be cheated even out of the one thing that our powerlessness can grant them: remembrance" (Adorno 1986, 117). That self-chosen immaturity relies on two related lies that one tells oneself and others. One lie assumes that reeducation of the complicitous generation through critically examining the received traditions could destroy the possibility of recovering one's national identity. The other lie suggests that Germans "aren't yet ready for democracy" (119). Through the Enlightenment-Kantian lenses, we already observed Habermas standing in the midst of the Historians' Debate, wherein he adopted the attitude, at some distance from his skeptical generation, as a critical social theorist bearing witness to the past disaster. If 1945 is reinterpreted later as a defeat or an interruption of the desired national continuity, then that year can never secure a responsible beginning. Adorno anticipates these nationalist revivals and historical revisions: "Insofar as the madness of nationalism manifests itself openly today in the reasonable fear of renewed catastrophes, to that extent is its diffusion promoted. Madness is the substitute for the dream that humanity could organize its world humanely" (124). As an antidote to self-chosen group madness, Adorno seeks an education for liberation in "a democratic pedagogy" (125).

Habermas makes the capacity for critical learning from history into the cornerstone for any future of democracy. This trust in learning empowers his approach with considerable strength and optimistic energy. Let me refresh my account with his more recent formulations. In his central post-1989 essay, "The Past as Future" (VaZ, chap. 3), Habermas affirms, against contemporary historical revisionists, the revolutionary contribution of the '68ers to democratizing the postwar Federal Republic of Germany:

> Even though this [W. German] republic owes its comparatively liberal climate to the broad change of attitudes set in motion by the student revolt of 1968, here's how the commentary of the generation of '68ers now reads: "History outfoxed them—and voted them out.... Their legacy will not be carried out. It has sunk out of view, opening up the vista—of that younger generation molded by the experiences of 1989 and 1990." (VaZ 85/63)[1]

The chapter title, "The Past as Future," comes from a West German election campaign slogan of the 1950s. Habermas employs it ironically after 1989. This irony in the service of critical pedagogy is to keep the repressed ghosts of the false German continuities at bay. "The futurity of the past could have been worked through with a self-aware creation of a constitution. Instead, the future is being perceived in the form of the past: 'let's get it over with, just as we did once before!'" (VaZ 89/66; there is no inner citation in the German original). Habermas distinguishes between *two kinds of future*: the future as a replica of the (repressed, traumatic) past and the future attained by a critically "worked through" past. The former future builds on repressing of the present: "the revisionist view of the world" engenders "the domination of the past over the future" (VaZ, afterword, 163). The latter future welcomes an unrepressed present through Adorno's admonition to critically work through the disastrous past: "Enlightenment about what happened in the past must work, above all, against a forgetfulness that too easily goes with and justifies what is forgotten" (Adorno 1986, 125).

Habermas' evolving skeptical integration of 1968 (the revolutionary core of the revolting generation) with 1945 (the democratic needs of the securing generation) not only defines my central thesis about his profile. It also achieves a crystal clear, indeed a prophetically beautiful, quality on the eve of the fiftieth anniversary of the Nazi surrender: "My thesis is that the Federal Republic has become politically civilized only to the degree that the obstacles to our perception of a heretofore unthinkable breach in civilization have been swept away. We had to learn to publicly confront a traumatic past." It is *here and now*, on May 7, 1995, at Frankfurt's Paulskirche, that Habermas both defines and situates his *contemporary post-1989 beginnings*. The title of his lecture encapsulates the world-historical instant that coincides with his existence, philosophy, and politics: "1989 in the Shadow of 1945" (NBR 170/164).

How can Auschwitz and radical democracy share the same historical present? Juxtaposing the Holocaust (*the* disaster) and democracy can acquire neither a religiously transcendent sense (as in the Easter *Exultet* where Adam's original sin is paradoxically welcome as necessary to deliver the Savior to the human race) nor a Kantian-transcendental sense (as the condition of the possibility of democratic Germany). Such interpretations of the Holocaust, and such formation of the Holocaust identity (Müller 2000, 44f., 143), would be as shamelessly indecent as any outright revisionism already is. Habermas' critical reflection on the historical present lies between facts and norms (FuG). "That a liberal political culture could develop in a culturally highly civilized society such as Germany only *after* Auschwitz is a truth difficult to grasp. The fact that it developed *because* of Auschwitz, because of reflection on the incomprehensible, is less difficult to understand if one considers what human rights and democracy mean at heart." In the democratic pedagogy of the oppressed, *we* learn to include everyone in her or his uniqueness in the human and "political community" (NBR 170/164).

If and when *we* learn how to begin, at that moment, May 8, 1945, will come to signify in every subsequent historical present "liberation in the political sense" (NBR 167/161). That momentous event depicts liberation likewise in an existential sense. Both the political and existential dimensions of that emancipatory instant deliver us to Habermas' contemporary beginnings from the hindsight of 1989 upon whose phantom Wall the shadows of 1945 are cast as invisible ghosts. These beginnings define what *coming to terms with the past after 1989 means for Habermas* for whom, too, "this retrospective interpretation resulted from a decades-long learning process" (168/162).

Without having been properly mourned, the disastrous past defines its future presents and gives its actual presents a bad conscience. The millennial (on the Christian calendar) Auschwitz debates indicate new uncertainties about the fragile post-Wall unity. What sort of World War II memorial or Jewish-German museum should be built in Berlin—the restored capital of the unified republic (afterword, in VaZ 157)? What memorial should be created at Buchenwald? Should a new supermarket, instead of a memorial, be built at Ravensbrück? These are two former concentration camps' sites (NBR 26/22). Should German identity in the third millennium still be tied to the history of its Nazi past, and so on?[2] The either/or questions and the issuing existential as well as political struggles for memory, memorials, and countermonuments read as follows: Will traumatic sites serve the future by erasing the memory of defeat in 1945? Will museums construct Auschwitz as a lie (59/53; 9/5)? Will historiography resume with 1989 false continuities, thereby faulty normality? Will memorials of forgetting, and the collective forgetting of memory, support the lie of normality (119–22/114–17)?

During Kohl's tenure in office, from 1982 to 1998, the politics of memory affected not only the ceremonial staging of forgetting, such as Bitburg, but also the architectural incarnations of revisionary history. Kohl's active politics of frenzied unification prolonged Germany's denial of melancholia for the loss of the beloved object (Hitler), as well as Germany's passivity and inability to mourn its loss (Mitscherlich 1975). Kohl's politics of memory was to undo the revolt of the 1960s, itself a delayed resistance against the pro-Nazi parents. He fashioned for his goal alternative forms of mourning through imperfect rituals and ritual sites fostered under his directives. Wiedmer (1999) and J. Young (2000), in their excellent studies of memorial politics in contemporary Germany, analyze crucial struggles over memory sites. Since Habermas mentions three such sites, I will briefly summarize their account of these alone.

In the refurbished East Berlin monument from the nineteenth century, the Neue Wache, Kohl honored on November 14, 1993, all victims of World War II tyranny. Here he achieved his Bitburg after all! He has done so in sync with the revisionist historians of the late 1980s as well as the history of the site. Besides being occupied by Prussian guards and then Nazis, the site served two regimes to memorialize the dead: the dead of World War I (Weimar period) and the dead fallen to Fascism and militarism (East German regime). Kohl placed Käthe Kollwitz's statue of a mother holding her dead son (a rendition of Michelangelo's pietà) as the center symbol of mourning and of unified Germany. Kohl's politics in Bitburg was to level the memorial field between victims and perpetrators; this site and its architectural as well as historical staging both now accomplish just that. Kohl negotiated his way out of the international controversy by promising to the late Ignatz Bubis, then president of the German Jewish community, that he would promote construction of a separate Berlin memorial to the Jewish victims. While Kohl placed at the Neue Wache site a plaque with the group names of various victims, he kept the design of the memorial (Wiedmer 1999, 115–19; J. Young 2000, 186–88; Kinzer 1993). Wiedmer (1999, 120) concedes that, ironically, there is something *true* in Kohl's obsession: "Is the Neue Wache to be read, then, as a disguised memorial to Hitler? This may not be as grotesque as it would sound to the memorial's sponsors, for just such a mourning has been called for, after all, by no lesser authorities than the Mitscherlichs, in order to remove the barrier to a full accounting by the German people of the damage done by that same absent father."

Daniel Libeskind's Jewish Museum Extension to the Berlin Museum has a long history of struggle over the design of the Jewish memorialization, lasting from the end of the Historians' Debate to 1997. Some of the struggle had to do with the issue whether to build a Jewish history museum or a Jewish extension of a German history museum (125). Libeskind, himself a second-generation child of surviving Polish Jews, reproduced his experience of loss in the museum's architectural conception of the void created by the destruction of Jews. German history would be interpreted and worked through by coming to terms with the loss, not primarily by mourning the victims themselves (131). A Jewish museum would accent Jewish culture, history, and its revival within contemporary Germany, and it would have a special place in the Jewish community (137). Thus the identities of those who construct memorial sites get invested in their very architectural and memorial conceptions and in "what is being mourned." The void experienced within Germany's fragmented identity is not the same as the pain of Jewish victims or survivors. Any identification between the two forms of absences could elevate Germans to the level of memorialization with the victims (139; cf. 138 with reference to La Capra 1994, 46; J. Young 2000, 152–83).

The third controversy surrounds plans to build a memorial for the murdered Jews of Europe, and the debate lasts from about 1988 past Kohl's end of tenure in 1998 to Schröder's approval of the memorial on June 25, 1999, "by a [Bundestag's] vote of 314 to 209, with 14 abstentions" (J. Young 2000, 222; cf. Wise 1999). Yad Vashem in Israel and the U.S. Holocaust Memorial Museum in Washington, D.C., would be the parallel models, though how to mourn Jewish dead in Germany has been far from obvious (Wiedmer 1999, 142). Discussion ensued whether it would be sensible to have a Holocaust memorial solely to the Jewish victims anywhere else but in Israel and whether or not other targeted groups—Sinti and Roma, Slavs, homosexuals, Jehovah's Witnesses, and disabled—should be also included (140–45). After the fall of the Berlin Wall, the memorial site was selected at the Potsdamer Platz, later at the Ministergärten in Berlin. Yet the controversy continued, with Ignatz Bubis pressing for a Jewish memorial site, where "rabbis and cantors could say kaddish [prayer for the dead] unobstructed" (147), hence it had to be separated from other memorials. With skinhead attacks on Roma and foreigners erupting all over Germany, Kohl decided to have two memorials built, one to

Jewish victims and one to Sinti and Roma (148). Objections were mounted against the idea by those who saw in it a reproduction of the Nazi labeling of various groups by symbolic triangles of different colors and shapes. There were two competitions for the monument in 1995 and 1997: the result of the first, a monumental tombstone-like design, was scrapped by Kohl who found it too big and not representative of all the disagreeing groups. So he ordered a brief period for reflection instead (159). The second competition was preceded by three colloquia about the meaning, site, and iconography of the proposed memorial. It was agreed that the project would be realized by January 27, 1999, the anniversary of the liberation of Auschwitz (160; J. Young 2000, 192), although that plan will not materialize before 2003. The most revealing, Wiedmer notes, was the calming effect of one of the presenters at the third colloquium, James E. Young (191–99), who broached the unspoken truth of "the universal difficulty of finding the appropriate form of mourning" (Wiedmer 1999, 161). The controversies about memory and commemoration themselves should be viewed as part of the larger mourning process, a countermonument or a vanishing monument (J. Young 2000, 90–151, 194). The winning project of the second competition, chosen by Kohl right before his electoral loss to Schröder, came from Peter Eisenman and Richard Serra. There was lingering dissatisfaction with all the finalists and serious skepticism about building the monument at all. Neither Schröder nor Michael Naumann, his new cultural minister, liked the design of the Field of Graves (161f.; see the photo on the back cover of Müller 2000; J. Young 2000, 211; typical is Augstein's [1998, 33] objection to Eisenman's "American aesthetic design" as a dictate to sovereign Germany of the memorial site, which will be in the future a "gathering point for the hooligans of all sorts in Berlin").

By the time Schröder and Fischer represent the "state reason of the '68er generation," the mood is "to end the Holocaust debate in the year 2000" as part of the normalization of the grown-up nation (Ertel et al. 1998, 31). The new Red-Green coalition now continues Kohl's politics of memory by other, social democratic, means. As Mohr (1998) drives home, not just Martin Walser, who in his speech at Frankfurt's Paulskirche on October 11, 1998, calls the winning proposal for the Berlin memorial "a big football field nightmare" (42), but also these former '68ers sound surprisingly like the revisionist historians. This is "the inverted world" in which the '68ers use the "conservative-patriotic vocabulary" to institutionally fund (liberate for the second time?) the new Berlin Republic. Thus Fischer longs for a Holocaust monument that "one would be glad to enter." He defends Germany's corporate interests against the "'unjustifiable' and at the same time globalized claims by the former concentration camp laborers," and with Schröder he tells Bill Clinton that "Germans are [now] normal people," a normal society just like any other. Germany has the "self-consciousness of a grown-up nation" (40f., 48). To all this, Bubis (1998, 50, 52) has but three things to say: (1) "Which visitor of Berlin does not go to the Neue Wache [memorial]?" (2) "I get shivers going down my spine" and "this appears to be a piece of [Schröder's and Fischer's] normality" when "the Memorial to the Holocaust must be such a place where one would be glad to enter"; and (3) "The end of the Holocaust debate will come [not as the new normalizers wish, in 2000, but] in the year 2030, when even the youngest survivors die." The revised design from June 1998, called Eisenman II (without Serra) and accepted a year later by the Bundestag, envisions a field of pillars (reduced from about four thousand to three thousand) and a small information center (J. Young 2000, 210–23).

In a telling footnote to the Holocaust memorial controversy, Habermas shifts the debate from "a purely aesthetic argument" to publicly performed existential self-choice (i.e., his political and discursive equivalent to antiredemptory countermonuments). He draws this distinction between an aesthetic drift and an existential ethic of an either/or self-choice from Kierkegaard.[3] The issue is not so much whether or not the World War II memorial built in Germany should include "the Christian (!) gestures of the Kollwitz Madonna" or remain an abstract, "inscriptionless" art that would remember generically all and offend none, Habermas reflects. "The real question—why the Holocaust memorial is in Washington [and Yad Vashem in Israel] and not Berlin—is utterly lost sight of." To examine "the political language" for such a memorial—in Germany—requires critical honesty. Germany's courage to create a memorial to the victims of the Holocaust, not a public lie, cannot be achieved without working off its monstrous past. Germany does not seem to have grown up from its catastrophe, not yet. Habermas' praxis of *anamnestic* solidarity with the victims of history and redemptive hope for another than this unjust world embraces an antiredemptory (i.e., disconsolate) countermonumentality in his Critical Theory:

> Only from the distance of a universalistic perspective—in the face of God, if such a formulation is permitted in a postreligious society—would the political-moral differences between culprits and victims, between "victims" of one kind or another, between the war dead and the resistance fighters, between the murderers, the collaborators, and the murdered, be indifferent.

Habermas concedes certain Jewish claims to have the Holocaust memorial built for Jewish victims alone: *"Only the state of Israel can memorialize its victims unambiguously"* (afterword, in VaZ 157; all citations above; italics added). But for all its manifest truth, even his sympathy with the Jewish survivors' need to honor their dead can provide a false alibi for failing to remember the victims of history unambiguously by Germans in Germany. J. Young's (2000, 191) words from March 1995 echo the core of Habermas' lifework sketched and chizeled by the strokes of a discursive countermonument: "Better a thousand years of Holocaust memorial competitions and exhibitions in Germany than any single 'final solution' to Germany's memorial problem.... Instead of a fixed icon for Holocaust memory in Germany, the debate itself—perpetually unresolved amid ever-changing conditions—might now be enshrined."

Wiedmer (1999) illustrates in one example how an unambiguous countermonumental memorialization in Germany can happen.[4] This is in an existing site at Berlin's Bavarian Quarter, which used to be a "Jewish Switzerland," boasting 16,261 distinguished Jewish residents during the 1920s. After the November 9, 1938, *Kristallnacht* pogrom, Jews were increasingly restricted, robbed of their houses, ghettoized, and finally deported to death camps. As Wiedmer notes, this process "has assumed the face of normality" (105). In the 1980s, new information about the extent of Aryanization of the quarter prompted the district council to create a memorial. From an initial idea of the working group for this memorial, in April 1992 the winning proposal for a decentralized memorial came forth from Renata Stih and Frieder Schonk. "Their concept, an installation consisting of eighty signs bearing stylized images on one side and inscriptions of Nazi laws and decrees on the other, incorporates these basic ideas into a memorial that re-creates on *a linguistic and pictorial level* the political violence that had characterized everyday life" (107; italics added; see 108f., 112 for the photos). I emphasize the linguistic and pictorial aspects of the struggle for genuine mourning and remembrance because they resonate with Habermas' interventions against normalization lies of postwar and post-Wall Germany, which are at once more abstract and more directly political. Stih and Schonk's memorial, composed of "sign language" (110), performs subversively against the accepted linguistic normalization and it does so on an existential level of everyday city life.

> The role of *Mitläufer* [fellow traveler] then literally unfolds as one walks along the memory lines created by the memorial. Realization of the extent of *Mitläufertum* among the former inhabitants of the quarter leads naturally to the question of what one's reaction might have been had one lived during that time, and finally of what one's reaction might be to the xenophobia potential in Germany today. (113; see photos in J. Young 2000, 112–16)

HABERMAS' LEARNING BY DISASTER AFTER THE WALL CAME DOWN

> Do we have to revise our understanding of the rupture of 1945 in the light of the events of 1989–1990? Or was it after all in vain that an abysmal irony of history lent a highly ambivalent meaning to the date 9 November, which continues to be remembered here in the Paulskirche as the anniversary of the night of the (*Kristallnacht*) pogrom? Does 1989 remain for us Germans in the shadow of 1945—for the time being—because it is only in light of the latter peripeteia that we can clearly understand the future of our political existence? (May 7, 1995, in NBR 171/165)

In taking up Adorno's questioning concerning the disastrous past, Habermas' twentieth-century philosophical-political profile becomes punctuated by four major post-Wall historical presents and his four corresponding interventions in them:

- October 3, 1990, the unification of Germany
- January 16–March 3, 1991, the Persian Gulf War
- August 1991–July 1993, the asylum debate and "a Second 'German Autumn'"
- March 24–June 20, 1999, NATO military intervention against Serbia (bombing suspended on June 10)

Habermas develops his core reflections on the first two events in 1990 (volume 7 of his small political writings, NR, sections 5–6) and between summer 1990 and March 1991 (the mail interview by Michael Haller, VaZ). He takes on the third series of events in three essays from 1992 to 1994 (FE = SR, the last two essays added to Haller's interviews only in the English translation of VaZ 121–65; cf. ZLB published in 1992) and further in his 1995 collection on Germany (NBR). The fourth event enters in his pivotal 1999 newspaper essay (BH; cf. Z for his response to objections from Peter Handke). The last decade of the twentieth century, the period of these four historical presents, is transformed by an ongoing drive to economic, political, and multicultural integration of Europe—what Habermas identifies as *Europe's second chance* (cf. VaZ and essays on the postnational constellation in PK; also EgA). What does this learning mean today *for Habermas*? The four post-Wall situations dramatize new possibilities for the self-corrective process of learning and learning by disaster to boot. I end my study in chapter 9 with two events that fall roughly within the period of NATO bombing: Habermas' March 31, 1999, reflections on the proposed Berlin memorial for the Jewish victims of the Holocaust and his indirect intervention against Peter Sloterdijk, who in July 1999 argues at Elmau for the genetic engineering of humans. I save this final discussion for my epilogue on discontents of 'Fascism'.

Re/Unification of Germany

I come from a small protestant corner of Rhein-Preußen, very far from Berlin. My family had no relatives over in the East. . . . On the other hand, I lived my first fifteen years in the German—indeed the "Great German"—*Reich*. That is why the events since 9 November 1989 are still able to awaken personal memories. . . . Most importantly . . . the demise of the GDR [East Germany] stirs up *other* pasts, whether we have personal memories of the prehistory or not, including pasts that ought not to serve as models for the future, pasts that shouldn't regain any power over the present. (VaZ 47–50/34–37)

Only two weeks after the November 9, 1989, opening of the Berlin Wall, Habermas (in then unpublished notes circulated among his friends) warns about the side effects of a hasty 'reunification' (NR 162, November 23, 1989). In his essay (DM) from the following March, he comes out in full force against the economic and political colonization of the East German territories. In May 1990, the economic treaty financially unifies two Germanies by establishing a 1-to-1 exchange rate between their two currencies. The economic union takes place in July. The final accounting for World War II transpires on September 12 among the two German states and the four victorious powers: France, Great Britain, the Soviet Union, and the United States. The terms of this 4 + 2 agreement (a de facto procedural version of Adorno's coming to terms with the past) paves the way for the political unification of Germanies, to be realized on October 3. New parliamentary elections are still held in East German states in October and again in all of "new" Germany in December of 1990. These December elections supervene on the October ones in the East: the July DM-colonization is followed by the October political annexation.[5]

I have already discussed the Bitburg debacle, which punctuated the fortieth anniversary of the Nazi defeat. That is one of those occasions when Habermas echoes Adorno ([1959] 1986), complaining that the revisionist 'defusing' *(Entsorgung)* replaces genuine 'coming to terms with' *(Aufarbeitung)* the past. It is worth recalling how Habermas' *profile* embodies his learning from history. We witness his twofold performative intervention:[6] first, by critically appropriating, in an immanent critique of the revisionist returns to normality, and, second, by publicly rejecting the false German continuities misremembered in the May events of 1945. On the first front, he cites Hermann Lübbe against Lübbe's intentions: Lübbe decries the '68ers for destroying Germany's historical healing and stability and for thereby opening the scars of the Nazi past; and Habermas cites him while approving exactly the opposite. On the second front, Habermas exposes the former chancellor Kohl's learning from history as a charade. In this unmasking of 1985, Kohl learned nothing from history, his claims to the contrary notwithstanding (EV 261/43).

I have been arguing that Habermas integrates the constitutional needs of 1945 with the revolutionary core of 1968. He critically appropriates traditions through their existential examination, and he positively rejects the 'normal' continuities established with the pernicious past. From the observation deck of 1998, he can afford softening his earlier criticism of Kohl. Kohl achieves *re*-unification of Germany, but he is also voted out. The key here is, Habermas claims, that

> Kohl achieved something else against his own intentions. The failure of his original talk of "a spiritual-moral change" acted as something of a litmus test. Once Kohl in office found that he could no longer do what he wanted at Verdun or Bitburg, or elsewhere, it was clear that the country has become a liberal society. (EgA 12/4)

Perhaps a mature political culture can be attributed more to the institutionalized democracy of Kohl's post-Wall Germany than to the feelings surrounding the unification itself (NR 157ff.). Democratic ideals represent in reality Habermas' critical utopianism—his hope for himself and his fellow citizens. Oddly, he identifies with Kohl: "People of my age also recognize Kohl as one of their own generation" (EgA 12/4). They are the more pragmatic and more skeptical in-between generation of the '58ers (neither the obfuscating generation of 1945 nor the hot-headed '68ers; NBR 84/80). They are characterized by the visceral aversion to any nationalist elitism, to all returns of the repressed forces of the pre-1945 ghosts (EgA 15/11).

When Habermas discusses the early uncritical drive for German unification, he has two primary concerns. First, he objects that West Germany's colonization of East Germany, although it was initially greeted by the DM-nationalism of East Germans,[7] jeopardizes the chances for sustaining genuine democratic political culture. Second, he worries that post-Wall German nationalism is built on a false sense of normality. On the one hand, it is symbolized by the shift from Bonn to Berlin and, on the other hand, it is supported by the new post-1989 defusion of May 8, 1945, beginnings. The ongoing debates about how Auschwitz should figure in the memorial to the victims of the Holocaust or in the Berlin museum are symptomatic of these new uncertainties about the fragile unified future. The past motivates the future; the repressed past remains this future's ghostly shadow.

Procedurally, the unification of Germanies bypassed the need for democratic consensus that would involve the citizens of both German states. According to Article 23 of the Basic Law of the FRG, East Germany can be directly incorporated (in the same manner East Germans who before the unification fled to West Germany were automatically citizens of the Federal Republic). According to Article 146 of the Basic Law of the FRG the unification would require a formal reconstitution of a new German state. In the first scenario, eastern German territories are annexed into an existing political entity without any need for a collective formation of meaning and will. In the second one, the two states end (hence also the Basic Law of West Germany is modified), and a unified state emerges in a constitutional convention, marking new collective beginnings. The latter scenario requires that a new constitution is supported by the entire German citizenry, East and West; the former one disregards East Germans and their self-determination.

The metaphor of *the past as future* becomes literally true of unified Germany since East Germans were not given any chance for a direct vote to constitute their political future. The latter option would have meant, on the contrary, that

> the will of the voting public is given precedence over an annexation cleverly initiated but in the final analysis carried through only at the administrative level—an annexation which dishonestly evades one of the essential conditions for the founding of any nation of state citizens: *the public act of a carefully considered democratic decision* taken in both parts of Germany. This act of foundation can only be carried out consciously and intentionally if we agree not to accomplish unifica-

tion via Art. 23 (which foresees the entry of "other parts of Germany") of our Basic Law. (NR 216; italics added)

The normative deficits of unification (see VaZ, chap. 2) are not offset by the eastward march of the deutsche mark. Perhaps someone could sketch a satirical portrait of the new DM-nationalism, Habermas suggests (NR 205). But it is the drive for the DM-empire that raises the real worry (210, 215). While overnight East Germany's savings and salaries are converted into West German currency, the richer western Germany retains the economic power and the salary base to buy goods and property in the new eastern provinces. To the equal (1:1) value of the currency union between East and West Mark corresponds neither political nor economic equality.

Would the shift from Bonn to Berlin as the capital of Germany symbolize new democratic beginnings or a resumption of the past as future? What would be the normality of this Berlin Republic (NBR)? We can notice now that Article 23 privileges the nationalistic interpretation of unification, while Article 146 foregrounds the constitutional rather than ethnic or cultural grounding of the state. The unification that takes place according to the first scenario comes to build the false sense of normality: it is rendered as a *re*-unification. From the observation deck of the crumbling Berlin Wall, annexing East Germany, without reconstituting the new German state, leads to the post-1989 defusion of the beginnings inherited from May 8, 1945. Kohl started this process in Bitburg and continued it through the post-Wall era. With Berlin as the symbol of this process, no wonder Kohl is sometimes compared to Bismarck.[8]

Unwittingly 1989 arrives in the shadow of 1945. The birth of the new millennium cannot step over its birth shadow. Habermas' existentially motivated philosophical and political birthday, on May 8, 1945, determines how he experiences, evaluates, and intervenes in the birth of unified Germany. He carries on his role of that Critical Theorist who becomes a postwar second-generation witness to the Holocaust. Says Habermas,

> Auschwitz can and should remind Germans, regardless of which state territory they may ever settle themselves ... that they cannot rely on the continuities of their history. With that monstrous break of continuity Germans have lost the possibility of grounding their political identity on anything else than the universalistic principles of state citizenship, in whose light the national traditions cannot be appropriated unreflectively but only critically and self-critically. (NR 219f.)

Identity secured in this posttraditional and postnational manner assumes a critical and discursive *mode* of one's allegiance to an examined political culture. Identity is not a permanent substance made of mythical origins (220).[9]

When Habermas invokes "the Hades of the nineteenth century" to describe those "*other* pasts" or the *past as the future* (VaZ 110f./83f.) of nationalism, anti-Semitism, and ethnocentrism, he does not merely take poetic license to characterize the post-1989 realities. His philosophical-political beginnings and situations define his profile and present interventions. Thus he conjoins his beginnings at fifteen in 1945 with the end of the twentieth century in 1989 (LD 71/310).

Of significance is Habermas' existentially inflected critique of any return to that "special consciousness" or that special way *(Sonderweg)* of greater Germany designated as the heart of Europe between the squeeze from west and east ("The Asylum Debate," in VaZ 134, 137, 140; afterword, in VaZ 161). Geographically, Central Europe does not lie in Germany but in the region that Germany coveted as well as dominated economically and culturally—Bohemia and Moravia. The *Sonderweg* already requires redrawing that map by the *Anschluß* (annexation) of Slavic and Jewish Central Europe. Symbolically, "the fairy-tale 'special path' hypothesis" (140) relies on a Big Lie. In fact, there were two Big Lies that Germans told themselves.

> *Big Lies are pathologies that stabilize themselves through their own existential usefulness.* During the Adenauer era, the Big Lie that we all had to deal with was issued from on high: "we're all democrats here." The Federal Republic needed a very long time to get over this. It took a youth revolt to free the Federal Republic from the devastating sociopsychological effects of this self-deception. If there really is a second Big Lie that has emerged since 1989, it's far more the lie that "we have finally become normal again." ("The Asylum Debate," in VaZ 136f.; italics added; cf. ZLB; NBR 161/156)

In an existential reversal of this special German version of the Platonic myth of the metals (Noble Lie),[10] Habermas harnesses the revolt of the '68ers to correct for the two (democratic and normalization) Lies of the '45ers. In his single intervention, he exposes the German political existentialists of the 1930s (ZLB) and contemporary historical revisions (the German Autumns of 1977 and 1983, the Historians' Debate of 1985–1987, the post-Wall era, 1989–). He is skeptical that there will be a second 1968 to awake unified Germany from its second Big Lie (last paragraph in ZLB).

Habermas' critical utopianism is shot through with a historical skepticism all but typical for his generation. It is understandable that he would seek to radically democratize the integration of the two watershed experiences of 1968 and 1945: the revolutionary questioning with democratic procedures. He identifies the nationalist myths that define modern states as nourishing the German Lie of achieved normality. He explains the rise of nationalist warfare by "the dominion of the past over the future." Beyond the "fictive unities" of nation-states and against the national maps drawn in *our* century, not by pen but by guns and ethnic cleansing, he embraces the multicultural model of political culture (afterword, in VaZ 163f.). This model requires minimally two achievements: first, the creation of a critical political culture and, second, "the creation of more complex unities through the simultaneous democratization of existing political institutions" (165). Again, we come to terms with the past by deciding which part of *our* past *we* shall continue and which *we* must jettison even while remembering it. And *we* may fashion the post-1989 era by working through the shadows of unmourned 1945, as these are symbolized by the either/or debates and by the radically democratic politics of memory.

The Persian Gulf War

> The Gulf War was at best a kind of hybrid. It wasn't carried out under the command of the United Nations.... And yet the Allies claimed the legitimation of the UN until the end. In theory, they acted as deputies of the world organization. That's better than nothing.... At least in regard to Israel ... the authorization for military sanctions against Iraq was justified. (VaZ 18, 23/11, 15)

If there are no doubts where Habermas was situated with regard to the historical revisions of the 1970s, 1980s, and 1990s, new questions arise now with his support for the two interventionist wars waged by the NATO alliance—the Persian Gulf War and the war over Kosovo/a.[11] I will return to both these events in a more critical vein in Part Three. Here I want to explain how his stance on the Persian Gulf War at the time of the interventions cannot be separated from his own beginnings: his evaluation of the Persian Gulf War (just as was Horkheimer's and Adorno's view of anti-NATO and anti–Vietnam War demonstrations in the 1950s and 1960s) is tied to Germany's postwar relation to the victorious Allies in 1945. Furthermore, his view makes sense in light of supporting (again with Horkheimer and Adorno) the FRG's westward orientation after 1945. Finally, he assumes consciously the debt of his unified country toward the Jewish victims of the Holocaust and, insofar as the memory of the victims can be passed on, toward the modern state of Israel. His conclusion from the discussion about the Berlin Holocaust memorial bears repeating: "Only the state of Israel can memorialize its victims unambiguously" (afterword, in VaZ 157).

Habermas appropriates the 'critical pedagogics' developed by Horkheimer and Adorno in the IfS during the 1950s–1960s as their contribution to the institutional and partly intellectual grounding of the FRG. Habermas' work takes over their three core founding values: democratization, west orientation, and reeducation (reflection on the past). He places much greater accents on the first two values as the key to the third one. By contrast, Adorno prevails over Horkheimer's concern for the first two values and emphasizes the third value. For Adorno, a new democratic republic is not founded once through its institutions but must be founded permanently. His view of revolutionary permanence does not lie in a constitutionally guaranteed democratic process or in a legal order alone, as this increasingly becomes so for Habermas, but in a permanently internalized, morally singular reflection or "critical intelligence" regarding the catastrophic past (Albrecht et al. 1999, 446f.; tab. 1.2).

As Habermas moves closer to Horkheimer's affirmative position and further from Adorno's negating skepsis, he is more prone to defend the U.S. and western Allied positions; more trusting of democratic institutions and legal procedures alone; and less willing to scrutinize the past by way of challenging the presumed innocence of western democracy and his participation in it. I will return to this in chapter 8.

If May 8, 1945, emerges out of the vanishing point of that traumatic past from which Habermas works through the Nazi legacy of his native country, then coming out against the Allies in 1991—as he did during the anti-NATO peace marches in 1957–1959 and 1981–1983 and against the Vietnam War in May 1966—would represent an obstacle. The Persian Gulf War is orchestrated in 1991 by the same victorious powers, except the Russian Federation, which defeated Germany in 1945. Moreover, the assault on Iraq is sanctioned by the United Nations. This international order, in Habermas' estimation, is built on the Kantian-Hegelian promise to embody Enlightenment courage, to become a mature civilization, to safeguard the self-determining moral point of view, and to institutionalize democratic procedures. That promise emerged in the aftermath of the disaster of World War II. The very existence of the UN represents, Habermas insists, one key global learning by disaster. Opposition to the Allies coming from the unified German soil would link (albeit unwittingly) 1991 to 1945, but in a revisionary historical narrative. Recall that right-wing historians such as Nolte would exploit such opposition to the Allies for revising the Nazi past. Opposing the Allies in 1991 would launch Germany back on its special path *(Sonderweg)*, recalling 1945 as defeat rather than liberation, turning Germany's westward orientation back to its Central European arrogance. Opting for *postnational political culture and democratic institutions*, Habermas sides with the allied west, and in 1991 he (quite consistently with this line of his profile but in contrast to his positions in 1957–1959, 1966, and 1981–1983) supports the intervention against Iraq.

Objections to Habermas' support for the Persian Gulf War must take into account the critical nuance in his position, lest we grossly misread him. He brings his vintage ambivalence into his expressed endorsement of the UN legitimation of this war. We must not lose sight of the fact that, in the aftermath of an extremely violent campaign against Iraq, his hesitation grows into expressed criticisms of the Allies. Yet even his ambivalence yields to an unequivocal support for the Allied intervention when the fundamental situation becomes linked to the fate of Israel. We must weigh the pros and cons regarding this position in the post-1945 terrain in which his philosophical-political profile gestates over a long period of time.

Habermas is not naive insofar as he is cognizant that the UN as we know it neither represents Kant's perpetual peace nor the Hegelian-Marxian institutionalization of radical democracy. The UN Security Council is in need of democratic reforms. As it stands, its membership replicates the arrogance of the dominant division of power in the present international order. The UN reality does not meet the ideal. The integration of an Enlightenment league of nations (Kant's regulative moral ideal) with a radically democratic institutionalization of this ideal (the Hegelian-Marxian political requirement) marks the core of Habermas' position from which he judges the imperfect reality in light of critical ideality (VaZ 17/10; 29/20; 32f./22).

We can explain his ambivalent yes-and-no position when it comes to the Persian Gulf War:

- "The Gulf War was at best a kind of hybrid. It wasn't carried out under the command of the United Nations. . . . And yet the Allies claimed the legitimation of the UN until the end" (VaZ 18/11). "The allies' military intervention in the Persian Gulf lay somewhere in the gray area between these two sides. It was carried out under the authorization of the UN, but under American command." (afterword, in VaZ 145)
- The UN legitimation, imperfect as it is, contains the seeds of a more rational ordering of the human affairs: "One can at least *appeal* to the norms that the superpowers invoked." (VaZ 20/12)
- "To try to make the best of the Gulf War" (18/11) means to foster the evolution of the conditions of the possibility of perpetual peace and of the requisite democratic institutions.
- "Surely, everyone today is in agreement that the idea of a just and peaceful cosmopolitan order lacks any historical and philosophical support. *But what other choice do we have, besides at least striving for its realization?* . . . The institutions of the UN, and the basic principle of international law expressed in the UN charter, embody what Hegel would have called a piece of 'existential reason'—a small portion of the idea that Kant had already clearly formulated two hundred years ago." (32f./22; italics added)

In reality the war was carried out by states and in a manner not accountable to the UN; nonetheless, the appeal to the normative horizon of legitimation draws a margin of sanity, Habermas reasons, for the future, when a more rational settling of human affairs can get its chance. This perpetual peace "is no longer merely a vague ideal." (Habermas sounds more poetic in German: "Sie schwebt nicht mehr bloß über den Wassern.") Normative implications arise from appealing to this discursive-democratic legitimation, however ideological and calculating such appeals to the UN by military powers may otherwise be. The more *we* render these very appeals "politically convincing," the more they become in the actual institutional performance "a piece of [*our*] reality" (33/22).

Contrary to a simplistic condemnation of Habermas, I hold out for a differentiated account of this thinker who tries to distill something out of a hopeless situation. In the Persian Gulf War, too, Habermas is learning by disaster: our international institutions, their (ab)uses, and the powers that be all indicate that we are very far from achieving a cosmopolitan world community, but *what other choices do we have, besides at least striving for its realization?* This retort is a true-to-reality portrait of a skeptical and yet pragmatic Habermas par excellence. What and where else can we go, what other either/or choices can we present to ourselves short of annihilation, what is the vanishing point of our future learning—except appealing to a democratic legitimation order and a cosmopolitan political culture in which we may evaluate the future of our traditions? These questions encapsulate, I think best, Habermas' way of dealing with any such objections.[12]

Habermas does not give himself or his compatriots any choice in one crucial instance: Israel coming under threat of a Scud missile attack by Saddam Hussein, with the warheads carrying deadly chemical gas produced by West German companies. With the historical record of Nazis using poisonous gas in the process of exterminating 6 million Jews, Habermas adamantly defends the Allied intervention against the prospect that Iraq would attack Israel with German-made lethal chemicals:

> Nobody can seriously doubt that Iraq's annexation of Kuwait and its announcement of its intention to open a war with Israel, even a war with nuclear, biological, or chemical weapons, constituted an injury to international law. (VaZ 19/12) . . . But I think that, at least in regard to Israel—that is the nightmare scenario of an Israel encircled by the entire Arab world and threatened with the most terrific kinds of weapon—the authorization for military sanctions against Iraq was justified. (23/15)

Regardless whether or not this is a defensible argument—and one would have some difficulty in applying it to the relation of Israel to the Palestinian struggle in the occupied territories—Habermas' position becomes consistent and intelligible from within his philosophical-political trajectory. My self-limiting task at present is to understand and elucidate how his profile and interventions are formed in response to his key situations. Why in the Persian Gulf War and not in 1957–1959 or 1981–1983, he learns this and not a radical pacifists' lesson from coming to terms with his past? Why is he inclined to support the *actual* extreme levels of the state monopoly on *violence and killing* in this (and Kosovo/a) case, but he defends state institutions and gradual reformism against the nonconformist *threat of violence* by the students in the 1960s, who were throwing at best rotten tomatoes and at worst street stones?

Historical revisionists want to rehabilitate the normality of Germany by rehabilitating its prewar special path in fighting Stalin. This revision would link the German pre-1945 past with certain Cold War aspirations of western Allies. For Habermas after 1945, witnessing to the memory of the victims of the Holocaust provides a caesura for making right judgments. "It's a matter of moral self-understanding, of remaining alert to the sensibility for incomparable injuries that are bequeathed to the next generation, and the one after that. And this means simply that these special duties ought to remain recognizable in the rational foundation of sober political judgments" (37/26). Even here Habermas applies to his German situation the nuance of his yes-and-no position on the Allied Persian Gulf War. Against the relief of Bitburg he worries that "the Gulf War serves as a catalyst for this reversal [to that special German path]." How could the Gulf War erase the traumatic German past? In some sense similarly as it did for George Bush and the U.S. trauma from the lost Vietnam War: if Germany could participate in some war on the side of the Allied forces, where Kohl's and historical revisionists situated Germany as a bulwark against the Asiatic barbarism, this would allow "for launching Greater Germany on the course toward a 'normalization' that will finally free us [Habermas identifies with Germany] from the trauma of mass crimes and give us back our national innocence" (42/29).

Consider this reversed plot: revisionists argue that it is the peace movement, not them, that seeks *a new special path* for Germany. The reversal of that critical term 'German special consciousness' allows now for an attack on the entire post-1945 democratic learning and even on the skeptical and revolting generations for their healthy postwar aversion to militarism. Habermas steers between pacifism conceived under "the trap of negative nationalism" (what in the United States is called insular protectionism) and the drive for Greater Germany (what Habermas should analyze under the rubric of imperialism) (38/27). 'Special consciousness' before implicated the revisionists; it is now turned upside down by them to discredit democratic consciousness (i.e., learning after 1945)—as "a new German special consciousness" (38, 44/26, 31). The hypocritical revisionist idea is that the grandchildren of the Nazis, siding with the peace movement, ally themselves with "the enemies of democracy for a second time" (44/31). The revisionists side with the Allies as they once did against Stalin and in Bitburg, so would reason the tendentious revisionist calculus.[13]

By adopting a yes-and-no relation to the Persian Gulf War, Habermas dances on a tightrope between false historical continuities and false universalisms. Yet by defending Israel under attack, he actively remembers the Nazi crimes and the Allied defeat of Germany in 1945. This double positioning seems virtually impossible: It was overdetermined in Habermas' fear of violence from the rebelling students, his fear justified, as he thought then, by their presumed lack of revolutionary situation and their presumed disrespect for the postwar democratic gains. It is overdetermined now in his endorsement, albeit reluctant, of George Bush's war, his endorsement justified by the implied normative appeals of the United States toward the legitimation of this war by the United Nations. I will return to this overdetermination of Habermas' profile by his past in Part Three. Suffice it to sum up here what he makes quite clear: to be able to resist the revisionist reversals of history, German identity must be oriented by western (read: democratic, critical, Enlightenment) civilizational values. In his distinction from both the strict pacifist of conviction and the militarist positions alike, he argues that any deployment of Germany's military outside of its borders—whether as peacekeeping units or as an international police force—must be placed under the 'legal pacifism' of the UN umbrella (see BH).

This is how Habermas fine-tunes his post-1989 learning by disaster—by linking the particular historical experience of Germany's catastrophe to the (moral) defense of universal human rights:

- "If after forty-five years the citizens of the Federal Republic are really to have learned something from the catastrophic mistakes of their fathers and grandfathers—and we can only hope for this with bated breath—then they would have made undeserved use of opportunities that themselves are connected with catastrophes and defeats." (VaZ 38f./27)
- "After Hitler and Auschwitz, the Germans have every reason for being particularly sensitive to universalism; that is, for the indivisibility of internationally recognized human rights and for a civilized mode of human interaction. One can take up and reflectively deal with specifically German experiences without ascribing a 'special role' to oneself." (40/28)

The Asylum Debate and a "Second 'German Autumn'"

Anyone who dissolves the connection between the question of political asylum and the question of immigration in flight from poverty is implicitly declaring that he or she wants to evade Europe's moral obligation to refugees from the impoverished regions of the world and is willing to tolerate instead a flow of illegal and uncontrollable immigration that can always be labelled "abuse of asylum" and used for domestic political purposes. (EdA 271/SR 143)

For the Wessies as much as for the Ossies (nicknames for West and East Germans), the *enemy* used to reside on the *other* side of the Berlin Wall. When the borders open after 1989, new waves of Germans arrive from the East and soon thereafter the stronger stream of refugees and immigrants. The *enemy* becomes, once again, the foreigner. In a more cynical manner, with Carl Schmitt, one might suggest that the state needs such an enemy to assure its founding and continued role as a protector. With the Wall tumbling down, the asylum seeker as well as the guest worker supplies this need for an enemy. Who says that the catch-up revolution (NR) takes place in Eastern Europe or the Balkans alone? Habermas knows that in the twentieth century Germany was the leading inventor and perpetrator of ethnic cleansing. Even in democratic Germany, now unified into a new nation-state, those old habits are difficult to unlearn.

During the increasingly violent right-wing attacks on foreigners, the very passivity of the German government, its political leaders, and the mainstream German society on both sides of the old Wall "constitute the phenomenon of a second 'German Autumn'" ("The Asylum Debate," in VaZ 127). The link between the *two autumns* leads from the attack on foreigners (September 1991) back to the German Autumn of 1977, when the Red Army Faction kidnapped and then murdered the head of the German Employers' Federation and one-time SS member, Hanns Martin Schleyer. In 1977, the West German government re-created the police state with an anti-Left "pogrom" atmosphere. In 1991, "the pogrom of Hoyerswerda" (MHFI 24, noted by Adam Michnik) and the benign reaction to it by both the general population and the regime echo that chilling atmosphere from 1977. In unified Germany, a new racist, murderous violence against *foreigners* (i.e., non-*Germans?*) reaches astonishing proportions. Wiedmer (1999, 146f.) lists "more than 1,000 arsons, 3,600 violent attacks on foreigners, 110 instances of cemetery defilement, and 500 cases of injury, to say nothing of 33 deaths, in 1991 and 1992."

The German asylum debate aims at the heart of Article 16 of the FRG's Basic Law from 1949, which states that "persons persecuted on political grounds shall enjoy the right of asylum" (VaZ, English translation, 178 n. 1).[14] The outcome of the debate leads to a drastic restriction of this article. But the controversy itself erupts in the wake of the radical growth of new asylum seekers in the first year after the Berlin Wall comes down—the 59 percent increase. In the second post-Wall year, Germany receives 193,000 applicants for asylum. By August 1991, some politicians call for sealing East German borders to prevent immigration from East-Central Europe. Only a thorough revamping of the quite liberal West German asylum law from 1949 could effectively close the borders to unwanted immigration. In September 1991 in Hoyerswerda a hostel for Vietnamese foreign workers is attacked by skinheads. Neither at the time nor during the following years when attacks occur is there even a "hint of moral outrage, sympathy, or democratic wrath against the return of the attitudes and affects that can only lead to the destruction of a political community" ("The Asylum Debate," in VaZ 126). Instead, in October 1991, a new reformed asylum policy is introduced with two provisions that would list countries free from political persecution (no seeker from these countries would be able to receive an asylum) and the secure third states (the seekers coming overland through the secure states—Czech Republic, Poland, and Austria—would not be allowed to enter Germany). In August 1992, the asylum shelters are burned down in Rostock. Still, there is no government outrage, although Chancellor Kohl worries that Germany's reputation might be damaged abroad (127). In November of the same year, at Mölln, a Turkish woman and two young girls die in their house as a result of a bomb attack by right-wing radicals. The conservative paper, *Frankfurter Allgemeine Zeitung*, only echoes Kohl's worry (see 127). Mass protest marches take place in Berlin and Munich, and in Frankfurt demonstrators gather in a political rock concert (140). Yet in December 1992 all political parties agree on the asylum compromise with the two above restrictions. The seekers from war-torn Yugoslavia are granted some exception from these provisions of the amended asylum law. In May 1993 the Bundestag approves the new asylum compromise, thereby affecting the Basic Law from 1949 with changes from December 1992. In July 1993, this law goes into effect: Article 16 of the Basic Law is now supplemented by a new Article 16a with the two provisions amending the original, more open asylum policy from 1949. Germany's most liberal asylum policies in Europe were an outcome of Germany's most atrocious barbarism in the twentieth century. Did the new asylum policy, instead of dissolving the fiction of an Aryan Germany into a multicultural society of immigrants, reintroduce purity-seeking hysteria as part of a politics of memory?

Habermas' maturing position on questions of political asylum, immigration policy, and multicultural coexistence could be counted (along with his earlier support for antinuclear and peace movements) among the most radically democratic, theoretical, and practical projects he embraced without hesitation during his lifetime. Against the backdrop of the foreigner bashing that resurfaced after 1989, he voices an optimism that the need for the Schmittian "Great Suspicion" of the Leftist "internal enemies of the state" can vanish along with "the bankruptcy of state socialism" and its Wall. "The left, for its part, has become pragmatic." Habermas mirrors here his own one-time wish coming now true (afterword, in VaZ 158).[15] With no global civil war between the Left and the Right on the post-Wall agenda, Habermas argues for a Left-liberal immigration policy. He holds out for a radically multicultural democratic coexistence (164). Both Left-liberal immigration policy (EdA 264–76/SR 135–48) and radical democratic multiculturalism (252–64/122–35) would rely on the possibility of harmonizing the future rights of world citizens with their universal human rights (NBR 155–58/151ff.; cf. xxi).

The radical character of Habermas' contemporary learning from Germany's disaster contains, in my view, two significant dimensions: (1) insight that deception can infect even this public democratic asylum debate *from within* and (2) admission that the politics of asylum cannot be separated from the historical question of economic immiseration.

With regard to a possible *deception within democracy,* Habermas concludes that not only the prior unification of two Germanies but now also the asylum debate proceeds "behind the smoke screen" of deceit. "This deceitful asylum debate" infects, he insists, the practices and judgments of the police, the prosecuting authorities, the courts, army officers, political parties, and the media. The increase in public deliberation only seems to entrench deception. "I can recall no other issue that has been so zealously dragged out and kept alive in the public media and yet, at the same time, has been made so obscure and unrecognizable" ("The Asylum Debate," in VaZ 127; cf. EdA 275/SR 146).

Habermas lists four aspects of "this obscured and obscuring debate." First, the debate introduces "false definitions," such as the misuse of asylum rights. The falsity consists, according to Habermas, in denying that Germany has been a nation of immigrants, that it is increasingly becoming a multicultural society, and that it needs an immigration policy distinct from asylum rights. The asylum compromise neither allows for an immigration policy nor for the naturalization of those guest workers who lived in West Germany for more than a decade ("The Asylum Debate," in VaZ 128). Second, there is a dishonest "politics of information." Although the problem is raised in terms of the growing post-Wall numbers of asylum seekers, Germany admits large numbers of immigrants of German descent. This is because being German is still defined along ethnic-blood lines (German as a *Volksdeutsche*) rather than by a legal, residential, or territorial definition (German as a citizen). Many asylum applicants already live in Germany, either as one-time guest workers or as children of immigrants. These so-called foreigners cannot be deported, but they are not granted citizenship. Third, "what pushes the asylum debate the furthest into the gray area between deception and self-deception is the suggestion that a change in the Basic Law could solve the problem" (129f.). Neither the agreed-on asylum compromise, which modifies the Basic Law, nor "an electronic Maginot Line" at the borders with Eastern Europe can stop immigration. Fourth, the asylum compromise bypasses the immigration and naturalization reform at home and dumps the problem of immigration at the door of the former Iron Curtain and the so-called persecution-free third states that are to function as a buffer (131).

Habermas' insight into the deceptiveness of the asylum debate shows that the post-Wall democracy will not be safe from its traumatic past, unless it learns from it self-reflectively. *He warns of deception in democracy by way of raising an either/or question for the democratic meaning and will formation:*

> Reactions to the reemergence of right-wing radicalism [the so-called second German Autumn]—and in this context, the emergence of the asylum debate as well—raise the question of *whether* the expanded Federal Republic is going to continue on the path toward political civilization, or *whether* it will reintroduce the old special consciousness in a new form. (134; italics added)

In order to render intelligible Habermas' insight that an established democracy is not safe from deception, I reintroduce the possibility of a doubly unspeakable dimension of the past affecting our present theory and practice. While I devote to this topic portion of Part Three and chapter 9 in particular, let me rehearse this notion in the present debate. There is the unspeakable trauma of the victims of history and the unspeakable denial of trauma by perpetrators of violence and bystanders. As to the trauma of victims, the plight of the guest workers should remind the contemporaries that German Jews were once before denied their citizenship along the same ethnic and blood thinking that survives from the SS files for the marriage permits of German officers and their families[16] in the present German provision for admitting *Volksdeutschen* but denying citizenship to guest workers. The plight of the refugees should be measured against the displacement of peoples caused by Germany between 1938 and 1945 and against the economic benefits from immigration experienced by the postwar West German boom. As to the deceptive unspeakability of those who are liable or personally guilty, Habermas warns about a threat to democratic procedures: "Today *the unspeakable*—something that a fifth of the population may have thought, but up until now never expressed in public—is cresting over the banks. . . . But this can gain a power of infection only within the milieu of a heartless prosperity chauvinism" (135f.; italics added). We come around the full circle to the "existential usefulness" of the two Big Lies, the postwar Lie of being always and already democrats and the post-Wall Lie of becoming once again a normal nation. The Two Lies, motivated by an inability to speak truth about the catastrophic past, express social pathology. Their existential usefulness to democracy consists in fortifying self- and other-deceptive, willed ignorance among its contemporary democratic practitioners (136f.).

Whether and how Habermas heeds his own critical social theorizing about deception within democracy is a question I leave for Part Three. I conclude here with the second dimension of his learning by disaster, that is, by *linking the politics of asylum with its economy*. Already his irritation with the European chauvinism of affluence indicates that Germany's desire to curb the tide of immigration is built on an amnesia of European history. He invokes the moral "obligation" of European countries or "a moral claim" against Europe by immigrants from poor countries. In his thinking, he hearkens to a twofold profit reaped by European modernity: from the primarily European emigration to the New World in the last two centuries and from the postwar immigrant work force entering Europe via other poor countries (EdA 269, 271/SR 141,143). Today's flood of migrants to Europe resembles the European economic migration in the nineteenth and twentieth centuries. There should be some form of reciprocity, if not also reparation, for the past fruits of emigration as well as for the effects of exploitation and colonization. This insight lies at the heart of Habermas' formulation of *the moral claim to reciprocal recognition:*

> From the moral point of view we cannot regard this problem [of immigration] from the perspective of the inhabitants of affluent and peaceful societies; we must also take the perspective of those who come to foreign continents seeking their well-being, that is, an existence worthy of human being, rather than protection from political persecution. (269/141f.)

Leaving aside the dubious formulation and assumption that NATO members and other Euro-Americans can be counted among truly "peaceful societies," it still remains a question whether or not the moral claim and the growing globalization of the capital markets alone can create pressures toward world (cosmopolitan) citizenship and "an existence worthy of human beings" (269/142) achieved "from the perspective of all parties involved." It would appear that unless Habermas' "moral basis for a liberal immigration policy" (271/142) is expanded consistently into an argument for economic democracy, his most radical impulses fall short of their own requirement. Once before the consistency of this sort was sought by Hegel against Kant and by Marx against both of them. Whether and how Habermas heeds his most radical insight in his critical social theorizing is a question I leave for the concluding part of the book.

The Conflict in Kosovo/a and NATO's Bombing of Serbia

The founding and proclamation of the human rights by the UN as much as the threat of punishment for the wars of aggression and the crimes against humanity—with the consequence of limiting, even if halfheartedly, the principle of nonintervention, these were the necessary and correct answers to the morally significant experiences of this century, to totalitarian political raging, and to the Holocaust. (BH 6/268; translation mine)

In the wake of the massacre of forty-five Albanians near Racak on January 16, 1999, and as the Rambouillet negotiations between Serbia, the Albanian Kosovars, and the Western Alliance broke down, the seventy-eight-day aerial bombing campaign against Serbia by nineteen states under the NATO military command began on March 24, 1999. During the NATO aerial war the Serb army, police, and paramilitary units completed their project of cleansing big parts of Kosovo/a from its Albanian majority. Over three-quarters of a million ethnic Albanian refugees left the Serbian-dominated Kosovo. The parties that prepared for the bombing strategy spent virtually no comparative money for material provisions to meet this human exodus. The refugees reported atrocities that Serbs perpetrated on the Albanian Kosovars. The international tribunal accused Slobodan Milošević, the besieged former Belgrade leader of Serbia, of war crimes; six of these atrocities named by The Hague tribunal occurred not only under his watch but also after the NATO bombing campaign began. The bombing meanwhile produced civilian casualties among the Serbs, destroyed the entire economic base of Serbia, and ecologically devastated the vast Balkan and Danube regions. Even many animals in the Belgrade Zoo suffered emotional breakdowns from the night raids and some caused physical harm to themselves in their anticipation of the infernal night. The democratic opposition in Serbia, whatever remained of it before the bombing, either was silenced or joined the prevailing anti-NATO sentiment. As NATO suspended the air strikes on June 10, more than 10,000 people, mostly military but including about 1,800 civilians, died as a result of the bombing—34,000 sorties and 25,000 missile strikes. The Serbian forces withdrew by June 20, ahead of the agreed-on schedule. But 60–90 percent of Serbs and Roma, fearing reprisals from the Kosovo Liberation Army, fled with them from their homes in Kosovo. As the UN reports of mass murders, torture, and other war crimes by Serbs against Albanian Kosovars began to surface, with the 40,000–45,000 Allied and UN units moving into the Kosova protectorate, neither multicultural democracy nor the rule of law and peaceful coexistence were established. Various factions of the former Albanian Kosovar fighters have more or less free reign in creating an ethnically pure region. The largest ethnic cleansing began under NATO command with its silent consent. Whereas the cost of intervention is a staggering $10 billion, and damage to Yugoslavia $60–100 billion, humanitarian aid to the ravaged region did not go over $1 billion (see n. 22 below). Ironically, Žižek (2000, 56f.; cf. Chomsky 1999) is correct that *we* should first unmask the "Orwellian oxymoron" in the expression "militaristic humanism" or "militaristic pacifism," then give up the *humanitarian* or moral pretense and finally admit fully the *military* nature of the intervention.

Habermas' position on the situation in Kosovo is remarkably consistent with the arguments he developed during the Persian Gulf War and the German asylum debate. Yet on a closer reading, we can detect a significant degree of learning insofar as he acknowledges that imperialism and hegemony, and not just universal human rights or humanitarian intervention, might have contributed to the basic motives of the United States and NATO. As the bombs begin to hurt Serbian civilians, Habermas heroically straddles the impossible and tries (again) to distill from the Serbian/NATO disaster a margin of rationality for the future to come. Still, heroism is a fallible virtue, and on a less charitable reading, which I cannot disallow myself to consider, Habermas joins the cluster bomb political liberals and social democrats in supporting, at least initially, just another major western-democratic war of intervention in this century. Admitting at the outset that the question of whether or not to intervene in Kosovo/a split liberals and the radical Left, as much as it divided the Right, should assuage any false impression that Habermas is singled out in my account as a punching bag for those who unilaterally opposed the NATO bombing of Serbia. To be fair, my aim here as in the Persian Gulf War is first of all to understand his thinking, which he shares not only with Madeleine Albright, Zbigniew Brzezinski, Bill Clinton, and Tony Blair but also with Václav Havel, Joschka Fischer, Michael Walzer, and Bogdan Denitsch, among others (Habermas' BH is reprinted in Buckley 2000, 306–16). Any thinker—from Plato in Syracuse to Vladimir Ilich Lenin in Russia to Martin Heidegger in Germany to Michel Foucault during the Iranian Revolution to Mihailjo Marković in Yugoslavia to Václav Havel in Central Europe—who takes influential public positions on the political conflicts of the day must assume the risks that come with enlisting his or her intellectual architectonic in support of a possible disaster in the making. To be sure, only some of the intellectual risk takers, just as only some among the activists, also learn by disaster or possible direct as well as indirect contributions to it. By contrast, the influential intellectuals who never dare to take a public stance or incur risk do not thereby escape the judgment of history. This hesitation to remain on the sidelines of history has never been Habermas' problem.[17]

I want to concentrate on Habermas' key questions: How does NATO's campaign answer Schmitt's starting point that humanity is always and already bestial (BH 6/267)? How is NATO's air war against Serbia's ethnic cleansing of Kosova "a war on the border between legality and morality" (1/263)? I noted that Habermas tried "to make the best of the Gulf War" (VaZ 18/11). What does he learn since then? What is *the best* that could be learned from the conflict over Kosovo/a?

More so in the Kosovo/a conflict than at the outset of the Persian Gulf War (I want to argue against rash polemics with him), Habermas is aware of a twofold possible disaster in play—Serbian units cleansing the Kosovar Albanians and NATO bombs killing innocent civilians. Western intervention, he admits, carries on its conscience the suffering caused by the bombing. This seems a humble and honest admission of human fallibility. Habermas raises to himself a serious concern that the military intervention could become a disaster that would arrest for a very long time any future attempt to elevate international relations to a new cosmopolitan coexistence. Isn't this just a dirty NATO war that might produce even greater catastrophe in its wake, he asks? Would not all the negative outcome "be grist for the mill of Carl Schmitt" (BH 6/266), the Nazi political theorist who always mistrusted humanity, making it coextensive with bestiality? In his most serious and self-directed doubt (one should be impressed knowing here how far he admits this fundamental threat to his overall project), Habermas worries that *the entire idea of a cosmopolitan world order among sovereign states* ("the legal pacifism *[Rechtspazifismus]* of a [German] Red-Green government," as opposed to the merely private "pacifism of conviction" BH 1/263f., translation altered) "*in the end itself may be the wrong project*" (6/267, italics added; cf. EdA 225/192). Pacifists of conviction, along with the more cynical political realists, by implying this negative sense of "'the' political" and of humanity, rely on the noninterventionist and merely instrumental international relations. This leaves us with the Schmittian struggle among sovereign nations, a struggle itself valued as an essential crusade against evil. Breaking down this impasse between the heroic and the meaningless fight unto death, Habermas inveighs against the simplistic moralization of politics. He aims to resolve Hegel's contradiction between ethical life, allowed only within the sovereign nation-states, and the violent state of nature, which Hegel affirmed as the only possible form of life among nations. From this Hegelian contradiction between ethics possible within a single nation and brute violence reigning among nations, Habermas hearkens back to the Kantian cosmopolitan peace and forward to its international equivalents in the present age. He holds out for a political future based on global cooperation in economy and politics (BH 6/267; cf. EdA 225–236/192–201; SR).[18] I would submit that the two salient insights from the asylum debate discussed above, insights surfacing already in the 1950s in the young Habermas' idea of radical democracy (SuP), reach their maturity in this vision of a more just international world order.

Habermas is critically aware that NATO bombing is not supported by any UN mandate and that therefore a different level of justification for NATO's war must be sought, if the war on the borderline between law and morality is not to be condemned as illegal international adventurism. Further, he warns against mixing humanitarianism and imperialism—the venerable U.S. tradition of a moralizing and sentimental power messianism (read: *saving the world* for democracy). This U.S. worldview confuses its moral values, promoted by power politics, with European federalism, which aspires to an international legal order with limits placed on the arbitrary uses of power (BH 7/269f.).

Such reservations and warnings empower Habermas' learning

- to oppose minimally NATO's unilateral action and to strive instead wholeheartedly for the UN mandate that would have included greater Russian and Chinese participation in conflict resolution
- to suspect more explicitly the overt humanitarian motives presented by the United States and the Euro-American alliance
- to resist the present disastrous facts that could set new normative legal precedents for an even more disastrous international future

This critical-suspicious learning is to be derived from Habermas' writings as much as from his native ambivalence about monological power politics, actionism, decisionism, and arbitrary violence in general.

- His stress on the discursive principle of inclusive participation can be met by the UN General Assembly or by the radically democratized Security Council, but never by NATO.
- His insight into the deceptive nature of the asylum debate within democracy becomes here directly relevant to judging the overt motives of any so-called humanitarian war.
- The legitimation of NATO's aerial war that took place, so to speak, between facts and norms becomes an utter disaster when one tries to universalize it—whether selectively (some victims are found more worthy than others) or globally (the United States becomes a global killer cop) or by Russia, China, Indonesia, Mexico, or any so-called rogue state that may assume the right to behave outside of international law the way NATO did.

Habermas argues critically for the Kantian ideal of perpetual peace, which, he realizes with healthy skepsis, lies far from NATO's campaign. But in his actual political recommendation, Habermas supports publicly, while restraining his ambivalence under a moral compulsion, the air bombing of Serbia:

- Habermas takes little or no critical distance on the media reporting of facts or on the German or other mainstream press. But some facts are arranged and others are excluded in this media in such a way as to stage the moral outrage and imperative to intervene.

- Habermas suspends the communicative principle of inclusion when opting for NATO over the UN, for war over continued and still-possible diplomacy. This suspension itself is decisionistic insofar as it lacks a rationally redeemable normative principle.
- Habermas' attempt to justify the outcome of the bombing campaign *post hoc factum* can become normative for the future only in a utilitarian, instrumental sense; one could have *possibly* achieved the same minimal end results in Kosovo/a through diplomacy and without an extensive loss of lives: the latter is universalizable, the former is not.
- Habermas fails to imagine positive communicative and nonviolent alternatives to both genocide and the NATO bombing: just as Hegel allowed for poverty and international wars, Habermas exhibits a failure of imagination and nerve when he falls behind the ideality of his communicative theory. Just as Hegel's ethical life in the nation-state provides a measure for pushing for an ethic of international relations, so Habermas' ethics of communication (see introduction) offers a measure for pushing beyond an interventionist war counsel. One option would be international brigades of human rights observers, activists, and encampments throughout Kosovo/a, in the same way these encampments exist, for example, in Chiapas, Mexico, where they continue to protect indigenous Mayans from massive expulsions and outright genocide by the Mexican military and paramilitary forces.
- Habermas does not return to scrutinize in full public view, and with ambivalence accorded by him to other events or theorists, his stance on the NATO bombing or support of the Persian Gulf War.

I make a disclaimer against Peter Handke's objection that "[Habermas'] entire essay [BH] is an apology for a blind-raging violence" (cited in Z). Handke's severe judgment of Habermas is made in the heat of the debate within the Left. The condemnation is inaccurate, since it overstates the case and misses the obvious. Habermas searches for the least violent and the most moral and legitimate path from a quagmire of either standing by while genocidal nationalism rages on next door or hurting innocents in the process of stopping that rage. I reject Handke's rash outrage for two already-indicated reasons, first, the high degree of learning that Habermas does between the Persian Gulf War and the Kosovo/a conflict. One could argue that he exhibits surprising levels of political naïveté during the initial stages of the Persian Gulf War in that he remains unmoved even by strong objections from his Leftist colleagues and friends.[19] The second is the list of doubts, all of which Habermas raised to his own reluctant support of the bombing. In his May 18, 1999, response to Handke [Z], he slightly qualifies this support by adopting the call of the Green Party for a conditional pause in bombing. We can measure his learning path by his critical note from 1993, the statement anticipating his later self-doubts during the Kosovo/a crisis:

Eurocentrism and the hegemony of Western culture are in the last analysis catchwords for a struggle for recognition on the international level. The Gulf War made us aware of this. Under the shadow of a colonial history that is still vivid in people's minds, the allied intervention was regarded by religiously motivated masses and secularized intellectuals alike as a failure to respect the identity and autonomy of the Islamic-Arabic world. The historical relationship between the Occident and the orient, and especially the relationship of the First to the former Third World, continues to bear the marks of a denial of recognition. (EdA 248/SR 119; italics only in English translation)

In my present rejoinder to Habermas, I want to focus on two dimensions in his profile:

- how his philosophical profile developed in the shadows of 1945 informs his theorizing of the Kosovo/a issue
- how the restrictions, self-imposed on his learning under the specters of 1968, in the end prevent him from developing a more robust critical social theory of international relations

First, this entire study implies both that theories emerge in historical forms of life rather than through value-free transcendental justifications (i.e., out of nowhere), and that Habermas' Critical Theory, more or less self-consciously, responds to key sociopolitical situations of his life. This insight into the internal relation between theory and praxis in itself portends neither a drawback for Habermas, as a critical thinker, nor for my study of him as both a thinker and an activist. On the contrary, I hold that discovering one's deeply motivating existential beginnings and defining historical situations, in which one's thinking emerges and is continually formed, can only deepen one's thinking. On the other hand, any such reflective strengths can become easily one's blind spots insofar as one can neither witness one's own beginnings nor think out of nowhere. Beginnings, lacking the guarantees of translucent origins, whether in theory or in practice, stay always difficult. This difficulty represents the radical limits of theory, even critical social theory, as well as of one's finite and fallible life journey.

The Kosovo/a conflict, lying at the utmost horizon of *our* temporal trajectory in this book, meets in an intensified mode also Habermas' philosophical-political returns to his existential beginnings.

"War is here," as if echoing the end of Hegel's *Philosophy of Right* (para. 331–34),[20] Habermas declares without embellishing the belligerent state of nature in Europe, just as NATO takes to the Serbian skies (BH 1/263). Yet we encounter another very curious pathos on the opening page of Habermas' essay on Kosovo/a. He begins by addressing Germany's historical consciousness. Perhaps this would be acceptable if written in German and published in a German intellectual paper, and thus primarily intended for the German public debate, as Habermas' piece was in all these regards. But this essay and the journal in which it appears, albeit German, by their very nature, carry international content and impact that transcend the German mentality. Habermas begins with neither the suffering of the Kosovar Albanians nor that of the Serbian civilians. His entry into Schmitt's and Hegel's wagers between bestiality or humanity is quintessentially through his German experience of the twentieth century. It would be much too easy to say that Habermas' horizon is German centered or that German political debate is inescapably turned insularly onto itself. Such a critique of Habermas, as true as it might be, would be too easy insofar as it presupposes that one could in fact abstract from one's own existential beginnings in history and experience. I have been claiming the opposite about Habermas and by implication about any theorizing. My rejoinder, therefore, does not imply that Habermas should not begin in the beginnings, but rather that any truly sober universalism must account for these beginnings in their strength as well as in greater awareness of their possibly disastrous blind spots. Habermas' strength lies in his responsibly adopted standpoint as a second-degree witness at the unloading ramp in Auschwitz. But the conflict in Kosovo/a does not parallel the Holocaust, the Serbs are not Nazis, and the Allied bombing of Serbia is not May 8, 1945, revisited. To think so is either to overreact to one's history in Germany or to fall prey to the ideological abuses of the Holocaust by the contemporary politics of memory and power (tab. 1.1).[21]

Habermas opens his essay on intervention in Kosovo by noting that the German army is fighting now for the first time since 1945 along with NATO and outside of its own and NATO's territory. (One factual correction is the former East German state that as part of the Soviet bloc and in a clear violation of the postwar agreements invaded Czechoslovakia in 1968.) Even though NATO's campaign *is* war, it is not "total warfare" of the twentieth century, which Habermas concedes as a historical step forward. The smart bombs and NATO's policy of avoiding the innocent civilian casualties carry "an important legitimizing function" even if for the Serbs, this value is all the same just a war. Luckily, then, Germany not only fights under the legitimating conditions of NATO's humanitarian, clean, and principled war, but with Germany's postwar reluctance to fight abroad, relinquished now to NATO, arrives the transformation of its heroic war mentality and rhetoric into a worthy cause. The "surgical precision" of the clean and distinct bombs eliminates the need for war rhetoric. With this progress, Germany can now be sober and pragmatic about war. What we find today in the debates between the supporters and the critics of the bombing is likewise the sobriety and pragmatism of "a crystal clear normative language." At the end of his preamble, Habermas sighs with a sound of relief that nobody any longer calls for a *Sonderweg* (special path) or *Sonderbewußtsein* (special consciousness) in the German discussions of this war. The Kantian tradition of legal pacifism is for the first time defended by Germany's Red-Green coalition government composed in great measure of the veterans of the 1960s revolt (1/263f.).

Ian Traynor wrote in the London *Guardian* (July 5, 1999) that there is "a generation war between the yuppies and hippies of Germany's Greens," thereby replaying the earlier generation rift of the 1960s. Now the founding fathers of the Greens (the '68ers, Joschka Fischer and Daniel Cohn-Bendit) are confronted by the revolting youth (those demonstrating, e.g., in November 1999 in Seattle, in April 2000 in Washington, and later in September in Prague against the World Trade Organization's globalization without both an environmental and a human face). There arises a new rift between the Greens and Gerhard Schröder's Red Social Democrats on the Kosovo issue. But the young generation of the progressive Greens wants their party to return from its present neoliberal cooptation to its roots in environmental, pacifist, and antinuclear issues. The roots are where Habermas once felt at home. Having opposed the students of 1968, he stands today with them on the same side as established Green politicians.

The problems with opening the debate on Kosovo[22] with the pathos for Germany's changing role in the international relations are legion. The key one, which I mention here, lies in making the German trauma into an entry point of the universal questions of human suffering and into the legitimacy and rationality questions of international conduct. Echoing his earlier concerns for the well-being of Israel in supporting the Persian Gulf War, Habermas hearkens now at one end to the Holocaust and at the other end to Germany's postwar history. At both ends, he joins with the Red-Green legal pacifists in support of NATO's action. Just as it is illegitimate for NATO to use this war for safeguarding its post–Cold War purpose, and just as it is illegitimate for the United States to find its meaning in the universe through an imperial messianism, so Germany could learn once and for all to grow up on its own and without needing to destroy others to do so. But who needs to care here and now about Germany's trauma, really, given that we speak about the Balkans? If Germany's learning from its terrible past were to be at issue, why not have the German army drop cluster bags filled with red paint on the skinhead or neo-Nazi communities in Germany, or why not deprive of profits the German corporations that made and kept income from slave labor during Nazi times? The bombing of Serbia is discussed in "a crystal clear normative language," but how do its "surgical precision" and the media accompanying propaganda differ, in principle (i.e., apart from the historical singularity of different events), from the instrumentality and propaganda of the instructions for a more efficient and humane gassing?[23] These are the parallels to Germany's disaster that I am less hesitant to invoke in light of Habermas' optimism about the crystal-clear discussion and surgically precise execution of war. However offensive and admittedly polemical these hyperbolic comparisons might be, and as much as I resist otherwise the said comparisons of the Yugoslav conflicts with the Holocaust, they are meant to offer an ironic mirror to the historical blindness of the opening paragraphs of Habermas' essay. Just as the Persian Gulf War was the wrong way to try to heal the U.S. trauma from the lost Vietnam War, so the action against Serbia can do little for Germany's lingering guilt over the Holocaust. There is no consolation in witnessing Germany's air force over Serbia, accompanied by nineteen western and democratic states (we *should* mock Habermas, just as Handke does, that these are "indisputably democratic" and "peaceful" states, Z; BH 7/270f.). Do *we* really honor in this bombing action Adorno's imperative that Auschwitz is not to happen again?[24]

Habermas' generational postwar trauma is written all over his opening passages. We can discern his philosophical profile, formed in response to the key formative events of his life (with May 8, 1945, at its core here), funding his very theorizing of the Kosovo/a conflict. Yet without greater sobriety about these beginnings, his optimistic pathos and relief about new Germany are not reassuring. His strengths, so magnanimously displayed in the first and second German Autumns and the Historians' Debate, blind him in the Persian Gulf War and the NATO bombing of Serbia, as they blinded him when he overreacted to the anarchic character of the West German student revolt. The revisionist echoes are scary: what the Bitburg ceremonies could not do, the mission over Serbia, side by side with those western Allies (whom also Horkheimer defended in the 1950s against the anti-American and anti-NATO protests and again in the 1960s during the anti–Vietnam War protests), united against a Holocaust-like event and against that last Communist Hitler, Milošević, will accomplish—fighting in a holy war against evil.[25]

> The group-fantasy of becoming an adult by punitive beating of naughty Milošević, must have a psychoclass basis—there must be a large portion of people sharing similar childhood experiences—and the leading figures of this war are just representatives re-enacting these experiences as delegates of the whole class. (Kurth 1999, 111)

Thus, when Fischer and Cohn-Bendit abandon the nonviolent position of the Greens (espoused by Habermas in the 1980s), this is mostly "celebrated . . . as 'mature', 'responsible', 'indicating the ability to govern'" (114). And "the identification of Milošević with Hitler, and of Kosovo with Auschwitz, was one of the main arguments used to justify the military intervention of NATO." The bombing "of Hitler" is a way to deal with the traumatic German past. Indeed, as Kurth points out, the memorial sites in Kragujevac and Novi Sad, where great massacres had been committed during World War II by the German army, were among the first to be bombed: "Did this happen by chance? Serbia is a traditional poison container for Germany—German troops attacked Serbia twice in this century and caused massive traumatizations with long-lasting effects" (118). If not at Bitburg or other memorial sites, then for real in Kosovo, "Germany now fights for the first time in its history on the right side" (119), says Fischer on April 22. Habermas writes (BH) affirmatively about Germany's participation in NATO out of the very same sentiment of reaching desired postwar maturity or adulthood.

Second, we arrive at the self-corrective "learning process," on which Habermas repeatedly places his greatest hope, even as *we*, born in the twentieth century, pass "across the trenches *[Gräben]* of an ongoing armed conflict" (BH 7/271, translation mine). Habermas, as a second-degree witness of twentieth-century disasters, admits that words alone might not be able to heal, what I called above the *doubly unspeakable* traumatic past. (It is doubly so, either because the horror simply cannot be spoken of directly by the victims and survivors, or because one wills to remain silently self-deceived about one's liability or personal guilt.) Yet he accentuates our ability to learn by disaster, even by *the* disaster (PK 74/LD 312), whose definite article indicates the literal translation of the Hebrew Shoah, the Holocaust. I submit that the relation between the two discoveries—of the *unspeakable* in the very inability to communicate about (rather than bear witness to) disasters and of learning by disaster—is worked out neither in Habermas' theory nor in his interventions. The ongoing tension between the two insights points to the blind spots or weaknesses of his achieved strengths in learning from the traumatic past *today*. I will resume this critical discussion in chapter 9. I want to encapsulate here other essential features of Habermas' affirmative learning.

He tends to respond to all those objections that push him into a corner, without leaving him obvious choices, by retorting, What other options do we have left? He learns, then, through a pragmatic destruction of dead ends. It is *our* history, he might reason in a discussion, that eliminates certain paths and brings the problems to us in a certain way. Neither experience nor problems, as we face them in history, comes to us unstructured. Grasping the way in which problems meet our understanding provides a pragmatically inflected material and a historical basis for their resolution. Habermas learns from his experience, existential situations, shared political history, and the limits of historical enlightenment.

Here emerges his idea of "domesticating the state of nature among states through human rights. With that [insight] is placed on the agenda the transformation of popular sovereignty into a right of world citizens" (BH 1/263, translation mine). Habermas discerns this ideal in greater depth through facing the critical problem of the Kosovo/a conflict. The problem comes to us as a choice between two equally bad options: the transgression of the sovereign, internationally recognized state rights and the moral defense of human rights without the requisite international legal order and sanction. Habermas' ideal envisions a sublation *(Aufhebung)* of the classical people's sovereignty into the cosmopolitan rights of a world citizenship. The critical problem at hand contains no easy path to this ideal. Enter his rebuke, What other options do we have left but. . . ? His question prompts us to fill in the blank spaces with NATO's air campaign—an action lying at the dead-end limit between law and morality. Yet this move to a problem solving of the Kosovo/a dead ends via NATO's war is far from obvious, especially given that Habermas aims at Kant's perpetual peace.

Habermas diagnoses an existing *postnational constellation* of the nation-state authority, which is increasingly diminished by the ethnic struggles erupting across its borders. From this correct evaluation of the fact of sovereign states and from the normative ideal of human rights, which would defend both universal and particular goals, Habermas concludes to the moralizing of international politics. Before we arrive at a moralized, cosmopolitan world order free from backward ethnic struggles, what becomes moralized is the ambivalent pathway of war. Namely, following the Persian Gulf War, we get another hybrid war, a *humanitarian war* of intervention. Concretely, Habermas' approach requires moralizing NATO's war as a humanitarian deed. So it is not so much that we have no other options than war in striving for a cosmopolitan world (he spends no time on diplomatic or other options). Rather, we must admit no explanation of NATO's action other than the humanitarian one. Even if sinister motives do exist, they cannot "explain the decision to undertake such a weighty, risky, and costly intervention" (BH 6/268).

As if trying to convince himself of NATO's humanitarian motives, Habermas collapses the normative argument—what other options do we have but evolving toward a more cosmopolitan world?—with a one-dimensional acceptance of presented facts—what other explanations for *this war* will work but the humanitarian one? I suspect that Habermas' self-imposed restrictions on a nuanced critique of imperialism (a specter of the 1960s) *and* genocide (a shadow of having a single overwhelming referent) block him from operating with a more robust critical social theory of international relations. In the degree that he, on the way to Kant's perpetual peace, retreats not only from Hegel's undertheorized internationalism but also from the critical internationalism of Marx, his learning suffers the blindness of cluster bomb (Left-) liberals. One need not be a pacifist of conviction in order to argue that NATO's unilateral intervention will carry far-reaching negative repercussions for international relations. We witness this outcome almost immediately in Russia's lawless insanity in Chechnya. Habermas admits that NATO's unilateralism can create havoc if other nations universalize this scenario in other areas of world conflict (cf. BH 7/271). Russia and China, the two nuclear members of the UN Security Council that were shunned by NATO, grow suspicious of the United States and the west beyond safe limits; moreover, any future reform of the UN (also shunned by NATO) is put on hold. The UN stands weakened and discredited by this war more than by any event since its founding. After the June suspension of bombing, Russia moved, ahead of NATO's peacekeepers, 200 soldiers into the Pristina airport; it also suspended disarmament talks with the United States and mandated during the bombing campaign that its entire nuclear arsenal be updated. Kant's perpetual peace calls for, among other things, abolishing standing armies, yet NATO's war rejuvenated the military-industrial complex of the G-8 countries, absorbing the peace dividend for years to come.

Habermas concentrates on the gap between the effectiveness and the legitimation of NATO's intervention: the UN is legitimate but weak, and NATO is effective but lacks the legitimacy of international law. He views the UN as the institution that is able to close the gap by moralizing and at the same time institutionalizing the global human rights politics.

Only when human rights have found their "place" within a worldwide democratic legal order in a similar manner as the basic rights in our national constitutions, only then will we be able to determine also on a global level that the addressees of these rights can understand themselves at the same time as their authors. (BH 7/270; translation mine)

Habermas comes close to questioning the political economy of the military industrial complex and of western imperialism when he worries that the United States wants to supplant the United Nations. Yet while he grows concerned about NATO's paternalism, he does not bother about its political economy. He restricts himself to an anticommunitarian argument that the United States confuses the legal implementation of human rights with promoting them as moral values. (In that sense, for example, the Iranian, initially progressive, revolution against U.S. imperial values, which were embodied in the shah's regime, degenerated into an adoption of regressive Islamic-fundamentalist values.) The antidote to U.S. imperial fundamentalism, masking itself under the rubric of democratic values, Habermas hopes, lies in learning processes whereby *we* become educated into an enlarged perspective, recognizing that "the self-authorization by NATO should not be allowed to become the general rule" (BH 7/271; translation mine).

That worldwide democratic order (on its way to becoming cosmopolitan and perpetual peace) ought to institutionalize rights to economic democracy; this move would require a critique of the rising imperial new world order and of its respective propaganda waged by the culture industry, the media, and the deceptive liberal discourse (the possibilities of deceptive democratic discourse are recognized by Habermas in the asylum debate). And yet this criticism of existing democracies and this move to economic democracy are both somehow absent from his mature architectonic; this reveals the conservatively skeptical side of Habermas' mature philosophical-political profile. I read this absence as the obverse side of his progressive profile or, more succinctly, the weakness of Habermas' strength.

NOTES

1. In this internal citation, Habermas refers to Antje Vollmer, *Frankfurter Allgemenine Zeitung*, December 12, 1990.
2. See Mohr 1998; Ertel et al. 1998, 31. See Müller (2000, 82, 203, 245-53, 255-59, 265, 272f., 283; also 44f., 76ff.) for a discussion of the problem of instrumentalizing Auschwitz in contemporary German politics.
3. Cf. Kierkegaard's (1988) distinction between aesthetic and ethical attitudes.
4. Another example comes from a defeated project in the second competition for the Berlin Holocaust memorial. This proposal, like the one in Berlin's Bavarian Quarter, is also by Renata Stih and Frieder Schnock. It is called *Bus Stop*, and it consists of "mobile monuments," namely, a bus station at the heart of Berlin with hourly buses destined to the nearby

concentration camps and weekly buses to other far-distant sites. These buses would be distinguished in color (red) and would travel through the city traffic with large signs of their destination to one of the factories of death. This less-grandiose proposal would not only intervene in the 'normality' of daily post-Wall life, but it would support the existing memorial sites, as well as those persecuted today, by connecting concrete Germans directly with the reality of persecution (Wiedmer 1999, 162–64, and the book jacket for the photo of the red memorial bus going to Sachsenhausen).

5. See Max Pensky's translation notes, which are rich in historical detail (VaZ 169–75).

6. Note how Butler (1993a) defines the performative in this twofold fashion. Cf. also Matuštík 1998a, 112–16.

7. DM = Deutsche Mark; this West German currency took over the East German territories.

8. See Hohendahl's foreword (in VaZ xv).

9. Sustaining the mode of postnational identity (Matuštík 1993) grounds the possibility of maintaining culture and politics in a postnational constellation (PK).

10. In Plato's *Republic*, citizens are told a Noble Lie of three metals that correspond to three natures and three classes in the state. The philosopher-kings, of the golden nature, are to follow and show the other two classes the special Platonic path to truth and justice in the state.

11. I use Kosovo/a as a name of the region shared by Serbs and Albanian Kosovars. The Serbs tried to cleanse the Albanian Kosova of the Albanian majority; NATO and the Albanian majority for the most part cleansed both Kosova and the Serbian Kosovo of its Serbs. Müller (2000, 254) mistakenly attributes to Habermas an oppositional stance toward the Persian Gulf War, as Habermas clearly defended the western Allied intervention against Iraq, minimally to defend Israel.

12. Habermas often displayed this answering strategy in his Frankfurt seminars that I attended in 1989–1991.

13. Diner (1991; cf. Wiedmer 1999, 86f.) argues against the antiwar, anti-American peace movements; he defends military intervention against Iraq from what he views to be a progressive position. He exposes the critique of the United States by the German Left as Germany's continued inability to mourn its Nazi past. Diner's thesis would support Habermas' complex thinking, though it would not explain the move made by the conservative revisionists. See Müller (2000, 38, 51, 54f., 60ff., 144f., 183, 188, 197, 202f., 205, 234, 269–71) on the original meaning of and the right-wing reversing of the so-called *Sonderweg* thesis.

14. I rely on Max Pensky's excellent translator's notes (VaZ 178–81) and on Habermas' own discussions.

15. Habermas painted the Stalinist-Fascist 'enemy' in objecting to the Spartakus Department of 1969.

16. I have in mind the "SS Collections of Rasse- und Siedlungshauptamt" of about 240,000 dossiers for individual SS personnel and their spouses (1932–March 1945). The job of this department was to guard the racial purity of the SS who applied for marriage licenses. The dossiers can be viewed in the Berlin Document Center.

17. For such accounting of the past risks and learning from disasters, see Arnason 1995; Lévinas 1981; or Blanchot 1995.

18. On Habermas' reading of Kant and Hegel, see Matuštík 1998a, chap. 6.

19. See note 11 in chapter 3 above.

20. See Matuštík 1998a, 135–38.

21. See "An Appeal" (1999): In their antiwar statement to the German Green Party, prominent U.S. Leftist-Jewish intellectuals argued against comparing the Kosovo/a conflict with the Holocaust. Cf. also Rosenthal 2000 and Kurth 1999. At the time of the appeal, Germany's foreign minister, Joschka Fischer, suffered a protest attack by a bag of red paint during the major showdown of the Red-Green coalition on the bombing of Serbia. Fischer kept his red-stained jacket during his Bundestag speech to dramatize his support for the victims of genocide and for the bombing of Serbia (see Kurth 1999, 115; and notes 86-89 for references to the daily press commentaries from 1999 in *Die Woche*, from April 29, p. 6; in *Die Zeit*, Leben sec., May 20, p. 13; and in *Der Spiegel*, May 24, p. 28). The most recent instrumentalizations of the Holocaust legacy surrounded the drama of the Cuban boy, Elián González, rescued by fishermen in the Gulf of Mexico after his mother died attempting to escape from Cuba. Elián's Miami relatives and the immigrant Cuban community compared his case to that of the Jewish children who needed to be given asylum from the persecution in Nazi Germany. By any other objective historical measure, but the one of Cuban ex-patriots, Fidel Castro is neither Adolf Hitler nor Joseph Stalin; to return to Cuba is not to arrive at Auschwitz. Bill Clinton on numerous occasions in conjunction with the Kosovo/a conflict dropped the Holocaust comparison to the plight of the Kosovar Albanians, positioning Serbia and the U.S. intervention in an analogy to World War II. Just as Habermas' generalized 'Fascism-Stalinism' invective against the protesting students in the 1960s, so also these references to the Holocaust are gratuitous. See references to Müller in n. 2 above.

22. One year after the NATO bombing, there is a vast array of informed discussion and evaluations on the mission in Kosovo/a. Postel's *Debating Kosovo* is a planned edited volume of original essays by the main protagonists and opponents of the war written during the bombing when the debate *did not* take place, and of later commentaries on those positions. This is a balanced and necessary volume. Habermas was invited to have his original essay (BH) reprinted and to write his rejoinder to a new critical piece by Douglas Cassel to be published here. Among other original essays to be included here with new critical exchanges are those by Noam Chomsky, Todd Gitlin, Michael Albert, Bogdan Denitch, Slavoj Žižek, Christopher Hitchens, Edward Herman, Branka Magas, Aryeth Neier, and Raiq Ali (compare with Buckley 2000, where Habermas' essay *is* included). Besides Habermas, among other supporters of the military intervention in Kosovo/a were Denitsch (1999); Havel (1999); and Walzer (1999); further *News and Letters* 44, no. 3 (1999): 1, 10; and 44, no. 6 (1999): 1, 10; and 44, no. 7 (1999): 1, 5, attempted to strike a balance in criticizing the Leftist one-sided opposition to the intervention, without taking into account the Serbian genocidal cleansing of Kosova, and exposing the brutality of NATO's action. For critical debates of the bombing, see Ally 1999; Chomsky 1999; Dienstbier 2000; Falk 2000; Herman and Peterson 2000; Judah 2000; Kurth 1999; Rosenthal 2000; Žižek 2000; and a review of other recent books on the Kosovo war, not mentioned here, by Hockenos 2000.

23. See Lanzmann 1985, 103ff., "Changes for special vehicles now in service at Kulmhof (Chelmno) and for those now being built" (signed by Just on June 5, 1942).

24. Adorno [1966] 1973, 365.

25. On the underside of the struggles against evil, see the work of the Frankfurt School–inspired social scientist, Becker 1975.

Part Three

IMPACT AND DISCONTENTS

In reconstructing Habermas' philosophical-political profile, I moved from *his* beginnings toward the beginnings that he shares with *our* contemporary generation. That path took me along a circular temporal trajectory from both sets of beginnings, through Habermas' key formative situations to the profiles shaped and the interventions motivated by reflections on these situations. I will consider next both the positive impact of Habermas' work and the discontents among his sympathetic readers as well as his most vocal critics. As I step back or aside in order to learn *today* from his strengths and weaknesses, my approach consists of the profile variations and views of Habermas taken from without. The guiding question of Part Three adopts a different angle from which to apprehend Habermas' profile: At what theoretical understanding do we arrive when we reconstruct Habermas' normative ideals (in ethics, morality, and politics) as complementary to his key situations and interventions in problems of his era? This way of questioning beckons us into a reverse motion along the path already taken. I shall proceed from the beginnings Habermas shares with *our* contemporary generation to *his* beginnings, and from the problems that face *us* in our critical understanding of the times to normative ideals by which to measure *our* theoretical and practical responses. Since this is a study with Habermas at its center focus, I would stray afar from the modest aim of grasping, integrating, and varying his profile, had I to reconstruct his theoretical architectonic in the same manner that numerous existing introductions to Habermas already do quite well. The next three chapters will endeavor instead to lay out the following:

- the relationship between Habermas' theoretical architectonic and political authorship, on the one hand, and his existential-political authoring on the other (his authoring occupies the central place between his theory and

politics, a dimension that at the same time accounts for the integrity of the profile I have been sketching)
- the Habermas effect in light of his pluralistic and interdisciplinary authorship and in relation to the unfinished debates
- the prospects for a *new critical theory*

Chapter Seven

ARCHITECTONIC AND AUTHORSHIP

I have taken an existential and political entry into Habermas' lifework, passing through the situations that shape his philosophical-political profile. Arguably it would be possible to take a high road of theory where his architectonic would be normatively justified. For me this was not a matter of some arbitrary choice, but rather a decision guided by balancing the received portraits of Habermas through a more integral profile. As I intimated in the introduction, in an existential passage from practice to theory, we can avoid both *the fallacy of induction* (i.e., deriving universals from an indeterminate collection of facts) and *the naturalistic fallacy* (i.e., deriving an ought from an is). I am not justifying Habermas' theory from his beginning motives or his historical situations. I do claim, however, that we can understand his theory much better by grasping his motivating life situations. The shorthand for this claim in the student vernacular would be that an unsituated Habermas is hard to digest, if not altogether dull. My approach to his philosophical-political profile is *dramatic and reconstructive rather than inductive or metaphysical*: Habermas did not have to become who he is now, yet we can rationally reconstruct the evolution of his thinking and thereby gain deeper insight into his work. This methodology is warranted by three additional areas of support.

First, the very idea of Critical Theory arises out of its difference from the positivistic notion of traditional theory (Horkheimer [1937] 1972). The latter separates the domains of facts from those of values. Critical Theory, learning as much from Kant as from the Hegelian-Marxist tradition, overcomes this division as arbitrary (there are no value-free facts out there to be found) and ideological (presenting any such facts is motivated, yet motives are left untheorized).

Second, numerous sympathetic readers of Habermas argue that the spheres of philosophy and politics become internally related for Habermas at least since his confrontation with Heidegger (Horster 1991, 8–9, 108–25), that we cannot grasp Habermas' Critical Theory apart from his political writings, that the original impetus for this theory comes from political and existential problems (Negt 1998), and that his political universalism, while normatively justified in democratic procedures, arises from and returns to his concrete and highly particular situation of being a polemical critic in postwar Germany (Pensky 1995).

Third, Habermas starts from social evolution and the human capacity to learn, reconstructs from both developments certain normative ideals, and complements in this fashion his formal justifications of theory (CES; TCA). From his contemporary vantage point, he checks his own learning and theoretical evolution against the sociohistorical and existential limits of other thinkers with whom he is in ongoing direct or indirect conversation (Kant, EdA, chap. 7; Hegel, FKH; Marx, TCA, chap. 8; or analytical philosophers, WuR).

By analogy, in my reconstruction of Habermas' profile, I have been applying Habermas' learning to Habermas. One may think with and at the same time against Habermas.

- In this chapter I will reconstruct, first, his architectonic from the integrative concepts discernible in his philosophical-political profile and, second, his integral lifework discernible through the main line of his debates with and learning from others.
- In the next chapter, I will consider how *we* may learn from his radical pluralism as well as from the discontents and unfinished debates with others.
- I will conclude in the last chapter with how *we* may learn from the sociohistorical and existential strengths, as well as from the limits of his authoring horizon.

HABERMAS' INTEGRATIVE CONCEPTS: SOCIAL CRITIQUE AND NORMATIVE IDEAL

There are no laws of history in the strict sense, and human beings, even whole societies, are capable of learning. (EdA 149/123)

The key integrative concepts of Habermas' lifework emerge in the historical present of his living profile. By the locution 'integrative' I designate their shared *praxial and ideal dimensions*. Since concepts do not emerge out of nowhere and vanish into nowhere, they have their praxial dimension. In critical social theory, concepts, the basic building blocks of theoretical edifices (ideal), emerge from a critical praxis in one's present age. We can trace the mature concept formation from the reconstructed profile of the thinker, who thought these concepts out, to the basic situations and their historical and existential beginnings. The idea of something existing a priori before having begun is possible in a thought experiment, but even then only as a comic conceptuality of an abstract thinker. Even the normative derivation or justification of concepts is thus a reconstruction by someone who lives somewhere in time. In this study, I reconstructed *three core praxial dimensions of Habermas' profile*. These are punctuated by the key dates: 1945, 1968, 1989. The last of these dates situates the most mature vantage point for the formation of corresponding integrative concepts. One can speak of correspondences insofar as there are ideal (normative, or philosophical) dimensions that correspond to certain praxial (critical, or existential-political) dimensions of the concept formation. *I claimed that Habermas integrates the democratic aspirations of the postwar securing generation (1945) with the revolutionary core demands of the protesting youth generation (1968).* The skeptical attitude of Habermas' generation accords him with the middle, corrective ground between the securing and revolting interests. The traumatic past prior to 1945 marks the historical vanishing point, while the caesura after 1989 marks the ideal vanishing point of Habermas' integration (tab. 7.1).

The concept of *constitutional patriotism* does not emerge for Habermas in 1945. At fifteen he is experiencing his philosophical-political birthday; ascribing to him this mature conceptual insight at that point in history would be, as it is done in some high Christology of the divine infant, existentially untrue. Habermas keeps developing his formulations all the way into the post-Wall era. The praxial dimension of the constitutional ideal is, however, traceable to 1945—in the postwar need to forge a polity gathered around the lasting democratic institutions, rather than under the colors of a national flag or to the sounds of a national anthem. We get at what is at stake in this ideal if we apply social criticism to the pre-1945 catastrophe. From the hindsight of the post-Wall Germany, Habermas integrates under his later notion of *deliberative democracy* the two praxial dimensions of 1945 and 1968.

The conceptuality of *postnational identity* becomes the motivating force required for the performance of constitutional patriotism. Yet this open and revolutionary identity emerges from the existential experience and the historical achievement of the '68ers. It is because the generation of the '45ers is initially incapable of inhabiting this praxial dimension that deliberative democracy too is at first only imposed on Habermas' Germany. The missing praxial dimension of the more fluid

Table 7.1 Habermas' Integrative Concepts

Praxial Dimension	Ideal Dimension
1945	Constitutional patriotism and deliberative democracy
1968	Postnational identity and postnational constellation
1989	Cosmopolitan world citizenship and radical democracy
Historical Vanishing Point	*Ideal Vanishing Point*
Learning after Auschwitz/ Learning by disaster	Permanent democratic revolution

identity formation is an outcome of the student movement. From the hindsight of the post-Wall Germany, Habermas integrates under his later notion of *postnational constellation* the two praxial dimensions of 1945 and 1968.

With the historically almost inevitable unification of Germany and the complementary post-1989 drive toward the union of European nation-states, further with the parallel unfolding of nationalist wars and the wars of intervention, the concepts of *cosmopolitan world citizenship* and *radical democracy* gain their ascendancy. The ideal of cosmopolitan world citizenship integrates two singular universals—constitutional patriotism and postnational identity. The ideal of radical democracy integrates two corresponding singular universals—deliberative democracy and postnational constellation. The most recent notions of cosmopolitan world citizenship and radical democracy thus represent the most generalized ideal responses to the particular praxial dimensions of historical experience. These later notions respond to Habermas' situation as well as the globalization problematic, whereas the earlier notions of constitutional patriotism and postnational identity are best applied to global contexts only through further abstractions under the more advanced concepts of deliberative democracy and postnational constellation.

The architectonic of these integrative concepts moves along two trajectories: from sociopolitical critique to normative ideal and from historical and existential particulars to philosophical and singular universals. At the particular historical and existential vanishing horizon—the horizon that recedes in the past—we run into the trauma of Germany's disaster; at the universalizing and philosophical ideal horizon—the horizon beyond which we cannot conceive of ideals—we situate ongoing normative theorizing of concepts and corresponding political practices. The existential modes of Habermas' and *our* contemporary historical presents are *learning by disaster* (LD) and *permanent democratic revolution* (VV 609/471).

If we draw on Habermas' reconstructed profile and his interventions in the public sphere, and if we trace both back to the key situations, we can easily reconstruct the genealogy of each of the aforementioned integrative concepts. The same approach can be adapted to introducing other concepts in Habermas' work. In this historically situated and materially existential approach to Habermas' Critical Theory and profile, we get at once an interesting, robust, and intelligible presentation of his entire architectonic. A normative theory is 'critical' in virtue of its emergence in confrontation with those historical situations and problems that face *our* age. The beginning student as well as any advanced specialist is thus accorded a presentation of critical social theory as a dynamic and living process. In such a living theory we may participate, since we are invited to make it our own. I will next illustrate the two above-mentioned trajectories—from existential-political critique to normative-philosophical ideal, and from the particular to the singular universal—by their core integrative concepts that were already introduced.

Constitutional Patriotism and Deliberative Democracy

We get at these two concepts when we begin from the critique of a particular German situation after 1945 and expand it into a universal notion. The first term is coined in 1979 by Dolf Sternberger in a specifically German context (Müller 2000, 92–98, 276–78): since postwar Germany had no democratic constitution, one was imposed on West Germany by the victorious Allies. Constitutional patriotism signifies, then, "a readiness to identify with the political order and the principles of the Basic Law" (EAS 168/NC 256), rather than with ethnically motivated nationalism. This patriotism is an imported ideality, administered from the top down; hence initially there is no corresponding (i.e., intrinsically motivated) consciousness to become constitutionally patriotic. From the praxial dimension of 1945, the social evolution toward constitutional patriotism contains an ideal form, but it lacks its existential core, which emerges as a social form of life after 1968. Only from that later context can Habermas define constitutional patriotism:

> This more sober political identity has detached itself from the background of a past centered on national history. The universalist content of a form of patriotism crystallized around the democratic constitutional states is no longer pledged to continuities filled with victories; this form of patriotism is incompatible with the secondary quasi-natural character of a consciousness that has no insight into the ambivalence of every tradition, into the concatenation of things for which amends cannot be made, into the barbaric dark side of all cultural achievements to the present day. (EAS 168f./NC 257)

Pensky (1995, 74) reminds us that while the postwar constitution applied to a specific historical situation, while it was meant as a short-term proviso for the West German state, it nonetheless survived all the way to the post-Wall unified Germany. "The Basic Law [*Grundgesetz* of the FRG] is one of the most liberal, universalistic, and democratic constitutions ever devised." Habermas accentuates how a particular response to a particular historical situation acquires an ideal and at the same time universal significance:

> The [1946 West German] constitution . . . gave in its general part . . . a political answer to the Nazi regime. In every of its 63 in detail developed human rights articles, there sounds the echo of the suffered injustice, which is at the same time negated word for word. These constitutional articles of the first hour not only achieve a determinate negation in the Hegelian sense; at the same time, they show the contours of a future social order. (EAS 18f.)[1]

> To be sure, every constitution which is not embodied in a living political culture remains abstract. We remember clearly the fate of the Weimar Republic. All the more, certain constitutional patriotism should be able to take root in the Federal Republic of Germany. (22)

Pensky (1995, 67) describes constitutional patriotism as an evolving universal mentality that arises from a "particular fate." Constitutional patriotism cannot be some given that is inscribed into the static document of the Basic Law. This patriotism is a dynamic and transformative sociopolitical task. I prefer an existential rendition of this task as set in Habermas' profile: his lifework, integrated in its praxial and ideal dimensions, embodies constitutional patriotism as a singular universal in postwar Germany. Pensky's reflections support my characterization:

> This *incorporation* of the spirit of the Basic Law on the level of motivations and mentalities (the political correlate of what Habermas's theoretical writings have described as the universalistic component of the discourse ethic) has for forty years been the primary question of Habermas's polemical writings. These have been guided by the consistent purpose of defending the fragile growth of "constitutional patriotism" in the Federal Republic from all threats. (75)

Pensky's analysis supports likewise my existential approach to Habermas. "For Habermas, the rare commodity of constitutional patriotism in the Federal Republic is a universalistic attitude that was only brought about by the particularity of Germany's fascist nightmare" (77). As his evidence Pensky cites from Habermas a portion of the text, which I reproduce here in greater length:

> For us in the Federal Republic constitutional patriotism means, among other things, pride in the fact that we have succeeded in permanently overcoming fascism, establishing an order based on the rule of law, and anchoring it in a reasonably liberal political culture. Our patriotism cannot suppress the fact that democracy has only been able to strike roots in the hearts and motivations of the citizens, at least of the younger generation, after Auschwitz, and in a certain sense only because of the shock of this moral catastrophe. For this anchoring of universal principles one always requires a *specific* identity. (NR 152/AS 239f.; cf. Pensky 2000)

When we are studying Habermas' architectonic, it is fitting to learn from Sartre's (1974) secular reading of Kierkegaard that the universal enters history through the particular. In my reconstruction of Habermas' profile, this existential insight, which I applied as my methodology in this study, carries several implications:

- The integrative universal concepts enter the architectonic through particular critical responses to the past trauma, for which one takes responsibility today (universal notions become embodied in a form of life).
- The integrative universal concepts enter the architectonic through the singular universal, whereby one communicates and deliberates with another while guided by the ideal of a shared future.
- The moral disaster represents Germany's and Habermas' vanishing past.
- Ethical-political discourses on the future of *our* traditions, on the one hand, and deliberative politics and law, on the other, come to embody the

popular and institutionalized forms of the collective meaning and will formation.

The Basic Law of Federal Germany, as a historical and yet living document, contains both the *reciprocal movement* between critique and ideal and the *temporal movement* between the past and future-oriented trajectories. Constitutional patriotism and deliberative democracy are the conceptualities that express these two trajectories. Movements from the particular to the universal and from the past trauma to a future liberation are recorded in Article 146 of the Basic Law. This constitutional article figured in Habermas' objections to the manner of German unification and in his critique of the deceptive asylum debate. That unification and that debate harkened to Article 23, which extends the Basic Law as in principle valid for all ethnic Germans. Article 23 (on the basis of which Helmut Kohl pushed through the unification of the Germanies; it still guarantees citizenship to ethnic "Germans" even if they live outside Germany and even if they do not speak German or possess substantial ties to the state territory) facilitates the blood-nationalist lines and not constitutional principles as the measure of political membership and rights. After the fall of the Berlin Wall, Germans missed their chance to make political peace with their traumatic past by making a deliberative and responsible self-choice of themselves as a constitutional republic rather than as a nationalistic state. This fact being a sore spot in Habermas' complaint, constitutional patriotism continues to inhabit its complex trajectories between critique and ideal and between the past and the future. Arising from the aspirations of Article 146 (the conclusion of the Basic Law), this constitutional ideality submits its own law to the ongoing democratic decisions of Germans, who alone are to legitimate their future in public and deliberative constitutional performance (NR 216–20).

From the post-Wall vantage point, Habermas extends the concepts born of the particular German historical context to the European nation-state; indeed, in his mature architectonic, these notions become universalized. Thus, we read the following generalized conceptual analysis:

> The political culture of a country crystallizes around its constitution. Each national culture develops a distinctive interpretation of these constitutional principles that are equally embodied in other republican constitutions—such as popular sovereignty and human rights—in light of its own national history. A "constitutional patriotism" based on these interpretations can take the place originally occupied by nationalism. (EdA 143/118)

The concept of *deliberative democracy* takes place in his architectonic as a multiple response to the failures of Weimar Germany and its continuities, further to the failures of Germany's unification and to the obscurity of the asylum compromise. Yet this concept addresses also the nationalistic democracies and their present discontents. People's sovereignty and their basic human rights are inscribed into the political process of self-determination. Learning to cherish such principles inspires a new patriotism. Rather than driven by national myths, demanding the exclusion of foreigners and at once the homogenization of members, this patriotism is celebrated in political-constitutional terms.

> Democratic self-determination does not have the collectivistic and at the same time *exclusionary* meaning of the assertion of national independence and of the realization of a unique national character. Rather, it has the inclusive meaning of self-legislation which involves all citizens equally. It is inclusive in that such a political order keeps itself open to the equal protection of those who suffer discrimination and to the *integration* of the marginalized, but without *imprisoning* them in the uniformity of a homogenized ethnic community. (EdA 166/139)

Responding to the question of whether Europe needs a constitution, Habermas defends a generalized "communicative understanding of democracy." This understanding arises from knowing that "the people" can never in their very origins constitute a homogeneous mass but rather are always and already a heterogeneous grouping. This understanding learns from criticizing the failed historical past, which wanted to ascertain a homogeneous ideal by making it a fact through cleansing all difference; it projects a permanently democratic and constitutionally anchored revolutionary ideal as its desired future:

> The ethical-political self-understanding of citizens in a democratic community must not be taken as a historical-cultural a priori that makes democratic will formation possible, but rather as the fluid content of a circulatory process that is generated through the legal institutionalization of citizens' communication. (EdA 191/161; all citations above)

The vanishing point of the constitutional ideality is, then, "the concept of deliberative politics." Habermas abstracts from the German praxial context with its "particular collectivity" and its "ethical questions." These particularities should have emerged in the instance of May 8, 1945, and again when all Germans would consider the mandate to choose themselves as political and deliberative people under Article 146 of the Basic Law. Habermas' present context is the normative ideal of democracy. Examining three models of democracy, he eschews the republican one, which requires strong national bonds and would thus follow Kohl at Bitburg and into *re*-unification. He rejects the market-liberal one, which leads to a fragmentary society of externally related entrepreneurs bereft of all normative social ties. The market model expresses the neoliberal, hands-off, minimalist state. He defends a procedural model of democracy, which expands beyond particular ethical questions (republican model) and yet moralizes the instrumental market society (neoliberal model) in order to raise universal "questions of justice." Neither the nationalist contexts of Germany and the civic religion of the United States nor the neoliberal markets can suffice. "Politically enacted law, if it is to be legitimate, must be at least in harmony with moral principles that claim a general validity that extends beyond the limits of any concrete legal community." Deliberative democracy "acquires empirical relevance only when we take into account the multiplicity of forms of communication in which a common will is produced, that is, not just *ethical self-clarification* but also the balancing of interests and *compromise*, the *purposive* choice of means, *moral justification*, and *legal* consistency-testing" (EdA 284/245; italics in German original).

Habermas' discourse theory of democracy thus travels the furthest distance in abstracting from the praxis of critique to a normative ideal by moving from the traumatic past to an ongoing democratic revolution. The discourse model of democracy operates concretely among people and functions as a regulative ideal in this world, never, therefore, as a world-transcendent principle. This model retains in its ideality the very praxial dimension from which it emerges and to which it addresses itself back.

> Making the proceduralist conception of deliberative politics the cornerstone of the theory of democracy results in differences both from the republican conception of the state as an ethical community and from the liberal conception of the state as the guardian of a market society. In comparing the three models, I take my orientation from that dimension of politics which has been our primary concern, namely, the democratic opinion and will formation that issue in popular elections and parliamentary decrees. (EdA 285/246)

Whether or not popular elections as we know them are for fools, as Sartre would have it, raises a critical question for radical democratic praxis. We should be mindful of this issue when we examine the discontents of Habermas' positive impact. At this juncture, suffice it to say that his architectonic integrates in the formal concepts of constitutional patriotism and deliberative democracy not some historical place or some concretistic utopian blueprint, but rather a self-corrective learning attitude, "an ideal procedure for deliberation and decision making" (EdA 285/246).

Postnational Identity and Postnational Constellation

As Habermas should know by now from his experience, ideals remain mere formal (if not empty) oughts unless they are supported by the requisite social forms of life and social consciousness. The ideals imposed on Germany after 1945 and prior to 1968 are for the most part precisely just that, formal principles (e.g., the Basic Law) and oughts in search of their citizens with suitable social identities and political cultures. The conceptualities of *postnational identity* (Matuštík 1993) and the most recent *postnational constellation* (PK) emerge as two responses to this gap between form and reality: the first concept responds to the generational gap between the '45ers and the '68ers and the second to the globalization trends of the so-called new world order (Matuštík 1998a).

The ideal of postnational identity responds to the praxial dimension of the student revolt, and it integrates that revolutionary upheaval with the constitutional requirements of postwar Germany. The notion of postnational constellation integrates the securing and revolting aspirations of two postwar generations; the notion abstracts from Germany's context to the universal trends toward economic globalization, multiculturalism, and political integration. Habermas' historical vanishing point is self- and other-destructive nationalism; his ideal vanishing point is a multiculturally differentiated society with a postnational political culture and democratic citizenship.

The linkage between these sets of concepts and the prior set is typically expressed by Habermas' post-Wall rumination on Germany: "Post-traditional identity loses its substantial, natural, character; it *exists* only in the mode of the public, discursive, struggle for the interpretation of a constitutional patriotism made each time concrete under our [German] historical conditions" (NR 220). The indicative voice, which grammatically defines these concepts, should not distract us from the fact that the new identity formation, even after 1968, is at best an ideal dimension rather than a full-fledged German or pan-European praxis. Posttraditional and postnational identity are roughly interchangeable ideal concepts (Matuštík 1993, 4, 20–27, 93f., 149); both make possible and also require a postnational constellation as an ideal form of life. That stabilizing such identity in free praxis and in a social form of life is precarious sustains these concepts only as regulative ideals and critical measures of what is.

Habermas would not wish to have his ideal architectonic run ahead of critically relating it to the historical present. As a member of the skeptical generation, he worries about the fragile motivating force of denaturalized individuals, who are unable to support constitutional patriotism in complex societies without forging sufficiently robust bonds of social integration (EdA 143/118; Matuštík 1993, 5f.). His concept of a postnational world constellation might strike one as naively utopian. Yet he is aware all too well that nationalism and religious fundamentalism remain formidable competitors to achieving political sobriety, communicative democracy, and existential freedom. He ventures with these ideal integrative concepts, while remaining at once cognizant of *his* traumatic past and hopeful for *our* difficult (yet the only possible) future. The passage from the Historians' Debate marks his hope-filled yet skeptically inflected realism:

> The current debate shows that this reading [you may easily use here the post-Wall text cited above] is a disputed one. In the same phenomena others see only indications of the pathology of a national identity that has been damaged. In either case, certainly, the beginnings of a postnational identity linked to the constitutional state could develop and stabilize only within the framework of more general tendencies [i.e., postnational constellation] extending beyond the Federal Republic. (EAS 169/NC 256)

And he specifies his inquiry into the possibilities of a postnational form of life after 1989:

> Under what conditions can a liberal political culture provide a sufficient cushion to prevent a nation of citizens, which can no longer rely on ethnic associations, from dissolving into fragments? (EdA 143/118)

If we glance at the trajectory between the praxial and the ideal dimensions and between the historical and the futural vanishing points, then we discover once again how Habermas situates the possibilities of aiming at postnational identity within Germany. "The trend toward what might be termed a 'postnational' self-understanding of the political community may have been more pronounced in the former Federal Republic of Germany than in other European states, given its peculiar situation and the fact that it had, after all, been deprived of fundamental sovereignty rights." He generalizes his findings, first, to include the European Union (read western Europe) and then the global cosmopolis. "But in most of the Western and Northern European countries, the welfare state pacification of class antagonisms had given rise to a new situation" (EdA 144/119). West Europeans have come to prioritize, Habermas concludes, basic rights ("the real nation of citizens") over blood or nationalist ties ("the imagined ethnic-cultural nation"). In this accent, they have created a broader postnational constellation (144/120; EgA; PK).

The trends toward "postnational democracy" (PK 134f.) follow both from the particular and the globalizing learning how to invent and inhabit nondestructive forms of life. The *postnational ideal* is just as much an invention nowadays as the *nation-state* once was. Yet the former is a political invention of a self-correcting attitude and social process, rather than a myth of pure origins. The invention of an attitude finds justification in history (critically) and as an ideal (normatively). In Habermas' historical past lies Germany's disaster; but the generalized future (Germany and beyond) projects the regulative ideal of postnational democracy:

> These experiences with successful forms of social integration are marked by the normative self-understanding of European modernity, an egalitarian universalism, which can make for us—the sons, daughters, and uncles of a barbaric nationalism—easier the transition to the demanding relations of recognition in a postnational democracy. (PK 156)

By intensifying their particularity (I presume doing so in life-enhancing and disastrous instances alike) Germany and Europe can learn to decenter insularity. Habermas stays hopeful:

> These sharp conflicts, which often reach the deadly peak, have provided—in their happier moments—also an urge to decenter their own perspectives, an impetus to reflect and take distance from presuppositions, a motive to overcome particularism. (155f.)

Given the rubble of Germany in 1945, the success of the welfare state compromise marks one of Habermas' own happier moments. "Within a single generation the status of citizens, however imperfect, was markedly improved in its legal and material substance" (EdA 144/119). Let us not be fooled, however; the West German economic miracle delivered Habermas into neither a socialist society nor an inclusive democracy. His descriptions capture something ideal and perhaps also real, but the latter transpiring only in his own philosophical seminar room and among equal participants in conversation. "Each individual could come to recognize and appreciate citizenship status as that which links her with the other members of the political community and makes her at the same time dependent upon and coresponsible for them" (145/120). The German miracle benefited from slave labor exploited under the Nazi regime and continued by exploiting guest workers, whom it granted virtually no cultural or citizenship rights.

The praxial dimension of 1968 does not make it into the postnational regulative ideal of 1989 in equal measure with the praxial dimension of 1945. There is here a skewed asymmetry. To generalize the student shakedown of the Fascist tradition in Germany would require expanding an impact of the '68ers on global trends. Unlike Marcuse, Habermas hardly ventures outside of the German context in thinking about the events of 1968. He is not alone among those who claim that the ideals of the '68ers have been lost in the geopolitical changes of 1989. To truly universalize the praxial dimension of 1968 would require a post-1989 project of radical economic democracy, social transformation, and liberation. As it stands, Habermas limits his hope to a postnational political culture empowering a lawful, democratic, and multicultural state or a federation of such states.

Habermas hopes that Germany can be saved from its worst self by developments beyond its borders. In the 1980s, he names four global trends that might stabilize postnational identity. (1) The self-destructive contradictions of the nationalist wars will encourage the trend from Hegel's ethical moment of war to Kant's perpetual peace. (2) The massive population movements due to war, oppression, and poverty will lead to greater learning about the limits of one's own tradition among all those affected by such population movements. (3) Both mass media and travel will bring the plight of distant countries into the living room, and this will give impetus to "the extension of moral consciousness in the direction of universalism." (4) The greater awareness of the fallibility of knowledges and interpretations will decenter the received forms of historical consciousness. He raises this integral (praxial and ideal) question:

> If we accept for the moment that these and other like tendencies do in fact indicate a change in the form of national identity, at least within the domain of Western industrial societies, how are we to understand the relationship between a historical consciousness that has become problematic and a postnational state identity? (EAS 169–71/NC 257–59; and all citations above)[2]

His architectonic answers this query by distinguishing, first, between the nation-state built on ethnic ties *(ethnos)* and the one emerging from the political notion of a citizen *(demos)* (EdA 129/154). Second, he differentiates between, on the one hand, multicultural differences to be preserved and nationalist principles of social integration to be jettisoned; on the other hand, between multicultural society and political culture, where the multicultural and political ideals are to complement each other in a postnational democracy (142–45/117–20). Postnational identity, democracy, and constellation are concepts of increasing abstraction. Yet all three result from the crisis of the ethnically based variants of the nation-state. The nation-state once played a progressive and integrative role; it provided a national home for the disintegrating feudal societies, and it stabilized borders, defined membership, and promised equal opportunities to all members (134/110f.). The other face of this *Janus-faced concept* (139, 157/115, 131)[3] is its *intra*-state homogenization of the membership and the *inter*-nationalist violence against nonmembers (136f./112f.).

Just as the feudal societies *learned* from their discontents, so can the nation-states learn in their present crises. The '68ers intimated postnational identity in their highly critical attitude toward those received traditions that became problematic. Many of this generation, and not only in Germany, have turned comfortable if not conservative since then. The global trends create new pressures toward a postnational constellation. This pressure calls anew for a social form of life that would be able to integrate a repeated achievement of postnational attitude in a nondestructive manner. What other options do we have? Habermas would most likely ask. Short of remaining "neurotic" (EdA 145/120)—and that means destructive on a large scale of ethnic or imperial cleansing—postnational thinking achieves existential sobriety. And there are possible active sociopolitical equivalents to this sobriety. Habermas is troubled by "too weak a bond to hold together complex societies" (143/118) and by the lack of "a binding force that extends beyond the level of the nation-state" (153/127). This absence of state or other fixed guarantees for communicative freedom is precisely the existential mark of postnational sobriety, a lucidity whose preservation remains a lifelong human task.

Habermas never allows himself and others a moment of rest that postnational identity and democracy have been achieved for all future generations. Postnational trends and possibilities did emerge in our history. Hegel's prognosis notwithstanding, unlearning an achievement of a prior generation is also possible; no universal progress is guaranteed: "Since 1989, a new sort of patriotic spirit has strengthened in the unified Germany, a spirit that regards the learning processes of the last forty years as already having gone 'too far'" (ÜöGH 21/20). The integral ideal of postnational identity and constellation recalls *us* constantly back to the praxial dimensions of 1945 and 1968 as well as to the vanishing points of the past failures and to the future task of permanent democratic (I would add: and existential) revolution (Matuštík 1993, 253–58; 1998a, 227–66). The ethical-political discourse on the future of our closed and open identities and traditions raises the existential question of "accountability" for the past and of freedom with regard to *our* future.

> The hermeneutic ability to recognize the true scope of responsibility and complicity for crimes varies with our understanding of freedom: how we value ourselves as persons, and how much we expect from ourselves as political actors. An ethical-political discourse of collective self-understanding raises just this pre-understanding as a topic of discussion. (ÜöGH 37/36)

Cosmopolitan World Citizenship and Radical Democracy

The fall of the Berlin Wall opened the world to the possibility of cosmopolitan citizenship, at least if *we,* like Habermas, view the world from Germany. There is nothing sinister in wanting to share the good thing, but Habermas' primary worry is that the good thing cannot remain good for long if unified Germany fails to become integrated into a larger project—"Europe's Second Chance" (VaZ 97–129/73–97). There is a long path from the Peace of Westphalia of 1648 to the Paris events of 1789 to Kant's idea of perpetual peace to the Central-East European events of 1989 to Habermas' idea of cosmopolitan order and radical democracy. Even if 1989 offers Europe a second chance to revisit that fragile peace among the warring religions and nation-states and a second chance for the idea of republican citizenship and radical democracy to take root—this alone does little for the world. Neither Europe nor the United States may replace the United Nations. Habermas exhibits an awareness of this global context (EdA 145/120) and supports the UN role; yet he reverts repeatedly to his particular place, which is now a slightly enlarged mentality of greater Germany inserted within the euro currency and the European administrative union.

He expects from the global trends new redemptive benefits for Germany (VaZ 94f./70f.; all citations below): "The changed world situation itself will make the unified Germany a new nation." Meanwhile, Germany, cognizant of its historical vanishing point, should strive for a post-Wall political consensus about its ideal future:

> There has to be a consensus over the future role of Germany in Europe, and over the sort of role of assistance that Germany, as the economic locomotive of the European Community, is to assume for a peaceful social and economic development within Eastern Europe. Further, I would wish for a consensus on a constitutional patriotism deeply rooted in the experiences of German history.... Also, naturally, the reminder that Germany is the only highly industrialized country in which an economic crisis led democratic state under the rule of law to collapse into a fascist dictatorship.

Germany must exercise a post-1989 either/or choice, integrating the experiences of 1945 and 1968:

> We have to know what it is that we want to defend: the crude economic chauvinism of a society as divided on the inside as it is walled off from the outside

world? or the integrity of a highly individualized society—a society that of course has to keep its damageable functional system intact, but only for the sake of implementing the demands of its universalistic constitutional principles?

Just as the praxial dimension of 1989 integrates its prior generational experiences, so also Habermas' later ideal concepts integrate the unfulfilled universal requirements of the prior concepts. The notions of cosmopolitan world citizenship and radical democracy address today's particular and global situations and Habermas' grasp of them in the post-1989 constellations. These conceptions, abstracted from the German soil and universalized to the world situation, function as ideals as well as critical alternatives for the present. When Habermas answers the question about the future of the Berlin Republic, the core of his expressed belief carries a world-historical significance:

> I believe we would *all* like to live in a civil country that is cosmopolitan in outlook and ready to play a thoughtful, cooperative role amongst other nations. We would *all* like to live amongst fellow citizens who are accustomed to respecting the particularity of strangers, the autonomy of individuals, and the plurality of regional, ethnic and religious identities. (EgA 15/12; italics added)

Again, that world-historical future refers Habermas' architectonic to a historical particular:

> The new republic would do well to remember the role of Germany in the catastrophic history of the twentieth century, but equally those rare moments of emancipation and achievement of which we can be proud. (15/12)

Habermas' historical particular marks the negative vanishing point—the insular and discontented nation-state, the regime that violates both citizen rights and basic human rights. The concepts of a cosmopolitan world citizenship and radical democracy represent the regulative ideals for a future social order. The anchor for this ideal dimension lies in the system of basic rights.

The rights are "absolute basic rights" (NBR 158/153) when they cannot be limited or abolished without thereby in principle violating the *beginning situation* of communicative freedom. "Communicative freedom exists only between actors who, adopting a performative attitude, want to reach an understanding with one another about something and expect one another to take positions on reciprocally raised validity claims" (FuG 152/119). "Morally grounded *human* rights" can be called basic rights in that they are grounded in the communicative freedom of participants who, in an effort to reach mutual understanding about something, may all equally raise, criticize, reject, or accept validity claims; these communicative rights acquire the form of "legal human *rights*" through enacted constitutions (NBR 157/152). The moral rights to individual autonomy and self-legislation are constitutive of the basic liberties that alone enable the functioning of legal norms; and the positive validation of legal liberties both presupposes and institutionalizes these communicative freedoms. "The key idea is that the principle of democracy derives from the interpretation of the discourse principle and the legal form. . . . Hence the principle of democracy can only appear as the heart of a *system* of rights" (FuG 154f./121). Basic human rights are universally inclusive, whereas citizens' rights, because constitutionally enacted by "a voluntary association under law" (155/122), are exclusive of nonmembers.

Habermas' architectonic establishes an internal, cooriginal link between two categories of rights: the legitimate moral norm of human rights (radical access to and the universal exercise of communicative freedoms) and the positive legal form of popular sovereignty. To reconcile legitimacy with legality, he invokes the regulative ideal of cosmopolitan world citizenship and radical democracy. This ideal integrates responses to concrete situations rather than the needs of theory alone: the critical ideal of radically democratic institutionalization of communicative freedoms is invoked within the praxial dimensions of problems coming to us from immigration and asylum requests, multicultural societies, human rights violations, wars of intervention against such violations, and the functioning of international law and the United Nations (FuG 157–65/123–31). From the angle of this book, an intelligible entry into Habermas' architectonic opens through the praxial dimensions to which his concepts are addressed in the first place.

Habermas argues with Kant's idea of perpetual peace against the perceived limits of Kant's moral idea of peace among the nation-states, set within his historical horizon, and against the limits of Hegel's international law, which admits of wars among the sovereign nation-states. The cosmopolitan law complements civic laws enacted within nation-states and international law among them. The ideal of a cosmopolitan law, beyond its merely moral imperative, introduces "a global legal order that unites all peoples and abolishes war." Kant's perpetual peace runs in this regard ahead of Hegel, who envisions ethical relations within the rational nation-state but relegates international relations to the premoral state of nature. Kant's thinking suggests that the international rules of war and the very right to wage wars are valid until "legal pacification" and elimination of war as such could be achieved. Kant's perpetual peace, unlike the Peace of Westphalia resulting from prior wars, or the Cold War's peace of deterrence, cannot emerge from legitimate wars. The new idea is to delegitimate the state of nature among states and warfare as a means of conflict resolution (EdA 192/165; cf. 195f./168).

Habermas ambitiously completes the Kantian project of moralizing this international state of nature: from Kant's moral imperative for a permanent union of nation-states, Habermas distills a requirement for a legally binding form in order to institutionalize radically democratic cosmopolitan freedoms of all. No longer depending "on each government's own *moral* self-obligation" (197/169) alone, he presses for "the project of a *constitutionally organized* community of nations" (198/170). Distrustful of the cognitive uncertainty of the international order, itself relying only on the weak goodwill of the sovereign nation-states, he calls for nothing less than "a cosmopolitan constitution." He explains Kant's limited theorizing of the cosmopolitan idea by the limited historical horizon of his times. The twentieth-century praxial dimensions of Habermas' horizon allow now for a new development of this Kantian idea.

> Because Kant does not transcend the horizon of his time, it is of course equally difficult for him to believe in any moral motivation for creating and maintaining a federation between free states dedicated to power politics. Kant sketches as a solution to this problem a philosophy of history with a cosmopolitan purpose which is supposed to lend plausibility, through a hidden "purpose of nature," to the improbable "agreement between politics and morality." (198f./171)

In concluding this section, I sum up the critical potential inscribed into Habermas' integral concepts of cosmopolitan world citizenship and radical democracy. I will return to discontents of his overall architectonic when, in the next chapter, I take up the Habermas effect and the unfinished debates.

Habermas, in an interim period between the Persian Gulf War and the Kosovo conflict, pleads his case for complex cosmopolitanism as a democratic, legal, and globally ethical ideal (see Pensky 2000, 64f., 75–78).[4] From *our* vantage point after both these *humanitarian* wars, *we* cannot but notice how Habermas' move partly exorcises the imperfect reality (i.e., sheer militarism) of such *humanitarian* wars of intervention (in the passage below, it is only the Persian Gulf War), how it thereby qualifies his public support for them. It would seem that he employs his theoretical ideal to criticize his own fallible praxis as a philosopher giving advice to the king. And yet we may not be able to silence the nagging question of whether or not he heeds his critical words before publicizing that—however otherwise careful, qualified, *and* ambivalent—support for NATO's *humanitarian* intervention in Serbia (BH; chap. 6 above). His own warning words, cited below, want to ward off any Schmittian or postmodern skeptic who would want to claim that the cosmopolitan democratic ideal can *never* correspond to a transformed future reality. The failed praxis (whether that of NATO or of one thinker) does not prove the impossibility of a more sane world. Habermas places great trust in the self-corrective processes of learning—even from disaster (NBR 17/12f.; EdA 149/123, 182/152, 206f./178, 217/186; PK 154ff.; ENPG 58; BH 7/271; and LD). With Feuerbach and Marx, he might retort to an absolute skeptic and to his own limited horizon (is there any other than a historically limited universal horizon *for us*?) that we must not only contemplate how concepts correspond to reality but also change our world from which they emerge to the one that they ideally project.

> It is because of their universal human rights content that the[se] basic rights are pushing—as if on their own—toward the realization of a form of world citizenship in which human rights everywhere acquire the status and the validity of positive law. Such a situation cannot be achieved solely through international

courts; for this we need a UN capable of reaching decisions and taking action, and that can, when it needs to intervene, employ military forces under its *own* command instead of delegating this function to the superpowers, which merely lend themselves UN legitimation for the conduct of their wars. (NBR 157/152)

The most interesting aspect of Habermas' mature formulation of the global cosmopolitan ideal (see EdA, chap. 7; PK 91–169; and ENPG) is its critical relation to the existing political praxis that he justified (cf. BH). In the Persian Gulf War, the U.S.-led armies did "merely lend themselves UN legitimation for the conduct of their wars" (NBR 157/152). In the bombing of Serbia, the UN was, de facto as well as normatively, bypassed as the sole international legitimating body. The tribunal in The Hague, by charging that war crimes were committed by the Serbian leadership, provided but a semblance of legitimacy for NATO's military action. Should not Habermas' regulative ideal (see the citation above), as much as his more sober conclusions about the real existing political praxis (see the citation below), have affected more consistently his public reflections on NATO's *humanitarian* war of intervention?

> It is one thing if the USA, however remarkable the political tradition at the root of its actions may be, plays the role of a hegemon guaranteeing the instrumentation of human rights. It is something else if we try to understand the precarious transition from classical power politics to a global civil society as a learning process with which all of us together are going to have come to terms, across the trenches [*Gräben*] of an ongoing armed conflict. This broadening of perspectives also admonishes us to take greater caution. NATO's self-authorization should not be allowed to become the general rule. (BH 7/271; translation altered)

THE STRUCTURE AND MODE OF HABERMAS' INTEGRAL LIFEWORK: POLITICS AND CRITICAL SOCIAL THEORY

> *Nihil contra Deum nisi Deus ipse.* Communicative reason is of course a rocking hull—but it does not go under in the sea of contingencies, even if shuddering in high seas is the only mode in which it 'copes' with these contingencies. (ND 184f./144)

> [*Nihil*] *contra Deum nisi Deus ipse*—which is not to appeal to some sort of deified reason, but on the contrary to say that it is only through reason that we can determine the limits of our own rationality. *This* is the fundamental figure of Kantian thought that was definitive for modernity. And modernity can't just be peeled off like a dirty shirt. It's in our skin. . . . It is existentially unavoidable. . . . This condition also implies a challenge, and not just disaster. (VaZ 125/94)

> I have a conceptual motive and a fundamental intuition. . . . The motivating thought concerns . . . the idea that without surrendering the differentiation that modernity has made possible in the cultural, the social and economic spheres, one can find forms of living together in which autonomy and dependency can

truly enter into a non-antagonistic relation. . . . The intuition springs from the sphere of relations with others; it aims at experiences of undisturbed intersubjectivity. . . . These . . . intersubjective relations . . . make possible a relation between freedom and dependency that can only be imagined with interactive models. (NU 202/AS 124f.)

Although the integrative concepts facilitate the architectonic of the authorship, the core situations, conversations, and interventions shape its dynamic structure. This relationship between concept formation and profile formation secures crucial evidence for the productive reciprocity between the particular and the universal, the praxial and the ideal, or the practical and the theoretical dimensions of Habermas' lifework. Because this study begins from particular praxial starting points, it is possible to reconstruct Habermas' authorship in light of his philosophical-political profile. Again, this approach does not mean that his theoretical edifice cannot be formally justified in ways that are independent of his motives, historical experiences, or fundamental intuitions. It does show that impartial justifications are never derivable in a historical vacuum, that is, with concepts and theories begotten without bodies, contexts, or limit horizons. By showing the limits of theories, even Habermas' criticisms of his predecessors and his contemporaries benefit from exposing the limits of particular contexts. By analogy (i.e., in principle and by doing justice to all involved), one should get the same benefits in studying Habermas' authorship.

Pensky (1995, 69) sums up the singularity of the political and theoretical faces of Habermas:

> Insofar as it takes its bearings from the particular historical and cultural *situation* of postwar Germany, Habermas's theoretical and political work is highly particular. And yet, because the dynamic that it derives from its own particular context has impelled Habermas's thought towards a thoroughgoing political universalism, he has become a *German* intellectual precisely by working against the Germanness of the political culture of the Federal Republic.

Continuing this thought, Pensky characterizes the *internal link* between Habermas' political and theoretical authorship as at once paradoxical and dialectical:

> This irony, what one might call this *dialectic of universality and situation* in Habermas's work, underlies the complex relation between theoretical and polemic writing that Habermas has produced over a career that, so far, has run exactly parallel to the curriculum vitae of the Federal Republic from its first hours to the moment of unification. "Universalism" is an abstract moral-political principle that nevertheless can be embodied only in particular cultural and political situations.

Yet Pensky (1999) writes more recently, like Metz in an earlier objection I introduced in chapter 5, that Habermas' lifework is propelled by an antinomy between its theory and praxis:[5]

> [TCA] offers no account of Fascist horror or genocidal violence.... (223) Given the divide between theory and nontheory that structures Habermas's work so powerfully, the political writings address themselves to the moral catastrophe only in so far as they insist on the status of the Holocaust as the nonnegotiable filter of ethical self-reflection through which all national traditions must pass. Hence these writings bear witness to the continuing effects of the Holocaust upon the lifeworld of which Habermas is a member ... while disavowing any attempt to link this causality back into the theoretical reconstruction of the modern, rationalized lifeworld of occidental civilization.... Indeed it is the uneffaceability and the unapproachability of the Holocaust as an object of writing that forms the point around which the antinomy between these two carefully distinguished sides of Habermas's work revolves—an antinomy that keeps them apart, but provides them with their unceasing productivity. (224)

If what Pensky calls an antinomy between the praxial and ideal dimensions existed in Habermas' authorship, it would disclose undertheorized or blind angles of his work. By focusing on the strengths of Habermas' integrative lifework, I bracket until the next two chapters Pensky's critical suggestion of an antinomy, as well as Metz's (1997, 152f.) earnest suspicion that there is an amnesia of Auschwitz within Habermas' theoretical architectonic even though it might pervade his political polemics and interventions. I accentuate below the positive conclusion to Pensky's analysis (1999), namely, that

> it is in essence a misreading of Habermas's career as a politically engaged intellectual to divide his political writings into this or that "debate"—the student debate, the historians' debate, the asylum debate and so forth. In fact, there has been a single, continuous debate with a *single* objective and a single, if constantly multiplying, opposition. (224)

The complaint about misreadings of Habermas renders Holub's (1991) very helpful introduction to the former's activist and critical role in the public sphere vulnerable. Holub divides his analysis according to Habermas' theoretical and political debates. It is, however, an existentially motivated reconstruction of Habermas' philosophical-political profile (the path I took in this study), rather than a focus on an antinomical model of his unpolitical theory *versus* nontheoretical politics (Pensky's concern), that facilitates my holistic reconstruction of his political and philosophical writings in this single account of lifework.

I organize my discussion of Habermas' integrative, philosophical-political lifework along its two structural dimensions: political polemic and critical social theory. These two dimensions are clustered around the three axes of the philosophical-political debates in which Habermas takes part at various times. The axes thus define the three areas of rational discourse, in which we may situate his philosophical-political thinking. But to conceive of this authorship in its unique singularity, we must circumscribe it holistically as an integral conversation. We can acquire an integral view when we reconstruct particular conversations, each addressing the historical vanishing point (Habermas' and Germany's past with their experiences of radical irrationality and disaster) and each projecting an ideal future (making all current historical problems available to rational discourse and to communicative freedom). The past-future axis of temporality, running through Habermas' path, takes place in many historical presents, within multiple discourses, in different voices, and through their interrelated problems. Otherwise, Habermas' Critical Theory, even as it embodies a unique singularity of his core motives and intuition, could not sustain its materialist, postmetaphysical, and radically pluralist orientation. The strength of my existential reading of Habermas' communicative rationality, ethics, and democracy are evident in *the integrative singularity of his authoring* within *the pluralist structure of his authorship* (tab. 7.2).

Habermas' authorship or lifework exhibits likewise two modes: basic intuitions or motives and their theoretical articulation. The two modes (tab. 7.3), in parallel to the two structures of praxial polemic and Critical Theory (tab. 7.2), cluster around three axes. Each articulation of Critical Theory (compare the right columns in tabs. 7.2 and 7.3) can be traced not only to certain problems of the present age (see the left column in tab. 7.2) but likewise to a pretheoretical mode contained in the basic intuitions or motives (see the left column in tab. 7.3).

The temporal vanishing points oscillate between the modes of melancholy or even despairing reason of an always and already lost myth and lost revolutionary hope, at one pole, and of an existential, multicultural, and democratic revolution in permanence, at the other pole.

Communicative Reason and Formal-Pragmatic Materialism

Habermas builds his communicative theory by answering to the problems that come to us in our mutual engagement about something in the world. By anchoring his theorizing in the problems of the present age, his authorship can be called historically materialist (ZRHM). He responds to the rationality deficits as

Table 7.2 The Structure of Habermas' Authorship

Polemic	Critical Theory
Rationality debates	Communicative reason and formal-pragmatic materialism
Communitarian-liberal debates	Communicative ethics and postmetaphysical normative theory
Struggles for recognition	Communicative democracy and the inclusion of the other
Historical Vanishing Point irrationality disaster	*Ideal Vanishing Point* validity domains of rational discourse communicative freedom

Table 7.3 The Modes of Habermas' Authorship

Basic Intuitions and Motives	Theoretical Articulation
Nihil contra Deum nisi Deus ipse	Communicative reason
ambivalence toward (an either/or choice of) traditions	Communicative ethics
rescuing future via *anamnestic* solidarity	Communicative democracy
Historical Vanishing Point witness: destruction of myth and reason; melancholy and despair	Ideal Vanishing Point recognition: multicultural enlightenment; permanent existential and democratic revolution

these become apparent through his various debates with other thinkers and positions. By anchoring his theory in conversations with contemporaries, his authorship begins in and returns to a performative and dialogic ground. The historical vanishing point of his theorizing runs up against the dead-end refusals to understand and against those myths that emphatically privilege irrationality over communicative interaction. The ideal vanishing point projects the validity domains of rational discourse or, expressing this notion more musically, "the unity of reason in the diversity of its voices" (ND 153–86/115–48).

That critical social theory responds to the problems of the age, rather than theorizing from nowhere, means that both its formal and substantive beginnings are material and historical. This is not to claim that the material base univocally determines the ideal superstructure. But it does mean that Habermas' theoretical architectonic concretely exists only within the responses to the problems that address us. The integral ground of the authorship is performative rather than either foundationalist or absolutist. To have a foundationalist beginning would mean that one would be able to begin in theory before one actually began in life. To have an absolutist angle would mean that one could reach a comprehensive, total view of truth at history's end. Although we cannot cease laying foundational grounds in order to make steps on the surface of something more or less stable and we cannot cease projecting ideality in order to take concrete steps somewhere, ordinary walking can still be a risky undertaking. It is risky especially after the German catastrophe of Auschwitz.

It should seem apparent that both foundationalist and absolutist guarantees pale in light of Habermas' historical vanishing point. To begin as he does, in the situations of his age and without any guarantees of the future progress, requires him to jettison both the foundationalist and the absolutist groundings of theory. Habermas adopts a peculiarly 'groundless' *performative holism*. It is holism, as opposed to foundationalism, since we always begin in media res, in a context of a preinterpreted life world. This holism is performative (without grounds secured apart from speech or action), since we can never reach an absolute point of view inside or outside history. In this position, he subverts the dual dangers of ahistorical foundationalism and hegemonic absolutism. Yet, Habermas will insist over and over, reason can recover from its blindness only by its own critical resources; history can recover from its disasters only with its own historical resources. Discovering the futility of a foundationalist Archimedean point from which one could lift the entire world does not mean that we do not and cannot walk here and now on some ground. Experiencing the failure of reaching an absolute totality inside or outside the temporal flux does not mean that we do not and cannot guide our actions critically by regulative ideals. *Nihil contra Deum nisi Deus ipse—nobody (can act) against God but God alone* (on this phrase, see Keulartz 1995, 13–15).

What does Habermas' sui generis combination of the Schwäbian and Jewish Cabalistic mysticism have to do with his communicative theory drawn from the resources of analytical, pragmatist, and Continental-European philosophy? Reading his theoretical works, one for sure does not get any impression that this could be an oeuvre funded by spiritual or mystical intuitions and motives. The now-dominant Anglo-American reception of Habermas, focused exclusively on his analytical apparatus and reproducing his thought in analytical-argumentative style, even further downplays this other side of Habermas. Yet formal pragmatics, the linguistic-communicative turn in philosophical methodology, and communicative reason ushering from both, are only somewhat drier, more technical terms for these other, rather mystical features of Habermas' authorship. *Formal pragmatics* refers to the praxial dimensions of problems from which Habermas' Critical Theory emerges; *communicative rationality* names the ideal that his Critical Theory invokes in dialogue with its theoretical contemporaries. The *linguistic-communicative turn* defines the domain of speech acts as the main sphere for normative investigation.

I will first sum up the technical meaning of this terminology. Since it has been explained well enough by other commentaries, I can be brief. I will then reconstruct the analytical-mystical dimension of Habermas' basic motives and intuitions behind these terms.

We can get at the meaning of *formal pragmatics* by an imaginary exercise: let us conceive past and future vanishing points of possible grounds on which we can walk with a fallible yet self-corrective sense of direction (however risky this might be) and without having to invoke foundationalist or absolutist crutches. A tightrope walker, for example, needs minimally a sense of direction, proper balance, and steadiness; and this would be true of such walking no matter where the rope were fastened. The vanishing points of the past and the future possible grounds become coterminous in the present: they define pragmatically (here and now) and yet formally (without reference to any concrete world) the possibilities of our actual performance. We could also call them the formal and pragmatic presuppositions of walking without which we would fall on our faces. Since Habermas takes communicative interaction to be the main medium of human intelligent motion, we may substitute speech acts for acts of walking.

The substitute question thus becomes, What are the minimal formal and pragmatic presuppositions of communicative interaction without which we would fall into incommunicable silence or sheer nonsense? Remember that we may not rely on crutches (a rock-bottom ground of communication or some ultimate horizon from which we then begin to communicate). Like the tightrope-walking example, Habermas' communicative reason moves with a fallible yet self-corrective sense of direction (however risky this might be). Habermas insists emphatically that it is possible to retrieve the general (read formal-pragmatic) sense of direction, balance, and steadiness for communicative interaction. Just as a tightrope walker might fall on his face if he focused on the fact that he was walking not on the ground but on a wobbly rope, so a human communicator might despair under the conditions of modernity. Out of this despair, she might either run for a set of crutches or declare motion impossible. Habermas' *rationality debates*—engaged by him at different times with positivists, social scientists, analytical philosophers, poststructuralists (and postmodernists), legal scholars, and neoconservatives—are the variations of his practical counsel against such despair as well as against faulty responses to this despair.[6]

The linguistic-communicative equivalents to the tightrope walker's ideal sense of direction, balance, and steadiness are the presuppositions of coming to a mutual understanding with another speaker about something in the world. Habermas' architectonic names three such ideal presuppositions of undistorted communication (i.e., presuppositions of walking and not falling down). These ideals invoke formal worlds of appeal and project an ideal communication community for the appeal. The idealities are formal (they do not exist in any ideal heaven) and pragmatic (they are invoked here and now by concrete communicative interaction in all natural or ordinary languages).

The three formal pragmatic presuppositions of communication are the appeals to truth, normative rightness, and sincerity; the ideal communication community marks the vanishing horizon (address) of those appeals. One cannot walk without (1) direction (even if wandering aimlessly), (2) balance (even if jumping), and (3) steadiness (even if walking with difficulty). Analogically, one cannot communicate, for the sake of reaching mutual understanding with another about something in the world, without (1) wanting to communicate something (sense of truth), (2) thereby wanting to ascertain something about something (sense of normative rightness), and (3) communicating that this entire act is earnest (sense of sincerity). The strategic modes of communication are always derivative of the basic mode.

The technical structure of making moves in communication defines the scope of formal pragmatics. The full scope of speech acts is performed from the first-vis-à-vis the second-person participant's perspective in communicative interaction. By standing outside, as external observers of static architecture, we can access only the third-person (i.e., descriptive) perspective. From within the internal performative attitude, we may reconstruct the formal validity of the claims to truth, rightness, and sincerity in all utterances raised in discourse. In theory, we only reconstruct them formally. But pragmatically, we have always and already performed the structure of the claims. If we play by the rules of the communication game, we cannot but raise, criticize, reject, or accept claims to validity. We should not ask for more help than this formal structure. To ask for more under the pluralist conditions of modernity, in which the formal and cultural and metaphysical crutches were previously reliable, would mean that we are appealing to something outside of communicative performance. In theorizing what takes place in communicative interaction, we admit that, unless we give up trying to understand one another (and fall on our faces instead), we can take recourse to these historically decentered and now rationally fallible forms of validity (ND 105–35/57–87; 153–86/115–48).

To take *the linguistic-communicative turn* requires employing in performance and reconstructing in theory all three dimensions of validity. The linguistic turn, while an advance over the prelinguistic forms of theorizing, abstracts from some praxial and some ideal dimensions alike; Habermas' linguistic-communicative turn learns from these advances and, in a Hegelian manner, dialectically builds on them. The turn to language depicts human self-relation and reason as thoroughly inseparable from their linguistic contexts. There is no 'I' that has not been always and already addressed by a 'Thou'; there is no self-relation apart from the structure of other relations; even the notions of subject, monologue, and inwardness reveal the structures of sociality or publicness from which each concept emerges and to which each is addressed.

Playing the communicative game with less than the performative attitude commits either the semantic and cognitivistic abstractions or the objectivistic fallacy (R 234; ND 178/139). The semantic abstraction results from the exclusive focus on the *architecture* of meaning and sentences; the cognitivist abstraction is a consequence of deriving meaning from *propositional and assertoric* types of claims alone; and the objectivist fallacy restricts truth conditions to sentences and their *semantic analysis*. In each analytical instance, what is being abstracted from, Habermas argues, is the threefold relation of hearers-speakers-sign. Thus the linguistic-communicative turn theorizes the *performative attitude* of the triple relation of coming to an understanding with one another about something in the world (ND 106/58; ND 63–103, English only).

Habermas rejects positivism as much as he jettisons appeals to metaphysical certainties. To view his authorship as foundationalist, absolutist, or fundamentalist represents thus a thorough mistake. But the fallible communicative reason, even as it frees itself from aspirations to its *apotheosis* (divinization), is more than nothing. Habermas rejects, albeit highly polemically, the antitheoretical discourses of postmodernity. Antitheory judges the failures of modern reason by the performatively and existentially false criteria of collective guilt: western logos failed to usher humans into more just forms of life, and western modernity produced many unenlightened instances of domination; hence all rationality is logocentric, dominating, violent; hence, we must learn to give up rationality for something else. These claims are at best caricatures of the mature positions held by Jacques Derrida or Michel Foucault. But the caricature suffices for the characterization of Habermas' own fears of and his consequent polemic with them. Given his theoretical sophistication, an unnuanced polemic with the complexity of postmodern thought remains the weakest part of Habermas' debates. He says in so many words that the discourses of postmodernity are an outcome of a disappointed desire (a tantrum argument, if you will) to achieve a successful absolute if not to become a god (PDM, lecture 7, n. 46). But the linguistic turn to postmetaphysical reason is accomplished not only by the generations of the twentieth-century Austro-Anglo-American analytical philosophers of language but, along the parallel time line, by Continental-European hermeneuticians, structuralists, and poststructuralists. I will note later how Habermas, in spite of his impatiently generalized reading of poststructuralist authors, effectively unravels the analytical-Continental/European-pragmatist divides in philosophy.

To say something about the analytical-mystical dimension of Habermas' basic motives and intuitions underpinning some of his technical terms, let us recall the citations that open this section. Here Habermas describes the ground after Auschwitz on which reason may still walk tall even if radically humbled: he names it a "shuddering in high seas" (ND 184f./144). This performative attitude, which recovers its ground even in the groundlessness of the era after a total disaster, is not a "deified reason." Habermas' appeal to existential groundlessness and to a God who acts against God contravenes Heidegger's ([1966] 1976) claim that only a God can save us now. For Habermas, reason in history, and no other divine principle, helps reason to redress its own bankruptcy and limits. Unlike the Manichaean dualists who balance two principles of good and evil, he travels on a single path, reason in history, on which human life transpires. This performative condition of modernity is "existentially unavoidable" (VaZ 125/94; both citations above). The very possibility that after a total disaster *we* may experience ourselves opening to something new and thus even reexperience certain innocence reveals a mysterious dimension of life. But this mystery is ascribed by Habermas to communicative reason in history, rather than to an apocalyptic myth of a saving 'God'.

Secularizing the mystical Protestant and Jewish traditions of Jakob Böhme and Isaak Luria, with the gnostic narrations of the salvation history, Habermas forms his intuitions about communicative nearness and distance, reciprocity and autonomy, vulnerability and separateness:

> In Lurianic mysticism the idea is developed of the universe's arising in virtue of a process of shrinkage and contraction; God withdraws into an exile within himself. In this way the primordial impenetrability and power of matter is explained, as well as the positive character of evil, which can no longer be facilely evaporated into a shadow side of the good.... This dark ground remains a nature in God.... [For Bloch, it follows from this insight that] Matter is in need of redemption. Since the time of that theological catastrophe described by the Zohar

in the image of the shattering of a vessel, all things bear within themselves a break.... The process of restoration was almost already completed when Adam's fall once again threw the world down from its proper stage and threw God back into exile. *The new age of the world,* with the ancient goal of the redemption of humanity, of nature, and indeed of the God knocked off his throne, *is now the responsibility of humans.* (PpP 60/39; italics added)[7]

This responsibility is slightly more active and hope-filled than the Sartrean speculative idea that even if God existed, it would make no difference to our responsible sense of freedom. For Habermas, even if God existed, even if only a God could save us now, in being dethroned in history, this God would need our help in liberation.

Since I made us enter Habermas' authorship through existential dimensions of his profile, it might be helpful to cite his biographical experience in which, after Germany's disaster, a future restorative path becomes possible (on this, see also Keulartz 1995, 14). The first, historical, experience comes "through the universal devaluation and insult that the Nazis have exerted to all who carry a human face"; the second, future-oriented, experience reveals "that after all that on the same ground, namely in the Federal Republic, still something *better* has come to be" (NR 32). His experience horizon stretches between, on the one hand, his deep ambivalence toward all social relations (NU 203f./AS 126) and the ambivalence of every uncritically received tradition (EAS 268f./NC 257) and, on the other hand, the Brechtian figure of "friendly living together." His originary intuition and motive build from his twofold experience of rupture and renewal, and reach back to "religious traditions such as those of the Protestant or Jewish mystics, also to Schelling" (NU 202f./AS 125).

We can trace the historically material grounding of formal pragmatics, and the communicative transformation of reason, to Habermas' core intuition about our shared radical historical responsibility. Reason might not fare better than "a rocking hull ... shuddering in high seas" (ND 184f./144). Kierkegaard (1988, 476) speaks of this dizzy freedom as an existential attitude of "simultaneously to be out on 70,000 fathoms of water and yet be joyful." Habermas does not consciously theorize this leap over the gap of irrationality and disaster to an undistorted, even solidary and joyful, communicative interaction. He only offers his two autobiographical experiences of disaster and liberation. Yet his *nihil Deum nisi Deus ipse,* even if profanized in Critical Theory, represents a leap within the space of communicative reason that, almost mysteriously, reconciles the gap between disaster and liberation. No matter how technically analytical the categories of the linguistic-communicative turn are, they invite us to work responsibly and also to await the arrival of some poetic, messianic (?) justice. We can imagine and even prepare but must wait, whether or not Bosnians, Croats, Albanians, and Serbs become capable of living once again as neighbors in a village that was cleansed, in a country that was bombed.

Following Jacob [Ger. Jakob] Böhme and Isaac [Ger. Isaak] Luria, Schelling correctly insisted that mistakes, crimes, and deceptions are not simply without reason; they are forms of manifestation of *the inversion* of reason [*verkehrter Vernunft*]. The violation of the claims to truth, correctness, and sincerity affects the whole permeated by the bond of reason. There is no escape and no refuge for the few who are in the truth and are supposed to take their leave of the many who stay behind in the darkness of their blindness, as the day takes leave of the night. Any violation of the structures of rational life together, to which all lay claim, affects everyone equally. (PDM 377/324; italics in the German original)

Communicative Ethics and Postmetaphysical Normative Theory

In examining the Historians' Debate and the basic integrative concepts of his architectonic, we witnessed how Habermas had responded to the perceived liberal-communitarian impasses in ethics, morality, politics, and law. Communicative ethics, just like communicative rationality, emerges through addressing the problems that come to us rather than through the in-house debates in normative theory. The historical and material grounds of communicative rationality extend to communicative ethics. His performative approach defines both the normative substance of communicative ethics and its postmetaphysical form. The historical vanishing point is Germany's moral disaster; the ideal vanishing point is the normative discourse based on a mutual respect for the process of deriving moral norms and for all those affected by these norms.[8]

The material and postmetaphysical grounds of Habermas' communicative ethics are discernible both in his technical terminology and in the existential project of his moral theory. Since I discussed some of the concepts already, I can be brief in this reconstruction: I will define his key technical terms and then situate communicative ethics in that larger project.

Communicative rationality defines the inescapable presuppositions of coming to an understanding with another about something in the world. *Communicative ethics* further specifies these presuppositions for the process of normative discourse. In normative discourse we derive, that is, justify, norms that would be generally valid for our conduct. With this in mind, we can clarify communicative ethics by the following composition that responds to the liberal-communitarian accents: Habermas learns both from the liberal accent on the self-determining individual and the communitarian accent on shared communal solidarities. But he does not grant primacy to one apart from the other. From Kant's liberal standpoint, Habermas accepts the categorically normative requirements of self-determination, self-legislation, and autonomy; from the Aristotelian-Hegelian communitarian standpoint, he derives the intersubjective requirements of mutual respect, recognition, and the normative (illocutionary) bonding effected through a consensual procedure. For communicative reason, there is no self-relation apart from other-relations; for communicative ethics, there are no privately valid norms. The rational error of *monologism* would be to assert 'I' or 'autonomy' apart from acknowledging the coconstitutive social world of linguistic interaction. The normative error of *decisionism* would be to assert moral norms form a pre- or extradiscursive standpoint. Only those norms can become valid that were accepted by all those to be affected by them.

It should be obvious why communicative ethics is considered a postmetaphysical normative theory. Insofar as metaphysics and linguistic interaction (or formal pragmatics) are exclusive conceptualities, the linguistic-communicative turn to communicative reason and ethics is a move away from metaphysics. Metaphysical presuppositions, by definition, lie outside of human performance, outside of what lies on *this side*[9] of the discursive world. Once metaphysical presuppositions enter discussion, they thereby become subject to the process of *linguistification*. This technical term designates a variant of tightrope walking without any props. The performative process, a walking on postmetaphysical ground, overtakes any purported metaphysical certainty or primacy.

While it might now be apparent why communicative ethics defines a postmetaphysical moral theory, it is not perfectly clear why this is still a normative theory. There are other postmetaphysical positions, from ordinary relativism to more complex forms of poststructuralism and here specifically deconstructionism. Common to these positions is an almost total collapse of the ideal dimension into the praxial one. Here even postmetaphysical normative language becomes suspect. Habermas' appeal to the force of the better argument, if suspected in this fashion, would amount to nothing better than Foucault's disciplinary power obsessed with managing what cannot be controlled by norms or law. In Foucault's view, the *illocutionary (binding) force* of the argument—moral norms and legal statutes as opposed to the *disciplinary* forms of institutionalized power (the countermorality and counterlaw)—could not be neatly separated into communicative and strategic kinds of actions.

But for Habermas, the possibility of ideally projecting and living in a normatively structured social world exists even after Nietzsche's death of God. *Postmetaphysical thinking*, like the Freudian unconscious, is not without an intelligible structure. Human ability to norm their shared world emigrates into the heart of language and practical discourse itself. The *liberal stress on individual rights* and autonomy, Habermas argues, contributes too little to this shared social project. The *communitarian request for the primacy of the communal good* over the liberal primacy of right falls back beneath metaphysics. Both rights and goods are redeemable and can become normative only within the intersubjectively shared consensual procedures and within their accompanying social forms of life. Habermas' communicative ethics has this existential, almost mystical quality of pointing to hope where all options have been exhausted.

Habermas admits that his model, which gets nourished by "the telos of reaching understanding, inherent in linguistic structures" (ND 131/81), profanizes the place once occupied by 'God' (LC, pt. 3, chap. 4; ÜGW 201–3, answer no. 8). Yet his model, even as it does not commit itself to a dogmatic atheism, a dogmatism that would be reminiscent of a fundamentalist conviction, employs an atheism methodologically. To repeat the opening of the second citation to this section: "*[Nihil] contra Deum nisi Deus ipse*—which is not to appeal to some sort of deified reason, but on the contrary to say that it is only through reason that we can determine the limits of our own rationality. *This* is the fundamental figure of Kantian thought that was definitive for modernity" (VaZ 125/94). Communicative reason and communicative ethics cannot console us for the catastrophes of our past, since they do not address collective guilt. Yet we are prompted to assume historical responsibility for our shared future.

> Communicative reason . . . neither announces the absence of consolation in a world forsaken by God, nor does it take it upon itself to provide any consolation. It does without exclusivity as well. As long as no better words for what religion can say are found in the medium of rational discourse, it will even coexist abstemiously with the former, neither supporting it nor combatting it. (ND 185/145; cf. 23/15, 34/25, 60/51; and ÜGW 203f., question and answer no. 9)

Communicative freedom redeems the ideality of God in social-historical terms. It bears repeating that Habermas' profanization of the redemptive promise of liberation, or his *linguistification of the idea of God*, contains core intuition and motive that things can get better in spite of disaster. His hope against hope reveals traces of waiting for the messianic future, which cannot be exhausted by our historical creation of the conditions for its arrival. Habermas does not explain the possibility of a leap from the irrational-disaster to the rational mode of discourse and to communicative freedom. He appeals to his experience, *that things do get better*, and to the mystical sources of his explanation, *Nihil contra Deum nisi Deus ipse*. The latter is not deified reason but a reason determining its own limits; communicative ethics, like its sibling existential ethics, wants to dance over 70,000 fathoms of water and yet be joyful. The analytical argument becomes funded by existential hope that communicative freedom can find resources for reconciling itself from within itself even after the disasters of modern life. God talk and Auschwitz are neither absent from Habermas' theory nor in an antinomical relation to it; rather, it is how they are linguistified that sets up an antinomy between Habermas' theoretical architectonic and core intuitions (cf. Pensky 1999, 224) or occasions Metz's (1997, 152f.) objection that Habermas' theory, in its redemptive aspirations, portends to heal all wounds.

Kierkegaard's existential ethics provides a suitable enhancement of Habermas' communicative ethics, just as his Schwäbian Protestant and Cabalistic Jewish sources fund the core intuitions behind communicative rationality. We encountered Kierkegaard's either/or choice deployed by Habermas in the Historians' Debate (chap. 5). Along with Jaspers's notion of collective liability, as distinguished from the faulty notion of collective guilt, Habermas continues to rely on

Kierkegaard's postconventional ethics to critically evaluate problematic traditions. Habermas takes Kierkegaard's existential self-choice of who I am and want to be and projects it into practical discourses of the future of *our* traditions. This either/or choice, now harnessed in terms of public discourse, at once allows for autonomy and solidarity, distance and vulnerability. Existentially self-reflecting individuals, like "the unanimity of separation . . . [in a] fully orchestrated music" and unlike the possessive individualists of the liberal kind and unlike the uncritical communitarians, find themselves in responsible solidary relations to tradition and to the community of others (Kierkegaard 1978, 62f.; see Matuštík 1993, pt. 3).

Communicative ethics, like its founding intuition, envisions vulnerable and yet highly individuated bonds among humans. That is why Habermas operates with a two-pronged normative theory: the moral point of view (practical discourse) and ethical-political discourses (the practical questions of individual and collective identity). This two-level model meets liberal and communitarian objections head-on. Normative practical discourse requires certain abstraction from the particular contexts in order to derive the moral point of view with universally valid norms. That level satisfies the liberal requirement of autonomy. The ethical-political discourse embodies an insight into the need for solidarity in order to socially integrate the autonomously self-determining and self-realizing individuals. This level satisfies the communitarian requirement of relationality (Matuštík 1998a, chaps. 1–2, 6). In this fashion Habermas can view autonomy and solidarity as co-original and reciprocal and yet distinct dimensions of human life.[10]

Communicative Democracy and the Inclusion of the Other

Just as the most recent among the integrative concepts (tab. 7.1) of Habermas' architectonic build exponentially on earlier historical experiences (praxial dimension) and theoretical projects (ideal dimension), so also the structural axes (tab. 7.2) and the modes (tab 7.3) of his authorship are internally related. Communicative democracy as a critical ideal embodies the procedural, political, and institutionalized forms for the deliberative exercise of communicative reason. The internal relationship between morality (communicative ethics) and politics and law (deliberative democracy) parallels the one between the concepts of universal human rights and citizens' rights, and between the popular democratic sovereignty of all humans and the civic sovereignty in the democratic state. The conceptions of communicative democracy and cosmopolitan world citizenship (or radical democracy) complement one another as the most generalized regulative idealities. Parallel complementarities exist between communicative rationality and deliberative democracy (or constitutional patriotism) and between communicative ethics and postnational identity (or postnational constellation).

The structural axis of the Habermasian *communicative democracy*, with its focus on the inclusion of the other, clusters around multicultural struggles for recognition.

These are both real social struggles of various peoples (i.e., the pragmatic-material dimension of the problems originating with ethnicity, race, gender, and, I should like to add, economic classes) and the debates among the liberal-communitarian-radical theoreticians of such struggles. It is not necessary to repeat here the prior accounts of such debates, nor can I do justice in this study to the complex nature of social struggles.[11] Rather, my aim was, first, to consolidate *the structure* of Habermas' authorship: his communicative model of critical, moral, and democratic theory. Second, I want to show how *the modal dimension of his authorship* discloses the commitment to the praxis of *anamnestic solidarity* with the victims of history. As I explained in chapter 5, Habermas' commitment bespeaks a core intuition, which he shares with Benjamin against Horkheimer, that the past is not closed. Our solidarity witnesses the tragic past of those whose struggles for recognition cannot be redeemed today without *our* weak messianic (Benjamin) or *anamnestic* (Habermas) power. Since *our* present praxis had been their future, *our* struggle and waiting for future liberation would be incoherent, if not incomplete, without working and waiting to rescue also that past. The structural (or ideal) vanishing point of *recognizing or including the other* must be, thus, traced to the modal (or temporal) vanishing point of *witnessing the other*. My distinction between the structural and modal dimensions of Habermas' authorship or lifework shows how witnessing and recognition are mutually implicated. I say more on certain absence of this implication in Habermas in the last two chapters.[12]

Through both his politically polemical and theoretical works, Habermas emerges as a situated critic of the present age. His communicative model of critical, moral, and democratic theory integrates what I call three axes of his responses to various problems and debates.

- Communicative reason responds to the fragmentation of the modern world, on the one hand, and to the monological (acommunicative) rejections of meaning or to the fundamentalist (acommunicative) assertions of foundations, on the other. The linguistic-communicative turn responds to the rationality debates (their perceived deficits) on the theoretical foundations in the aftermath of modernity; formal pragmatics preserves the insights of historical materialism—that problems address us first and that theory responds to and translates back to praxis.
- Communicative ethics responds to the discontents of modern individuals, who are left without the shared ethical worldview, and to the discontents of homogeneous communities, who are bereft of individual freedom for authentic self-realization and moral self-determination. Postmetaphysical thinking reconciles the liberal-communitarian debates in a higher-level intersubjectivity. The validity claims, which are presupposed by any communicative interaction, become specified in the discursive procedure for validating moral norms.

- Communicative democracy responds to the anomie and the fragmentation of modern forms of life and to the communal wars of nationalist-ethnic struggles for recognition that lead to the cleansing of the alien other. Multicultural, communicative, and radical democracy projects the performative ideal of the polis. Habermas' inclusion of the other and his focus on the global institutions of the UN are his two responses to the discontents of the nation-states.

Habermas' authorship structurally and modally operates with key arguments and motives. First, Habermas distinguishes argumentatively the following *rationality domains:*

- validity claims (truth, rightness, sincerity)
- discourses (pragmatic, moral and legal, ethico-political)
- institutional and democratic procedures (e.g., science, courts, museums)

Habermas *argues* that by keeping to these distinctions, *we* can deliver on the ability of communicative reason to limit itself by its own resources. In communicative freedom, reason exhibits its unity within the diversity of its voices.

Second, Habermas refers his theory to the following *basic motives:*

- transcendence of rational limits within the limits of reason
- nonviolent relation between vulnerability and autonomy
- the liberating role of dangerous memory

Habermas is *motivated* by the unique possibility of establishing perpetual peace on the same grounds where disasters struck: his experience-based hope communicates that even after a disaster something better could come about. When wolf and lamb (e.g., the Serbian civilians and NATO soldiers, the Kosovar or Bosnian Muslims and the Serbian and Croatian Christians) learn to live in peace or minimally coexist in the same village in which they before sowed death, then Habermas' intuition becomes fulfilled in this particular instantiation.

The *argument* for a new multicultural enlightenment (Matuštík 1998a, chap. 3) and for the democratic politics of recognition (SR) proceeds by resolving the discontents of the nation-states in the direction of the world cosmopolitan citizenship and communicative democracy. Just as the linguistic-communicative turn addresses the rationality debates, and just as the postmetaphysical thinking of the moral point of view aims to resolve the liberal-communitarian debates, so also legal pacifism (BH) is to bring relief to the struggles for recognition (SR).

The project of a revolution in permanence, what I have called elsewhere permanent existential and democratic revolution (Matuštík 1993, 253–57), invokes a living *motive,* which funds the works of communicative freedom. But this "revolutionary project overshoots the revolution itself; it eludes the revolution's own concepts." The internal link between *the argument (structure) and the motive (mode)* of Habermas' authorship or lifework can be located at this very intersection of the revolutionary project, which is both categorically inescapable and instrumentally elusive (VV 609/471).

The existential and democratic project of communicative freedom is instrumentally elusive because neither the past nor its unrequited suffering can be directly redeemed through rationality domains. Indeed, the politics of recognition cannot but fail to give justice to the victims of history. Paradoxically, Habermas' recurrent recourse to certain Protestant and Jewish mystical narratives locates the fate of a dethroned God among these victims for whom an ordinary politics of recognition may not bring any relief. And yet he returns also to his basic motivating intuitions: that things get better even where disasters once took place; that we can choose ourselves responsibly even if each one was individualized through a socialization in totally bankrupt traditions; and that the traumatic past can be redeemed through *our* actively working and waiting for liberation. His basic motivating intuitions, therefore, cannot be based directly in his arguments for communicative reason, ethics, and democracy. Rather, his motivating intuitions address the historical vanishing point and the implied disaster of our possible future with the destruction of myth (motivating narrative) and reason (enlightenment). The complement to the argument for a worldwide cosmopolitan recognition that would constitute communicative democracy is the attitude of witnessing. The witness is oriented to the doubly unspeakable past—the past's melancholy of loss and the past's motivated despair to deny that loss. The witness can rescue the future by actively learning now from the past disaster. Habermas' own learning addresses this universal (generalized) tension within the revolutionary project (VV 609f./471): Melancholy is inscribed in the revolutionary consciousness—a mourning over the failure of a project that *nonetheless cannot be relinquished.*[13]

Writing only some months before the fall of the Berlin Wall (1989), he links the impact of the French revolutionary ideal (1789) to the postwar situation (1949) of his experience:

> In view of the double anniversary of the years 1789 and 1949—and stung by *other* "anniversaries"—a leftist in the Federal Republic must consider this undertaking an imperative: the principles of the Constitution will not take root in our souls until reason has assured itself of its orienting, future-directed contents. (VV 609f./471)

Yet reason's self-assurance is itself motivated by a messianic-historical project: "It is only as a historical project that constitutional democracy points beyond its legal character to a normative meaning—a force at once explosive and formative" (VV 609f./471).

The main title of the essay on "Popular Sovereignty as Procedure" expresses in a different manner the notion of a constitutionally anchored communicative freedom. Still another way of expressing this performative ideality is recorded in permanent revolution institutionalized in the political and legal procedures of cosmopolitan, deliberative, radical, and communicative democracy. Habermas concludes this essay with an astonishing and indeed direct evidence for what I distinguished as the structure and the mode of his authorship or lifework.

> One reservation still remains. The sobriety of a secular, unreservedly egalitarian mass culture does not just defeat the pathos of the holy seriousness that seeks to ensure social status to the prophetic alone. The fact that everyday affairs are necessarily banalized in political communication also poses a danger for the semantic potentials from which this communication must still draw its nourishment.... Even the moment of unconditionality insistently voiced in the context-transcending validity claims of everyday life does not suffice. *Another* kind of transcendence is preserved in the unfulfilled promise disclosed by the critical appropriation of identity-forming religious traditions, and *still another* in the negativity of modern art. The trivial and everyday must be open to the shock of what is absolutely strange, cryptic, or uncanny. Though these no longer provide a cover for privileges, they refuse to be assimilated by pregiven categories. (VV 630f./490)

NOTES

1. Unfortunately, Pensky's (1995, 74) insightful essay, which translates one portion of the above-cited passage from Habermas, suffers from both factual errors and the wrong textual attribution.

2. For a detailed answer to Habermas' question asked above, see Matuštík 1993.

3. The god Janus is Habermas' favorite figure of pagan divinity with two faces, front and back. Janus is a metaphor of always looking with two profiles or faces in two opposite directions. This metaphor incarnates Habermas' profound ambivalence into his concepts: Janus-faced socialism (NR 195; PK 131); Janus-faced nation (EdA 139, 157/115, 131; PK 153); Janus-faced validity claims (R 243); or "the Janus face of youth protest" (KPS 291/TRS 45). Other notions suffer St. Paul's (more erotic) thorn in the flesh: "the realist thorn in the flesh of the politics of human rights" (BH 7/267); or "the thorn of skepticism [that] must have penetrated deeply enough into the normative flesh" (NBR 136/132). And still other concepts undergo painful passages. The biblical passage to socialism today leads through a self-critique by neoliberalism as the "only eye of the needle through which everything must pass" (NR 203); the passage "using the devil to drive out Satan" (NBR 187/180); the passage of "cleansing self-reflection" (44/39); the passage through nationalism as "the Hades of the nineteenth century" (VaZ 110/83); or "original sin" (89/67) as a passage through Germany's "collective repetition compulsion" (92/69).

4. Pensky (2000) makes a very interesting proposal that Habermas' "*legal* cosmopolitanism" (64), by inserting a wedge of universal democratic rights between national and popular sovereignty, requires "a substantial support—a global ethics, as opposed to a universal morality." Pensky's notion of "cosmopolitan solidarity as a global ethical discourse" invokes the Adornean-Benjaminian 'coming to terms with the past' but omits making explicit what I called with Habermas the Kierkegaardian existential responsibility for the future (77). I argued much earlier (1993, 1998a) that Habermas' cosmopolitanism intimates such complementary need for postconventional yet substantive existential ethics, which would be available to all individuals in every generation and across national and cultural boundaries. Neither Habermas (not even in PK) nor Pensky—who in his essay discovers now this very idea of "a global ethical discourse" as a publicly enacted existential discernment of who we were, are, and want to be—develops this need in requisite depth.

5. See chapter 5 n. 30; and chapter 1 n. 3 above.

6. On the key debates, see the detailed discussions and references in Holub (1991, chap. 2 on the positivist debate [cf. Habermas, ZLS], chap. 3 on the debate with Gadamer, chap. 5 on the debate with Luhmann [cf. Habermas, TGS], and chap. 6 on the debate with Lyotard [cf. Habermas, PDM]). See also Honneth and Joas 1991, McCarthy 1982, Thompson and Held 1982, and Wiggershaus 1989, 628–62/1998, 566–96.

7. For other key formulations of the same insight, see chapter 6, "Between Philosophy and Science: Marxism as Critique," subsection "Critique and Crisis," in TP; PDM 377/324; and the most revealing recent interview, ÜGW 201–3, answer no. 8, in which Habermas admits directly that his communicative categories translate in profane language the core religious intuitions about human emancipation. While Habermas names Gershom Scholem as the origin of his interest in Jewish mysticism, his Protestant upbringing likely gave him insight into Schwäbian pietism. See also Mendieta's introduction to RaR.

8. For our purpose, I need not discuss here the distinction between the normative discourses of justification and application (see JA; Matuštík 1993, chaps. 2, 4; Rehg 1997).

9. Habermas often uses this phrase when speaking about transcendence (cf. his title TiTD).

10. I argued repeatedly that a three-pronged model, with an existential mode as the third term, is needed to satisfy Habermas' own requirements (Matuštík 1993, 1998a, 1999). Habermas' most recent return to Kierkegaard (KE) is a bit more nuanced since 1987, but it is in the end still set up with a two-pronged model.

11. On the debate between Charles Taylor and Habermas, see SR and EdA; cf. Matuštík 1998a: chaps. 1–2; see also SnI and VV; on the Habermas/Rawls debate, see EdA, pt. 2.

12. Oliver (1998, xi–xiii, xv, 80, 88–94, 173–78) introduced the category of witnessing as a corrective to the Hegelian struggle for recognition (cf. Honneth 1992; Matuštík 1998a, chap. 1).

13. Cf. Derrida 1993.

Chapter Eight

THE HABERMAS EFFECT

The Habermas effect is felt in every major discipline of the human and social sciences. Habermas towers over the contemporary fields of communication, ethics, hermeneutics, law, linguistics, philosophy, political theory, sociology, and critical social theory. His contributions to interdisciplinary research in social and human sciences, cultural studies, and philosophy are groundbreaking. The ease with which he moves across divisions erected among and within these various fields challenges his readers to loosen their disciplinary constraints and open their intellectual territories. While the academy guards its intellectual property with jealous eyes and often with a partisan provincialism reminiscent of petty nationalisms, Habermas takes the liberty to transgress the conventional frontiers erected between analytical and Euro-Continental as well as pragmatist approaches to philosophy. He draws on philosophical reflection, legal analysis, and sociological research, and he constantly learns from his collaborators and critics; by conversing with both, he keeps amending his ongoing research program. Despite the many forceful criticisms, his theory expands and adjusts with perspectives brought by new waves of students and interlocutors. Among the most significant of these, we find the contributions from feminist and postcolonial theorists. Habermas' impact cannot be diminished by the discontents with it, since it is the latter that testifies to the growing significance of the former. Three generations of students on all continents—third, fourth, and fifth generations after the Frankfurt Institute originated in 1924—do not merely replicate but creatively transform his work. His theoretical architectonic challenges both beginners and advanced specialists in several ways at once:

- Habermas' linguistic-communicative turn dislodges the divides among analytical, Continental-European, and pragmatist orientations in philosophy entrenched in the latter part of the twentieth century, mainly in the

Anglo-American universities, from which they spread to other countries like Germany.
- His interdisciplinarity overcomes the insularity of sociology, political science, and philosophy and establishes intelligent communication lines across the disciplinary borders.
- The communicative unity of reason within the methodological complexity of his authorship responds to post/modern fragmentation and anomie by envisioning the project of radical democratic freedom.

I will divide my discussion of Habermas' impact and discontents, accordingly, into the contributions of his pluralism and his unfinished debates with other thinkers and positions.

RADICAL PLURALISM

> From the outset I viewed American pragmatism as the third productive reply to Hegel, after Marx and Kierkegaard, as the radical-democratic branch of Young Hegelianism, so to speak. Ever since, I have relied on this American version of the philosophy of praxis when the problem arises of compensating for the weaknesses of Marxism with respect to democratic theory. (NU 215/AS 148f.)

Habermas challenges his readers to become masters of thought across disciplinary and methodological divisions once before fashioned for cogent grounds but often kept intact as part of administrative or institutional power politics. He renders present and future attempts to hold on to such divisions for unsound philosophical-political reasons difficult. Once tasting the richness of mutual understanding that can be achieved across the analytical, Continental-European, and pragmatist divides, one is no longer able to turn back from one's enlightenment to the inter- and intradisciplinary battles without experiencing a harm to one's critical intelligence. The most talented students influenced by Habermas become incapable of respecting such divisions as in themselves worthy of distinction. Just as his architectonic is composed of the core integrative concepts (tab. 7.1), and just as his authorship comprises structural and modal dimensions (tabs. 7.2, 7.3), so likewise his pluralist effect is cumulative (tab. 8.1).

That Habermas' methodologically rich Critical Theory carries a cumulative effect (*radical pluralism is nurtured by the polyphonic unity of reason in the diversity of its voices,* ND, chap. 7/chap. 6) can be glimpsed from the temporal perspectives of two vanishing points. At the critical vanishing point of pluralism would be both the loss of *our* competence to communicate and the accompanying loss to act with communicative freedom. Max Weber calls this dual loss—its anomie (meaninglessness) and fragmentation—the iron cage of rationalized modernity. He depicts the iron cage as a situation with disenchanted gods and demons in their mutual struggle,

Table 8.1 Habermas' Radical Pluralism

Situation in the Present Age	The Habermas Effect
Divide among analytical, Continental-European, and pragmatist philosophies	The linguistic-communicative turn in philosophy
Disciplinary insularity	Interdisciplinary conversations
Post/modern fragmentation and anomie	The project of radical democratic freedom

Critical Vanishing Point
  the loss of communicative competence
  the loss of communicative freedom
	Ideal Vanishing Point
	  critical social theory
	  critical praxis

with their strife both unhinged and irreconcilable, like the value orientations of modernity. The Weberian cage has encircled both western (democratic) and eastern (Soviet) variants of historical modernity, from the positivist dogma of scientistic truth to the emotivist assertion of values. The dual loss of meaning and freedom fuels what Horkheimer and Adorno ([1944] 1987) define as the dialectic of myth and enlightenment. The myth, once it is told, must be always and already conceptually mediated. The Enlightenment's quest for self-certainty and lucidity always and already falls back into precritical myth: the more enlightenment (the more rationalized traditional life worlds become in modernity), the more anomie; the greater any individual's practice of liberty (as opposed to traditional forms of solidarity), the more intense the feeling of social fragmentation and separation. Habermas' oeuvre and politics respond to Weber's pessimistic realism, to the early Frankfurt School's tragic critique of modern culture, and to the postmodern variations and intensifications of such critiques of modern reason (PDM).

But communicative competence and freedom, Habermas argues, are the conditions of the possibility of critical social theory and praxis. The dialectic of myth and enlightenment in Adorno and Horkheimer, as well as the charges against modernity by Nietzsche, Weber, and postmoderns—Habermas often links these gloomy critics of modernity together (PDM, lecture 5)—violate in their very criticisms the performatively inescapable conditions of critique. Habermas' adopted mystical formula, *Nihil contra Deum nisi Deus ipse* (*nobody [can act] against God but God alone,* see chap. 7) leaves its distinct imprint on his radical pluralist response to the post/modern discontents. Set against Weber's iron cage, against Horkheimer and Adorno's dialectic of myth and enlightenment, and equally against the perceived postmodern and positivist abdications of critical rationality, Habermas' pluralism is procured from within communicative competence and freedom and against the posited radical others of reason.

In other words, Habermas is *monotheistic* in communicative freedom (reason and freedom can learn only from their own resources) and *polytheistic* in performance (there is no absolute synthesis that could unify all diverse voices). In this dialectical unity of rational freedom in the polyphony of its voices, he respects the

Judaic prohibition (see ÜGW 200f., answer no. 7) on the carved images of G-d: there are to be no concretistic blueprints for rational or democratic ideals of communicative freedom.

> We have to let ourselves *learn* from our own feelings. Only further enlightenment—*docta spes*—has grown from the devastation of enlightenment. Totalizing critiques of reason—which reason itself brings to confusion—are worthless. (VaZ 125/94)

Habermas' fundamental motive carries further implications for his sociopolitical analysis:

> Europe must use one of its strengths, namely its potential for self-criticism, its power of self-transformation, in order to relativize itself far more radically vis-à-vis the others, the strangers, the misunderstood. That's the opposite of Eurocentrism. But *we* can overcome Eurocentrism only out of the better spirit of Europe. (127f./96)

Resisting all blueprints of justice and carved images of divinity, he rejects along with them any version of the Hegelian absolute, as well as the concretistic variants of the Soviet or certain applied Heideggerian utopias. Even if philosophy should contribute to changing the world (Marx's eleventh thesis on Feuerbach), rather than just thinking about it (Hegel), philosophers on their own cannot accomplish much:

> I've got a tin ear for Heideggerian melodies. "Only a god can save us" [see Heidegger (1966); chap. 1 above]—that's the kind of noble tone in philosophy that already got on Kant's nerves. Philosophers don't change the world. What we need is to practice a little more solidarity: without that, intelligent action will remain permanently foundationless and inconsequential. (128/96)

The philosopher in the fallible task of a stand-in and interpreter (MkH, chap. 1), rather than some intellectual "great man" speaking from on high, answers dogmatic Hegelians, Marxists, and Heideggerians in one breadth. The wide-ranging Habermas effect can be attributed to his role as an engaged public intellectual. His direct impact on public debates, especially in all of Germany and on the pan-European scene, cannot be stressed enough. Like Sartre in France, Habermas takes personal risks in entering various public debates; he is willing to take defined positions even before the dust of the heated controversies settles down and before any theoretical architectonic can elucidate praxis. More reminiscent of Foucault than Hegel, Habermas builds bridges across disciplinary boundaries, and unlike global intellectuals acting in a dogmatically absolutist or dogmatically negating monologue, he engages and learns from others in ongoing conversations (cf. OSSA).[1] Yet learning from the problems that come to us (i.e., from historical and personal experiences) comprises equally historical, pragmatist, critical, and existential dimensions. Habermas' agitation for the coming of that "better spirit of Europe" may be easily described as a pragmatist and Kantian Hegelianism, or a pragmatist and Hegelian Kantianism, or a Hegelian and Weberian Marxism.

The Habermas effect can be summed up in positive terms by his radical pluralism and public intellectual and political engagement. Because his communicatively funded Critical Theory is motivated by learning from experience, there is an internal link between the praxial (existential, political, critical) and theoretical (ideal) dimensions of his architectonic and authorship (tabs. 7.1, 7.2, 7.3). *The internal link between Habermas' theory (philosophy) and praxis (politics)*

- is established at first through his critique of Heidegger in 1953
- remains in his work in spite of his critique of the students for mixing theory and active politics (i.e., politicizing science or university) in the 1960s
- is invoked directly when he takes recourse to state power in consenting publicly to the Persian Gulf War and NATO bombing of Serbia

In his confrontation with student 'actionism', Habermas distinguishes sharply the apolitical role of scientific theorizing from the practical role of citizen, journalist, activist, peaceful protester. Yet recall also that he takes recourse to police power, even if, unlike Adorno in January 1969, he only indirectly makes space for it by a prior argument on December 1968. In later endorsing *humanitarian* wars of intervention, he deploys communicative democratic theory to clarify the requisite politics of power and justify his own public stance. Hohendahl's perceptive introduction to Habermas' post-Wall political essays confirms my analysis of this *internal* link:

> As diverse as the essays [in NBR] are ... they are written with the author's more systematic work in mind. They mediate between concrete historical situations and more general theoretical claims. For this reason they differ from Adorno's essays, which are by definition antisystematic and subversive. Habermas's conception of the intellectual, while it rejects the claim for leadership and exclusive knowledge, holds on to a paradigm of rational pedagogy.... This paradigm is not to be confused with dry instruction based on a deductive method. Typically, their procedure is one of dialogue or of immanent criticism. (in NBR xxiii)

Habermas unites post-Hegelian and neo-Kantian Continental-European thought with the pragmatist tradition that learns equally from Hegel and Kant; and he joins both with his communicative transformation of Critical Theory. Suffusing Habermas' integrative architectonic is his analytical-linguistic clarification of the normative presuppositions of communicative interaction. His theoretical pluralism, his recourse to the linguistic turn of analytical philosophy in particular, politically intervenes in the received intra- and interdisciplinary divisions of theory.

I was fascinated both by Chomsky's program for a general theory of grammar, and by Austinian speech-act theory, as systematized by Searle. All this suggested the idea of a universal pragmatics, with the aid of which I wanted above all to deal with the awkward fact that the normative foundations of the Critical Theory of society were entirely unclarified. Having rejected the orthodoxy of the philosophy of history, I had no wish to lapse back either into ethical socialism, or into scientism, or indeed into both at once [cf. Althusser]. (NU 215/AS 149)

The ideal vanishing point of Habermas' linguistically anchored theory and praxis does not project the ascetic priest. Rather, it resists in one stroke the self-declared minimalism of Anglo-American analytical philosophy, whose linguistic turn would bar from philosophy all 'nonphilosophical' questions that Critical Theory asks, and the totalizing claims of Continental-European postmodernism, whose antinormative, at times apocalyptic, antiutopia would render critical social theory and praxis equally impossible (ND 242–63/205–27; PDM; R 233–50).

Habermas' communicative turn integrates at least *three linguistic turns* taking place almost side-by-side in analytical, continental-European, and pragmatist philosophies. The *linguistic turn proper* defines one of the main domains of analytical philosophy as such. In the simplest sociological terms, analytical philosophy is the turn of certain Anglo-American philosophy away from certain other ways of doing philosophy on the European continent, notwithstanding the analytical amnesia of its historical and geographical, Austro-German-Czech origins in pre-Hitlerian Vienna and Prague—cities that at the time also welcomed Edmund Husserl.[2] The turn signifies the shift from philosophy focused on consciousness to the study of meaning and reference, propositions, and linguistic practices. Continental-European phenomenology, both in its Hegelian and Husserlian branches and in their later combinations, undergoes its own waves of the turn to language. In Hitler's shadow, Heidegger initiates *the hermeneutical turn* from the phenomenological subject to the contexts of interpretation. The legacy of that first wave defines hermeneutical and existential phenomenology from Gadamer to Merleau-Ponty to Ricoeur. *Structuralism and poststructuralism* in Russia, Central Europe, Scandinavia, and later more prominently in France and the United States, mark the other two waves of the turn from the study of Cartesian or Hegelian consciousness to the contexts of interpretation and structures of signifiers and signifieds. Peirce's study of signs (semiotics) effects an even earlier turn to language in pragmatism, and this one antedates all the above turns (TCA 2, chap. 5).[3]

Habermas' deliberate undoing of the rigid divides among analytical, Continental-European, and pragmatist ways of thinking about and doing philosophy arises through a triangulation of the above three linguistic turns. The *communicative turn* addresses all three sides of the divide with the same formally pragmatic appeal to the performative character of linguistic interaction. I noted in the preceding chapter how Habermas argues against forms of linguistic analysis that limit themselves to one or two of the three pragmatically necessary structural components of communication; he develops a parallel argument against the hermeneutical, poststructuralist, or deconstructive models (and against the Hegelian and Husserlian variants of phenomenology) insofar as these too may omit one of the performative structures of communication.[4]

The Habermas effect is practically historical and theoretically cumulative. His effect is historical in that it revisits the shared philosophical conversation before it was interrupted, first, by Hitler's era (Dummett 1994, ix, 1–3; cf. 5, 26, 28–42) and, then, by the Cold War period (McCumber 1996; Albrecht et al. 1999).[5] His effect is theoretical insofar as the performative attitude of the first person vis-à-vis the second person in coming to an understanding about something in the world (*the linguistic-communicative turn*) resolves the incompleteness perceived in each preceding linguistic turn and thus integrates their insights across the philosophical divide. Habermas' communicative turn is as much political (praxial) as it is theoretical (ideal); its effect cuts in both directions. Turning to Anglo-American and pragmatist resources provides the postwar German students with alternatives, first, to existing German philosophy, still dominated by its insular debates and by the impact of the later Heidegger (this motive inspired also the IfS of the 1950s to turn to U.S. sociology) and, second, to the poststructuralist transmutations of Heidegger's turn to language. Habermas furthermore reconnects his Anglo-American analytical and pragmatist sources with their European cousins in hermeneutics (itself of Heideggerian-Gadamerian lineage) and poststructuralism (of a mixed Franco-German lineage) in order to resume the conversations interrupted by the geographical disasters, dislocations, and theoretical cleansings of the twentieth century.

Habermas' recovery of the richer philosophical conversation of the west represents without any doubt his single most important philosophical-political impact and achievement. He bequeaths to the present and future generations of students, who engage with his questions, that unique chance to acquire a renewed existential, political, and theoretical sense of philosophical purpose, direction, and shared dialogue. This truly revolutionary effect sets slowly into its long march through the institutions. Yet we know, at least since Plato, about the lasting pedagogical effects achieved through internalized learning. Judging Habermas' long-term impact, there is now concrete hope that in the future work of those who engage with his ideas, whether they agree or not, some of the political and disciplinary divisions that debilitated the twentieth-century philosophy and social sciences might gradually lose their entrenched institutional stronghold.

For all the architectonic complexity of his trajectory, Habermas' anchor remains primarily that of a social theorist. His lifework serves to find possible yet fallible answers to normative and social problems of liberation. His communicatively transformed Critical Theory is both pragmatic and analytical, and in both regards it is soberly guarded:

> If there is any small remnant of utopia that I've preserved, then it is surely the idea that democracy—and the public struggle for its best form—is capable of

hacking through the Gordian knots of otherwise insoluble problems. I'm not saying that we are going to succeed in this; we don't even know whether success is possible. But because we don't know, we at least have to try. Apocalyptic moods sap the energies that nourish these initiatives. (VaZ 128f./97)

Hope for alternatives to failed socialism and capitalism leads today though a narrow strait:

> After the bankruptcy of state socialism is [radical-democratic self-critique of a capitalist society] . . . the only eye of the needle through which all [das alles] must pass. (NR 203)

Nonetheless, Habermas does not tire of emphasizing the human capacity to learn by disaster (LD):

> The year 1989 is a break that also opened even the blindest eye to the rise, fall, and crimes of the Soviet Union. . . . Still written in the stars is the date that—one day—may mark the shipwreck of another regime exercised anonymously throughout the world market. . . . *Can we learn from history?* (NBR 17/12f.; italics added)

UNFINISHED DEBATES

Where would any of us be without our Kant? (VaZ 152/115)

After fifty to sixty years of Soviet Russian development, no one can fail to see that Max Weber was right . . . that the abolition of private ownership of the means of production in no sense does away with class structures as such. Personally, I no longer believe that a differentiated economic system can be transformed from within in accordance with the simple recipes of workers' self-management. (NU 255/AS 182f.)

My theoretical works also have as their vanishing point the demand for conditions that are worthy of human beings, in which an acceptable balance between money, power, and solidarity can come into normal practice. (NBR 97/92)

We have to let go of interpretations that have become dear to us, including the idea that radical democracy is a form of self-administering socialism. Only a democracy that is understood in terms of communicative theory is feasible under the conditions of complex societies. (NBR 137/133; translation altered)

Die Zeit: So there are no alternatives? *Habermas:* Not at all. (EgA 12/5)

The citations introducing this section variously circle around the question of the material conditions of the possibility of communicative rationality, ethics, and democracy. The material conditions—insofar as they pertain to embodied theorists and not to talking heads, to human beings living somewhere and sometimes rather than nowhere and outside of time—ground integrally theory and praxis alike. As conditions of the possibility of one's free exercise of communicative reason and specifically of the radically democratic project, they meet categorically Habermas' own "demand for conditions that are worthy of human beings" (NBR 97/92). He admits that there are the minimal material conditions of possibility that must be met for communicative ethics, freedom, and multicultural democracy:

> My sense is that multicultural societies can be held together by a political culture, however much it has proven itself, only if democratic citizenship pays off not only in terms of liberal individual rights and rights of political participation, but also in the enjoyment of social and cultural rights. The citizens must be able to experience *the fair value of their rights* also in the form of social security and the reciprocal recognition of different cultural forms of life. Democratic citizenship can only realize its integrative potential—that is, it can only found solidarity between strangers—*if it proves itself as a mechanism that actually realizes the material conditions of preferred forms of life.* (EdA 143/119; second italics added)

Finally, as constitutionally anchored, such minimal material conditions are categorially required in order to realize the basic system of rights—the systemic elaboration of a basic *"right to the greatest possible measure of equal individual liberties"* (FuG 155/122):

> Basic rights to the provision of living conditions that are socially, technologically, and ecologically safeguarded, insofar as the current circumstances make this necessary if citizens are to have equal opportunities to utilize the civil rights. (FuG 156f./123)

In sum, if Habermas *really* means what he says above, then communicative reason, ethics, and democracy must account in theory (ideally) and praxis (critically) for the material conditions of their possibility. Honneth (1986, 192; Matuštík 1993, 56f.) suggests just as much: communicative ethics presupposes a concept of material justice (i.e., fulfilling the conditions that allow communicative freedom to become actual). The categorial requirements invoked by communicative performance, as Habermas cogently argues in his case for formal pragmatics, cannot be relegated to applied disciplines, empirical considerations, political ethics, legal stipulations, acts of civil disobedience, or even the so-called humanitarian warfare. All these latter venues are already some applied instances of the formally normative and pragmatic thinking envisioned under the ideal conditions of interaction. The notion of minimal material justice pertains to concrete thinkers and must thus be a concretely operative part of the regulative ideal.

I enter into some of the discontents with Habermas via immanent criticism. That strong discontents are elicited by his equally strong impact should be considered as praise. I too unfold my critical reflections throughout the book as part and parcel of my overall receptive disposition to and fascination with Habermas' engagement with the twentieth century and its legacy. Since none of us is a god, not shying from the weaknesses of this thinker's strengths is a human, all too human matter. Criticisms and discontents, just as affirmations of positive impact, are inevitably incomplete, fallible, and open to revision.

Analogically to tables 7.2 and 7.3, I organize the Habermasian discontents under the structure of unfinished debates (tab. 8.2) and the modes of learning and blindness by disaster (tab. 8.3). The present structural analysis (tab. 8.2) takes up the three axes of Habermas' authorship in order to study how the discontents of the Habermas effect in turn affect his key theoretical constructions. This procedure is both immanent and dialectical. Immanently, we can evaluate how his project requires certain elements, which are either undertheorized or entirely missing. Dialectically, each turn of the discontents impacts the Habermas effect, thereby suggesting either a revision of or a corrective to his project. The present modal analysis (tab. 8.3) enlarges the focus on the vanishing point of discontents where the mode is but one of the dimensions. With each strength of Habermas' learning we can pair, on the obverse side of his fallible horizon, what he does not or cannot grasp, his blind spots. For each critical learning by disaster, a warning is raised about that very disastrous past returning, as if behind *our* backs, *as our* possible future. There is an epilogue to this learning and blindness in the continued hysteric transmutations and projections of 'Fascism' through Germany's discontented historical presents (tab. 1.1 and the epilogue in chapter 9).

The Postcolonial Turn against Imperialism

The success of West Germany in making its own the democratic constitutional rule and the impact of the industrial miracle within which a new welfare state becomes the fact of the postwar life in Germany are indisputable. One must

Table 8.2 The Structure of Unfinished Debates

The Habermas Effect	*Dimension of Discontent*
Communicative reason and the linguistic-communicative turn as responses to the rationality debates	The postcolonial turn and effects of persistent imperialism on formal pragmatics
Communicative ethics and interdisciplinary conversations as responses to the liberal-communitarian debates	The turn to the margins and effects of new social movements on postmetaphysical thinking
Communicative democracy and communicative freedom as responses to struggles for recognition	The postsecular turn and effects of radical existential, multicultural, and economic democracy on the inclusion of the other
Vanishing Point of the Effect validity domains of rational discourse and communicative freedom	*Vanishing Point of Discontents* structure: recognition mode: witness

Table 8.3 The Modes of Habermas' Learning and Blindness by Disaster

Learning by Disaster	Blindness by Disaster
Auschwitz: unmasks the two Big Lies of uninterrupted democracy and renewed normality	Defeat of Germany on May 8, 1945: uncritical of the western Allies and Euro-American imperialism
Student revolt: unmasks the false German cultural continuities and the securing postwar generation	Hitler Youth: hypercritical of anarchy and violence in revolutionary social movements
The fall of the Berlin Wall: unmasks the discontents of the nation-state	Auschwitz: uncritical of 'humanitarian' wars of intervention
Disastrous Past as Future	*Disastrous Past as Future?*
critique of neoliberalism and state socialism critique of revisionist returns of Fascism	capitalism with a human face? cosmopolitanism bereft of economic democracy?

wonder if it is not this turning of life for *the better* on the same soil where the disaster took place (1945 liberation is not synonymous with the postcolonial turn) that blinds Habermas to the persisting need for "economic democracy" (Schweickart 1996, 60–77; Postone 1993; cf. ENPG 54f., 51; PK 140ff.). Habermas is aware of the material conditions of the possibility of realizing communicative rationality, ethics, and democracy. But he is enamored with the welfare state compromise, with constitutional law and order, with peaceful democratic European citizenry (EdA 144f./119f.; EdA 269/SR142; BH 7/271; Z; ENPG 47). Coupled with the enduring memory of the war trauma and with the reality of bankrupt socialism next door, Habermas' horizon may explain why he would think, and then generalize in theory, how life has become *better* in postwar Germany. Within this horizon of experience—from liberation to affluent constitutional welfare state—and for certain strata of Germans, *life did turn for the better*. Insofar as both Hegel and Marx trace ideas to their historical forms of life, could not one's comfort with West Germany's liberal welfare state easily mirror also the conventional view of one's middle class? Could it not reflect the peaceful and orderly conversation of an established German philosophical seminar? Any finite horizon transmits a background pool of inclinations out of which one tends to respond conservatively to unprecedented future problems that shatter that horizon.

If I may leave my observation deck once again and enter into the debate for a brief moment, I can provide a contrasting example to sharpen this discontent with Habermas. One similar challenge was raised to my inconsistent consideration of socialist markets (see Matuštík 1993, 90). Martin (1999) brands the "western dream" of the liberal welfare state comfort as "'Swedenism,' the pleasant Volvo factory or whatnot, even if much of this is being abandoned even in Sweden." His objection to me illustrates by contrast how far Habermas ventures nowadays even from the ideal of socialist markets, whose cogency Martin questions in my account.

Habermas ridicules that ideal as "the simple recipes of workers' self-management" (NU 255/AS 182f.); and more recently he adopts an even more condescending tone, speaking now of "the venerable doctrinal quarrel over the relationship between social justice and market efficiency" (ENPG 51; the same in PK 140ff.). What seems to most trouble the critics is not that Habermas does not consider the relationship between economy and democracy or that he hardly worked in any serious manner on the former. (By analogy, one should not blame Hegel for not being Marx, for writing *Philosophy of Right* and not *Capital*.) His monumental achievement in democratic political theory blinds him to the need for a theory of economic democracy and justifies him in disparaging such need as a regression to utopian socialism. Nothing he has accomplished in democratic theory warrants this hegemonic gesture of appropriating the socialist ideal of economic democracy under the "terms of communicative theory" alone (NBR 137/133, translation altered; cf. NR 199f.). Such a gesture, perceived by critics as dogmatic, triggers the discontents on the socialist Left. Without any doubt for the neoliberal mainstream, he is already too much of a Left-liberal theorist, who smuggles the old ideals of socialism into democracy—wearing now the trendy communicative clothing. Habermas traverses here a difficult path among his critics.

The need for economic democracy exists in Habermas' horizon neither as a theoretical nor as a practical possibility. He compensates for the perceived "weaknesses of Marxism with respect to democratic theory" and law with an "American version of the philosophy of praxis" and with his major communicative theory of law (NU 215/AS 148f.; FuG). Yet he does not consider it important to compensate from the other side for the weaknesses of the Left-liberal imaginary—its procedural democracy and law with respect to the need for economic democracy. This oversight or disregard is explainable only under the assumed guiding regulative idea of *capitalism with a human face*[6] (i.e., the communicatively structured welfare state compromise). The communicatively structured life worlds (human faces and their communicatively democratic demands) would compensate for and resist the encroachments by an otherwise efficient (read: all that we can demand of markets to be acceptable is that they be efficient) but anonymous media of money and administrative power. Existing capital, labor, and investment markets are left undisputed by Habermas: they are designed for efficiency by the market economists and utilized by entrepreneurs since efficiency cannot be translated into the language of social justice and vice versa. By capitalism with a human face, I mean this coexistence between free markets (efficiency) and democratic institutions (curbing the globalization of markets by expanding the project of the welfare state compromise on a global-domestic scale). In sum, capitalism and democracy are not a contradiction, since for Habermas there is nothing undemocratic about efficiency and nothing economic about democracy. He is a political liberal. His earlier interest in socialism immigrates from the sphere of political economy into the communicative project of democratic politics and law. He stands here much closer to John

Rawls or even Richard Rorty than James Marsh, Kai Nielsen, Moshe Postone, David Schweickart, Tony Smith, or Patrick Murray.

> Politics will succeed in "catching up" with globalized markets only if it eventually becomes possible to create an infrastructure capable of sustaining a global domestic politics without uncoupling it from democratic processes of legitimation.... The criteria for the legitimate uses of power differ from those used to measure economic success; for example, *markets, unlike polities, cannot be democratized.* A more appropriate image here would be that of competition between different media [nonlinguistic, systemic, media of money and power, and the communicative-linguistic media of interaction]. (ENPG 54; italics added)

Habermas follows in Marx's footsteps insofar as he demands the "conditions that are worthy of human beings, in which an acceptable balance between money, power, and solidarity can come into normal practice" (NBR 97/92). With the early Frankfurt School, he rejects the dogmatic Soviet model of DIAMAT (dialectical and historical materialism), that is, "the idea that radical democracy is a form of self-administering socialism." For a socialist or even a social democrat, his demand for balancing the efficient media of money and power with the communicative media of democratic meaning and will formation sounds at best hollow. Although this demand is always and already too much for fiscal or market conservatives as well as for market liberals, it says too little about economic democracy after 1989. The 1968 ideal of socialism with a human face, unlike the ironically renamed capitalism, was not incoherent insofar as it envisioned the need to democratize both the polity and the workplace. Habermas' balancing act within the basically intact capitalist forms of life seems very consistent for the good-feeling Left-liberals, but it is just this good feeling that is incoherent with the social reality of immiseration. Neither Kant nor Hegel was Marx, who demanded economic democracy where the former two left intact within their moral ideals the surd of an unjust social world with either hunger or war or the violence of both. Habermas intimates the ideal of radical democracy already in 1958 (SuP). Yet he limits this ideal, "under the conditions of complex societies" (read: anonymous capital, efficient labor markets, and corporate and private bank investment structures are here to stay), to institutionalizing the formal-pragmatic and the moral 'terms of communicative theory'.

Habermas' most recent turn to democratic theory and law ushers the institutional grounding of the 'republican' state ideal into its second wave—with the first wave taking place in the democratic turn of the 1950s (Albrecht et al. 1999, 137, 168). He leaves the revolutionary aspirations of the '68ers in the vestibule. The West German 1960s can be characterized by the rediscovery of the early critical theory and the Café Marx of the 1920s; the 1950s are marked by turning away from socialist democracy; and the era after 1989 attempts to win a new respectability for Critical Theory within the project of globalization. The 'democratic turns' of the 1950s and of the 1990s propel, in tandem, regressively restorative aims: they move away from the revolutionary ideals of the 1920s and 1960s in order to protect against the perceived dangers of reaction in the 1930s, 1970s–1980s, and again at the turn of the twentieth century.

That alternative economic structures—from democratic and public investment institutions to democratically structured workplace and socialist markets—were successfully developed and could be democratically sought by wider new social movements (Schweickart 1996), does not enter Habermas' cosmopolitan imaginary. So when Love asks, "What's left of Marx?" (White 1995, 46–66), the answer of discontents most likely will be: really, not much! We learn here more about Habermas than Marx, and that itself should not be a cause for discontent, lest Habermas insisted on having the last and best word on grasping what can or should remain of Marx *today*.

> I am very wary of neo-liberal philippics against the alleged dead-weight of our [German] welfare state. More flexibility means—decoded—that labor-power should be stripped of every specific or personal quality and treated as merely commodity like any other. Have we not learnt from Marx that one cannot simply be converted into the other? (EgA 15/10)

This citation might strike us as quite faithful to Marx if it were not for Habermas' rejection of *the labor theory of value* that is here hidden beneath a seeming praise. Habermas' oeuvre is not the place for innovatively thinking *with Marx,* and that again might be an uncontroversial claim today. The discontents have to do with the added impression that Habermas offers a radical critical social theory and with the claim that he not only continues but also improves on the legacy of the early Frankfurt School.

In fact, the above citation, which on the face of it appears to be a Marxist critique of neoliberalism, might be read as Habermas' thinking with Marx *against Marx*: that labor and market values "cannot simply be converted [one] into the other" means that one can no longer criticize efficient market profits as forms of alienated labor either. The labor theory of value analyzes the accumulation of capital as a form of surplus labor for which the worker is not compensated; profit is alienated labor. Although Marx's labor theory requires contemporary revisions, Habermas' architectonic offers no explicit place (though internal critique of it can radicalize what remains implicit as a possibility) for thinking of noncapitalist economic structures; he admits only that an existing welfare state compromise can be expanded into a globally cosmopolitan domestic order. *Habermas self-assesses his Critical Theory in non-Marxian terms:* "I don't consider the retention of the labor theory of value to be feasible. That's one of the reasons, by the way, why many people don't consider me a Marxist" (KPS 527/AS 91).

Consistently with this perhaps generational failure of imagination is Habermas' very vague and unconvincing critique of such neoliberal international institutions as NAFTA (the North American Free Trade Agreement) and the most devastating ones—MAI (the Multilateral Agreement on Investments) and WTO (World Trade Organization). He notes that MAI does not really aim at "taming capitalism" but rather at "institutionalizing markets." He grasps that MAI is to be a global structure of legal protections for investments and markets parallel to the ones existing in each nation-state and among the blocs of them, as NAFTA is now for Canada, the United States, and Mexico. His general awareness of the far-reaching consequences of MAI misses the point of the needed critique: "Difficult problems of this kind require supranational agreement over environmental, social and economic measures" (EgA 14/7). Even with his well-intended liberal ideal of global institutions for a possible cosmopolitan-domestic welfare, no supranational agreement or global-domestic democratic institutions offset the market function of NAFTA, MAI, and WTO. These are designed at their core to be undemocratic economic bodies without elected government. The cosmopolitan democratic order and the undemocratic movement of capital investments, raiding resources and cheap labor, are in principle incompatible. Perhaps *these* two orders are not translatable into one another? I realize that a yes to this last question would inevitably lead from Habermas (and from both Kant and Hegel) forward to a rereading of Marx. Economic democracy defines the missing step between (1) the praxial beginnings and (2) the Critical Theory ideal as these are conceived by Habermas below:

> [1] For the first time in its history, capitalism did not thwart fulfillment of the republican promise to include all citizens as equals before the law; it made it possible. For the democratic constitutional state also guarantees equality before the law, in the sense that all citizens are to have an equal opportunity to exercise their rights. . . . If we read our constitutions in this material sense, as texts about achieving social justice, then . . . (ENPG 47)

> [2] A politics of that kind would have to be conducted with a view to bringing about harmonization. . . . The long-term aim would have to be the gradual elimination of the social divisions and stratification of world society without prejudice to cultural specificity. (ENPG 59)

A much more uncomplicated truth is voiced, for example, by the Mayan communities of Chiapas rising up in January 1994 against NAFTA. It might be of benefit to contrast *the truth, rightness, and sincerity of their two validity claims* with Habermas' accommodating position:

> [1] NAFTA is the death sentence on the indigenous communities. (Katzenberger 1995, 67)

> [2] Basta ya! Enough already! (*La Revuelta* 1999, 28)

Recall the long citation from chapter 4 (my commentary on Habermas' fourth thesis regarding the West German student movement): when Dews queries

Habermas in 1984 on the possible links of communicative theory to postcolonial struggles, the latter takes a raincheck (NU 255f./AS 184). In the same interview, which contains not only his disappointing answer but also the quip about the "simple recipes of workers' self-management," Habermas makes nonetheless two astonishingly promising admissions. This very fact dramatizes the vintage profile of Habermas: every discontent brings from around the corner one more reason to think with Habermas of radical alternatives; the portrait that is emerging in this study tells us that he is both too complex and too skeptical to allow us just one way (even his preferred one) of reading him.

- First, he suggests between the lines that the vanishing point of holding on to the systemic imperatives of efficient markets under a radically democratic check would lead to "a gradual abolition of the capitalist labor market"! Some balance between "plan and market" could result, which, in principle, could issue in a qualitative change beyond mere welfare tinkering within otherwise intact capitalist markets. In principle (Habermas confesses here with a keen sense of finitude to have only a rudimentary knowledge of economics), developing some version of market socialism would *not* be inconceivable on the basis of an ongoing learning process.
- Second, Habermas concedes that he "should not talk about socialism only in interviews"! (NU 255, 257/AS 183–184)

He does not return in a significant way to redeem either of these two promises in his later work, resting instead with the philosophical and political conclusions he reached in the 1960s.

Habermas' interpretation horizon of the German catastrophe of 1945 seems to restrict him, as a member of the in-between skeptical generation, in how much he learns from the aspirations of the '68ers and how much he commits to any new social movement. "I belong more to the generation of 1958, and cannot speak for the generation of 1968" (NBR 84/80). He says yes only to those aspects of the student movement that fit within his horizon. Among these he lists consistently the challenge of the '68ers to the '45ers. This is also his learning by the disaster of Auschwitz; his learning is heightened by the generational aspect of the student rebellion. He misses the core of the worldwide student movements, the core inspired by the postcolonial turn and its constitutive liberation struggles by various oppressed gender, sex, race, and economic *classes*. His partial no to the student movement expresses his own blindness to this main student challenge. His no is born from his blindness by disaster—his *blindness by the light of liberation* in 1945 and by the fact of the Allied liberation of Germany. In both instances he downplays the struggles against growing Euro-American political and economic imperialism. As this student lesson was underestimated and even shunned from on high, that gap in learning haunts his later positions. He once belonged to a Fascist youth organization and he was fooled by its rhetoric of action before waking up in the Allied defeat of Germany. Could his reluctance to belong to and learn from the youth movement in the 1960s—both without falling back on a deeply skeptical ambivalence (at best) and harsh antagonism (at worst)—have at least some of its seeds in the moment of liberation from that first preadult allegiance?

If we revisit Habermas' objections to the students from chapter 4, one of his critical theses discards the internationalist perspective of the new social struggles. He thinks that imperial exploitation, even if originally a factor contributing to poverty in the developing countries, no longer offers an adequate assessment of the causes of poverty. Even as he acknowledges in 1968 the "American barbarism in Vietnam" (SiK 256), perpetrated in the name of freedom and democracy, he drops the language of colonialist and imperialist exploitation. That language would commit him to the idea of economic democracy, a framework at odds with his already evolving linguistic-communicative turn in social and democratic theory. He speaks instead about relations of dependency of the former colonies on Euro-American democracies (255). He learns from new social movements insofar as they learn from the constitutional-democratic, enlightenment framework. This includes not only erecting checks on administrative power but also appropriating the postwar gains by Germany's capitalist miracle (260). His post-Wall restatement of the socialist project absorbs the postcolonial and the anti-imperial challenges under the rubric of deliberative democracy. Finally, he makes in various places claims that do not even try to gloss over the emphatic Eurocentrism of his position (NBR 90f./85f; NU 256/AS 183). He dons pan-European and German-centered glasses in his praise of Europe's second chance (VaZ; PK 156, 167ff.; ENPG).

However tendentious and polemical the response of the German Left to Habermas was at the heat of the movement (Negt 1968), it balanced his polemical offense at student activism. Together with Negt's (1989) public apology to Habermas, for having published the tendentious volume of Left answers to Habermas, and with Habermas' more affirmative reformulation of the idea of socialism after 1989 (NR), we acquire a bit more careful and less frustratingly ambivalent sketch of the present discontents with him.

We should keep in mind that there are two sides to these discontents, at least since the time of his confrontation with the student movement: Habermas accepts the Marxian charge that because he jettisons the labor theory of value (KPS 527/AS 91), he must be a "radical liberal" (NU 240f./AS 171) rather than a Marxist. Yet he values being "considered a Marxist" (KPS 516/AS 82). Thus Habermas speaks of "a certain oscillation" in his yes and no to Marx:

> I'm not a Marxist in the sense of believing in Marxism as a surefire explanation. Still, Marxism did give me both the impetus and the analytical means to investigate the development of the relationship between democracy and capitalism. (KPS 517/AS 82)

Holub's (1991, 94–105) assessment of the discontents from the 1960s elucidates Habermas' confrontation with Marxism and his consequent reconstruction of historical materialism as what I named materialism within formal pragmatics. The Left objections to Habermas are standard fare, and for anyone reading Habermas from other than socialist sympathies, they are nowadays unproblematic characterizations of his evolving, Left-liberal position, something he continues to hold with genuine comfort. What the critics object to—that Habermas gives up on the Marxist theory of economic crisis of capitalism, the labor theory of value, class analysis, and the internationalist analysis of imperialism—coincides with his politically liberal rump Marxism. Yet Holub notes (95) that Habermas, unlike Marcuse in his leadership role in the New Left, overlooks more differentiated, nonorthodox, and progressive dimensions of the student movement. Habermas' yes and no to Marx becomes in this instance problematic for different reasons.

First, he is unable to reconcile himself to the communicative and democratic import of nonrational and even extraparliamentary protest. In the 1960s, he brands this actionism. Second, his thinking presupposes a classical theory of revolutionary change, which functions as a straw man against which he then unfolds his criticism. Holub suggests (98f.) that in originating his polemic from such an orthodox theory, Habermas must become either "a reformist liberal" with no revolutionary subject (students, women, blacks, gays, Greens, etc., cannot be the subject of the classical revolutionary scenario) or "a disillusioned socialist" with a waning, because absolute, utopian dream. Thus the presumed orthodoxy of Habermas' parting with Marx did not undergo the postcolonial turn. His polemic with students in the 1960s misses the links between the less orthodox early critical social theory (and, e.g., Marcuse, Krahl, Dutschke, Negt) and the complex (even postmodern) resources of the new social movements. He not only undermines his leading role within the ranks of the SDS but also misdiagnoses the complex revolutionary—postcolonial and anti-imperialist—needs of the present global situation.

When Habermas returns his attention to the new social movements (NU 249/AS 177f.; TCA 2, chap. 8, p. 3; and NR 188–203), their role is inscribed into the parameters of the liberal reformist response to the rationality, motivation, and legitimation crises of his postwar generation—crises of the cherished welfare state compromise (LC). Yet even after 1989 he holds out for the socialist ideal in name at least. This post/Marxian ambivalence of his earlier period continues in his mature thinking, thereby fueling discontents from the Left as well as from the mainstream liberal center and the Right. His ideal does not govern the rationality domain of possible economic democracy, only "the principles of constitutional state" (NU 254/AS 182). Peirce's "logical socialism" and the pragmatist tradition of "radical-democratic humanism," from Dewey to Mead, together inform his communicative corrective to and his radically democratic and legal variant of the Marxian praxis philosophy (AS 189). If there would be a 'third way' socialism (Habermas dislikes, just as today East Europeans do, the notion of any third way, ENPG 52;

PK 3), it would be pragmatist socialism (see NR 191). Unlike the revisionist Marxian reforms (the envisioned reforms by the praxis philosophers of the 1960s in Yugoslavia, Czechoslovakia, Hungary, and Poland were more complex in theory and experimental implementation than Habermas' own 'simple recipes' for neoliberal economies curbed by communicative democracy and law are today), Habermas' ideal would be 'socialist' only in a pragmatic-procedural sense. His pragmatist socialism projects no regulative ideal of economic democracy.

Habermas reiterates after 1989 his various criticisms of Marx's thinking. And here his list of objections and rejections is reminiscent of his critical theses against the student movement (SiK). When he provides the laundry list of a DIAMAT orthodoxy, the more complex thinking of the early critical theorists, Marcuse and Adorno, and of Western Marxists, Sartre, Lukács, Gramsci, or Merleau-Ponty, as well as of those in the New Left and in the new social movements really do not fit with his characterizations (NR 189–91, points a–f). The postcolonial turn requires the shift to a broader theory of social change. Yet that complex basis, even as a materially conceived formal pragmatics of problems that come to us, seems to be more nuanced than Habermas' procedural pairing down of "Marxism as critique" (187). His Marxism or socialism as critique, to become *our* ruthless criticisms of everything existing, may not be restricted to "normative expectations of rationality . . . in democratic process" (195). To imply that demands for postcolonial thinking, economic democracy, and anti-imperialist praxis are "concretistic" would be to miss the point of these discontents with Habermas' political restriction on Critical Theory. Marcuse's (1966, 37; May 22)[7] question raised at the Frankfurt protest against the Vietnam War is still worth pondering, even though Habermas, who was present, for all practical purposes, set it aside:

> Is a noncapitalist form of industrialization possible in these countries, a form of industrialization that avoids the repressive, exploitative industrialization of early capitalism, which constructs its technological apparatus *à la mesure de l'homme* and not in such a way that it has power over people from the start and that they need to submit to it?

For Marcuse and the student critical social theorists and activists of the 1960s, the liberation movements in developing countries offered both powerful imagination of a more just world and actual resources for liberation. An international solidarity remains even more true and necessary under the conditions of today's globalization than it was when Habermas offered his theses (SiK).

Habermas rejects the Marxist-Leninist orthodoxy that postulates the causal material base of the economy and its effect of cultural-political superstructure. He articulates in their place a noncausal, fallible, and permanent democratic revolution, a "placeless place" of "popular sovereignty" (NR 196). He bypasses the experiments in workers' self-management and in market socialism along with the failures of self-administering state socialism, even though the former experiments represent inventive reformulations of the latter as well as alternatives to neoliberalism. He erects his own dual-systems model: material reproduction (i.e., the neoliberal systems of money and power, capitalism as we know it) and symbolic reproduction (i.e., the life worlds imbued with deliberative political culture). The latter's communicative imperatives are to curb the former's functional imperatives of efficiency.

The discontents object that instead of entering what he discounts as a venerable dogmatic dispute of market efficiency with social justice (PK 140),[8] Habermas entrenches the liberal dogma against the impossibility of economic democracy. His counterintuitive mantra bears repeating: "markets, unlike polities, cannot be democratized" (ENPG 54). In the interview from 1994 (NBR 144ff./140ff.), Habermas once more dodges very direct questions that would impel him to think creatively about the possibilities of economic democracy. And yet these very possibilities are implied by his most recent system of basic rights (in FuG) and by the incompatibility between deliberative democracy and the devastation sown by capitalist production. Notwithstanding all this, Habermas sticks to his theses: decoupling of the efficient economic and power media from the traditional life world; the consequent colonizations of the life-world imperatives of communication by systemic imperatives of efficient steering; and the reformist need to curb the latter. He offers little that sophisticated theorists of economic democracy and of anticolonial struggles can add to their efforts. His thesis of 'internal colonization' is only a distant, perhaps even misleading, word cognate of these latter struggles against the new colonialism.

As in George Pullman's experiment with the company town (see Matuštík 1998a, 86), Habermas insists that democracy enters through the political or legal doors because there is nothing democratic or undemocratic about efficiency and noncommunicatively circulating money or administrative power. He invites deliberative democracy into the symbolic sphere of communicative interaction but not into the nonlinguistic, material spheres of work or relations with nature (ecology). He thus vacates for the post-Wall neocolonial economy and imperial politics an autonomous place for their neoliberal reign. His 'socialism as critique' for the twenty-first century and his admonition to "the non-Communist left" against "melancholy" (NR 188) and "depression" (203), while salutary and well-taken, remain without the postcolonial turn at best contentless and at worst powerless oughts. The regulative ideal of radical democracy is projected communicatively and morally in a materially unjust world. Critics should not wish to overlook that Habermas plays a crucial critical role against the growing neoconservative trends in the west and in the post-Communist east. And perhaps one cannot say more within the Euro-American conservative mainstream of *today* than Habermas does. Yet why does he turn out to be so unattractive a European resource for anticolonial struggles against the ascendancy of the Euro-American world order, someone who is hardly even cited in postcolonial studies as an ally in these struggles? His praise for the productive and steering capacity of the postwar capitalist conjunctures blinds him to the more robust critique of the humane and ecological destruction wrought by capitalism (NBR 145, 162/141, 157; ENPG 46f.). In this failure to analyze the inherent destructiveness of global capitalist economies, he reproduces the productivist bias under the guise of 'complexity-fetish' (i.e., complex markets and power structures render the ideals of economic democracy obsolete). Today he shares this bias not only with the welfare state liberals but also with the crowd of discredited state socialist planners (cf. NR 189).

"But *we* can overcome Eurocentrism only out of the better spirit of Europe" (VaZ 127f./96). The mystical underbelly of this phrase about the dethroned goddess Europa, who must save herself from her own resources alone, gives too little to those who have never been part of the European project. It comes too late to curb the imperial reach of the new world order that *promises* to replace that project (Matuštík 1998a, chap. 9). It is true enough that "occidental rationalism also produces the cognitive positions that allow us to take a self-critical attitude towards Eurocentrism" (NBR 91/86). It is, however, true that any decentering by Europe's hegemonic center alone does not yet require *us* to meet those who are excluded. *We* learned that Europe's ongoing reformation not only does not escape but also accelerates the spirit of capitalism. Moreover, the idea of Federal Europe and its political institutions is quite compatible with Europe's once more expanding imperialism. Unless we expose this sinister compatibility, why should Europe's second chance be the rallying chant rather than the gasoline on the flames of discontent? Habermas dodges the question about the links of his communicative-democratic ideal with anticolonial and social struggles on those occasions when this issue is posed to him directly (NU 256/AS 183; NBR 144ff./140ff.). That he wears emphatically bifocal pan-European and German-centered glasses in his main focus on "Europe's Second Chance" (in VaZ; cf. PK 156, 167ff.; ENPG; Matuštík 1998a, 51–54, 135–41, 228, 247, 265) stirs discontents. His discussion of the cosmopolitan world order reverts repeatedly to Europe's project. This project *is* local insofar as Europe's universalism is partial for most postcolonial critics: Europe is not the world, and European modernity is not the only historical modernity (West 1993).

Habermas takes his place within the hegemonic center of power, that is, among those "powers which can act globally at all" (PK 167). Echoing Marcuse, he inveighs against the post-Wall melancholy among the progressive Left, hoping for a better future. Unlike Marcuse (1991, 257), he does not invoke the Benjaminian hope for the sake of those without it. The wretched of the earth (Fanon 1963) are powerless to communicate globally in the cosmopolitan manner prescribed by Habermas from the institutional centers of Euro-America. He envisions the "cosmopolitan consciousness" to come about within the European Federation—"here in Europe and in the Federal Germany" (PK 168). To hope in the "European actions playing field" in order "to fashion social Europe" (169)—is not this an image of the cosmopolitan world, which is still shrouded in the idea of Europe, an idea as old if not older than St. Augustine's (1981) ruminations at the time of the ethnic invasions of ancient Rome?[9]

The Turn to the Margins

Habermas learns over time from his sympathetic feminist and cultural critics to pay greater attention to the new liberation movements (TCA 2, chap. 8; FuG, chap. 9, sec. 2.3). Yet it appears that for all his articulated sensitivity to gender, race, and economic issues, he is often challenged by many specialists in these fields to be more descriptively and politically concrete. Revisions of his model of communicative reason and ethics have been attempted or at least suggested by feminist, Marxist, postcolonial, and queer theorists.[10] I must underscore that even the most serious among these critics do not simply overlook Habermas' accomplishments. Quite a few stress that his communicative model marks a great advance in social theory as well as great promise for various liberation movements. However strong are the disagreements from the margins, they should be measured against the sustained commitments to the overlapping consensus that the communicative turn in Critical Theory is a step forward.

Insofar as Habermas learns from the challenges made by the new social movements, he brings them under the overarching roof of his intact theory. What he does not think that he needs to learn stays outside of the rationality domains of his model either as a particular, an empirical, or an applied issue. Insofar as concerns with gender, sex, race, or economic classes can be raised as valid claims under the formal-pragmatic presuppositions of his communicative model, does he need to learn from feminist and postcolonial authors? Does he need to cross (in principle, i.e., in an enlarged theoretical ideality) over those complex class boundaries and turn to the margins? The general conclusion from the discontents at the margins of his theorizing is that the challenges of the 1960s and of the new social movements, emerging since those rebellious years, do not *intrinsically* affect the architectonic of his communicative theory.[11]

The above questions produce the Janus-faced learning *and* blindness by disaster (tab. 8.3). The defeat of the Nazi regime and the liberation of Habermas' world by the western Alliance both inoculate him against the Fascist continuities and blind him to the point of not being able to criticize the ascending imperialism of that alliance. We can locate Habermas between Horkheimer's wholly uncritical defense of the U.S. postwar policies, whether in Europe or in Vietnam, and the forceful criticisms of western imperialism by the student theorists and activists of the 1960s and by today's postcolonial movements. Such criticisms evoke frightful pre-1945 memories: the shared liability in defeat and the gratitude for liberation can negatively overdetermine any robust evaluation of the western powers. The student revolt in 1968 unmasks the false continuities lingering since 1945. But the memory of once before belonging to and being fooled by Fascist lawlessness and anarchy can blind one to the point of shrinking away from the revolutionary dimension of new social movements. Habermas endorses their 'unruly practices' (cf. Fraser 1989) only insofar as they challenge the false normality and as they are willing to become pacified by democratic procedures, law, and civil order. The case of civil disobedience, as I explained in chapter 4, marks his outer point beyond which he is unable to tolerate extraprocedural social discord. In the theoretical domain parallel to the praxial domain of the new social movements, the subsumption of all postmodern and poststructuralist innovations under the neoconservative turn reveals more about Habermas' youthful trauma of being once part of a Fascist cultural anarchy than about the post-1960s politics of difference. If traumatic memory can occasion biased readings and blanket judgments (this is typical especially for his essays on Derrida in PDM), the blindness by disaster can turn fear itself into an entrenched conserving attitude.

These discontents reveal the search for the material conditions of the possibility of Habermas' communicative turn. The turn to the margins itself affects how we conceptualize the unity of reason in the plurality of its voices (i.e., what he vouches for as postmetaphysical thinking). The heart of the discontents is the question whether or not socialism is that ideal vanishing point to be envisioned as worth striving for on this side of the world or merely a formal ideal of critique on this side of the pacified but unjust world. Habermas' formula 'on this side of the world' indicates the postmetaphysical nature of this question. The formula itself does not decide *the how* of this postmetaphysical question. His socialism is pragmatically democratic, rather than sociopolitically and economically transformative. His project can be expressed in terms of the tension between normative ideal and social critique within postmetaphysical thinking: "For Habermas, socialism is to be attainable as a 'discourse-in-exile'. What's left of Marx in this is the tradition of Jewish mysticism" (Love 1995, 46). But does not the turn to the margins transpire in the life world, with the historical exile of those left without hope? "Marx understands that liberal politics, as well as capitalist economics, leaves humanity in exile. This is partly because it asks us to be gods, to abstract from our creaturelike aspects" (61). While Habermas' Marxism as critique and 'discourse-in-exile' continue to remove "the beam in liberalism's eye," the new social movements show that he shares with liberal universalism that very beam. The turn to the margins removes the beam blinding Habermas' eye (58).

To keep my present discussion focused on Habermas, I restrict my way through the vast and diversified fields of feminist and postcolonial studies to the core dimensions of discontents with Habermas. Risking some oversimplification, I nonetheless propose the following road map:[12]

The discontents from the margins of Habermas' theoretical edifice develop along two complementary trajectories. (1) There are those who raise problems in regard to his universalism (Butler 1997; Cornell 1992; Benhabib et al. 1995; Young 1990, 1994, 1996). (2) Others fault his position for not being universalist enough (Benhabib 1994; Benhabib and Cornell 1987, chap. 4; Fleming 1997; Fraser 1989, pt. 3; Outlaw 1996).

Taking up an issue with any universalism that is either too abstract or problematically particular (i.e., partial), there are two types of responses. (1) Some answers come from existential and social phenomenology *after* the linguistic-communicative turn (Bartky 1990; Gordon 1995a,b, 1997; Huntington 1998; Marsh 1988, 1995; Matuštík 1993, 1998a; Outlaw 1996; Schrag 1989). (2) Complementary and at times overlapping responses are articulated within the debates between the proponents of the politics of difference (Cornell 1987, 1991, 1992; Benhabib et al. 1995, chaps. 4, 7; Huntington 1998; Oliver 1998; Young 1990, 1994, 1996, 1997a,b) and those who seek the articulation of a more concrete communicative ethics (Benhabib 1992, 1994; Benhabib and Cornell 1987, chap. 4; Braaten 1991; Meehan 1995, chaps. 1, 5; Fraser 1989, 1997a,b; Honneth 1992; Taylor 1989, 1991; Taylor et al. 1994).

Benhabib (Benhabib and Cornell 1987, chap. 4) begins to remove the beam from Habermas' eye by distinguishing between the generalized and the concrete other. Habermas starts in theory with the formal other, thereby attaining the generality of an ideal discourse; the new social movements commence in theory with the concrete other, thereby reaching to the specificity of oppressed human beings and social groups. Benhabib's distinction between these two versions of the other defines two theoretical starting points for social critique and emancipatory ideals. The concrete other is neither a point of application of communicative ethics nor an individual category opposed to its social complement. Habermas' ideal of discursive equality corrects on an ongoing basis for the imbalances between liberal politics and neoliberal economy and power. But, as Love notes, this corrective—even though working hard on this (i.e., postmetaphysical) side of the world—holds out for that ideal in a discursive exile from our human world. Patriarchy, racism, sexism, and economic immiseration exile real humans from material justice. The ideal of human equality unmasks the misnomer of a 'capitalist democracy' at its material core, thereby calling for "a 'politics of return' [from exile] as a politics of difference" (Love 1995, 63; cf. Fischman 1991). The turn to the margins of the new social movements materially affects Habermas' postmetaphysical thinking.

Fraser's influential essay (Meehan 1995, 21–55) sharpens these discontents by asking Habermas directly, "What's Critical about Critical Theory?" (cf. Matuštík 1998b). She frames her query as "The Case of Habermas and Gender" (subtitle is in the original publication of the same essay, Fraser 1989, chap. 6). Against Habermas' continued insistence on the separation between noncommunicative (material) labor and communicative (symbolic) interaction (e.g., RC 220–29), Fraser characterizes work and its specific case, child rearing, as "a 'dual-aspect' activity" (Meehan 1995, 24f.). She drives a wedge into the distinction between system and life world. Workers in the workplace, nurturers caring for children, educators, and agents in the marketplace are active at the same time in the domains of symbolic and material reproduction. "Thus, the capitalist economic system has a moral-cultural dimension" (Fraser in Meehan 1995, 26; cf. Ingram 1995, 203, 236–46; Marsh 1995, 161–76, 239, 252ff., 261, 271; Matuštík 1998a, 87f.). Reifying that life-world dimension apart from the workplace, Habermas robs himself of the lived access to the marginalization and immiseration of labor that would require a more robust criticism than his dual-systems model permits. Fraser contends that he splits the private and public realms along the lines of economic labor and domestic child rearing (in Meehan 1995, 30f.). In the system/life-world distinction, he entrenches the gender subtexts of valued (male) and unvalued (female) labor and the unquestioned "gender-neutral money" and power (33).

What I have named blindness by disaster (i.e., Habermas' fear of the revolutionary side of new social movements), Fraser introduces under the heading of "the gender-blindness of Habermas's model" (36). Indeed, introducing gender and race categories into the heart of his communicative model would be nothing short of revolutionary; it would challenge the patriarchal and racial contracts written into modern democracies (Pateman 1988; Mills 1997). Fraser identifies "conceptual dissonance between femininity and the dialogical capacities," and we could add the dissonance between raciality and the dialogical capacities, as being "central to Habermas's conception of citizenship" (Meehan 1995, 35). The citizen in capitalist societies is defined by his white male roles; the links between the economy and state power, on the one hand, and the public sphere and family, on the other, are never gender and race neutral (35–37).

Habermas holds a version of dual-systems theory: first, he theorizes the notion of decoupling. This means that due to societal rationalization, the nonlinguistic systems media of money and power split off from the life world. Subsequently he elaborates a critical concept of colonization, which depicts the case when these nonlinguistic systems encroach upon the life world. The dual relations between system and life world prevent him from complementing the form with the substance of social struggles by women as well as by other racially and sexually oppressed groups. Human needs, human bodies, social identities, and formations of gender, race, and sexual orientation all include the substantive contents of social struggles. Yet bodies cannot "be dismissed as particularistic lapses from universalism" (45; cf. 44, 48 n. 8, 49 n. 16, 52 n. 34), and they cannot be adequately theorized under the hegemonic roof of Habermas' colonization thesis. The new social movements embody the basic lines of struggle, at the gender and color lines of the turn of twentieth century. The front lines lie "between the forms of [white] male dominance linking 'system' to the life world" (47; cf. Du Bois 1995; Huntington 1997). Fraser (Meehan 1995, 47) concludes her critique by summarizing Habermas' three key blind spots: he holds to a categorial opposition between the systemic and life-world institutions; he derives that opposition by analytically severing the domains of material and symbolic reproduction; and he severs the two action contexts of social and system integration.

Butler (1993a, 1997, 86–102), unlike Fraser or Benhabib, contests the very notion of universalism. In an earlier essay (1993a) she analyzes the case of a white jury interpreting the visual evidence of Rodney King's beating by the Simi Valley police. That jury is wearing particularly white racialized glasses. She develops a phenomenology of perception of this particular *we* (white jury) in order to unmask its purported universal we (that the video evidence truly, rightly, and sincerely shows how the black man assaulted the police officers). In her later treatise, Butler (1997) studies various cases of injurious, excitable, or deformative speech (e.g., the status of pornographic and hate speech or of prohibition on gays speaking openly of their gay identities within the U.S. military). These case studies trouble the abstract universality of Habermas' ideal communication community.

Butler's (1997, 86f.) universals-trouble demonstrates how claims to a universal 'we' mask an ambiguity and partiality:

> The ideal of consent, however, makes sense only to the degree that the terms in question submit to a consensually established meaning. . . . Habermas insists that reaching consensus requires that words be correlated with univocal meanings. . . . But are we, whoever "we" are, the kind of community in which such meanings could be established once and for all? Is there not a permanent diversity within the semantic field that constitutes an irreversible situation for political theorizing?

She makes her challenge on the basis of her Derridean and Foucaultean amplification of the Austinian performatives. That is, she invades Habermas' territory to make trouble with his analytical tools, now inflected through a radical slippage between utterance and meaning:

> The disjuncture between utterance and meaning is the condition of possibility for revising the performative, of the performative as the repetition of its prior instance, a repetition that is at once a reformulation. Indeed, testimony would not be possible without *citing* the injury. (87) . . . The anticipated universality, for which we have no ready concept, is one whose articulations will only follow, if they do, from a contestation of universality at its already imagined borders. (91)

Because there is a gap between utterance and meaning, performatives (even if citing a prior use) offer "the linguistic occasion for change" (102). This gap, not an abstract universality, enables the critical discourses of transgressive repetition and the resignification of injurious words (1993a).

Cornell's (1992, 13–38, 55, 60f., 85f.) and Young's (1990, 1997a) notions of asymmetry raise another difficulty to Habermas' universal ideal of communicative symmetry. While all three desire some form of ethical or communicative reciprocity, Habermas insists on symmetry as the conditions of its possibility, whereas Cornell distinguishes between phenomenological symmetry of our basic humanity and (with Young) ethical and political asymmetry governing any ideal of justice (cf. Matuštík 1998a, 122–25). Young formulates the normative ideal of communicative ethics as that of asymmetrical reciprocity and Cornell as that of ethical asymmetry (cf. Cornell, "What Is Ethical Feminism?" in Benhabib et al. 1995, 75–106; Huntington 1998, chap. 8). Reasons for these discontents with Habermas' universalism are articulated succinctly by Young (1990, 106f.):

> The alternative to a moral theory founded on the assumption of impartial reason, then, is a communicative ethics. Habermas has gone further than any other contemporary thinker in elaborating the project of a moral reason that recognizes the plurality of subjects. He insists that subjectivity is a product of communicative interaction. Moral rationality should be understood as dialogic. . . . Yet even Habermas seems unwilling to abandon a standpoint of universal normative reason that transcends particularistic perspectives. . . . In a democratic discussion where participants express their needs, no one speaks from an impartial point of view, nor does anyone appeal to a general interest.

Young's strongest criticisms rest on her otherwise sympathetic assessment of Habermas' achievements. She shares with Cornell and Butler some of the same sources of suspicion. Among the earlier ones is Sartre's existential notion of singular universality (rather than the Hegelian speculative and generalized notion) as the irreducible vanishing point of any reciprocity and ethical solidarity. Among the later resources are other post-Hegelian theorists of singularity, notably Adorno, Derrida, Foucault, Lévinas, as well as the feminist poststructuralist critics of masculinist universality, such as Kristeva and Irigaray. It would be a mistake to place either Young or Cornell—because they disagree with Habermas—outside of the larger project of new social criticism. Young's (1990, 7) self-evaluation is representative:

> Though my method is derived from Critical Theory, I reject some tenets of critical theorists. While I follow Habermas's account of advanced capitalism and his general notion of communicative ethics, for example, I nevertheless criticize his implicit commitment to a homogeneous public. . . . From . . . [the] postmodern orientation, in which I include some writings of Adorno and Irigaray, I appropriate a critique of unifying discourse to analyze and criticize such concepts as impartiality, the general good, and community.

It is quite instructive if we now consider the above criticisms from an opposite angle. Fleming (1997, 1, 225), like Fraser and Benhabib, argues that "Habermas's theory is not universalist enough" because "the basic categories of the theory are gender-coded." Outlaw implores us to "move from universality via conceptual strategies to universality in the form of democratically based shared unity as an existential project" (1996, 182). Habermas prematurely junks the insights from existential and social phenomenology *after* the linguistic turn, on the one hand, and those gained from the poststructuralist turn to language, on the other. He favors anchoring his communicative turn almost exclusively, with the exception of pragmatism, in the formal linguistic analysis. For all his pluralism,

Habermas needlessly reduplicates the Anglo-American prejudices that still prevail toward the Continental-European philosophical tradition. To be sure, while the linguistic turn requires radical methodological revisions of the phenomenological subject-centered starting point, analytical philosophy's access to the lived dimension of the life world is rather limited. In that self-limitation Habermas severs his ideal concepts from concrete universalism attained in existential and social phenomenology *after* the linguistic turn (cf. Taylor 1989, 1991; Matuštík 1998a, chaps. 1–2). A robust universalism attends to the particularity (Outlaw 1996, 179) of theorizing from the margins. New critical theorizing must be developed from the margins, whether conceived in a politics of difference (Cornell, Young) or as concrete communicative ethics (Benhabib, Honneth); it must envision in its ideality postpatriarchal and postcolonial singular universalism. Otherwise *we*, as critical social theorists and activists, have nothing to write home about.

Contemporary critical feminist and race theorists often utilize the insights of existential and social phenomenology (e.g., Bartky 1990; Gordon 1995a,b; Honneth 1992; Huntington 1998; Ingram 1995; Marsh 1995; Matuštík 1998a; Outlaw 1996) as well as of poststructuralism (Butler 1993b; Cornell 1991, 1992; Young 1990, 1997a). With a more concrete starting point situated in the life world, they can offer evidence for Fleming's (1997, 6f.) claim that the androcentric subject is transported to and reproduced in Habermas' intersubjectivist model, which depicts the life world in terms of the generalized other (Benhabib and Cornell 1987, 77–95). Reinforcing Fraser's argument discussed above, Fleming (1997, 7) contends that

> [since] all knowledge is produced by embodied and interested human beings, in relationship with each other and in history . . . [then], contrary to what Habermas might think, there is a connection between gender and rationality in his theory that he does not acknowledge, and it is a connection that he cannot acknowledge without abandoning important parts of his theory.

Fleming objects to Habermas that since he views feminism as a "particularistic" (1) new social movement, he accords no moral status to gender: he says next to nothing about it, and it has next to nothing to contribute to the question of rationality (2). Since the links between gender and rationality are assumed in a problematic way in his theory, they make his universalism deficient (7). Fleming neither wishes to get rid of the communicative rationality, unlike some feminists might do in taking an emphatically poststructuralist turn against Habermas (6), nor does she adopt a ping-pong move from universalism to particularism (220). Rather, like Outlaw and others (e.g., Sartre 1974; Schrag 1989; Young 1990), she argues for a new methodology that would integrate the particular perspectives in a differentiated manner within the projected universal rationality. Habermas' view of competent speakers in the public sphere is ideologically "genderless," Fleming worries (221), since those who are given a way to speak are liberal, white, and male heads of households. Habermas professes Enlightenment universalism and makes his theory into a vintage bastion against the perceived postmodern dismantling of that ideal; and yet "for someone who has universalist aims, . . . his theory actually promotes the identification of male and human being in its retention of a gender-structured family" (221). In his unreconstructed partiality (blindness), he is badly universalist and particularist at once, elevating his social location into a universal.

We can follow Marx, then Pateman or Firestone, and then Gordon, Mills, or Outlaw in gradually breaking down the western contractual identifications of human beings with bourgeois subjects, patriarchal subjects, and white subjects. The linguistic-communicative turn alone can break down none of these false continuities and sham democratic normalities. Again, *this* rupture of false continuities requires nothing less than a revolutionary change in social consciousness (however otherwise postmetaphysical it has become) and its institutionalizations. Habermas' linguistic-communicative turn accomplishes a shift from the subject-centered phenomenology to a communicative paradigm of intersubjectivity. But in this turn, he takes with him uncritically all the problems of an untheorized embodied subject. He abandons existential and social phenomenology for correct formal reasons (the need for a linguistic turn) and yet with disastrous substantive oversights due to his atemporal and analytically disembodied model of communication. The phenomenological perspective in the life world, *after* the linguistic-communicative turn, detects the structurally hidden untrue claims of the bourgeois, patriarchal, and white subject. For this reason, even after the turn to communication, an existential-phenomenological methodology of embodied communicative praxis (Schrag 1989) corrects the formally analytical turn with a still more radical turn to the margins.

The Postsecular Turn, Ethnic Cleansing, and Humanitarian Warfare

What is entailed in the notion of the inclusion of the other? The politics of difference requires that we shed once and for all the illusion of being able to assume the position of the other as other (Young 1994, 1997a; cf. Benhabib 1994). The future of *this* self-divinizing illusion yields a disenchantment with the ideal of symmetrical reciprocity. What the postsecular turn teaches is that *every* other is wholly other (Derrida 1995, 77f.). To fail this lesson in singularity is to cleanse the other either by erasure or by inclusion. The fall of the Berlin Wall enables Habermas to unmask the ethnic cleansing of the other that is carried out by the erasure of difference within and among the nation-states. The demand to act in such a way as to make a future Auschwitz impossible, however, can blind one to the cleansing of the other by a *humanitarian* war of intervention. Does not one run the frightening danger of cleansing the other by including him or her in that globally reenchanted hegemonic ideal of the new world order? These dangers mark an extreme point of discontents with Habermas.

Already Benhabib (1992, 1994) and Honneth (1992) articulate their concerns that Habermas' model of communicative ethics and democracy needs to be rendered more concrete. They search for the concrete ethical form of life that would avoid the pitfalls of the nation-state or ethnic homogenization, at one end, and the pitfalls of hegemonic, unsituated moral agents at the other end. They call this form of life a postconventional *Sittlichkeit* (Benhabib 1992, 11, 165; Honneth 1992, 274–87; Matuštík 1993, 259–64; 1998a, chap. 1, 142–44). That notion is derived by pruning the branches of the Habermasian communicative competence, itself derived from the moral subjects, onto the trunks of the ethical life of communities or larger nation-states. A postconventional identity formation should be able to resist both the homogenizing and the hegemonic abstractions, thereby facilitating critical relations to one's traditional culture as well as to the deliberative procedures of political culture.

Fraser (1997a) expands this search for a postconventional ethical life into the domain of material justice. She distinguishes the culturalist struggle for recognition (see Taylor 1994; cf. Honneth 1992; and SR) and the economic need for redistribution. By assigning each domain its proper nonreducible task (recognizing the needs arising from gender, sex, and race vs. those of economic redistribution), Fraser wishes to overcome the false "postsocialist" antithesis between "the cultural" and "the social" Leftists (1997a, 3; cf. 207–23). Ironically, her sophisticated distinction between recognition and redistribution might unwittingly reproduce the dual-systems theorizing that she earlier criticized in Habermas. While Fraser (198f.; 1997b) suspects Young's (1990, chap. 2) "five faces of oppression," Young theorizes an integral, materialist-cultural model of social criticism (1997b).

I employed before the notion of communicative democracy as a political equivalent to Habermas' linguistic-communicative turn. But it is Young's politics of difference (1990) and, in particular, her move (1996, 120–35) from Habermas' generalized deliberative model of democracy to a more concrete one that gives us the more integral conception of communicative democracy. To render communicative ethics and democracy concrete in the ways envisioned already by Benhabib, Fraser, or Honneth, the ideals of ethical community and democratic polity must preserve the vanishing point of difference. This can be done only if the ideal of communication community does not divinize even its postmetaphysical voice of the people. Not to worship its own echo, the communicative ideal must nourish the other not only by recognition but also by witnessing the other as other (cf. Oliver 1998). This reformulation of the ideal affirms the postsecular intuition that regards every other as a wholly other (cf. Derrida 1995). Each and every one is saved here from homogenizing erasure and hegemonic inclusion (i.e., cleansing).

The notions of the politics of difference, asymmetrical reciprocity, and ethical asymmetry aim to correct the Hegelian homogenizing and hegemonic gesture insofar as it too survives within Habermas' communicative ideal and even within some of its reformulations by sympathetic critics. Disagreeing with Habermas' ideal, as well as Benhabib's reformulation of it (1992, 1994), Young corrects for two perceived problems: the culturally biased restriction of democracy to argument and the biased presupposition of unity as the beginning or end of communication

(1994; 1996, 122). The first bias assumes a universality, which is partial to Eurocentric and "male speaking styles" (1996, 123). The second bias appeals to the unitary interest as an ideal outcome of discussion, but this tends to hegemonize positions and interests and even languages of those with some privilege in the discussion (125f.). Young, like Cornell (1992, 55, 85f., 60f.), holds that in spite of the shared phenomenological symmetry (as humans we are not *that* wholly other that we could not share any bodily, economic, and cultural experiences and languages), "each position is aware that it does not comprehend the perspectives of the others differently located, in the sense that it cannot be assimilated into one's own." Thus "communicative democracy is better conceived as speaking across differences of culture, social position, and need, which are preserved in the process" (Young 1996, 127; cf. 1994; 1997a).

Outlaw strives for "a rehabilitated notion of reason that preserves universality while also preserving particularity of historically situated life-worlds" (1996, 179). After affirming the promise of Habermas' communicative ideal, Outlaw points out how racial minorities occupy the place of erased or excluded difference within European modernity.

> In part this is a function of the subtle, but pervasive, racism mediated in the liberal and Marxian voices that narrated periods of the histories of particular European peoples as though, on the one hand, they were the histories of *all* peoples, and, on the other, as though Hegel had in fact provided the definitive word on Africans: a people without history because a people not yet sufficiently developed as to be makers of history. (181)

There arises what Dussel calls an offense of disclosing the racist heart of the philosophical discourse of Euro-American modernity (1996, 20):

> Modernity was born in 1492 with the "centrality" of Europe.... The "I" which begins with the "I" conquer of Hernán Cortés or Pizarro, which in fact precedes the Cartesian *ego cogito* by about a century, produces Indian genocide, African slavery, and Asian colonial wars. The majority of today's humanity (the South) is the other face of modernity.

There is also the offense of placing Euro-American modernity alongside the other New World African modernity (West 1993, xii; Matuštík 1998a, 229). This is the offense of including the voices of difference within the inclusion of the other achieved in a priori terms of Europe's second chance.

> The excursion through "difference" involves, potentially, more than a concern on the part of women, peoples of Amer-Indian, African, Hispanic, Asian descent, gays, etc., to tell our own stories and, in doing so, to re-affirm ourselves. The important point is *why* the histories and cultures—the modalities of being, the life-worlds—are meaningful and important, *why* they have an integrity worth preserving and struggling for while subjecting them to progressive refinement. (Outlaw 1996, 181f.)

The offense of the postsecular turn is the question that challenges the very thought of Europe's second chance held today in the midst of those without hope (Fanon 1963; Marcuse 1991, 257). This question projects radical existential, multicultural, and economic democracy. The project calls us, for Adorno ([1966] 1973) and Lévinas (1981) since Auschwitz, to think otherwise than being, otherwise than Eurocentrically, to think the other of Europe's heading (Derrida 1992; Matuštík 1998a, chap. 2).

Given that Habermas' second-degree witnessing of his own and his nation's past manifestly reaches repeatedly back to the unloading ramp at Auschwitz, some very hard questions resurface. Why does he bequeath us no radically transformative ideal of liberation, even shrinking away from the mere thought of a revolutionary social movement? But then why does he incarnate his last vestiges of utopian hope for the cosmopolitan world in his two endorsements (where did his healthy skepticism vanish?) of the dreadful *humanitarian* wars of intervention?[13]

I raised these questions to Habermas so far only immanently. It appears now from this late moment at the turn of the twentieth century that his one-time allergy to student actionists had already in the 1960s more to do with his preferential sensibility for stable law and order—the marks of his war trauma—than with preferences for nonviolent, radically democratic ways. Any answer I can give will prove inadequate and even unfair to the complexity of his profile that motivates his thinking and actions. And yet I may not shrink from asking questions that face *us* here. I want to avoid equally the blanket condemnation and simple affirmation of his published views on the Allied assaults against Iraq and Serbia. In search of greater understanding, taking seriously discontents with his militarist-humanist turn, I press in two directions at once. I endorse Habermas' cosmopolitan ideal and thereby think with him against his stated positions on the Persian Gulf War and on the conflict over Kosovo/a. By appealing to the postsecular hope of those without hope (i.e., by appealing genealogically to the margins of Habermas' texts and of his philosophical-political profile), I can recover the politically more inclusive and existentially more concrete dimensions of his lifework. I move in an opposite direction to the one adopted at the outset of this study. I begin with Habermas' theory and critically test it against his political assumptions. I traverse this path from his essay on Kant's "Perpetual Peace" (EdA) to the Kosovo/a event (BH) in order to rationally reconstruct what his thinking *should* have been from the present point in time. I refer to his earlier treatment of the Persian Gulf War where this is helpful for my discussion.

Any Left critique of imperialism should be balanced by a critique of nationalism, fundamentalism, and the consequent cleansings of political, ethnic, and religious opponents. In the two post-1989 Euro-American wars of intervention, against Iraq and Serbia, the Left as well as the Right split at the precise juncture when this balance was lost. This division occurred more so during the NATO bombing. Many of those who were outraged at the Serbian regime's policy of suppression of the Albanian-Kosovar autonomy said next to nothing of the Allied diplomatic intransigence and NATO's hegemonic designs in the region. Those who spoke up against U.S. and pan-European imperialism kept more or less silent about the threat of genocide, lest they would offend their Serbian comrades and find themselves supporting the official policy of NATO intervention.

To Habermas' credit, his position on the Kosovo/a conflict (BH), unlike his assessment of the Persian Gulf War (VaZ), manifests a concern for both these sides of the imperialism-genocide divide. He is among those few who, whether on the liberal or radical Left, were willing to think about both these difficult questions at once and had the courage to condemn equally western imperialism and the Serbian nationalism. I state at the outset that I inhabit the same standpoint of a dual condemnation of imperialism and genocidal nationalism, though I do not subscribe to Habermas' stated conclusions. The overall discontents with him arise from his instrumental yielding to war.

Facing a conundrum here between imperialism and genocide, one is likely to err on each side in trying to prevent imperialism while doing nothing about genocide, or trying to stop genocide and exponentially entrenching long-term imperial designs. We face here and in future conflicts a tragic situation and a difficult task. The situation of tragedy and the difficulty of beginnings as such do not legitimate certain positions or actions. The imperialism-genocide conundrum should have been obvious in Iran's anti-imperialist revolution, which exiled or suppressed its progressive social movement and ushered Iran into despotic theocracy; at the other end, an outcome of the *humanitarian* wars, whether against Iraq or Serbia, was not democracy but rather 100,000 dead Iraqis, continued tyranny in Iraq with the moneyed oligarchy in Kuwait, and 10,000 dead in NATO's war with then continued authoritarian rule in Serbia and NATO's protectorate in ethnically cleansed Kosova. We must measure any counsel to the war parties not only against these disastrous consequences but by envisioning the possibility of disaster as the end inscribed into the very means of such *humanitarian* wars.

Kant envisioned perpetual peace among the associated nation-states, Hegel thought that giving up the right to go to war *(ius ad bellum)* among sovereigns was a bad idea, and Habermas thinks that his cosmopolitan ideal can square this Kantian-Hegelian circle. Yet the twentieth century did not learn how not to dance to the beat of the war drums. Habermas seems to be aware of this tragic fact when he speaks its truth *after* the Gulf War: "Surely, everyone today is in agreement that the idea of a just and peaceful cosmopolitan order lacks any historical and philosophical support." He gives his honest existential assessment by assuming his own difficult responsibility to think the impossible: "But what other choice do we have, besides at least striving for its realization?" Does his next move redeem these sober reflections? I see no advance in places, where Habermas, after the Persian Gulf War, detects the dawn of a new era, "a piece of reality" with "normative implications." His claims here no longer discern the tragic dimensions of the unevolved social consciousness of human freedom, nor do they assume existential responsibility for the impossible freedom that we must strive for, often against all odds. His existential sobriety yields to a Kantian wish for the moral reality of the regulative ideal in an unjust world, now coupled with a Hegelian thinking of this reality *as if* it were already "a piece of 'existential reason'" at hand (VaZ 32f./22; all citations above).

So why should Habermas at the end of his hard-thinking days endorse the assault on Baghdad and Belgrade as coherent with his own, at times quite astonishing, existential sobriety and with his pragmatically concrete ideal of a global cosmopolitan democracy? Could he possibly be wrong in trying to match his ideal, almost word for word, to the conflict situations (compare the key concepts used in VaZ, EdA, and BH)? Or is his ideal a mismatch for *our* reality? Or is his political judgment of the ground theater out of touch with empirical reality? Or are his ideal and his political intuitions both correct, and the events under discussion are thus their correct, albeit disastrous, applications and complements?

Habermas thinks with Kant against Kant. He reasons that Kant did not transcend his historical time horizon when intimating perpetual peace though Habermas allows *us* today to think through that Kantian intuition dialectically, thereby arriving at the idea of cosmopolitan world citizenship. In that same manner we may push through the limits of Habermas' horizon, motivated as it is by the key experiences that shape his profile. That horizon allows for a still more radical embodiment. In imitating Habermas' sympathetic reading of Kant against Kant, I resist diminishing Habermas' achievement.

Just as Kant overlooked indoctrination and "deception *by means of* language" invading the "*global* public sphere" (EdA 204/176), and just as he had yet to learn of market capitalism (201/173), so likewise Habermas unlearns these lessons as he falls back behind the nineteenth-century learning by suspicion. Habermas cogently reformulates Kant's optimism about international peace through Hegel's concern for ethical life in the state and he then projects that ideal globally. Yet he does so manifestly against Hegel's endorsement as well as against Schmitt's glorification of war among sovereign states (the title of BH). Still he leaves out the lessons learned after Kant and Hegel (EdA 208/179), thereby rendering that optimism somewhat naively detached rather than filled with hope for the sake of those without it. Habermas forgets the lessons of class and the racial and patriarchal conflicts of modern nation-states as they expand into imperial violence. The nation-states and the empires are produced by cleansing the difference within their respective territories.

This is how such naive optimism materializes: manifestly, it has a positive side. In reinterpreting Kant, Habermas envisions international peace "as a *process*, which unfolds in a nonviolent manner and which aims not merely to prevent violence but to satisfy the real preconditions for a peaceful coexistence of groups and peoples." In conflict, short of resorting to military *(humanitarian)* force, he permits "nonviolent intervention designed to promote processes of democratization" (EdA 216/185). He trusts that the "accommodating" trends will continue beyond the imperfect Kantian association of free nation-states, as well as beyond the post-Hegelian world wars among them "to a transitional stage between international and cosmopolitan law" (213/183). Sharing global dangers favors adopting peaceful and cosmopolitan scenarios. That idea inspired the United Nations. "Those who do not completely despair of the learning capacity of the international system have to rest their hopes on the fact that the globalization of these dangers has in fact long since united the world into an involuntary community of shared risks" (217/186).

Then there is the negative side of this naive optimism. It arrives with the question of the right of foreign intervention, such as the one legitimated by the UN against Iraq in 1991 or the one assumed by NATO against Serbia in 1999 without the UN's blessing and with a free-floating moral argument. In contrast to Kant's "'there is to be no war,' the 'heinous waging of war' must come to an end" (EdA 193/166), we have Habermas' "war is here" (BH 1/263) and his view of the latter as a coherent accommodating trend toward the former. Habermas compellingly underscores the gap between the effectiveness and legitimacy of military intervention. He correctly evaluates the need for an international procedures of a functional, reformed UN Security Council. He rightly concludes that since international human rights have a weak institutional basis, the border between moral appeals to them and legal procedures based on them is left unclear (6f./266–71). And yet—is closing that gap with the UN's cosmopolitan human rights policy on the same path as closing it via NATO's bombing of Serbia or via similar acts of *humanitarian* wars of intervention? There is a gap, all right; but there is likewise a non sequitur in both the theoretical and the praxial dimensions set in the same gap between the two paths: out of Kant's moral ideal and out of Hegel's pseudoexistential and pseudomaterial reality we get neither Kierkegaard's existential freedom nor Marx's social liberation. There is no way we can get normatively (in regulative ideal or in gradualism) from the state of nature among sovereign nation-states via the wars of intervention against the wars of genocide into a cosmopolitan world order. This entire move would cause a short circuit. We do discern the gap between the first two wars in the state of nature and the latter order. NATO's war against Serbia does not lie on the border between law and morality, since that war was both illegal and immoral—the genocidal Serbian nationalism notwithstanding. The gap reveals the need for a qualitative achievement of existential freedom and social liberation. This achievement to come separates the beginnings in our present individual and social evolutions (from one kind of war to another kind of war) from those other, cosmopolitan beginnings. Bridging this gap represents an existentially and sociopolitically transformed form of life. Of that path *we,* the keepers and inheritors of the twentieth-century hope for a more just world, have not yet been capable. Habermas does not make a dent in overcoming this failure.

Habermas nonetheless shares the mainstream "western interpretation [according to which] the war in Kosovo could signify *a leap* from the classical international law of states to a cosmopolitan law of a global civil society" (italics added).

Moreover, he argues, "this development was initiated by the founding fathers of the UN and was accelerated by the Gulf War and other interventions after a long period of stagnation caused by the Cold War" (1/264). For sure, Habermas must confuse here the decisionistic, rationalist-quantitative leap, which he mentions above, with the self-transformative, existential-qualitative leap to responsible freedom and social liberation, which he fails to thematize. Is not the conflation of the two paths—between the ideal of Kant's perpetual peace and the post-Hegelian wars of intervention, at one end, and the cosmopolitan world of communicative and democratic freedom at the other end—obvious in Habermas' great leap forward that abstracts from needing to achieve a qualitatively transformed concrete existence?

Habermas' naive optimism rears its ugly head in his lack, even shunning, of any capacity for the "suspicions based on the critique of ideology. The case at hand shows that universalist justifications do not by necessity always function as a veil for the particularity of unconfessed interests. The results of the hermeneutics of suspicion are quite meager in the case of the attack on Yugoslavia" (6/268). Is he not so blinded by the memory of Auschwitz and by the memory of the Allied liberation of Germany that he is unable to distance himself from the media, the deceptive public debate, and the mismatch (or gap) between his ideal and the means to it? Is he so concerned not to play onto the Fascist and antihumanist "mills of Carl Schmitt" and so unable to grasp this war otherwise than as a feat "magnanimously undertaken by NATO for the community of nations" (6/266), that he deliberately wills his own ignorance—convincing himself, making himself literally blind and deaf to NATO's underlying motives?

> Neither the motive of securing and extending its sphere of influence ascribed to the United States, nor the motive of finding a new role attributed to NATO, and not even the motive of establishing a "European fortress" as a way of preventing waves of immigration, can explain the decision to undertake such a serious, risky, and costly intervention. (6/268)

Blackburn (1999), in the same issue in which Habermas articulates a recent version of his regulative ideal of the cosmopolitan world citizenship (ENPG 57ff.), demonstrates how NATO's bombing of Serbia was indeed a war of expansion.[14]

Thus, while Habermas appeals to "a critique of ideology" against Schmitt's cynical equation of humanity with bestiality, he forgets to bring that very critique against the bestiality at hand. His valid fear of the Schmittian or even Hegelian internationalism becoming our future does not inversely legitimate or prove right the path of NATO's war. And what about that minimal "Hegel's 'honor of war,'" which Habermas detracts from "Lenin's Hegel" and from Schmitt (EdA 232/198) but implicitly grants to "the World Spirit" (207/178)? I am not saying that Habermas holds on to a notion of divine providence revealing itself in and making us learn through war. Still, his argument carries a Hegelian echo, now rendered fallible in the "learning process with which all of us together are going to have to come to terms, across the trenches of an ongoing armed conflict" (BH 7/271, translation mine). This echo too must be the meaning of Habermas' "trying to make the best of the Gulf War—the best not only for the Middle East but for the order of international relations as such" (VaZ 18/11). Such wars of intervention, once again, carry within them "what Hegel would have called a piece of 'existential reason'" or a convincing "piece of reality" with "normative implications" (32f./22).

Yet to become 'existential' in this Hegelian sense is to conflate one's concrete freedom with speculation and to conflate *our* social liberation with its moral ideal. Habermas stays closer to reality by seeking to institutionalize the cosmopolitan ideal. Given that Germany never had a successful social revolution, and that its political existentialists of the 1930s were rather confused about democratic institutional politics, Habermas' appeals to law and order and to existential reason in the same breath should be subject to the hermeneutics of suspicion. In resisting Germany's past coming back as future, he sensibly unmasks the discontents of the nation-state. In endorsing the *humanitarian* wars of intervention, are not we revisited by that past *as* future?

Habermas' keen sensitivity to the Fascist past renders his evaluation of the Kosovo/a conflict more balanced than the summary silence about ethnic cleansing in various other criticisms of NATO's imperial policy. Yet were not the stakes of Habermas' ideal placed as high as they are, and were not the key contradictions between the failing reality and that ideality so glaring, would also Habermas' war counsel be one among many other fallible claims. True, silence and inaction might have been just as pernicious in light of ethnic cleansing. It is also true that making *no* criticism of ethnic cleansing might have been just as complicitous for a social critic as writing a front-page piece that in the end provides moral arguments in an imperfect world of NATO's bombing for the cause of human rights. Cleansing was in progress in the former Yugoslavia since the west, with the Federal Republic of Germany in the lead, unilaterally recognized the breakaway Yugoslav republic of Croatia and then, postgenocidally, negotiated the Dayton peace deal with Slobodan Milošević. Thus a social critic need not be naive about NATO's motives: the victims of genocide were not decisive for making the war over Kosovo/a now, and they were not decisive for saving the victims of Sarajevo before. Moreover, compelling evidence exists that the bombing escalated genocidal acts. The Kosova protectorate, without an independent Kosovar future, might have been a minimalist outcome of diplomatic negotiations before the war.

When the full story is eventually told, Habermas' dual endorsements of the *humanitarian* wars will most probably continue to be subject of discontents. His fear of student street activism and revolutionary aspirations in the 1960s and his panic over their purported Left Fascism both pale in contrast to the thousands of dead Iraqis and thousands of dead inhabitants of the former Yugoslavia. Will the twenty-first century learn to suspect those Fascist continuities that, as Adorno (1986) and Marcuse (1991) feared, now invade our cherished lawful democracies? The incongruity of Habermas' harsh rebuke to the revolutionary Left students along with his yes to the wars of intervention, just because the latter appeal to constitutional human rights and the former adopt extraprocedural or act-up politics and even street anarchy, will perhaps continue to raise some eyebrows. At worst, then, Habermas' enthusiasm for the interventionist bandwagon might undermine his theoretical ideal of the UN, since instead of reforming it, these wars debilitated the very institutional fabric of the UN. At best, Habermas might be prompted to revise his theory or admit that he misassessed how the ideal fits the situations, which his Critical Theory should have apprehended with a more adequate skepticism.

When a protester hurled red paint at Germany's foreign minister, Joschka Fischer, to dramatize Germany's Red-Green governmental support for NATO's bombing of Serbia, the uncivil and even injurious force of this body politics manifested aggravated discontents with the deceptively democratic discourse and even with its force of the better argument. The demonstrators from Seattle in November 1999 might ask, Life has become better, but for whom and in which context? Should the good feelings of Germany within the European Federation be *our* measure? Perhaps these queries are unfair if addressed to Habermas alone. The questions present *us, the children of the twentieth century,* with a radical self-choice: Either *we* will learn by disaster to witness ourselves as finite and even powerless theorists and actors, thereby learning to think and act in solidary ways, rather than as imperial gods; or the blindness by disaster will continue to frustrate any new beginnings one may take. With this either/or choice arises the question that prompts one to step back from any easy self-assurance one, as a critical social theorist and activist, may still have: Will *we* learn how to think and how to embody *our* working off the traumatic past otherwise than *as our* disastrous future?

NOTES

1. There is one exception to my words of praise that, minimally, numerous contributors to the originally planned volume on Habermas in the Library of Living Philosophers series might raise. Habermas is to date perhaps the only world-famous thinker who was invited to be part of this prestigious series (founded by Arthur Schilpp and then edited by Lewis E. Hahn for Open Court), who accepted the invitation and signed a contract with the publisher but then withdrew from the project. In the course of several years over thirty people from around the world wrote original essays for the volume. Habermas was supposed to respond individually to each contributor after writing an extended intellectual autobiography, which accompanies all volumes in the series. Many distinguished living philosophers are typically invited to have a book about them as part of the series (e.g., Davidson, Gadamer, Ricoeur, Sartre, or Quine). After Habermas' unprecedented withdrawal from the project, perhaps on account of his poor health, he continued to be both prolific and active in other debates, but the plan for this work had to be redesigned as a self-standing book with most of the original and a few new contributors, yet without Habermas (Hahn 2000).

2. Husserl (1970) gave his lecture on the crisis of European sciences in Vienna and Prague in 1935. Carnap ([1932] 1959) gave his critique of Heidegger while living in Prague. Quine spent a postdoctoral year with Carnap in Prague in 1932–1933 and returned to lecture in Prague, like Richard Rorty or Sir Karl Popper, after 1989. Horkheimer's key essay (1972) on Critical Theory appears in 1937. The Nazis attacked with the same venom the Vienna Circle, the Frankfurt School, and the phenomenological movement. The diaspora in Great Britain and North America of these complex Central European philosophical origins opened the space for the later Cold War invention and entrenchment of the analytical-Continental split (cf. McCumber 1996).

3. I cannot discuss here Habermas' elaboration of Peirce's semiotics through Wittgenstein's language-game theory, Austin's speech acts theory, or Mead's thesis of individualization through socialization (see TCA 2, chap. 5; the essay on Peirce in the English translation of ND; on Mead, see ND, chap. 8/chap. 7; see also Habermas' polemic with Derrida vis-à-vis Austin's and Searle's speech acts theory in PDM, chap. 7; and Derrida's [1988, 156ff.] response). Cf. the polemic with Habermas by Butler (1997) who adopts a poststructuralist appropriation of Austin. See Matuštík (1998a, on Derrida and Habermas, 65–96; on Butler and Foucault, 112–22).

4. Habermas recalls the earlier German resources for his communicative-theoretic approach in Karl Bühler's threefold structure of speech (1934, 28; cited in ND 105/58) and in Wilhelm Humboldt (ND 191/152f.; 245/208).

5. Dummett, McCumber, and authors in Albrecht's volume show from very different angles how the Nazi and Cold War periods contributed to the breakdown of philosophical conversation not only on both sides of the Atlantic but also within very different traditions. McCumber expands his essay, cited above, in a forthcoming book-length study.

6. I am hardly the only one who uses this term to ironize the new bedfellows, democracy and capitalism. Another East-Central European, Žižek (2000, 62f.) writes: "Is not the true message of the notion of the Third Way therefore simply that *there is no second way*, no actual *alternative* to global capitalism, so that in a kind of mocking pseudo-Hegelian negation of negation, this much praised 'Third Way' brings us back to the *first and only* way— the Third Way is simply *global capitalism with a human face*, that is, an attempt to minimize the human costs of the global capitalist machinery, whose functioning is left undisturbed." In my time, socialism with a human face was a hopeful ideal (before crushed by the Soviets) of the Prague Spring of 1968.

7. Cited in Wiggershaus 1989, 681; 1998, 614.

8. In the absence of his own contribution to the field of political economy, Habermas' tone is surprising if not presumptuous. That same tone appeared in his derogatory and psychologizing characterizations of the students' motives in the 1960s (see SiK, theses 3, 5; Negt 1968; cf. Holub 1991, 94–98).

9. Compare Habermas' position with Derrida's (1992) critique of the idea of Europe (cf. Matuštík 1998a, chaps. 2–4, 9).

10. See, for example, Benhabib 1992; Benhabib and Cornell 1987; Benhabib et al. 1995; Braaten 1991; Butler 1990, 1997; Fleming 1997; Fraser 1989, 1997a,b; Ingram 1995; Marsh 1995; Matuštík 1998a,b; Meehan 1995; Outlaw 1996; Postone 1993; and Young 1990. Alison Jaggar and Drucilla Cornell are developing correctives to Habermas' communicative democratic and legal theory.

11. This crucial difference from Marcuse is evident again in PK 232–39.

12. See my discussion of these positions (Matuštík 1998a, 112–25, 129f., 142–58, 227–66).

13. And dreadful these wars were. In the Persian Gulf War, 88,000 tons of bombs were dropped on Iraqi soldiers and infrastructure to protect the Kuwaiti monied oligarchy. Along the "highway of death" in Kuwait lay hundreds of charred bodies incinerated by napalm, mangled by cluster bombs and fuel-air explosives. The U.S. used depleted-uranium shells against tanks. This was the so-called turkey shoot or "shooting fish in a barrel" of the U.S. high-tech war. On March 2, 1991, General Barry McCaffrey ordered shooting at the retreating Iraqi army two days after the official ceasefire was signed: in the Battle of Rumaila, the Battle of Causeway, and the Battle of Junkyard, the U.S. Twenty-Fourth Division engaged in one of the biggest assaults of the war, "some seven hundred Iraqi tanks, armored cars, and trucks, and killing not only Iraqi soldiers but civilians and children as well. Many of the dead were buried soon after the engagement, and no accurate count of the victims could be made" (Hersh 2000, 49). Two hundred prisoners of war were shot dead in another My Lai–like incident reported by Hersh. What could "making the best" of this massacre possibly mean? In Kosovo, the greatest exodus of Albanian Kosovars, as well as the most serious acts of ethnic cleansing against this ethnic group, began after NATO bombing of Serbia started. Under NATO protection, almost 90 percent of Serbs and Roma left Kosovo.

14. Cf. Kellner's (1992) study of the Persian Gulf War; "An Appeal" (1999); Walzer 1999; Denitsch 1999; and Ally 1999 and notes 21–22 to chapter 6 above.

Chapter Nine

AT THE CROSSROADS OF A NEW CRITICAL THEORY

> I am ... ambivalent because I have the impression that something is deeply amiss in the rational society in which I grew up and in which I now live. On the other hand, I have also retained something else from the experience of 1945 and after, namely that things got better. *Things really got rather better.* One must use that as a starting-point too; and I then go on to look for a prehistory which too lightly disposed of with the concept of "Enlightenment." (NU 203f./AS 126, translation altered, italics added)

A typical conclusion to a book would recapitulate the salient topics or events mentioned in it. The conclusion would likewise derive some implications for further study. In these regards the preceding two chapters have done this already. I will inhabit the conclusions through the beginnings, resuming both of them with a new sense of the path traversed. Just as the clusters of biographical events followed a dramatic narrative in Part One and then reversed the linear order in Part Two, so also the entire book moves within a circular sense of time. The lived angle from within which this profile is written transpires in a nonlinear movement. From this circular perspective, to move at all, and to move at the beginnings and ends in particular, I must intensify my standpoint on the spot existentially. Moving forward or backward cannot bring out anything new by way of conclusions either.

To grasp this freedom of movement, I shift my perspective from the conceptual structure of the *authorship* or lifework, its impact and discontents, to reading Habermas' *authoring* as his singular integrative series of actions, as his fundamental life project. It is this existential axis of authoring, rather than the structure of authorship, that I want to reread at this end. Intensifying the standpoint of beginnings and ends delivers communicative freedom to the difficulty of speaking about the unspeakable. Two queries and an epilogue will guide my conclusions:

- Why and how should *we* read Habermas *today*?
- What can *we* learn from *our* coming to terms with the unspeakable?

- What do *our* discontents about the past disclose about *our* historical present?

WHY AND HOW TO READ HABERMAS?

There are some felicitous and some not-so-interesting answers to the question that motivates any beginner, whether one is a specialist or not: Why read Habermas? The *why* questions are raised often when students plan courses for the upcoming semester or when professors justify academic offerings to curriculum committees or their departments and universities. It is customary in the publishing industry or in advertising a new course to describe the importance of a theorist or an oeuvre for some field of studies, specialization, advanced degree, and general education. The conventional answers and the disciplinary borders tell us, however, more about how *not* to than *why* read anyone. And Habermas is no exception. Such answers give us but a conventional Habermas.

Why read Habermas? This question becomes more meaningful after the conventional answers have been taken care of. The question can now voice disappointment with the conventional answers. This question could suddenly betray something unspoken, something noticeable by the inflection of disappointment or boredom among the questioning readers-to-be. The undertone is recognizable by an intonation or the context of the questioner, as if the mood of a question said, Why *bother* reading Habermas?

By having my book start here rather than conventionally, I wished to attract the attention of such disappointed or bored questioners, of those who are ready to jump the ship of Critical Theory for other seas. I should not have had to convince the Habermasian readership about advantages of postconventional beginnings. Conventional borders are, at least in principle, disrespected by the postconventional attitude implied in the very definition of Critical Theory. Yet the established variants of Critical Theory can lose their path and aim. Like any revolutionary research program, Critical Theory can become a normal science, if not a new convention. This postconventional distance on received views of Habermas informs my study, written unencumbered by an unnecessary need for polemics or an uncritical need to follow. With a postconventional profile of Habermas, *we* arrive at today's crossroads of *a new critical theory*.[1]

Two significant features have come to dominate and define the received conventions of Habermas scholarship. First, the view of Habermas as a philosopher in the German idealist and critical traditions, from Kant to Hegel and Marx to the Frankfurt School, prevails among the Euro-Continental as much as among the analytical philosophers. Second, the mainstream Anglo-American reception of his work is forcefully shaped by the methods of formal analysis rather than those of existential and social phenomenology or current American pragmatism. I think that these features, accentuated as much in the conventional receptions of Habermas as in translations of his texts, eclipse the richer existential and political dimensions of his lifework.[2] Yet these dimensions motivate him to challenge the notorious methodological and political splits among analytical, Euro-Continental, and pragmatist orientations.

A fresh look at Habermas reveals a theorist in the ways he is neither received within the North American sociopolitical debates (e.g., among liberals and communitarians) nor conceptualized within mainstream Critical Theory. In the United States Habermas is profiled philosophically as a liberal theorist in the Anglo-American and mainly analytical tradition. After 1989, his political profile as a Left-liberal socialist became even less pronounced. What moves to the foreground is the sketch of a reformist social democrat. Rawls and Rorty, rather than Marcuse and Sartre, provide parallel even if not very exact points of comparative reference. It is not surprising that most readers would not classify Habermas first and foremost as an existential thinker or a revolutionary activist. Despite these received interpretations, any reading of Habermas that does not attend to the existential and sociopolitical dimensions of his lifework remains incomplete. Even a very solid, helpful scholarly introduction to Habermas, if produced through the dominant received orientation of only one philosophical orientation, sketches at best a truncated profile of a complex and interesting thinker.

Here is an example of *how not to read Habermas:* by restricting his corpus to the questions raised by Anglo-American analytical philosophy and the prevalent liberal politics. A broader portrait of Habermas would give us a thinker who does not fit the conceptual straitjacket of such schools, who may not be easily co-opted if not hijacked by any disciplinary mold even as he deeply learns from and impacts them. Settling on a normalizing and now respectful Habermas (e.g., an analytical and liberal social theorist) would impoverish not only his but also our beginnings.

Reading Habermas against the received view of him should not disregard the benefits of those interpretations that opened the doors for his reception in Germany, the United States, and elsewhere. Yet admitting these benefits, one need not begin from the vantage points of his literal interpreters or of those who merely react to these interpretations in critical readings. I commenced instead in concrete historical situations of Habermas' present age, focused on his philosophical trajectory, and examined both in light of the defining political events of his generation. Therein lies a twofold advantage and a twofold tension of discussing his profile. One advantage of starting with situations consisted in the possibility of extricating his thought from the (no longer productive) one-sidedness to which dominant receptions and even helpful criticisms of him can be prone. The other advantage came with the considerable freedom this study gained in forging a set of observations and reflections developed independently of the received view of Habermas.

With regard to the tension, first, this study can be regarded by some readers as an intervention. Any corrective, even as it offsets preexisting one-sidedness, is itself inevitably partial and one-sided. Admittedly, although a corrective reading procures what appears as violence to certain interpretations, the corrective's force (as a plausible and even interesting reading) is validated by a more wholesome portrait. The hermeneutically superior and more comprehensive story claims, in the end, to offer a better argument. In hoping to have offered such better arguments, my profile of Habermas can be defended by vintage Habermasian moves. This study becomes one candidate for such 'a better argument' about Habermas; minimally, it should get a hearing among those who value these moves in the first place.

Second, if the corrective reading produced a narrative that was aesthetically more wholesome and beautiful, and argumentatively better and even more truthful, then we would obtain an increasingly interesting profile of Habermas. This tension not only aims to win the minds and hearts of various readers (whether they are Habermasian Critical Theorists or not) for another Habermas; it also wishes to introduce the next generation of thinkers and activists into their fresh beginnings in critical social theory. At this point the book transcends an ordinary intellectual biography or concerns of this or that thinker. This reading against the grain of the mainstream foregrounds the emancipatory, indeed, revolutionary and liberating ideals of Habermas' lifework in order to preserve them—from safer and even normalizing readings—for a critical theory to come.

To ascertain how *not* to read Habermas cannot be sufficient for answering the skeptics *why* read him at all. To accept the latter challenge, one must change how one poses the question, Why read Habermas? And unless we question in this other manner, even at the end, we have not begun yet. In questioning the beginnings, I do not seek a normative justification of why one should or should not read Habermas. *Only questioning that does not concern itself with such justifications merits the subtitle I chose for this book:* A Philosophical-Political Profile. *I studied the relationships between the genealogy of Habermas' ideas and values, his existential and political experiences, and his engagements in the present age.* Clarifying this linkage is all the more important with Habermas, since it defines the methods and contents of an ongoing interdisciplinary program of a social and political theory with practical intent.

On Authorship and Authoring

I discern minimally two possible readings in Habermas' own public narrative of his lifework. First, there is his overall existential-political interest in a more just form of life. This distinct self-choice infuses his lifelong concerns across personal and historical discontinuities, and it defines his recurring beginnings from early to mature work. His autobiographical interviews, interventions, and political texts disclose an active author of this self-choice. Second, a growing influence on his self-reading comes from secondary commentaries on his completed authorship. His authorship comprises likewise his particular reactions to various commentaries or direct criticisms. The study of an authorship in itself can be beneficial. Yet without raising the question of one's existential-political authoring, an exclusive focus on authorship can eclipse his publicly stated self-choice or his active authoring as well as self-reading. Authorship gives us some received justification for the question, Why read Habermas? Active authoring attests to an author's beginnings, and it matters in sketching Habermas' philosophical-political profile.

Habermas, in spite of ever seeking a nuanced differentiation of his views from Rawls or Rorty, is not entirely uncomfortable with being placed along the lines of their analytical and liberal authorship. With the fall of the Berlin Wall in 1989 and the subsequent demise of the Soviet empire, an almost permanent truce between liberal politics and neoliberal markets has been supported by certain strains of minimalist analytical methodology in philosophy and political theory. This mainstream focus adapts to Habermas' critical yet comfortable Left-liberal platform from which he can speak to his Anglo-American peers. Such a platform too could justify the author's own, now conventional response to the question, *Why read me?*

Developing a *new critical theory* of liberation, striving for radical socioeconomic democracy, would appear badly utopian (read: out of fashion if not embarrassingly Marcusean, Benjaminian, Sartrean, Fanonian, Marxian, etc.) among today's liberal social theorists and in the global neoliberal economic climate. Being non- or post-conventional in this regard, one would have to eschew the need to justify oneself to such neo/liberal establishments, one would have to embrace instead the discomforts of being critical of them.

Only insofar as Habermas internalizes the narrative of a respectful liberal theorist, sober analytical philosopher, and safe democratic reformist—shying away from his lifelong, more radical philosophical-political impulses—I am not compelled to accept this reading, even were it to be Habermas' preferred self-reading, as the full story. I do not consider my refusal to accept at face value this received view of Habermas (instead of attesting to his beginnings) as doing violence to the author. With my singular partiality to my own existentially motivated philosophical-political beginnings on August 21, 1968 (the day I woke up to the Soviet invasion of Prague), and in writing for *a critical theory to come*, I meet him through a holistic, dramatic, and open profiling of his beginnings. In such a conversation, I can gain an existential and a philosophical-political contemporaneity with him as a critical social theorist and activist. My profile of Habermas is inevitably unfinished. It is the events of his authoring, rather than the second-level readings of his received authorship, that can form an entry into Habermas' beginnings, beginnings with Habermas.

From the side of Critical Theory, there should be in principle no contradiction between existential (philosophical-political) motivations and analytical methods. Yet, given the Ockhamian razor of certain philosophical approaches, the Habermas of existential questions tends to be bracketed in the commentaries on his work. These are not Husserlian phenomenological brackets whose *epoche* would guide us to an even greater concretion. Rather, attending to Habermas' concrete life would seem to fall outside of 'philosophy', that is, outside of what any study restricted to propositions and arguments would decide to 'understand' as philosophically interesting and legitimate. For better or worse, Habermas' social theory, even once he adopts the linguistic turn of analytical methodology to clarify the linguistic-communicative turn in the normative foundations of Critical Theory, begins in living situations, or it would not have begun as a critical social theory. The tension with some analytical views of what counts as philosophically legitimate explains their secondary need to downplay these existentially motivated philosophical and political beginnings, thereby often restricting his or any Critical Theory to a species of rationality debates.

If we free up Habermas from this contrived need to justify him as philosophically relevant to some establishment, while we highlight how his work masterfully steers the course across the analytic-(Euro) Continental-pragmatist divide, a twofold benefit accrues. Students and general audiences get a more exciting, motivating entry into Habermas' corpus. And we obtain a more robust view of philosophy and social sciences, including politically relevant and existentially motivating applications of analytical and empirical methodologies. If there need not be in principle any contradiction between existential motivation of philosophical thought and an analytical attention to argumentative logic, then we are not compelled to choose between them. One of the significant, often overlooked fine qualities of Habermas' work lies in operating as a Trojan horse in the theoretical warfare between these approaches, as many of the divisions still rage on both sides of the Atlantic. Introducing new generations of students to Habermas in an institutionally irreverent fashion makes a great stride toward, first, existentially demotivating, second, theoretically delegitimating, and, finally, politically dismantling one of these ideological walls of the bygone Cold War era. *Why and how to read Habermas?*—these questions turn the boring quip, which could have masked sheer disinterest, into activist concerns. They present the reader with such questioning *today* in order to nurture a critical social theory with *liberation* intent.

THE UNSPEAKABLE AND COMMUNICATIVE FREEDOM

When we run through Habermas' scattered autobiographical statements, some of them cited earlier in this book, we can experience how the temporal instants, of what are now but still-life portraits, communicate his rich profile as if in a motion picture. What is new at this juncture concerns the emphasis I placed in different significant parts of his journey on a certain *difficulty of speaking about the unspeakable*:

- "I'd rather not say terribly much about my youth. A true retrospective can only be made at seventy [that date passed on June 18, 1999].... I grew up in Gummersbach, in a small town environment." (KPS 511/AS 77; italics added)

- "There is nothing at all to which I have an unambivalent attitude, at least apart from very rare moments. For this reason even my naive connection to social relations is not really naive, but profoundly ambivalent. This has to do with *personal experiences, which I would rather not speak about,* but also with *critical moments*—for example with the coincidence of great events and my own puberty in 1945." (NU 203f./AS 126; italics added; cf. the opening citation for this chapter)
- "The political climate in our family home was probably not unusual for the time. It was marked by a bourgeois adaptation to *a political situation with which one did not fully identify, but which one didn't seriously criticize either.*" (KPS 511/AS 77; italics added)
- "*I was in the Hitler Youth*; at fifteen *I was sent* to man the western defences." (KPS512/AS 78; italics added)
- "At the age of 15 or 16 *I* sat before the radio and *experienced what was being discussed* before the Nuremberg tribunal; when *others, instead of being struck silent* by the ghastliness, *began to dispute* the justice of the trial, procedural questions, and questions of jurisdiction, there was *that first rupture, which still gapes.*" (PpP 62/41; italics added)
- "When I was a student, in 1953, I wrote a comparable article on Heidegger's 1935 lectures, because *I was outraged by the inability of the protagonists* (such as Heidegger . . .) *to utter even one word admitting a political error. But I avoided any confrontation with my father, who was certainly only considered to be a passive sympathizer* [*Mitläufer*]." (NR 23/AS 231; italics added)
- "Partisanenprofessor im Lande der *Mitläufer*." (The partisan professor in the country of sympathizers [fellow travelers]: the main title of the essay for Wolfgang Abendroth's sixtieth birthday, *Die Zeit*, April 29, 1966, only in German PpP 249–52; italics added)
- "All the professors *who had any importance to me* were already professors before 1933." (KPS 514/AS 80) "*My own two teachers,* under whom I wrote my dissertation—Ernst Rothacker and Oskar Becker—were cases in point." (AS 192; italics added)
- "*Painful revelations of the conduct of one's own parents and grandparents can only be an occasion for sorrow; they remain a private affair between those intimately involved. . . .* An awareness of *collective liability* emerges from widespread individually guilty conduct in the past. This has nothing to do with the ascription of collective guilt." (ÜöGH 25, 27/24, 26; italics added)
- "Now our responsibility extends to the past as well. This cannot simply be accepted as something fixed and over and done with. Walter Benjamin has probably defined most precisely *the claim which is made by the dead on the anamnes[t]ic power of living generations.*" (NR 155/AS 242; italics added)
- "This newspaper has the title *Libération*, and Sartre knew as much as Marcuse did what is to be understood under that heading." (NR 33)

I want to resume now the topic left unfinished from chapters 5–7. In chapter 5, I introduced Metz's objection that insofar as the event of Auschwitz does not affect Habermas' communicative theory *as* theory, and only enters into his political essays and interventions, his architectonic suffers the contemporary amnesia about Auschwitz, as communicative theory might be aspiring to heal all wounds of history. Pensky reiterated this contention insofar as he suggested that there is an antinomy between Habermas' theory, which seems unaffected by the Holocaust, and his politics, which is shaped by coming to terms with Germany's disaster. At the outset of chapter 6, I stated that since no beginnings are innocent, critical questioning opens to what remains *unspeakable* in them. I asked, What does coming to terms with the past mean *today* and for the future? In the preceding two chapters, I began to show how this question communicates the unspeakable dimension in Habermas' temporal beginnings, situations, profiles, interventions, as well as in his entire authorship, that brings them historically and structurally together.

I argued throughout the book that *in each defining moment, though explicitly only since the 1960s, Habermas increasingly integrates the key experiences of 1945 and 1968, thereby meeting the constitutional-democratic grounding of the postwar generation and the revolutionary-existential grounding of the '68ers*. The obverse side of this integration is what remains unspeakable in these defining situations. Here my integrative thesis solicits a critical corrective: *Insofar as certain dimensions of the past remain unquestioned, that past motivates the present in ways that stand in the blind spots of theory and praxis.* My corrective attests to the unspeakable dimension in Habermas' own critical acts by which he wards off future disasters, (i.e., of "the past as future"—VaZ 89/66; afterword, in VaZ 163).

Adorno ([1959] 1986, 115) makes the following key observation, which strongly impressed Krahl during the 1960s: "I consider the continued existence of National Socialism *within* democracy potentially more threatening than the continued existence of fascist tendencies *against* democracy." Adorno curiously anticipates Marcuse's critical analyses of western one-dimensional democracies. I say curiously because, unlike Marcuse, who unmasks the sham democracies in the 1960s with an equally forceful consideration, neither Adorno nor Habermas (sharing some of the sobriety during the asylum debate) would extend this insight into a careful evaluation of the student movements around the world. In spite of Adorno's momentary idea that the rebellious students are placed by history in the role of the absent Jews in German society, for him and Habermas the Fascist ghosts of Weimar are reincarnated in new Leftist fashions, threatening to appear in Germany as the phantom revolutionaries of 1968. Taking to heart Adorno's analysis from 1959, one would have to exorcize those other, in Habermas' critique barely audible, phantoms, namely, those of imperial democracy. This did not happen in 1969, when Adorno and Friedeburg called the police on the rebelling students. Marcuse, as if we could hear his echo from 1969 in our heated debates about the Persian Gulf War and the Kosovo conflict, reveals in a Hamlet-like stance that there is something decaying in western democracies, namely, "American imperialism": "I really can see no reason to be allergic to the use of this concept" (Adorno and Marcuse 1999, 133; chaps. 2, 4 above).

The new obscurity, and this I admit is a contentious deployment of Habermas' phrase (from NU; cf. Lau 1999), of the imperial phantoms of the present age results from the sharpness of the sight focused single-mindedly on the ghosts of 1945. Habermas' autobiographical sensibility and his philosophical acumen and political courage all *can* become at other moments his weakness. The agility of anti-Nazi vision, trained by Adorno and his student Habermas in their witnessing against the Nazi disaster, perhaps became distorted in the 1960s and gave way to an aggravated blindness during the Persian Gulf War and the Kosovo conflict. We must question whether or not the fear of the ghosts of 1945 and the specters of 1968 casts a shadow over and conjures up phantoms in the democratic state. I argued that insofar as some dimensions of the past motivate Habermas' attitude in the 1960s, they can also motivate his future attitudes in 1991, the Persian Gulf War, and, in 1999, NATO's campaign against Serbia.

In a *phantom democracy*—and this too is a contentious transfiguration of Habermas' term 'phantom revolution'—Fascism can survive in the most pernicious forms, Adorno warns. His critical pedagogy confronts the two-pronged lie about the need for pristine national origins and the need for total transparency in democracy. If no origins are innocent, and Adorno and Habermas did learn this historical lesson once before, how could democratic meaning and will formation ever be transparent? Adorno has amnesia about this lesson when it comes to the student movement. Habermas consistently ignores it because of his wholehearted struggle to establish basic democratic procedures and laws.

It is not that Habermas simply forgets to question the ability of democratic structures to check the residues of Fascism infecting the same structures from within. His horizon of what is speakable or visible must be read against the relief of his astute generational sensibilities. He believes that deliberative democracy— because in its form it appeals to an unforced force of a better argument—already gives us this check on Fascism in principle. 'Fascism' stands here for coercive, dominating, and violent uses of strategic argument or brute force. Adorno's distinction between Fascism without and within democracy, and his concurrent Platonic question, present this falsifying case: who will "educate the educators" (1986, 126)? Who will educate democracy to ward off Fascism *within* its democratic procedures? Adorno and his student Habermas are remarkably sensitive to the forms that Fascism takes in the postwar generation; they are inflexible and oblivious to its truly disastrous forms in the 1960s. At its worst, they claim to find Fascism where the objective conditions for its emergence are missing.

Habermas singles out the role of Jewish thinkers within German culture, recall from chapter 1, as those who in Germany are among the most sensitive to the ways that culture fooled us (KPS 470f./AS 46; NR 150/AS 238; see Adorno 1986, 126f.). In his effort to bring about public enlightenment, he no longer feels compelled to raise such radical suspicions about his own postwar democratic socialization. In overreacting to the rebelling students who question the professed democracy of their parents, and in his post-Wall valuations of the *humanitarian* wars of intervention, he stands in his generational blind spots. I called these blind spots the specters of 1968 and the shadows of 1945. Their phantoms and ghosts dramatize those vanishing points of the past, which remain unspeakable (in Metz's estimation: left out from theory and thus indicative of an amnesia if not trauma) in Habermas' present philosophical-political profile.

Learning by disaster is another expression for learning how to begin, since the character of the end points is foreshadowed by their beginnings. The unspeakable marks the possibility of disastrous beginnings. This possibility can be *doubly disastrous* and hence *doubly unspeakable*. Insofar as one is ignorant of that possibility, either (self-) deceptively (it is unspeakable because one will have none of it) or because of an overdetermined trauma (it is unspeakable because one is unable to speak of it directly), disasters invade communication either as *the monstrously unspeakable* or *the traumatically unspeakable*. The opposite of disastrous beginnings would be the beginnings in existential-communicative freedom and sociopolitical liberation. Yet existentially free and socially liberated beginnings represent, in human terms, a lifetime task. In human terms, they cannot eliminate once and for all the apprehension and the possibility of disaster. By learning of that possibility and in taking on this task, one resists naive and motivated ignorance; by witnessing to the unredeemed claims of the past generations, one begins to rescue communicative freedom from trauma pertaining to that past and to one's living present. That critical and existentially sober resistance, paired with witnessing, are other expressions for learning by disaster, learning through *anamnestic solidarity* with the victims of history and through existential responsibility for the shared future present—learning how to begin.

Metz and Pensky are correct in raising the tension between the disaster of Auschwitz and Habermas' Critical Theory. Yet they are both wrong about the nature of this relation in Habermas' profile. It is neither true that Auschwitz is simply absent from Habermas' theoretical works, nor is it obviously true that its presence in his politics stands in an antinomian relation to his theory. Rather, the motivation of learning by disaster is both present in his authoring profile and internal to his authorship. I defend Habermas' integral profile against the above objections to amnesia or antinomy because they suggest greater incoherence than what would allow me to affirm the strengths and blind spots in one and the same person. Only an integral profile renders the motivation by a present (even if somehow hidden from oneself) trauma intelligible. *The unspeakable to which one is not related either by critically resisting one's naive and motivated ignorance or by responsibly witnessing to the dimension of the unspeakable in communicating anything exceeds both self-understanding and theory. That excess can take root either deceptively or through traumatic motivation.* The following are some of the notions discussed in the book that seem overdetermined in ways that exceed Habermas' communicative theory:

- The notion that all can be communicated (or translated into the structure of communication and one of its validity claims) if placed within the proper rational category (e.g., ethics, politics, therapy; morality and law; aesthetics) of discourse.
- The notion that symmetrical recognition secures the ideal of communicative ethics and democracy (i.e., its requirements of reciprocity and justice).
- The notion that an unforced force of the better argument, as institutionalized in lawful democracy, suffices to check deceptive discourses.
- The notion that the ideal of cosmopolitan world citizenship, in principle, resolves the problems brought about by economic and political colonialism and imperialism, by patriarchy, or by technological rationality.

By recognizing the unspeakable dimension *of* communicative freedom, we must qualify the above notions:

- The twofold relation of critical resistance (to one's naive or motivated ignorance) and of responsible witnessing (to the traumatic past) attests to the unspeakable dimension within the constitutive priority of communicative freedom.
- The ideals of communicative freedom and justice, in order to fulfill their condition of possibility, require both symmetrical and asymmetrical reciprocity, both recognition and witnessing; otherwise the past of the victims of history would be closed and their suffering could not claim from the future generations their solidarity, remembrance, and rescue.
- Being critically related to the possibility of disaster allows one to learn how to resist that deception which is deployed within the structures of communicative interaction. Becoming a responsible witness allows one to learn how to restore voice to speech and to its validity claims when both are traumatized by disaster.
- Appeals to consensual and cosmopolitan ideals protect neither these ideals nor their future chances from the deceptive blindness by disaster within democracy itself. Only by relating to the *possibility* of disaster actively may we begin and continue to witness responsibly as well as resist critically its return.

To sum up: *communicative freedom and its unspeakable dimension exhibit an internal relation. That relation performs a positive effect through facilitating our learning by disaster. That relation performs a negative effect when it exceeds theory and praxis in blinding each by disaster.*

Another way of articulating this thought would be to develop the Benjaminian-Kierkegaardian and the Marcusean-Sartrean rejoinders to Habermas. The last three citations from the series with which I introduced this section foreshadow these rejoinders. Had Habermas not himself provided at least partial ground for this reading of his profile and its motives, which is at once more existential and redemptive and revolutionary, it would be difficult to press his Critical Theory in this direction. That existential, redemptive, and revolutionary direction is emphasized by the extent of the discontents with Habermas. The discontents, when harnessed constructively to enhance rather than shipwreck Habermas' project, can offer the fertile ground for a renewed dialogue with him.

With Benjamin, we learned in chapters 5 and 7 that the past is not closed; therefore, *we* can learn to speak also about the unspeakable trauma. In Benjamin's nonlinear view of time, the future can affect the past and ingress into the present. Indeed, past generations wait for the redemptive rescue of their traumatic present (*our* historical present) through *our* weak power of remembrance. *We* too may encounter this rescue, but not through some linear progress, which for Benjamin names a form of disaster. Rather, we meet it through *our* future present whose temporal effect on us has an intensifying circular character. Or, as Habermas endorses this thought from Benjamin and against Horkheimer, we can perform *our anamnestic solidarity* with the victims of history and thereby responsibly affect the continuation or transformation of our inherited traditions. We learn from Kierkegaard about radical possibilities to reshape our future by choosing ourselves within the received tradition. This existential choice infuses communicative freedom with a radically open futurality. With regard to the unspeakable, such freedom invokes an impossible hope that things do get better even where disasters struck. Habermas learns in both ways from Benjamin and Kierkegaard, yet he assumes more about the transparency of communicative reason and about the continuity of communicative freedom than either one of them would. They, unlike him, inhabit that dimension of wonder, gratitude, and impossible hope that is never in *our* power, no matter how linguistified and secularized that power would become. This postsecular sensibility almost entirely escapes Habermas.

From Marcuse and Sartre, we learn about anticolonial struggles and the need for postcolonial solidarity. We learn from Marcuse about the problems of technological rationality and from Sartre about the ongoing dangers of imperialism. While Habermas as a Gymnasium student was inspired by Sartre and while he continues to admire a Marcusean existential variant of critical social theory, the transformative vision of liberation drops out from his mature articulation of the communicative model of Critical Theory. One can accept Habermas' wise sobriety that counsels *us* against expecting Critical Theory to console for death. How does he honor his own wisdom? Could it be that even his disconsolate and postmetaphysical Critical Theory, as Metz's objection to its amnesia about Auschwitz drives home, projects a purpose that it can neither explain nor possess in its own ideal standpoint? In being endowed with unhelpful ambivalence, could it be that his theorizing hinders the transformative hope of liberation? These questions too point to the unspeakable dimension of communicative freedom. The ideal of communicative freedom, to meet its concrete requirements, presupposes qualitative change on the way to existential freedom and social liberation. In both instances, the ideal likewise presupposes the material possibility of rescuing the past by *our* liberating hope for the future.

If the new social movements represent the praxial dimension of a *new critical theory*, then the ideal dimension needs to account for them in principle, not as an afterthought, not as an empirical issue alone, not in application of already justified norms, and not by admitting them into an already fully furnished communicative architectural edifice. By bearing witness to the traumatic-unspeakable (i.e., those instants found along Habermas' path in contemporary Germany), here and now we begin to rescue it in explicit conversation. In this fashion I hoped to nurture in Habermas' philosophical-political profile its radical existential, redemptive, and revolutionary promise. Gathering such fragments of the traumatic past begins to redeem *today* the unfulfilled promise, the unmet hope of the past generations. In each instance, from Habermas, whose incredible and exciting journey we followed, to ourselves as witnesses in this study, to each person in every generation, such promissory hope does not seem to be an outcome of one's sheer effort. It comes as a wondrous gift. Even Habermas' incredible hope, that things can get better where disasters struck, raises a form of redemptive expectation, no matter how linguistified and secularized becomes that expectation to be able to speak at all and then *redeem* validity claims.

Benjamin (1968) expresses this incredulous hope when he invokes the future affecting our present by redeeming the past. That past opens into the temporality of the now time *(Jetztzeit)* "of the present as the 'time of the now' which is shot through with chips of Messianic time" (263).[3] In *anamnestic solidarity* with the victims of history, in remembering the unfulfilled promise of personal freedom and social liberation, in gathering the fragments of hope, *we* always already embody existential, redemptive, and revolutionary praxis.

In the circular movement of this study, we witnessed how the unmet promise of the '45ers had been redeemed by the weak messianic power of the '68ers. Inversely, we witnessed how the '68ers had exercised *anamnestic solidarity*, acts of responsible rescue, and critical resistance vis-à-vis the '45ers. The '68ers performed their task for the living as well as the victimized generation of their parents. Yet 1989 no longer redeems the promise of 1968. Why is this so? Why would not Habermas or many of his contemporaries assume greater solidarity with the unfulfilled hope of that generational revolt and promise? Why does 1989, in Habermas' periodization, end the short twentieth century bereft of that rescuing and resisting hope invoked by the protesting generation?

At this crossroad I wish to resume my reflections from the end of chapter 3. What if there is a past that carries the chips of redemptive time coming from the future of the not-yet of existential freedom and social liberation? What if the answer to the above questions is another question that the skeptical generation misrecognizes as its own and *our* hope and expectation? If there is no generation that would rescue the orphaned hope of the '68ers, if that very generation joined now the main road of the established institutions (Lau 1999), how can the future of that promise, no matter how linguistified and secularized that expectation has become, turn to be *our* own *today*? Can one become blind to one's future? What if 1968 came too early for its own generation as well as for the '89ers? If 1968 arrived too early in its own time, then *our* later promissory hope could still come from the protesting generation of 1968. Yet this hope of '68ers would be coming *to us* from the future and not from the past. The expectation would come from a future perfect: not the past *as* future, but rather as a future that before arrived misrecognized. The rescue of this promise for the post-1989 generations would redeem that impossible hope of the worldwide revolutionary time in 1968.

This path is not taken by Habermas or the Critical Theorists who work within the received view of his architectonic. They pass over 1968 as a strange era that no longer has much new to offer in our complex world. This situation, and not because I say so, is the reason why *we* find ourselves at certain crossroads of a critical-social theory to come.

The memorials of the centennial of Marcuse's birth in 1998 were marked by this mixture of nostalgia for a strangely distant era and the presently still misrecognized promise (PK 232-39). What if after 1989, at the end of what Habermas (LD) names the short twentieth century, the joint future of existential freedom and social liberation comes from the unfulfilled hope of 1968? I ask this question as a member of the so-called lost generation, for whom 1968 represents his own existentially motivated philosophical-political birthday. The question is addressed to Habermas, whose own existential beginnings in May 1945 present him with a very different set of tasks. His great legacy in taking the early and postwar critical social theory into its sophisticated theoretical seriousness and wider reception stands as success beyond dispute. Yet the deeply troubling absence in that legacy of his Critical Theory is the concrete struggle for free and liberated existence. His positive impact remains far-reaching, established, and here to stay: the linguistic-communicative turn in the methodology of social theory, radical pluralism in thought and interdisciplinary dialogue, and the radical democratic project for the world cosmopolitan citizenship. The absence of a more radical liberating promise is, however, evident in that he jettisons the transformative ideal of economic democracy and meets only externally the aspirations of new social movements (as applied topics within his theory), such as the gender and race relations or the struggle against the destruction of the environment by the hegemonic technological rationality. The absence of this liberating promise within the core of his democratic theory becomes evident in his translation of the postmetaphysical dictum, that theory cannot console for death, into his silence about the postsecular question of hope: What is the point of communicative freedom if not to express the yearnings of the suffering age, striving to liberate the entirety of personal and social existence? In a solidarity of remembrance with that unfulfilled revolutionary aspiration of the '68ers, with their claim arriving from the future as their weak redemptive power for *us*; with each new social movement acting on *our* tired twentieth-century remnant as so many chips of redemptive time; may *we* not learn to imagine and become empowered to work for a *new critical theory* and praxis of liberation, thereby springing in existential freedom over that troubling absence of hope to its impossible promise?

EPILOGUE: 'FASCISM' AND ITS DISCONTENTS

Certain discontents of 'Fascism' in the context of contemporary Germany dramatize the continued 'hysteria' of the past that will not let itself pass. Habermas' role in these discontents has been singular, and his public voice testifies both to his greatness as a human being and to his exemplary place in the postwar founding of Germany. I will follow the reverse sequence of several seemingly minor events at the turn of the twentieth century, starting with the most recent from the standpoint of this epilogue to the more distant ones:

June 29, 2000

- Helmut Kohl, who was accused of illegally financing his party in 1999, compares his plight to that of the Jews under Hitler.
- On the same day Erich Nolte (along with Horst Möller's Laudatio for Nolte) inaugurates a new wave of the Historians' Debate.

July–September 1999

- Peter Sloterdijk lectures at the Bavarian castle in Elmau on the genetic engineering of humans, "Regeln für den Menschenpark" (published September 16).
- September 2 and 6, Sloterdijk is attacked by Habermas' supporters (Thomas Assheuer, "Das Zarathustra-Projekt" and Reinhard Mohr, "Züchter der Übermenschen").
- September 9, Sloterdijk responds with two open letters ("Die Kritische Theorie ist tot"); one is addressed to Habermas and one to Assheuer and indirectly to Mohr.

March 31, 1999

- Habermas publishes a deeply thoughtful contribution to the national discussion of the Holocaust memorial in Berlin, "Der Zeigefinger: Die Deutschen und ihr Denkmal."

October 11, 1998

- Martin Walser receives the "Friedenspreis" of the German publishers; in his speech he warns against "the routine of guilt," suggesting that one should not speak of Auschwitz.

There is no need to elaborate on Kohl's financial scandals that irrupted on November 4, 1999, with the revelation that in 1991 about 1 million German marks passed into the coffers of the CDU without taxation and that Kohl took almost DM2 million in illicit donations between 1993 and 1998 to support the party's activities in East Germany. Since then an avalanche of information led to Germany's greatest postunification political scandal for Kohl and his conservative party. Among the questions under scrutiny are undeclared contributions to the party, kickbacks for favorable sales (such as the thirty-six German Fuchs tanks to Saudi Arabia), advantageous price-fixing of privatized state businesses in East Germany (such as the oil-processing plant, Leuna-Werke, sold to the French Elf Aquitaine), or the lost records from Chancellor Kohl's office files (Hildebrandt et al. 2000; the chronology of the scandal, 26f.). One can be astonished at the arrogant claim Kohl made to reporters after the special hearing before the Bundestag on June 29, 2000: "This had been an unprecedented attempt to defame through inaccurate reports, insinuations, and twisting of the facts to criminalize me." One can be bemused by his stubborn refusal to name the secret donors of undeclared funds, even risking jail for this contempt of court. And yet one can only call it a hysterical self-defense when Kohl "compared the ostracism he believes he is suffering to that of the Jews under Hitler." When he is queried about this highly charged stylization of his case next to the Holocaust, he defiantly insists on having learned the correct lessons from history: "I do not need any private tuition on history. As far as the relationship with the Jews is concerned, I suggest you go to Jerusalem or Tel Aviv. There you will find out who among living German politicians is held in highest regard" (Cohen 2000).

Revisionist historians and politicians were productive bedfellows during the Bitburg rituals and in the Historians' Debate. In their new number at the turn of the twentieth century we find such historians not far from Kohl's millennial June hysteria. Nolte's speech upon receiving the Konrad Adenauer Award from the conservative Germany Foundation is unwittingly supported by the director of the prestigious Munich Institute of History, Möller. Nolte in his acceptance speech and Möller in his Laudatio speech, in tandem, inaugurate a second wave of the Historians' Debate (Herzinger 2000; Ullrich 2000). They likewise echo, at one end, German writer Martin Walser's warning (from October 11, 1998) against "a routine of guilt" and his recommendation that therefore 'normal German folks' should go into the next German century without needing to speak or hear of Auschwitz (Harpprecht 1998; Baumgart 1998). At the other end, they intervene in the decade-long debate (among historians, architects, archivists, religious leaders, and politicians) about the plans for the Berlin Holocaust Memorial (see chap. 6 above). A provocative editorial in *Der Spiegel* suggests that perhaps Nolte intends the Berlin Holocaust Memorial "for the SS"! That provocation shows the instant in which a historian's revisionist 'hysteria' comes to birth: Nolte remarks in his acceptance speech for the June award that the proposed Berlin memorial is "a work of a self-appointed all-knowing minority," and if this is so, then the historical and political intention of the monument should be regarded "as if it were dedicated to all victims of the ideology states of the twentieth century" ("Mahnmal" 2000, 18; Herzinger 2000). No matter how carefully veiled his praise for Nolte is, Möller wins no friends whether in his own Munich Institute of History or in the person of Berlin's cultural minister, Michael Naumann. While Möller does not subscribe to Nolte's repeated thesis that the Nazi regime evolved as a defensive reaction against the Asiatic terror of Bolshevism and Hitler's real enemy in world Jewry, he does not condemn it outright either. He wishes in an undifferentiated manner to "historicize" National Socialism. Indeed, his "unreflective application of the concept of 'red Holocaust' must have risen a suspicion that the crimes of National Socialism and of Communism should be not only compared, but also set on equal footing" (Ullrich 2000).[4] Thus "what [in Nolte's work] remains, then, worth praising in the emphatic judgment [of Möller's] about 'a lifework of high degree and of irreplaceable uniqueness?'" (Herzinger 2000, citing Möller). Berlin's cultural minister, Naumann, recognizes that this praise by the director of the historical institute cannot serve anyone and worries that the Laudatio brought the institute into questionable company. Since Möller's Institute receives about DM3 million for research from the government (see "Mahnmal" 2000, 18), this new 'hysteria' infects German democracy as if from within.

If we return to July 1999, we find Peter Sloterdijk (1999a), a well-known German postmodern philosopher from Karlsruhe, lecturing at the Bavarian castle in Elmau about the genetic engineering of human moral behavior. His imagined rules for a new human park offer a posthumanist answer to Heidegger's letter on humanism in light of the new genetic technologies and the antihumanist tragedies of the twentieth century. Sloterdijk proposes that the next generation formulate and develop a nonelitist moral code for anthropological biotechnologies. He is very smart and thus must have known that this would be a strange science fiction to relate anywhere, but eminently in Germany and to an assembly of Jewish theologians and philosophers! Habermas, upon learning of the talk, becomes at first alarmed and then acts with great urgency if not panic (while on a trip in Jerusalem) to encourage, so it seems, two of his supporters, Assheuer (1999) (Sloterdijk claims this was Habermas' former student) and Mohr (1999), to write rebuttals. To be expected, both writers charge Sloterdijk's speech as scandalous, suffused with Fascist rhetoric, and continuing the worst of German traditions, including Nazi appropriations of Nietzsche as well as the one-time Nazi sympathies of Heidegger. Sloterdijk (1999b) responds with an open letter, the first part addressed to Habermas and the second to Assheuer (indirectly Mohr). My objective is not to dwell on the ins and outs of the Elmau essay, but on its hysterical fallout.

Sloterdijk's (1999b) first four objections (listed as A below) charge Habermas with performative contradiction (saying x and doing y); the last four objections are more rhetorical in nature as they close his open letter with a provocative *ad hominem* (objecting to the person Habermas is) charges (listed as B below).

A. Sloterdijk objects that

- Habermas spoke with many people about Sloterdijk but never with him.
- Habermas made numerous telephone calls on his way from Hamburg to Jerusalem in order to move others to his view.
- Habermas distributed unauthorized copies of Sloterdijk's text (which was given to him in private) with instructions on how to read it and how to act in light of that reading.
- Habermas instructed Assheuer and Mohr to raise alarm about Sloterdijk's speech in their articles but not name Habermas.

These objections charge that Habermas falls into a contradiction with his professed (theorized and performed) ethics of discourse. First, he treats Sloterdijk strategically from the third- (impersonal) rather than the first-person (personal) perspective. Second, he employs strategic action to prevent mutual understanding with others about Sloterdijk's speech. Third, he violates Sloterdijk's integrity as an author and a speaker by intervening in the autonomy of his text. And, fourth, "even after becoming professor emeritus," Habermas acts behind the scene in "the role of the sovereign of the German discourse production."

B. Sloterdijk objects that

- "*The era of hypermoral sons of National Socialist fathers is running out of time.* A bit freer generation advances.... The retrospective tendency of postwar children, conditioned by trauma, cannot be any longer its [that new generation's] concern (with the exception of those among the young, who took over the Jacobin neurosis from their parents—sons from sons, a chapter in Left social psychology).... Whom does it surprise anyway that in this situation the dictators of an old mentality protect themselves from being replaced and with last-ditch efforts try to lay their guilt and unfreedom onto the next generation? *They want to build a memorial [Denkmal] to their own hypermorality*, and they want one more time, as once before, to set out on a hunt on Fascists, as if no dead dictator could be safe from our resistance" [italics added].
- "Oh, dear Habermas, I would like to say, it is all over now."
- "*Critical Theory died* on this September 2." (1999, the publication date of Assheuer's essay)
- "We will gather at the tomb of an epoch in order to take an account of it, but also to reflect on *the end of a hypercrisis*. To think means also to thank, said Heidegger. I mean, rather, to think means to breathe out." (italics added)

Ironically, this second series of objections cannot be raised if we let stand both Metz's worry about the perceived amnesia of Auschwitz and Pensky's reading of

A New Critical Theory   295

antinomy into Habermas' authorship. Yet playing one set of charges against another set would be a Pyrrhic victory for understanding Habermas. Sloterdijk's ad hominem objections (B) to Habermas are more serious and more personally injurious than the charges of contradicting in practice the theory of discourse ethics (A). Indeed, Habermas (PvbG), in his open reply to Sloterdijk (1999b), successfully deflects the unfair treatment suffered under Sloterdijk's attack. Habermas shows one by one that Sloterdijk either did not get adequate information about Habermas' actions or had his facts wrong (e.g., Assheuer was not Habermas' student as Sloterdijk asserts). And yet, even as he implicates Sloterdijk's tone in an "unreflective" knee-jerk reaction (really an echo of the German conservative cultural aversion to "hypermoralism" ascribed to postwar German intellectuals on the Left), Habermas manages to reverse only the charges of having violated professional or discourse ethics, the charges I grouped under (A). But he does not directly address the severe implications of Sloterdijk's ad hominem argument (B).

Sloterdijk's last four claims not only try to dislodge the founding role of critical social theory in postwar Germany, but they also take aim, calculatedly, at the heart of Habermas' life, self-understanding, and self-choice as a public intellectual and second-degree witness to Germany's disaster.

Habermas makes three assertions about his father: (1) he headed the Bureau of Trade and Industry in Gummersbach (KPS 511/AS 77) and (2) he was considered a "fellow traveler" (sympathizer) of the Nazi regime. (3) Habermas did not confront him at the time he exposed Heidegger in 1953 (citations in the previous section and chap. 1 above). Either Sloterdijk takes extremely risky license, insinuating in his ad hominem attack unsupported facts about Habermas' father, or in Germany one can comfortably make such sweeping assumptions about the entire securing generation. Although I find the latter possibility just as crass as the thesis of collective guilt, I cannot avoid at this juncture the question broached by Sloterdijk's astonishing assumption about Habermas' father. So I am compelled to complete Habermas' profile by explaining why Sloterdijk's highly publicized open letter (as damaging as the first four charges of purported ethical violation of professional ethics might be) raises assumptions about who Habermas is and wants to be—assumptions that not only are at their core 'hysterical' but also lead to wrongheaded conclusions. I will proceed in the last two dramatic acts of this journey, first, by disclosing the record invoked by Sloterdijk's assumptions and, second, by letting Habermas speak for himself through his penetrating reflections on Germans and their Holocaust memorial (ZDD).

Habermas is the son of Ernst Habermas and Grete Köttgen. Ernst Habermas worked (at least between 1939 and 1941, as I was able to establish with some precision) as the district director *(Geschäftsführer)* of the industrial-commercial office for leather products in the Third Reich.[5] In his commercial post Ernst Habermas was responsible for leather and luggage products in the district of Rheinland and Westfalen. His position subordinated him directly to the central district office in Offenbach (Main). Both his local and the central district offices received in turn their directives from the Third Reich headquarters for the twenty-fifth industrial group of "leather industry."⁶ Karl Guth was then the chief superior *(Hauptgeschäftsführer)* for all thirty-one departments of industrial commerce in the Third Reich (see *Gliederung* 1939, 11), and thus a main superior to whom both the district in Offenbach and the local office in Gummersbach, where Ernst Habermas worked, would have had to answer. Guth (1941, 14–41) describes in great detail the centralized organizational structure of the industrial leadership in the Third Reich. In an almost Foucaultean yet approving fashion, he traces the disciplinary matrix of industrial power in Nazi Germany: Every industrial group must have a leader *(Leiter)*. Under the leader's direction at each central, district, and local level stand one or more directors of industry *(Geschäftsführer)*. The aim of the leader is to promote the Nazi objectives, and the leader has at his disposal various ways of eliciting obedience from his subordinates. The leaders are appointed directly by the Berlin ministry of industry. Guth insists that the "principle and the thought of leadership are not merely technical means of an orderly society, but that they establish a concrete community; and only this one can lead to the truth" (34). Thus next to the industrial leaders (and Guth had one above him as well) are lined up the directors of commerce *(Geschäftsführer)*. The relationship between the leader and the local director at all levels of authority is to be one of military subordination. It is the leader who appoints the commercial director "with the permission of the [Berlin] ministry of industry." Those who are chosen by the industrial leaders to fulfill the role of the district or local commercial directors "must be the chosen men of special trust" (33). At this juncture the Nazi Party plays the "decisive" role as "the vehicle of the political will-formation of the nation." Both the industrial leaders and the directors of commerce are to be the "men" who get the approval of the Nazi Party organization. "Thereby it should be assured that only those men would be appointed [in the role of industrial and commercial directors], whose character comportment expresses the worldview of National Socialism" (34). Whether or not Ernst Habermas, as local director of commerce in Gummersbach, fit the ideal requirements, I cannot ascertain from afar. I relate only bare facts.

According to research material from the Berlin Document Center,[7] recently made available for public use also through the U.S. National Archives II in College Park, Maryland, I was able to establish the following facts: Dr. Ernst Habermas, born on August 30, 1891, was a card-carrying member of the NSDAP (Nationalsozialistische Deutsche Arbeiterpartei = National Socialist German Labor Party) from May 1, 1933, until the defeat of the Third Reich.[8] The same name appears on five documents described below. Four of these documents contain in addition to the name of Dr. Ernst Habermas also his date of birth and the identical NSDAP membership number. These are the five documents:

1. the NSDAP "Ortskartei"[9]
2. the title page for the file or dossier

3. the letter from the Köln registration of the NSDAP to the Munich central registration, asking the latter to enter a correction of the name in their registration records[10]
4. the letter response from the Munich party registration of the NSDAP to Köln about having made the requested change[11]
5. the corrected registration card with the relevant data[12]

None of the documents that I was able to locate and examine provides any other information about the NSDAP responsibilities of Ernst Habermas. Besides the established general fact of his belonging between 1933 and 1945 in Gummersbach to a mass criminal organization (i.e., NSDAP), then legally in existence in the Third Reich, I found no record of his possible personal involvement in specific criminal activities as a Nazi Party member or a local district director of commerce. From the available documents of the Berlin Document Center I was not able to make any other determination regarding the World War II activities of other members of Jürgen Habermas' immediate or extended family. As an overall assumption behind Sloterdijk's invective, we can safely accept that Habermas' father most likely would not have been able to keep and perform his highly visible industrial post without being at least a nominal member of the Nazi Party and on fairly good terms with the Nazi establishment in Gummersbach as well as in the Berlin headquarters at the ministry of industry. Habermas told the public as much when he said in one of his printed interviews that his father was, like the great majority in that generation, Hitler's "fellow traveler." Indeed, a man with this past would have been someone whom Habermas had thought of confronting already at the time of intervening against Heidegger.

Habermas publishes an essay on Germans and their memorial (ZDD) seven days after the onset of NATO's bombing of Serbia, a month before publishing an essay on that war (BH), and about four months before the controversy over Sloterdijk's lecture erupts. It befits this dramatic ending to let Habermas' deeply moving text speak the last word of this profile.

Ten years after the fall of the Berlin Wall, two competitions, repeated postponements, and a break for thought in the spring of 1998, writes Habermas in March 1999 (ZDD), and Germans are still discussing the why, for and by whom, where, and how the Berlin Holocaust Memorial should come about. He refers this present situation back to Walser's backpedaling intervention against conscious acts of coming to terms with the past as well as to "the courage of prominent Jews" in Germany who again are the ones who would "free the political public" by looking the past squarely in the face. Habermas insists at this time that one should not be deceived that the democratic process in the Bundestag (Federal Parliament) will have the courage to meet the hurdle after the summer break of 1999. (As noted in chapter 6, the Bundestag approved Eisenman II on June 25, 1999). He means the summer one year prior to Nolte's and Kohl's latest tantrums. Habermas reminds Germans that the timeliness of their coming to terms with themselves—as peoples they were, are, and want to be—is passing by. This countermonumental passage of the right time (*kairos* and not *chronos*) lies at a 180-degree angle from where Walser, Nolte, Kohl, and, yes, Sloterdijk wish to get themselves and other Germans:

> In the 50 year long history of the Federal Republic [of Germany], this is the first time in which a Parliamentary vote for a sign [such as the Holocaust memorial] of refined collective German identity with unforeseeable consequences in the future really becomes a possibility. It also appears to be the last time in which this is still possible. A Berlin Republic that would be dedicated to the mistaken, monumental past casts its shadows into the future. (ZDD)

After setting this radical, existentially motivated, and, in that, political and philosophical either/or choice before the German public, Habermas returns to the one remaining question: "whether the memorial should be dedicated only to the murdered Jews." This question breaks down into subquestions: (1) What is the meaning of the memorial? (2) Who makes the memorial? (3) What purpose will the memorial serve? (4) For whom will the memorial exist?

The meaning is inscribed into the ongoing existential either/or question of "who we are and want to be." That is why a genuine memorial is neither a monument to something in the past nor a political manipulation of the present and future, as for example Kohl's Bitburg or the site at Neue Wache (see chap. 6). A genuine memorial would be a countermonument: I claim that Habermas' lifework, even as it incarnates *anamnestic* solidarity and redemptive hope, erects such an antiredemptory countermonument in words and deeds. Habermas follows the above citation with a one-sentence overview of the key existential situations in postwar Germany, as I have discussed most of them in the course of this book: from the protests against the Veit Harlan films and the struggle against the rearmament of the FRG in the 1950s, to suspending the time limits on prosecuting Nazi criminals and the Auschwitz trial in Frankfurt, to the antinuclear demonstrations of the 1980s. In the next sentence he transports us to the contemporary horizon of debates about ordinary German collaboration with the Nazis (see Goldhagen 1996; ÜöGH), reparations for the stolen bank accounts and unpaid insurance claims, and the slave labor in the Nazi camps and factories, and so on. All these moments in postwar Germany point in a "concentrated" manner to one and only one existentially motivated, philosophical-political question. The question about the memorial is addressed by the first and last point in time that existential self-choices involve. Indeed, the question underlines that this is the urgent time of existential self-choice to be made by every German and not, therefore, one made by Habermas for others. Note, therefore, how Sloterdijk's own self-choice in postwar Germany is evaded in his later accusing act of raising a 'hysterical' invective against Habermas' perceived hypermoralism, supposedly inherited with the Nazism of Habermas' father and his generation. This question about proper mourning is one that Habermas has been raising and answering to himself throughout his life—no matter where the political winds would blow or what career choices his stance would affect or what risks to his prestige in German society his answer would raise for him. He has been raising this question with a wholeheartedness that one can witness in his life as if it were a lifeline on the palm of his hand:

> Shall we take over, we who as the citizens of the Federal Republic of Germany stand in the political-legal and cultural succession to the state and the society of the "perpetrator-generation," a historical liability for the consequences of their acts? Shall we make the self-critical remembrance of "Auschwitz"—the vigilant reflection on the event connected with this name—explicitly into an integral part of our political self-understanding? Shall we accept the disquieting political responsibility—which will accrue to those born later from the civilizational break exercised, supported, and tolerated by Germans—as an element of a ruptured national identity? [It is] "ruptured" insofar as this responsibility signifies the will to discontinue the misleading ways of thinking [enshrined] in the continuity of their own traditions. (ZDD)

In one regard, then, Sloterdijk is right that Habermas *wants to erect a memorial* to the civilizational break, not only in Berlin, unified Germany's capital, but also, as he has done repeatedly, with his work and in his very life. The ad hominem type of charge carries its own existential check and revenge against abuse, and the charge turns here on Sloterdijk. Critical Theory dies only and only with him or with others who would be evading or outright silencing, for the first or the last time, the existentially motivated philosophical-political question of radical self-choice. Such questioning inhabits a countermonumental impulse (e.g., to blow up the Brandenburger Tor in Berlin proposed by Horst Hoheisel's for the Berlin memorial to the murdered Jews of Europe, see J. Young 2000, 92f.). One cannot sidestep this questioning by chiding someone else's hypermorality, by externalizing existential and social hypercrisis, by projecting a Jacobin-like neurosis into another's interiority, or by assuming in an entire generation an existence of a desire to engage in a witch-hunt on Fascists used nowadays as scapegoats for aging postwar guilt. "The planned memorial should be the answer to these [above] questions" (ZDD).

As such an answer, then, the memorial is not made by Germans for the Jews (in some analogical sense to Yad Vashem, the Holocaust memorial in Israel, or the U.S. Holocaust Memorial Museum in Washington, D.C.). Rather, Habermas continues, the Berlin memorial is to shape the political self-understanding of present and future generations about crimes against humanity, "and with that is introduced the tremor about the *unsayable,* inflicted on the victims, as a persisting disquietude and reminder" (italics added). To follow with the related question of who creates this memorial, Habermas insists that the essential responsibility falls primarily with those in Germany who have inherited, with their history, culture, and citizenship, liability for the generation of the perpetrators. This liability, if responsibly assumed, requires that victims are not instrumentalized in a general act of abstract and self-stigmatizing accounting, or by running away, of those who feel guilty. This insight, shared with Jewish leaders, drives home an existential point that turns the tables on various revisionist moves from Kohl to Nolte to Walser to Sloterdijk's letter. They are turned on the dual 'hysteria' of false self-pity and gratuitous denial:

> The value of the weak, yes futile power of anamnestic solidarity is first truly lost, when [one's] self-relation is rendered narcissistically and when the memorial turns into a "stigma." Those who consider Auschwitz as "our shame" are interested in the picture that others hold about us, but not in the picture, which the citizens of the Federal Republic form out of themselves in relief to the civilizational rupture in order to be able to look themselves in the face and act with one another. (ZDD)

The memorial for the murdered Jews would serve Habermas in his singularity; it would serve his fellow Germans in whose face he often stands as an angry biblical prophet—it would serve their self-responsible and truly democratic public sphere "to come clean with ourselves"! The past divides the descendants of the perpetrators from those of the victims. Yet a genuine memorial also "expresses a civil consideration for the descendants of the victims."

Lest this existential motivation is confused with the 'hysteria' of false self-pity and gratuitous denial, Habermas explains that the aim of the memorial cannot be "the Holocaust as a 'grounding myth of the Federal Republic.'" This confusion would somehow make learning from and after Auschwitz instrumental if not also necessary for the essential self-understanding of German history and culture. To remain "fixed at the unloading ramp in Auschwitz," Habermas emphasizes, is not the same as to witness one's liability for the civilizational break, thereby taking responsibility for the personal and political future. The difference lies between genuine remembrance and narcissistic wallowing, between genuine new beginnings and running away from responsibility in evasion or denial, between monumental history and repeated acts of remembering.[13]

In the last two sections of his essay, called "The Unreasonable Demand" and "The Open Question: For Whom?" Habermas tackles the issue whether or not the Berlin Holocaust Memorial should be dedicated to all of Hitler's victims or to the Jews alone. (Nolte's provocation from the following June that would broaden the dedication to include, perhaps, even the SS from Bitburg, does not arise in this question.) Is the memorial too much for Germans to bear, given their desire for a normal Berlin Republic? Will the memorial foster resentment or vandalism by skinheads? Habermas demands the 'unreasonable'—the memorial must have a "massive police protection round the clock." This is the only normality "that is for the time being possible in our land." Without this guarantee of protection, there can be no talk of achieved German normality. The monument at Neue Wache did not need such protection, since it allowed all groups and all revisionists to identify with some victims of war and dictatorship. This is where the discontents of Fascism were resolved in the direction of yet another 'hysterical' politics of memory.

And this backward memorialization politics was at the origin of the request for creating in Berlin the memorial to the murdered Jews of Europe.

Must this memorial mean, then, an exclusion of the universal and noncomparative suffering of all victims of Hitler's annihilation policies? Or is there some ground for having a specifically Jewish Holocaust memorial in Germany? "There is no moral justification for a differential treatment of victims, which shared in the end the same destiny." What is, however, relevant is the unique place of Jews in German history, culture, and politics. This fact does not "neutralize" the equal consideration of all victims of the Holocaust, as Habermas follows the careful path of this argument. And yet it is this "relevant difference" of Jews in German traditions that would seem to "validate a nonexclusive dedication of the memorial" to the murdered Jews. "I am not sure," Habermas walks a fine line, "whether the 'Auschwitz memorial' can express both [intuitions]." Perhaps the revised design by Peter Eisenman (see Wiedmer 1999, 161; and photo in "Mahnmal" 2000, 18, and on the back jacket of Müller 2000; cf. J. Young 2000, 185, 213ff.), by carrying no name and no sign on this memorial, besides the names of the extermination camps—or simply one name, "Auschwitz"—could serve this dual purpose. The "collective name" of Auschwitz, Habermas concludes, became identical with the Holocaust. As such, the word implies that "this covers not only the fate of the Jews" but all those who perished in Hitler's extermination camps. "As *Pars pro toto* it [Auschwitz] signifies the totality of the complex event of annihilation" (ZDD).

★ ★ ★

If the greatness of a person's life could be encompassed by its narrative lines, then the dramatic axis of one's lifework could be conveyed through a philosophical-political portrait of its architectonic. The temptation of a biographical sketch such as this one is to pretend to achieve this fullness. Yet a life transcends any of its profiles. This transcendence marks the silences as varied as those of Thomas Aquinas, Ludwig Wittgenstein, Emmanuel Lévinas, and the more materialist silences of Walter Benjamin or Merleau-Ponty. Common to them is the dimension of the unsaid and even unspeakable that evades the possession by any single author of a life.

Toward the end of his illustrious life, Thomas Aquinas is reported to fall into silence, writing nothing, dictating nothing, setting aside the architectonic of his *Summa Theologica*, and finally answering his friend, Reginald of Piperno, who worried about the mental state of his great master: "Reginald, I can write no more. All that I have hitherto written seems to me nothing but straw" (Pieper 1966, 39). Without a doubt Aquinas's silence was quickened by his spiritual intimation of another than this unjust world, and critical social theorists and activists are unmoved by such yearnings, as they do not always or necessarily share the underlying spiritual motives. Yet even the manifestly secular silence can speak with postsecular resonances that any single lifework transcends its particular achievements. In this sense Merleau-Ponty found the best historical writing done in the present existential, lived historical tense and Benjamin strained against the untranslatable dimension of language and the messianic, redemptive dimension of time.

Had Jürgen Habermas done nothing else in the course of his adult years than stand as a witness and a loud, bothersome nuisance reminding Germans not to avert their faces from their disaster in the twentieth century, perhaps it would have been enough for one lifetime. For this singular reason, Germany in the twentieth century is not thinkable without Habermas. My profile of Habermas' philosophical-political life attests to this repeated instant of his singular pathos that in some unquantifiable measure transcends his major theoretical achievements. One can always criticize his theory just as much as any other fallible position he took. In a paradoxical but not cynical sense, if the architectonic-transcending meaning of Habermas' lifework would amount to nothing else than his gaining sufficient visibility and audibility, prestige and recognition, so that his voice could be heard loud and clear; had he used that platform to prick the conscience of postwar Germany, would that not be worthy of being called a magnanimous achievement? Perhaps the greatness of this or any life lies not in the architectural edifice one has constructed in theory, even as one can truly marvel at its magnificence, but in trying to communicate a deeply existential passion for living in truth.

NOTES

1. The term *New Critical Theory,* when capitalized, names the book series by Rowman & Littlefield. As a general term, it is coextensive with new social movements and defined by the range of authors, topics, and practices of new critical social theorists and activists. This umbrella concept refers to spaces in which existing social movements and novel trends in critical social theory inform and help articulate each other. This study not only begins but also ends with this consideration.

2. To place accents on certain features does not mean the same thing as making a mistake. I am not saying that Habermas was mistakenly received or poorly translated. I am, however, saying that the U.S. reception may have prevented discovering Habermas' rich existential and political dimensions. This reception influences some analytically focused North American translations of Habermas that do not pick up on the German terminology and phraseology that disclose his more distinct existential and revolutionary leanings. For example, Habermas' *Faktizität und Geltung* does not communicate the same thing as the English title *Between Facts and Norms.* The latter title echoes debates with John Rawls and various positions in political, legal, and social sciences in the United States. The former title, literally, "Facticity and Validity," echoes in addition debates with Martin Heidegger, Hegel, Max Weber, and the positions influenced not only by critical legal studies but also by hermeneutics, phenomenology, and poststructuralism. Cf. the English translation of KFnT.

3. See chapters 5, 7; and Matuštík 1999.

4. There is some family resemblance between the concepts 'red Holocaust' and 'Left Fascism,' but it is the former notion that really unmasks the instability of the latter one.

5. The business office for "Lederwaren- und Kofferindustrie" (leather products and luggage industry) was located at Körnerstrasse 33 in Gummersbach; the listed telephone number in 1939 was 2337 (see *Gliederung* 1939, 125; 1941, 171).

6. The headquarters of the twenty-fifth (out of thirty-one groups existing in the Third Reich) industrial group (for leather production) were located in Berlin (see *Gliederung* 1939, 123) under the direction of Alfred Gauer. The fascinating spider's web of specialized and district leadership of the industrial organization in the Third Reich is appended at the very end of the above publication. All districts were subordinated to the "Reichswirtschaftministerium" (the ministry of the industry in the Third Reich). The thirty-one industries of the Reich were directly subordinated to the Berlin ministry and its "Reichswirtschaftskammer," located at Neue Wilhelmstrasse, 9-11, in Berlin NW 7.

7. Bundesarchiv, Finckensteinallee 63, Postfach 450569, 12175 Berlin-Lichterfelde, Germany. To utilize the archival material directly from the Bundesarchiv in Berlin, it is necessary to first disclose how the information is to be used; only then can one obtain the data as well as permission to use the material for the stated purpose (see Kurzinformation für Benutzer provided by the Bundesarchiv). Since the U.S. National Archives require no such prior contract for using the historical data, in my research, I am utilizing only the openly available U.S. microfilms of the Berlin Document Center. I neither sought nor received permission from the Bundesarchiv. I want to thank Rita Simmersbach Scheirer, from the ROOT Search in Washington, D.C., for her assistance in helping me locate the data from the U.S. National Archives II in Maryland.

8. The Central Index Card of the Berlin Document Center, found in the National Archives II, College Park, Maryland, lists "Dr. Ernst Habermas." His position is noted on the card as folows: the director of the Bureau and Trade Industry in Gummersbach (i.e., the person Habermas describes in the cited interview). Dr. Ernst Habermas (with his occupation) is listed as Habermas' father in several Who's Who encyclopedias of contemporary leading German personalities.

The full text on the BDC index card reads:
HABERMAS,   Ernst
Dr.
Leiter der Zweigstelle Oberberg, Sitz:
Gummersbach der Bergischen Industrie-
und Handelskammer Wuppertal/Remscheid

9. Berlin Document Center, NSDAP Ortskartei, A 3340-MFOK-roll G 59, frame 1674. This document lists the name, Dr. Ernst Habermas, NSDAP membership 2102565, date of birth, 30.8.91, entry date 1.5.33. The surname "Habermas" is written above another name "Habenner" that is crossed out. This correction occasioned the NSDAP party correspondence (see below).

10. Berlin Document Center, Partei Korrespondence (party membership correspondence), A 3340-PK-D277. The following two documents are relevant. Frame 0618 lists the title page for the party file of Dr. Ernst Habermas in the BDC (date of birth 30.8.91). Frame 0622 contains the letter from the Köln NSDAP registration to the Munich's central NSDAP registration, dated on April 16, 1934. The first line of the letter asks to correct the two registration cards (names are listed below the instruction); the third line orders the following correction to be made: "Dr. Ernst Habenner, Nr. 2102565, es muss heissen Habermas."

(Change the name of Dr. Ernst Habenner, no. 2102565, to Habermas.) The letter ends with the usual party greeting and is signed by "Gauschatzmeister."

11. Berlin Document Center, Partei Korrespondence (party membership correspondence), A 3340-PK-D277, frame 0620 contains the letter from Munich to Cologne dated 25.4.34. The first line of the text indicates that in response to the request from 16.4.34, the NSDAP registration in Munich changed the names of the below-mentioned NSDAP party members. The fifth line then reports this change: "Dr. Ernst Habermas (. . . [bisher] Habenner) . . . [Nr.] 2102565." ("Dr. Ernst Habermas [... {formerly} Habenner] . . . [Nr.] 2102565.") The words *bisher* (before) and *Nr.* (no.) are meticulously omitted (I list these above in parentheses) because Dr. Ernst Habermas is listed on the line below another name change. The last line of the letter notes that the changes were made on the NSDAP party membership cards of the above-named members and that, therefore, their names are now correctly registered. There is an unidentified handwritten note on the left margin next to the check mark by "Dr. Ernst Habermas": the handwritten note (it is part of the microfilm record of the BDC document) indicates the date of birth: 30.8.91. The letter is signed with initials and ends with the usual party greeting, which I find against my taste reproducing here or above.

12. Berlin Document Center Microfilm, Partei Korrespondence (party membership correspondence), A 3340-PK-D277, frame 0624. The handwritten card lists on line 1: "Habermas, Ernst Dr." Line 2 lists the date of birth: "geb. 30.8.91." Line 3 contains the NSDAP membership number "2 102 565."

13. Habermas refers to two German words for the memorial, *Denkmal* and *Mahnmal*, indicating that the former took on the added meaning of monument only in the seventeenth century. It would be beneficial to read Müller's (2000) suggestion that we critically correct the undifferentiated political impact of the so-called Holocaust identity, particularly as this has become formative of Grass and Habermas and their cohorts, against Sloterdijk's polemic with Habermas' generational hypermoralism. It is not obvious that either Müller's suggestion or Sloterdijk's invective easily evade Walser's charge of instrumentalizing Auschwitz, or that Bohrer's justification of unified Germany on the ground of shared repentance for the crime of Auschwitz gets around the problem of nationalism. I agree with Müller that the strength of Habermas' conscience, what I called his learning by disaster, occasions certain blind spots, what I named his blindness by disaster (see tab. 8.3). Yet in my profile of Habermas I attempted to attain an even sharper nuance that shows his sui generis position within his postwar generation. Most of what Habermas expresses in his remarkable essay (ZDD) already answers, at least indirectly, Müller's later criticisms of the pitfalls of the Holocaust identity prevalent among the members of the skeptical generation. If at fifteen, May 8, 1945, marks Habermas' *philosophical–political birthday*; if at twenty-four, the year 1953 records his *signature event* in which he confronted in Heidegger the generation of his father; then in his seventies, March 1999 dramatizes a *discursive and performative* counterpart to artistic *countermonuments*. His lifework is antiredemptory in that it embraces its own existential finitude, it is countermonumental by affirming in every historical present an ongoing *anamnestic* task to come to terms with the past for the sake of our lived responsibility and redemptive hope today.

HABERMAS BIBLIOGRAPHY AND ABBREVIATIONS OF WORKS CITED

All references in text and notes that begin with an abbreviated title are to Habermas. Where possible, both German and English page numbers, following the abbreviation of the German original, are given. Some English editions do not correspond to the German originals, some English translations are compiled from several different German originals, and some publications exist only in the German original or only in the English original. Abbreviations, followed by page numbers, are given only for works written or edited by Habermas; all other citations follow the conventional author-date style. References in the main text and in notes follow the samples given below:

NR/AS	(Die Nachholende Revolution/Autonomy and Solidarity)
EAS/NC	(Eine Art Schadesabwicklung/The New Conservatism)
EdA/SR	(Einbeziehung des Anderen/Struggle for Recognition)
ND 106/58	(Nachmetaphysiches Denken/Postmetaphysical Thinking; pages in German/English)
ND 63–103	(Nachmetaphysiches Denken; pages in the German edition)
R 234	("A Reply"; pages in the English publication only)
Afterword in VaZ	(Afterword in the English edition of *The Past as Future*)

AG   "Das Absolute und die Geschichte: Von der Zwiespältigkeit in Schellings Denken." Ph.D. diss., Universität Bonn, 1954.

AS   *Autonomy and Solidarity: Interviews with Jürgen Habermas.* Ed. Peter Dews. Rev. and enl. London: Verso, 1992.

BEE   "Brief an Erich Fried." July 26, 1967. Originally in PuH, 149–51. Cited from Kraushaar 1998, 2: doc. 146. This highly relevant piece is excluded from the reprint of PuH in KPS. It is not available in English.

BH   "Bestialität und Humanität: Ein Krieg an der Grenze zwischen Recht und Moral." *Die Zeit,* April 29, 1999, 1, 6–7./"Bestiality and Humanity: A War on the Border between Legality and Morality." Trans. Stephen Meyer and William E. Scheuerman. *Constellations* 6, no. 3 (1999): 264–72. Consult the new annotated translation of BH by John Torpey and approved by Habermas in William Joseph Buckley, ed., *Kosovo: Contending Voices on Balkan Interventions*, 306-16. Grand Rapids, Mich.: Eerdmans, 2000. Here "Recht" in the title of BH is translated as "Law" rather than "Legality."

CD "Civil Disobedience: Litmus Test for the Democratic Constitutional State." *Berkeley Journal of Sociology* 30 (1985): 95–116. Translation of NU 79–99.

CES *Communication and the Evolution of Society.* Trans. Thomas McCarthy. Boston: Beacon, 1979. Comprises translation of ZRHM and WhU.

DE "Diskursethik: Notizen zu einem Begründungsprogramm."/"Discourse Ethics: Notes on a Program of Philosophical Justification." In MkH 53–126/43–115.

DM "Der DM-Nationalismus: Weshalb es richtig ist, die deutsche Einheit nach Artikel 146 zu vollziehen, also eine neue Verfassung anzustreben." *Die Zeit,* March 30, 1990, 62–63. Cited from NR 205–24, in which this essay is mistakenly listed as previously unpublished.

DTFS "Drei Thesen zur Wirkungsgeschichte der Frankfurter Schule." In Axel Honneth and Albrecht Wellmer, eds., *Die Frankfurter Schule und die Folgen: Referate eines Symposiums der Alexander von Humboldt-Stiftung vom 10.-15. Dezember 1984 in Ludwigsburg,* 8-12. Berlin: Walter de Gruyter, 1986.

EAS *Eine Art Schadensabwicklung: Kleine Politische Schriften VI.* Frankfurt a/M: Suhrkamp, 1987. Partially translated in NC.

EdA *Die Einbeziehung des Anderen: Studien zur politischen Theorie.* Frankfurt a/M: Suhrkamp, 1996./*The Inclusion of the Other: Studies in Political Theory.* Ed. Ciaran Cronin and Pablo De Greiff. Trans. Ciaran Cronin. Cambridge, Mass.: MIT Press, 1998.

EgA "Es gibt doch Alternativen!" Interview with Günther Hofmann and Thomas Assheuer. *Die Zeit,* October 8, 1998, 12, 14–15./"There Are Alternatives." *New Left Review* 231 (September–October 1998): 3–12.

ENPG "The European Nation-State and the Pressures of Globalization." Trans. G. M. Goshgarian. *New Left Review* 235 (May–June 1999): 46–59. Originally published in *Blätter für deutsche und internationale Politik,* April 1999, 425–36; some themes and formulations appear in PK 91–169.

EuI *Erkenntnis und Interesse.* Frankfurt a/M: Suhrkamp, 1968./*Knowledge and Human Interests.* Trans. Jeremy J. Shapiro. Boston: Beacon, 1971. Inaugural lecture, "Knowledge and Human Interests," appears in the appendix. It was delivered on June 28, 1965.

EV "Entsorgung der Vergangenheit: Ein kulturpolitisches Pamphlet." *Die Zeit,* May 17, 1985. Cited from NU 261–66/"Defusing the Past: A Politico-Cultural Tract." Trans. Thomas Levin. In Geoffrey H. Hartman, ed., *Bitburg in Moral and Political Perspective,* 43–51. Cambridge, Mass.: Basil Blackwell, 1986.

EzD *Erläuterungen zur Diskursethik.* Frankfurt a/M: Suhrkamp, 1991. Partially translated in JA.

FE "Die Festung Europa und das neue Deutschland." *Die Zeit,* May 28, 1993, Politik sec., 3. This essay is expanded in SR.

FKH "From Kant to Hegel and Back Again: The Move towards Detranscendentalization." *European Journal of Philosophy* 7, no. 2 (1999): 129–57.

FuG	*Faktizität und Geltung: Beiträge zur Diskurstheorie des Rechts und des demokratischen Rechtstaats.* Frankfurt a/M: Suhrkamp, 1992. The German original (541–99) contains the English translation of LM/*Between Facts and Norms: Contributions to a Discourse Theory of Law and Democracy.* Trans. William Rehg. Cambridge, Mass.: MIT Press, 1996. The English translation contains PFG but omits LM.
GpI	"Geschichtsbewußtsein und posttraditionale Identität: Die Westorientierung der Budesrepublik."/"Historical Consciousness and Post-Traditional Identity: The Federal Republic's Orientation to the West." In EAS 161–79/NC 249–67.
GuS	"Gerechtigkeit und Solidarität: Eine Stellungnahme zur Diskussion über 'Stufe 6.'" In Wolfgang Edelstein and Gertrud Nunner-Winkler, eds., *Zur Bestimmung der Moral: Philosophische und sozialwissenschaftliche Beiträge zur Moralforschung,* 291–318. Frankfurt a/M: Suhrkamp, 1986./"Justice and Solidarity: On the Discussion Concerning 'Stage 6.'" In Michael Kelly, ed., *Hermeneutics and Critical Theory in Ethics and Politics,* 32–52. Cambridge, Mass.: MIT Press, 1990.
GW	"Die grosse Wirkung: Eine chronistische Anmerkung zu Martin Heideggers 70. Geburtstag." *Frankfurter Allgemeine Zeitung,* September 26, 1959./"Martin Heidegger: The Great Influence." Cited from PpP 76–85/53–60.
HB	"Herbert Marcuse über Kunst und Revolution."/"Herbert Marcuse: On Art and Revolution" (1973). In KuK 345–51/PpP (English) 165–70.
Hil	Letter to the *Frankfurter Allgemeine Zeitung,* August 11, 1986. Habermas' rebuttal to Klaus Hildebrand (1986a).
HRPS	"Human Rights and Popular Sovereignty." Northwestern University, September 23, 1992. Public lecture.
ICI	"An Intersubjectivist Concept of Individuality." Paper presented at Brighton: World Congress of Philosophy, August 24, 1988. This is an early version of ND 187–241/149–204 without Habermas' later Kierkegaard discussion.
ILH	"Im Lichte Heideggers." *Frankfurter Allgemeine Zeitung,* July 12, 1952.
IuA	"Israel und Athens Oder: Wem gehört die anamnetische Vernunft? Zur Einheit in der multikulturellen Vielfalt." In VsE 98–111./"Israel and Athens, or to Whom Does Anamnestic Reason Belong? On Unity in Multicultural Diversity." Trans. Eduardo Mendieta. In David Batstone et al., eds., *Liberation Theologies, Postmodernity, and the Americas,* 243–52. New York: Routledge, 1997.
JA	*Justification and Application: Remarks on Discourse Ethics.* Trans. Ciaran P. Cronin. Cambridge, Mass.: MIT Press, 1993.
KE	"Kierkegaard's Ethics." Course description for the Habermas seminar, Studies in Contemporary Philosophy. Northwestern University, fall quarter, 2000.
KFnT	"Kommunikative Freiheit und negative Theologie." In Emil Angehrn et al., eds., *Dialektischer Negativismus: Michel Theunissen zum 60. Geburtstag,* 15–34. Frankfurt a/M: Suhrkamp, 1992./"Communicative Freedom and Negative Theology." Trans. Martin J. Matuštík and Patricia J. Huntington. In Martin J. Matuštík and Merold Westphal, eds., *Kierkegaard in Post/Modernity,* 182–98. Bloomington: Indiana University Press, 1995.
KNV	"Keine Normalisierung der Vergangenheit" ("Der Intellektuelle ist mit seinem Gewissen nicht allein)," *Süddeutsche Zeitung,* November 19–20, 1985. Cited from EAS 11–17. Not available in English.

KPS   *Kleine Politische Schriften (I–IV).* Frankfurt a/M: Suhrkamp, 1981.
KuK   *Kultur und Kritik: Verstreute Aufsätze.* Frankfurt a/M: Suhrkamp, 1973.
LC   *Legitimationsprobleme im Spätkapitalismus.* Frankfurt a/M: Suhrkamp, 1973./*Legitimation Crisis.* Trans. Thomas McCarthy. Boston: Beacon, 1975.
LD   "Learning by Disaster? A Diagnostic Look Back on the Short 20th Century." Trans. Hella Beister. *Constellations* 5, no. 3 (1998): 307–20. Translation of PK 65–90.
LJPS   "Jürgen Habermas on the Legacy of Jean-Paul Sartre." Interview conducted by Richard Wolin. *Political Theory* 20, no. 3 (1992): 496–501.
LM   "Law and Morality" (October 1–2, 1986). Trans. Kenneth Baynes. *The Tanner Lectures on Human Values.* Vol. 8. Salt Lake City: University of Utah Press, 1988, 217–79. Translated from English to German in FuG 541–99.
LzDM   "Literaturbericht zur philosophischen Diskussion um Marx und den Marxismus." *Philosophische Rundschau* 5, no. 3–4 (1957): 165–235. Not included in the English translation of TaP.
MHFI   "More Humility, Fewer Illusions: A Talk between Adam Michnik and Jürgen Habermas." *New York Review of Books,* March 24, 1994, 24–29.
MHgH   "Mit Heidegger gegen Heidegger denken: Zur Veröffentlichung von Vorlesungen aus dem Jahre 1935." *Frankfurter Allgemeine Zeitung,* July 25, 1953. Cited from PpP 67–75/"Martin Heidegger: On the Publication of Lectures from the Year 1935." Trans. Dale Ponikvar. *Graduate Faculty Philosophy Journal* 6, no. 2 (1977): 155–64.
MkH   *Moralbewußtsein und kommunikatives Handeln.* Frankfurt a/M: Suhrkamp, 1983./*Moral Consciousness and Communicative Action.* Trans. Christian Lenhardt and Shierry Weber Nicholsen. Cambridge, Mass.: MIT Press, 1990.
MP   "Modernity versus Postmodernity." Trans. Seyla Benhabib. *New German Critique* 22 (Winter 1981): 3–14.
MS   "Moralität und Sittlichkeit: Treffen Hegels Einwände gegen Kant auch die Diskursethik zu?" In Wolfgang Kuhlmann, ed., *Moralität und Sittlichkeit: Das Problem Hegels und die Diskursethik,* 16–37. Frankfurt a/M: Suhrkamp, 1986./"Morality and Ethical Life: Does Hegel's Critique of Kant Apply to Discourse Ethics?" In MkH 195–215.
NBR   *Die Normalität einer Berliner Republik: Kleine Politische Schriften VIII.* Frankfurt a/M: Suhrkamp, 1995./*A Berlin Republic: Writings on Germany.* Trans. Steven Rendall. With an introduction by Peter Uwe Hohendahl. Lincoln: University of Nebraska Press, 1997.
NC   *The New Conservatism: Cultural Criticism and the Historians' Debate.* Ed. and trans. Shierry Weber Nicholsen. With an introduction by Richard Wolin. Cambridge, Mass.: MIT Press, 1989. A partial translation of EAS and NU with essays from other volumes.
ND   *Nachmetaphysisches Denken: Philosophische Aufsätze.* Frankfurt a/M: Suhrkamp, 1988./*Postmetaphysical Thinking: Philosophical Essays.* Trans. William Mark Hohengarten. Cambridge, Mass.: MIT Press, 1992.
NR   *Die nachholende Revolution: Kleine politische Schriften VII.* Frankfurt a/M: Suhrkamp, 1990.

Bibliography and Abbreviations 309

NU Die neue Unübersichtlichkeit: Kleine politische Schriften V. Frankfurt a/M: Suhrkamp, 1985. Partially translated in NC.
OSSA Observations on "The Spiritual Situation of the Age." Ed. and with an introduction by Jürgen Habermas. Trans. and with an introduction by Andrew Buchwalter. Cambridge, Mass.: MIT Press, 1985. German text of Habermas' introduction in KPS 411–41.
PDM Der Philosophische Diskurs der Moderne: Zwölf Vorlesungen. Frankfurt a/M: Suhrkamp, 1985./ The Philosophical Discourse of Modernity: Twelve Lectures. Trans. Frederick Lawrence. Cambridge, Mass.: MIT Press, 1987.
PFG "Postscript to Faktizität und Geltung." Philosophy and Social Criticism 20, no. 4 (1994): 135–50. Cited from FuG 447–62.
PK Die postnationale Konstellation: Politische Essays. Frankfurt a/M: Suhrkamp, 1998. A translation is forthcoming in 2001 from MIT Press: The Postnational Constellation: Political Essays.
PpP Philosophisch-politische Profile. Frankfurt a/M: Suhrkamp, 1971./ Philosophical-Political Profiles. Trans. Frederick G. Lawrence. Cambridge, Mass.: MIT Press, 1983. Incomplete edition of the German text.
PT "Psychic Thermidor and the Rebirth of Rebellious Subjectivity" (1980). In Richard J. Bernstein, ed., Habermas and Modernity, 67–77, 218 n. Cambridge, Mass.: MIT Press, 1985.
PuH Protestbewegung und Hochschulreform. Frankfurt a/M: Suhrkamp, 1969. Partially reproduced in KPS.
PvbG "Post vom bösen Geist. Peter Sloterdijk, 'Die Kritische Theorie ist tot': Offener Brief an Thomas Assheuer und Jürgen Habermas, Die Zeit 37 (1999)" [Habermas' response to Sloterdijk (1999b).] Die Zeit, September 16, 1999, 68.
PZ "Ein Plädoyer für Zurückhaltung aber nicht gegenüber Israel." Die Zeit, February 8, 1991.
R "A Reply." In Axel Honneth and Hans Joas, eds., Communicative Action: Essays on Jürgen Habermas's The Theory of Communicative Action, 214–64. Trans. Jeremy Gaines and Doris L. Jones. Cambridge, Mass.: MIT Press, 1991.
RaR Religion and Rationality: Essays on Reason, God, and Modernity. Ed. and with an introduction by Eduardo Mendieta. Cambridge, U.K.: Polity, forthcoming.
RBpB "Reflexionen über den Begriff der politischen Beteiligung." Introduction to SuP; reprinted in KuK 9–60.
RC "A Reply to My Critics." Trans. Thomas McCarthy. In John B. Thompson and David Held, eds., Habermas: Critical Debates, 219–83. Cambridge: MIT Press. Later German translation in VuE 475–570.
SiK "Die Scheinrevolution und ihre Kinder: 6 Thesen über Taktik, Ziele, und Situationsanalysen der oppositionellen Jugend." In KPS 249–60.
SnI "Staatsburgerschaft und nationale Identität: Überlegungen zur Europäischen Zukunft" (1990)./"Citizenship and National Identity." In FuG 632–660/491–515.
SÖ Strukturwandel der Öffentlichkeit. Frankfurt a/M: Suhrkamp, 1962. Vorwort zur Neuauflage, 1990, 11–50./ The Structural Transformation of the Public Sphere: An Inquiry into a Category of Bourgeois Society. Trans. Thomas Burger with the assistance of Frederick Lawrence. Cambridge, Mass.: MIT Press, 1989.

SR	"Struggles for Recognition in the Democratic Constitutional State." Trans. Shierry Weber Nicholsen. In Charles Taylor et al., *Multiculturalism: Examining the Politics of Recognition,* 107–48. Ed. and with an introduction by Amy Gutmann. Exp. 2d ed. Princeton: Princeton University Press, 1994. German text in EdA 237–76.
SuP	With Ludwig von Friedeburg, Christoph Oehler, Friedrich Weltz. *Student und Politik: Eine soziologische Untersuchung zum politischen Bewußtsein Frankfurter Studenten.* Neuwied/Berlin: Luchterhaud, 1961.
TaP	*Theory and Practice.* Trans. John Viertel. Boston: Beacon, 1973.
TCA	*Theorie des kommunikativen Handelns.* 2 vols. Frankfurt a/M: Suhrkamp. Vol. 1, *Handlungsrationalität und gesellschaftliche Rationalisierung,* 1981. Vol. 2, *Zur Kritik der funktionalistichen Vernunft,* 1985./*The Theory of Communicative Action.* 2 vols. Trans. Thomas McCarthy. Boston: Beacon. Vol. 1, *Reason and the Rationalization of Society,* 1984. Vol. 2, *Lifeworld and System: A Critique of Functionalist Reason,* 1987.
TgKM	"Thesen gegen die Koalition der Mutlosen mit den Machthaber: Kritik an der Großen Koalition auf einer vom Sozialdemokratischen Hochschulbund veranstalten Podiumsdiskussion." (Discussion took place at the end of November.) *Diskus* 16, no. 8 (1966): 2. Cited in Kraushaar 1998, 2: doc. 108, pp. 216–17.
TGS	Jürgen Habermas and Niklas Luhmann. *Theorie der Gesellschaft oder Sozialtechnologie: Was leitet die Systemforschung?* Frankfurt a/M: Suhrkamp, 1971.
TiTD	"Transzendenz von innen, Transzendenz ins Diesseits." In TuK 127–56./"Transcendence from Within, Transcendence in This World." Trans. Eric Crump and Peter P. Kenny. In Don S. Browning and Francis Schüssler Fiorenza, eds., *Habermas, Modernity, and Public Theology,* 226–50. New York: Crossroad, 1992.
TP	"Theorie und Politik." In *Gespräche mit Herbert Marcuse,* 9–63. Frankfurt a/M: Suhrkamp.
TpS	"Triebschicksal als politisches Schicksal: Zum Abschluss der Vorlesungen über Sigmund Freud an den Universtäten Frankfurt und Heidelberg." *Frankfurter Allgemeine Zeitung,* July 14, 1956, 10.
TRS	*Towards a Rational Society: Student Protest, Science, and Politics.* Trans. Jeremy J. Shapiro. Boston: Beacon, 1970. Incomplete and abridged translation of PuH and TuW.
TuK	*Texte und Kontexte.* Frankfurt a/M: Suhrkamp, 1991.
TuW	*Technik und Wissenschaft als 'Ideologie.'* Frankfurt a/M: Suhrkamp, 1968.
UeB	"Unruhe, erste Bürgerpflicht: Römerbergrede gegen die Atombewaffnung der Bundeswehr." *Diskus* 8, no. 5 (1958): 2. Cited from Kraushaar 1998, 2: doc. 50, pp. 104–6.
ÜGW	"Über Gott und die Welt: Eduardo Mendieta im Gespräch mit Jürgen Habermas." In Jürgen Manemann, ed., *Befristete Zeit,* 190–209. Münster: Lit Verlag, 1999. Written answers to Mendieta's fourteen questions.
ÜMS	"Über Moralität und Sittlichkeit: Was macht eine Lebensform Rational?" In Herbert Schnädelbach, ed., *Rationalität: Philosophische Beiträge,* 218–35. Frankfurt a/M: Suhrkamp, 1984.
ÜöGH	"Über den öffentichen Gebrauch der Historie: Warum ein 'Demokratiespreis' für Daniel Goldhagen?"/"On the Public Use of History: Why a 'Democracy Prize'

	for Daniel Goldhagen?" German-English ed. In Karl D. Bredthauer and Arthur Heinrich, eds., *Aus der Geschichte Lernen—How to Learn from History: Verleihung des Blätter-Demokratiepreises 1997.* Trans. Max Pensky. Bonn: Blätter Verlag, 1997.
VaZ	*Vergangenheit als Zukunft.* Zürich: Pendo, 1990./*The Past as Future.* Interview by Michael Haller. Trans. and ed. Max Pensky. Lincoln: University of Nebraska Press, 1994. "The Asylum Debate (Paris Lecture, 14 January 1993)," 121–41, "Afterword (May 1993)," 143–65, and translator's notes, 167–81, appear in the English edition only.
Vpem	"Vom pragmatischen, ethischen, und moralischen Gebrauch der praktischen Vernunft."/"On the Pragmatic, the Ethical, and the Moral Employment of Practical Reason." In EzD 100–118/JA 1–17.
VsE	*Vom sinnlichen Eindruck zum Symbolischen Ausdruck: Philosophische Essays.* Frankfurt a/M: Suhrkamp, 1997.
VuE	*Vorstudien und Ergänzungen zur Theorie des kommunikativen Handelns.* Frankfurt a/M: Suhrkamp, 1989.
VV	"Volkssouverentität als Verfahren" (1988). In FuG 600–631/463–90.
WaW	"Work and Weltanschaung: The Heidegger Controversy from a German Perspective." Trans. John McCumber. In NC (English) 140–72.
WhU	"Was heißt Universalpragmatik?" In Karl-Otto Apel, ed., *Sprachpragmatik und Philosophie,* 174–273. Frankfurt a/M: Suhrkamp, 1976. Cited from VuE 353–440/CES 1–68.
WuR	*Wahrheit und Rechtfertigung: Philosophische Aufsätze.* Frankfurt a/M: Suhrkamp, 1999.
Z	"Zweifellos." *Süddeutsche Zeitung,* May 18, 1999, 17.
ZDD	"Der Zeigefinger: Die Deutschen und ihr Denkmal." *Die Zeit,* March 31, 1999, Feuilleton sec., 42–44.
ZG	"Zum Geleit." In *Antworten auf Herbert Marcuse,* 9–16. Frankfurt a/M: Suhrkamp, 1968.
ZLB	"Die zweite Lebenslüge der Bundesrepublik: Wir sind wieder 'normal' geworden." *Die Zeit,* December 11, 1992, 48. The text partially overlaps with "The Asylum Debate (Paris Lecture, 14 November 1993)," in VaZ (English), 136–41.
ZLS	*Zur Logik der Sozialwissenschaften.* Frankfurt a/M: Suhrkamp, 1985.
ZRHM	*Zur Rekonstruktion des Historischen Materialismus.*

REFERENCES

Adorno, Theodor W. [1966] 1973. *Negative Dialectics.* Trans. E. B. Ashton. New York: Continuum.
———. [1955] 1984. *Prisms: Cultural Criticism and Society.* Trans. Samuel Weber and Shierry Weber. Cambridge, Mass.: MIT Press.
———. [1959] 1986. "What Does Coming to Terms with the Past Mean?" In Geoffrey H. Hartman, ed., *Bitburg in Moral and Political Perspective,* 114–29. Indianapolis: Indiana University Press.
Adorno, Theodor W., and Herbert Marcuse. 1999. "Correspondence on the German Student Movement." Trans. Esther Leslie. *New Left Review* 233 (January–February): 123–36. German correspondence is cited from Wolfgang Kraushaar, ed. 1998. *Frankfurter Schule und Studentenbewegung.* Vol. 2. Hamburg: Rogner & Bernhard.
Adorno, Theodor W., et al. 1950. *The Authoritarian Personality.* New York: Harper.
Albrecht, Clemens, et al. 1999. *Die intellektuelle Gründung der Bundesrepublik: Eine Wirkungsgeschichte der Frankfurter Schule.* Frankfurt: Campus.
Ali, Tariq, and Susan Watkins 1998. *1968: Marching in the Streets.* New York: Free Press.
Ally, Matthew C., ed. 1999. "Special Symposium on NATO's War in Yugoslavia: Reflections and Critiques." *Radical Philosophy Review* 2, no. 1: 1–49.
Angehrn, Emil, et al., eds. 1992. *Dialektischer Negativismus: Michel Theunissen zum 60. Geburtstag.* Frankfurt a/M: Suhrkamp.
"An Appeal from American Jews to the Green Party of Germany." 1999. Signed by Noam Chomsky, Edward Herman, Robert Weissman, Michael Albert, Mitchel Cohen, Michael Brün, Mark Weisbrot, Dean Baker, and Robert Naiman. May 9. <http://www.preamble.org>.
Apel, Karl-Otto, ed. 1976. *Sprachpragmatik und Philosophie.* Frankfurt a/M: Suhrkamp.
Ardagh, John. 1995. *Germany and the Germans.* 3d ed. New York: Penguin.
Arendt, Hannah. [1963] 1965. *Eichmann in Jerusalem: A Report on the Banality of Evil.* New York: Penguin.
Arnason, Ronald. 1995. *After Marxism.* New York: Guilford.

Assheuer, Thomas. 1999. "Das Zarathustra-Projekt: Dr Philosoph Peter Sloterdijk fordert eine getechnische Revision der Menschheit." *Die Zeit,* September 2, 31–33.
Augstein, Rudolf. 1986. "Die neue Auschwitz-Lüge." *Der Spiegel,* October 6, 62–63.
———. 1998. "Wir sind alle verletzbar." *Der Spiegel,* November 11, 32–33.
Augustine. 1981. *The City of God.* Trans. Henry Bettenson. Ed. and with an introduction by David Knowles. New York: Penguin.
Bark, Dennis L., and David R. Gress. 1989. *A History of West Germany.* 2 vols. Oxford: Oxford University Press.
Bartky, Sandra Lee. 1990. *Femininity and Domination: Studies in the Phenomenology of Oppression.* New York: Routledge.
Batstone, David, et al., eds. 1997. *Liberation Theologies, Postmodernity, and the Americas.* New York: Routledge.
Baumgart, Reinhardt. 1998. "Sich selbst und allen unbequem: Der Weg des Martin Walser als 'geistiger Brandstifter.'" *Die Zeit,* September 10, 53.
Becker, Ernest. 1975. *Escape from Evil.* New York: Free Press.
Becker, Oskar. 1942. *Gedanken Friedrich Nietzsches über Randordung, Zucht, und Züchtung.* In *Kriegsvorträge der Friedrich-Wilhelms-Universität.* Vol. 97. Bonn a. Rh.: Scheur.
Benhabib, Seyla. 1992. *Situating the Self: Gender, Community, and Postmodernism in Contemporary Ethics.* New York: Routledge.
———. 1994. "In Defense of Universalism—Yet Again! A Response to *Critics of Situating the Self.*" *New German Critique* 62 (Spring–Summer): 173–89.
Benhabib, Seyla, ed. 1996. *Democracy and Difference: Contesting the Boundaries of the Political.* Princeton: Princeton University Press.
Benhabib, Seyla, and Drucilla Cornell, eds. 1987. *Feminism as Critique.* Minneapolis: University of Minnesota Press.
Benhabib, Seyla, et al. 1995. *Feminist Contentions: A Philosophical Exchange.* With an introduction by Linda Nicholson. New York: Routledge.
Benjamin, Walter. 1955. *Ausgewahlte Schriften II.* Frankfurt a/M: Suhrkamp.
———. 1968. *Illuminations: Essays and Reflections.* Edited and with an introduction by Hannah Arendt. Trans. Harry Zohn. New York: Schocken.
———. 1979. *One-Way Street and Other Writings.* Trans. Edmund Jephcott and Kingsley Shorter. With an introduction by Susan Sontag. London: Verso.
———. [1937] 1982. "Eduard Fuchs: Collector and Historian." In Andrew Arato and Eike Gebhardt, eds., *The Essential Frankfurt School Reader,* 225–53. New York: Continuum.
———. [1928–40] 1989. "N [Re the Theory of Knowledge, Theory of Progress]." Trans. Leigh Hafrey and Richard Sieburth. In Gary Smith, ed., *Benjamin: Philosophy, Aesthetics, History,* 43–84. Chicago: University of Chicago Press.
Berlin Document Center Microfilms. 1933–1945. NSDAP Partei Korrespondence [NSDAP party membership correspondence]. A 3340-PK-D277, frames 0618-0624. National Archives II. College Park, Md.
———. Central Index Card. National Archives II. College Park, Md.
———. NSDAP Ortskartei. A 3340-MFOK-roll G 59, frame 1674. National Archives II. College Park, Md.
Bernstein, Richard J., ed. 1985. *Habermas and Modernity.* Cambridge, Mass.: MIT Press.
Blackburn, Robin. 1999. "Kosovo: The War of NATO Expansion." *New Left Review* 235 (May–June): 107–23.

Blanchot, Maurice. 1995. *The Writing of the Disaster.* Lincoln: University of Nebraska Press.
Braaten, Jane. 1991. *Habermas's Critical Theory of Society.* New York: SUNY Press.
Bredthauer, Karl D., and Arthur Heinrich, eds. 1997. *Aus der Geschichte Lernen—How to Learn from History: Verleihung des Blätter-Demokratiespreises 1997.* Trans. Max Pensky. Bonn: Blätter Verlag. Side-by-side German-English publication.
Bronner, Stephen Eric. 1994. *Of Critical Theory and Its Theorists.* London: Basil Blackwell.
Browning, Don S., and Francis Schüssler Fiorenza, eds. 1992. *Habermas, Modernity, and Public Theology.* New York: Crossroad.
Bubis, Ignatz. 1998. "Moral verjährt nicht." *Der Spiegel,* November 30, 50, 52, 54. A *Spiegel* interview about the Auschwitz debate, including exchanges with Martin Walser and Klaus von Dohnanyi.
Buckley, William Joseph, ed. 2000. *Kosovo: Contending Voices on Balkan Interventions.* Grand Rapids, Mich.: Eerdmans.
Bühler, Karl. 1934. *Sprachtheorie.* Jena: Gustav Fischer.
Butler, Judith. 1990. *Gender Trouble: Feminism and the Subversion of Identity.* New York: Routledge.
———. 1993a. *Bodies that Matter: On the Discursive Limits of "Sex."* New York: Routledge.
———. 1993b. "Endangered/Endangering: Schematic Racism and White Paranoia." In Robert Gooding-Williams, ed., *Reading Rodney King: Reading Urban Uprising,* 15–22. New York: Routledge.
———. 1997. *Excitable Speech: A Politics of the Performative.* New York: Routledge.
Calhoun, Craig, ed. 1992. *Habermas and the Public Sphere.* Cambridge, Mass.: MIT Press.
Carnap, Rudolf. [1932] 1959. "The Elimination of Metaphysics through Logical Analysis of Language." Trans. Arthur Pap. In A. J. Ayer, ed., *Logical Positivism,* 60–81. New York: Free Press.
Chomsky, Noam. 1999. *The New Military Humanism: Lessons from Kosovo.* Monroe: Common Courage.
Cohen, Roger. 2000. "Kohl Is Defiant before Panel Probing Scandal." *Chicago Tribune,* June 30, sec. 1, p. 3.
Cornell, Drucilla. 1987. "Two Lectures on the Normative Dimensions in the Law." *Tennessee Law Review* 54: 327–43.
———. 1991. *Beyond Accommodation: Ethical Feminism, Deconstruction, and the Law.* New York: Routledge.
———. 1992. *The Philosophy of the Limit.* New York: Routledge.
Critchley, Simon, and William R. Schroeder, eds. 1998. *A Companion to Continental Philosophy.* Oxford: Basil Blackwell.
Davis, Angela. 1988. *An Autobiography.* New York: International.
Denitsch, Bogdan. 1999. "A Botched Just War." *Dissent,* Summer, 7–10.
Derrida, Jacques. 1988. *Limited, Inc.* Evanston, Ill.: Northwestern University Press.
———. 1992. *The Other Heading: Reflections on Today's Europe.* Trans. Pascale-Anne Brault and Michael B. Naas. With an introduction by M. B. Nass. Bloomington: Indiana University Press.
———. 1993. *Specters of Marx: The State of Debt, the Work of Mourning, and the New International.* Trans. Peggy Kamuf. New York: Routledge.
———. 1995. *The Gift of Death.* Trans. David Wills. Chicago: University of Chicago Press.

Dews, Peter, ed. 1999. *Habermas: A Critical Reader.* London: Basil Blackwell.

Deutschland im Herbst [Germany in autumn]. 1978. Photography by Michael Ballhaus. Edited by Beate Mainka-Jellinghaus. Available from World Artists Home Video, Los Angeles, Calif. Motion picture.

Dienstbier, Jiří. 2000. Report of speech in *CTK National News Wire,* April 20.

Diner, Dan. 1991. *Der Krieg der Erinnerungen und die Ordnung der Welt.* Berlin: Rotbuch.

Du Bois, W. E. B. 1995. *The Souls of Black Folk.* New York: Penguin. With a new introduction by Randall Kenan.

Dummett, Michael. 1994. *Origins of Analytic Philosophy.* Cambridge: Harvard University Press.

Dussel, Enrique. 1996. *The Underside of Modernity: Apel, Ricoeur, Rorty, Taylor; and the Philosophy of Liberation.* Atlantic Highlands, N.J.: Humanities.

Duvenage, Pieter. 1999. "The Politics of Memory and Forgetting after Auschwitz and Apartheid." *Philosophy and Social Criticism* 25, no. 3: 1–28.

Edelstein, Wolfgang, and Gertrud Nunner-Winkler, eds. 1986. *Zur Bestimmung der Moral: Philosophische und sozialwissenschaftliche Beiträge zur Moralforschung.* Frankfurt a/M: Suhrkamp.

"Erfahrungen am eigenen Leib: Der Architekt Peter Eisenman über die Walser-Debatte und die neue Kritik an seinem Entwurf für das Holocaust-Mahnmal." 1998. Interview with Eisenman conducted by Hanno Ravterberg. *Die Zeit,* Feuilleton sec., December 10, 51–52.

Ertel, Manfred, et al. 1998. "Schuld und Schlußstrich." *Der Spiegel,* November 30, 30–38.

Evans, Richard J. 1989. *In Hitler's Shadow: West German Historians and the Attempt to Escape from the Nazi Past.* New York: Pantheon.

Falk, Richard. 2000. "Kosovo Revisited." *The Nation,* April 10, 3–5.

Fanon, Frantz. [1961] 1963. *The Wretched of the Earth.* Trans. Constance Farrington. With a preface by Jean-Paul Sartre. New York: Grove. German translation published in 1966.

Farias, Victor. 1989. *Heidegger und der Nazionalsozialismus.* Trans. Klaus Laermann. Frankfurt a/M: Fisher.

Felman, Shoshana. 1994. "Film as Witness: Claude Lanzmann's Shoah." In Geoffrey H. Hartman, ed., *Holocaust Remembrance: The Shapes of Memory,* 90–103. Cambridge, Mass.: Basil Blackwell.

Felman, Shoshana, and Dori Laub, M.D. 1992. *Testimony: Crises of Witnessing in Literature, Psychoanalysis, and History.* New York: Routledge.

Fest, Joachim. 1986. "Die Geduldete Erinnerung: Zur Kontroverse über die Unvergleichbarkeit der nationalsozialistischen Massenverbrechen." *Frankfurter Allgemeine Zeitung,* August 29, 23–24.

Firestone, Shulamith. 1979. *The Dialectic of Sex: The Case for Feminist Revolution.* Introduction by Rosalind Delmar. London: Women's Press.

Fischman, Dennis. 1991. *Political Discourse in Exile: Karl Marx and the Jewish Question.* Amherst: University of Massachusetts Press.

Fleming, Marie. 1997. *Emancipation and Illusion: Rationality and Gender in Habermas's Theory of Modernity.* University Park: Pennsylvania State University Press.

Flynn, Thomas. 1984. *Sartre and Marxist Existentialism: The Test Case of Collective Responsibility.* Chicago: University of Chicago Press.

Foucault, Michel. 1984. *The Foucault Reader*. Ed. Paul Rabinow. New York: Pantheon.

Fraser, Nancy. 1989. *Unruly Practices: Power, Discourse, and Gender in Contemporary Social Theory*. Minneapolis: University of Minnesota Press.

———. 1997a. *Justice Interruptus: Critical Reflections on the "Postsocialist" Condition*. New York, London: Routledge.

———. 1997b. "A Rejoinder to Iris Young." *New Left Review* 223 (May–June): 126–29.

Geiss, Imanuel. 1988. *Die Habermas Kontroverse: Ein deutscher Streit*. Berlin: Siedler.

Giesen, Bernhard. 1998. *Intellectuals and the German Nation: Collective Identity in an Axial Age*. Trans. Nicholas Levis and Amos Weisz. Cambridge: Cambridge University Press.

Gliederung der Reichsgruppe Industrie. 1939. 2d ed. Leipzig: Lühe. Published by the directorate of business.

Gliederung der Reichsgruppe Industrie. 1941. 23d ed. Leipzig: Lühe. Published by the directorate of business.

Goldhagen, Daniel Jonah. 1996. *Hitlers willinge Vollstrecker: Ganz Gewöhnliche Deutsche und der Holocaust*. Munich: Siedler Verlag.

Gooding-Williams, Robert, ed. 1993. *Reading Rodney King: Reading Urban Uprising*. New York: Routledge.

Gordon, Lewis R. 1995a. *Bad Faith and Antiblack Racism*. Atlantic Highlands, N.J.: Humanities.

———. 1995b. *Fanon and the Crisis of European Man: An Essay on Philosophy and the Human Sciences*. New York: Routledge.

Gordon, Lewis R., ed. 1997. *Existence in Black: An Anthology of Black Existential Philosophy*. New York: Routledge.

Gruppenexperimente über Integrationsphänomene in Zwangssituationen. 1953. Hectographed research report of the Institute for Social Research, Frankfurt a/M.

Guth, Karl. 1941. *Die Reichsgruppe Industrie: Standort und Aufgabe der industriellen Organisation*. Berlin: Junker & Dünnhaupt.

Habermas, Jürgen, ed. 1968. *Antworten auf Herbert Marcuse*. Frankfurt a/M: Suhrkamp.

Hahn, Lewis E., ed. 2000. *Perspectives on Habermas*. Chicago: Open Court.

"Haltung gegenüber den Juden." 1952. *Neue Zeitung,* January 12. Resolution of the student parliament of Johann Wolfgang Goethe-Universität, issued on January 9, 1952.

Harpprecht, Klaus. 1998. "Wen meint Martin Walser?" *Die Zeit,* October 15, 1.

Hartman, Geoffrey H., ed. 1986. *Bitburg in Moral and Political Perspective*. Indianapolis: Indiana University Press.

———. 1994. *Holocaust Remembrance: The Shapes of Memory*. Cambridge, Mass.: Basil Blackwell.

Hass, Aaron. 1990. *In the Shadow of the Holocaust: The Second Generation*. Ithaca: Cornell University Press.

Haug, Wolfgang Fritz, ed., *Deutsche Philosophen 1933*, 125–59. Hamburg: Argument-Verlag.

Havel, Václav. 1999. "Kosovo and the End of the Nation-State." *New York Review of Books,* June 10, 6.

Hegel, G. F. W. 1967. *Philosophy of Right*. Trans. T. M. Knox. London: Oxford University Press.

Heidegger, Martin. 1953a. *Einführung in die Metaphysik*. Tübingen. English edition, 1959. *An Introduction to Metaphysics*. Trans. Ralph Maneheim. New Haven, Conn.: Yale University Press.

———. 1953b. "Heidegger on Heidegger." *Die Zeit,* September 24, 10.

———. 1962. *Being and Time.* Trans. John Macquire and Edward Robinson. New York: Harper & Row.

———. [1966] 1976. "Nur noch ein Gott kann uns retten: Spiegel-Gespräch mit Martin Heidegger am 23. September 1966." *Der Spiegel,* May 31, 193–219.

"Heidegger warnte vor der Gentechnik." 1999. Letters to the editor responding to Sloterdijk 1999a,b. *Die Zeit,* October 7, 61–62.

Herman, Edward S., and David Peterson. 2000. "Kosovo One Year Later: From Serb Repression to NATO-Sponsored Ethnic Cleansing." *ZNet Commentaries.* <sysop@zmag.org>, June 23.

Hersh, Seymour M. 2000. "Overwhelming Force: What Happened in the Final Days of the Gulf War?" *New Yorker,* May 22, 49–82.

Herzinger, Richard. 2000. "Totalitäre Dynamik: Vorschau auf einen neuen Historikerstreit? Wie Ernst Nolte in München mit dem Adenauer-Preis geehrt und von Horst Möller vergeblich laudiert wurde." *Die Zeit,* Feuilleton sec., June 8, 42.

Hildebrand, Klaus. 1986a. "Das Zeitalter der Tyrannen, Geschichte und Politik: Die Vewalter der Aufklärung, das Risiko der Wissenschaft und die Geborgenheit der Weltanschauung. Eine Entgegnung auf Jürgen Habermas." *Frankfurter Allgemeine Zeitung,* July 31, 17.

———. 1986b. "Wer dem Abgrund entrinnen will, muss ihn aufs genauste ausloten. Ist die neue deutsche Geschichsschreibung revisionistisch?" *Die Welt,* November 22, GW1.

Hildebrandt, Tina, et al. 2000. "Die Bundeslöstage." *Der Spiegel,* July 3, 22–30.

Hillgruber, Andreas. 1986a. "Mangel, an elementarer Redlichkeit beim Zitieren." Letter to the *Frankfurter Allgemeine Zeitung,* August 23.

———. 1986b. "Jürgen Habermas, Karl-Heinz Janssen und die Auklärung Anno 1986." *Geschichte in Wissenschaft und Unterricht,* December, 725–38.

———. 1986c. *Zweirlei Untergang: Die Zerschlagung des Deutschens Reiches und das Ende des europäischen Judentums.* Berlin: Corso bei Siedler.

Hockenos, Paul. 2000. "Human Wrongs." *In These Times,* August 7, 26–30.

Hoffman, H., ed. 1987. *Gegen den Versuch, Vergangenheit zu verbiegen.* Frankfurt a/M: Suhrkamp.

Hofmann, Günther. 1998. "Wegsehen oder Weggehen: Ignatz Bubis, Deutscher jüdischer Glaubens." *Die Zeit,* Politik sec., December 10, 3. With added newspaper heading: "Walser, Bubis und die Folgen: Wen die Erinnerung einholt."

Holub, Robert C. 1991. *Jürgen Habermas: Critic in the Public Sphere.* New York: Routledge.

Honneth, Axel. 1986. "Diskursethik und implizites Gerechtigkeitskonzept: Eine Diskussionsbemerkung." In Wolfgang Kuhlmann, ed., *Moralität und Sittlichkeit: Das Problem Hegels und die Diskursethik,* 183–93. Frankfurt a/M: Suhrkamp.

———. 1992. *Kampf um Anerkennung: Zur moralischen Grammatik sozialer Konflikte.* Frankfurt a/M: Suhrkamp.

Honneth, Axel, and Hans Joas, eds. 1991. *Communicative Action: Essays on Jürgen Habermas's* The Theory of Communicative Action. Trans. Jeremy Gaines and Doris L. Jones. Cambridge, Mass.: MIT Press.

Honneth, Axel, and Albrecht Wellmer, eds. 1986. *Die Frankfurter Schule und die Folgen: Referate eines Symposiums der Alexander von Humboldt-Stiftung vom 10.-15. December 1984 in Ludwigsburg,* Berlin: Walter de Gruyter.

Honneth, Axel, et al., eds., *Zwischenbetrachtungen: Im Prozeß der Aufklärung*, 733–38. Frankfurt a/M: Suhrkamp.
Horkheimer, Max. 1958a. "Mitte Mai 1958." In Wolfgang Kraushaar, ed. 1998. *Frankfurter Schule und Studentenbewegung.* Vol. 2, doc. 49. Hamburg: Rogner & Bernhard.
———. 1958b. "Zur Funktion der Atombewaffnung." In Wolfgang Kraushaar, ed. 1998. *Frankfurter Schule und Studentenbewegung.* Vol. 2, doc. 52. Hamburg: Rogner & Bernhard.
———. 1958c. September 27. "Brief an Theodor W. Adorno." In Wolfgang Kraushaar, ed. 1998. *Frankfurter Schule und Studentenbewegung.* Vol. 2, doc. 53. Hamburg: Rogner & Bernhard.
———. 1967. May 7. "Amerika heute im Bewußtsein der Deutschen: Zum Problem der Verständigung." Diskus, June, 10. In Wolfgang Kraushaar, ed. 1998. *Frankfurter Schule und Studentenbewegung.* Vol. 2, doc. 115. Hamburg: Rogner & Bernhard.
———. [1937] 1972. "Traditional and Critical Theory." Trans. Matthew J. O'Connell. In *Critical Theory*, 188–243. New York: Herder & Herder.
Horkheimer, Max, and Theodor W. Adorno. [1944] 1987. *Dialectic of Enlightenment.* Trans. John Cumming. New York: Continuum.
Horster, Detlef. 1991. *Jürgen Habermas.* With a bibliography by René Görtzen. Stuttgart: J. B. Metzlersche Verlagsbuchhandlung.
Huntington, Patricia. 1997. "Fragmentation, Race, and Gender: Building Solidarity in the Postmodern Era." In Lewis R. Gordon, ed., *Existence in Black: An Anthology of Black Existential Philosophy*, 185–202. New York: Routledge.
———. 1998. *Ecstatic Subjects, Utopia, and Recognition: Kristeva, Heidegger, Irigaray.* Albany: SUNY Press.
Husserl, Edmund. [1935] 1970. *The Crisis of European Sciences and Transcendental Phenomenology.* Trans. David Carr. Evanston, Ill.: Northwestern University Press.
Ilsemann, Mareike. 1998. "Die Elfjährigen und die SS: Junge Deutsche finden sich unweigerlich in einem Dilemma: Sie wollen einem normalen Volk engehören, sie wollen aber auch Erinnerung an den Nationalsozialismus wachhalten." *Die Zeit*, Politik sec., December 10, 4. With added newspaper heading: "Walser, Bubis und die Folgen: Überdruß am Gedenken?"
Ingram, David. 1995. *Reason, History, and Politics: The Communitarian Grounds of Legitimation in the Modern Age.* Albany: SUNY Press.
Irigaray, Luce 1985. *Speculum of the Other Woman.* Trans. Gillian C. Gill. Ithaca, N.Y.: Cornell University Press.
Jaspers, Karl. 1931. *Die geistige Situation der Gegenwart.* Berlin: Gruyter.
———. 1933. *Man in the Modern Age.* Trans. Eden Paul and Cedar Paul. New York: Holt.
Jay, Martin. 1973. *Dialectical Imagination: A History of the Frankfurt School and the Institute of Social Research, 1923–1950.* Boston: Little, Brown.
———. 1984. *Adorno.* Cambridge: Harvard University Press.
Judah, Tim. 2000. "The Unfinished War." *The Observer* (London), February 20, 24–25.
Kant, Immanuel. [1784] 1959. "What Is Enlightenment?" In *Foundations of the Metaphysics of Morals*, 85–92. Trans. Lewis White Beck. Indianapolis: Bobbs-Merrill.
Katzenberger, Elaine, ed. 1995. *First World, Ha Ha Ha! The Zapatista Challenge.* San Francisco: City Lights.
Kellner, Douglas. 1992. *The Persian Gulf TV War.* Boulder: Westview.

Kelly, Michael, ed. 1990. *Hermeneutics and Critical Theory in Ethics and Politics.* Cambridge, Mass.: MIT Press.

——. 1994. *Critique and Power: Recasting the Foucault/Habermas Debate.* Cambridge, Mass.: MIT Press.

Keulartz, Jozef. 1995. *Die verkehrte Welt des Jürgen Habermas.* Hamburg: Junius. Translated from the Dutch by Inge van der Aart.

Kierkegaard, Søren. 1978. *Two Ages: The Age of Revolution and the Present Age.* Ed. and trans. Howard V. Hong and Edna H. Hong. Princeton: Princeton University Press.

——. 1980a. *The Concept of Anxiety.* Ed. and trans. Howard V. Hong and Edna H. Hong. Princeton: Princeton University Press.

——. 1980b. *The Sickness unto Death.* Ed. and trans. Howard V. Hong and Edna H. Hong. Princeton: Princeton University Press.

——. 1985. *Philosophical Fragments.* Ed. and trans. Howard V. Hong and Edna H. Hong. Princeton: Princeton University Press.

——. 1988. *Stages on Life's Way: Studies by Various Persons.* Ed. and trans. Howard V. Hong and Edna H. Hong. Princeton: Princeton University Press.

Kilian, Michael. 2000. "Lynne Cheney's Time at Humanities Agency in Spotlight." *Chicago Tribune,* July 28, sec. 1, p. 6.

Kinzer, Stephen. 1993. "The War Memorial: To Embrace the Guilty, Too?" *New York Times,* November 15, A4.

Klemperer, Victor. 1999. *I Will Bear Witness: A Diary of the Nazi Years, 1933–1941.* Trans. Martin Chalmers. New York: Modern Library.

Koch, H. W., ed. *Aspects of the Third Reich,* 17–38. New York: St. Martin's.

Krahl, Hans-Jürgen. 1971. *Konstitution und Klassenkampf.* Frankfurt a/M: Suhrkamp.

Kraushaar, Wolfgang. 1990. *Revolte und Reflexion: Politische Aufsätze 1976–87.* Frankfurt a/M: Verlag Neue Kritik.

Kraushaar, Wolfgang, ed. 1998. *Frankfurter Schule und Studentenbewegung.* Vol. 1, *Chronik, 1946–1995* [cited by page or date]. Vol. 2, *Dokumente* [cited by document number and page]. Vol. 3, *Aufsätze und Kommentare, Register* [cited by page]. Hamburg: Rogner & Bernhard.

Kristeva, Julia. 1984. *Revolution in Poetic Language.* Trans. Margaret Waller. New York: Columbia University Press.

Kuhlmann, Wolfgang, ed. 1986. *Moralität und Sittlichkeit: Das Problem Hegels und die Diskursethik.* Frankfurt a/M: Suhrkamp.

Kurth, Winfried. 1999. "The Psychological Background of Germany's Participation in the Kosovo War." *Journal of Psychiatry* 27, no. 2 (Fall): 100–123.

La Capra, Dominick. 1994. *Representing the Holocaust: History, Theory, Trauma.* Ithaca: Cornell University Press.

Landgrebe, Ludwig. 1952. *Philosophie der Gegenwart.* Bonn: Athenäum Verlag.

Lanzmann, Claude. 1985. *Shoah: An Oral History of the Holocaust.* With a preface by Simone de Beauvoir. New York: Pantheon.

La Revuelta de la Memoria: Textos del Subcomandante Marcos y del EZLN sobre la Historia. 1999. San Cristóbal de las Casas, Chiapas: Centro de Información y Análisis de Chiapas.

Lau, Jörg. 1999. "Die Verräter sind unter uns." *Die Zeit,* April 22, 17–19.

Leaman, George. 1993. *Heidegger im Kontext: Gesamtüberblick zum NS-Engagement der Universitätsphilosophen.* Hamburg: Argument-Verlag.

Lenhardt, Christian. 1975. "Anamnestic Solidarity: The Proletariat and Its Manes," *Telos* 25: 133–55.
Lepeniens, Wolf. 1967. "Vorbild einer studentischen Minorität." *Frankfurter Allgemeine Zeitung,* July 19, 18.
Leslie, Esther. 1999. "Introduction to Adorno/Marcuse Correspondence on the German Student Movement." *New Left Review* 233 (January–February): 118–23.
Lévinas, Emmanuel. 1969. *Totality and Infinity: An Essay on Exteriority.* Trans. Alphonso Lingis. The Hague: Martinus Nijhoff.
———. 1981. *Otherwise Than Being, or Beyond Essence.* Trans. Alphonso Lingis. The Hague: Martinus Nijhoff.
Lewalter, Christian E. 1953. "Wie liest man 1953 Sätze von 1935: Zu einem politischen Streit um Heideggers Metaphysik." *Die Zeit,* August 13, 6.
Love, Nancy S. 1995. "What's Left of Marx?" In Stephen K. White, ed., *The Cambridge Companion to Habermas,* 46–66. Cambridge: Cambridge University Press.
Lübbe, Hermann. 1983. "Es ist nicht vergessen, aber einiges ausgehielt: Der Nationalsozialismus im Bewußtsein des deutschen Gegenwart." *Frankfurter Allgemeine Zeitung,* January 24, 9.
Lukács, Georg. 1971. *History and Class Consciousness: Studies in Marxist Dialectics.* Trans. Rodney Livingstone. London: Merlin.
"Mahnmal für die SS?" 2000. *Der Spiegel,* July 3, 18.
Maier, Charles S. 1997. *The Unmasterable Past: History, Holocaust, and German National Identity.* With a new preface. Cambridge: Harvard University Press.
Malanowski, Wolfgang. 1986. "'Vergangenheit, die nicht vergehen will,' Das politische Buch." *Der Spiegel,* September 1, 66–67, 70.
Manemann, Jürgen, ed. 1999. *Befristete Zeit.* Münster: Lit Verlag.
Mannheim, Karl. 1993. "The Problem of Generations." In Kurt H. Wolff, ed. *From Karl Mannheim,* 351–98. New Brunswick, N.J.: Transaction.
Marcuse, Herbert. 1965a. "Aufhebung der Gewalt: Max Horkheimer zum 70. Geburtstag." Süddeutsche Zeitung, February 13. In Wolfgang Kraushaar, ed. 1998. *Frankfurter Schule und Studentenbewegung.* Vol. 2, doc. 92. Hamburg: Rogner & Bernhard.
———. 1965b. "Repressive Tolerance." In Robert Paul Wolff, Barrington Moore Jr., and Herbert Marcuse. 1969. *A Critique of Pure Tolerance,* 81–117. Boston: Beacon. German translation published in 1966.
———. 1966. "Vietnam: Die Analyse eines Exempels." *Neue Kritik* 36–37 (June–August): 30–40.
———. 1968. "Postscript 1968." In Wolff, Moore, and Marcuse, *Critique of Pure Tolerance,* 117–23.
———. [1958] 1969a. *Soviet Marxism: A Critical Analysis.* New York: Columbia University Press.
———. 1969b. *Essay on Liberation.* Boston: Beacon.
———. [1955] 1974. *Eros and Civilization: A Philosophical Inquiry into Freud.* Boston: Beacon. With "Political Preface 1966." The German translation was published in 1957.
———. 1978. *Gespräche mit Herbert Marcuse.* Frankfurt a/M: Suhrkamp.
———. 1988. *Negations: Essays in Critical Theory.* Trans. Jeremy J. Shapiro. London: Free Association Books. Originally published as *Kultur und Gesellschaft.* 1965. 2 vols. Frankfurt a/M: Suhrkamp.
———. [1964] 1991. *One-Dimensional Man: Studies in the Ideology of Advanced Industrial Society.* With a new introduction by Douglas Kellner. Boston: Beacon Press. [Ger. trans. 1967.]

Marsh, James L. 1988. *Post-Cartesian Meditations: An Essay in Dialectical Phenomenology.* New York: Fordham University Press.
———. 1995. *Critique, Action, and Liberation.* New York: SUNY Press.
Marten, Rainer. 1987. "Ein rassistisches Konzept von Humanität: Überlegungen zu Victor Farias' Heidegger-Buch und zum richtigen Umgang mit Heideggers Philosophie." *Badische Zeitung,* December 19–20, 14.
Martin, Bill. 1999. "Existential Marxism, the Next Chapter: Martin J. Beck Matuštík's *Specters of Liberation.*" *Radical Philosophy Review* 2, no. 2.
Marx, Karl, and Friedrich Engels. [1848] 1964. *The Communist Manifesto.* Trans. Samuel Moore. New York: Washington Square.
Matuštík, Martin J. 1988. "Review of Habermas." *Auslegung* 14, no. 2 (Summer): 225–28.
———. 1993. *Postnational Identity: Critical Theory and Existential Philosophy in Habermas, Kierkegaard, and Havel.* New York: Guilford.
——— Martin J. Beck. 1998a. *Specters of Liberation: Great Refusals in the New World Order.* Albany: SUNY Press.
———. 1998b. "What Does Critical Theory Have to Do with It?: In Retrospect and Prospect." *Radical Philosophy Review* 1, no. 1: 46–53; 1–2: iv–v.
———. 1999. "Existence and the Communicatively Competent Self." *Philosophy and Social Criticism* 25, no. 3: 93–120.
———. 2000. "The Critical Theorist as Witness: Habermas and the Holocaust." In Lewis E. Hahn, ed., *Perspectives on Habermas,* 339–66. Chicago: Open Court.
Matuštík, Martin J., and Merold Westphal, eds. 1995. *Kierkegaard in Post/Modernity.* Bloomington: Indiana University Press.
McCarthy, Thomas. [c. 1978] 1982. *The Critical Theory of Jürgen Habermas.* Cambridge, Mass.: MIT Press.
McCumber, John. 1996. "Time in the Ditch: American Philosophy and the McCarthy Era." *Diacritics* 26, no. 1 (Spring): 33–49.
Meehan, Johanna, ed. 1995. *Feminists Read Habermas: Gendering the Subject of Discourse.* New York: Routledge.
Metz, Johann Baptist. 1989. "Anamnetische Vernunft: Anmerkungen eines Theologen zur Krise der Geisteswissenschaften." In Axel Honneth et al., eds., *Zwischenbetrachtungen: Im Prozeß der Aufklärung,* 733–38. Frankfurt a/M: Suhrkamp.
———. 1994. *Diagnosen zur Zeit.* Düsseldorf: Patmos. The Metz *Festschrift,* June 16, 1993.
———. 1997. "Zwischen Erinnern und Vergessen: Die Shoah im Zeitalter der kulturellen Amnesie." In *Zum Begriff der neuen Politischen Theologie,* 1967–1997, 149–55. Mainz: Matthias–Grünewald.
Mills, Charles W. 1997. *The Racial Contract.* Ithaca, N.Y.: Cornell University Press.
Mitscherlich, Alexander, and Margarete Mitscherlich. 1975. *The Inability to Mourn: Principles of Collective Behavior.* Trans. B. Placzek. With a preface by Robert Jay Lifton. New York: Grove.
Mohr, Reinhard. 1998. "Total Normal?" *Der Spiegel,* November 30, 40–48.
———. 1999. "Züchter der Übermenschen." *Der Spiegel,* September 6, 268–69.
Müller, Jan-Werner. 2000. *Another Country: German Intellectuals, Unification, and National Identity.* New Haven, Conn.: Yale University Press.

Negt, Oskar. 1989. "Autonomie und Eingriff." *Frankfurter Rundschau*, Feuilleton, June 16, ZB 3.
Negt, Oskar, ed. 1968. *Die Linke antwortet Jürgen Habermas*. Frankfurt a/M: Europäische Verlagsanstalt.
Negt, Oskar, and Alexander Kluge. 1981. *Geschichte und Eigensinn*. Frankfurt a/M: Zweitausendeins.
News and Letters. 1999. 44, no. 3 (April 1999): 1, 10; and 44, no. 6 (July 1999): 1, 10; and 44, no. 7 (August–September 1999): 1, 5.
Nolte, Ernst. 1985. "Between Myth and Revisionism? The Third Reich in the Perspective of the 1980s." In H. W. Koch, ed. *Aspects of the Third Reich*, 17–38. New York: St. Martin's.
———. 1986a. "Vergangenheit, die nicht vergehen will: Eine Rede, die geschrieben, aber (bei den Römerberggesprächen) nicht gehalten werden konnte." *Frankfurter Allgemeine Zeitung*, June 6, 25.
———. 1986b. Letter to the *Frankfurter Allgemeine Zeitung*, December 6.
Oliver, Kelly. 1998. *Subjectivity without Subjects: From Abject Fathers to Desiring Mothers*. Lanham, Md.: Rowman & Littlefield.
Outlaw, Lucius. 1996. *On Race and Philosophy*. London: Routledge.
Pateman, Carole. 1988. *The Sexual Contract*. Stanford, Ca.: Stanford University Press.
Pensky, Max. 1989. "On the Use and Abuse of Memory: Habermas, 'Anamnestic Solidarity,' and the Historikerstreit." *Philosophy and Social Criticism* 15, no. 4: 351–80.
———. 1995. "Universalism and the Situated Critic." In Stephen K. White, ed., *The Cambridge Companion to Habermas*, 67–94. Cambridge: Cambridge University Press.
———. 1999. "Jürgen Habermas and the Antinomies of the Intellectual." In Peter Dews, ed., *Habermas: A Critical Reader*, 211–37. London: Basil Blackwell.
———. 2000. "Cosmopolitanism and the Solidarity Problem: Habermas on National and Cultural Identities." *Constellations* 7, no. 1 (March): 64–79.
Peukert, Helmut. [c. 1984] 1986. *Science, Action, and Fundamental Theology: Towards a Theology of Communicative Action*. Trans. James Bohman. Cambridge, Mass.: MIT Press.
Pieper, Josef. [1957] 1966. *The Silence of St. Thomas: Three Essays*. Trans. John Murray, S.J., and Daniel O'Connor. Chicago: Regnery.
Pirandello, Luigi. 1958. *Six Characters in Search of an Author*. Trans. Frederick May. London: Heinemann.
Postel, Danny, ed. "Debating Kosovo: Left Intellectuals on Opposing Sides of NATO's Intervention." Unpublished manuscript.
Postone, Moshe. 1993. *Time, Labor, and Social Domination: A Reinterpretation of Marx's Critical Theory*. Cambridge: Cambridge University Press.
Rasmussen, David M. 1990. *Reading Habermas*. Cambridge, Mass: Basil Blackwell.
Rawls, John. 1971. *A Theory of Justice*. Cambridge: Harvard University Press.
Rehg, William. 1997. *Insight and Solidarity: The Discourse Ethics of Jürgen Habermas*. Berkeley: University of California Press.
Ricoeur, Paul. 1970. *Freud and Philosophy: An Essay on Interpretation*. Trans. Denis Savage. New Haven: Yale University Press.
Rosenthal, John. 2000. "Kosovo and the 'Jewish Question.'" *Monthly Review* 51, no. 9 (February): 24–42.

Rothacker, Erich. 1934. *Geschichtsphilosophie. Handbuch der Philosophie.* Munich: Oldenbourg.
Sartre, Jean-Paul. 1974. "Kierkegaard: The Singular Universal." In *Between Existentialism and Marxism.* New York: New Left Books.
———. 1976. *Critique of Dialectical Reason.* Vol. 1. Trans. Alan Sheridan-Smith. London: New Left Books.
Schelsky, Helmut. 1957. *Die skeptische Generation: Eine Soziologie der deutschen Jugend.* Düsseldorf: Diederichs.
Schnädelbach, Herbert, ed. 1984. *Rationalität: Philosophische Beiträge.* Frankfurt a/M: Suhrkamp.
Schrag, Calvin O. 1989. *Communicative Praxis and the Space of Subjectivity.* Bloomington: Indiana University Press.
Schweickart, David. 1996. *Against Capitalism.* Boulder: Westview.
Secor, Laura. 1999. "Testaments Betrayed: Yugoslavian Intellectuals and the Road to War." *Lingua Franca* 9, no. 6 (September): 26–42.
Sherman, Scott. 1998. "Remembering Tlatelolco." *The Nation,* December 7, 22–24
———. 2000. "Left Out: A Militant Student Strike Sidelines Mexican Intellectuals." *Lingua Franca* 10, no. 5 (July–August): 32–42.
Showdown in Seattle: Five Days That Shook the WTO. Motion picture produced by independent filmmakers for Deep Dish TV, 1999.
Sloterdijk, Peter. 1999a. "Regeln für den Menschenpark: Ein Antwortschreiben zum Brief über den Humanismus—Die Almauer Rede." *Die Zeit,* September 16, 15, 18–21.
———. 1999b. "Die Kritische Theorie ist tot: Peter Sloterdijk schreibt an Assheuer und Habermas." *Die Zeit.* September 9, 35–36. Two open letters to Habermas and Assheuer.
Smith, Gary, ed. 1989. *Benjamin: Philosophy, Aesthetics, History.* Chicago: University of Chicago Press.
Sternberger, Dolf. 1979. "Verfassungspatriotismus." *Frankfurter Allgemeine Zeitung,* May 23.
Stürmer, Michael 1986a. "Geschichte in geschichtslosem Land." *Frankfurter Allgemeine Zeitung,* April 25, 1.
———. 1986b. "Suche nach der verlorenen Erinnerung." *Das Parlament,* May 17–24, 1.
———. 1986c. *Dissonanzen des Fortschritts: Essays über Geschichte und Politik in Deutschland.* Munich: Piper.
Taylor, Charles. 1989. *Sources of the Self: The Making of the Modern Identity.* Cambridge, Mass.: Cambridge University Press.
———. 1991. *The Ethics of Authenticity.* Cambridge: Harvard University Press.
Taylor, Charles, et al. 1994. *Multiculturalism: Examining the Politics of Recognition.* Edited and with an introduction by Amy Gutmann. Exp. 2d ed. Princeton: Princeton University Press.
Thompson, John B., and David Held, eds. 1982. *Habermas: Critical Debates.* Cambridge, Mass.: MIT Press.
Tiedemann, Rolf. 1989. "Historical Materialism or Political Messianism? An Interpretation of the Theses 'On the Concept of History.'" In Gary Smith, ed., *Benjamin: Philosophy, Aesthetics, History,* 175–209. Chicago: University of Chicago Press.
Traynor, Ian. 1999. "Generation Split Bleeds German Greens." *Guardian* (London), July 5.

Trey, George. 1998. *Solidarity and Difference: The Politics of Enlightenment in the Aftermath of Modernity*. Albany: SUNY Press.

Turner, Henry Ashby, Jr. 1992. *Germany from Partition to Reunification*. New Haven, Conn.: Yale University Press.

Ullrich, Volker. 2000. "Ein Institut im Zwielicht." *Die Zeit*, June 21, 41–42.

Walzer, Michael. 1999. "Kosovo." *Dissent*, Summer, 5–7.

Weber, Th. 1989. "Arbeit am Imaginären des Deutschen." In Wolfgang Fritz Haug, ed., *Deutsche Philosophen 1933*, 125–59. Hamburg: Argument-Verlag.

Weck, Roger de. 1999. "Der Kulturkampf: Günter Grass, Jürgen Habermas—und ihre Widersacher." *Die Zeit*, October 7, 1.

Weinreich, Max. [1946] 1999. *Hitler's Professors: The Part of Scholarship in Germany's Crimes against the Jewish People*. New Haven, Conn.: Yale University Press. With a new foreword by Martin Gilbert.

West, Cornel. 1993. *Keeping Faith: Philosophy and Race in America*. New York: Routledge.

White, Stephen K., ed. 1995. *The Cambridge Companion to Habermas*. Cambridge: Cambridge University Press.

Wiedemann, Conrad. 1998. "Der Erwälte: Eine Antwort auf Robert Leichts Leitartikel." *Die Zeit*, Politik sec., December 10, 5. With added newspaper heading: "Walser, Bubis und die Folgen: Moralisch sein oder Moralisieren?"

Wiedmer, Caroline. 1999. *The Claims of Memory: Representations of the Holocaust in Contemporary Germany and France*. Ithaca, N.Y.: Cornell University Press.

Wiesel, Elie. 1998. "Ohne Schande: Offener Brief von Elie Wiesel am Martin Walser." *Die Zeit*, Politik sec., December 10, 4.

Wiggershaus, Rolf. [c. 1986] 1989. *Die Frankfurte Schule: Geschichte, Theoretische Entwicklung, Politische Bedeutung*. Munich: Deutsche Taschenbuch. English translation: [c. 1994] 1998. *The Frankfurt School: Its History, Theories, and Political Significance*. Trans. Michael Robertson. Cambridge, Mass.: MIT Press.

Wise, Michael Z. 1999. "Totem and Tabu: The New Berlin Struggles to Build a Holocaust Memorial." *Lingua Franca* (December/January): 38–46.

Wolff, Kurt H., ed. *From Karl Mannheim*, 351–98. New Brunswick, N.J.: Transaction.

Wolff, Robert Paul, Barrington Moore Jr., and Herbert Marcuse. 1969. *A Critique of Pure Tolerance*. Boston: Beacon.

Wolin, Richard. 1998. "Critical Reflections on Marcuse's Theory of Revolution." Lecture presented at the Conference on the Legacy of Herbert Marcuse. University of California–Berkeley, November 7.

———. 1996. "Left Fascism: Georges Bataille and the German Ideology." *Constellations* 2, no. 3: 397–428.

Young, Iris M. 1990. *Justice and the Politics of Difference*. Princeton: Princeton University Press.

———. 1994. "Comments on Seyla Benhabib, *Situating the Self*." *New German Critique* 62 (Spring–Summer): 165–72.

———. 1996. "Communication and the Other: Beyond Deliberative Democracy." In Seyla Benhabib, ed., *Democracy and Difference: Contesting the Boundaries of the Political*, 120–35. Princeton: Princeton University Press.

———. 1997a. "Asymmetrical Reciprocity: On Moral Respect, Wonder, and Enlarged Thought." *Constellations* 3, no. 3: 340–63.

———. 1997b. "Unruly Categories: A Critique of Nancy Fraser's Dual Systems Theory." *New Left Review*, no. 222: 147–60.

Young, James E. 2000. *At Memory's Edge: After-Images of the Holocaust in Contemporary Arts and Architecture*. New Haven: Yale University Press.

Žižek, Slavoj. 2000. *The Fragile Absolute or, Why Is the Christian Legacy Worth Fighting For?* London: Verso.

INDEX

Abendroth, Wolfgang, 23, 35, 37–38
absolute basic rights, 215–16
actionism, 109; Habermas, 51–52, 99; student movement, 107; terrorism, 67
Adenauer, Konrad, 11–12, 31, 39–40
Adorno, Theodor W., xxii, 19, 31, 109; *The Authoritarian Personality,* 27; correspondence on student movement, with Marcuse, 60–61, 119–20; death, 47, 57, 60; *Dialectics of Enlightenment* (with Horkheimer), xxvii, 22, 139, 239; Nazi past, 6t–7t; *Negative Dialectics,* 25t, 44; postwar grounding of FRG, 25, 25t, 26; student movement, 35–63;"What Does Coming to Terms with the Past Mean?," 162–63
Adorno Prize lecture, 127–28
Albrecht, Clemens, et al., xiii, xx, 4, 24, 33n16, 35
ambivalence of Habermas: causes, 8, 12, 83; criticism, 103–4, 265–74, 288; German reunification, 77–85; Habermas, 90; integration, 91–92; Kosovo/Serbia, 188; learning after disaster, 139–40; Persian Gulf War, 176–77; religion, 9; student movement, 42–43, 45–61; violence, 115–16
amnesia: historical, 138–39; silence, 155; triumph, 143

anamnestic solidarity, 11, 126–27, 139–50, 289; existential self-choice, 152; praxis, 232
Anglo-American philosophy, 242; view of Habermas, 223, 278–79
anticolonialism, 43, 118
antinomies, xxv, 219–20
antinuclear movement, 25t; Habermas, 28, 30–31, 101; in '80s, 71–72, 74–75
anti-Semitism: Germany, 31, 181; Harlan, 23; university, 18–19
antitheory, Habermas, 225
Apel, Karl-Otto, 32n8, 80
APO. *See* extraparliamentary opposition
architectonic, 201–36
Ardagh, John, 40
Arendt, Hannah, 21, 39
Assheuer, Thomas, 291, 293, 295
Association of Socialist Sponsors of the Friends, Sponsors, and Former Members of the SDS, 38
Asylum Debate, 180–85
atheism, 10–11
"The Attitude toward the Jews" (student parliament of Goethe-Universität), 23
Auschwitz. *See* Holocaust
Austin, J. L., xvii
authoring, xx–xxii, 277, 280–82; relationship to authorship, xxi

327

Index

The Authoritarian Personality (Adorno), 27
authorship, xxii–xxxvi, 201–36, 221*t*,
   280–82; relationship to authoring, xxi

Baader-Meinhof Gang, 67, 85n3
Bachman, Joseph, 54
Barnés, Francisco, 117
Basic Law of FRG, 81, 115, 205, 207;
   Article 16, 181–82; Article 17, 40; Article
   23, 207; Article 146, 207; reunification,
   172–73
Baynes, Kenneth, 86n11
Beauvoir, Simone de, 22
Becker, Oskar, 17–18
Behrmann, Günther C., 44
Being and Time (Heidegger), 13, 15
Benhabib, Seyla, 260
Benjamin, Walter: anamnestic solidarity, 11,
   126–27; coming to terms with the past,
   147–48; Habermas, 22, 288; memory,
   76–77
Berkeley, California, 47, 61
Berlin Holocaust Memorial, 166–69,
   196n4, 291–93; Habermas, 297–301
Berlin Museum, Jewish Museum
   Extension, 166
Berlin Wall 39, 65, 77–85
"Bestiality and Humanity: A War on the
   Border between Legality and Morality"
   (Habermas), 48, 185–88, 190, 194–96,
   217–18, 268–71
Bierman, Wolf, 54
Big Lies, 174, 184
Bitburg ceremonies, 65, 75–77, 133–34
blind spots, 9; of Habermas, 261, 284–91,
   294
blindness by disaster, 252–53, 287; gender,
   261; modes, 247*t*
Bloch, Ernst, 22, 47, 56
Bohemia, 174
Böhm, Franz, 30–31
Bohman, James, 86n11
Böhme, Jakob, 226–28
Bohrer, Karl Heinz, 81
Brandt, Willy, 41, 60, 70

BRD. *See* Federal Republic of Germany
Brecht, Bertolt, 132
Brezhnev, Leonid, 56
"Brief an Erich Fried" (Habermas), 52,
   62n15
Buback, Siegfried, 72
Bubis, Ignatz, 165–68
Buchwalter, Andrew, 71, 130
Bush, George, 179
Butler, Judith, 262

capitalism, 256–57; human face, 248–51
CDU. *See* Christian Democratic Union
Charles University, 19
Cheney, Lynne, 85n4
Chiapas, Mexico, Mayan uprising, 115–17,
   189, 251
Christian Democratic Union (CDU), 39,
   41–42, 70
Christian Social Union (CSU), 39, 41–42,
   70
civil disobedience: 74–75. *See also*
   nonviolence; protests
"Civil Disobedience: Litmus Test for the
   Democratic Constitutional State"
   (Habermas), 30, 74–75, 112–15, 125, 130
class struggle, 96
Claussen, D., 108
Clinton, Bill, 167, 198n21
Cohn-Bendit, Daniel, 57, 94, 120, 192–93
Cold War, xxiii, 12, 31, 90
collective liability, 144–46; versus personal
   guilt, 141–42
coming to terms with the past, 125–59;
   Adorno, 162–63; Asylum Debate, 183;
   German reunification, 171; meaning,
   161, 284; monuments, 162–69; versus
   settling accounts, 134–35; witnessing,
   146, 173
communication, 224
communicative action. *See* theory of
   communicative action
communicative democracy, xix, 231–35
communicative ethics, xix, 228–32;
   anamnestic solidarity, 148–49; criticism,

262–63; definition, 228; nonviolence, 115
communicative freedom, 20, 239–40, 290–91; beginning situation, 215
communicative rationality: definition, 223, 228; normative theory, xvii; possibility, material conditions, 244–45
communicative reason, 129, 221–28, 232
communicative turn, 242–43
communism. *See* Left; Marxism
concentration camps, 76
conservatism, 109, 126
Conservative Party, Germany, 11
constitutional patriotism, 154, 205–7; definition 205; development of concept, 203
continuities, 17–18, 73, 132; attitudes toward, 154–55; liabilities, 147; lost, 141; reunification, 80–81
conventionalism, 154–55, 266
convergence thesis, 129
Cornell, Drucilla, 262–63
cosmopolitan world citizenship, 46*t*, 187, 194, 204, 214–18
countermonumentality, 167–69, 298–99; witnessing, 156
Criminal Code, FRG, 71–72, 110, 130
The Crisis of European Sciences (Husserl), 42
critical questioning, xv–xvi, xviii–xix
critical social theory: definition, xxiv; early movement, xxv, 22–25; future prospects, xxv; Marcuse, 42–44; politics, 218–35; student movement, 102–9; witnessing, 156
critical theorist as witness, 143–50, 152–53, 156, 173
Critical Theory, xxii; definition, xxiv; existentialism, 152; genealogy, xxv–xxvi; Habermas' introduction, 23–31; influence, 238; institutional grounding, 25*t*; Mexico, 118; Sloterdijk, 291, 294; student movement, 47, 50–51, 57, 59. *See also* Frankfurt School
CSU. *See* Christian Social Union
Czechoslovakia, 56, 63n20, 191

Davis, Angela, xxiii, 48, 52
deception, 5, 10, 16–17, 20–21, 84, 146; Big Lies, 174, 184; within democracy, 182–83; Jewish thinkers, 285; Plato, 197n10
decisionism, 21, 229; and either/or, 154
decoupling, 261
Decree against Radicals *(Radikalenerlass)*, 71
defiance, 156
"Defusing the Past" (Habermas), 75, 132–33, 162, 171
deliberative democracy, 205, 207–9, 231, 285; development of concept of, 203
democracy: communicative, xix, 231–35; deception, 182–83; deliberative, 203, 205, 207–9, 231, 285; discourse theory, 207–9; existential self-choice, 151–52; Fascism, 104–5, 107–8, 284–85; learning from history, 163; models, 208; phantom, 285; postnational, 211, 213; radical, 27, 29, 204, 214–18, 249–50, 256
demos, 213
Derrida, Jacques, 129, 225–26
despair, 20, 159n40, 162
Dews, Peter, xx
dialectical atheism, 11
Dialectics of Enlightenment (Horkheimer & Adorno), xxvii, 22, 139, 239
difference, politics of, 266–67
disaster. *See* blindness by disaster; learning by disaster; unspeakable
discontents, 199–200
discourse theory: of democracy, 207–9. *See also* theory of communicative action
"Der DM-Nationalismus" (Habermas), 171
dramatic axis, xx–xxii
Dregger, Alfred, 68, 109, 135
Dresden, 80
Dubček, Alexander, 54, 81
Durkheim, Emile, 22
Dussel, Enrique, 267
Dutschke, Rudi, xxiii, 28, 47, 51–52, 73–74; assassination attempt and death,

48, 54, 60, 74; critical social theory, 102, 104–6; terrorism, 68–69

East Germany. *See* German reunification
economics: Asylum Debate, 184; imperialism, 196
education, Adorno on, 163
Eichmann, Adolf, 21, 39
Eisenman, Peter, 167
either/or: choice of traditions, 150–56, 214–15; types, 154. *See also* existential self-choice; existentialism
emancipatory praxis, 108, 152
Emergency Laws, 50, 53–55, 68
"The End of Utopia" (Marcuse), 51
Enzensberger, Hans Magnus, 55, 100
Erhard, Ludwig, 39–41
Eros and Civilization (Marcuse), 43
Essays on Liberation (Marcuse), 44, 61, 81
etatism, 104, 112
ethical-political discourses, 10
ethnic cleansing, 180, 195; critique of Habermas' views, 265–74
ethnos, 213
Eurocentrism, 257
"The European Nation-State and the Pressures of Globalization" (Habermas), 217, 247–49, 251, 253–54, 256–57, 272
European Union, 211
evil, 142
existential questioning, xv, xvii, 5
existential self-choice, 10, 20; communicative ethics, 230–31; democratization, 150–56; Habermas, 8–9; post-Wall, 214–15; in twenty-first century, 274
existentialism: choice of traditions, 150–56; types, 20–22
extraparliamentary opposition, 44, 50, 53; versus terrorism, 69. *See also* public sphere

Faktizität und Geltung (*Between Facts and Norms*, Habermas), xxvi, 101, 164, 215–16, 248, 256

Fanon, Frantz, 97, 112, 118
Farias, Victor, 13
Fascism: danger, 120; within democracy, 104–5, 107–8, 284–85; discontents, 291–302; generational confrontations with Nazi past, 5, 6t–7t; Habermas' sensitivity, 73, 121, 126; student movement, 55–58. *See also* violence
FDP. *See* Free Democratic Party
Federal Republic of Germany (FRG; BRD): Cold War, xxiii, 12; economic miracle, 40, 212; Habermas, 302; NATO, 191; political shifts, 71–72; postwar government, 11–12; postwar groundings, 24–26, 25t, 35–36, 46t; recent events, 291–302; reunification, 172; special way, 174, 176, 191; violence, 110
Feenberg, Andrew, xxiii
feminist criticism of Habermas, 258, 260–64, 266–68
Fest, Joachim, 135–36, 138, 158n23
Filbinger, Hans Karl, 68
Fischer, Joschka, xxiii, 57, 81, 122n1, 192–93, 198n21
Fleming, Marie, 264–65
formal-pragmatic materialism, 221–28
formal pragmatics: definition, 223–24; grounding, 227
Foucault, Michel, 129, 225–26, 229
Frankfurt School, xxii; Habermas, 23–30, 36–37; Nazis, 19; RAF terrorists, 66–70, 109–10. *See also* Critical Theory
Frankfurt University: Habermas, 37–38, 41–42, 66, 74; student occupation, 54–55, 57–60
Fraser, Nancy, 259–61, 266
Free Democratic Party (FDP), 70–71
Free University of Berlin, 47, 50–51, 92
Freiburg University, 17, 19
French Revolution, 28, 46, 78; Habermas, 140
Freud, Sigmund, 22
FRG. *See* Federal Republic of Germany
Fried, Erich, 52, 62n19

Friedeburg, Ludwig von, 49–50, 58–59
future: anachronism of student movement, 81–82, 289–90; past as, 163–64, 172–73, 247t; types, 163–64

Gadamer, Hans-Georg, 37
Garrido, Luis Javier, 118
Gehlen, Arnold, 18
generational cohorts, xxii–xxiii, 4–5; anamnestic solidarity, 289; blind spots, 294; coming to terms with the past, 148–49; confrontation, 6t, 9, 50; Green Party, 192; Habermas, 91, 101–2; Kosovo/Serbia, 193; nonviolence, 109–22. *See also specific generation*
genetic engineering, 291, 293–96
German Autumn, 66–75, 85n4, 127; political positions, 70f; Second, 180–85
German culture: changes, 151; post-Wall, 171–72; postwar, 12, 66, 140; self-criticism, 10
German Democratic Republic (GDR; DDR). *See* German reunification
German identity, 130; struggle over, 153
German Research Association, 37
German reunification, 77–85, 85n1, 161–98; coming to terms with the past, 171; continuities, 80–81; Habermas, 170–75
German Socialist Student League (SDS), 38, 48–49, 52–54, 59, 104; Leather Jacket faction, 106–7
Germany. *See* Federal Republic of Germany; liberation of Germany; Nazi Germany
Gerstenmaier, Eugen, 40
Geyer, Michael, 141–42, 153, 155–56, 159n32
globalization: protests against, 103, 105, 192; UNAM, 117
God: communicative ethics, 229–30; issues regarding, 218, 223, 226–27
Goethe House, 53, 101
Gonzalez, Elian, 198n21
Gorbachev, Mikhail, 80

Göttingen Manifesto, 30
Grand Coalition, 39, 41–42, 53
Grass, Günter, 57, 81, 101, 107
great refusal, 106
Green Party, Germany, 49, 192–93, 198n21
guilt, 139–50; collective liability, 141–42; survivors, 141–44
Guth, Karl, 296

Habermas, Ernst, 3–4, 295–97, 303nn8–10
Habermas, Jürgen: architectonic and authorship, 201–36; critiques, xviii–xix, 244–74, 246t, 287–88; deception, 11–17; Dutschke, 73–74; existentially motivated birthday, 3–11; existential self-choice, 8–9; fundamental project, 84; German reunification, 77–85, 161–98; Holocaust, 143, 284–91; incubation and revolt, 35–63; influence, 237–76; intellectual formation, 17–23; liberation of Germany, 3–33; Nazi past, 6t–7t; phantoms of student movement, 89–123; political engagement, xix–xx, 30–31, 80; political position, 29, 70f, 126; sensitivity to Fascism, 73, 121, 126; signature, 17; staging for return to politics, 66–75; student movement, 36–61, 46t, 92, 95–102; timeframe of life, 78–79. *See also* ambivalence; integration
Hahn, Lewis E., xxi
Haller, Michael, 170
Handke, Peter, 170, 189, 193
Hansen, Miriam, 141–42, 153, 155–56, 159n32
Harlan, Veit, 23
Havel, Václav, 80
Hegel, G. W. F., xxv, 45, 151, 176–77, 213, 216
Heidegger, Martin: *Being and Time*, 13, 15; Habermas' break, 12–17, 153; Nazis, 5, 12–17, 32n6
Heller, Agnes, 56
hermeneutical turn, 242
Heydrich, Reinhard, 69

Hilberg, Raul, 76
Hildebrand, Klaus, 135, 158n23
Hillgruber, Andreas, 133, 135–37, 154
Historians' Debate, 131–39, 291–92; alternative, 156; end, 167–68; postnational identity, 210; seeds, 72–73; terms, 132
historical materialism, 147–48
historical responsibility, 227
Hitler Youth, 4, 31n1
Hoheisel, Horst, 299
holism, performative, 222–23
Holocaust: beginning after, 11; centrality to Habermas,143, 284–91; coming to terms, 125–59; films, 138; Kohl, 292; revisionism. *See* Historians' Debate; revisionist historians
Holocaust identity, 78, 143; definition, 10
Holub, Robert C., xx
Honecker, Erich, 80
Honneth, Axel, xxiii
hope, 8, 11, 81–82, 244, 289; Habermas, 82–85; learning after disaster, 139–50
Horkheimer, Max, 31; *Dialectics of Enlightenment* (with Adorno), xxvii, 22, 139, 239; emigration, 19; on Habermas, 28–30, 36; Nazi past, 6t; postwar grounding of FRG, 25, 25t, 26; securing generation, xxii; student movement, 23–24, 29, 35–63; "Traditional and Critical Theory," xxvi
Horster, Detlef, xx, 73
Hoyerswerda, 181
human rights, 195–96; Habermas, 215–18; postnational identity, 211
humanitarian wars of intervention, 187, 195; cosmopolitan citizenship, 217; critique, 265–74; resistance, 119
Hussein, Saddam, 178
Husserl, Edmund, 19, 42

IfS, 23–31
"Im Lichte Heideggers" (Habermas), 13
impacts, xviii–xix, 199–200, 237–76
imperialism, 186, 195, 284–85; postcolonial turn against, 246–57

inclusion, of other, 231–35
inductive fallacy, xxi, 201
Ingram, David, xxiii
Institute for Social Research, xxii, xxiii–xxiv. *See also* Frankfurt School; IfS
institutional grounding of FRG, 24; Critical Theory, 25t; student movement, 46t
integration by Habermas, 91, 164, 203; break with Heidegger, 12, 17; civil disobedience, 114; existentialism, 151, 153; Holocaust, 284; questions, 127; reunification, 171, 174–75; structure and mode, 218–35, 221t-22t
integrative concepts, 202–4, 203t
intellectual grounding of FRG, 24, 35–36; student movement, 46t
intellectuals: Habermas, 35, 310. *See also* student movement
interdisciplinarity, 237–38
intersubjective liability, 141–42, 144–46
interventions, 87, 91–92
Iranian revolution, 196
iron cage of rationalized modernity, 238–39
Israel, 178
"Israel and Athens" (Habermas), 143

Janus-faced concept, 213, 235n3
Jaspers, Karl, 126, 128–29, 150, 153
Jay, Martin, xx
Jewish Museum Extension. *See* Berlin Museum
Jewish thinkers: Habermas, 9–10, 21, 285–86; Kosovo, 198n21
Johann Wolfgang Goethe-Universität, 19, 23, 41, 55, 94
Jünger, Ernst, 18
Jürgen Habermas: A Philosophical-Political Profile (Matuštík): axes for viewing, xx–xxvii; methodology, 201; syllabus, xv–xx; tense used, xxvi–xxvii; writing, xiii–xv, xxi

Kant, Immanuel, xxv, 244; concept of perpetual peace, 31, 176–77, 188, 191, 216–17; Habermas, 270

"Keine Normalisierung der Vergangenheit" (Habermas), 76, 132, 138
Kellner, Doug, xxiii
Kierkegaard, Søren: anamnesis, 145; constitutional patriotism, 206; critique of Habermas, 288; despair, 20; existentialism, 10, 150–56, 159n40, 230–31; Habermas, 126, 150
Kiesinger, Kurt Georg, 41
King, Martin Luther, Jr., 118
Kohl, Helmut: Bitburg ceremonies, 70, 74–76, 133, 135; memorials, 165–66; scandal, 291–92; xenophobic violence, 181
Kollwitz, Käthe, 165, 168
Kosovo/a, 7t, 83, 185–96, 276n13; critique of Habermas' views, 270–73; evaluation, 198n22; Habermas, 190–91; term, 197n11
Köttgen, Grete, 295
Kragujevac, 193
Krahl, Hans-Jürgen, xxiii, 28, 33n20, 47, 53–58, 60, 100; on critical social theory, 102–6; Habermas, 107–8
Kraushaar, Wolfgang, xiii, xx; early student movement, 23–24; Left Fascism, 53; student movement, 57, 104–6; terrorism, 69
Kristallnacht, 77, 169
Kuby, Erich, 47
Kurras, Karl-Heinz, 50, 53

labor theory of value, 250
Landgrebe, Ludwig, 13
language, violence and, 111
Lanzmann, Claude, 138
Leaman, George, 18–19, 32n5
learning: from feelings, 240; Habermas, 82–85, 103, 189–90, 202–18; after Holocaust, 139–50; postnational identity, 212–13
learning by disaster, 204, 244, 286–87; Asylum Debate, 182–85; Kosovo/Serbia, 186–89, 194; meaning, 161; modes, 247t; Persian Gulf War, 176–78, 180; post-Wall, 169–96

learning by suspicion, 270
learning from history: democracy, 163; Kohl, 133
Leather Jacket faction, 106–7
Left: FRG, 110, 120–21; Habermas, 27–28, 99, 101, 110–11, 127–30, 254–56; Kosovo, 186; Nazi Germany, 18–19, 38; political position, 69; terrorism, 68–69. *See also* Marxism
Left Fascism, Habermas, 7t, 49, 51–54, 61, 62n19, 67–68
Leipzig, 80
Lepenies, Wolf, 102
Lewalter, Christian E., 14
liability, collective, 141–42, 144–46
liberalism, 229; phantom, 104
liberation, 164–65; criticism of Habermas, 288; new critical theory, 281–82
"Liberation from the Affluent Society" (Marcuse), 52
liberation of Germany, 3–33, 164–65; critical social theory, xxiv–xxv; ghosts, 125–59; revisionism, 77
Libeskind, Daniel, 166
Library of Living Philosophers, xxi, 274n1
linguistic-communicative turn, xix, 225, 243; definition, 152, 223; influence, 237–38
linguistic turn proper, 242
linguistification of sacred, 135, 143, 229; idea of God, 230; solidarity, 146
Löwith, Karl, 22, 37
Lübbe, Hermann, 171
Lukács, Georg, 22
Luria, Isaac, 226–28

Maier, Charles S., 133
MAI. *See* Multilateral Agreement on Investments
Marcuse, Herbert, 19, 106, 290; correspondence on student movement, with Adorno, 60–61, 119–20; critique of Habermas, 288–89; *Eros and Civilization,* 43; *Essays on Liberation,* 44,

61, 81; Frankfurt School, 42–43; generational cohorts, xxii–xxiii; Habermas, 22, 26–27, 97; *One-Dimensional Man,* xxvi, 26, 43–44, 93–94, 148; "Philosophy and Critical Theory," xxvi; "The Problem of Violence in the Opposition," 51, 118–19; "Repressive Tolerance," 43–44; student movement, 6*t*, 26, 43–44, 46*t*, 48, 51–56, 94; theory/practice issues, 118–21; violence, 69, 116*f*, 121

Marcuse, Inge, 91

margins, turn to, 258–65

market economy, 96

market-liberal democracy, 208

Marković, Mihailo, 32n6

Marten, Rainer, 15

Marxism: criticism of Habermas, 258–59, 266, 268–70; Habermas, 14, 22, 95–96, 99, 250, 253–56. *See also* Left

Marx, Karl, xxv, 176–77

materialism: formal-pragmatic, 221–28; historical, 147–48

Matuštík, Martin J. B., xxi, 21; Habermas, 79–82

Max Planck Institute, 66

Mayan uprising in Chiapas, 115–17, 189, 251

May Events, 54, 81, 94

McCarthy, Joseph, 74

McCarthy, Thomas, xx, 86n11

Meinhof, Ulrike, 72

melancholy, 142–43, 234

memoration, 147

memorials: in Berlin, 165–68, 196n4, 291–93, 297–99; in Serbia, 193

memory: Benjamin, 76–77; Habermas, 10–11, 89–90, 146; manipulation, 77; politics, 75, 165; struggle over, 153; unmourned, 142

Mescalero, 72

methodological atheism, 10–11

Metz, Johann Baptist, 143

Mexico: Mayan uprising, 115–17, 189, 251; student movement, 115, 117–18; Tlatelolco, 56, 117

Mexico City, 63n21

Michnik, Adam, 181

Milošević, Slobodan, 32n6, 185, 193

Mitläufer, 4, 62n5, 169

Mitschelrich, Alexander, 8, 58–59

Mitterand, FranVois, 75

modernity: Habermas, 218; voices, 267–68; Weber, 238–39

Mohr, Reinhard, 291, 293

Möller, Horst, 291–93

Mommsen, Wolfgang, 158n23

monologism, 228–29

moral catastrophe, 139–50. *See also* Holocaust

Moravia, 174

mourning: absence, 142; for lost continuities, 141. *See also* coming to terms with the past; memorials

Müller, Jan-Werner, xxi, 77–78, 158n31, 159n32; Holocaust identity, 9; Persian Gulf War, 197n11

multiculturalism, 213, 232–33, 245

Multilateral Agreement on Investments (MAI), Habermas, 251

NAFTA. *See* North American Free Trade Agreement

Nasser, Gamal, 31

National Autonomous University of Mexico (UNAM), 117–18

nationalism, 135; Adorno, 163; Habermas, 151, 213. *See also* postnational

NATO. *See* North Atlantic Treaty Organization

naturalistic fallacy, xxi, 201

Naumann, Michael, 167, 293

Nazi Germany: adolescence, 8; defeat of, 3–11; Ernst Habermas, 295–97; generational confrontations, 6*t*–7*t*; German politicians, 41; Heidegger, 5, 12–17, 32n6; university professors, 18–20, 33n10, 38

Negative Catalogue, 57–58

Negative Dialectics (Adorno), 25*t*, 44

Negt, Oskar, 28, 48, 50, 55, 85n2, 100; critical social theory, 102–4, 110–11

Nelson, Benjamin, 43
neoconservatism, 72–73, 75, 129
neoliberalism, 82, 84, 250–51
Neue Wache, 165–67
new critical theory, xxv, 277–304, 302n1
New Left, 67
new social movements, 130, 153;
  Habermas, 113–14, 128, 254, 258–65;
  new critical theory, 289
Nihil contra Deum nisi Deus ipse, 218, 223, 227, 230, 239
nineteenth century, 78
Noerr, Gunzelin S., 28
Nolte, Ernst, 135, 137–38, 154, 158n23, 291–93
nonviolence: generational cohorts, 109–22, 193; Habermas, 52, 74–75, 115; phantom, 110
normality: definitions, 132; monuments, 167, 169; revisionist historians, 131–39
normative ideal, 202–18
normative rightness, 224
normative theory of communicative rationality, xvii
North American Free Trade Agreement (NAFTA), 250–51
North American pragmatism, xix
North Atlantic Treaty Organization (NATO): bombing of Serbia, 83, 185–96; protests against, 74–75
Novi Sad, 193
NSDAP. *See* Nazi Germany

"Observations on 'The Spiritual Situation of the Age'" (Habermas), 128–30
Ohnesorg, Benno, 49–50
One-Dimensional Man (Marcuse), xxvi, 26, 43–44, 93–94, 148
other: inclusion of, 231–35; versions of, 260
Outlaw, Lucius, 32n6, 263, 267

pacifism, 198n21; legal, 180, 187, 191, 216; militaristic, 186
Paris. *See* May Events

Parks, Rosa, 118
Parsons, Talcott, 22, 43
past: contradictory attitudes toward, 141; as future, 163–64, 172–73, 247t; Habermas, 175; Historians' Debate, 132–33; revisionists, 138. *See also* coming to terms with the past
Patočka, Jan, 19, 33n10
Peace Award, 57
peace movement, 115, 197n13
Pensky, Max, xx–xxi, 158n29, 205–6, 219–20, 236n4, 284
performative holism, 222–23
permanent democratic revolution, 204, 213, 233–34, 255
Persian Gulf War, 7t, 83, 86n11; critique of Habermas' views, 269–73; Habermas, 175–80; humanitarian intervention, 119, 187–88
Pestel, Eduard, 72
Peukert, Helmut, 148–49
phantom democracy, 285
phantom liberalism, 104
phantom nonviolence, 110
phantom revolution, 55, 57
phantoms: of revolution, 92–102; of student movement, 89–123
Philosophical-Political Profiles (Habermas), 60
philosophical-political questioning, xv, xvii–xviii
"Philosophy and Critical Theory" (Marcuse), xxvi
Plato, 197n10
pluralism, radical, 238–44, 239t
Pöggeler, Otto, 15, 32n8
police: student movement, 50, 53, 55–56, 59, 94; surveillance, 71, 130
political action: Habermas, 58. *See also* extraparliamentary opposition; theory/practice issues
political correctness, 85n4
politics: critical social theory, 218–35; of difference, 266–67; of information, 183; of memory, 75, 165
Ponto, Jürgen, 67

popular sovereignty, 216, 235, 255
positivism, 225
postcolonialism, 246–57; criticism of Habermas, 258, 261–62, 288–89
postconventional identity, 154–55, 266
postmetaphysical thinking, 10–11, 15, 228–31
postmodernism, 128, 225–26
postnational constellation, 204, 209–14
postnational identity, 10, 194–95, 209–14; development of concept, 203–4; global trends, 212–13; Persian Gulf War, 176
postsecularism, 142, 146–47, 149, 223, 226–27; criticism, 265–74
poststructuralism, 242, 264
posttraditional identity, 10, 210
Prague, 19, 56, 79; globalization protests, 103, 105, 192; Spring, 54, 56, 81
praxis philosophy, 32n6, 56
"The Problem of Violence in the Opposition" (Marcuse), 51, 118–19
protesting generation, xxii, 4; coming to terms with the past, 133; Habermas, 89, 91, 98; Nazi past, 6*t*–7*t*; skeptical generation, 45, 50. *See also* integration by Habermas; student movement
protests, 47, 56–57; Asylum Debate, 181; Emergency Laws, 54–55; globalization, 103, 105, 192; Habermas, 95, 113; police violence, 50; Vietnam, 48–49
public sphere, 27, 93; criticism, 264–65; global, 270; Habermas, 35, 38–39

queer criticism of Habermas, 258
questioning, types of, xv–xvi

race theory criticism of Habermas, 261–62, 264, 267
radical democracy, 204, 214–18, 249–50, 256; development of concept, 27; social, 29
radical pluralism, 238–44, 239*t*
Radikalenerlass. *See* Decree against Radicals
RAF. *See* Red Army Faction

Rasmussen, David M., xx
rationality, 234; debates, xix, 224; domains, 233
Ratzinger, Joseph, Cardinal, 68
reading Habermas, 278–82
Reagan, Ronald, 61, 75–76, 135
Red Army Faction (RAF), 65–69, 72
Red–Green coalition, 49, 167, 187, 191
redemption, 147–48, 227, 289; hope, 8; need, 142; waiting, 155–56. *See also* anamnestic solidarity
reeducation, 11, 175
regulative ideal of communicative reason, 129
religion, 9, 11
remembrance. *See* memorials; memory
repressed past, Horkheimer on, 29–30
"Repressive Tolerance" (Marcuse), 43–44
republican democracy, 208
resistance, right of, 51–52, 56, 61n1; humanitarian intervention, 119; relationship to violence, 112, 115, 121
responsibility, 227. *See also* liability
restoration, 3–33
revisionist historians, 65–86, 131–39; Adorno, 163; Bitburg ceremonies, 75–77; memory, 142; Nazi past, 7*t*; Persian Gulf War, 178–79
revolution(s): of 1848, 121; fall of Berlin Wall, 80, 82; Habermas, 28–29, 111–12, 126, 137; Iran, 196; Krahl, 108; permanent democratic, 204, 213, 233–34, 255; phantom, 55, 57; phantoms of, 92–102; Velvet, 63n20
revolutionary consciousness, 45
Ricoeur, Paul, 141
Right: Habermas, 127–29; Kosovo, 186
rights. *See* absolute basic rights; human rights; resistance, right of
Rothacker, Erich, 17–18, 32n8

Rüegg, Walter, 53
sacred. *See* God; linguistification of sacred; postsecularism
Sartre, Jean-Paul, 22, 43–44, 46, 54, 97, 206; critique of Habermas, 288–89
"Die Scheinrevolution und ihre Kinder" (Habermas), 55–56, 94–95, 99–102, 105, 112–13
Schleyer, Hanns Martin, 66–67, 69
Schmid, Carlo, 53
Schmidt, Alfred, 48
Schmidt, Helmut, 70
Schmitt, Carl, 18, 180, 186–87
Schnock, Frieder, 169, 196n4
Schröder, Gerhard, 166–67, 192
SDS. *See* German Socialist Student League
Seattle protests, 103, 105, 192
securing generation, xxii, 4, 9, 16, 20; Nazi past, 6t. *See also* integration by Habermas
Seebohm, H., 11
self-choice. *See* existential self-choice
self-critical culture, ideal, 10
Senghor, Léopold Sédar, 57
Serbia, bombing, 83, 185–96, 276n13; humanitarian intervention, 119, 187–88, 195
Serra, Richard, 167
settling accounts, versus coming to terms with the past, 134–35
Shoah (film by Lanzmann), 138
silence, 301; Habermas, 16; postwar government, 12; revisionists, 137; securing generation, 9, 16, 20; types, 155
sincerity, and communication, 224
situations, xx–xxii, 1
skeptical generation, xxii–xxiii, 4–5, 8; ambivalence, 83; Nazi past, 6t; protesting generation, 45, 50
Sloterdijk, Peter, xiii, 291, 293–96; Habermas' response, 295
social critique, 202–18
Social Democrats (SPD), 30, 38–39, 41–42, 70–71, 192
social justice, 109–10, 187

socialism: Habermas, 96; third way, 254–55, 275n6. *See also* Left
socialization, 3–5
solidarity, 240–41
Sonning Prize lecture, Copenhagen (Habermas), 126, 141–43, 145, 153, 156
Sontheimer, Kurt, 67–68, 109–10
Sorel, Georges, 52
Soviet Revolution, 28
SPD. *See* Social Democrats
Spiegel protest, 39–40
Springer Verlag, 39, 54
Sternberger, Dolf, 205
Stih, Renata, 169, 196n4
Stojanovič, Svetozar, 56
Strauss, Franz Josef, 40–41, 134–35
strikes: Frankfurt, 57–58; Mexico, 117–18
structural axis, xxii–xxxvi
structuralism, 242
Structural Transformation of the Public Sphere (Habermas), 39
student movement, 35–63, 81; actors, 46–47; anachronistic, 1–82, 289–90; critical social theory, 102–9; demands, 57–58; early, 23–25, 30–31; end, 59–60, 106; generations, xxiii; Habermas, 36–61, 46t; Habermas' critique, 92, 95–102; Marcuse, 6t, 26, 43–44, 46t, 48, 51–56, 94; Mexico, 115, 117–18; Nazi past, 6t–7t; phantoms, 89–123
Student und Politik (Habermas et al.), 27–28
Stürmer, Michael, 135, 137, 154
Subversive Action, 47
suspicion, 154, 188; hermeneutics, 141; learning, 270
systems rationality, 96

terrorism, 66–69, 72; Habermas, 67–69; Left, 68–69. *See also* violence
theory of communicative action, xvii, 96; and nonviolence, 115
The Theory of Communicative Action (Habermas), xxvi, 96, 220, 242, 254

338 Index

theory/practice issues: coming to terms with the past, 148; generational cohorts, 109–22; Habermas, 218–35, 240–41; Mexico, 117–18; violence, 115
theory, stages of, xxv
"Theses against the Coalition of the Despondent with Dictators" (Habermas), 41–42
third way socialism, 254–55, 275n6
Third World: Habermas, 96–97, 112, 257; Marcuse, 120; student movement, 93
Thomas Aquinas, 301
Tiedemann, Rolf, 148
Tillich, Paul, 19
Tito, Josip Broz, 56
Tlatelolco, Mexico, 56, 117
"Traditional and Critical Theory" (Horkheimer), xxvi
traditionalism, 154
traumatic loss, 8–9
Traynor, Ian, 192
trust, 155
truth, 224
twentieth century, 78–79; legacy, xiv; life of Habermas, xiii–xv
twenty-first century, 81–82

UNAM. *See* National Autonomous University of Mexico
United Nations, 195; Habermas, 175–77, 185, 214, 218
United States: Habermas, 83, 86n11,176; Holocaust Memorial Museum, 166, 168; Horkheimer, 29–30, 48–49; worldview, 188
universalism, 259–62
University and Democracy: Conditions and Organization of Resistance (conference), 50
"University in a Democracy—Democratization of the University" (Habermas), 92
university professors: Mexico, 118; Nazi party, 18–20, 33n10; terrorism, 72. *See also* student movement

"Unruhe, erste Bürgerpflicht" (Habermas), 35
unspeakable: Asylum Debate, 183–84; definition, 286; Habermas, 16, 282–383; Kosovo, 194; memorials, 299; speaking about, 282–91; witnessing to, 148–49

V-E Day, 3–11, 77, 164–65; ghosts, 125–59
Velvet Revolution, 63n20
victims: claims, 148–50; Habermas, 143–44
Vienna circle, 19
Vietnam—Analysis of a Model (conference), 48
Vietnam War, 48, 53, 179
violence: Critical Theory, 68; generational cohorts, 109–22; Habermas, 52, 56, 61, 110–12, 115–16, 116f; language, 111; Marcuse, 69, 116f, 121; monuments, 169; resistance, 112, 115, 121; student movement, 105; xenophobic, 181. *See also* anti-Semitism; Fascism
Vonnegut, Kurt, 81

waiting, redemptive, 155–56
Walser, Martin, 159n32, 167, 291–92
war, humanitarian. *See* humanitarian wars of intervention
Washington, D.C.: protests, 103, 105, 192; U.S. Holocaust Memorial Museum, 166, 168, 299
weak anamnestic (messianic) power, 148–49, 232
Weber, Max, 22, 43, 238, 244
Weizsäcker, Carl Friedrich von, 66
welfare state, 211–12, 247–48
Wellmer, Albrecht, 68
"What Does Coming to Terms with the Past Mean?" (Adorno), 162–63
Wiggershaus, Rolf, xx
witnessing: critical theorist, 143–50, 152–53, 156, 173; to Other, 232; to unspeakable, 148–49
Wolff, Reinhart, 58
World Bank, 117

World Trade Organization, 192, 251
The Wretched of the Earth (Fanon), 43–44

xenophobia, 181

Yad Vashem, 166, 168, 299
yes or no. *See* ambivalence of Habermas

Young, Iris M., 262–63, 266–67
Yugoslavia, 181

"Die Zeigefinger: Die Deutschen und ihr Denkmal" (Habermas), 297–301

ABOUT THE AUTHOR

Martin J. B. Matuštík is professor of philosophy at Purdue University, where he has been teaching since 1991. In August 1968, as an eleven-year-old, he witnessed the Soviet invasion of his native Czechoslovakia. At twelve, he published as his first piece a photo from the funeral march for Jan Palach, the philosophy student who in 1969 immolated himself in protest against the Soviet crushing of the Prague Spring. At nineteen, as a student of psychology at Prague's Charles University and a participant in Jan Patočka's "flying university," he signed *Charta 77*, the manifesto for human rights in Czechoslovakia. He immigrated to Santa Monica, California, from an Austrian refugee camp in 1978. He studied with Jürgen Habermas as a Fulbright doctoral fellow in Frankfurt a/M during the time of the fall of the Berlin Wall and the Velvet Revolution in 1989 until the summer of 1991. He taught as a Fulbright scholar in Prague during 1995. He is author of *Postnational Identity: Critical Theory and Existential Philosophy in Habermas, Kierkegaard, and Havel* (1993) and *Specters of Liberation: Great Refusals in the New World Order* (1998), and coeditor with Merold Westphal of *Kierkegaard in Post/Modernity* (1995) and with William L. McBride of *Calvin O. Schrag and the Task of Philosophy after Postmodernity* (forthcoming).